YAKUZA

P9-BJI-666

YAKUZA

JAPAN'S CRIMINAL UNDERWORLD

EXPANDED EDITION

DAVID E. KAPLAN AND ALEC DUBRO

UNIVERSITY OF CALIFORNIA PRESS   BERKELEY   LOS ANGELES

The excerpt on pp. 6–7 is reprinted with permission from *The East*, October 1981, Tokyo, vol. xvii, nos. 9 & 10, pp. 47–48.

The excerpt on p. 9 is reprinted with permission from an article entitled "Delinquent Groups and Organized Crime," in the *Sociological Review Monograph*, no. 10, 1966, published by Routledge & Kegan Paul plc, London.

University of California Press
Berkeley and Los Angeles, California
University of California Press, Ltd.
London, England

Copyright © 2003 by the Center for Investigative Reporting and David E. Kaplan

Library of Congress Cataloging-in-Publication Data

Kaplan, David E., 1955–
 Yakuza : Japan's criminal underworld / David E. Kaplan and Alec Dubro.—Expanded ed.
     p.   cm.
 Includes bibliographical references and index.
 ISBN-13 978-0-520-21562-7 (pbk. : alk. paper)
 ISBN-10 0-520-21562-1 (pbk. : alk. paper)
   1. Yakuza—Japan—History. 2. Yakuza—History. 3. Organized crime—Japan—History. 4. Crime—Japan—History. 5. Gangs—Japan—History. I. Dubro, Alec. II. Title.
 HV6453.J33 Y355 2003
 364.1'06'0952—dc21   2002007138

Manufactured in the United States of America

15 14 13 12 11 10 09 08 07

12 11 10 9 8 7 6 5

The paper used in this publication is both acid-free and totally chlorine-free (TCF). It meets the minimum requirements of ANSI/NISO z39.48–1992 (R 1997) ⊗.

CONTENTS

ACKNOWLEDGMENTS

THIS BOOK IS A COLLABORATIVE EFFORT. OVER THE COURSE OF OBSERVING
the yakuza for nearly twenty years, we were helped by so many people in so
many ways that it is, quite literally, impossible to thank them all. Our work
on the first edition was aided by at least fifty researchers and reporters
spread across five continents. The revised edition relied on dozens more.

We have, in addition, drawn on the work of countless others from aca-
demia, the media, law enforcement, and the underworld. Many of our
sources cannot be named due to concern over job security and, in some
cases, personal safety. We regret if others' contributions pass unnoticed
here; this book would have been an impossible task without the assistance
of all those friends and colleagues, and our heartfelt thanks go to all who
helped in any way.

Our foremost thanks go to our old colleagues at the Center for Investigative Reporting, who made this book happen. Our gratitude goes out to
Dan Noyes, Sharon Tiller, and David Weir; to Mark Schapiro for saving the
project when it nearly died an unnatural death; and to the rest of the CIR
family who so enthusiastically supported this work.

We owe three of our colleagues in Japan an equally important debt.
Glenn Davis and the late, great John Roberts, two veteran Tokyo correspondents, contributed enormously at virtually every step of this project—from
commenting on our initial proposal to arranging interviews, performing
research, and critiquing our manuscript. Their expertise and experience
helped produce the vast store of information that forms the heart of this
book. In addition, their friendship, and that of their families, greatly
warmed what was an otherwise freezing Tokyo winter. In addition, we are
enormously grateful to the remarkable Michio Matsui, our friend, collabo-

rator, and cultural guide. Matsui-san first translated *Yakuza* into Japanese and proved to be an extraordinary resource and colleague.

Our colleagues at Nippon Hoso Kyokai (NHK), Japan's public broadcasting system, also are deserving of great thanks. Their careful arrangements secured interviews with leading yakuza, allowing American journalists an unprecedented look at the Japanese underworld. Despite countless cultural blunders on our part, NHK producers patiently and skillfully guided us along a sometimes treacherous path. Thanks to Sadaharu Inoue, who helped from the beginning, and to Hajime Suzuki, Atsushi Karube, and Yasuo Onuki.

Our translators and interpreters performed admirably both at home and abroad. Thanks to Reiko Makeuchi for courage far beyond the call of our meager payments; Professor Yuzuru Katagiri, Ike Matsuzaki, and K.T. for offering invaluable help in understanding not only a difficult language but a complex culture as well; and James Chun, Jon Joseph, and Taka Yamada for filling in at critical moments. On the revised edition, three others were similarly heroic and generous with their time: Hiroshi Suto, Kyoko Matsuda, and Michiko Toyama.

In Tokyo, our sincere gratitude goes to Ryuma Suzuki of the Sumiyoshi-kai. Special thanks also to Chuk Besher, who proved a constant source of ideas and encouragement. In addition, we were helped immeasurably over the years by many in the Japanese law enforcement community. Most prefer not to be named, but we would be remiss in not thanking Hiroto Yamazaki for his suggestions and hospitality, and Kanehiro Hoshino for his patience and wisdom. Two former top cops, Seiji Iishiba and Raisuke Miyawaki, also offered invaluable guidance. And a handful of friends there were terrific resources over the years: David Bong, Andrew Marshall, Mark Schreiber—thank you so much.

Also in Tokyo, a hearty thanks goes to the estimable Bernard Krisher for his unique contributions to our project. Many others offered their time and suggestions: Dave Butts, Harry Godfrey, Brad Martin, Peter Shigeta, Fred Schmidt, Howard Snyder, Greg Starr. From Nippon Television, thanks much to Hisao Adachi, Yuko Fuse, Atsushi Hatayama, and Toshiya Sugimoto. Jeanne Sather contributed mightily with research and news clips. We extend thanks to the staffs of the Foreign Press Center (especially Shigeyoshi Araki) and the Foreign Correspondents Club of Japan. Hajime Takano and Takao Toshikawa were generous with needed advice and research assistance, and Goro Fujita and Kenji Ino provided invaluable insights. And Tom Gill—thank you for helping on the Japanese edition.

Special thanks go to those around the globe who helped with research and interviews: Stan Correy in Australia, Mike Kepp in Brazil, Ramon Tulfo in the Philippines, Kay Landmann in Germany, Toshimitsu Shigemura in South Korea, and others in Thailand, Hong Kong, and elsewhere who must

remain unnamed. Our researchers at the Center for Investigative Reporting also deserve enormous credit for digging up and compiling key sources
of information: Susan Moran bore the brunt of this work. The efforts of
Frances Dinkelspiel, Jennifer McNulty, and Brenda Sunoo are also greatly
appreciated. And John Sweeney, librarian extraordinaire, thanks for your
generous efforts over the years.

In the San Francisco Bay Area, we were helped by Professors Harumi
Befu and Chalmers Johnson, who made available their considerable expertise in Japanese culture and politics. Lowell Bergman made invaluable contributions over the years. Thanks also to Sasha Besher, Brad Bunnin, Bon-
nie Burt, Tony Crittenden, Barbara Faison, Loren Kelly, John McKenna,
Karl Schoenberg, Mike Sterrett, and others unnamed.

In Honolulu, special thanks go to Bill Sweet, Mike Fleming, and others
who worked with the U.S. Customs Service there. Also in that city, we owe
a good bit of Japanese *giri* to Professor Joe Tobin of the University of Hawaii, who painstakingly went over our original manuscript and made much-
needed suggestions. Jim Dooley and Keith Kaneshiro also helped a great
deal over the years. And thanks to Bernie Ching and Ron Higa, formerly of
the Honolulu Police Department; Hilton Lui, Don Carstensen, Steve Lane,
Naomi Sodetani, and Ken Szymkowiak.

In Los Angeles we thank the many veterans of the LAPD who have
helped, in particular Yoichi Ikuta, George Min, John Vach, and Jimmy Sakoda. Also in L.A., thanks to Dwight Chuman, Shigeharu Higashi, and
Kurashima-san. In New York, thanks to Marnie Inskip and the late Charles
Kades, and to our law enforcement sources in the region.

In Washington, D.C., we thank Russell Adise, Don Goldberg, Pharis Harvey, Larry Johnson, John Mintz, Raphael Perl, and Gordon Witkin; Manuel
Gonzalez and John Leonard, formerly with the President's Commission on
Organized Crime; Tom Melcher for helping sort things out at a critical time;
and many others. David Kaplan extends special appreciation to his editors
at *U.S. News,* Peter Cary and Susan Headden, for tolerating a sometimes
crazed schedule and interests on the other side of the globe.

Our friends at the International Association of Asian Crime Investigators
were helpful to a fault, offering everything from guidance to protection.
Thanks most of all to the SFPD's Tom Perdue, who is sorely missed; and
to so many others, among them Bill Cassidy, Cord Hart, Ken Sanz, Mike
Watson, and Jack "Wo Fat" Willoughby. Elsewhere, thanks go out to Fred
Gushin, Braith Hill, Rich LaMagna, Bertil Lintner, Bill O'Reilly, Spencer
Sherman, and Mark West; Frank Joseph Shulman and Tamiko Cooke of the
University of Maryland; Fred Pernell of the National Records Center,
Thomas Burkman of Old Dominion College, and the late Howard Schon-
berger of the University of Maine.

We are greatly indebted to Howard Bray and the Fund for Investigative

Journalism, who generously supported this project at the beginning. Our gratitude also goes to the PEN Writers Fund for its important contribution. And many thanks to those who supported Kaplan's research for the revised edition: the U.S.-Japan Fulbright program, especially David Adams, Mizuho Iwata, and Sam Shepherd; the East-West Center and its congenial hosts, Dick Halloran and John Schidlovsky; and the Woodrow Wilson International Center and Mary-Lea Cox.

Thanks, too, to our editors and others who have made the various editions of *Yakuza* happen. And, of course, our wonderful agents: Bless you Leslie Breed and Gail Ross.

Alec Dubro extends a personal note of thanks to Ruth Dubro, Leon and Shirley Becker, Ben and Toni Coplan, Lee Hamilton, Steve Krinsky, Julie and David Marino, Jim Tobias, and, of course, Kim Fellner for her support over the years. David E. Kaplan gives thanks to his pals Phil Cook and Rocky Kistner, to the Kaplan and Eichner families, to his loving wife Pam and daughter Adi, and to his parents, who made it all possible.

DAVID E. KAPLAN is deputy editor of the investigative team at *U.S. News & World Report* in Washington, D.C., where he covers organized crime, terrorism, and intelligence. In addition to *Yakuza,* Kaplan is author of the critically acclaimed *Fires of the Dragon,* on the murder of journalist Henry Liu, and co-author of *The Cult at the End of the World,* on the doomsday sect behind the nerve gassing of Tokyo's subway. His work has won more than a dozen awards, including honors from Investigative Reporters & Editors, the American Bar Association, Overseas Press Club, and World Affairs Council.

ALEC DUBRO has written professionally since his first music review in *Rolling Stone* in 1968. Since then, he's gone on to write hundreds of newspaper and magazine articles, as well as scripts, position papers, speeches, reports, and comic books. He has worked as a private investigator, editor, television news writer, and consultant to state and federal crime commissions. He currently lives and works in Washington, D.C., where he divides his time between journalism and communications consulting for the labor movement and NGOs. He is past president of the U.S. National Writers Union.

THE CENTER FOR INVESTIGATIVE REPORTING, founded in 1977, is the only independent, nonprofit organization in the United States established as an institution to do investigative reporting. From their offices in San Francisco, the CIR staff write for leading newspapers and magazines and work closely with television news programs in the U.S. and abroad. Center stories have helped spark congressional hearings and legislation, U.N. resolutions, public interest lawsuits, and changes in the activities of multinational corporations, government agencies, and organized crime figures. Its stories have won numerous honors, including an Emmy, a Polk Award, a National Magazine Award, and a National Press Club Award. For more information contact CIR at 131 Steuart Street, Ste. 600, San Francisco, CA 94105 or at www.muckraker.org.

PREFACE TO THE NEW EDITION

THE ORIGINAL EDITION OF YAKUZA WAS FIRST PUBLISHED IN 1986 BY Addison-Wesley in the United States. Sales were modest at first, but the book earned a place as a standard reference on Japanese organized crime. Foreign publishers also took interest in the work and eventually *Yakuza* was translated into nine languages. Along the way, the authors encountered some rather odd experiences which added measurably to our understanding of Japanese crime.

A British edition went to three printings and over 30,000 copies worldwide, becoming a best-seller in the Far East. Despite these sales, in 1989 the book's publisher, Robert Maxwell, suddenly ordered our entire inventory shredded, over the protests of his staff. The authors, unaware of all this, were rather puzzled as to why the books so quickly disappeared from shelves around the world. Maxwell, we later learned, was doing a favor for his Japanese friend and backer, philanthropist Ryoichi Sasakawa. This book had reported on Sasakawa's imprisonment as a Class A war criminal and tied him to Japan's underworld and ultranationalist movement. Both Maxwell and Sasakawa are now dead, and no legal challenge was ever made to this book. Unfortunately, the international English edition died an unnatural death.

The authors also had high hopes for marketing *Yakuza* in Japan, where books by foreigners about the Japanese sell well, as do books about the yakuza. But after expressing great interest in the book, publisher after publisher turned down the work. In all, some eighteen houses passed on *Yakuza,* much to our dismay. Our Japanese literary agent finally wrote from Tokyo, attempting to outline the problem. "The content of book presents some possibilities of trouble," he telexed, "as some words refer to racial segregation (our historical problem with Koreans) and references to particular figures in certain political parties and organizations are mentioned in the book. Most of the publishers fear that when published, they would meet some hindrances and pressures as the book touches taboos of our society."

A friend in Tokyo suggested the book had become a victim of *mokusatsu*, or death by silence. In 1988, co-author Kaplan gave a talk at the Foreign Correspondents Club of Japan, at which he accused Japanese publishers of in effect blacklisting the book. His talk was widely covered by the Western press, and virtually ignored by the Japanese news media. But from that event, the authors were put in touch with a small, radical house in Tokyo, Daisan Shokkan, whose publisher was determined to release the book. Finally, in 1991, a Japanese-language edition of *Yakuza* was published—five years after the American edition. The Japanese version hit bookstores just as huge scandals tied to the gangs were making headlines, and the book became a best-seller.

By then, though, the book was seriously out of date. Research for the original edition spanned the years 1981 to 1985, and since then the gangs have gone through extraordinary change. *Yakuza* was first published just before Japan's Bubble Economy took off, inflating stock and land values to dizzying heights and pouring billions of dollars into yakuza coffers. Concern about Japanese gangs spread to police throughout the Pacific Rim, who worried about huge investments and criminal activity. Scandals following the Bubble's collapse revealed a level of yakuza infiltration into Japan's top corporations that surprised even the authors. At the same time, the yakuza began to capture imaginations in the West, becoming standard fare in popular culture. They became occasional villains on TV cop shows and in feature movies (*Black Rain, Rising Sun, American Yakuza*). They appeared as shadowy figures in novels of crime and suspense (Van Lustbader's *Angel Eyes* and van de Wetering's *The Japanese Corpse*). They have even been hurled into cyberpunk futures by writers of science fiction (Gibson's *Neuromancer* and Besher's *Rim*).

Many of these depictions are fanciful at best, but the fascination with Japan's colorful underworld is understandable. Indeed, it has drawn the authors back into the field after years of watching the gangs from afar. In an attempt to pull together developments from the last fifteen years, we have completed several new rounds of interviews and research. Readers will find this edition of *Yakuza* considerably expanded, with three additional chapters on the gangs' economic impact and expansion overseas. Several other chapters have been heavily revised and the entire book updated. We trust that these changes will meet the approval of disgruntled godfathers and reluctant publishers worldwide.

David E. Kaplan
Alec Dubro
Washington, D.C.
Fall 2002

ENTER THE YAKUZA

IF YOU WANT THE *YAKUZA* STUFF TAKEN SERIOUSLY, THE MAN FROM JUSTICE said, start by getting rid of those stories about tattoos and missing fingers. That was the message from Washington, D.C., to Michael Sterrett in Hawaii.

It was the spring of 1976 and Sterrett, a sharp young federal prosecutor, was making headlines in Honolulu. For three years he had journeyed to Hawaii to initiate a remarkable set of prosecutions. Working out of any available desk in Honolulu's old federal building, Sterrett obtained a series of convictions that set back organized crime in the islands for years. Now he was pushing hard to open the federal government's first Organized Crime Strike Force office in the fiftieth state, but some of his organized crime reports were generating considerable skepticism.

It had been difficult enough just to gain permission for the flights to Hawaii. Unlike trips to other states, travel to the islands required approval from the number two man at the Department of Justice, the assistant attorney general. And it didn't help that Sterrett's home office at the San Francisco regional headquarters wasn't always taken seriously, or that Hawaii was hardly a priority for Washington policy makers. The state's criminal gangs—an array of Asians, whites, blacks, and Pacific Islanders—received little attention from a federal agency preoccupied with the traditional American mob. No one in Washington had ever built a career on chasing crime around the mid-Pacific.

But Sterrett was getting results. Capitalizing on a rare moment of cooperation between local and federal law enforcement, he had prosecuted and put away "Nappy" Pulawa, the Hawaiian gambling kingpin whose connections included top Las Vegas mobsters. And Sterrett had successfully gone after Pulawa's successor, Earl K. H. Kim, and the members of his gambling syndicate.

It was during his work on those cases, as he pored over police reports, that Sterrett first began to notice the presence of Japanese nationals. Federal officials in Honolulu already were concerned over the growing ties between mainland and Hawaiian crime syndicates. Now a third leg of an underworld triangle began to emerge, one that had been apparent to local police since the late 1960s.

The tattoos and missing fingers comprised the most striking, immediate features of these new criminals. They were not ordinary tattoos, but magnificent, full-color designs of samurai warriors, flowers, and dragons that stretched across the body from neck to calf. And the mutilated fingers—these were the ceremoniously severed tops of the smallest digit, lopped off at the joint and presented to the gang leader as a mark of atonement. Sterrett's memos to Washington, filled with such bizarre descriptions, accurately depicted the classic traits of Japanese organized crime syndicates. After 250 years of crime in the Far East, the yakuza had finally arrived in the West.

At first, Sterrett was puzzled by the appearance of the yakuza. What were they doing in Honolulu, and who did they know? One fact was clear, however—the islands hosted the right elements for organized crime to flourish: machine party politics coupled with a tough labor movement; a hedonistic culture with widespread acceptance of prostitution, gambling, and drugs; and a massive tourist industry that each year gathered millions of visitors from around the world and turned them loose on Honolulu streets.

Perhaps most important was Hawaii's geographic position in the mid-Pacific, a convenient stopping-off point for international trade and travelers from throughout the Orient and North America. It was here that the much-heralded era of the Pacific Basin could be seen firsthand. Trade among the Pacific Rim nations was booming, threatening to overtake the North Atlantic as the world's major market area. The rapidly expanding economies of East Asia, the steady growth of Japan and California, and the emergence of China left little doubt about the region's potential.

Hawaii itself comprised an ethnic mirror of the entire basin. Once populated solely by Polynesians, the islands were now one-third white and one-quarter ethnic Japanese. An assortment of other Asians and Pacific Islanders made up much of the rest. Asian investment capital streamed into the islands from Hong Kong, Japan, and Singapore; investors bought up hotels, banks, real estate, and, in the eyes of the locals, anything that could be purchased.

If this was the dawn of the Pacific Era, reasoned Sterrett, it would follow that the rapid development of legitimate business might be paralleled by an equally burgeoning underworld economy. The American Mafia, after all, had gone international years before with their investments in Europe and the Caribbean, and through their ties to the Italian Mafia, the Corsican mobs, and heroin refiners from Bangkok to Marseille. It seemed logical, then, that the linking of the Pacific Rim economies would bring new criminal groups into the picture. Reports were already coming into Honolulu about counterfeiters from Taiwan, drug dealers from Hong Kong and Thailand, and suspect investors from Las Vegas, Tokyo, and Seoul. Another set of Asian crime syndicates—the Chinese triads—was also beginning to cause trouble for authorities in both Europe and America.

The potential for organized crime to expand in the Pacific was enormous. Already in the region there existed the power of what Sterrett liked to call shadow governments—underworld states that collect their own taxes and enforce their own laws. Sterrett could see future glimpses of a vast criminal empire that would reach across national boundaries, accountable to no one but the underworld, in which drugs and guns and huge amounts of money would move across the Pacific. The possibilities were endless; who could estimate the impact of a U.S.-Japan crime syndicate on the $85 billion worth of goods shipped between the two countries each year? What might be the effect of a "yakuza connection" on both sides of the Pacific?

The scenario, though intriguing, seemed a bit too far off and alarmist for a young prosecutor already having trouble getting his memos read. So at first Sterrett hedged, refusing to exaggerate the possible importance of a few Japanese crooks lurking around Hawaii. But in time he changed his mind. "It took a lot of learning to understand what was involved," he recalled. "Slowly, though, it began to dawn on us that we were dealing with a completely different kind of organized crime problem."

Detailed information in English about the yakuza was at best scarce. There were translation problems, and, strangely, the Japanese police appeared reluctant to cooperate. Much to the amazement of U.S. law enforcement, requests for information were answered slowly and incompletely. Japanese authorities refused to provide their American counterparts with a list of known yakuza members. Apparently, there were some formidable legal—and cultural—obstacles at hand. What little intelligence did become available, however, raised eyebrows around the old federal building.

Sterrett leafed through a handful of reports on the yakuza from Japan's National Police Agency and scanned the sketchy profiles then developed by police in Honolulu. The figures cited were striking: 110,000 gangsters lived and worked in Japan, neatly organized into 2,500 "families" and federations. In the United States, with twice Japan's population, the Justice Department estimated that there were only 20,000 members of the Mafia. It seemed a remarkable statistic for Japan, a country famous for its low crime rates. Yet even the figure of 110,000 gangsters, according to Japanese police, was down from a peak of 180,000 only fifteen years earlier. The huge yakuza syndicates, furthermore, seemed well financed and highly organized—the criminal counterpart to the country's efficient, finely tuned corporations.

Sterrett found that, like the American mob, the yakuza service the covert vices: prostitution, pornography, drugs, gambling. He learned that the Japanese gangs share other similarities with their American equivalents: large chunks of the construction and entertainment industries lie under their control, including movie studios, nightclubs, and professional sports. A third of the Japanese mob's sizable income comes from drug dealing, say police, particularly in methamphetamines—what the Japanese call "awakening drugs." The yakuza portfolio also includes loan sharking, trucking, and an array of strong-arm, smuggling, and extortion rackets. According to the National Police Agency, the yakuza control thousands of legitimate businesses and countless illegal ones; their impact is felt from small streetside businesses to the country's largest corporations. And, for a price, they break strikes and help silence dissenters. The gangs are politically powerful as well, extending their influence through shadowy figures to the highest levels of Japanese government.

That, however, is where the similarities with the American mob end. The yakuza are accepted into Japanese society in a way that confounded Sterrett and the few other U.S. officials who bothered to investigate them. Yakuza groups, for example, for years kept offices that prominently displayed the gang emblem on their front doors, much as if they were the local loan company (which, in fact, they often are). This is equivalent to a New Jersey crime family opening an office in Newark emblazoned with the sign MAFIA HEADQUARTERS, LOCAL 12. Yakuza members are also in the practice of sporting on their suits lapel pins that identify their gang, displaying them with the same pride as Rotarians and fraternity brothers. Several of the largest gangs publish their own newsletters or magazines, complete with feature articles, legal advice, and even poetry written by gang members. After gang wars, the feuding leaders have even called press conferences, announcing that the fighting has ended and apologizing to the public for any inconvenience they might have caused.

Clearly, there was a very different tradition of organized crime at work here, one that Western cops had never encountered before. Some of the material Sterrett came across seemed pretty far-fetched. The yakuza appeared to be living anachronisms, samurai in business suits. They cast themselves as the moral descendants of Japan's noble warriors, the last upholders of the nation's traditional values. The Japanese public, furthermore, seemed to accept this. The gangsters had somehow developed an enduring image as patriots and Robin Hoods. They seemed not so much a Mafia as a loyal opposition, the honorable members of Japan's criminal class.

Out of all his research, though, what struck Sterrett most were the reports of ritual finger-cuttings—the very items he was told to keep out of his memos to Washington. They symbolized to him in one act the radically different nature of the Japanese gangsters. "Here were individuals so devoted they were willing to endure amputating their own fingertips for the boss," he said. "The motivation, the loyalty of these people were things we'd just never seen before."

Impressed with their organization, their size, and reports of their increasing activity in Hawaii, Sterrett began building a file. He soon learned that his vision of a trans-Pacific criminal cartel might not be so far off the mark. Yakuza members had been seen by Honolulu police mixing with both local and mainland organized crime figures. They had become involved on the islands in prostitution, pornography, extortion, and gunrunning. Apparently, they were venturing to the mainland as well—to San Francisco, Los Angeles, and Las Vegas. Other reports showed that, since the early 1970s, the Japanese mob had gone international, expanding into South Korea, Southeast Asia, and a host of other regions around the Pacific Rim. By the early spring of 1976, Sterrett was finally convinced that the yakuza did in fact pose a problem meriting federal attention.

The watershed event for Sterrett, though, occurred in May of that year, when Wataru "Jackson" Inada was found murdered in his Honolulu apartment. Inada, a small, tough ex-boxer, got caught up in Hawaiian rackets and drug dealing upon his arrival from Tokyo in 1972. He bore on his back the ornate tattoos of a yakuza, which he acquired as a soldier in the 6,000-member Sumiyoshi federation, one of Japan's largest syndicates. Police believe Jackson's murder was a result of an ambitious, though ill-fated, heroin deal involving West Coast Mafiosi.

The Inada case was what Mike Sterrett later called the beginning of the institutionalization of the yakuza in the United States. Within two short years, Jackson Inada had made connections to high-ranking members of the mainland Mafia. He had allied himself with the leading figures of Hawaiian organized crime, while maintaining his relationship to the yakuza in Japan. And he had made American law enforcement take a hard, second look at the potential impact of the tattooed men. Sterrett's Strike Force office was opened a year later, in 1977.

It had been a frustrating fight for recognition, Sterrett recalled. "You have to remember," he said, "that it had been only ten or eleven years since the Mafia's existence was officially even acknowledged by the FBI and Justice. They didn't want to hear about non-Mafia activity; their priority was La Cosa Nostra. Now imagine: there I was, someone who took over twenty trips from, of all places, San Francisco, to Honolulu, warning the Justice Department about yet another organized crime group whose members amputated their own fingers . . ."

Sterrett's work, however—including his exotic memos—began to get closer attention from Washington, and in 1979 he was given charge of the San Francisco regional office. Before leaving, he would see his hunches about the yakuza start to come true.

By 1979, the Japanese gangs had become big news in Hawaii, with extensive press and television coverage of their involvement in drugs, gambling, and prostitution. But it took a second smuggling case, after Inada, to really set off the alarm. In May 1979, a trio of yakuza "mules," or couriers, were arrested at Honolulu International Airport. Each man held one pound of white Asian heroin stuffed into his carton of Dunhills. A passport check revealed a total of sixteen trips to Bangkok, Thailand—the probable source of the heroin—and twelve subsequent journeys to Hawaii, Guam, and San Francisco. A search of their homes in Tokyo by Japanese authorities turned up a strange set of instructions carefully spelling out the duties of the smugglers: "You should obey whatever you are told to do by your group leader," the document read. "You have no choice, you cannot refuse or complain of the leader's instruction. The above instructions are given at the request of the financier in order to protect ourselves and to accomplish our work."

U.S. officials were alarmed. According to a classified report by the Drug Enforcement Administration, the arrests "clearly demonstrate" that the yakuza are "furiously engaged in heroin smuggling . . ." The DEA's fears were echoed by federal investigators at a 1981 congressional hearing, who warned: "It's only a matter of time before the yakuza groups become seriously involved in the smuggling of heroin into the United States." Authorities had become justifiably concerned that, given the yakuza's excellent organization and reserves of cash and men, they could develop into the most efficient importers of narcotics into the West Coast.

American law enforcement, meanwhile, began finding extensive yakuza investment in Hawaii and California. Hidden by the vast movement of capital between Japan and the United States, the yakuza's illicit profits were being laundered through American real estate, hotels, and what the Japanese call *mizu shobai*—literally, "water business"—bars, restaurants, and night-clubs. Using souvenir shops as fronts, the yakuza muscled into the lucrative Japanese tourist trade in Los Angeles and San Francisco. They developed as well a multi-million-dollar racket in the smuggling of hard-core pornography and handguns to Japan. There were also charges of white slavery rings in which fraudulent talent scouts recruited young female entertainers in the United States and, once in Japan, forced them to work as prostitutes and sex show performers.

By 1981, the yakuza had begun earning their share of attention from the American public as well as the police. A parade of stories on the coming of Japan's Mafia marched out of the media. In *Newsweek*, the *Los Angeles Times*, Jack Anderson's column, and on local and national television, the groups were profiled, their activities exposed. Most of the coverage, while at times sensational, was accurate, quoting police about the extent of yakuza heroin dealing and dwelling on the huge size of the gangs and their strange customs.

Predictably enough, a handful of reports began to surface, laced with what might charitably be called latent racism. One news headline, summoning fears of another era, spoke of Japanese criminals "invading" the West Coast. Another publication went further, depicting on its cover a monstrous gangster looming out of Japan, enshadowing Hawaii and threatening Los Angeles. It was the yakuza as yellow peril, an easy jump for people needing scapegoats for U.S. foreign trade problems. In liberal San Francisco, a popular radio talk show focused on the yakuza one day, only to attract callers denouncing the Japanese as the cause of America's economic malaise, with one enterprising woman suggesting a full trade boycott until "these people" stop sending their criminals abroad. There was the porno magazine cover story, featured in bold headlines: "First came the Japanese televisions, stereos and radios that flooded the American marketplace. Next was the invasion of Japanese-made autos that helped cripple our economy. Now an even greater threat to America has arrived—the Yakuza."

The yakuza do indeed pose a threat to the United States, but this threat hardly merits archaic racist stereotypes bound up in the frustrations of an economic trade war. The problems, of course, are more complex, involving what Mike Sterrett called the institutionalization of the yakuza. It is the prospect that, like other organized crime groups, once entrenched in a host country, the yakuza will be extremely difficult to dislodge. They will have found a home abroad.

There is another, equally compelling reason for the West to be wary of the yakuza, a reason more profound, yet at first perhaps less alarming: organized crime in Japan is extraordinarily politicized. The modern history of the yakuza is intertwined with that of Japan's extreme right wing, a bizarre group of emperor-worshipping activists who were the most virulent force behind that country's rise to domestic fascism and military expansion. Although currently less powerful than in the prewar period, the ultranationalist right still makes waves in Japan. So closely associated with the yakuza are these extremist bands that at times the groups are indistinguishable. There is no near analogy in American society. In some respects it is as if the Ku Klux Klan and the Mafia formed an enduring, politically potent alliance.

Over the years, this often violent coalition of rightists and gangsters has served as a paramilitary force for Japan's Liberal Democratic Party, the LDP, which has exercised an enduring hold over the nation's postwar politics. It is a history that rivals the worst traditions of corruption in America. So rooted in Japanese culture are these practices that at times they defy the very meaning of *corruption* as used in the West. More important, the political workings of the yakuza have over the years influenced critical events in Japan, at one point with the active complicity of U.S. intelligence agencies. Today, their activities continue to bear heavily on the future of America's chief Pacific ally and largest overseas trading partner, influencing key issues that include, foremost, the rearming of Japan.

When Michael Sterrett first investigated Honolulu's Japanese gangsters, he could not have realized how true his intuition would prove: the yakuza are not simply another organized criminal gang. But then, they have always been something more.

PART I

CHAPTER ONE

THE HONORABLE OUTLAWS

ONE MIGHT CALL GORO FUJITA THE BARD OF THE YAKUZA AND HE WOULD NOT object. His business card, ornate even by Japanese standards, introduces the man by asking for forgiveness, explaining in humble terms that he drinks too much but is devoted to his work. He is a short, round fellow whose bushy hair hangs around a face that might belong to either a comedian or a thug, depending on his mood. He is, in fact, a former gangster, a veteran of the Tosei-kai, the largely ethnic Korean gang known for its ruthless control of nightclubs in Tokyo's famous Ginza district. But Goro Fujita no longer patrols the night streets for the "Ginza Police," as they once were called. He is now something of a celebrity among the yakuza, as novelist, historian, and storyteller of Japan's underworld.

Fujita is the proud author of some thirty novels about the yakuza, romantic works that dwell on a particularly Japanese brand of virility, bravery, and fatalism, of noble values that can be traced back to the samurai warriors of feudal Japan. They are books with names like *Big Gambler, Cemetery of Chivalry, Poetry of the Outlaw,* and *I Don't Need My Grave.* He is master of the sword fight scene, interpreter of arcane custom, and archivist of criminal history. He beams while presenting, alongside his many novels, three encyclopedic tomes that comprise the core of his lifework: the first, a massive genealogical dictionary of the complex kinships among the yakuza; the others, two volumes of a treatise on right-wing politics and organized crime in Japan. It is a history, says the author, that dates back over three hundred years.

At his comfortable home on the outskirts of Tokyo, Fujita carries on a rare seminar for special guests on the history of the yakuza. He lovingly pulls out old photos of early bosses, pressed between the pages of a dozen hardbound volumes stored on his fine wooden shelves. His office library bulges with a unique Japanese literary collection—books on swords, guns, martial arts, general history, regional history, war, and the right wing.

Fujita is a man who spins a good yarn, tells long-winded jokes, and can hold even the demanding attention of a yakuza boss. He writes fiction because he doesn't like to use real names. "Too many demands would be placed upon me," he explains. Fujita's characters, nonetheless, manage to convey his profound feelings for the yakuza world, sentiments that have found a welcome audience among the Japanese reading public. His work belongs to a genre of Japanese literature that has long extolled the image of the romantic gangster. The yakuza, in fact, form a central theme of popular culture in Japan, with heroes and anti-heroes enshrined in countless movies, books, ballads, and short stories.

For Fujita and his colleagues, the history of organized crime in Japan is an honorable one, filled with tales of yakuza Robin Hoods coming to the aid of the common people. The heroes of these stories are society's victims who made good, losers who finally won, men who lived the life of the outlaw with dignity. These tales stand at the heart of the yakuza's self-image—and of public perception as well. Yakuza experts challenge the accuracy of these portrayals, as do most scholars of Japanese history, but the feeling persists among Japanese—including many police—that organized crime in their country bears a noble past. To understand this romantic image of the gangster, one must go back nearly four centuries to the country's Middle Ages, the source of countless modern legends that in Japan take the place of the frontier West in American culture—where the sword replaces the six-shooter and the cowboy is a samurai.

Samurai Bandits and Chivalrous Commoners

To the commoners of feudal Japan they were known as *kabuki-mono,* the crazy ones, and as early as 1612 they began attracting the attention of local officials. Like rebels of a more recent era, they wore outlandish costumes and strange haircuts; their behavior was often equally bizarre. At their sides hung remarkably long swords that nearly trailed along the ground as the outlaws swaggered through the streets of old Japan. Terrorizing the defenseless townspeople almost at will, these outlaws were not above using them to practice *tsuji-giri,* a hideous rite in which a samurai would waylay a passerby to test a new blade.

The kabuki-mono comprised the legendary crime gangs of medieval Japan, eccentric samurai warriors known also as the *hatamoto-yakko,* or, loosely, the servants of the shogun. They made heavy use of slang and adopted outrageous names, such as Taisho Jingi-gumi, or the All-Gods Gang. They displayed an unusual loyalty among themselves, swearing to protect one another under any circumstance, even against their own parents.

It was the Tokugawa era, the time of the shogunate. Centuries of civil war had come to a historic end when Ieyasu Tokugawa unified the island country in 1604, thereby becoming the first great shogun. But Japan was not yet stable. Peace in the nation meant that as many as 500,000 samurai were suddenly unemployed, workers whose best skills lay largely in soldiering and the martial arts. Eventually, most samurai joined the growing merchant class, as large villages like Osaka and castle towns like Tokyo and Nagoya were transformed into bustling urban centers. Others found jobs in the expanding civil bureaucracy, or as scholars and philosophers. But not all were success stories. The kabuki-mono—nearly all of them samurai of good standing—found themselves caught within a rigid medieval society about to enter a two-hundred-year period of self-imposed isolation, with few opportunities beyond those offered by street fighting, robbery, and terror.

Such a life was not a new one for the *ronin,* or masterless samurai. In earlier times, many had turned to banditry when their lords were defeated in battle, looting the towns and countryside as they meandered across Japan. Traditionally, these renegade warriors were taken into the armies of the feudal lords then warring over Japan, but now, in the relative peace of Tokugawa society, these new groups of outlaw samurai began to take on a life of their own. (The gangs of roving bandits from this era would later be brought to life in the Japanese movie *Seven Samurai,* which in turn inspired the American Western *The Magnificent Seven.*)

While these criminal servants of the shogun—the hatamoto-yakko— might appear to be the true forebears of the Japanese underworld, today's yakuza identify not with them but with their historic enemies, the *machi-yakko,* or servants of the town. These were bands of young townsmen who, as fear and resentment grew, formed to fend off the increasing attacks by hatamoto-yakko. At times they sported the same odd habits as their opponents, but their leaders were often of different stock—clerks, shopkeepers, innkeepers, artisans. Others were laborers rounded up by local construction bosses, including a good many homeless wanderers and stray samurai. Like the gangs of today, the machi-yakko were adept at gambling and developed a close relationship with their leaders that may well have been a precedent for the tightly organized yakuza.

The townspeople naturally cheered on the machi-yakko, elated to watch fellow commoners stand up to the murderous samurai. Indeed, among the citizens of Edo, as Tokyo was then called, the town servants quickly became folk heroes. It is understandable, then, that the yakuza—who see themselves as honorable outlaws—have chosen to look upon the machi-yakko as their spiritual ancestors. But a direct connection is difficult to make. Kanehiro Hoshino, a criminologist with Japan's Police Science Research Institute, points out that both yakko groups disappeared by the late seventeenth century after repeated crackdowns by an alarmed shogunate. Tokyo's All-

Gods Gang, for example, met its fate in 1686 when officials rounded up three hundred of its members and executed the ringleaders. Although occasionally the gangs no doubt performed honorable acts, they seem largely to have been what one scholar called "disorderly rogues."

Like most Robin Hoods throughout history, the machi-yakko owe their reputation not to deed but to legend, in this case the numerous eighteenth-century plays in which they are invariably portrayed as heroes and champions of the weak. So popular were these dramas that the Japanese theater itself owes much of its early development to the depiction of these marauding bands of eccentrics. They were further heralded in assorted folktales and songs that remain among the most popular of Japan's past. In these stories and plays they are billed as the *otokodate*, or chivalrous commoners. There is the tale, for example, of Ude no Kisaburo, or One-armed Kisaburo, immortalized in a kabuki play. Kisaburo, a skilled swordsman who protects the townspeople, is excommunicated by his fencing teacher after having an affair with a woman. Seeking his teacher's forgiveness, he severs his right arm in an act of remorse and then goes on to battle the thugs of Tokyo.

The most celebrated tale of the machi-yakko is that of Chobei Banzuiin. Born into a ronin family in southern Japan, Chobei journeyed to Tokyo around 1640, where he joined his brother, who was the chief priest of a Buddhist temple. Chobei became a labor broker, recruiting workers to build the roads surrounding Tokyo and to repair the stone walls around the shogun's palace. Using a ploy that would become a yakuza mainstay, Chobei opened a gambling den. The betting not only served to attract workers, but also enabled him to retrieve a portion of the salaries he paid them.

According to the stories and kabuki plays about his life, Chobei became the leader of Tokyo's machi-yakko. The tales are filled with his great deeds—a town girl rescued from assault, the marriage of two lovers once unable to wed because of their different social classes. Whenever thanked by those he helped, he would answer: "We have made it our principle to live with a chivalrous spirit. When put to the sword, we'll lose our lives. That's our fate. I just ask you to pray for the repose of my soul when my turn comes." As his words predicted, he was put to the sword, slain by his archenemy Jurozaemon Mizuno, the leader of Tokyo's hatamoto-yakko. Although the circumstances leading to Chobei's death are uncertain, one kabuki play offers the following finish:

> One day, Mizuno invites Chobei through his messenger to come to his residence and have a drink together in a token of reconciliation. Chobei and his many followers immediately determine that the invitation is a trap. Not listening to his followers, who ask him not to go, Chobei goes to Mizuno's house alone.
>
> Mizuno receives Chobei respectfully at his home, and before long, a ban-

quet begins. At the banquet, one of Mizuno's followers spills sake from a large cup on Chobei's kimono under pretense of a slip of his hand. As planned, another of Mizuno's followers takes Chobei to a bathroom, suggesting he have a quick bath and change his kimono. When Chobei becomes defenseless in the bathroom, four or five samurai, all Mizuno's followers, attack him. But being proud of his physical strength, he defeats them without any difficulty. Holding a spear in his hand, Mizuno himself then appears in the bathroom. Looking into the eyes of Mizuno, Chobei says calmly, "Certainly, I offer my life to you. I'm ready to throw away my life, otherwise I'd never have accepted your invitation and come here alone; I'd have listened to my followers who worried about my life. Whether one lives to be a hundred or dies as a baby depends on his fate. You are a person of sufficient status to take my life because you are a noted hatamoto. . . . I offer my life to you with good grace. I knew I would be killed if I came here; but, if it was rumored that Chobei, who had built up a reputation as a machi-yakko, held his life so dearly, it would be an everlasting disgrace upon my name. You shall have my life for nothing. I have iron nerves, so lance me to the heart without the slightest reluctance!"

Though tough, Mizuno shrinks from these words and hesitates to spear him. His followers urge him. Finally, he makes up his mind and stabs Chobei through the heart with his long spike. The curtain falls with Mizuno's line: "He was too great to be killed."

Another play climaxes with the gallant Chobei being sliced to death "like a carp on a chopping block." Whatever the hero's final fate, his story has made quite an impression on today's yakuza, who claim him as one of their own.

The Yakuza Emerge

The legends and traditions of the machi-yakko were inherited by a later generation of "chivalrous commoners." Among them were Japan's old firemen—gutsy, quick-tempered fellows who usually did construction work but also served as the community's volunteer fire department. Other common heroes included police detectives, leaders of labor gangs, sumo wrestlers, and the members of Japan's eighteenth-century crime syndicates.

These early yakuza would not appear until a hundred years after the death of Chobei Banzuiin, in a society still bound by the feudal laws of the shogun. They were the enterprising members of a medieval underworld who today are widely seen as the true ancestors of the modern yakuza: the *bakuto,* or traditional gamblers, and the *tekiya,* or street peddlers. So distinctive were the habits of the two groups that Japanese police today still often classify yakuza members as either bakuto or tekiya (although the gangs are now diversified into countless rackets). The ranks of both groups were largely filled from the same quarters—the poor, the landless, and the delinquents and misfits found in any large society. Each group, however, stuck closely to its unique area of control to such an extent that different groups could operate within the same small territory without conflict: the bakuto along the busy highways and towns of old Japan, the tekiya amid the nation's growing markets and fairs.

It is to these rustic bands of itinerant traders and roadside gamblers that Goro Fujita traces back yakuza genealogy in his *One Hundred Year History*. Through his oral histories with yakuza elders, research at Japan's modern libraries, and even field trips to the tombstones of ancient yakuza, Fujita claims to be able to link today's godfathers to a criminal lineage extending back to the mid-1700s. The accuracy of the genealogical charts within Fujita's books, however, is less certain than the degree to which they illustrate the preoccupation with history among the varied yakuza clans. Alongside the pictures of great godfathers that adorn the walls of gang headquarters today are family trees that link the group, however precariously, to these noble outlaws of old. What is unusual is that such ancestral connections are invariably made not by blood, but through adoption.

Like the Italian Mafia, the yakuza began organizing in families, with a godfather at the top and new members adopted into the clan as older brothers, younger brothers, and children. The yakuza, however, added to that structure the unique Japanese relationship known as *oyabun-kobun,* or, literally, "father role–child role." The *oyabun* provides advice, protection, and help, and in return receives the unswerving loyalty and service of his *kobun* whenever needed.

In the feudal society of eighteenth-century Japan, the oyabun-kobun system often provided the basis for relations between teacher and apprentice, between lord and vassal, and, in the nascent underworld, between boss and follower. It was a mirror of the traditional Japanese family in which the father held great and final authority, including the power to choose marriage partners and occupations for his children. Within the early yakuza gangs the oyabun-kobun relationship created remarkable strength and cohesion, leading at times to a fanatic devotion to the boss. Today, despite encroaching modernization, it continues to foster a level of loyalty, obedience, and trust among the yakuza unknown within American crime groups except between the closest of blood relatives. Sociologist Hiroaki Iwai, an authority on delinquent groups in Japan, wrote of the devotion to the oyabun: "New kobun will be expected to act as *teppodama* ('bullets') in fights with other gangs, standing in the front line, facing the guns and swords of the other side, risking his life. . . . On occasion he will take the blame and go to prison for a crime committed by his oyabun."

Like other organized crime groups, the early yakuza developed an elaborate ceremony to initiate new recruits into the organization. Within the triad societies of the Chinese underworld, the rites involved the killing of a young rooster, the reciting of thirty-six oaths before an altar, and the drawing of blood from a recruit's fingers. The cutting of a new member's skin, done to symbolize blood relations, was also heavily practiced by the Sicilian Mafia until the 1930s. The old Mafia initiations had religious overtones as well. As paper was burned, representing the immolation of a saint, the recruit swore an oath pledging his honor, loyalty, and blood to the Mafia.

Within the yakuza, bakuto and tekiya began using a formal exchange of sake cups to symbolize the blood connection. These rites, however, have represented not only entry into the gang, but also entry into the oyabun-kobun relationship. The ceremony holds religious significance as well, typically being performed before a shrine devoted to Shinto, the indigenous religion of Japan. The amount of sake in the cups depends upon one's status. If the participants are not father and child, but brother and brother—as in treaties between gang bosses—equal amounts are poured into each cup. If the relationship is one of elder brother and younger brother, the elder brother's cup is filled six-tenths and the younger brother's cup four-tenths. Various other combinations exist, each coming with its own carefully prescribed set of duties within the "family."

Such ceremonies continue today, although usually in abbreviated form, and commemorate not only initiations but promotions, peace treaties, and mergers as well. One ceremony between oyabun and kobun, held in its full formality, was described by sociologist Iwai:

> An auspicious day is chosen, and all members of the organization will attend, with torimochinin or azukarinin ("guarantors") present as intermediaries. Rice, whole fish, and piles of salt are placed in the Shinto shrine alcove, in front of which the oyabun and kobun sit facing each other. The torimochinin arrange the fish ceremonially and fill the drinking-cups with sake, adding fish scales and salt. . . . They then turn solemnly to the kobun and warn him of his future duties: "Having drunk from the oyabun's cup and he from yours, you now owe loyalty to the ikka [family] and devotion to your oyabun. Even should your wife and children starve, even at the cost of your life, your duty is now to the ikka and oyabun," or "From now on you have no other occupation until the day you die. The oyabun is your only parent; follow him through fire and flood."

The oyabun-kobun system reached its peak around the turn of the twentieth century, influencing the structure of political parties, social movements, the military, business and industry, and the underworld. Today it remains a concept with which most Japanese are intimately familiar, and while it continues to carry certain responsibilities, the relationship is generally treated far less seriously than in the past. An oyabun, for example, is now often a senior at work with whom one is especially close—the equivalent, perhaps, of a mentor in the West. It is almost exclusively within the yakuza that the oyabun-kobun system remains unchanged from its past, existing in a world where kobun will kill others or even kill themselves for the sake of the oyabun. An old adage still popular among gang members goes: "If the boss says that a passing crow is white, you must agree." It is this relationship that stands at the heart of the present, and future, of the Japanese underworld.

Tekiya: The Peddlers

There are various theories offered about the origin of the tekiya. Goro Fujita believes they began as nomads, peddling their goods at castle towns and trading centers. Other ideas center around the word *yashi,* an earlier name used for the peddlers. Because *yashi* connotes banditry, tekiya may have begun as ronin outlaws roaming the countryside. The most widely accepted theory, though, is tied to the yashi's patron god Shinno, a Chinese god of agriculture believed to have discovered medicine to help the sick and poor. This account holds that the yashi were groups of medicine peddlers, something akin to the traveling snake-oil salesmen of America's Wild West (the word *shi* can mean medicine and *ya* a merchant or peddler). Over time the name became a catchall for peddlers of various kinds.

Whatever their origins, by the mid-1700s the tekiya had banded together for mutual interest and protection from the perils of Tokugawa Japan. The gangs were able to establish control over the portable booths in market fairs held at temples and shrines. They were men with a well-deserved reputation for shoddy goods and deceptive salesmanship, a tradition that survives today among the nation's thousands of tekiya members. The early peddlers developed a proven repertoire of cheating techniques: they would lie about the quality and origin of a product; act drunk and make a show of selling items cheaply so customers would believe they didn't know what they were doing; or delude the customer with such enterprising tricks as selling miniature trees (*bonsai*) without roots.

The tekiya were organized according to feudal status, with members falling into one of generally five ranks: the boss or oyabun, the underboss, officers, enlisted men, and apprentices. The gang became a sophisticated operation in certain respects. The oyabun's home served as both gang headquarters and training center for new members, who began by living in the boss's home and learning the business. They would later join the enlisted men, who were required to peddle the boss's goods through the countryside. Only after they returned with good results were they admitted as full-status members. All members, however, were bound by a strict organization, a domineering oyabun, and, among most groups, the following "Three Commandments of Tekiya":

Do not touch the wife of another member (a rule established because wives were left alone for long periods while their husbands went peddling).

Do not reveal the secrets of the organization to the police.

Keep strict loyalty to the oyabun-kobun relationship.

The boss controlled not only his kobun, but the allocation of stalls and even the availability of certain goods. He would collect rents and protection money, and pocket the difference between them and the rental payment required by the shrine or temple. It was a kind of extortion that would continue to the present day: tekiya bosses demanding payment from street peddlers for the privilege of opening their stalls. Those who refused would find their goods stolen, their customers driven away, and risk being physically assaulted by gang members anxious to maintain their monopoly over the region. Disagreements between tekiya bosses over territory led to frequent fights. Nevertheless, a good deal of cooperation existed among the gangs, for as the peddlers trekked from fair to fair they inevitably fell under the care of other bosses, who, upon payment, would see to it that the vendors were assigned a favorable place to open their stalls.

Unlike the gamblers, the tekiya by and large did legal work. Indeed, feudal authorities greatly increased the power of tekiya bosses by granting official recognition of their status between the years 1735 and 1740. In order to reduce the widespread fraud among tekiya vendors and to prevent future turf wars, the government appointed a number of oyabun as "supervisors" and allowed them the dignity of "a surname and two swords," symbols of near-samurai status. With such legitimacy, and with the rapid growth of towns over the next century, the gangs began to expand. Some started organizing additional fairs of their own, becoming, in a sense, the "carnival people" of Japan. They put on festivals resembling circuses with colorful sideshows, and numerous tekiya stands selling food, gifts, housewares, and whatever might attract a buyer. Despite their newfound legitimacy, however, the gangs continued to nurture some thoroughly criminal traits. They would take into their vast network wanted criminals and other fugitives; their protection rackets expanded along with their territory; and their frequent brawls with other gangs often turned tekiya meeting places into armed camps.

Although the early tekiya were made up largely of the same types of misfits as their gambling cousins, the bakuto, they also attracted members of Japan's ancestral class of outcasts. These were the *burakumin,* or "people of the hamlet," who comprised a separate caste somewhat similar to the untouchables of India. The burakumin were an arbitrary class, consisting largely of those who worked with dead animals, such as leather workers, or in "unclean" occupations such as undertaking. Discrimination directed against the burakumin was cruel and relentless. They were popularly referred to as *eta* (heavily polluted) or *hinin* (nonhuman). Just as the samurai were able to abuse the commoners, so were the commoners allowed to torment the burakumin.

In his book *Peasants, Rebels, and Outcasts,* historian Mikiso Hane describes the conditions under which the burakumin lived:

> They were restricted in where they could live, quality of housing, mobility in and out of their hamlets, clothing, hairdo and even footwear. . . . In some areas they were required to wear special identification marks, such as a yellow collar. They were banned from the shrines and temples of non-eta communities, and intermarriage with other classes was strictly forbidden.

In relation to the underworld, the system seemed to feed on itself. Under the Tokugawa regime, those who violated laws or customs could be relegated to the status of eta or hinin; some tekiya members, therefore, already were branded as nonhuman. At the same time, many born into burakumin families joined the tekiya gangs, which provided a path out of abject poverty and disgrace. Peddling offered the burakumin one of the few opportunities to leave their birthplace, where they would forever be known as outcasts. It was a significant pool of potential outlaws; by the end of the Tokugawa era in 1867, the burakumin numbered about 400,000 of Japan's 33 million people.

Legal discrimination against the burakumin was officially ended in 1871 by a government decree. However, the abuse and victimization of these people remains to this day, and continues to drive substantial numbers of burakumin into the hands of the yakuza.

Bakuto: The Gamblers

Much as Japan's outcasts helped swell the ranks of the tekiya, the bakuto also had little trouble finding members. The first gambling gangs were in fact recruited by government officials and local bosses who, under the Tokugawa administration, were responsible for a variety of irrigation and construction projects. These efforts required the payment of substantial sums to the workers, money that their employers schemed to get back in much the same way as Chobei Banzuiin a century earlier: by hiring a motley crew of outlaws, laborers, and farmers to gamble with the workers.

The hired gamblers gradually began attracting misfit merchants and artisans, as well as Japanese of higher status, such as samurai and sumo wrestlers. As they organized into disciplined bands, these early gamblers found their niche along the nation's great trunk roads, where their colorful lives formed the basis for countless tales of old Japan. Their contribution, though, would be far greater than enriching Japanese folklore: the bakuto became what Tokyo criminologist Hoshino calls "the kernel of organized crime groups" in Japan. They would give that country's underworld not only its central tradition of gambling but also its customs of finger-cutting and the first use of the word *yakuza.*

The highways of feudal Japan proved a benign environment for the gamblers. As a deterrent to misbehavior in the provinces, the Tokugawa government decreed that all lords visit Tokyo once a year and that their families reside in the city permanently. The main highways thus became the political lifelines of the country, carrying frequent processions of nobles and servants, as well as an almost constant stream of couriers. Spaced at convenient intervals along the road were stopping places where the traveler might find a night's rest and some entertainment, including the chance to wager a coin or two. Japan's most famous route, the Tokaido Highway, was built in 1603, joining Kyoto—the ancient capital and home of the emperor—with Tokyo, seat of the shogun and real power of the Tokugawa government. In all, there were fifty-three of these way stations along the highway; most of these, by the mid–nineteenth century, played host to a local bakuto gang.

It was along the Tokaido and other highways that the gamblers first began using the word *yakuza.* According to the most widely held belief, the term derives from the worst possible score in the card game *hanafuda* (flower cards). Three cards are dealt per player in the game, and the last digit of their total counts as the number of the hand; therefore, with a hand of 20—the worst score—one's total is zero. Among the losing combinations: a sequence of 8-9-3, or in Japanese, *ya-ku-sa.*

The losing combination of ya-ku-sa came to be used widely among the early gambling gangs to denote something useless. It was later applied to the gamblers themselves, to mean they were useless to society, born to lose. For years the word was limited to the bakuto gangs—there are still purists today among the Japanese underworld who insist that the only true yakuza are the traditional gamblers. As the twentieth century progressed, however, the word gradually received wide use by the general public as a name for bakuto, tekiya, and a host of other organized crime groups in Japan.

Like the tekiya, the early bakuto groups developed a set of rules that included strict adherence to secrecy, obedience to the oyabun-kobun system, and a ranking order determining one's status and role within the group. It was a feudal organization with almost total control resting with the oyabun. Promotions were likely to be based on members' performances during gang fights; gambling skills and loyalty to the oyabun also figured greatly. For the lowly kobun, promotion through the ranks could be an arduous task. He would generally be assigned such jobs as polishing dice, cleaning the house of the oyabun, running errands, and baby-sitting.

The gamblers dealt severely with those who broke the gangs' rules. Cowardice, disobedience, and revealing gang secrets were treated not only as acts of betrayal but also as affronts to the reputation and honor of the gang. Certain offenses were particularly taboo, including rape and petty theft. Short of death, the heaviest punishment was expulsion. After banishing the transgressor, the oyabun notified other bakuto gangs that the gambler was no longer welcome in his group; by general agreement, the outcast could not then join a rival band. It is a tradition that survives today. In the event of expulsion, the gang sends a volley of open-faced postcards via regular mail to the various underworld families. The cards comprise a formal notice of expulsion and ask that the gangs reject any association with the former member.

For serious violations not meriting death or expulsion, the bakuto introduced the custom of *yubitsume,* in which the top joint of the little finger is ceremoniously severed. The practice of finger-cutting was not confined to the bakuto. Others in the lower rungs of Tokugawa society later employed it, including the prostitutes of Tokyo's famous Yoshiwara district, who saw it as a mark of devotion to their special lovers. The yakuza, however, used the ritual amputations more practically. Finger-cutting reportedly began as a means of weakening the hand, which meant that the gambler's all-important sword could not be as firmly grasped. Such an act, whether forced or voluntary, succeeded in making the errant kobun more dependent on the protection of his boss.

When amputated in apology, the severed phalanx is wrapped in fine cloth and solemnly handed to the oyabun. The oyabun generally accepts, for great merit has traditionally been accorded this act. Further infractions, however, could mean another amputation at the second joint of the same digit, or at the top joint of another finger. Often yubitsume occurs just prior to expulsion, as a lasting punishment inflicted by the gang.

The practice of finger-cutting spread to the tekiya and other crime groups, and, according to Japanese authorities, has actually increased since feudal times. A 1993 survey by government researchers found that 45 percent of modern yakuza members had severed finger joints, and that 15 percent had performed the act at least twice.

The other great trademark of the yakuza, the tattoo, also won widespread acceptance among the bakuto during Japan's feudal period. The yakuza's tattoo originally was a mark of punishment, used by authorities to ostracize the outlaws from society; criminals generally would be tattooed with one black ring around an arm for each offense. There is, however, a nobler tradition of tattooing in Japan. Its remarkable designs, considered by many to be the world's finest, date back hundreds of years. As early as the third century, a Chinese account of the Japanese noted: "Men both great and small tattoo their faces and work designs upon their bodies." Over the years the patterns grew more complex, blending a striking array of famous gods, folk heroes, animals, and flowers into one fluid portrait. By the late seventeenth century, intricate, full-body designs became popular with the gamblers and with laborers who worked with much of their bodies exposed: porters, stable hands, carpenters, masons. Occasionally, the *geisha* (Japan's professional female entertainers) would indulge, as did the prostitutes of Tokyo and Osaka, who would tattoo the name of a favored client on their arm or inner thigh. The Tokugawa government, which tried periodically to prohibit tattooing, was unable to curb its popularity.

The traditional tattooing process is an agonizing one. Using a tool carved from bone or wood, and tipped with a cluster of tiny needles, the artist punches into the skin with a succession of painful jabs. The thrusting action of the tattooer is particularly stinging to such sensitive parts as the chest and buttocks. The operation, furthermore, is a prolonged one. A complete back tattoo, stretching from the collar of the neck down to the tailbone, can take one hundred hours.

Such extensive tattooing, then, became a test of strength, and the gamblers eagerly adopted the practice to show the world their courage, toughness, and masculinity. It served, at the same time, another, more humble purpose—as a self-inflicted wound that would permanently distinguish the outcasts from the rest of the world. The tattoo marks the yakuza as misfits, forever unable or unwilling to adapt themselves to Japanese society.

As with ritual finger-cutting, the tattooing spread from the bakuto to the tekiya and other Japanese gangs, and the practice became increasingly confined to the underworld. So closely associated with the yakuza is the custom today that saunas and public baths, wanting to protect their clientele from gangsters, hang signs reading "No tattoos allowed." Today an estimated 68 percent of the yakuza bear some tattooing, although many employ modern electric needles, which are faster and less painful. Still, it is a mark of great respect within the underworld to have endured the torture of the traditional method.

The bakuto's contributions to criminal history extend to traditions other than tattoos and finger-cutting. Certain early gangster bands were granted a measure of official sanction and became adept at working with authorities, though less formally than the tekiya. Some oyabun were even deputized. Such agreements with the police often allowed the gangs to consolidate and expand their power. Other gangs, however, viewed cooperation with the police as contrary to the gambler's code of conduct and often attacked the errant bakuto. Nevertheless, these early moves by authorities to recognize, work with, and even co-opt the underworld broke important ground. Similar agreements later formed the basis for political corruption that would reach the highest levels of Japanese government.

Despite official cooperation by some groups, and occasional bloody disputes over territory by others, the early bakuto generally helped one another. Indeed, at times they resembled an underworld mutual aid society. Of particular note was the bakuto's system of "travelers," a custom by which itinerant gamblers would visit the boss of each region on their route, stay for several days, and receive a small amount of money for expenses. The traveler was treated with the great courtesy reserved for an invited guest: according to bakuto etiquette, although host and visitor were strangers, they were in the same profession.

The travelers were among the most colorful figures of the Tokugawa era; even today their outfits are easily recognized by most Japanese through the countless plays and movies about their lives. They wore hats of sedge that almost covered their faces, caped overcoats that flapped in the wind as they walked, straw sandals and gaiters, a strapped pair of bundles slung over their shoulders, and a single sword at their side (as opposed to the two blades worn by samurai).

Ritual and custom pervaded the life of the bakuto, and the travelers were no exception. Upon arrival at the house of the oyabun, the traveler introduced himself, using archaic Japanese, to the kobun answering the door. "I was born in so-and-so place. I am so-and-so of the so-and-so group. I am a humble man, and as we have now made acquaintance, I would like you to support me from today onwards." The traveler then presented a hand towel to the kobun as a gift and, according to etiquette, it would be returned with a small amount of money and the phrase, "Your courtesy is enough appreciation." In exchange for his meals, the traveler would do menial tasks in the oyabun's house, such as cleaning or drawing bath water from the well. The boss, for his part, would treat the traveler as his guest. In the event the traveler was a wanted man—which was often the case—the oyabun would take responsibility for sheltering him.

The Gambler as Hero

The bakuto in general, and the travelers in particular, became the basis for the leading characters in the *matabi-mono* (stories of wandering gamblers), a genre of Japanese literature that has enjoyed great popularity since the early 1900s. Among the authors was Shin Hasegawa, a pulp novelist whose widely read works beginning around 1912 turned the yakuza into popular heroes. His stories depicted the gamblers as faithful and humane people, men whose loneliness and sorrow few outsiders could understand. Like Goro Fujita's novels of seventy years later, Hasegawa's stories portrayed men of questionable backgrounds who fought as hard as they gambled, yet maintained a philosophy of supporting the underdog and never troubling the common folk. Above all, they remained loyal to those who helped them. A virtuous traveler would be willing to sacrifice his life for the oyabun who for one day had opened the gang's home to him.

The aggressive yet compassionate outlaw, useless to mainstream society but willing to stand up for the common man—these are the essential components of the yakuza legend. It is a tradition inherited not only from the machi-yakko but from the samurai as well, and it spread through the feudal underworld.

The yakuza were especially keen on the values embodied in *bushido,* the much-heralded code of the samurai. Like the warriors, they would prove their manliness by the stoic endurance of pain, hunger, or imprisonment. Violent death for the yakuza, as for the samurai, was a poetic, tragic, and honorable fate. But the value system developed by the early yakuza endured because it went far beyond a mere reflection of the samurai's code. At its heart rested the concepts of *giri* and *ninjo,* two terms not easily translated into English. The ideas behind giri and ninjo had a formidable impact on the samurai and continue to exert a powerful influence on Japanese society at large.

Giri loosely means obligation or a strong sense of duty, and is tied up with complex Japanese values involving loyalty, gratitude, and moral debt. In a sense, giri is the social cloth that binds much of Japan together; its observance figures centrally in such matters as the oyabun-kobun system. Still, such explanations fall short of conveying the intricacies implied by the word. Ruth Benedict, in her classic 1946 account of Japanese culture, *The Chrysanthemum and the Sword,* cited the country's old saying that "Giri is hardest to bear." Wrote Benedict, "There is no possible English equivalent and of all the strange categories of moral obligations which anthropologists find in the cultures of the world, it is one of the most curious. It is specifically Japanese." The obligations encompassed by giri range from "gratitude for an old kindness to the duty of revenge."

Ninjo is roughly equivalent to "human feeling" or "emotion." Among its many interpretations is generosity or sympathy toward the weak and disadvantaged, and empathy toward others. It is typically used in conjunction with giri, and the tension created by these two forces—obligation versus compassion—forms a central theme in Japanese literature. By adopting giri-ninjo, the yakuza greatly enhanced their standing in society, showing that, like the best samurai, they could combine compassion and kindness with their martial skills.

Among those who follow the yakuza there is a spirited debate about whether these old values still exist. The oyabun of Japan's great syndicates, cast in their Confucian-like roles as teachers and preservers of tradition, are outspoken on the yakuza's position. In a 1984 interview, Kakuji Inagawa of the Inagawa family, at the time Japan's most respected oyabun, put it this way: "The yakuza are trying to pursue the road of chivalry and patriotism. That's our biggest difference with the American Mafia, it's our sense of giri and ninjo. The yakuza try to take care of all society if possible, even if it takes 1 million yen to help a single person." A ranking boss from the rival Sumiyoshi syndicate agreed: "In the winter we give the sunny half of the street to the common people because we survive on their work. In the summer we yakuza walk on the sunny side, to give them the cool, shaded half. If you look at our actions, you can see our strong commitment to giri-ninjo."

Nowhere do the old values shine brighter than in the tale of Shimizu no Jirocho (Jirocho of Shimizu). This is the story, taught to millions of Japanese children, about the man who is undoubtedly the country's most famous gangster.

Jirocho was the third son of a sailor, born, according to legend, on New Year's Day of 1820 in the thriving seaport of Shimizu. His hometown lay along the great Tokaido Highway, on a stretch between Tokyo and what was then a quiet fishing village called Yokohama. Because of a local superstition that New Year's babies grew up to be either great geniuses or hopeless villains, his father took no chances and gave the boy up for adoption by a wealthy relative. As a young boy, Jirocho was a terror, but eventually he settled down to become a model rice merchant in his adoptive father's business.

Soon his father died, however, and at sixteen Jirocho inherited the business. There he stayed until age twenty, when one day he encountered a wandering monk standing in his doorway. The monk warned him he would die before his twenty-sixth birthday, a prediction Jirocho took to heart. Jirocho, by then bored with his job, considered joining up with the bands of gamblers that flourished in Shimizu and up and down the Tokaido. After a drunken brawl with local hoodlums, he finally left his wife and business, and took to the road for three years as a "traveler." During that time he made a name for himself as an exceptional fighter, mediator, and leader of men.

Upon returning to Shimizu, he set about organizing his own gang, and soon attracted gamblers and would-be gamblers from miles around: there were street toughs, construction workers, ronin; Jirocho put together the classic bakuto gang. According to one account, at his peak he commanded an army of six hundred gamblers and held sway over the heartland of the Tokaido, stretching along eight coastal stations from the Fuji River near Tokyo to the Oi River toward Kyoto. Jirocho's men, in fact, became the law of the land along their stretch of the Tokaido, for the Tokugawa police were often undisciplined and notoriously corrupt. Under Jirocho's able leadership, his men would fight heroic battles against dishonorable gamblers and thieves, and guard the common people against the brutal ways of the samurai and their lords.

Jirocho's heyday spanned the turbulent years of the mid–nineteenth century in Japan. The Tokugawa shogunate was in decline, weakened by assaults from every side: there were powerful nobles and merchants who wanted change and recognition; foreign navies demanding that the country open its doors to the West; repeated uprisings by an oppressed peasantry; and a growing hostility from the imperial court in Kyoto, whose own power over Japan was fast increasing. A mighty movement was gaining strength to install the emperor as actual head of state. (His role heretofore had been largely symbolic.) Among its supporters were those who hoped to keep the nation closed to foreigners, for the shogun had bowed to Commodore Perry's demands in 1854 and was gradually opening Japan's ports to the West. Spouting the slogan "Revere the emperor, expel the barbarians," these traditionalists would inadvertently hasten the end of over two hundred years of isolation, for the emperor would swing Japan's doors open far wider than the shogun ever did.

This was to be the final chapter of the Tokugawa era, the end of Japan's long immersion in feudalism. It was in these confused final days of near civil war that Jirocho, like many yakuza, finally chose sides, lending his support to help enshrine the emperor as the divine ruler of the Japanese islands. The motivation was not ideological: gamblers that they were, the bakuto were merely playing the odds, hoping to win political advantage from the victors.

Jirocho's gamble was a wise one, for all his past crimes were pardoned, and he became a powerful man in his community. The bakuto boss promoted improvements in farming, fishing, and the development of the city of Shimizu. In keeping with the new surge toward modernization, Jirocho started one of Japan's first English schools. To the likely amazement of his old colleagues, he even established a penitentiary. His followers, meanwhile, continued to keep order and run the gambling games in the region.

Jirocho died in 1893 at the age of seventy-three. Thousands today still visit his grave each year, where he lies buried with his followers in a local temple. It is said that at the foot of Mount Fuji there stands still another monument to the old outlaw, a Shinto shrine dedicated to Jirocho, built by farmers who work the land he once reclaimed.

That, more or less, is how Japan's most famous yakuza has been depicted in countless ballads and tales over the years. But not everyone agrees with the legend. Among the dissenters is Japan's prestigious newspaper, the *Asahi Shimbun*, which ran a story in January 1975 entitled "'Robin Hood' of Shimizu Was Nothing but a Thug." According to old administrative documents discovered in a town next to Shimizu, says the story, Jirocho, far from inspiring worship among the people, "was in truth nothing but a gangster who oppressed the farmers." The documents reveal that Jirocho, who was entrusted to rule over the area by the government, remained a gang boss at heart, controlling Shimizu through violence and intimidation. Like most of the world's great outlaws, Jirocho is best remembered through legend, not history.

The Yakuza Modernize

The forces of historical change swirling around Jirocho's life climaxed in 1867, when, bowing to the inevitable, the fifteenth and final shogun of the Tokugawa family resigned and was replaced by the young Emperor Meiji. It was the dawn of the Meiji Restoration, in which all the pent-up commercial and intellectual power of Japan would be released and the Japanese would perform their first economic miracle, breaking the last bonds of feudalism and swiftly transforming their country into an industrial power.

By the turn of the century, Japan had evolved into a complex, rapidly modernizing society populated by some 45 million people. Between 1890 and 1914, the country's total industrial production doubled, while its share of factories more than tripled. Politically, too, the country was fast changing. The Japanese witnessed the birth and maturation of their first parliament and political parties, and the growth of a powerful, autonomous military that would invade China, annex Korea, and in 1905 defeat the Russians in war.

As the country modernized, the yakuza expanded their activities in step with the growing economy. The gangs gained a foothold in organizing casual laborers for construction jobs in the big cities and in recruiting stevedores for the booming business on the docks. Also, with the introduction of the metal wheel, the underworld influenced control of the new carts, called rickshaws, which by 1900 numbered 50,000 in Tokyo alone.

Gambling remained the center of life for the bakuto gangs, although better police control forced them to take their games farther underground into urban hideaways and private haunts. Many bosses started legitimate businesses to act as fronts for the gangs' rackets and began an enduring custom of making payoffs to local police. The tekiya also maintained their traditional livelihood, the street stalls. The peddlers were able to expand their territory more easily, for unlike the gamblers, they worked in a legal trade. Determined police efforts, however, were making it clear to both groups that the all-out open brawls and territorial wars of the past would be far less tolerated in the new state.

The bakuto and tekiya gangs also continued to play politics, and gradually some gangs developed close ties to important officials. These gangs wanted some measure of government sanction, or at least freedom from government harassment, and saw cooperation as the key. On the other side, the government continued to find uses for the organized gangs, as it had since before Jirocho's day.

At first, the use of this muscle was somewhat haphazard, as it had been with Jirocho's men, and ideology had little to do with the association between politician and hit man. It remained as pure opportunism on both sides. There was always a strongly conservative cast to the relationship, but late in the nineteenth century that conservatism began to veer to the right. Japan now began its climb to militarism abroad and its descent into repression at home, for just as the nation began experimenting with democracy, an ominous new force was being born—the ultranationalists.

Patriotic Gangsters

Modern ultranationalism, the force behind Japan's swing to the extreme right, harks back to the 1880s. It was first defined in Kyushu, the southernmost of the four major islands, and at the time a poor fishing and coal mining region. Kyushu was home to a large community of disgruntled ex-samurai, many of whom had taken part in rebellions against the new social order. The discontent of these soldiers was exploited by patriots and politicians critical of the new regime's corruption and disregard of tradition. Particularly affected was the city of Fukuoka, in the corner of the island closest to the Asian mainland. The city developed into a breeding ground for antigovernment thought, and within a few years became the center of a new militarism and patriotism in Japan.

Out of Fukuoka emerged a leader who would forever change the course of both organized crime and politics in Japan, joining those two forces together in a way that would endure to the present day. He was Mitsuru Toyama, born the third son to a family of obscure samurai rank. Information on his early years is difficult to verify. It is said that Toyama spent his childhood in poverty, peddling sweet potatoes on the streets of Fukuoka, and developed into a tough, streetwise teenager who idolized the samurai tradition.

By the time Toyama reached his twenties, his activities turned political. He took part in one of the final samurai uprisings, earning a three-year jail sentence from the Meiji government. Upon his release, the young patriot enlisted in his first nationalist group, the Kyoshisha (Pride and Patriotism Society), and for the first time began to gather a following. Toyama took to the streets and set about organizing the listless toughs of Fukuoka. His men became both a disciplined workforce and a tough fighting force used to keep labor unrest at a minimum in the region's coal mines.

Like others before him, Toyama gained a reputation as a local Robin Hood, handing out money to his followers on the streets of Fukuoka without bothering to count it. He became known as "Emperor of the Slums" and earned the respect of local politicians, who knew and feared his frequent use of violence.

Toyama's rise to national power came with his founding of the Genyosha, or Dark Ocean Society, in 1881. Genyosha, a federation of nationalist societies, would be the forerunner of Japan's modern secret societies and patriotic groups. The articles of its charter were vague: revere the emperor, love and respect the nation, and defend the people's rights. The ambitious Toyama, however, knew exactly what the organization was about—tapping directly into the powerful sentiment among the ex-samurai for expansion abroad and authoritarian rule at home. Even the name Dark Ocean suggested expansion, symbolizing to Toyama and his followers the narrow passage of water separating Japan from Korea and China.

It was Toyama who foresaw and formed, almost single-handedly, a new patriotic social order that would be used as a paramilitary force in Japanese politics. Through a campaign of terror, blackmail, and assassination, the Dark Ocean Society's work would prove highly effective, exerting particular influence over members of the officer corps and the government bureaucracy and playing an instrumental role in sweeping Japan into East Asia and, ultimately, into war with the United States.

Genyosha members worked as bodyguards for government officials, as strong-arm persuaders for local political bosses, and as skilled laborers in legitimate jobs—as plumbers, carpenters, masons—in unions affiliated with the society and its successors. These new yakuza considered themselves at the opposite end of the underworld spectrum from the bakuto and tekiya, as high-class gangsters imbued with the righteousness of Toyama's superpatriotic politics.

The society's agents were sent abroad to China, Korea, and Manchuria as spies. They operated schools where an entire generation of ultranationalists were trained. Through studies in the martial arts, foreign language, and spying techniques, Genyosha graduates formed the basis of a sophisticated intelligence network created by the Japanese prior to World War II.

In Japan, Toyama deployed his men with equal skill. They were used to foment or subdue public unrest, intimidate both political candidates and voters, suppress dissident laborers, and punish anyone of whom their bosses disapproved. The Dark Ocean Society and its ilk were especially useful to mining and manufacturing companies, who employed them not only as strikebreakers but as hired political muscle who helped promote or shatter the careers of would-be politicians.

Toyama and his Dark Ocean followers held a larger agenda, however. Using money gained from their growing rackets, Toyama launched a campaign of terror and assassination aimed at achieving a new social order in Japan. Genyosha activists hurled a bomb into the carriage of Foreign Minister Shigenobu Okuma, who lost a leg to the explosion; stabbed the liberal politician Taisuke Itagaki; and murdered Toshimichi Okubo, perhaps the Meiji era's most brilliant statesman.

The year 1892 saw a new phenomenon in Japan: a national election. Toyama and company greeted it with the first large-scale cooperation between rightists and the underworld. The society, already making deals with conservatives inside the Meiji government, launched a violent campaign in support of like-minded incumbents.

Fearing that his forces might not be adequate, Toyama called on the leader of a gang in nearby Kumamoto, who sent three hundred of his men to Fukuoka as reinforcements. This combined force was joined by the local police, who had been mobilized by none other than the minister of home affairs to assist the gangsters in harassing antigovernment opponents. The result was the bloodiest election in Japanese history, with scores dead and hundreds wounded. Genyosha, for its part, stated openly in its official account that the purpose of the Fukuoka campaign was to uproot all democratic and liberal organizations in the region.

Genyosha's next mission was more ambitious. Toyama, acting on a secret request from the minister of war, was to "start a fire" in Korea, creating a pretext for Japanese troops to move in. In 1895, a squad of Genyosha agents, trained as assassin-spies in the martial arts of the *ninja*, infiltrated the Korean Imperial Palace and murdered the queen. This act, in part, precipitated Japan's invasion of that country. The Japanese would not leave for fifty years.

From then on, ultranationalism became a more or less permanent fixture on the political landscape. The Dark Ocean Society provided the model for hundreds of secret societies reaching into every corner of Japan and, eventually, through much of East Asia as well. They sported such colorful names as the Blood Pledge Corps, the Loyalist Sincerity Group, the Farmers' Death-Defying Corps, and the Association for Heavenly Action. Some groups were supported by wealthy patrons; others financed their work through an array of crimes that today still form the daily bread of yakuza gangs: gambling, prostitution, protection rackets, strikebreaking, blackmail, and control of labor recruiting, entertainment, and street peddling. The secret societies attracted the bosses of local tekiya and bakuto groups and began a process that a hundred years later would continue to blur the distinction between gangsters and rightists in the minds of Japanese.

Initially, the more traditional yakuza groups had no real ideology and seemed to stand at some distance from the Genyosha and its successors. But the similarities among them were very strong. All shared a mystical worldview that worshiped power, resented foreigners and foreign ideas (especially liberalism and socialism), revered a romanticized past, observed Shinto as the core of their belief systems, and deified the emperor as a living Shinto god. Equally important was structure: the groups traditionally organized along rigid oyabun-kobun lines and used similar ceremonies to tighten those ties. Many of the ultranationalist groups, then as now, were often nothing more than gangs of violent thugs whose "patriotic" purpose tended to be as much financial as political.

Ultimately, these social patterns produced virtually identical politics among most rightists and gangsters. Local gang bosses—whether they controlled dockworkers, street stalls, or village politics—realized that the entire basis of their authority was threatened by left-wing attacks on traditional society. With the emergence of a noticeable left and labor movement at the turn of the century, this understandable fear among the oyabun made them easy converts to the new ultranationalism.

Among the groups that the yakuza found appealing was a successor of Genyosha called Kokuryu-kai, or the Amur River Society, founded in 1901 by Toyama's right-hand man, Ryohei Uchida. The name of this secretive group hinted at its purpose: the expansion of Japanese power to the Amur River, the boundary between Manchuria and Russia. The group would become far better known by a different title, however: the characters for the name Kokuryu-kai could also be read as the "Black Dragon Society," a name that caught the fancy of Western journalists.

The ultimate objective of the Black Dragons was no less than the domination and control of all Asia. To the more fanatic visionaries, the society was destined for the calling of Hakko-ichi-u—the Eight Corners of the World under One Roof. The roof, of course, was that of the Emperor of Japan, descended from the Sun God in an unbroken line. The Black Dragon Society became the natural successor to Toyama's Dark Ocean, taking over its followers, its policies, and its goals. Under the patronage and guidance of Toyama, it would push Japan into a victorious war with Russia, commit political assassinations, and do for China what the Dark Ocean activists had done for Korea—help create the conditions for a Japanese invasion. For some thirty years the organization flourished, exhorting the Japanese to wage a holy war against capitalism, bolshevism, democracy, and the West. Through it all, Toyama and Uchida would reign as the Marx and Lenin of the Japanese ultranationalist movement.

The 1920s, the so-called period of Taisho democracy, represented the peak of Japan's prewar liberalism. Despite a political climate plagued by assassination, police repression, and an increasingly renegade military, the country continued to prosper. Universal suffrage was introduced, labor unions grew, and, spurred on by further economic growth, the middle class greatly expanded. But ominously in the background stood Toyama, who had continued to increase in stature. The patriot was courted by leading politicians, and even received money from the imperial family.

Toyama's next underworld achievement—the first national federation of gangsters—occurred in 1919, with the formation of the Dai Nippon Kokusui-kai (Great Japan National Essence Society). This organization of more than 60,000 gangsters, laborers, and ultranationalists was the brainchild of Toyama and Takejiro Tokunami, then minister of home affairs. The new federation fit neatly into the mold set nearly forty years earlier by Toyama's Dark Ocean Society. Its platform spoke vaguely of honoring the emperor, the "spirit of chivalry," and ancient Japanese values. Practically, however, the Kokusui-kai served as a massive strikebreaking force and introduced an unprecedented level of violence into the ultranationalist movement. Headed by Tokunami himself, with Toyama as chief adviser, the organization functioned quite similarly to its Fascist contemporaries in Italy—Mussolini's Black Shirts. The Kokusui-kai operated with the strong support of the Home Ministry, the police, and certain high-ranking military officials. Its numbers were deployed not only against strikers but also against any target deemed subversive by Toyama and friends. Among the group's many actions was an attack on the 28,000 men who had walked out in the great 1920 Yawata Iron Works strike. The Kokusui-kai gangs worked side by side with police, military gendarmes, firemen, veterans, and muscle men of other ultranationalist groups to break the strike.

Tokunami's Kokusui-kai evolved into the paramilitary arm of the Seiyu-kai, one of the two dominant political parties of the day. By the end of the decade Seiyu-kai's principal opposition, the Minseito Party, had organized its own gangster force: the Yamato Minro-kai, filled with yakuza also drawn largely from construction gangs. So integrated into their respective political parties did these gangs become that more than a few bosses ran successfully for national office. Their presence in the Diet, Japan's parliament, was but another sign that all did not bode well for Japan's future.

By the 1930s, rightist groups had proliferated tremendously. The country was destabilized as moderate politicians fell victim to assassination or withdrew completely from public life. From 1930 until the end of the war, Japanese police would officially record a total of twenty-nine rightist "incidents." Among them were attempted coups d'etat by military officers and ultranationalists and repeated attacks on leading politicians and industrialists—including the assassinations of two prime ministers and two finance ministers.

Toyama's star continued to rise through the tumultuous 1930s as the practice of democracy nearly vanished in Japan. The aging leader, now possessing great prestige and wealth, arranged cabinets as well as assassinations. He was invited to dinners at the imperial palace and at ultranationalist societies. He addressed key patriotic gatherings, at which he would invariably be asked to lead the three cheers for the emperor. Symbolic of Toyama's new power was his introduction to the Japanese of their new prime minister, Prince Konoe, before a crowd of 18,000 in 1937. With many of Toyama's allies now in power, the country slid deeper into a decade of repression known to many Japanese as Kuroi Tanima, the Dark Valley. As the Nazis seized control in Germany and the Fascists rose to power in Italy, a ruthless militarism erupted in Japan. Every sector of society was organized for political regimentation and indoctrination. The era was at hand of the Greater East Asia Co-Prosperity Sphere, in which Japanese might would sweep over the Western colonies of the Orient. To the aging Toyama and his fellow ultranationalists, their dream was coming true.

The varied yakuza and strong-arm gangs continued to contribute men and muscle to the patriotic cause. Yakuza groups cooperated with the militarists by going to occupied Manchuria or China to participate in "land development" programs. For Japan's gangs, the exploitation of resource-rich Manchuria meant open season on the Chinese. It was, as one scholar put it, "the heyday of the yakuza, a return to the good old days of feudalism." Among the vocations attractive to the gangs was assisting the government's Opium Monopoly Bureau in its dual job of making money and weakening public resistance by fostering drug addiction. It was a page taken from British colonial handbooks of a century earlier, and the Japanese employed it skillfully. The military estimated its revenue from Japan's narcotization policy in China at $300 million a year. (Note: All yen-to-dollar conversions are given in rates current at the time.) When not spent on graft and corruption, the money went into the industrial development of the occupied lands.

Outside their political pursuits, the more traditional yakuza gangs were busy expanding their financial base at home. Military expansion brought more money into Japan, and the yakuza were well situated to grab a large share of the booty. Like Tokunami's labor bosses and their construction gangs, the yakuza organized the laborers along Japan's waterfronts. In the port city of Kobe, for instance, yakuza gangs gathered up groups of otherwise unemployable men and sold their labor cheaply to longshore firms in need of docile, unskilled workers. So lucrative was this racket that various oyabun fought over contracts and territories. The Kobe group that emerged victorious was the Yamaguchi-gumi, under the able leadership of Kazuo Taoka. Over the next quarter-century, he would transform his waterfront gang into the largest yakuza syndicate in Japan, reaching a peak of more than 13,000 members in thirty-six of Japan's forty-seven prefectures. (A prefecture is roughly equivalent to a U.S. state.) The infamous Yamaguchi syndicate would become a household word in Japan, and Taoka the undisputed godfather of Japanese crime.

While Taoka was organizing the docks and laying the ground for the future of the yakuza, a remarkably similar process was occurring in the United States. The Lucky Luciano mob had taken over much of the Manhattan and Brooklyn waterfronts, acting through "Tough" Tony Anastasia and Joe "Socks" Lanza, and work on the docks functioned in an almost oyabun-kobun fashion. So tightly did the mob control the waterfront that during the war, the Office of Naval Intelligence felt it prudent to make a deal with Luciano, then in a New York prison, to make sure the docks remained free of saboteurs.

In other respects, though, the American mob had outstripped its Japanese counterparts. Despite the widespread integration of gangsters into the ultranationalist movement, city or neighborhood gangs were still the rule in Japan. American gangs, meanwhile, flush with the huge cash reserves generated by liquor sales during Prohibition, were growing into a sophisticated national syndicate. Equally important, U.S. gangsters were learning how to invest their newfound capital and manage it according to modern corporate practice. These historic changes came about when Luciano joined forces with the gangsters under Meyer Lansky and Benjamin "Bugsy" Siegel and, for the first time, organized crime moved beyond strictly ethnic groupings. These New York gangsters combined with Cleveland's Mayfield Road Gang, Detroit's Purple Gang, the Chicago mob, and others to apportion large sections of the country for specific rackets, such as gambling, drugs, and labor racketeering. By the 1930s, the mob was so strong a force that it had influence in presidential elections.

The bombing of Pearl Harbor, however, changed life radically for both the U.S. and Japanese Mafias. With the advent of war with the West, the Japanese government's love affair with the far right and the yakuza came to an abrupt end. The wartime government, having moved as far to the right as big business and the army wished, no longer needed the rightists or gangsters as an independent force. Upper-echelon rightists either worked for the government or were imprisoned. Likewise, yakuza either put on a uniform or saw the war from the inside of a cell. Among those spending time in prison was the waterfront boss Kazuo Taoka, who passed his time reading books about Toyama and the Dark Ocean Society.

Mitsuru Toyama finally died in 1944 at the age of eighty-nine, but not before seeing his beloved Japan conquer much of Asia and the Pacific. His influence would live on through innumerable gangster-rightist organizations, and two generations later his portrait adorns the walls of nearly all rightist offices and of many yakuza ones as well. Unfortunately, this grand old man of the Japanese right did not see the final result of his long years of militancy, as the war thrust Japan to both the height and depth of its political power, all within four years. By August 1945, the Americans had dropped the atom bomb and the Soviets had invaded Manchuria, and within a few days the Japanese had finally had enough.

PART II

THE KODAMA YEARS

CHAPTER TWO

OCCUPIED JAPAN

THE RANKING MILITARY OFFICERS OF THE U.S. OCCUPATION OFTEN GAVE press conferences, but this one was a bit out of the ordinary. It was not held in the General Headquarters building, and it was unusually combative in tone. The date was September 19, 1947, and the place was Tokyo.

The principal speaker told the press that he had just finished addressing a meeting of Japanese public procurators—the equivalent of district attorneys—and he was now taking his case to the people. The speaker was Colonel Charles L. Kades, a former New York attorney, the assistant chief of Government Section, and one of the most influential men in the Occupation hierarchy. Colonel Kades told the journalists that he had warned the procurators of a web of criminal gangs and influential gangsters throughout Japan that formed "a massive underground network extending from the smallest rural village to the highest echelons of the national government."

The statement may have been a revelation to the American journalists present, but it was hardly a surprise to the Japanese. This was a part of their culture that most citizens, and all journalists, knew at least by reputation.

Kades, a genial yet forceful New Dealer who had been the principal architect of the new Japanese constitution, concluded to the press, "This clannish and clandestine combination of bosses, hoodlums, and racketeers is the greatest threat to American democratic aims in Japan." At the time, Kades was only dimly aware that this same combination had been a threat to democratic aims of the Japanese people for the past fifty years. The American press found the story titillating. The Hearst papers began grinding out breathless crime stories that sounded very close to wartime propaganda. There was an "invisible government" in Japan. The gangs were a threat to the Occupation forces. They would bring back militarism and ultranationalism. In other words, more yellow peril. Exaggerated and alarmist as these articles were, they were also naively prescient. The mobs would indeed help steer Japan backward and to the right, but not by attacking the Occupation directly. On the contrary, like other Japanese, gangsters knew who was in charge and wanted to form alliances with the people in power. In fact, Kades himself was approached by a gang leader and asked if he needed anyone beaten up.

Occupation officials decided to look into the threat. Investigations, some of which had been begun prior to Kades's announcement, yielded piles of evidence attesting to the power of the gangs. Occupation offices poured forth a stream of press releases and fact packets. In November 1947, the *Christian Science Monitor* devoted a full page to the topic, in which reporter Gordon Walker considered the prospects for a concerted campaign against organized crime in Japan. "If these and other measures are [not] effective in breaking down the labyrinth of undercover controls and influences now operating behind the scenes," wrote Walker, ". . . many occupation authorities frankly admit the long-term prospects for a truly free Japan are endangered."

The reaction of the Japanese officials was a loud, dull thud. The procurators made a few cases—if the Occupation police led them by the hand. But the political hierarchy tied the hands of the procurators and ignored the issue publicly. Prime Minister Katayama simply denied the existence of underground organizations, much as J. Edgar Hoover was then denying that any Mafia functioned in the United States. By the beginning of 1948, the gangs began to disappear from the newspapers. The campaign against the underworld diminished in intensity, and soon it was dead.

Paradoxically, while the Occupation's Government Section was fulminating about the yakuza and the press was drawing some trenchant conclusions about the peril posed by the gangs, other forces in the Occupation were aiding the yakuza. For one thing, American policies in Japan—particularly in regard to food rationing—helped perpetuate the black market, which brought many gangs wealth and power. Also, the complete disarming of the civil police allowed the gangs to run free. But most disturbing is the fact that some Occupation officials actively aided the gangs, encouraged them, and even paid their leaders.

Japan in Ruins

Officially, the U.S. Occupation of Japan began on September 2, 1945, with the signing of the surrender aboard the USS *Missouri* in Tokyo Bay. On September 8, General Douglas MacArthur flew from Okinawa and arrived at Atsugi Air Base, which had been rebuilt for his coming in four days. He drove solemnly through the charred streets of Tokyo to the American embassy. There, he raised the American flag and directed the Eighth Army to occupy and administer the defeated nation.

The widespread devastation wreaked on Japan was staggering. Virtually every major city except historic Kyoto had been severely damaged by high explosives, firebombs, or nuclear weapons. The military of Japan was in disarray, its soldiers disgraced and hungry. Over 4 million remained in East Asia, outside of Japan. The civilian population was suffering, uncertain, stunned. Never before had an enemy conquered the home islands. In the city of Tokyo, 1 million out of 1.65 million buildings had been demolished, mostly by the 1945 fire raids. Nationwide, one-quarter of the wealth, one-third of the manufacturing machinery, four-fifths of the shipping, one-fifth of the vehicles had been destroyed.

But there was a great deal left. American industrialist Edwin Pauley, in surveying the damage for the Occupation, found that "in spite of extensive destruction, especially in the closing phases of the war, Japan retains more industrial capacity than she needs or has ever used for her civilian economy." This was a fact not lost on either the Americans or the neighboring Soviets. While the Western European allies scrambled to regain their lost Asian colonies, America had plans for Japan itself.

It was clear from the beginning that the running of Japan was going to be an American show. In theory, the supreme power over the defeated Axis combatant lay in the Allied Council for Japan, a group consisting of the foreign ministers of the U.S., the USSR, China, and three Commonwealth countries (Britain, Australia, and New Zealand). It was supplemented by the thirteen-member Far Eastern Commission. Neither organization accomplished much more than the maintenance of offices in Tokyo. The real seat of government was the office of the Supreme Commander for the Allied Powers (SCAP), General Douglas MacArthur, who assumed the post on August 15, 1945.

MacArthur's mission was simple in concept: remake Japan. As summarized by Justin Williams in *Japan's Political Revolution under MacArthur,* SCAP had to accomplish the

> quick demobilization of Japan's military forces, total destruction of her war equipment, complete closure of her war factories, arraignment of Gen. Tojo Hideki and other wartime leaders, arrest and trial of hundreds of war criminals, institution of a far-reaching purge in all walks of Japanese life, abolition of secret societies and the thought-control police, removal of all restrictions on civil liberties, release of Japanese political prisoners, the outlawing of a state-supported Shinto religion, the large-scale shake-up of the Japanese school system, free discussion of the Emperor system, cleanup of the Japanese press, breakup of the large industrial and banking combinations, sale of large landholdings to Japanese peasants, legalization of labor unions and encour-

agement of collective bargaining, enfranchisement of women, liberalization of the election law, adoption of a democratic constitution and a general election of members to the lower house of the Diet (Parliament).

The tools MacArthur used were orders, called SCAPINS, which dropped from his office at the Dai Ichi Building as if bearing revealed truths. To interpret these truths to the Japanese, some 6,000 civilians, including a host of Japanese American translators, supplemented the U.S. military, which numbered 200,000 in early 1946.

SCAP was an American bureaucracy and had the usual political divisions and cliques, which the Japanese learned to exploit for their own ends. Above it all, MacArthur reigned serenely, a latter-day American shogun. Just below him, General Courtney Whitney headed Government Section. A successful Manila lawyer, Whitney felt that implementing the Post Surrender Directive, the comprehensive plan for the Occupation, meant inhibiting Japan's war-making desires and capabilities. This, in turn, meant strengthening the Japanese left—unions, liberals, socialists, and Communists. Whitney was opposed by General Charles A. Willoughby, head of intelligence, or G-2. Willoughby feared the Japanese left, Chinese and Soviet Communists, and American liberals. He used G-2 to give aid, comfort, money, and position to precisely those Japanese whom Whitney and Kades sought to remove from public life—the ultranationalist right.

Whitney and Willoughby were, in a sense, merely actors in a larger drama. Through much of the war, the New Dealers in the Roosevelt administration were lobbying for elimination of the emperor and a general suppression of Japanese nationalism when the war ended. On the other side were American conservative business interests, who feared a leftist Japan and lobbied to keep the socioeconomic structure more or less intact. SCAP was generally effective in running the defeated and destitute Japan. It was, by and large, a humane and generous way to treat a vanquished enemy. It is much more doubtful whether the Occupation achieved its other aim— cleaning up Japanese politics. Japanese institutions, including corrupt ones, proved far more hardy than anyone had expected. Some undesirable elements, such as the yakuza, seemed not only to survive but to flourish, even in the dismal wreckage of the bombed-out cities.

The first year of the Occupation was a very grim one for most Japanese. Ten yen was a typical day's salary for a working Japanese, enough to buy a dozen sardines or one small orange. The Americans saw no need to provide more than a bare minimum of food while shortages plagued their wartime allies. With the demobilization of Japan's huge army, and industry at a standstill, there were plenty of people eager to deal in black market rice and other goods. There was money to be made this way. It gave rise to a host of nouveaux riches, called the New Yen class.

Another new class arose in the Occupation years: the newly liberated Asian minorities living in Japan, the so-called *sangokujin*. Literally "people of three countries," the sangokujin were Chinese, Taiwanese, and Koreans who had been brought into Japan to replace the many workers who had been drafted into the army. Working in what were often conditions of virtual slavery, the sangokujin served as forced labor in factories and various unskilled jobs. An estimated 2.6 million Koreans and 50,000 Chinese entered wartime Japan, and eventually some 2 million were repatriated. The others stayed behind to try their luck under the American administration.

After the surrender, the rage of the minorities—a rage built up from years of prejudice and exploitation—exploded into vicious attacks on Japanese citizens. Those sangokujin who remained in Japan, still excluded as they were from the economic mainstream, built up a flourishing business controlling many of the nation's major black markets. Initially, they had a leg up on the native Japanese black marketeers. The occupiers distrusted the Japanese and favored other nationals; the sangokujin became aides and informers to U.S. officials. At the same time, SCAP literally disarmed the civil police, as swords were replaced with night sticks. In addition, SCAP purged the upper echelons of the police force. Some had been members of the feared Tokko, or "Thought Police," while others had connections to the ultranationalist right. Lacking effective leadership, the Japanese police became too confused or timorous to act against the sangokujin.

Into this breach strode the yakuza. It is difficult to say whether the yakuza were at the time more outraged by the sangokujin attacks on Japanese or by the usurpation of lucrative black market space by the "foreigners." In either case, yakuza groups openly clashed with the sangokujin, often under the eyes of the beleaguered police.

In Kobe, a group of some three hundred sangokujin invaded a police station and held hostages as a show of force. According to Yamaguchi-gumi boss Kazuo Taoka, the mayor of Kobe approached the yakuza leader for help. Taoka and his allies ambushed the sangokujin at the police station, stampeding them with swords, guns, and grenades. The yakuza's reward was twofold: the hated sangokujin were undercut, and the police owed the yakuza a long-term debt of giri.

In Tokyo, the sangokujin were strong enough to parade in front of the emperor's palace. They had also managed to take over the rackets along the Ginza, where they clashed with furious yakuza gangs. Another pitched battle took place in the summer of 1946 in a nearby section known as Shimbashi. In the bombed-out area near the train station, a black market had been established, with a group of Taiwanese taking control of the street stalls.

Goro Fujita tells the tale of how tekiya gangsters fought back with a machine gun salvaged from a crippled fighter plane. The peddlers crept to the top of a nearby elementary school, mounted the gun, and began firing volleys at the sangokujin, forcing them to scatter, leaving behind their new businesses in the Shimbashi market. Fujita and other champions of the yakuza would consider the fight over Shimbashi, like the Kobe police station fracas, a major battle of a great patriotic stand. Among many older Japanese today, the battles are fondly remembered, with the yakuza cast as embattled heroes saving a prostrate Japan from evil foreigners. It was, once again, the yakuza as champion of the common people. These stories would be retold until, like a tattered news clip, they were blurred and indistinct.

Although American military police were aware of the "Korean problem" and the armed clashes, they did not really understand the nature of the conflicts. Public Safety Division police investigator Harry Shupak changed all that when he arrived in Shimbashi in late July 1946.

Shupak found that Giichi Matsuda, boss of a local gang battling the sangokujin, had been shot by one of his own men, apparently in an abortive coup attempt. Matsuda's wife, Yoshiko, then took over the day-to-day operation of the Kanto Matsuzakaya Matsuda-gumi, as the gang was formally known. On August 26, she was called before the Metropolitan Police Board for questioning and provided Shupak and his PSD associates with their first explanation of the way things actually worked in Tokyo. She freely and proudly described the workings of what the Americans began to call the oyabun-kobun system.

According to Mrs. Matsuda, Giichi had organized the gang in 1945 when it became evident that the outdoor market business was, in her words, "very booming." The gang established itself after driving out the other thugs. As stalls rapidly increased in number, Matsuda installed his kobun in the marketplace and, in cooperation with the ward office and the police, formed all the stalls into the open-air stall market, or black market.

Matsuda, in the time-honored tekiya fashion, ordered his lieutenants to charge the stall operators for their licenses and to bill them monthly for leases, cleaning, and electricity. The Matsuda-gumi also kept the competition away—until the sangokujin decided to make a stand. Giichi Matsuda had gotten his feet wet in the coming yakuza wave and was already riding the crest when he was assassinated. The tekiya business was very booming, indeed.

Black Market Underworld

Although the Occupation police could not see it easily, a new type of oyabun-kobun group was forming, one that would be a model for most of the yakuza groups soon to follow. This was the *gurentai,* a far more ruthless form of yakuza than the traditional gamblers and peddlers. The Occupation had, by sweeping away the top layer of control in government and business, left a power vacuum. The results were described in Gordon Walker's 1947 *Christian Science Monitor* story: "Into this vacuum has sprung a degenerate 'boss' system reminiscent of the Capone gangster days. Largest and strongest of these organized gangs are the so-called Gurentai, or armed hooligan mobs, which have sprung up like mushrooms all over Japan. Drawing upon demobilized young men without jobs, repatriates without incomes, and capitalizing upon the lowered moral standards resulting from military defeat, the gangs operate through the use of threat, extortion, and violence."

One of the most visible gurentai had been the subject of a Counter Intelligence Corps (CIC) investigation as early as February 1946: Akira Ando. Although Ando was convicted by a military court of possessing black market items, he continued to receive money, work, and friendship from many high-ranking Occupation officials. Apparently, many Americans needed him, as the Japanese government had once needed him. In 1941, for instance, the Tokyo Metropolitan Police named him "Guardian of Korean Laborers and Protector of Korean Juveniles." This seemingly benevolent title was an acknowledgment that Ando controlled Korean labor—a valuable commodity in labor-short wartime Japan. With this workforce, Ando's outfit, the Dai-An Construction Company, built infrastructure and moved factories for the government after the air raids began.

When Japan surrendered, Ando was commissioned by the Americans for construction work. In 1945 he spruced up Atsugi Air Base in preparation for MacArthur's landing. That same year, Ando received additional contracts and, while millions of Japanese barely survived on less than a thousand calories a day, he made a tidy multi-million-dollar profit.

Ando was something of a prototype of the modern yakuza leader. Born in 1901, he was forty-four years old at the war's end. He headed the Ando-gumi, a cross between a gurentai gang and a construction company, and was on close terms with the black market oyabun in the major cities. Equally important, he was on more than speaking terms with Prince Takamatsu, the emperor's brother, as well as with wartime politicians of national stature.

Favors did not, of course, come free; Ando had to reciprocate. Japanese politicians who wanted to ensure the position of the emperor system used Ando to help in lobbying the American brass. Ando ran a string of eighteen clubs—expensive whorehouses, actually. The most famous was the Dai-An, which was closed by SCAP and reopened under another name, the Waka-tombo. At his Ginza clubs, Ando's frequent guests included a handful of the highest-ranking officials of the Eighth Army.

It is doubtful that Ando alone swung MacArthur to a pro-emperor position, but his work didn't hurt. Ando's motivation, one that would be heard ad nauseam, was simple. "I shall fight communism as long as I live," he explained. "I stand for democracy and the preservation of the imperial system."

Although Ando's blend of hustle and graft played very well as an Occupation tactic, Ando himself disappeared into obscurity in the mid-1950s. And, although he may have been the most successful gang boss of the Occupation, he certainly wasn't the most famous. That honor probably goes to Kinosuke Ozu, the tekiya boss of Tokyo. Ozu was actually oyabun of just one section of Tokyo, Shinjuku, but like Al Capone, who officially ran only the West Side of Chicago, Ozu's power and fame went much further. In fact, in October 1947, *Saturday Evening Post* reporter Darrell Berrigan profiled Ozu in a story entitled "Tokyo's Own Al Capone." Ozu was a garden-variety thug until the end of the war. He then capitalized on the death of Giichi Matsuda, taking over the Shimbashi market and other neighborhoods. Ozu amassed considerable money and power, but like so many gangsters, he wanted respectability as well. His base remained in the tekiya groups, where he controlled hundreds—even thousands—of street peddlers; he also established control over the various bakuto and gurentai gangs operating in Tokyo's Shinjuku district. With this base, he forced his way onto the Tokyo Chamber of Commerce, which he proceeded to terrorize for his own uses.

Ozu cowed the Chamber of Commerce, but he failed to do the same to the people of Shinjuku. He ran for the Diet seat from that district in 1947, and lost. His opponent was Sanzo Nozaka, the popular Communist leader. Ozu promised during the election to donate most of his millions to the poor, but somehow his brand of socialism was less appealing than Nozaka's. Ozu, however, did get 12,000 votes.

Most of the time, the links between the mob and politicians were too strong and too obvious for anyone to ignore entirely. Yet as late as 1950, some Occupation personnel were still marveling over these links. That year, the Office of the Political Advisor (POLAD), the State Department's provisional office under SCAP, cabled Washington concerning gang activities in the Tokyo area. The telegram stated that a well-organized band of gangsters, headed by Masajiro Tsuruoka and Kakuji Inagawa and supported by unidentified high-level rightist politicians, had been operating on a large scale throughout the Tokyo–Yokohama Shizuoka area since the end of the war. Exactly why Tsuruoka and Inagawa could claim this patronage becomes clear later in the cable. Apparently, the gang had collected some 50,000 yen for building construction, repair of streets and roads, and other work. With rebuilding of cities moving ahead rapidly, gangs with this sort of muscle could make a lot of yen. And this was just one gang.

This was not a case of simple extortion. Construction companies themselves were traditionally so similar to gangs as to be often indistinguishable. Both groups employed the same word, *gumi* (gang or association), to describe their organizations. The construction companies, furthermore, often exerted political influence in their own right. In the northern island of Hokkaido, for instance, a gumi boss and public works builder, Chiizake Usaburo, gave money to the Liberal Party, ordered his newspaper to support the Communists, and ran himself as an independent, all in one Diet election. Usaburo's influence would be felt no matter who won, and he would most likely continue to draw lucrative public works contracts.

There were, of course, times when politicians didn't want to get into bed with the gangs, and many times when businesses didn't want to make payoffs. Often, such refusals brought fires in the night, or brutal attacks. So entrenched and widespread were these practices that SCAP's order that "all the people of Japan must be urged to stop paying tribute to bosses and gangsters" was futile. SCAP, furthermore, was hardly taking steps to remedy the situation. Indeed, between 1945 and 1950, the Occupation failed miserably to protect the Japanese people from the gangs. Even the Eighth Army did not stop the sangokujin, and in all, little was ultimately done about the power of the gurentai. Furthermore, American GIs fed the black markets with an endless supply of goods. Nevertheless, for a brief period, SCAP did make an effort to combat the gangs.

In September 1947, SCAP's Controls Coordinating Committee established the Oyabun-Kobun Subcommittee, composed of representatives from fourteen major and minor SCAP staff sections. Although established primarily to look into criminal activity, the subcommittee found itself exploring the larger structure of Japanese society. Oyabun-kobun was, as pointed out, a structure that included many legitimate relationships, such as owner-manager, editor-reporter, and others. SCAP was surprised. The subcommittee issued a full report on the oyabun-kobun within two weeks, perhaps a peacetime bureaucratic record. Some of the findings were startling.

According to the report, of the 14-million-person labor force in Japan, 3 million were part of the oyabun-kobun system. Two-thirds of these were construction gangs, and the rest mainly casual labor. However, it was discovered that a 20,000-man workforce was kept confined in the Hokkaido coal mines under terms that hovered between indentured servitude and slavery. A Tokyo newspaper concluded that workers were held in virtual slavery and would be freed when their contracts ran out. The subcommittee also found that the oyabun were engaged in anti-union activity, controlling the black market rice and using it as an economic weapon to force new kobun to join and remain outside of any labor union.

A related report by the Public Safety Division analyzed the three major oyabun-kobun groups—bakuto, tekiya, and gurentai—observing that "political pressure often prevented effective action on the part of the police." In summation, the analysis concluded that the oyabun-kobun system "extends into politics, controls the price of everyday commodities, controls the flow of goods through regular channels, and performs local government functions in the issuance of licenses and the collection of taxes. In addition to these functions the Gurentai terrorize a large portion of the population of the large cities who are engaged in the restaurant business and other public amusement enterprises."

The subcommittee found that the gurentai groups had grown more than anyone had anticipated. The report of the Public Safety Division calculated that the centers of gurentai strength were Tokyo, with 7,400 kobun in the employ of 181 oyabun, and Kobe, with 6,400 kobun working beneath 82 oyabun. Living was good for the gurentai, said the report, with shakedowns of small and medium-sized businesses bringing in a large and constant income. "The average take seems to be about 5,000 to 10,000 yen for each establishment," noted the PSD report, enough to make rich men out of those living on the criminal fringe.

The tekiya did not slip by uncounted. Said the PSD, the tekiya "grew to amazing proportions, controlling 88 percent of the 45,000 stalls in Tokyo and having partial interest in the remaining 12 percent." Known as the Street-Stall Tradesmen's Cooperative Union (Roten Dogyo Kumiai), it comprised at the time 200 bosses, 4,000 followers, and 22,557 lesser followers under the leadership of Kinosuke Ozu, "a ruffian of the lowest type." The reports were reasonably accurate and presented a picture of crime out of control. Kades's efforts to publicize the problem, though, were repeatedly thwarted. When the reports were taken to the Dai Ichi building for MacArthur's perusal, they never got past his aides. Frequent weekly and monthly reports also died in the antechambers.

It soon became clear that the United States high command had no real desire to root out organized crime, despite the efforts of men like Kades and a number of Government Section officials. It wasn't just the Japanese police who were constrained; the problem simply wasn't a priority for American MPs. Although the alarm sounded that the yakuza were working hand-in-glove with remnants of ultra-rightist groups—groups that were illegal under the Occupation—MacArthur apparently didn't want to be bothered. Inertia and a desire to look good were two reasons to avoid the yakuza problem, but there were far more disturbing reasons.

Basically, elements in the Occupation were finding it expedient to go easy on the right side of the Japanese political spectrum. Among the components of the right were the yakuza gangs, many of which were tied to conservative politicians ranging from right-centrists to closet ultranationalists. The gangs were almost always thoroughgoing anti-Communists, and this, for some SCAP officials, was good enough. The fact that they made life miserable for a sizable section of the Japanese public was merely an unfortunate side effect.

But why? The extreme right had just plunged the Pacific Basin into its most destructive war ever, and the Americans were determined to make Japan pay in one way or another for that war. How policy changed, and how the right and its yakuza allies found the climate improving over the course of the Occupation, is a story that begins not in Tokyo but in Washington.

SCAP Changes Course

Long before the Occupation began, a critical diplomatic struggle broke out in State Department circles over the administration of Japan and the rest of East Asia after the war was won. Basically, there were two distinct factions: the so-called China Crowd, left of center and disciples of *Amerasia* magazine; and the Japan Crowd, centering around associates of the former American ambassador to Japan, Joseph Clark Grew.

Simply put, the China Crowd wanted China, and a China under Mao at that, as the centerpiece of American foreign policy in East Asia. Mao's opponent, Chiang Kai-shek, had through the years generated great antipathy and distrust among American liberals because of his corruption and indifferent war effort against the Japanese. With Mao's China as a U.S. ally, reasoned these strategists, Japan's future was that of a neutral country. Japan would be reduced to a nonmilitary power, shorn of its emperor and purged of its bellicose right wing. The nation, if it behaved itself, would be allowed to become the Switzerland of East Asia.

The Japan Crowd, on the other hand, wanted Japan's military power to be reduced and realigned, not eliminated. They wanted the economic structure to be left largely as it was before the war. Japan would be the keystone of America's Asian interests, and Japan would provide a line of defense against the Soviet Union, clearly a rival for the riches of northeast Asia. Japan could also partially counter the threat posed by a Communist China, if it came to that.

The appointment of MacArthur as administrator of Japan initially delighted the Japan Crowd. MacArthur—Republican, anti-Communist, scourge of the Bonus marchers—was an ideal conservative. But they were quickly disappointed, for two reasons. One, MacArthur had suffered military defeats and personal humiliations at the hands of an ultranationalist Japan. Two, MacArthur and his staff simply disliked the Japan Crowd's old-boy network and generally disregarded their advice. As a result, MacArthur approved, although he did not initiate, reforms for Japan that might in another context be considered anti-capitalist. Some of his non-economic measures were not overly controversial, at least to Americans, although they were often misunderstood by the Japanese: human rights, female emancipation, freedom of the press, elimination of secret police. But the simultaneous enactment of labor rights, land reforms, and the attempted breakup of Japan's huge financial combines—the *zaibatsu*—sent American conservatives into a frothing rage.

In the first months of MacArthur's tenure, pressure was kept on the right. Some zaibatsu were forced to divest. The Kempei Tai, the internal military police, were disbanded, as were the Thought Police. Meanwhile the Japanese left was actively encouraged. All political prisoners—including the Communists—were released, and exiles returned home. Labor was encouraged by the New Dealers in SCAP to flex its muscle. Within a year, Japanese organized labor grew from nothing to 5 million members, ten times its prewar high.

Then there were the purges. SCAP's Post Surrender Directive, the 1945 mandate for carrying out the Occupation, ordered the incarceration of high-ranking wartime political and military leaders. In addition, read the order, "Persons who have been active exponents of militarism and militant nationalism will be removed and excluded from public office and from any other position of public or substantial private responsibility." Eventually, over 200,000 persons were purged.

The purges had not a vestige of democratic process, convicting men on unsupported word and denying the accused a fair trial. But the punishment, for the most part, was neither harsh nor lengthy. By 1947, SCAP began to indicate that enough social reorganization was enough. A return to normalcy, minus the military expansionism, was called for: it was time for Japan to take its rightful place as the linchpin of U.S. strategy in the Far East.

The Cold War was beginning. Chiang Kai-shek was losing ground and the Russians were seizing territory in Eastern Europe. Suddenly, anything that served to strengthen the American position vis-à-vis world Communism was deemed good and proper. By 1948, the New Dealers in Government Section, men such as Kades and T. A. Bisson, had resigned or been sent home. The China Crowd was discredited, shortly to be blamed for the "loss" of China.

Japanese of all political persuasions were somewhat bewildered by this apparently arbitrary change. Later the term *gyakkosu*, or reverse course, was coined to explain America's political about-face. Some historians have doubted that such a reversal took place, citing that the United States never intended to allow a social revolution in the first place. But internationally, the change was noted; the Soviets believed that Japan was about to be used as a springboard for an attack on the USSR, according to a 1947 CIA report. And, from the perspective of Japanese liberals and leftists, a change most certainly happened, no matter what SCAP stated. SCAP, it appeared, had suddenly acquired a fear of the left.

The fear wasn't SCAP's alone. The conservative government of Japan, headed by Shigeru Yoshida, an aristocratic anti-Communist, also wanted the left dealt with, and quickly. In April 1949, SCAP responded with the so-called Red Purge. Leftist unions and groups were forced to register under the Organizational Control Ordinance.

The primary object of the Red Purge, from SCAP's point of view, was the Japanese Communist Party (JCP), which was seen by the Americans as not merely a civil disrupter but an instrument of the Soviets and others. The JCP's membership had grown from 8,000 in 1946 to 100,000 in 1949, and the party controlled to varying degrees an estimated half of organized labor. Despite its growth, though, politically the JCP never won more than 10 percent of the electoral vote in any Diet election. Yet so alarmed were SCAP officials, there was consideration of banning the party altogether. Although this never occurred, measures were enforced against it, and, much as in the United States, the legal position of its members grew increasingly precarious.

Even though the JCP was the prime target, a wholesale purge took place against anyone found annoying or dangerous by the increasingly dominant conservatives. Labor unions were undermined with growing regularity, their leaders harassed and assaulted, and membership declined; 20,000 civil servants and schoolteachers were dismissed; newspaper and radio offices were the subject of police raids; universities were urged to rid themselves of leftist professors. There were other changes as well. The breakup of the huge financial combines like Mitsui and Mitsubishi was discontinued; the emperor, it was decided, would not be tried as a war criminal; SCAP officials began to make plans for "housebreaking the unions"; and the original policy for complete demilitarization of Japan was abandoned as unrealistic.

Why was SCAP so willing to acquiesce to the Japanese rightists, the very group responsible for the war that had cost the United States so dearly? Foremost, it was a strategic move: use the rightists to help secure Japan while fighting Communism on the Asian mainland. It was imperative that Japan's demobilized army of nearly 6 million—the largest in Asia—not pose the slightest risk to American aims. But partly, it was the reluctance of the U.S. military to socially reform Japan. SCAP became far more interested in reducing the economic burden on the United States, and saw stability rather than reform of the nation as the key. Equally important, wealthy American businessmen, many of whom filled SCAP's higher ranks, were anxious to stake out shares in Japan's future. The country's defeat provided a historic opportunity to influence or control one of the world's great industrial systems.

Given these American motives, and the self-preserving instincts of the Japanese conservatives, it is unsurprising that no tactic in support of these motives was rejected as too brutal or unfair. The problem was how to form a phalanx of loyal troops who could counter the threat, both real and perceived, from the left. This force, which would continue to function in some form up to the present, was a loose, familiar assemblage of rightists and yakuza.

Gangsters and Dirty Tricks

A strikingly similar set of events was then unfolding half a world away in Western Europe. The CIA was paying Corsican gangsters in France, particularly in the city of Marseille, to disrupt Communist strikes and help break the back of the French Communist Party. As was the case in Japan, much of France lay in ruins. Unemployment was high, wages low, and amid shortages of every kind, the black markets had become a way of life.

Alarmed by electoral gains of the French Communists and by Soviet expansion into Eastern Europe, U.S. officials quickly began a secret war against the far left on the Continent. Only months before the 1947 strike in France, the Truman administration had established the CIA and introduced the multi-billion-dollar European Recovery Plan, popularly known as the Marshall Plan. The small, sophisticated Corsican gangs were a tough lot. Some, like the yakuza, were accustomed to doing battle with leftists and labor unions. The French Fascists had used them to battle Communist demonstrators in the 1930s, and during the war, the Gestapo had found them useful for spying on the Communist underground. (Others, though, had served with the Resistance.) But it was the Corsican mob's alliance with the CIA that proved most significant to its criminal future, according to Alfred McCoy. In his *The Politics of Heroin in Southeast Asia,* McCoy wrote that as the CIA funneled cash and arms to the French underworld, the Corsicans were put "in a powerful enough position to establish Marseilles as the postwar heroin capital of the Western world and to cement a long-term partnership with Mafia drug distributors." Some scholars disagree, arguing that evidence is scant and that the U.S. role was negligible. But clearly the CIA's backing didn't hurt. Within a year of the agency's 1950 operation, the Corsican mob opened Marseilles's first heroin labs and began shipments that over the next twenty years would dump thousands of pounds of heroin onto American streets—a pipeline of drugs that would later be called the French Connection.

The French story has been told before; but few understand that Americans were hiring mobsters in Japan as well, in a secret war against the left that began as early as 1946. At its helm stood Major General Charles Willoughby, MacArthur's intelligence chief both during the Pacific campaigns and under SCAP, where he headed G-2 (intelligence). Willoughby and his trusted aides in G-2 worked to directly repress the left, as did G-2's Counter Intelligence Corps, and to indirectly repress it, by aiding and financing rightist thugs or yakuza to do the job. To help run his covert operations, the general followed another pattern similar to that which U.S. officials were then secretly employing in Europe: recruiting for intelligence use key members of the enemy who probably should have been tried as war criminals. Willoughby succeeded in freeing from the purge in Japan certain well-placed officers from the Imperial Army and Navy. Many of these held extreme right-wing views, and their attitudes toward Communism would be put to good use. Just as U.S. agents made life easier for Nazis like Klaus Barbie (the "Butcher of Lyon") and General Reinhard Gehlen (the Wehrmacht's intelligence chief in Russia), so Willoughby recruited such men as Lt. General Seizo Arisue, former chief of military intelligence for the Japanese General Staff. Arisue and other officers were incorporated into G-2's "Historical Section" and into a number of secret agencies. In addition to supplying U.S. officials with intelligence gleaned from years of work on Korea, China, and the Soviet Union, Willoughby's new recruits made a second career spying on and disrupting the left in Japan.

Major General Charles André Willoughby seems to have been naturally inclined toward the role of guardian of the extreme right. Born Adolf Weidenbach in Germany, Willoughby was called by one fellow officer "our own Junker general." His mentor, General MacArthur, referred to him as "my lovable Fascist." Willoughby had functioned under MacArthur in Manila, and there became close to the Falangist Spaniards who supported Franco. After the war, Willoughby served as promoter for Franco, perhaps paid, perhaps not. He devoted himself to far-right causes in the United States, too, such as Billy James Hargis's Christian Crusade; he also edited American anti-Communist newsletters and wrote for *The American Mercury*. For years he sought, in vain, to obtain an official posting with the CIA or some other U.S. spy agency.

During his tenure in Japan, Willoughby was forever discovering Communist spy plots, some of which, particularly those revolving around the Soviet liaison offices, did exist. But his paranoia and sense of drama tended to blur his perceptions. According to one former colleague, Kenneth Colton of Government Section, Willoughby circulated memos on blue paper— called Willoughby Chits by staffers—that were sometimes "far-fetched." One SCAP veteran asserted that Willoughby was "horribly involved with the right wing."

The full scope of spying and disruption under Willoughby's command is difficult to assess, let alone prove, and the answer may have died with Willoughby in October of 1972. American researchers have been stymied in their attempts to locate and review Willoughby's own G-2 files, which seem to have disappeared. Asked what became of them, an official at the MacArthur Memorial Archive asserted that "Willoughby was a burner."

Perhaps Willoughby was somewhat embarrassed by G-2's frequent ineptitude. One former military intelligence officer who worked under the general recalled, "We were supporting every right-wing jerk who came along. It was so chaotic in the postwar years that American agents were stumbling over each other. Five different guys were running one Japanese, and the Japanese were collecting money from each of them. Most of them [the Japanese rightists] had their own agendas anyway. It was hard to say who was running who."

Nonetheless, there emerged a series of highly suspicious incidents that discredited the left, particularly the JCP, which critics in Japan have long blamed on "dirty tricks." The most famous of these incidents is the Matsukawa case. In August 1949, saboteurs derailed a Japan National Railways train in the town of Matsukawa, killing three people and injuring many more. The case came to be known as the greatest cause celebre in the history of lawsuits in Japan. In a highly politicized atmosphere, twenty workers—all but one either Communists or trade union leaders—were charged and convicted of the crime. Their case assumed the proportions of the Rosenberg, Oppenheimer, and Hiss cases in the United States, with support committees, demonstrations, and enormous press coverage. The convictions were overturned by the Japanese Supreme Court in 1963, but legal proceedings dragged on for another seven years until, in 1970, the accused were paid damages by the Japanese government for possibly having been the victims of a frame-up by the prosecution.

It has never been proven exactly who did sabotage the Matsukawa train; fingers have pointed at both U.S. and Soviet intelligence agents, as well as the JCP. All had conceivable motives for creating such an incident. One persistent theory, introduced by defense lawyers in the case, maintains that the saboteurs—all men—were attached to an obscure traveling band, the Japan Girls' Opera Troupe (Nihon Shojo Kageki Dan). Typical of the yakuza's tekiya-style operations, the troupe had mysteriously appeared for an unscheduled one-night stand in Matsukawa the day before the incident.

Matsukawa, though, was but one of a whole string of mysterious incidents blamed on the JCP and the labor movement. One month before the Matsukawa train careened off its tracks, the president of the National Railways fell—or was pushed, as many believed—in front of a train, an event known as the Shimoyama incident. Blame was laid upon the JCP. An earlier train crash, known as the Mitaka incident, was also attributed to JCP sabotage; finally, the murder of a policeman (the Shiratori incident) was again blamed on the JCP.

It is possible, of course, that the JCP was involved in one or more of these incidents. It was a time of great labor unrest in the railroad industry, with widespread layoffs aimed at leftist organizers as part of GHQ's purge. The Communists were engaged in an often violent battle for control of the labor movement, and their leaders talked loosely about the inevitability of armed struggle in the country. The JCP leadership, however, previously had shown a significant talent for successful manipulation of the public, so it seems unlikely that it would have engaged in mass murder—hardly a public relations coup. In any case, the perceived link between these incidents and the JCP—whether actual or G-2 inspired—couldn't have suited G-2 better: the bad publicity and court trials turned public opinion against the Communists.

There was one case in which Japanese rightists and American intelligence were caught red-handed. This was the Kaji affair, which began in late 1951. A leftist writer named Wataru Kaji was kidnapped by G-2 and handed over to the newly ensconced CIA. Up until this point Willoughby had assiduously refused to allow the CIA or its predecessor, the OSS, to operate freely in his domain. Intelligence in Japan was an Army affair. But Kaji was held incommunicado for more than a year by the CIA and was allegedly subjected to torture. He was apparently suspected of working as a Soviet spy, although the U.S. embassy claimed he was a double agent. When the affair came to light, the Japanese were outraged because Kaji's detention lasted past April 1952, when Japanese sovereignty was restored. The press also discovered the existence of a Japanese espionage group that had aided the Americans in the kidnapping.

This group was one of several operating under Willoughby and G-2, and was named for its principal officer, ex-Colonel Takushiro Hattori, a former aide to General Tojo. His group, the Hattori Kikan (Hattori Agency), was made up of a dozen colonels and three hundred of lower ranks. Another group, the Cannon Agency, named for American colonel J. Y. Cannon, was also accused of involvement in the Kaji affair, although here the hard evidence was lacking. Perhaps the least-known was the Katoh Agency, whose name was an acronym of five Japanese rightist officers. One of these was General Arisue, who had formerly been assigned to G-2's Historical Section. Katoh was so shadowy that Government Section assigned Major Jack Napier to conduct an investigation into its purpose. Napier, in turn, handed the assignment over to the Japanese attorney general, who pursued the matter. One report, dated December 23, 1948, connected Arisue with Major General Willoughby. A later report noted that Arisue worked inside G-2 and that the "contents of [his] business are supposed to be related to information on the Soviet situations and the 'Red' activities within Japan."

Katoh, Cannon, and the other agencies operated under the unofficial mandate of protecting Japan from internal and external Communism. But while Willoughby's officers were undoubtedly helpful to G-2's plans, for certain uses they were not always practical. Dirty tricks were one thing, but countering street demonstrations and strikes took another breed. For really unpleasant work, men without commissions had to be discreetly called upon. In 1947, for instance, Chinese in Yokohama were abusing the Japanese population. For reasons not apparent, SCAP officials did not take action against the sangokujin. However, one member of the Cannon

Agency, a Korean Navy commander, took care of the disturbance. He appealed for help to a Korean Japanese named Hisayuki Machii, who was then in the process of forming one of the major gangs of the yakuza, the Tosei-kai. In spite of the Chinese being fellow sangokujin, Machii told his followers to gather rifles and machine guns and end the problem. Apparently, a show of force was all that was necessary.

Machii had sufficient strength, and solid connections through the Cannon Agency and elsewhere, to be useful to G-2. The aging oyabun currently presents himself as a legitimate businessman, although, according to Japanese police, he still maintains close ties to his old fellows. Mr. Machii does not grant interviews, but his American business partner, former California assemblyman Kenneth Ross, told the authors that his partner was no gangster, that his Occupation activities were limited to "strong-arm" tactics used to "break up Communist demonstrations, kind of like union busting. It was illegal in the pure sense, but it was done under the quasi-jurisdiction of our Occupation forces."

Among the groups that exercised "quasi-jurisdiction" was the Counter Intelligence Corps of G-2. "You had to be lily white to get into CIC and turn coal black to stay in," recalled the late Harry Brunette, who served as a special agent with CIC during the Occupation. "That CIC badge was your authority to do anything. If they told you to break in and steal some documents, you did it. We'd trade with the devil if we had to." Brunette remembered the specially commissioned agents affiliated with the Cannon Agency and similar outfits. "They were almost always linguists, Japanese Americans, and they were directly responsive to CIC headquarters. They'd only come into our field office to get paid and drop off sealed reports for Tokyo."

At times CIC's special agents intervened directly in disturbances. *Chicago Sun* correspondent Mark Gayn, reporting in Japan from December 1945 to May 1948, described their work as part of a "campaign of union busting." In his remarkable account of the Occupation years, *Japan Diary,* Gayn makes note of the hypocrisy of SCAP's labor policy. As early as October 1946, wrote Gayn, while "the Labor Division was talking in pious phrases to Japanese union leaders, Counterintelligence agents were breaking up labor demonstrations." Indeed, Japan's famously cooperative company unions are due more to the anti-labor activities of some SCAP officials than to the supposedly docile nature of Japanese workers.

There also existed a growing force of other thugs and gangsters that certain Occupation officials could count on in their campaign against the left. These were the new ultranationalist gangs. In the same tradition of earlier yakuza-rightist gangs, they were organized along the traditional oyabun-kobun lines and engaged freely in the black markets, racketeering, and extortion. But most conspicuous of their activities were strikebreaking and murderous attacks on trade union and leftist leaders. The new gangs were characterized by an ideology that was simultaneously anti-Communist, anti-Korean, and anti-American.

Despite the official condemnation by SCAP, during much of the Occupation the gangs freely launched attacks on leftists and labor unions. The fact that the Americans in 1946 originally banned all ultranationalist groups and purged their leaders appears to have been a minor inconvenience for the extreme right. The agency responsible for enforcing the ban on such groups was none other than G-2, which was not only unenthusiastic about the whole program, but was accused of actually using the gangs in its own campaigns to spy on and disrupt the left.

By 1947, the purge against the right seems to have been thoroughly undercut. Mark Gayn, writing in May of 1948, summed up the sorry state of affairs. "The purge, as of this date, has become a sham," he wrote. "War criminals sit in the Diet, the Cabinet and the imperial court, draw new 'democratic' legislation and administer the purges to fit their political ends. War criminals are 'revising' the textbooks, running the press, dominating the radio and moving picture industries. Thought Control agents, purged and purged again, keep reappearing in positions of responsibility—often with American encouragement."

By 1949, policy crept even with reality as SCAP launched its full-scale depurge. It was to be one of the last formidable acts of the reverse course: by the start of the Korean War, SCAP had released 10,000 people from purge restrictions, and over the next year and a half freed a total of some 200,000.

The official lifting of the purge added even more recruits to the rightist gangs, which by the end of the Occupation numbered as many as 750 separate groups. The new gangs of rightists sported evocative names reminiscent of the organizations founded by Mitsuru Toyama and fellow ultranationalists in the 1920s and 1930s. There was, for example, the New and Powerful Masses Party, begun in June 1946 in Tokyo by a gambling boss. In response to the growing labor movement, the enterprising "party" leader expanded the gang's interests to violent anti-union and anti-Communist activity. In 1946, a truckload of its members, militantly adorned with white headbands and shoulder sashes, arrived at the headquarters of the National Railway Workers Union to persuade them to cancel their threatened strike. Within the year, the gang would be involved in a more highly publicized incident. Two members paid a visit to Katsumi Kikunami, a JCP Diet member and chairman of the Congress of Industrial Unions, and exhorted him to use his influence to call off a planned general strike. To emphasize their point, they slashed Kikunami's forehead with a dagger.

In the face of such blatant acts of violence, SCAP officials had little choice but to take action. In 1947, the Masses Party had the distinction of being the first postwar rightist group to be specifically ordered to disband.

But the gang persisted. Over the next few years, its members would be arrested for gambling, extortion, assault, robbery, murder, fraud, and other crimes.

Another such group was the aptly named Japan Goblin Party (Nihon Tengu To), whose aims seemed to weigh heavily on the gangster side despite its avowed political beliefs. The group was founded in 1945, with its headquarters located in Tokyo's Ginza district; among its most prominent members were local political bosses and gamblers. Its known political acts included plastering public places with anti-Communist posters. This sort of activity was not very lucrative, and the Goblins moved on to more remunerative work, such as robbing a post office, stealing Occupation cigarettes, and various acts of extortion, robbery, and fraud, until their party, too, was finally banned.

Although the rightists' political acts were no doubt appreciated by certain U.S. officials, no one in SCAP, not even Willoughby, really wanted to soil his hands dealing with the country's gangs of rightists and crooks. If hired muscle for intimidation or worse was needed, SCAP could usually count on the many rightists on G-2's payroll to arrange something. But while the staffs of Willoughby's clandestine agencies played a major role, they were not always effective. What G-2 needed was a central go-between, someone who had power in his own right, and who would not succumb to anti-American sentiments; someone brutal, but not too treacherous. It turned out that SCAP had just the man.

G-2, the CIA, and Mr. Kodama

From 1946 until late 1948, Yoshio Kodama languished in Tokyo's Sugamo Prison, the holding tank for many of the accused war criminals awaiting trial or sentencing by the International Military Tribunal for the Far East. Kodama was Class A, a designation reserved for cabinet officers, military men, and ultranationalists. On December 23, 1948, the Class A criminals were separated into two groups: seven of those convicted by the tribunal, including former prime minister Tojo and four military men, dropped from the gallows. Hours later, sixteen others, including Kodama, stepped out into the cold night air.

It had not been Kodama's first incarceration, but it was undoubtedly the most profitable. In his three years behind bars, Kodama wrote two books, *I Was Defeated,* a turgid political analysis of his life on the right, and *Sugamo Diary,* an amusing and perceptive report of life in prison. More important, Kodama made or solidified friendships with other Japanese rightists who would some day run the country. When Kodama left Sugamo at age thirty-seven, he was just starting a new phase of his old work. Through his ties to the right, the underworld, and American intelligence, Kodama would become one of the most powerful men in postwar Japan—and the master-mind behind the yakuza's rise to political power.

He began life in 1911, the fifth son of a Nihonmatsu City gentleman who was down on his luck. In 1920, at age eight, Yoshio was placed with distant relatives in Korea, where he suffered through isolation and child labor in a variety of exceedingly unpleasant industrial jobs. In his teens, young Kodama, sensitive to the exploitation of the worker, turned first to socialism and then to ultranationalism as a solution to personal and social problems. As a theorist, he was less than convincing, but he turned out to be extremely adept at organizing, profiteering, and violence.

Beginning in the late 1920s, Kodama enlisted in a series of ultranation-alist groups, apprenticing himself to the infamous Mitsuru Toyama of the Dark Ocean Society. In 1929, he joined Kenkoku-kai (Association of the Founding of the Nation), begun by Dr. Shinkichi Uesugi and Bin Akao, one of Japan's best-known, most virulent rightists. Kenkoku-kai had a reputation as the most radical of the rightist groups. Upon joining, Kodama tried to hand the emperor a written appeal urging increased patriotism. Kodama was seized by the police at a motorcade before he could serve Hirohito with the papers, and drew six months in jail. Three years later Kodama founded the Dokuritsu Seinen Sha (Independence Youth Society). This group col-laborated with Tenko-kai (Society for Heavenly Action) in 1934 in an abortive attempt to assassinate cabinet members, including Prime Minister Admiral Saito. Kodama was caught but sentenced to only three and a half years in prison.

Kodama was released from Fuchu Penitentiary in 1937. He had served a total of six years in various prisons and jails. "During my six years of impris-onment," he wrote in *I Was Defeated*, "the rightist movement had been com-pletely castrated while the reform ideals that had risen all over the country since the Manchurian incident [1931] had been completely canalized into the field of foreign policies."

Not one to miss an opportunity, Kodama used his rightist connections to move into the world of "foreign policies." According to the book *Uyoku Jiten* (Right-wing dictionary), after becoming a staff officer at Army headquar-ters, Kodama entered the Foreign Ministry's information bureau. He later joined the expeditionary force to China and the East Indies, and was also attached to the Navy, Air Force, and Ministry of the Interior as a nonregular.

Kodama's talents were recognized by his superiors, and from 1939 through late 1941 the young rightist toured East Asia, spying for the gov-ernment. His frequent trips between China and Japan caught the attention of U.S. Army intelligence agents, who credited him with setting up a net-work of Manchurian spies and collaborators that stretched across China. On December 8, the day after the Japanese attack on Pearl Harbor and much of Southeast Asia, the thirty-year-old Kodama set up shop in Shanghai. He started an operation called Kodama Kikan (Kodama Agency) with an exclusive contract from the Navy Air Force to supply strategic materiel needed for the war effort.

Kodama operated as a sort of imperial Japanese version of *Catch-22*'s Milo Minderbinder, buying tungsten here, guns there, reselling them, and peddling vast stores of radium, cobalt, nickel, and copper. He obtained the materials in China and Manchuria, forcing the Chinese at gunpoint to sell at pitifully low prices. It was an incredibly lucrative effort, one that might easily be termed looting. Kodama, however, saw it differently. His enterprises, unlike other so-called development firms in the conquered territories, grew out of an ill-suppressed idealism. His agency, said Kodama, was "an organization with no thought of profit and since it was simply composed of a group of self-sacrificing youths, I was only able to continue my work through the sincere efforts of the men cooperating with me." Such "sincere" efforts apparently pay off; by the end of the war, Kodama Kikan had become a financial giant with a working capital of $175 million in industrial diamonds and platinum, as well as banknotes. With so many "self-sacrificing youths" working for him, Kodama found time to continue his intelligence work. He ran operations for Section Eight of the General Staff office in Shanghai, which handled intelligence. In addition, he financed the Shanghai office of the Kempei Tai—the Japanese secret police. Still, the demands of his industrial kingdom must have left increasingly little time for spy missions. By the early 1940s, according to U.S. intelligence reports, the Kodama Kikan controlled iron, salt, and molybdenum mines, and operated farms, fisheries, and secret munitions plants through much of central China. And, although it might not have been his usual line of work, he at times acted as a go-between in major heroin-for-minerals deals.

The end of the war saw Kodama, by then a thirty-four-year-old rear admiral, back in Japan as an adviser to the prime minister, Prince Higashikuni. Kodama did use his influence to help implement the surrender with a minimum of violence, but the Americans were not impressed. In the first days of 1946, he was rounded up with other high-ranking Japanese and sent to Sugamo Prison to await trial. During his three-year imprisonment, he was interrogated at great length concerning his operations in China. In a key report of May 1947, at least one G-2 official argued strongly for Kodama's continued internment. Concluded the report:

> In summary, Kodama appears to be a man doubly dangerous. His long and fanatic involvement in ultranationalist activities, violence included, and his skill in appealing to youth make him a man who, if released from internment, would surely be a grave security risk. In addition, there is the outstanding probability . . . that, as a result of his hearty co-operation with the war effort, he has a large fortune to back up whatever activities he might see fit to undertake . . . [and] could very easily become a big-time operator in Japan's re-

constructional period. . . . Kodama's past performance indicates that he is the sort of man G-2 considers more dangerous than either the superannuated ideologists or the professional men who aided Japan's war-time effort for reasons of patriotism or survival of their professional interests . . .

Like many veteran ultranationalists, however, Kodama was never tried, or even formally charged. According to SCAP's chief of Legal Section, Alva C. Carpenter, the "suspected" Class A war criminal was released because the international tribunal had found other civilians not guilty, and Legal Section — expecting acquittal for Kodama — declined to bring charges. But the historical record is not that simple.

It appears that Kodama's release also may have involved a deal he had struck with G-2 officials, then increasingly obsessed with Communism, to share both his wealth and his considerable intelligence on China and the Japanese left. If not in prison, it was shortly after his release that Kodama's work began with U.S. intelligence.

At the time of his release from Sugamo, Kodama had already begun the machinations that would soon create a powerful rightist bloc inside and outside the government. In fact, prior to his arrest, Kodama entrusted a good part of his fortune — he was the second-richest man among the 644 suspected war criminals — to another influential rightist, Karoku Tsuji. Occupation officer Harry Emerson Wildes, in a 1946 internal report on Tsuji, called him the "mystery man of Japanese politics" because of his ability to make lavish campaign donations without any visible means of income. Only later would it be revealed how Tsuji used Kodama's booty to finance the founding of the Liberal Party. That money firmly established the close relationship that would exist between Kodama and the ruling conservatives in Japan for the next thirty-five years. In 1955, the Liberal Party merged with the Democratic Party to form the Liberal Democratic Party, or LDP, which then wielded a nearly unbroken hold on postwar Japanese politics. From that point on, over the next two decades, Kodama was perhaps the most powerful single individual within the LDP.

Kodama's work dovetailed nicely with that of the Americans. From the beginning, U.S. agents had been making surreptitious payments to the emerging Japanese conservatives. Although both Americans and Japanese denied it for decades, the facts were laid bare in a 1994 *New York Times* story based on recently declassified documents. It was entitled simply "C.I.A. Spent Millions to Support Japanese Right in 50's and 60's." The CIA refused official comment, naturally, but various retired officials went on the record. Alfred C. Ulmer Jr., who ran the CIA's Far East operations from 1955 to 1958, told the *Times*, "We financed them. We depended on the LDP for information." Ulmer added that the CIA had used the payments both to support the party and to recruit informers within it from its earliest days.

Upon release from Sugamo, Kodama found two bases of power that would serve him well—the yakuza and American intelligence. Kodama quickly showed that he had the support of the yakuza legions whenever he needed it. In 1949, for instance, he led the Meiraki-gumi against labor unions at the Hokutan Coal Mine. These unions had been the most effective and militant of the miners' unions, and all the governing forces, Japanese and American, wanted them brought into line. When a frontal assault on the union proved insufficient because of the miners' willingness to do battle, Kodama's men tried to foment internal strife, also with limited success. By 1950, it appears that Kodama had solidified his position as a principal go-between for G-2 and the various yakuza bands. One aging gangster, the retired boss of Tokyo's Takinogawa gang, summed up Kodama's work in a 1984 interview: "None of us gang bosses had much connection with GHQ. Kodama was the one who did that." Kodama was able to swing that much weight because he knew the essential element of power—money. Not only did he have a lot of it, but he knew how to move it around as well.

Kodama also retained an interest in another major component of political power—intelligence. However, his first known venture in concert with G-2 did not turn out to be particularly auspicious for either party. Kodama was involved in an operation to send a spy ship, sailing under merchant marine cover, to Shanghai to gather intelligence on the new Communist regime. Kodama was of particular interest to G-2 because of his extensive China background. However, when the *Choshu Maru* docked at the port city in January 1951, it was promptly seized by the suspicious Chinese.

In 1949, the Central Intelligence Agency had begun to take over Japanese intelligence operations despite General Willoughby's objections. Kodama's next venture was with the Agency and, despite his earlier failure, he was assigned another maritime black-bag job. This time he was given $150,000 up front to smuggle a cargo of tungsten out of China. An official, later with the CIA, who was involved in the deal said that the ship never arrived. Kodama, he said, kept the money and told the U.S. embassy that the ship had sunk.

One might think that these fiascoes would be enough to make the Americans drop Kodama altogether. Far from it. This was the beginning of a long-standing relationship between Kodama and the CIA. Kodama's approach wasn't original—rightists around the world had used it for generations—but it was effective: cry red and the Americans will usually pony up. In fact, it was *highly* effective. The use of organized crime and ultranationalists by the Occupation kept the Japanese left on the defensive and off balance, just as the CIA's use of the Corsican mob did against the French Communists. But such policies create unwanted side effects. In France, the CIA's use of the underworld helped the Corsican gangs establish the French Connection for massive heroin shipments to the United States. And in Japan, the aftereffects were at least as profound. The money, the favored treatment, and the privileged relationships accorded to rightists and their gangster allies by U.S. officials created a corrupt power structure that would last for decades. The yakuza now resumed their role in Japanese politics—providing money and muscle—in a stronger position than ever. They continued to act as company goons and strikebreakers. Their strength enabled them to grab increasingly larger segments of the economy, drawing money from the Japanese people far in excess of any services they provided. And the country's rightist politicians benefited from having a private yakuza army at their disposal.

Colonel Kades was prescient in his 1947 press conference when he claimed, "This clannish and clandestine combination of bosses, hoodlums and racketeers is the greatest threat to American democratic aims in Japan." The colonel also might have noted that this was the greatest threat to Japanese democratic aims, and would continue to be for years to come. It is an unfortunate fact that American misuse of power helped undermine Japanese democratic goals. It is not an exaggeration to say that the Occupation gave the yakuza its biggest lease on life. The best for the yakuza was yet to come.

CHAPTER THREE

NEXUS ON THE RIGHT

AS THE OCCUPATION DREW TO A CLOSE, MANY JAPANESE, ESPECIALLY THOSE on the political right, were fearful of a leftist move toward power. One of those worried was Tokutaro Kimura, the powerful minister of justice under Prime Minister Yoshida.

As 1952 began, Kimura was nervously anticipating the April signing of the peace treaty with the United States. He called together a group of influential rightists to discuss the future. In his book *The Great History of the Right Wing,* rightist historian Bokusui Arahara re-created that scene in a Tokyo meeting room. Kimura spoke in ominous tones to his assembled colleagues:

> "It is clear as day that Communists will rise in revolt all over Japan and a bloody revolution will begin. I already have information that a standing government of the Communist Party would be formed in Nagano Prefecture.
>
> "There is information that the police are infiltrated by the reds, and there are many Communist Party members among high ranking officers of the Reserve Corps [the forerunner of the Self-Defense Forces, or army]. Furthermore, there are many who are not regular members of the Communist Party but have pledged loyalty to the Party. If so, we cannot depend on the police, and there is a strong possibility that the Reserve Force will become our foe.
>
> "Can't you call together men with common beliefs to fight desperately against the Communist Party, to preserve the national policy?"

Kimura's plea was quickly answered by his henchman Nobuo Tsuji:

> "Justice Minister, there is nobody who would risk their lives but gamblers, racketeers, and hoodlums. If the Communists should arise in revolt, those who talk about theories are not useful when it actually comes to a fight. There are none but those fellows, who risk their lives for their bosses. However, we

may have difficulty in recruiting them since their bosses were hunted and the groups dispersed by the Occupation policy."

Tsuji estimated to the minister that if money were available, he could possibly organize a special attack unit of criminals, and that of the number of bakuto, tekiya, and gurentai—whose population he generously estimated at several million—he thought that 200,000 could be considered reliable, dedicated anti-Communist fighters. Replied Kimura: "Oh, 200,000 courageous persons can be called! Thank God! It's providential. If they can be gathered, the nation can be saved!"

Kimura then shook hands with his three closest cronies and said through his tears of joy, "I beg you to work for the country. I will never let you worry about money."

The Minister of Drawn Swords

The meeting may not have taken place precisely as Bokusui Arahara depicted it, for Arahara, a former yakuza and a Christian pastor, was a rightwing partisan as well as a writer. But less biased historical sources confirm that such an event did indeed occur, and preparations were made to launch a 200,000-man force. It was to be called Aikoku Hankyo Battotai, or the Patriotic Anti-Communist Drawn Sword Regiment. The Japanese Youth Guidance Association, Nihon Seishonen Zendo Kyo-kai, would be used as a front group, and Kimura planned that ultimately the Japanese government would take the whole project under its wing.

Kimura was unusual not because he sought to reinstitute the rightist/ gangster nexus from inside the Japanese government, but because he sought to do so during the American Occupation, and in such a crude prewar fashion. Kimura's success, though, was due in part to the same SCAP policy that let Kodama and other prewar ultranationalists back out on the streets and into the elective offices and the corporate boardrooms.

Much as Tokunami had done thirty years earlier, by the end of the Occupation Kimura would sweep across the nation, organizing postwar Japan's first national alliance of gangsters and rightists. It was a remarkable feat: the nation's highest-ranking law enforcement official attempting to form the splintered yakuza bands into a single cohesive underworld force.

Kimura rose to prominence as a lawyer. He hung out his shingle in 1911, and after functioning as a private attorney, became chairman of the Japan Lawyers' Association. During the war, he assumed the directorship of one of the many ultranationalist groups, the Dai Nippon Butoku-kai (the Great Japan Military Virtue Society), as well as a local post in the Imperial Rule Assistance Youth Association.

At the war's end, Kimura entered the Yoshida government, first as procurator general, then as attorney general (later retitled minister of justice) from May 1946 until a year later, when his past caught up with him. The rightist attorney was pronounced a Class D war criminal and purged from public life. He didn't suffer too badly, as he resumed his private practice and served on the boards of two Tokyo industrial firms.

By the summer of 1948 Kimura was itching to return to power, and his former boss, Prime Minister Yoshida, tried to pull some strings. A SCAP Government Section investigation was less than complimentary: "The entire record of Mr. Kimura's association with SCAP has been one of opposition, of recalcitrance, and of defiance by delay and misfeasance. . . . He is undesirable for any position of power and influence over the people of Japan." MacArthur himself wrote to Yoshida saying that he could do nothing, "regardless of the fine reputation for personal integrity which you tell me Mr. Kimura enjoys."

Less than a year later, in May 1949, Yoshida was again asking for Kimura to be granted reinstatement, claiming that Japan's recovery was seriously impeded by a lack of talent. Kimura, claimed Yoshida, was not a rightist, but had been merely head of the fencing division of Butoku-kai, a position offered to him "because of his preeminence as a citizen and his hobbies of fencing and sword collection which of course have nothing to do with militarism and aggression." This time it worked, for SCAP's reverse course had begun and thousands of rightists were being depurged. On October 13, 1950, Kimura was reinstated and became once again justice minister.

From there it was a short hop to the Drawn Sword Regiment, a name chosen no doubt by the fencing buff. For a justice minister, Kimura showed less interest in justice than in cozying up to powerful gangsters. According to Arahara, Kimura met with tekiya leader Eiji Sekiguchi and helped create the nationwide Street Peddlers Union, which was loyal to the justice minister. Kimura also engineered the release of "Tokyo's Al Capone," Kinosuke Ozu, who then joined with the Drawn Swordsmen. Kimura went straight to the top as well, securing the loyalty of perhaps the most influential of Occupation-era bosses, Kanbei Umezu, who at the time was in prison. From there, Japan's highest lawman urged a consortium of Tokyo oyabun to create a new association, the Nippon Kokusui-kai, and received their support in the fight against Communism.

Kimura had underworld support, but he failed at the other end. His main stumbling block was Prime Minister Yoshida, who knew better than Kimura that the Americans—though suddenly tolerant of the old ultranationalists—were not prepared to let the reverse course run back to 1937. Somewhat dismayed at his minister's zeal, Yoshida squelched the Drawn Sword Regiment. Complicating matters for Kimura, major funding failed to appear, and what money was raised somehow didn't make it to the various rightists and yakuza. Kimura, it seemed, had his faults. In fact, among the legal profession he was called the "Sweetfish of Tamagawa" because he promised colleagues this delicacy and then neglected to make good. He was also known as "Venerable Ready Consent, Man of Non Performance," a phrase that flows better in Japanese.

Although stymied in his plan to create a private army, Kimura did not retire in defeat. In 1954, Yoshida appointed him to head the National Defense Agency, overseeing the new Self-Defense Forces and sniffing out Communists in the nascent army and throughout Japan: he would, in fact, become known as "Japan's Joe McCarthy." Kimura, who lived until past ninety, was also an unreconstructed militarist. In 1953, he put together a coalition of thirty-seven rightist organizations under the name Hoyu-kai and used it as a pro-military lobbying group. He was later elected to the upper house of the Diet, where he pushed for a number of perennial planks in the rightist platform: a sovereign emperor, elimination of the MacArthur constitution, textbook revision, and a strengthened army.

Kimura was by no means the most important postwar rightist; he was merely one fish in a whole school of ex-officers, old ultranationalists, new rightists, yakuza bosses, and others. His career in public service, though, was a clear indication of just how lenient the Occupation and the new independent Japan would be with the personnel and the ideas that had steered the nation to disaster. The failure of his Drawn Sword Regiment was merely a tactical defeat, and others picked up the banner.

The 1950s were a time of rapid and bewildering changes for the Japanese. The country began to regain its industrial base, and the social system moved rapidly into the realm of the Western industrial democracies, although Japan would never become westernized per se. Nonetheless, great changes swept through Japanese society: women began to work outside the home in greater numbers; labor continued to organize; elections were regularly held; and the old order lost much of its control over individual citizens. At the same time, though, the zaibatsu, Japan's massive financial combines, regained much of their hold on the national economy, and the conservatives continued to run the government.

The San Francisco Peace Treaty came into force in April 1952 and marked the formal end to the Occupation, although many Japanese regarded it as just that—a formality. There was, for one thing, the rather suspect nature of the treaty: the three major Asian powers—China, India, and Russia—were nonsignatories, and a number of smaller Asian countries also refused to ratify. The treaty provided only a partial end to the Occupation, since American military bases on the home islands and complete American control over Okinawa were mandated, and the basic instrument of government, the American-written constitution, remained in effect. Moreover, there is little argument over the fact that Japanese foreign policy, particularly regarding China and Russia, was closely bound up with American aims.

But if Japan had a semicolonial status, it was hardly an exploited nation. Freed from the burden of equipping and maintaining a large standing army—indeed, enjoined from it under the terms of the constitution—the nation could devote most of its energies to improving the material lot of its citizens. This, as the world already knows, Japan did, emerging from the ruins in 1945 to become the world's third-largest economy by 1968.

Politically, Japan's governments have largely been middle-of the-road conservative since the surrender. In spite of pressures from the left, the conservatives strengthened their hand in the 1950s. In 1955, the Liberal Party, begun with funds from Yoshio Kodama's hoard of plundered wealth, merged with the Democratic Party, and under the leadership of Nobusuke Kishi, together they formed the Jiyu-Minshuto, or Liberal Democratic Party, the LDP. The Socialist Party often mounted well-organized challenges to conservative rule, but except for the brief period from April 1947 to February 1948, it never participated in any government until 1993. The Japanese Communist Party was held in check by the deep-seated conservatism of the rural Japanese, and by legal, economic, and physical force directed by the LDP and the far right.

In spite of relative political stability—relative certainly to many other Asian nations and to the previous two decades in Japan—there was a good deal of public disorder from both the right and the left in the 1950s. Issues such as the contamination of a Japanese fishing vessel in the mid-Pacific by American nuclear tests in 1954 touched off a lengthy round of leftist protests. The right, on the other hand, found it more convenient to agitate against the Soviet Union, and there was a good deal to complain about: continued internment of Japanese prisoners of war; seizure of the Kurile Islands to the north; harassment of the Japanese fishing fleet.

The left in the 1950s maintained control of large sectors of the labor movement, such as the Nikkyoso, or Japan Teachers' Union, and the Sohyo, or General Council of Trade Unions. The right, on the other hand, could muster far less support than even the Communist Party, but the country's arch-conservatives found that grassroots support wasn't the only way to power. There were, as there had been before the war, the old-line political bosses in the countryside, and better yet, the gangsters in the cities.

When Tokutaro Kimura's friend Nobuo Tsuji claimed that there were millions of hoodlums in Japan, he was exaggerating, but not by much. In 1952, there were still millions of people plugged into the black markets and oyabun-kobun rackets that grew up in the war's aftermath. As conditions improved, most of these men drifted off into less precarious pursuits; those who stayed became the core of the new emerging yakuza empire.

From their strongholds in Osaka/Kobe in the west, and Tokyo/Yokohama in the east, gangsters began to consolidate their forces. Out of the thousands of gangs, some began to dominate. In the Kanto region, around Tokyo, names like Kinsei-kai, Tosei-kai, and Sumiyoshi-kai began to sound familiar to newspaper readers. In the Kansai region around Osaka and the nearby port of Kobe, the Yamaguchi-gumi and the Honda-kai began to overshadow their competitors.

As Japan recovered from defeat and destruction, the gangs were forced to move from control of necessities to control of luxuries. The yakuza were no longer needed in the black market, for credit and abundant foodstuffs were again available. But the yakuza found that even before prosperity fully arrived, there was big money to be made in non-essentials—drugs, prostitution, and entertainment. During the war, Japan, like other countries, discovered that weary soldiers could be kept going on amphetamines, and produced large stocks of the drug. The most famous military users of amphetamines were *kamikaze* pilots (who would at least not suffer through the excruciating comedown that amphetamines produce). In any case, stocks of speed were appropriated from military stores and sold during the Occupation, finding a market among the dispirited people of defeated Japan. Although Japanese morale improved as time went on, the demand for amphetamines persisted, fluctuating with supplies and periodic crackdowns by police. It is an extremely lucrative market that the yakuza have come to monopolize, and one that would play a key role in financing the gangs' expansion at home and abroad.

Prostitution, too, became yakuza business. Traditionally, many forms of prostitution were respectable in Japan, and were certainly not the domain of crude gangsters. But the war's end changed all that. Out of economic desperation many women were sold by their families to yakuza, who used them as prostitutes in the cities—often for American customers. Public solicitation and management of prostitutes were finally outlawed in 1958, after which time nearly all organized vice fell into the hands of the yakuza and their associates.

Gambling, on the other hand, was in part taken out of the hands of the bakuto, at least as exclusive operators of the games. Most of the popular forms of public gambling were legalized: horse racing, bicycle racing, and later, speedboat racing. The government found them a convenient source of needed revenue. The enterprising bakuto then were suddenly reduced to scalping tickets, touting at races, and running illegal bookie shops. Those bakuto with any vision soon expanded into vice, drugs, or businesses such as bars and restaurants.

The Korean War gave a huge boost to the Japanese economy, sparking a boom that continued through the 1950s. Large construction projects and heavy demand for shipping impacted areas controlled by the yakuza and poured money into the underworld. Some gangs started their own contracting firms; others functioned as labor brokers and hired muscle. As the Japanese gained both money and leisure time, entertainment also became popular again, and the yakuza moved to control much of this growing field, with its lucrative potential for extortion and protection rackets. Professional sports, from ancient sumo to the more recent import of baseball, came under mob influence. Theater, cabarets, and the burgeoning movie industry were all, to some degree, forced to yield control to the gangs.

Government reaction to the growing power of the yakuza was mixed. At the police level, there was a strong response to gang power, and crackdowns and arrests were frequent. But high officials, particularly those in the right wing of the LDP, were less concerned with the day-to-day rackets of the yakuza, and often more interested in making alliances with them. Throughout the 1950s, the right and the new, powerful gangster organizations once again began to assume each other's coloration. By 1959, the national newspaper *Yomiuri* could headline an article "Hoodlum Gangs Become Rightist Organizations." Some gangs, said the paper, had changed into rightists in order to avoid the police crackdown then in progress. The largest of the three new "political parties" was the Kokusui-kai, the same group that had been founded by Kimura's associates. According to the article, "The setup of the three organizations is patterned after the Liberal-Democratic Party. . . . These organizations are anticommunist and fervently support the emperor system."

Perhaps the comparison with the LDP was tongue-in-cheek, perhaps not. In any case, it was often very apt. Although this confluence of rightist and gangster was appalling to most Japanese, there were others, including some of the most powerful men in the country, who prospered because of their ties to the gangster/rightist organizations. The gangs played an essential role in the creation of several immense fortunes and helped others in shaping political careers that reached, in some cases, to the very top.

The Kuromaku Come of Age

Since the late nineteenth century, the *kuromaku* has been a pivotal figure in Japanese politics. Literally "black curtain," the word originated in classic Kabuki theater, in which an unseen wirepuller controls the stage by manipulating a black curtain. Today it connotes a powerful godfather or fixer who operates behind the scenes. Although most political arenas have their kuromaku, the term traditionally has applied to those men on the right who serve as a bridge between the yakuza/ultranationalist underworld and the legitimate world of business and mainstream politics. Most famous of the early kuromaku was Mitsuru Toyama, doyen of the extreme right and head of the Dark Ocean Society.

In postwar Japan, a number of men rose to fill the position of kuromaku, and perhaps the best known of these was a trio of Class A war criminals, all former residents of Sugamo Prison: Yoshio Kodama, Ryoichi Sasakawa, and Nobusuke Kishi. Prewar ultranationalists all, these men lost no time in bringing the right wing up to date and using it to influence business and the ruling Liberal Democratic Party.

Kodama, as noted earlier, had spent the war largely in China, procuring strategic materials for the Imperial Navy, dealing in looted goods, occasionally brokering heroin, and operating an intelligence net. His activities landed him in Sugamo, but SCAP's G-2 section found him a valuable contact after the war, and Kodama's links to American intelligence, as well as his renewed involvement in Japan's extreme right, began as soon as he was released from prison at the end of 1948.

Kodama brought with him skill at organizing, a fair ability for political theorizing, and immense personal charisma, all of which stood him in good stead with the emerging postwar right. He was only thirty-four at the war's end, and Kodama hit the ground running upon his release. As the eminent historian Ivan Morris wrote in 1960: "Kodama is considered to be extremely influential as an undercover man in conservative and financial circles. At the same time he maintained links with former military men and rightists . . ." Among Kodama's many associates in the "New Japan" were yakuza boss Karoku Tsuji, Prime Minister Ichiro Hatoyama, political wheeler-dealer Ichiro Kono, and ultranationalist Bin Akao. (The last named was linked to the dramatic 1960 stabbing assassination of Socialist Party leader Inejiro Asanuma, and as late as that year Akao was calling himself the "Hitler of Japan.")

Kodama had been introduced to party politics by Ichiro Kono before the end of the war, and both men immediately afterward began planning new paths to power. During the Occupation, Kodama contributed a healthy slice of his vast fortune to the Liberal Party, and by 1954 he had helped engineer the election of Hatoyama as prime minister. He owned outright a real estate firm and several nationally distributed sports (gambling) newspapers; he was suspected of possessing interests in a film company, a baseball team, and a shipping line. In addition, Kodama reportedly owned part of the Ginza nightclub empire that was controlled by his strikebreaking pal, Korean gang boss Hisayuki Machii. He also returned to his wartime sidelines of intelligence-mongering and running black-bag jobs. By 1958, six years or so after he had left the direct employ of G-2, Kodama was placed on the CIA payroll, with many lucrative spinoffs coming his way. And, from his talents as a strikebreaker, nurtured by General Willoughby's organization, Kodama went into private practice. He hired himself out to industrialists to protect them against undue labor problems—a job that kept him in close contact with underworld bosses.

Kodama worked well with most of the various groups and individuals he cultivated—politicians, businessmen, yakuza, rightists, and spies. During the 1950s and 1960s, he strengthened his ties to the traditional right and forged new links to the growing gangster conglomerates. Kodama organized, theorized, and moved huge sums of money around. He paid politicians and they paid him—if not with money, then in giri, or favors and obligations. But he was certainly not the only kuromaku following such a path. One of Kodama's former cellmates accumulated enough money and power to also alter Japan's postwar history.

Ryoichi Sasakawa used a slightly different road to power than did Kodama, and placed a greater emphasis on money over loyalty to ideals. But both men would inhabit essentially the same circles, and both came from the very same roots. Not merely an ultranationalist before the war, Sasakawa was an open admirer of Mussolini, and ordered his private militia to don black shirts in imitation of the Italian Fascists. Among his followers was an ardent young rightist named Yoshio Kodama.

Sasakawa served time in Sugamo in 1945 for three years where, for a time, he shared a cell with Kodama. It was there he learned an important lesson that he could continue to build upon: cultivate the Americans. But not all the Americans in SCAP were enamored of Sasakawa. The final prison report on the Fascist leader admonished: "In summary, Sasakawa appears to be a man potentially dangerous to Japan's political future. . . . He has been squarely behind Japanese military policies of aggression and anti-foreignism for more than twenty years. He is a man of wealth and not too scrupulous about its use. He chafes for continued power. He is not above wearing any new cloak that opportunism may offer."

The report was not well heeded, for Sasakawa took precisely that course. He moved steadily toward a less aggressive form of foreign intervention, making friends around the world with right-wing despots and ministers. He would also find that once the liberals from SCAP departed, the Americans weren't such bad fellows after all. He began making trips to the United States, spreading largesse among influential Americans for both personal and political advantage.

Sasakawa began his postwar life of opportunism while still in Sugamo, where he devised a plan to make it big in the gambling business. Upon leaving the prison in December 1948, he approached various local governments in Japan. Would they consider splitting the take with him from motorboat races? They were only too glad to have the income. Over the next thirty-five years, Sasakawa built an enormous gambling empire, the Japan Motorboat Racing Association, which sets up the racecourse, operates the stands and the boats, pays the drivers, pays the pari-mutuel windows, and cleans up—in every sense. In 1980, Sasakawa's company grossed

$7.4 billion—an extraordinary sum in those days. At the same time, Sasakawa won over the various bakuto gangs. He bragged publicly that he was a drinking companion of Japan's leading godfather, Yamaguchi-gumi head Kazuo Taoka. In the kuromaku tradition, Sasakawa also reportedly served as a mediator between feuding yakuza gangs. And, like his cohort Kodama, he employed squads of financial racketeers to push along his controversial investments.

Sasakawa also resumed his right-wing activities, taking care to adapt his schemes to changing conditions. For instance, his prewar group, the Kokusui Taishuto, or Patriotic People's Mass Party, was transmogrified into the postwar Zenkoku Kinrosha Domei, or All-Japan White Collar Workers' League. Sasakawa also found it expedient to ally himself with non-Japanese rightists. He counted himself among the founders of the Asian People's Anti-Communist League and its stepchild, the World Anti-Communist League (WACL), along with such early supporters as Syngman Rhee and Chiang Kai-shek. In 1963, Sasakawa became an adviser to the Japanese branch of Reverend Sun Myung Moon's Unification Church, known in Japan as Genri Undo. Moon and Sasakawa brought a number of Japanese rightist groups together in a WACL subsidiary known as Kokusai Shokyo Rengo, the International Federation for Victory over Communism, and Sasakawa assumed the roles of both patron and president. He continued to advise and fund rightist groups until, by the late 1970s, he could claim to have the allegiance of some 8 million Japanese.

This huge number, however, included the entire membership of groups that were simply traditionalist rather than politically right, organizations ranging from karate federations to sword dancing groups. As he was funding these groups, Sasakawa was also marching off to regions not even rightists could easily comprehend, promoting the "science" of Waterology, a collection of crackpot ecological notions. He also bought up huge blocks of television airtime to exhort youngsters to honor their parents and keep the earth clean. He embarked on a fifty-year career of shameless self-aggrandizement, running hundreds of print and television ads bearing his smiling visage and reminding Japan of his beneficence. "Formerly I had Yoshio Kodama and many other roughnecks around me," he once said. "I was their leader. So, some may call me a rightist. But I am not a rightist, I am a humanitarian." But as late as 1974, *Time* magazine would quote him as repeatedly boasting, "I am the world's wealthiest Fascist."

The names of Kodama and Sasakawa would become synonymous in Japan with the dark side of the nation's politics. Both men would exert enormous influence over the LDP and have a say in the naming of cabinet ministers, even the prime minister himself—much as Kodama did with the third Sugamo power, Nobusuke Kishi.

In some ways, Kishi's story is the most remarkable of the three. He began his political career as a follower of the influential Fascist Ikki Kita in the early 1930s, and by the end of the decade had moved into a position of power within the government. Kishi's real base of power was Manchukuo, the Japanese puppet state in conquered Manchuria. From 1936 to 1939, Kishi was officially the second-highest-ranking civilian in Manchukuo, although some referred to him as the ruler of the province. There, he maintained office with the help of those rightists and gangsters who came to help with the "development" of Manchukuo. After leaving the province, Kishi went on to hold the offices of minister of trade and industry, as well as vice munitions minister in Tojo's wartime cabinet.

Kishi was held as a Class A war criminal by the Americans, but left Sugamo along with Kodama and the others who were released on December 23, 1948. Kishi then staged one of the world's greatest political comebacks. He was depurged in 1952 and immediately entered politics. By allying himself with key rightists within the government, and through a series of shrewd maneuvers, Kishi soon moved to center stage. He became secretary-general of the LDP in 1955 and pushed on to become deputy prime minister under Yoshida's successor, Tanzan Ishibashi. But when Ishibashi was forced to resign after only three months for health reasons, Kishi went all the way. Backed by Kodama's money and influence, he staged an unstoppable run for prime minister. Kishi assumed the nation's highest post in March 1957, only five years after being depurged and nine years after release from war criminal status. This mutual assistance among the Sugamo graduates would mark Japanese electoral politics for years to come.

Kishi managed to help return to center stage a whole galaxy of prewar rightists and yakuza allies. Among them were two symphonious, and notorious, names—Ichiro Kono and Bamboku Ohno. Kono was a part of many major LDP decisions, including those to name Prime Minister Kishi and his successor, Eisaku Sato. Kono himself was minister of agriculture and was an elected member of the Diet. He was also a sworn brother to Yoshio Kodama.

Perhaps even more critical to the rightist alliance was Bamboku Ohno, an old-line rightist who controlled an important faction in the LDP. Backed by Kishi and Kodama, Ohno assumed the secretary-general post in the party, where he remained until his death in 1965.

In 1963, Ohno revealed his connections by publicly addressing a gathering of Kobe yakuza. The occasion was a reception for Katsuichi Hirata, godfather of the Yamaguchi-gumi subgroup, the Honda-kai. Over 2,500 people crowded into the plush Shin-Seiki Club to hear Hirata take the oath of office. Ohno arrived to speak to the crowd; he was accompanied by six husky bodyguards wearing black suits and sunglasses. In a rousing speech, the LDP's secretary-general told the assembled that *ninkyo*, or chivalry, was part of Japan's best traditions, and that this very tradition was being kept alive by the Honda-kai gang. Said Ohno, "Politicians and those who go the way of chivalry [yakuza] follow different Occupations. But they have one thing in common and that is their devotion to the principles of giri and ninjo." He concluded, "I offer my speech of congratulations by praying that you would further exert yourself in the ways of chivalry in order to make the society and our country better." He led the crowd in three *banzai*—cheers for the emperor—and received a thunderous ovation. The guests then moved on to a reception where they were entertained by a host of geisha.

Ohno and Kono were merely the most visible members of the right to be helped by the Kishi regime. Many of those in Kishi's Manchuria crowd, for instance, received offices under his stewardship. For three years, from 1957 until 1960, Kishi strengthened the position of the far right in the LDP and fostered antipathy to the constitution. He kept an eye toward the future as well: the youngest member of the Kishi cabinet was Yasuhiro Nakasone, a member of the Kono faction and a protege of Kodama, with whom he shared a secretary-adviser. Twenty-two years later, in 1982, the hawkish Nakasone finally became Japan's prime minister with the help, not surprisingly, of Kodama.

But despite Kishi's seemingly firm hold on the right and on the prime ministry, he would, during his term, encounter furious opposition from an unexpected quarter—the student left.

The Ampo Struggle

In 1960, there erupted a prolonged period of demonstrations and conflict in Japan that would strain the LDP hold on the country, threaten briefly the relationship between the United States and Japan, and prove that the old alliance between rightist and gangster was more valuable than ever to those in power.

The Americans had been attempting to renegotiate the U.S.-Japan Security Pact, the mutual defense treaty between the two nations. Although it stipulated that America would continue to maintain bases in Japan, as it had under the terms of the peace treaty, the security pact put little actual burden on Japan. America was required to come to the aid of Japan if the latter were attacked, but Japan had no responsibility to help the Americans if that country were under attack elsewhere in the world. The Kishi government was anxious to see that the pact be swiftly concluded and ratified, but the treaty contained a number of provisions that many Japanese, particularly anyone even slightly left of center, thoroughly disliked.

The pact allowed American forces in Japan to be equipped with nuclear weapons—a matter of grave concern to the Japanese after Nagasaki and Hiroshima. It also allowed the United States to take action within Japan if the Japanese government requested aid to quell any internal disturbances, something the left believed was aimed at them. Basically, American interests were an outgrowth of later Occupation goals—protecting its flank against Soviet and Chinese Communism, and keeping Japan in the American orbit. American aims, though, did not necessarily sit well with the Japanese.

In the spring of 1960, an international incident polarized Japanese and American interests. On May 1, the Soviet Union shot down an American CIA reconnaissance plane, the U-2, over Russian territory. Although this particular overflight originated in Pakistan, another major U-2 base was at Atsugi, Japan. Japanese who were opposed to the stationing of the U.S. military on Japanese soil saw the U-2s as a magnet for Soviet bombers.

But even before the U-2 incident, grassroots opposition to the security pact had been brewing in Japan. By March 1959, in fact, a wide-ranging progressive coalition had formed—the People's Council for Preventing Revision of the Security Treaty, the Ampo Joyaku Kaitei Soshi Kokumin Kaigi, generally called simply Ampo. This coalition contained every left-of-center group and then some. There were labor, education, women's, and Marxist groups, ranging from the Japan Anarchists League to the Executive Committee of the Japan Group Singing Association. But when it came time to take the case to the streets of Tokyo, Ampo drew its troops primarily out of the city's huge student population, from the leftist movement known as Zengakuren.

Quickly, the right responded, and it was immediately evident that the old alliance was working. According to a contemporary newspaper account, "In an attempt to cope with rallies staged by leftist forces against the security pact, rightist bodies organized a number of public meetings favoring the pact. Among them were a rally sponsored by the Patriotic Party at the Hibiya Public Hall on July 25, 1959, and another held by the Matsubakai [The Pine Needle Association, a major yakuza gang] at the same site on September 25."

The appearance of the yakuza group was the first indication that the right might not be content merely to sway public opinion. By themselves, rightists and yakuza would get nowhere with the public, who, for the most part, supported the leftist position. But the momentum produced by the Ampo forces frightened the more conservative elements in the business and political communities. Kishi, in particular, had a lot of personal ambition staked on the passage of the treaty, and did not want the left he so despised do anything to endanger its ratification.

On May 19, 1960, amid a series of massive public demonstrations by the Ampo people, the LDP took the extraordinary step of physically barring the socialists from the Diet chambers and ramrodding the treaty through to ratification. All that remained was the formal signing in June. This was to coincide with a state visit from President Eisenhower. The demonstrations, however, did not subside and the government was forced to take the Ampo factions seriously. Not that the treaty should be reconsidered, but that the demonstrators ought to be silenced, or at least contained.

By the May 19 ratification, events had grown noisy, with frequent fighting between demonstrators and police or, often, rightist thugs. But there had been a certain restraint on both sides and no loss of life on either. The Kishi people, though, were not at all confident that their police and rightist supporters could contain the Ampo demonstrators at a critical time. With Ike's visit imminent, the LDP's top leadership took a historic step backward—it turned to the underworld in the hopes of fashioning a criminal reserve army comprised of the yakuza and the far right.

The initial conduit between the LDP and the mob was Yoshio Kodama, who pledged his support and assured the politicians that this could indeed be accomplished. The LDP then sent its emissary, the head of the party's "Welcome Ike" committee, Tomisaburo Hashimoto, to a meeting of gangster bigwigs. Hashimoto contacted a number of influential yakuza: Kakuji Inagawa, head of the huge Kinsei-kai; Yoshimitsu Sekigami, oyabun of the Tokyo-based Sumiyoshi-kai; and "Tokyo's Al Capone," Kinosuke Ozu, still leader of the massive tekiya association. All agreed to help. To make sure the organization was tight, Kodama remained the linchpin of the operation. To him, it must have been the call of the wild: the government of Japan was once again, as in prewar days, summoning a patriotic underworld army. It was as if the Black Dragon Society itself had been reborn.

In a sense, the government had no choice. Eisenhower was expected to arrive on June 21 and to drive from the Tokyo airport accompanied by the emperor in an open limousine. The idea of an attack on the car was horrifying to the LDP politicos planning the motorcade. In the face of the anticipated demonstration, authorities planned to mobilize 18,000 police—enough to line the route with cops stationed every two yards. There were up to 15,000 Tokyo police available, and there were plans to requisition police from cities hundreds of miles away, but the LDP decided to rely on irregulars as well.

Three rightist coalitions were called upon for troops. One, the New Japan Council, organized in 1958 by Kishi himself and headed by Tokutaro Kimura, was to be a source of nonviolent types, people who would mass themselves in support of Ike. For heavier action, the government could draw on the All-Japan Council of Patriotic Organizations, composed of rightists and gangsters. In the distant reserve were some 300,000 members of the Japan Veterans League, a group that included some of the ultranationalist wartime leaders.

The final plans for June 21 were described by veteran Tokyo journalist Koji Nakamura, writing in the *Far Eastern Economic Review:*

> Kodama persuaded yakuza leaders of organized gamblers, gangsters, extortionists, street vendors and members of underground syndicates to organize

an "effective counter-force" to ensure Eisenhower's safety. The final plan called for the deployment of 18,000 yakuza, 10,000 street vendors [tekiya], 10,000 veterans and members of rightist religious organizations. They were supported by government-supplied helicopters, Cessna aircraft, trucks, cars, food, command posts and first-aid squads, in addition to some 800 million yen [about $2.3 million] in "operational funds."

It was a remarkable feat of organization, and from the point of view of the Japanese government, concluded none too soon. Eleven days before Eisenhower's scheduled arrival, the Japanese got a taste of what the president's visit might be like. U.S. ambassador Douglas MacArthur II (nephew to the general) met Eisenhower's press secretary, James Hagerty, at the Tokyo airport, and on the return drive their limousine was cut off, surrounded by angry demonstrators. MacArthur and Hagerty had to be rescued by military helicopter.

Five days later, MacArthur cabled State Department headquarters and conveyed the Japanese plans to protect Ike, although his notion of these plans was at some divergence with reality. In addition to police, wrote MacArthur, waiting along the route would be welcoming groups of Boy and Girl Scouts, as well as adults friendly to the president. These, he said, "will be in sufficiently great numbers to overwhelm any unfriendly demonstration and will ensure that [the] president receives [a] proper welcome." But in case the scouts failed to deter the Ampo demonstrators, MacArthur wrote, "30,000 young men of various athletic organizations and strongly opposed to zengakuren [the students] are being issued arm bands for identification and will, if required, assist police."

The "athletes" never got the call, because at the very same time as MacArthur was cabling Washington with the good news, the demonstrations reached a new peak. The left did not back down in the face of the rightist threats, but pushed on against the treaty. Finally, on the evening of June 15, the demonstrations outside the Diet building reached another peak, and this time events went too far. Gangsters and rightists battling the students seriously injured a number of protesters and killed a young coed from Tokyo University.

It was enough. The Japanese government withdrew the invitation to Eisenhower, fearing more deaths and even greater embarrassment. The confrontation between left and right over the visit would probably have been more disastrous than the shame of cancellation. But the drama was not yet over.

Three days later, 300,000 leftists moved through the streets of Tokyo shouting "Ampo hantai" (Down with the treaty) and "Kishi taose" (Overthrow Kishi). But at midnight on the 18th of June, the treaty was automatically afforded final ratification, and on the 21st, the emperor's seal was fixed upon the security pact. It is very unlikely that the United States would have removed its bases had the treaty been rejected, but with ratification, both the LDP and Washington were satisfied.

Someone still had to pay for the massive anguish and disruption the country had suffered through, and on June 23, Kishi announced that he would resign as prime minister, an act that indeed defused the Ampo demonstrations. Three weeks later he turned the government over to another conservative, Hayato Ikeda. The Ampo forces at the time believed that they had effected an important change, but the LDP was returned to office by a wide margin at the next election, and the security pact remained in effect.

Kishi had not been personally popular as prime minister, and never recovered his position of public power, but he continued to work behind the scenes. By giving the coalition of rightists and yakuza the official imprimatur of the government, Kishi reinstated a tradition dating back to the dark days of ultranationalism. His actions, furthermore, legitimized the postwar ties between the government and the underworld and ushered in a new era of gangster-rightist cooperation.

Perhaps the most enduring institution on the right stemming from the Ampo period is the Zen Nippon Aikokusha Dantai Kaigi, the All-Japan Council of Patriotic Organizations. By the early 1960s, Zen Ai Kaigi, as it was invariably known, had quickly grown into the leading Japan-wide federation of rightist groups, with a total membership of over 150,000. It was from the outset a true coalition, with 440 groups ultimately participating. In the subsequent years, Zen Ai Kaigi provided both political theory and political muscle to the right, and many of its ventures were under the direction of Kodama and his close allies.

Kodama did not create Zen Ai Kaigi by himself. He was only one of a network of influential rightists behind the organization, all aided by a number of yakuza leaders as well. The oyabun of Nippon Kokusui-kai, Matsuba-kai, Gijin-to, and others were "advisers" to the group. And on the board of directors were names out of the past: Tatsuo Amano, who led an abortive coup in 1933; Kozaburo Tachibana, who was involved in the prewar assassination of a prime minister; and Tadashi Onuma, the murderer of Finance Minister Junosuke Inouye. Ryoichi Sasakawa, with his growing financial clout, sat on the board, as did former G-2 sidekick Giichi Miura.

Although Zen Ai Kaigi adhered to general rightist principles, it did not have a clear program. It did, however, launch actions that went beyond mere advocacy. Early in its existence, for instance, Zen Ai Kaigi received a request from a steel fabricating firm in Chiba, a prefecture near Tokyo, to help the company with its labor problems. Specifically, it was asked to break up a strike. So well did Zen Ai Kaigi tackle the task that the union was broken up and 680 people were hospitalized. These were obviously not theoreticians at work.

In fact, so prevalent were yakuza among Zen Ai Kaigi's membership that some observers called it Yakuza Kaigi. It was fitting, then, that the organization chose its leadership with an eye to holding the yakuza within the coalition. The organization's second chairman and longtime boss was a Buddhist priest named Keizo Takei, a man who had been a yakuza in his youth and a spy and saboteur in the 1930s.

Factions within the huge coalition were common. In April 1961, yakuza groups within Zen Ai Kaigi—Matsuba-kai, Nippon Kokusui-kai, Nippon Yoshihito-to—withdrew from the alliance and formed an all-yakuza rightist coalition, the Nippon Jiyu Shugi Renmei. That same year, a more activist group loyal to Yoshio Kodama formed within the Zen Ai Kaigi. This was the Seinen Shiso Kenkyu-kai, known as Seishi-kai, the Youth Ideology Study Association. Despite its innocent-sounding name, Seishi-kai was far more criminally inclined than the parent group. Its chairman and actual organizer was one Tomeo Sagoya, the former head of the Fatherland Protection Corps, who was implicated in the 1930 assassination of Prime Minister Osachi Hamaguchi and imprisoned in 1955 for extortion. Seishi-kai had its subgroups as well; one of these was headed by a former boss of Tokyo's huge Sumiyoshi syndicate, and another by the Korean crime boss Hisayuki Machii.

Kodama assumed greater control over Seishi-kai in the 1960s until, at the end of the decade, amid intense factional infighting, he withdrew the organization from Zen Ai Kaigi. Shortly thereafter, 120 Seishi-kai stalwarts headed for the mountains of Niigata Prefecture, north of Tokyo. There they established a military training camp and learned the basics of street fighting, physical fitness, and bomb throwing. Kodama maintained a watchful eye on his troops, and at the end of the training, he sent them off with an inspirational message: "I hope that each of you will kill one hundred enemies for one, instead of one for one."

Just how many enemies, if any, Seishi-kai killed is unknown, but Kodama's efforts were not in vain. Instead of being used on the front lines against Communist revolution, Seishi-kai members fought against unfavorable publicity in Japan. In early 1971, a journalist named Hisatomo Takemori was in the process of publishing a book on Kodama and friends, entitled *Black Money*. When Seishi-kai chairman Masayoshi Takahashi heard of this blasphemous act, he leaned rather heavily on the publisher, preventing the printing and distribution of the work. He was subsequently charged with threatening the publisher, but the message came through—no books about Kodama unless the boss agrees.

The legacy of Ampo, then, was a power base that could not actually seize the reins of government, but was a constant, simmering force. Men like Kodama could use it either for their own personal ends—such as silencing an unfriendly book publisher—or for larger political aims—breaking a strike, collecting funds for candidates, intimidating leftists. The real winners were Kodama and those aligned with him.

Rise of the Gangster Shoguns

The war's aftermath continued to produce changes in yakuza methods and structure. For one thing, the yakuza became individually and collectively more violent. The older bakuto gangs were often appalled at the lack of ceremony in the newer mobs, the so-called gurentai, but there was usually little anyone could do. Swords were on their way out and guns were coming in. Ordinary citizens now could be the targets of yakuza as robberies and street shakedowns increased. The yakuza did not necessarily walk in the shadows as they traditionally claimed to do, while the commoners walked in the sun.

The yakuza also began to look different. Under the steady influence of the Americans, both during and after the Occupation, the yakuza began to assume some of the characteristics of their American gangster counterparts. Yakuza who swore to uphold traditional values were as entranced with American styles as any Japanese, but as often was the case, Japanese perceptions of Americans were somewhat skewed. Since yakuza didn't know any real American gangsters, they turned to the movies instead. They seemed to focus on gangster parodies, and the result was that the characters of *Guys and Dolls* rather than *White Heat* or *The Petrified Forest* were their models. The kobun took to dressing in dark suits, dark shirts, and white ties. Sunglasses were de rigueur, and in the 1960s, yakuza affected crewcuts and kept them for a longer time perhaps than anyone else in the world. To match their outfits, they affected a leer and a swagger that set them apart from the ordinary citizens. Yakuza leaders also acquired a taste for an imported luxury that might seem ironic today—foreign (principally American) cars. Even today, yakuza leaders are among the few customers for large American sedans in Japan.

The structure of the gangs started changing as well. Out of the chaos of the Occupation, some syndicates began to enlarge and dominate their regions through war or alliance. Whereas prewar gangs tended to remain small—an oyabun and up to fifty kobun—postwar gangs began to swell up to hundreds, sometimes thousands, of members overseen by dozens of sub-oyabun. The postwar tekiya gangs had already formed into the massive Roten Dogyo Kumiai under Tokyo boss Ozu, but by the time of the peace treaty, the new gangs had begun to make moves to consolidate the underworld. Observed the newspaper *Mainichi* in 1964, "As Japan's economy

grows, the big companies expand their markets and absorb smaller enterprises under their control and become mammoth in size. So does the same
process take place in the world of violence."

In addition to centralization of power, the gangs added numbers. The
Tokyo Metropolitan Police estimated that in 1958 there were 70,000 yakuza
in the whole of Japan; five years later the number had swelled to 184,000,
more men than in Japan's entire army that year. The actual number was
probably less than the number of people engaged in criminal activity under
the Occupation, but these were not mere black-market swindlers. Most
were committed criminals in some 5,200 gangs, preying upon an economy
growing at breakneck speed.

Some analysts, such as noted yakuza expert Kenji Ino, a Tokyo-based
journalist, believe that the high membership was due in part to large numbers of shop owners and operators of entertainment businesses who joined
as associates. This period saw the entertainment districts more crowded
than ever, and club and restaurant owners were anxious to avoid trouble
with the gangs, so they enlisted. By the time the 1964 Tokyo Olympics rolled
around, though, the police had finally begun a systematic crackdown on the
gangs, ending the postwar period of official tolerance.

During the twenty years following the war, there was one gang that prospered mightily under the new regime of violence and acquisition—the
Yamaguchi-gumi. Beginning life as an ordinary Kobe waterfront mob,
the Yamaguchi-gumi grew rapidly during the Occupation. Like many of
the others, it was patterned on the structure of the ancient bakuto gangs,
but used the violent tactics of the newer gurentai. Within five years of the
end of American rule, the gang came to control most of the area around the
nearby metropolis of Osaka, and by the end of the decade had begun to expand nationally. The story of the postwar Yamaguchi mob begins before the
war and is very much the story of its longtime boss, Kazuo Taoka.

Born in a small village on the southern island of Shikoku in 1913, Taoka
was orphaned at a young age and sent to work at a Kobe shipyard. There, at
age fourteen, he began to associate with members of a small gang headed
by Noburu Yamaguchi, a gang that took its name from its titular head. For
nine years, Taoka was basically an apprentice member and ran errands,
waited on the boss, and worked himself up to regular gang tasks. He earned
a reputation for ferocity in fights, gouging opponents' eyes out with his fingers. Taoka's comrades soon nicknamed him Kuma, "The Bear." In 1936,
he became a blood member of the group and the same year found himself
looking at an eight-year prison sentence for slashing to death a rival gang
member.

Kazuo Taoka spent half the war in prison, and when he walked out in

1943 he was welcomed back to a gang decimated by police crackdowns and the military draft. Shortly after the war, in October 1946, Taoka, thirty-three, assumed the mantle of oyabun when Noburu Yamaguchi died of natural causes. The young boss had only twenty-five devoted kobun, but he had developed a remarkable talent for organization. Those resources, combined with his legendary ruthlessness, would propel him to greatness in the underworld.

The Bear learned that enterprise was as valuable as brutality, and he quickly discovered new ways to prosper. On the Kobe docks, he founded the Yamaguchi-gumi Construction Company and began work on local projects with his obedient workforce. At the same time, he moved to grab a greater share of the local gambling and extortion rackets. In the late 1940s, he formed an alliance with the largest local bakuto gang, the Honda-kai, but Taoka was too ambitious to remain locked in a relationship of parity. The ensuing gang war showed the superiority of Taoka's killers over traditional gamblers, and Taoka took over Honda-kai's rackets, incorporating the weaker gang into his own. A Korean mob, the Meiyu-kai, was next, and Taoka took over their Osaka territory. Then the Miyamoto-gumi fell to Taoka's men. He operated like a smart guerrilla leader, concentrating his forces and attacking savagely when the time was right.

Taoka also expanded the role of the traditional Osaka underworld and vastly increased his income. He launched into show business, forming a talent agency that pushed Osaka-area performers. Taoka put together a package of performers called Home Run Hit Parade and sent them on the road around Japan. The heart of his operation, however, remained in the Kobe docks. He continued to broker day laborers and even took a financial interest in a number of cargo firms. By the mid-1960s, the Yamaguchi syndicate controlled an estimated 80 percent of all cargo loading on the Kobe docks. At the same time, Taoka had a piece of some fourteen firms in the area—mostly cargo transport companies—that grossed him nearly $17 million in 1965 alone.

By 1964, Taoka controlled 343 different gangs under the Yamaguchi umbrella, and at the end of the decade could boast 10,000 kobun. His success was noted by political figures on the right. Taoka's front company, the Association of Harbor Stevedoring Promotion, received financial backing from Tokyo rightist Seigen Tanaka and political support from Kodama ally Ichiro Kono, then minister of transportation. Taoka was viewed as a controller of labor, one who could keep leftist unions off the docks. By the late 1950s, Taoka was a political power to be reckoned with and was feared and courted widely.

In the area around Tokyo, no one gang came to dominate as the Yamaguchi-gumi had done in Osaka. But even in this competitive situation, a very few gangs rose to the top, either through muscle, influence, or both. One of the premier gangs was that of Kakuji Inagawa, a Yokohama bakuto with talents that in many ways equaled those of Kazuo Taoka.

During the Occupation, ethnic Koreans and Chinese became particularly powerful in the port city of Yokohama, outside Tokyo. Not only did they control that city's black market, but they expanded their operations down the coast to the hot springs resort of Atami. Dismayed at the influence of these "foreigners," Inagawa decided to help his mentor, Yokohama oyabun Masajiro Tsuruoka, whose territory included Atami. Inagawa organized a small gang to fight the Chinese and Koreans alongside Tsuruoka's men. Inagawa's gangsters displayed a legendary ruthlessness in chasing the non-Japanese from the area, and within several years Inagawa had built his own gang to equal that of Tsuruoka. Together, their activities expanded through the region, including among other places Shimizu, historic fighting ground of that most famous of all yakuza, Jirocho of Shimizu.

By 1950, both Inagawa and Tsuruoka had come to the attention of the Occupation authorities. The American consul general in Yokohama cabled Washington with this observation: "The activities of this gang ranged from blackmail and intimidation, in connection with the collection of 'protection' money, to control and direction of bands of thieves which were regularly placed aboard foreign merchant ships calling at Yokohama and Shimizu in the guise of cleaning crews."

Inagawa weathered the displeasure of the American authorities. By the early 1960s, Inagawa and his gang, the Kakusei-kai, had spread from their initial territory in Yokohama and Atami to Tokyo and even to parts of the northern island of Hokkaido. By 1964, more than 2,700 yakuza stood under his command. The gang's major source of money came from gambling enterprises. Despite the widespread legalization of betting on races, cards and casino gambling were still forbidden, and bakuto such as Inagawa could make a sizable fortune running such games. According to the Tokyo Metropolitan Police, Inagawa took in $175,000 from one high-stakes card game in 1965, a fee just for running the game.

By 1963, Inagawa was feeling the heat of too much police attention and changed the name of his gang to Kinsei-kai. (He would later change the name yet again, to Inagawa-kai.) The new name would go along with his new status—he applied for the registration of Kinsei-kai as a political party. Political solidarity for the gangs was usually problematic. Although Inagawa's syndicate, like others, shared a gut-level ideology of anti-Communism and a rightist outlook, alliances were hard to come by. The day-to-day enemy most gangs dealt with was certainly not the remote threat of a Communist takeover of Japan, but that of other gangs, a factor that made yakuza unity a pleasant fiction. At least one person, though, had the vision and the power to deal with the factionalization in the underworld. He would forge alliances and speed the modernization of the yakuza, ensuring that the political and financial development of Japan's underworld kept pace with the nation's rapidly expanding economy. That person was Yoshio Kodama.

Kodama saw that the gangster coalition he put together during the Ampo crisis could perhaps be reconstituted as a permanent entity. It would also provide Kodama with a valuable source of power. Certainly Kodama would strengthen his own hand with the LDP by showing an ability to control both the far right and the warring gangster clans. That control would soon alarm much of the Japanese government.

In December 1963, an unusual leaflet was sent out to all national LDP legislators. It warned Diet members:

> While the Liberal-Democratic Party is occupied incessantly in factional feuds, the leftist influences in Japan are accumulating their energy for revolution.... You should realize that what is contaminating Japan the most today is the factional policies of the Liberal-Democratic Party and its intra-party feuds.... Before the public's goodwill toward the party changes into a feeling of hatred, all of you should cease intra-party feuds.

Several members of one LDP faction were identified by name in the leaflet, but that was not the most startling thing about it. Such alarmist statements from the right were common enough, and would ordinarily be ignored. But the signers of the statement were a combination of seven yakuza groups, some of the most powerful in Japan. Japanese Diet members were stunned. That gangsters were involved in politics was no surprise, but that a giant federation had formed and was pointedly suggesting national policy was a new and generally unwelcome development.

These seven participating gangs were the components of a coalition formed in December 1963 at the Tsuruya Hotel in Inagawa's resort town of Atami, under the guidance of Kodama. After the meeting commenced with the singing of the national anthem and three hearty banzai, Kodama got to the crux of the matter:

> When we have scuffles, before we shed our blood, let us solve them by discussion. Let us only use our physical strength when we are in danger of a leftist revolution in Japan or when some natural calamity visits us. I hope with this as a starting point, each group would try to maintain friendly relations with the others, and thus try to improve the character of your organizations.

It was true that there were "scuffles" among the gangs, although murderous vendettas would better describe them, and perhaps Kodama genuinely deplored the violence. But he was motivated more by a political vision than anything else. The ideology behind the new alliance grew out of the prewar rightist concept of a Toa Doyu-kai, or Asian Federation, to be used "as a breakwater against communism in time of national crisis," as one commentator put it. The fact that Japan in 1963 was not by any stretch of the imagination facing that sort of national crisis did nothing to deter Kodama.

Rather than a pan-Asian federation, Kodama now envisioned an all-Japan gangster coalition. But in February 1963, when Kodama was holding preliminary talks on the subject, Kazuo Taoka abruptly withdrew his Osaka gang from any proposed federation. From all-Asia, Kodama eventually wound up with an all-Tokyo coalition—the Kanto-kai, named after the Kanto Plain encompassing Tokyo. Nonetheless, it was a formidable organization, comprised of 13,000 gangsters from seven major gangs and headed by Kakuji Inagawa. If Kodama could now pull the gangs together as a functional unit, he would have one of Japan's strongest organizations at his disposal.

Kodama was aided in his task by a group of rightist theorists who bombarded Kanto-kai with messianic dogma. One popular theory was the Showa 45 Crisis theory, which stated that in 1970 (Showa 45, or the forty-fifth year of Emperor Hirohito's reign) Japan would face a leftist revolution. The right, the gangsters were told, had to present a united front. But for most of the members, rightist thought was uncomplicated and direct. Perhaps Kakuji Inagawa said it most eloquently: "We gamblers cannot walk in broad daylight. But if we unite and become a wall to stop communism, we can be of service to the nation. If anything happens, we would like to stake our lives for the good of the country."

Not all participants found these political aims worthy or even necessary. Yoshimitsu Sekigami, president of the Sumiyoshi-kai, said: "We are in the Kanto-kai with the idea that it is an association for amity. I do not believe that Japanese politics is in such a poor state that gamblers must interfere with it."

For some of the gangs, though, political action and posturing were long a part of their repertoire, and Kanto-kai represented no more than a formalization of that tactic. Uichiro Fujita, boss of the 2,400-member Matsuba-kai, for instance, publicly fulminated against the "subversive" nature of the Japan Teachers' Union—a favorite target of the right—and demanded that the government fund a school for military arts. The Matsuba-kai also threatened the leadership of the communications workers for daring to engage in a strike. And Fujita took his members to a mass rally of 3,000 gangsters and rightists protesting the Tokyo visit of Soviet deputy premier Anastas Mikoyan. Matsuba-kai was of course criminally active as well; members averaged one arrest for every day of the year, the second-highest rate of any Tokyo-area gang. This record led police to conclude that Fujita's political involvement was largely a smoke screen for his far more lucrative criminal activities.

Kodama's attitude toward the overtly criminal activities of the gangs was ambivalent. On the one hand, he saw fit to attack the growing problem of street crime, the *gyangu,* or teenage wolf packs. (*Gyangu* can mean "stupid," "pigheaded," or simply "gang.") "There are too many petty hoodlums," Kodama said. "It made me angry to see them loitering around and causing trouble to passersby. . . . That is why I tell the oyabun to rectify their own character first and control the petty hoodlums themselves." Clearly, organized rackets did not fall into the same category; these Kodama did not condemn.

Kodama walked a thin line with Kanto-kai, trying to whip the gangs into a unit, but ultimately it was beyond even his organizational abilities. In slightly more than a year the federation began to fall apart under the strain of competing interests. In January 1965, the thirty executive members of the seven bodies voted to dissolve Kanto-kai, after only fifteen months. But if the organization failed, Kodama did not go down with it.

During the mid-1960s, everything seemed to turn Kodama's way. Not only top LDP figures, but business, professional, and even academic people paid him honors with their presence. His house in Tokyo's Setagaya district was the scene of constant meetings and audiences before the great Kodama *sensei* (teacher). Kodama sometimes received prominent foreign visitors. With a surgeon, he would discuss how to raise money for a research facility, while with a politician he would offer help in campaigning.

To the oyabun who stopped by, Kodama was a towering figure. Said Inagawa: "I am sometimes made to wait for seven hours at his house, but when I listen to his talk, I come to understand the world." Even Taoka, who refused to join Kanto-kai, found Kodama a figure worthy of some respect. "I am positively opposed to the idea of his reigning as the boss of the yakuza," said Taoka, "but if he stays a patriot, I am most willing to become his companion." In fact, Taoka would come to depend on Kodama for more than ideological inspiration.

Kodama's pivotal role as a bridge between the gangs and the echelons of legitimate power was understood by many, but not generally acknowledged. It was, therefore, something of a milestone when, in July 1964, the national *Mainichi* newspaper published an exhaustive fourteen-part series on the underground gangs and their relation to aboveground power. Investigative reporting in Japan does not have the tradition that it enjoys in the United States, and for a major daily to commit itself to a six-month investigation and risk treading on the toes of some dangerous and powerful people was a major accomplishment. Although the paper was attacked for the series, it had its supporters. In its final segment, *Mainichi* quoted Toshio Eguchi, director of the National Police Agency (NPA). Eguchi took to task what he perceived as the hypocrisy of Japanese power:

> Although our political and financial circles ever complain about organized vi-
> olence, they continue to contribute money to the various groups. In order to
> eradicate violence from our society, we must give the underworld no political
> consideration. It must be relentlessly smashed from all directions.

It was a courageous statement, but it had little effect on those rightist
politicians and financiers who customarily worked with the yakuza. Police
did crack down on the gangs, but otherwise it was business as usual, and Kodama, for the time being, remained untouched. The structure of the gang
world continued to change in the 1960s. Previously, Taoka's Yamaguchi-
gumi had confined their predatory activities to the Kansai area around
Osaka and Kyoto, generally avoiding Tokyo and its surrounding regions.
One of the purposes of Kanto-kai, from the point of view of the participants,
if not of Kodama, was to present a united front to any moves Taoka might
make into Kanto. There was more than just economic interest at play. Residents of Kansai and Kanto foster a great regional rivalry, like Americans on
opposite sides of the Mason-Dixon line. There are cultural and political differences, of course, but they are not usually a serious issue. In a gang war,
though, these differences can be expected to exacerbate matters.

Kanto-kai did not have any deterrent effect on Taoka. During the short
tenure of the alliance, Taoka's syndicate, Yamaguchi-gumi, began sending
people into Yokohama and incurring the wrath of Inagawa. There was, in
fact, such friction between Inagawa's men and the arriving Yamaguchi thugs
that an armed battle known as the Grand Palace incident took place on the
streets of Yokohama.

Kodama viewed the warfare as deplorable, a threat to anti-Communist
unity, and used his connections to secure a truce. His solution was to facilitate an expedient alliance between Taoka and Machii, Korean boss of
Tokyo's Tosei-kai. Machii traveled to Kobe for the ceremony uniting the two
gangs, and the ensuing alliance helped break Kanto-kai for good. Again Kodama used his good offices to mediate between Inagawa and his Kanto allies, and Taoka. A truce was called, and Taoka accepted a limitation of no
more than ten men in the Yokohama area.

Taoka sought to evade this restriction by an elaborate ploy devised by his
friend Seigen Tanaka, rightist and Kodama rival. Together they created the
cynically named League for the Stamping Out of Drug Traffic, and promoted it in both Kansai and Kanto. Taoka asserted that he began the organization because of the damage to his men caused by drug use during the
Occupation. "It was simply agonizing to see them when they were out of the
drugs," he claimed. "Their wives had an awful time, and they tried to have
their husbands recuperate by imprisoning them in the house, but half of
them died and half of them became invalids."

In the Osaka area, Taoka used some of Tanaka's connections and found unusual allies. President Masatoshi Matsushita of Rikkyo University and Masako Hika, head of the Kansai Housewives Association, joined with the gang boss in publicly demonstrating against drug use. Taoka then sent his men to the Tokyo area under the guise of fighting the drug menace. In Yokohama, Yamaguchi men were in the streets in October 1963 attempting to gather signatures for a petition denouncing drugs, an act that infuriated the Inagawa gang.

The police and the public, as well, rightly viewed with some suspicion a notorious crime syndicate vowing to stamp out drug traffic. It was a remarkable display of yakuza nerve, but it worked. The Yamaguchi-gumi maintained their presence in the Tokyo-Yokohama area and continued to pressure the other gangs, especially Inagawa's Kinsei-kai.

The anti-drug campaign took a new turn in November 1963 when Tosei-kai member Haruo Kinoshita shot and seriously wounded Seigen Tanaka, architect of the campaign. Kinoshita had seen that Taoka, by allying himself with the Tosei-kai boss Machii, had forced the Korean gang into an isolated position in Tokyo. Other Kanto gangs were now blaming Tosei-kai for the Yamaguchi move into the capital region, so Kinoshita tried to remedy the situation.

Taoka took the assassination attempt as a personal attack, although Tanaka made a remarkable recovery and left the hospital after only four months. Machii felt himself responsible for the assassin's action, even though the latter had acted on his own. Machii traveled to Kobe to make his amends. With him he brought two items that would prevent a possible gang war: 2 million yen for Tanaka, and his fingertip for Taoka.

Tensions between Taoka and Inagawa remained high, however, until the Tokyo oyabun was found guilty of operating an illegal gambling casino and sentenced to three years in prison. Taoka took stock of the situation and directed all Yamaguchi-gumi members in Fukushima Prison to help make Inagawa's stay as pleasant as possible, reasoning that Inagawa would then be in his debt. When Inagawa was released in January 1969 he found that his gang had been seriously reduced by disorganization, mutiny, and arrest. In fact, three-quarters of his members had been arrested in the previous year. The situation called for strong action: first, through a series of decisive moves, he subdued the unrest among the various gangs in his fiefdom. Of far greater importance to Japan's underworld, Inagawa decided that the Yamaguchi-gumi was too powerful to fight any longer. Inagawa, faced with both the carrot and the stick, found that an alliance with Taoka was both reasonable and possibly beneficial.

To lay the groundwork for the alliance, Inagawa turned to Kodama, who then made the arrangements. On October 24, 1972, the long-range plans came to fruition. That day, ten men wearing crewcuts and dark suits got out of four black American cars in front of Taoka's Kobe house. Because of the heavy police surveillance, no bosses from other gangs were invited to the ceremony.

In Taoka's living room, his two top men, Kenichi Yamamoto and Yoshio Masuda, faced off against Inagawa-kai lieutenants Susumu Ishii and Hsiao Chun-shu. It was a classic rite of sakazuki, the choreographed exchange of sake to create a blood brotherhood between two forces. Small altars, called *sambo,* were placed before Yamamoto and Ishii, and the go-between said solemnly: "The ritual to tie the bond of brotherhood between Kenichi Yamamoto, representing leader Taoka of the Yamaguchi gang, and Susumu Ishii, representing the Inagawa gang, will now commence."

> Sake was poured into unglazed ceremonial cups and drunk. The two then wrapped the cups in special paper and put them into their kimono. They then clasped each other's hands. The go-between held their clasped hands and announced: "The sake cup ritual on even terms is now over."

A quiet reception followed, almost masking the enormity of the occasion. Between them, the two syndicates controlled or had alliances with gangs in virtually all of Japan; only four prefectures were wholly independent of a Yamaguchi-Inagawa combine. To yakuza watchers at the time, it seemed as if the consolidation among the gangs that began in the early 1950s was reaching its peak, and Yoshio Kodama, the underworld's visionary godfather, was reaping the benefits.

Kodama himself always scoffed at the notion of being boss of the yakuza, but then he also denied that he enjoyed immense power. His goal, as he told the newspaper *Mainichi* in 1964, was simply to retire. "I would like to wash my hands of the worthless everyday world and enjoy my life fishing, for instance," he said. In fact, Kodama was quite the fisherman. He even included a photo of himself flycasting from a boat midstream on the flyleaf of his autobiographical *Sugamo Diary.* Given the purpose of the photo, it's unlikely that Kodama's mind at the time was only on trout or carp. For him, the period from 1960 to the middle of the 1970s was one where nearly every cast brought in a fish. He, and the organizations he represented—from the thugs in the streets, to the yakuza, to his minions inside the government— had reached the summit of power. Kodama had an army of rightists and gangsters at his call, millions of dollars in his hands, and a government both corrupt and complicit. The underworld's scowling power broker had become the most powerful man in Japan.

CHAPTER FOUR

THE BLACK MIST

AS THE LIGHTS GLARED IN ROOM 4221 OF THE DIRKSEN SENATE OFFICE
Building, the Honorable Frank Church pored over his voluminous notes.
Assembled before him stirred a huge, expectant crowd of reporters, spec-
tators, and the investigative staff of his own Subcommittee on Multinational Corporations. It was Wednesday, February 4, 1976, and Frank Church,
Democratic senator from Idaho and presidential aspirant, was ready to de-
liver the fruit of six months' labor.

At 10:01 A.M., Church called the hearing to order:

"We will hear today first from Lockheed's accounting firm, Arthur Young and
Company, and then from the responsible Lockheed executives themselves,
about bribes and questionable political payments made in Europe and Japan.

"We will find that the company has used an off-the-books account to buy
business intelligence and pay the officials of major European consortia . . . we
will see that Exxon and the CIA have not been the only ones making million-
dollar political contributions to parties and government ministers in Italy . . .
and, most disturbing of all, we will show that Lockheed has for many years employed as its agent a prominent leader of the ultra-right wing militarist faction
in Japan and has paid him millions of dollars in fees and commissions over the
last few years.

"In effect, we have had a foreign policy of the U.S. Government which has
vigorously opposed this political line in Japan and a Lockheed foreign policy
which has helped to keep it alive through large financial subsidies in support
of the company's sales efforts in the country."

To the witness stand that week in Washington, D.C., Church summoned
forth a nervous handful of top officials and accountants representing the
Lockheed Aircraft Corporation. The witnesses for the first time publicly
testified how during the past twenty years Lockheed had secretly funneled

more than $12.6 million into Japan, much of it apparently spent on illegal payoffs to the country's most powerful political figures. This huge sum was expended in an effort to sell more than $1 billion worth of Lockheed aircraft to Japan's number two airline, All Nippon Airways, and to the defense agency of the Japanese government. Roughly $7 million of the amount, most of it in yen bills packed in cardboard boxes, had been covertly passed to Lockheed's secret sales agent in Japan—the ubiquitous Yoshio Kodama.

Headlines raced across Japan's newspapers about the "Rokkiedo jiken" (Lockheed incident), and for the next year the scandal dominated the country's affairs. Lockheed became Japan's Watergate, at the time the biggest scandal in the nation's postwar history. The Japanese press recounted in minute detail the testimony of the subcommittee's star witness, Lockheed president Carl Kotchian, who reluctantly detailed the company's long history of secret payments to Kodama. Spurred by Kotchian's admissions, investigators would soon reveal that Lockheed's men had bribed their way into deals with Japan's leading politicians. Before the scandal subsided, the list of bribed officials included Prime Minister Kakuei Tanaka, the secretary-general of the LDP, the ministers of industry and transportation, the chairman of the LDP's Special Committee on Aviation, and the current and former parliamentary vice-ministers of transportation. In addition, said investigators, Lockheed had thrown in a kickback of $50,000 to the president of All Nippon Airways on each airplane sold.

The revelations should not have come as a shock to the Japanese, given the postwar history of collusion between the nation's political and criminal underworlds. But the Japanese public had studiously ignored the warning signs. Although some journalists in Japan knew of the Lockheed payoffs as far back as the early 1960s, the press showed little interest in pursuing such a controversial story. The scandal brought up too much of what the Japanese had come to call *kuroi kiri* (black mist), the dark history of dirty tricks, corruption, and organized crime in Japan.

By 1976, however, the political system that Kodama helped create had begun to unravel. The Lockheed revelations struck in an atmosphere already charged by the resignation fourteen months earlier of Prime Minister Kakuei Tanaka. Tanaka had been stung, in November 1974, by a two-part exposé in *Bungei Shunju,* a prestigious and widely read monthly. A team of investigative reporters detailed for the first time the enormous sums of so-called black-money running through Tanaka's political network—more than $250 million channeled through dummy corporations from big business to members of his party faction. The reporters further estimated that some $15 million of this amount was used for payoffs within the LDP to secure the post of prime minister for Tanaka.

These revelations, coming only three months after Nixon's resignation over Watergate, threatened to cause heavy political damage to the prime minister. But Tanaka, nicknamed "The Computerized Bulldozer" for his political and financial skill, seemed undaunted. The prime minister, after all, had only expanded and shrewdly employed an already existing system of political gifts and payoffs.

Tanaka had good reason to believe that, like other postwar scandals, this one would pass quickly. Indeed, for the next week the Japanese press refused to touch the story. That changed, however, with Tanaka's appearance before the Foreign Correspondents' Club of Japan, where he was subjected to questions unusually direct and probing for the Japanese. The prime minister, humiliated and unnerved, stormed out of the club, but with the world's press onto the story, the scandal could no longer be ignored. Now, with a vengeance, the Japanese went after Tanaka's politics, his personal finances, and his evasion of income taxes.

Two weeks after the *Bungei Shunju* story first appeared, Tanaka resigned as prime minister. If the Japanese were getting ideas that even the office of prime minister could be bought and sold, the Lockheed scandal confirmed them. The Lockheed scandal went far beyond Tanaka's "money-power politics" to expose in three dimensions the extent of corruption in Japan. One authority on Japan, political scientist Chalmers Johnson of the University of California, summed up the scandal this way:

> The details were shocking not so much because the Lockheed Company had smoothed the way for its sales of airplanes in Japan—there was plenty of evidence that Boeing, McDonnell Douglas, and Grumman were engaged in similar operations—but because the case took the Japanese back in time, to periods and people they would have liked to forget, to rightwingers and gangsters. . . . The case was serious since it deeply implicated officials of the transportation ministry, plus one of Japan's leading trading companies and the prime minister himself. Worst of all, it brought up the name Yoshio Kodama.

The Lockheed Corporation and Mr. Kodama

Kodama's relationship with the Lockheed Corporation dates back to early 1958, when the forty-seven-year-old rightist was expanding his political power over both the rapidly growing yakuza gangs and the increasingly entrenched Liberal Democratic Party. Kodama's contact was Taro Fukuda, a close friend from his postwar stay at Sugamo Prison. An interpreter by trade, Fukuda was born and educated in the United States and went to Japan to attend Waseda University. U.S. officials revoked his American citizenship upon learning that he had worked for the Japanese government in occupied Manchuria.

Fukuda translated and published Kodama's rhetorical autobiography, *I Was Defeated,* and later, with Kodama's financial backing, founded a public relations agency. That agency was hired by Lockheed's man in Japan, John

Kenneth Hull, to conduct a press campaign. Hull had arrived in Tokyo in December 1957, when his company moved into Japan to sell its F-104 Starfighter. Hull also put on Lockheed's payroll an assistant named Yoshi-yoshi Oni, who would later become Lockheed's Tokyo office manager. Oni had served as an espionage agent in China during the war and later worked for the U.S. Occupation, apparently as one of General Willoughby's re-cruits in G-2.

Worried that the Starfighter sales campaign was not going well, Hull asked Fukuda to suggest Japanese politicians who might help Lockheed present its case to the government. Instead, Fukuda recommended Ko-dama, and arranged for the two men to meet. Kodama subsequently agreed to become Lockheed's secret "consultant," with Fukuda as the go-between. This arrangement would last for the next eighteen years.

Kodama went to work and performed admirably for his new American client. By using his political connections, he lobbied successfully for Japan's defense agency to choose Lockheed's Starfighter over the Grumman F-11F. His key contacts in the government centered around three of Japan's most yakuza-tainted politicians: Bamboku Ohno, a leading Diet member and, at the time, the LDP's vice president; the powerful Ichiro Kono, another se-nior LDP official; and Nobusuke Kishi, who, with Kodama's backing, had risen to become prime minister.

Lockheed continued to rely on Kodama's services through the mid-1960s, although the company's demands were relatively light. That was probably just fine with Kodama, who had many other tasks before him. Infighting then plagued Zen Ai Kaigi, his national alliance of gangsters and rightists, until in 1969 the group's most activist members splintered off into the even more radical Seishi-kai, taking Kodama with them. But turning the yakuza into superpatriots was not always very lucrative, so when Lockheed had further plans for Japan, Kodama was glad to be of assistance.

By the end of the decade, Lockheed had renewed Kodama's contract and extended it to include South Korea as well. Soon he was at work again, this time unsuccessfully lobbying for the government purchase of yet another jet fighter. His failure may well have been due to a weakening hold over those controlling the LDP. Both Ohno and Kono had died in the mid-1960s, and Kodama had less influence over Prime Minister Kishi's succes-sors, Eisaku Sato and Kakuei Tanaka. But Kodama was not easily discour-aged. To underscore his sincerity to the prime minister, Kodama wrote Sato an open letter in 1968, stating: "If there was the smallest act of corruption among the parties directly or indirectly concerned with the selection of Japan's next fighters, it should be denounced severely as immoral conduct corrupting the politics of this country."

It was at about this point that Lockheed approached Kodama with its most critical task yet: the sale of its new wide-bodied passenger plane, the TriStar L1011. A large sale in Japan was deemed crucial by Lockheed executives, who needed it to help overcome financial problems elsewhere in the company. It was to be the jumbo-jet sales war of the 1970s, with Lockheed going up against both Boeing and McDonnell Douglas in Japan. In January 1969, Lockheed apparently began its first formal contract with Kodama, and from then on the money poured in. Kodama received $138,000 a year for "consultation" and was guaranteed a commission of $4 million for an initial order of three to six TriStars to any major Japanese airline. Kodama was also promised $120,000 each for the sale of the seventh through the fifteenth TriStars, and $60,000 more for each additional plane.

With the Kodama machinery now well oiled, Japan's leading power broker went into action. Lacking close connections to certain key LDP leaders, Kodama began to rely increasingly more on money to make things happen. A major problem was how to get to Tanaka, then chief of the powerful Ministry of International Trade and Industry and a candidate to succeed Sato as prime minister. Not having a close relationship with Tanaka, Kodama turned to a mutual friend, Kenji Osano.

Osano, one of Japan's wealthiest men, was a formidable kuromaku in his own right. He was a close friend and the largest individual backer of Tanaka. Osano was also the largest private shareholder in Japan Air Lines and a major investor in All Nippon Airways (ANA). So successful was Osano that the press, in tribute to his financial skill, had dubbed him with a host of titles: "The Takeover King," "The Business Sphinx," "The Ambulatory Cashbox," and "Monster Osano."

As Tanaka rose in political might after the war, Osano scored business success after success. By the mid-1950s, Osano had parlayed a dilapidated fleet of charcoal-burning buses into a fortune, in good part by supplying U.S. forces during the Korean War. In 1964 he bought his friend Tanaka's faltering construction firm for $6 million, an incredibly good deal for Tanaka.

It was at about the time Osano picked up Tanaka's company that he apparently became close to Yoshio Kodama. The newspaper *Asahi*, citing court records, states that in 1965 Osano provided Kodama with 200 million yen (about $550,000). "Mr. Kodama needed money for political purposes and asked for my help," reportedly testified Osano, "so I gave him a 200 million yen bill . . ." Kodama, then busily organizing yakuza into rightist groups, no doubt put the money to use quickly.

By the time Kodama approached Osano in 1972—this time on behalf of Lockheed—the latter had become a billionaire. Kodama's fellow kuromaku had built up a financial empire of real estate, hotels, airplanes, and banks. The $6 million development company he had bought from Tanaka in 1964 was by 1972 producing some $330 million in revenues. Osano's flagship company—Kokusai Kogyo—boasted thirty-eight subsidiaries, all under his personal control. By the early 1970s, Osano's assets included nearly forty hotels in Japan, Hawaii, and California, as well as ski areas, bowling alleys, taxi and bus companies, and restaurants. Osano's companies traded across the Pacific in everything from golf clubs to automobiles.

As he did in business, Osano made his political investments aggressively. Over the years, the tycoon had gained a reputation for making massive contributions to political candidates of both the LDP and the Socialist Party, contributions that rarely appeared on official lists of campaign spending. In the tradition of the kuromaku, Osano was owed a lot of debts by a lot of people. So when Kodama came knocking with a lucrative proposal regarding U.S. aircraft sales, Osano listened intently.

Of Money Changers and Mobsters

By 1971, the jumbo-jet war was in full swing and Lockheed's president, Carl Kotchian, had arrived in Japan to personally take charge of the TriStar sales campaign. Although Kotchian had visited Japan at least once a year since 1961, it was only now that he finally met Kodama. Kotchian had read Kodama's *Sugamo Diary* before their first meeting, and although he knew his salesman bore an unsavory reputation, it hardly mattered to the corporate chieftain. In a 1976 interview with the newspaper *Asahi*, Kotchian admitted, "I was not much concerned about Mr. Kodama's political ideas or behavior. It was enough to be told that he had an excellent record as an agent . . ."

Kodama had indeed been confirming his worth during the past year. One of Lockheed's biggest obstacles was the president of All Nippon Airways, Tetsuo Oba, who had already taken an option for the McDonnell Douglas DC-10. Kodama knew that for Lockheed to be successful, Oba would have to go.

First, Kodama turned to Osano and advised his friend to move up as an ANA stockholder from twenty-eighth to tenth place, thus guaranteeing inside information on the company's affairs. (This cost Lockheed more than $200,000 in payments to Osano.) Next, Kodama activated one part of a large force of *sokaiya* under his command, financial racketeers who specialize in the extortion of Japanese corporations. The day before the ANA stockholders' meeting that year, Kodama's people leaked embarrassing information about a bogus $1 million loan with which president Oba was connected. Kodama's racketeers then packed the shareholders' meeting, demanding information about the loan.

That was enough to topple Oba, who never showed up at the meeting and resigned the following day. In Oba's place Kodama installed a more pliable candidate, a recently retired vice-minister of transportation.

At one point, when Lockheed seemed in danger of losing the TriStar sale, Kodama pulled into the fray other movers and shakers in Japan. Among those he contacted, according to Kotchian, was Kodama's old friend and sometime rival, Ryoichi Sasakawa. Godfather of Japan's multi-billion-dollar boat racing industry, Sasakawa was, like Kodama, no stranger to political and financial intrigue. Kodama had asked his former cellmate to intervene on behalf of Lockheed, for there were protests over landing the TriStar at Osaka's already too noisy Itami Airport. Sasakawa, among his many titles, was chairman of the Aircraft Nuisance Prevention Association, and although no payment was ever revealed, he saw to it that the TriStar would have no trouble meeting the airport's noise control levels.

Kotchian must have been impressed with these feats, for between 1970 and 1972 Kodama's fees jumped more than twentyfold, to more than $2.2 million. Kotchian soon came to call Kodama his "Department of State" in Japan. Although the deal was yet to be clinched, Kotchian could see the wind shifting in Lockheed's favor.

In July of 1972, Kakuei Tanaka became prime minister, and events began to unfold rapidly. At a summit meeting with President Nixon in Hawaii the following September—in a hotel owned by Osano—Tanaka promised that Japan would buy $320 million worth of civil aircraft to help alleviate the U.S. trade deficit. Japanese officials, according to press accounts, stated that Nixon actually suggested that the aircraft come from Lockheed. Upon his return home, the prime minister summoned the president of All Nippon Airlines and there immediately followed reports in Japan and the United States that the company would buy the TriStar.

Lockheed suddenly began to covertly move large sums of money through its Tokyo office to Kodama. Within days of Tanaka's meeting with the ANA president, Kodama was signing receipts for more than $3 million in payoff money. The receipts were ably translated into English by Taro Fukuda, Kodama's old friend and longtime Lockheed connection. In addition, several million flowed to Lockheed's acknowledged sales representative in Japan, the giant Marubeni Trading Company. Marubeni executives signed coded receipts for "100 peanuts" or "120 pieces," each unit signifying 1 million yen (then worth about $3,000). The money, like much of that sent to Kodama, was used to bribe leading government and airline industry officials.

By 1973 the TriStar sale was secure, but Lockheed payoff money continued to flow into Japan. The reason: an even more lucrative deal loomed ahead—the sale of Lockheed's P-3C Orion antisubmarine plane to the Japanese Air Force. The order, for some one hundred planes, could have been worth as much as $1 billion. Kodama reportedly stood to take in $9 million, partly as his commission and partly for use as bribes. The deal was just about to go through when Lockheed officials were summoned before Congress and began telling U.S. senators about their payoff practices overseas.

There were logistic problems for Lockheed in moving so much unattributable cash into Japan. The vast amount of the more than $12.6 million Lockheed sent to Kodama and Marubeni was transferred from Switzerland or Los Angeles through Deak and Company, a New York–based firm of international currency dealers. Kodama may well have known of Deak before his payments from Lockheed, because for years the company had served as a covert channel for moving CIA funds. The firm was founded before World War II by Nicholas Deak, a Hungarian emigré who had belonged to the CIA's wartime predecessor, the OSS (Office of Strategic Services). After the war he built up Deak and Company to fifty-nine offices worldwide and earned a reputation for discreetly handling the funds of those who wished to avoid the regulations and paperwork of ordinary banks. Ten million dollars of Lockheed money passed through Deak's Hong Kong office between 1968 and 1976, most of it from Switzerland.

Some analysts have speculated that the CIA may have lent a guiding hand to Lockheed's efforts in Japan. Veteran reporter Tad Szulc, writing in *The New Republic* in 1976 on Lockheed's Deak connection, suggested that the millions of dollars funneled to Kodama were not entirely Lockheed's idea. "It appears," wrote Szulc, "that the Nixon and Ford administrations, and specifically [the] CIA, may have used Lockheed as a leading edge in the execution of American policies in Japan, particularly in support of ultra-conservative groups." Lockheed officials, in fact, had no knowledge of the ultimate use of their payoff money, and Kodama certainly never let on as to what happened to the cash he received. As one intelligence source told Szulc, "Lockheed . . . would have been a perfect channel for the CIA to move funds secretly to people like Kodama." The involvement of Deak as a conduit would only have made it easier for both Lockheed and the CIA.

Whatever the CIA's role in the Lockheed case, it is clear that almost from the beginning the agency knew of the payoffs and the involvement of Kodama. As early as 1958, a CIA official at the U.S. embassy had been apprised of the situation, and in turn contacted Washington. The CIA, for the record, has claimed that it has no files of any agency involvement with the Lockheed bribes, and has denied any role in the scandal. Lockheed officials have similarly denied that their company had any dealings with individuals in Japan known to be CIA officers.

The immediate—if unintentional—effect of the Lockheed payoffs, guided by Kodama's well-greased hands, was to bolster the position of America's key ally inside Japan, the LDP. Evidence suggests that much of the Lockheed money was used not only as bribes, but as election funds as well, bankrolling LDP candidates in the 1974 upper-house election campaign. Kodama chose his friends carefully, though, and some of Lockheed's millions may well have ended up in the hands of his pals on the far right and, of course, in the yakuza.

Kodama and Osano soon found other challenges besides Lockheed to keep them busy. By 1973, with the TriStar deal well in hand, they were at work together again; this time, Kodama was helping Osano in his successful takeover of the Kokumin Sogo Bank. It had been a profitable relationship between the two kuromaku, but obviously not one that was meant to go public. Three years later, under the floodlights of the scandal, Osano would testify before the Diet that his relationship with Kodama had never gone beyond "sitting for tea" several times a year.

Osano could say whatever he liked, but for the first time he would have to contend with reporters and prosecutors who displayed an uncharacteristic zeal for investigating powerful figures. And it was not only Osano they were suddenly after. Each Lockheed payment led to different politicians and power brokers, and to a different stratum of a corrupt society. Lockheed's dealings with Osano, Kodama, and others ultimately brought into public view a broad cross section of the black mist enveloping the nation, where leading politicians met gangsters and questionable financial payments seemed a way of life.

Next to Kodama, perhaps the best example of underworld connections could be seen in the case of his powerful protégé, Dietman Koichi Hamada, a close ally of Tanaka, a rising star in the LDP, and a "former" member of the Inagawa crime family.

Hamada, then forty-three, lost an incredible $2 million playing baccarat during a series of Osano-sponsored tours to Las Vegas between 1972 and 1974, losses that were covered by Osano using Lockheed money. Osano's tours had become something of a legend among certain circles in Tokyo and Nevada. One such trip, in April 1974, was a nine-day, all-expense-paid junket of twenty-eight people to Honolulu, San Francisco, and Las Vegas. The guests, to put it charitably, were a rather diverse lot.

Government prosecutors and critics in the Diet later accused Osano and Hamada of including in the tours three top executives of the Inagawa syndicate, as well as a leading racketeer associated with Kodama. Another alleged participant was the notorious Susumu Ishii, the number two man in the 4,300-member Inagawa-kai. The FBI later questioned those who kept company with Osano and friends in Las Vegas, including reputed members of the U.S. Mafia.

How did Hamada end up in such good graces with Osano and Japan's ruling party? According to press reports, the wily politician had a police record dating back to 1952, when he was convicted of assault and embezzlement and served a year in prison. Upon his release, Hamada found that his old gang was among many around Tokyo being absorbed by the rapidly growing Inagawa syndicate. In the mid-1950s, Hamada consulted with Inagawa about succeeding his recently deceased boss. Inagawa advised his ambitious kobun to consider another path, and, when Hamada expressed an interest in politics, Inagawa introduced him to Kodama.

For two to three years Hamada stayed with Kodama, working as secretary and servant, and learning the art of politics, Kodama-style. With Kodama's backing, the enterprising candidate worked his way through a succession of local offices and finally to the national Diet. It was as a prefectural assemblyman that Hamada first met Kenji Osano, and over the next fifteen years the two men speculated together in a series of highly lucrative, and often questionable, real estate deals. Hamada soon came to call Osano *oyaji* (father) and Kodama *sensei* (teacher).

Once made, a relationship with the yakuza is very difficult to end, and Hamada's was no exception. Throughout his career, yakuza, reportedly from the Inagawa-kai, have helped fund-raise and campaign for candidate Hamada. His tactics certainly didn't bother the rest of the LDP, many of whom also employed yakuza as campaign workers. In fact, at the peak of his power in 1980, Hamada held office as the LDP's campaign chief.

Hamada enlisted in Kodama's favored faction in the Diet, the intensely nationalistic Summer Storm Society (Seiran-kai), whose financial backers also included gambling czar Ryoichi Sasakawa and Korean gang boss Hisayuki Machii. Eventually, Hamada served as the group's secretary-general. By the time the Lockheed scandal broke, he had become a leading LDP member and was appointed vice-minister of the Defense Agency, a prime spot from which to push his views on rapidly rearming Japan. Along with his newfound political power, Hamada remained close to his old gang. As late as 1978 he would boast, "One of the men whom I respect most is the chief of the Inagawa-kai."

Despite his rather open ties to the yakuza, Hamada seems to have enjoyed popularity with his constituents. It was only his involvement in the Las Vegas gambling trips—and their connection to Lockheed—that temporarily derailed his political career. In April of 1980, Hamada resigned his seat in the Diet rather than face public exposure of his activities with Osano in Las Vegas. He quickly reemerged, however, as an independent candidate in his old district, and won back his place in the Diet. In 1984, after a poor electoral showing by the LDP, he was among nine independent conservatives recruited by a frantic Prime Minister Nakasone to keep control of the Diet's lower house. Hamada rose to become chair of the powerful Budget Committee in the House of Representatives; he resigned the post in 1988 after publicly branding the chief of Japan's Communist Party a murderer.

He finally left the Diet in 1993 and became a fixture on Japanese TV talk shows, touting a tell-all memoir and crooning sentimental ballads.

The Fall of Kodama

Although Hamada survived the Lockheed scandal, his mentor did not fare as well. After Kotchian's 1976 Senate testimony in Washington, the Japanese press unleashed a merciless crusade against Kodama, atoning for its too many years of silence about the man and his influence. Investigators raided his house—a heretofore unthinkable act—and seized vast quantities of his personal files (those he hadn't burned). Tax officials began probing his labyrinthine financial dealings, searching for evidence of the Lockheed money and possible tax evasion.

The scandal may have taken its physical toll on Kodama as well. Shortly after Kotchian's initial testimony, the sixty-five-year-old Kodama suffered a stroke and was confined to his home. But even Kodama's mansion was no escape now. Demonstrators from both right and left protested outside his house. Leftist radicals even tried storming his gates, but were repulsed by police and still-loyal yakuza. Ultranationalist groups—once Kodama's deepest admirers—sent the bedridden fixer suicide notes, suggesting that he commit *hara-kiri* for having stained Japan's honor. Rumors even floated around that the Yamaguchi-gumi was plotting his assassination.

But the worst was yet to come. Indeed, Kodama himself could not have planned a more dramatic gesture. On the chilly Tuesday morning of March 23, 1976, Mitsuyasu Maeno, a twenty-nine-year-old film actor, arrived with three friends at Chofu Airport on the western outskirts of To-kyo. All were dressed in the style of kamikaze pilots. Maeno, a qualified pi-lot, told flying club officials that he wanted to rent two aircraft to film a se-quence on kamikaze fliers.

Maeno had once idolized Kodama. Five years earlier, according to one account, he was part of a select band of ultranationalists gathered in Tokyo's elite Okura Hotel to hear the premiere recital of a proposed new national anthem, "Song of the Race." The anthem, writes Lockheed historian David Boulton, called for "a kamikaze coup d'etat to restore the glories of Imperial Japan." The composer of the song was Yoshio Kodama.

Maeno was then a struggling actor with a large film company in Tokyo. (He had discovered that more money could be made starring in porno-graphic movies, and by 1976 he could be seen in dozens of seedy theaters lining the back alleys of Japan's entertainment districts.) When he and his friends, clad in kamikaze outfits, approached airport officials with their camera crew, they were convincing enough to obtain the rental of two planes.

Maeno knew the route well. The week before, he had made three flights around Kodama's neighborhood. Before climbing into the cockpit of his Piper Cherokee, he strapped on a headband emblazoned with the Rising Sun, as kamikaze pilots did before their suicide flights during the war. Shouting the kamikaze war cry, "Tenno heika banzai!" (Long live the emperor), Maeno flew off, followed by his friends, and they proceeded to circle Tokyo in formation for about an hour. Maeno then changed course, telling his cohorts he had some business in Setagaya—a Tokyo suburb and home to Yoshio Kodama.

Maeno approached Kodama's house at low altitude and circled twice, shouting the war cry over his radio. Aiming his aircraft nose first, he dove into Kodama's house, smashing into a veranda and dying instantly—but missing his intended victim, who lay in bed in another part of the house. The attack set the building ablaze, however, and Kodama's yakuza guards worked frantically at dousing the fire. So enraged were Kodama's bodyguards that later in the day they attacked newsmen outside the house. (Reporters later complained that ten riot police stood by during the assault, warning the newsmen not to "excite the young men.")

Police concluded that Maeno had acted alone, that he was not, as feared, part of a rightist plot. But Kodama's woes were far from over. He survived the kamikaze attack only to face trial in June 1977 for tax evasion and violation of foreign exchange laws. It was Kodama's only appearance in court, and he pleaded not guilty to all charges. From then on he refused to leave his home, claiming ill health. Prosecutors, though, were unimpressed and persistently arrived at his bedside, questioning him on seventy different occasions, according to one account. Worse, in addition to seizing his files, tax officials attached most of his property and assets—including a sizable Asian art collection—to ensure the collection of any back taxes and penalties.

The Lockheed revelations, and the subsequent arrest of Kodama, ended an era in Japan. CIA operative, ultranationalist financier, yakuza godfather, political kingmaker—for a generation, no one could lay a finger on Yoshio Kodama. "Kodama never worried about the police, the tax agency, or the prosecutor's office," said one prominent ex–cabinet minister to a reporter. "He was confident that no one could touch him . . ." But now, investigating and writing about Kodama's affairs were no longer taboo. Japanese publishers issued some fifty books on the man's life, many of them best-sellers. Scores more were published about the Lockheed scandal and its principal characters, and a host of plays and movies appeared.

Along with Kodama and his private secretary, fourteen other individuals involved in the scandal were finally indicted, including Kenji Osano. Among the charges: perjury, bribery, and violation of foreign exchange laws. Although at least eight politicians were clearly implicated, prosecutors felt they had enough evidence to indict only three: the prime minister, the LDP's secretary-general, and the parliamentary vice-minister of transportation. Prosecutors in 1981 demanded for Kodama a three-and-a-half-year prison term and a fine of about $3 million, but the trial was postponed due to Kodama's worsening health.

The aftermath of the scandal was decidedly mixed. U.S. relations with Japan were not noticeably harmed, despite early fears by American officials. Key records of the case remained sealed in U.S. federal court, after Secretary of State Henry Kissinger argued their release would damage American foreign policy interests. Meanwhile, Lockheed's money changer, Deak and Company, encountered troubles of its own. By early 1985, the firm had filed for bankruptcy, a move caused largely by a run on deposits by customers after the President's Commission on Organized Crime publicly linked the company to money launderers. Nicholas Deak's troubles ended several months later when the aging spook was murdered in his Manhattan office, apparently by a demented drifter.

The Lockheed revelations did prompt Congress to pass into law the Foreign Corrupt Practices Act of 1977, outlawing overseas bribes by U.S. corporations, but controversy lingers around that event as well. According to political scientist Chalmers Johnson, the well-intentioned law has instead had the effect of "worsening the American balance of payments while enriching several large American law firms . . . [and ensuring] that much future business will probably go to America's competitors instead." Still, the law has been used as a model by other nations in the hope that an honest and transparent business climate might yet prevail overseas.

In Japan as well, the impact of the Lockheed scandal was mixed. All but one of the politicians implicated in the payoffs scored resounding victories in the following general election. They were not as fortunate, however, in the courts. Excluding Kodama, all those indicted were found guilty. The last conviction, in October 1983, fell on former prime minister Tanaka. The Tokyo District Court found that Tanaka had accepted $2.1 million to arrange the purchase of Lockheed's TriStar by All Nippon Airways. He was sentenced to four years in jail and ordered to pay a fine equaling the amount he received as a bribe. Tanaka and the other defendants remained free while appealing their verdicts; it would be nineteen years until Japan's painfully slow Supreme Court upheld the last of the original decisions.

Osano seemed largely unaffected by his conviction and continued investing and making vast sums of money. In 1983 he displayed for the press his latest acquisition—the thirtieth hotel under Osano management. The plush five-hundred-room hostelry sat right across the street from Tokyo Eki, Japan's Grand Central Station. Among the guests at his lavish opening were noted corporate leaders and his old pal, former prime minister Ta-

:d and out of jail, Osano would pass away in 1986, leaving be-
dollar estate.

:omeback story, though, lay with Tanaka himself. As the
;un" of the LDP, he controlled through his "Tanaka faction"
22 LDP seats in the Diet. So powerful did Tanaka remain that
he became the party's undisputed kingmaker, ensuring, among other
things, the election of Nakasone as prime minister in 1982 and again in
1984. His long years of lavishing huge public works projects on his home
district had paid off. Despite opinion polls, front-page newspaper editori-
als, and widespread calls from both opposition and LDP members suggesting that he resign, Tanaka held onto the Diet seat he had kept for thirty-six
years. Just two months after his conviction, in an election that centered
around his continued influence over the LDP, the sixty-five year-old Tanaka
won his home district by one of the largest vote margins in Japanese history.
The rest of his party did not fare as well; the election nearly cost the LDP its
postwar hold over the nation's politics. The press was not kind either, dub-
bing the new administration the Tanakasone cabinet. But Tanaka was unfazed. Until hobbled by a severe stroke in 1985, the former prime minister
reigned as the most powerful man in all Japan. After his death in 1993, Tanaka's appeal of the Lockheed case—still on appeal—was quietly dismissed
by the Japanese Supreme Court.

Kodama could no longer keep up with his old pals, although the aging
kuromaku claimed to have had a hand in Nakasone's ascendancy to the
LDP throne. Kodama had in fact once said that his last endeavor from the
sickbed was to make Nakasone—his old protégé—the prime minister. But
under indictment, with his assets frozen and his followers leaving, Kodama's
power slipped even further. Many businesses cut off their payments of many
years to Kodama's financial racketeers. Lockheed had long ago canceled his
once lucrative contract. Scores of politicians and businessmen who once
boasted of their friendship with the man claimed to no longer see him. Tax
officials and Tokyo police, meanwhile, accused Kodama of tax evasion on
1.36 billion yen (about $6 million) he had received in business deals un-
connected to Lockheed.

Kodama spent the next three years hospitalized, his health failing and his
empire crumbling. During one bedside interview, Kodama told a prosecutor he had received "divine punishment" for serving a U.S. aircraft company
that had killed so many Japanese during the Pacific War. His chief physician
later told the press that Kodama's mind had deteriorated to the point of being "deranged." By then, however, the powerful kuromaku was seventy-two
years old, and he had made his mark on the world. On the evening of January 17, 1984, Kodama suffered another stroke and silently passed away.

For several days, mourners streamed to Kodama's mansion. The visitors
represented a cross section of Kodama's life: leading businessmen, rightists,

gangsters, entertainers. Curiously missing, though, were many of his close political allies over the years, politicians he had once funded and even controlled, but who now felt it unwise to publicly honor the man to whom they owed so much. Not so constrained was yakuza godfather Kakuji Inagawa, who repeatedly and rightfully proclaimed, "The world will never see the likes of Yoshio Kodama again."

The Kuromaku Legacy

The "black mists" of Japan did not die with Yoshio Kodama. In the spirit of the late kuromaku, questionable payments and mob connections still stretch far and wide among Japan's elected officials, affecting not only moral standards but public policy as well. Although not as blatant as it once was, the political use of organized crime members in Japanese politics goes well beyond what would now be possible in the United States. Reports of mob ties do create a sensation in Japan, much as they would in the United States, but politicians appear far more able to ignore the allegations and get on with their work. Such smugness is in part the price paid by the Japanese for tolerating the closed political system that has dominated the postwar era. Another reason lies in the much more public role the yakuza play in Japan, with openly identified members and offices, and a grudging acceptance of the gangs by the society at large. Whereas political careers are made in the U.S. by prosecuting gangs, little or no political advantage is gained in Japan by publicly fighting the yakuza.

One key to the yakuza's political influence can be found in rural areas, long a bulwark of LDP support. One veteran Tokyo prosecutor explained how the system works:

> Under the LDP system, if you investigate corruption in an election, you typically find yakuza acting as brokers. In rural areas, often the local LDP campaign chief is a yakuza boss. In most cases of election fraud we find these campaign chiefs are yakuza who head the local nokyo (agricultural cooperative).
>
> In back of the nokyo are construction companies, which are often headed by yakuza. The rice growers can't survive on rice alone, so they work in the cooperative and get construction jobs. The power of nokyo and the construction companies is very strong—they control hundreds of votes. Without the blessing of the local construction company, candidates may find their campaigns disrupted.

In the big cities, too, for many politicians the yakuza presence is a fact of life during election time. Gang members are widely employed as fundraisers, bodyguards, and campaign workers. Local yakuza bosses bring crowds to political rallies, provide security, and, when needed, "extra" votes on election day. In return, the gangs receive access to many of the nation's leading politicians, and gain through this a host of benefits, not the least of which is legitimacy. These connections have prompted some gang bosses to brag about their influence over the political system. "We provide reliable blocks of votes," explained Tokutaro Takayama, chairman of Kyoto's large Aizu Kotetsu syndicate, who boasted of delivering 30,000 votes to elect a prefectural governor. "Politicians always come to pay their respects at election time," another top yakuza told the press. "They bring gifts of sake and money. You see, I represent 4,000 votes."

Such statements are not unfounded. A public record exists of these gangland ties to Japan's parliament; it is a remarkable account for a country that some consider the most crime-free in the modern world. Perhaps the most striking is that some of the nation's senior political figures have consciously and publicly demonstrated their support to members of the underworld.

Japanese were stunned when, in 1971, former prime minister Kishi, accompanied by former education minister Umekichi Nakamura and a third politician, guaranteed bail for a Yamaguchi-gumi boss convicted of murder. All three politicians were current LDP members of the Diet; Nakamura was then chairman of the Diet Court Indictment Committee. Such connections apparently did not bother the former prime minister. In December 1963, three years after leaving office as prime minister, Kishi had acted as vice-chairman of a committee in charge of arrangements for a yakuza funeral. Later, in 1974, he was among scores of prominent guests invited by Yamaguchi godfather Kazuo Taoka to the lavish wedding of his son. Unable to attend, Kishi made sure the family received a congratulatory telegram, as did Ryoichi Sasakawa and Eitaro Itoyama, Sasakawa's relative and an LDP Diet member. Itoyama apparently saw himself carrying on a noble tradition. After twenty years in the Diet, he retired in 1996 and publicly boasted of his underworld ties. "Among Japanese politicians with the most influence with the yakuza, I have to say it's me," he told the *Washington Post*.

Although police have grown accustomed to such connections, it still dismays them to learn of prime ministers associating with known gangsters. Kishi is not the only one. During the term of Prime Minister Masayoshi Ohira in the late 1970s, police raiding the home of a Yamaguchi-gumi boss made an unexpected discovery: a huge, blown-up photo, proudly displayed, of Mr. Ohira hobnobbing over drinks with the gangster, apparently taken at a party. Then there was the case of Toshiki Kaifu, who become prime minister in 1989. Five years earlier, while education minister, he was photographed shaking hands with a well-known racketeer, and had his name engraved on a commemorative stone to mark the occasion. Then there were the news reports in 2000 accusing then–Prime Minister Yoshiro Mori of being "married to the mob" after he admitted joining five lawmakers at a 1996 wedding reception for the son of a former godfather. At the reception, Mori allegedly served as the "nakodo," or go-between, for the bride and groom—

a major role in Japanese weddings. Mori insisted he had "no personal relation" with the ex-yakuza and knew nothing of the man's background. His
closest aide, Chief Cabinet Secretary Hidenao Nakagawa, resigned months
later after facing allegations, among others, that he had ties to the leader of
a rightist group. Even if all this is true, it paled in comparison to Noborū
Takeshita, who, as will be shown, rose to become prime minister with the direct help of one of Tokyo's top godfathers.

Many of Japan's politicians do, of course, scrupulously avoid involvement
with the underworld. But association with the yakuza appears quite widespread, and is not limited to the LDP. In 1990, Keigo Ouchi, leader of
Japan's opposition Democratic Socialist Party, was caught on film visiting
a top Inagawa-kai boss in his district during election time. Ouchi later
claimed he thought the godfather was actually "president of a small company," despite the gang insignia and portraits of notorious godfathers that
adorned the walls. That same year, the Japanese press reported that Socialist Dietman Kenichi Ueno was joined by a Sumiyoshi-kai boss on a three-
week summer's tour of Africa and Europe.

Within Japanese politics, however, it is in the long-ruling LDP that mob
influence finds its fullest expression. Consider the case of Akira Ohno, minister of labor during the Nakasone government's first term. Ohno, son of
the notorious LDP powerhouse Bamboku Ohno, apparently meant to follow in his father's footsteps.

The younger Ohno became something of a power in his own right. By
1982, the seasoned fifty-four-year-old politician had been returned to
Japan's lower house seven times, and had held such important posts as
deputy secretary-general of the ruling party. But the public took a second
look upon revelations that from 1980 to 1982 Ohno's office had raised
some $435,000 in campaign funds from a loan sharking group closely tied
to the Yamaguchi-gumi. Ohno again came under fire for a series of visits to
mob leaders. Concerning a speech he gave at the wedding of a son of a recently "retired" Yamaguchi boss, the *Mainichi* newspaper cited a secretary to
the minister who stated that Ohno's ties to the man were close before the
mobster's retirement, and that the man "helped Ohno win elections and
promote business." Ohno, however, firmly denied any yakuza connections.

Other leading lights of the LDP allegedly have made use of characters
from the underworld. In 1976, for example, the late Rokusuke Tanaka—
then the LDP's chief cabinet secretary—admitted that a "former" gangster
actually ran one of his campaign groups. The thirty-four-year-old yakuza
strongman had once headed a gang in the conservative Tanaka's home district in Fukuoka, birthplace of Japan's modern yakuza-rightist groups. Although the man had recently served time in prison in connection with a
manslaughter case, Tanaka reportedly welcomed him, arguing, "It is the responsibility of a politician to rehabilitate ex-convicts."

Apparently Tanaka's responsibility extended to present gang members as well. In late 1983, two yakuza campaigners for the politician were arrested for violating Japan's Public Offices Election Law. The men belonged to the 330-member Kusano family, which holds sway over Tanaka's district. In the election, Tanaka was returned to the Diet for his eighth consecutive term. His yakuza campaigners didn't seem to bother the LDP hierarchy, which subsequently appointed the sixty-year-old Tanaka as secretary-general of the party.

Sometimes mob contacts are used by Japan's leading politicians for purely personal reasons—to intimidate errant relatives, for example. But the yakuza seem to be most widely employed in political campaigning and fund-raising. One revealing videotape showed LDP Dietman Kazuki Motomura at a 1986 New Year's party hosted by the Dojin-kai, the largest yakuza syndicate on Japan's southern island of Kyushu. The syndicate's boss, Isoji Koga, led a shout of three banzai cheers for his guest, praying for Motomura's success in his forthcoming election. Motomura did not forget the show of support; after Koga was imprisoned on racketeering charges, Motomura paid a jailhouse visit to express his sympathy.

Yet another noteworthy case comes from LDP stalwart Juichiro Tsukuda. Among the man's credentials: former minister of posts and telecommunications, former governor of Niigata Prefecture, and longtime member of the Diet's upper house. By 1970, the sixty-seven-year-old Tsukuda had come under fire at least once, for attending the funeral service of a noted gangster. But by 1981, the politician had gone a step farther by offering yakuza members not only condolences but employment as well. Tsukuda had hired Takashi Jo, a fifty-year-old ranking member of the huge Sumiyoshi syndicate. Jo's task was to collect about $1 million worth of unsettled bills and checks Tsukuda had issued on behalf of the owner of a "Turkish bath" as part of a bizarre fund-raising scheme gone awry. Tsukuda told a *Mainichi* reporter he was unaware that his bill collector had a violent record. "Many bills and checks are now held by gangs," said the former minister, "so I hired him." Jo took his job seriously. Police arrested him for punching in the face a Tokyo financial broker trying to cash a 2.1-million-yen check drawn on Tsukuda's name at a bank near the Diet building. Jo was released the same day, thanks to a personal visit by Tsukuda to the police.

Tsukuda did not apparently play favorites among the varied yakuza gangs. Eight months later, he was in the news again for intervening in a police investigation on behalf of another syndicate. This time the yakuza was one of the top eight lieutenants of the Yamaguchi-gumi—Shigemasa Kamoda, the same oyabun whom ex–labor minister Ohno admitted knowing. Tsukuda stopped in on Osaka police officials to advise them that Kamoda— then under suspicion of violating gambling laws—had in fact a good alibi.

Similar tales of political corruption and mob connections appear through much of Japan. Considering the pervasive and open dealings between the yakuza and national politicians, it is not surprising that Japan's "black mist" also operates in smaller towns and cities. In some communities, the yakuza today exert enormous influence over local politics, much as the Mafia traditionally has in parts of America. Recent years have seen city officials and gangsters involved in a long list of bribery, intimidation, and fraud cases, as well as the public sponsoring of "retirement" parties for the community's leading thugs.

The widespread ties of gangsters to public officials in Japan are not without risk. One Diet member from Fukuoka, now dead, borrowed so heavily from a yakuza-tied finance company that the gang's debt collectors showed up at his funeral. In Shimizu, three members of an Inagawa-kai gang strangled to death a former city councilman in 1977. He, too, had failed to repay millions of yen he had borrowed from the mobsters to win reelection. Occasionally, local yakuza engage in their own lobbying campaigns. In 1997, frustrated at a town council member's opposition to sales of boat racing tickets in Saitama Prefecture, two Inagawa-kai thugs dragged the forty-seven-year-old woman from her house and beat her with an iron rod.

The Political Yakuza

Although cases of mob-connected politicians are not unfamiliar to Americans, at times the yakuza go well beyond simply aiding the candidate of choice—they run for office themselves. Ever since Mitsuru Toyama's Dark Ocean Society blurred the distinction between gangster and rightist in the late nineteenth century, the yakuza have been organizing their gangs into political parties.

Even during the Occupation, often under the nose of U.S. officials, yakuza bosses were running for office in communities where they wielded power. Tekiya strongman Kinosuke Ozu, "Tokyo's Al Capone," garnered 12,000 votes in a 1947 bid for the Diet. In 1952, the oyabun of the Asano-gumi successfully ran for a seat on the city council of a town on Japan's Inland Sea. The election no doubt boosted the gang's plans for expansion; by 1964 the Asano-gumi had doubled in size (to eighty members) and had become the most powerful gang in Okayama Prefecture, an area inhabited by more than 1 million people. In 1980, one gang ran a Yamaguchi-gumi boss for the Diet. The godfather, an associate of LDP Dietmen Ohno and Tsukuda, vowed to halt drug abuse across the nation, claiming that he was "a monk following the path of chivalry" laid down by Yamaguchi-gumi boss Kazuo Taoka.

Perhaps most remarkable is that, occasionally, yakuza candidates have won office. At least one of these yakuza councilmen bore a prior conviction for murder: Eiji Sadaoka, oyabun of the Sadaoka-gumi in southern Japan.

In a town outside Nagasaki, the forty-one-year-old gangster won a seat on the city council in 1975, checking in with the largest number of votes in that town's election. Several days later, police arrested Sadaoka on a drug trafficking charge and revealed that their man had a record of five previous convictions, including murder.

Ideology often plays a secondary role in the yakuza's political efforts. The gangs are typically far more interested in maintaining the status quo to continue their assorted underworld pursuits. This attitude is shared by organized crime syndicates worldwide. As Chicago's Al Capone reportedly said more than sixty years ago, "I'm a hundred-percent supporter of the American free enterprise system." A survey of yakuza political views by criminologist Kanehiro Hoshino found that more than 50 percent supported the ruling Liberal Democratic Party. Nevertheless, there is a strong, very conservative bent to those the yakuza support. Invariably, their candidates are well to the right of center, staunch anti-Communists, and highly nationalistic. The involvement of prominent, yakuza-tainted politicians like Koichi Hamada in the ultranationalist Summer Storm Society is no accident.

The effect of the yakuza on public policy is difficult to gauge. The structural corruption that pervades so much of Japanese society is often inspired and lubricated by the gangs. Certainly, regulatory reforms in yakuza-dominated industries, such as longshoring, construction, and moneylending, have long been delayed, due in part to influence by yakuza and their friends in the Diet. But it is in the rightist-yakuza nexus that the gangs' political impact is most severely felt. The yakuza are so closely entwined with Japan's modern ultranationalist movement that it is frequently hard to tell the groups apart.

Zen Ai Kaigi, the mobbed-up rightist federation once favored by Kodama, still claims thousands of followers and scores of affiliated offices across Japan. Its members continue to sponsor paramilitary exercises and demonstrations around the country. Using a tactic dating back to the Dark Ocean Society—the nation's first modern ultranationalist group—Zen Ai Kaigi exacts money from many leading corporations in Japan. Past issues of the group's tabloid *Kaibyaku* (meaning "foundation" or "beginning") reveal impressive advertising. There were many of Japan's largest banks: Fuji, Mitsubishi, Mitsui, Sanwa, Sumitomo, and others. Leading financial brokers such as Daiwa, Nikko, Nomura, and Yamaichi Securities were represented, as well. Kawasaki Heavy Industries, Kawasaki Steel, Iwatate Road Company, and many others also added to the group's coffers.

Rightist groups do more than carry on an old tradition among the gangs: because they are tax-free and not targeted by anti-gang laws, they offer a convenient front for other activities. By 1992, Japanese authorities reported that more than half of the country's 1,400 ultranationalist groups—comprising some 22,000 members—were yakuza front organizations. "The major syndicates all have affiliated rightist groups," explained one top NPA official. Reminders of a dark past, these ultranationalist groups bear names like the Great Japan Harmonious Association and the Spiritual Justice School. And like more formal yakuza syndicates, many enjoy close ties to political figures. During the 1980s, one group in Gifu Prefecture boasted an LDP Diet member as an "adviser," according to the newspaper *Asahi*. In Ehime Prefecture, on the eastern island of Shikoku, several members of the prefectural assembly reportedly were advisers to a new "rightist" group.

These rightist gangs, often staffed by yakuza and others on the criminal fringe, are a common sight in Japan's major cities. In a culture that lays great emphasis on harmony, these modern ultranationalists are the nation's most notorious violators of the public peace. Clad in helmets, battle fatigues, and sunglasses, they dart about town in steel-plated trucks sporting military banners and flags adorned with the Rising Sun. Atop the vehicles stand huge loudspeakers blaring martial music in all directions, with breaks in the score to call for strident anti-Communist measures, repeal of the constitution, a crash military buildup, and restoration of the dignity of "the Japanese race."

Most are not formal members of the yakuza syndicates, but are frequently used by them for such odd jobs as collecting protection money from recalcitrant nightclub operators. For about $1,000 per day, a gang can rent a rightist sound truck and crew and have them harass their target of choice. Indeed, the business of the rightist gangs is so bound up with that of the yakuza that they are often one and the same. Yakuza gangs disguise themselves as rightist organizations, while rightist groups can be so involved in extortion, hired muscle, and other mob business that even police are hard pressed to explain the difference. "Today the far-right wing isn't what it used to be," observed Sasakawa, the ultranationalist veteran, in 1986. "For the last fifteen to sixteen years, they've all been gangsters."

One prominent gangster with an ultranationalist bent was Kusuo Kobayashi, a powerful boss of Tokyo's Sumiyoshi-kai. Until his death, Kobayashi for years ran his own paramilitary troop that trained each month on the streets of Tokyo. Kobayashi's gang was deeply enmeshed in drug dealing, extortion, and gambling, but that didn't stop him from flaunting his views on Japanese politics. "This I say as a warning to politicians," he told an American TV crew in 1988. "If the difference between the rich and the poor were really great, we would not hesitate to assassinate the Prime Minister."

The rightists are known for their dramatic touches. Most famous is Yukio Mishima's 1971 ritual suicide, in which the novelist called for a coup d'etat before disemboweling himself at a military base. While there is surprising sympathy for much of the far right's agenda, the great majority of Japanese look upon the gangs as an oddity, as relics of an era that was long ago and rightfully buried. Nonetheless, Japan's ultranationalist gangs are too dangerous to ignore. They comprise an active force that is at once anti-foreign, violent, and unpredictable, and enforce an unwelcome censorship on a disturbing range of topics in Japan. Those who write or speak critically about the emperor system, wartime responsibility, or the far right can expect assaults, bombings, and death threats. Between 1980 and 2000, ultranationalists were responsible for scores of attacks on politicians, journalists, and businessmen.

With the end of the Cold War and a new, modern postwar emperor installed, the ultranationalist movement has been forced to shift its thinking. Communism is no longer the threat, or the easy target, it once was. But there are other targets. Foreigners—both inside and out of Japan—have become convenient scapegoats. Russia and China are still not to be trusted, and the United States is generally viewed with suspicion. For others, the "enemy within" is the nation's corrupt political system. And those who question the far right's view of history and politics do so at their own risk.

Nervous curators have canceled art shows, publishers have withdrawn books, and politicians have ceased to speak out. In 1997, the ethnic Korean winner of one of Japan's most prestigious literary prizes, the Akutagawa Prize, had to cancel her book signings after bomb threats from a rightist. Some 1997 showings of a film on the Rape of Nanking had to be canceled because of protests by rightists, including one who slashed the screen with a knife. Indeed, broaching taboo subjects can have fatal consequences. Consider the fate of Nagasaki mayor Hitoshi Motoshima after he suggested in 1988 that the ailing Emperor Hirohito bore some responsibility for World War II. First came the death threats and the cutting off of support by his own LDP; then in December a man burst into city hall with a gasoline container but was arrested. Two months later, a knife-wielding rightist was stopped before attacking the mayor. In March shots were fired at city hall. Finally, in January 1990, in front of city hall, a rightist shot Motoshima in the back, nearly killing him. The assassin belonged to the Seiki Juku, or Spiritual Justice School, a shadowy group involved in blackmail, extortion, and emperor worship.

Japan's top politicians are not immune. In 1971, the forty-year-old leader of a Fukuoka yakuza gang sent a .22-caliber pistol and 175 bullets to Prime Minister Sato. Included was the following appeal: "You have allowed policemen to be killed, let students storm the Imperial Palace and caused trouble for the Emperor, all because you have remained Prime Minister. Herewith I send you a pistol so you can kill yourself honorably with it." Such practices have not faded into the past. In 1992 a right-wing protester slit his stomach on Prime Minister Kiichi Miyazawa's doorstep after Miyazawa approved an imperial visit to China. Also that year, a rightist gunman wearing a headband and sash bearing the Rising Sun charged into LDP headquarters, shot out a window, and demanded Miyazawa dissolve his scandal-plagued government and resign. Two years later, shortly after Morihiro Hosokawa resigned as prime minister, a gunman approached him from behind and fired into the ceiling of Tokyo's Keio Plaza Hotel—in protest of Hosokawa's admission of Japan's role as a World War II aggressor.

Another target was LDP power broker Shin Kanemaru, whom the far right saw as soft on North Korea and a key force behind Japan's corrupt political system; in 1991, his home was firebombed. One year later, Kanemaru escaped three bullets fired at him by a member of Seiwa-kai, a rightist group deeply implicated in extortion rackets. Political parties and the Diet itself are also fair game. One March day in 1995, ultranationalists threw a firebomb at the main office of Japan's Socialist Party and crashed a gasoline-soaked car into the Diet gates. Eight months later, a smoking rightist van packed with gasoline rammed the main gates of the Diet as the new legislative session began. In 1997, another rightist crashed his van into the front gate of Daijiro Hashimoto, governor of Kochi Prefecture and brother to then prime minister Ryutaro Hashimoto. Daijiro's crime: questioning whether Japan should keep the song "Kimigayo" (His majesty's reign) as Japan's national anthem.

"Occasionally violence is needed," explained Hakobu Konishi, head of the rightist Kokuyu-kai. Konishi practiced what he preached. In 1989 he cut off his little finger and sent it to then prime minister Noboru Takeshita, to protest political corruption.

Westerners are vulnerable, as well. In 1992, after the crash of Tokyo's stock market, an anonymous letter was sent to foreign securities houses in Tokyo:

Foreigners beware.

You are being watched. You have plotted to send stock prices lower and thus have profited greatly.

You have manipulated the market so that stock prices love to move up and down. How many times will you repeat this? This has already caused hundreds of people to commit suicide. Do you wish for more? . . .

The country is now caught up in a vicious circle, where companies go into the red and bankruptcies greatly increase, unemployment sharply rises, robbers cheat and murders multiply, suicides rise and numerous other incidents occur. All this because of foreigners. Confess your sins.

The media is another target of ultranationalist rage. In one famous 1961 incident, a seventeen-year-old rightist burst into the home of the editor of *Chuo Koron,* a respected news monthly which had published a story that treated the imperial family as less than divine. The maid was killed and the editor's wife severely injured. In 1993, rightists opened fire at the offices of publisher Takarajima, whose magazine had run a story critical of the imperial household. The liberal newspaper *Asahi* has suffered more than its share of attacks, enduring firebombs, shootings, and frequent harassment. In 1987, an *Asahi* reporter was killed and another critically wounded by a masked attacker who opened fire with a shotgun. An obscure rightist group, citing a campaign against "anti-Japanese elements," claimed credit for that attack and three others that year, including a time bomb.

Stories on the imperial family and the far right are not the only ones Japan's press must be wary of. The gangs can be rather sensitive to reporting on the underworld. In 1990, crime writer Atsushi Mizoguchi published a book on the Yamaguchi-gumi, after being warned not to. He was stabbed in the back. One year later, a lone yakuza smashed phones and windows at a local Yomiuri newspaper bureau after it reported on the arrest of his boss. In 1992, two Yamaguchi-gumi members used metal pipes to attack editors at *Friday,* a popular newsweekly, after the magazine ran a story suggesting the crime syndicate was on the decline. And in 1994, a gangster fired shots into the ceiling of *Mainichi* to protest the report of *Sunday Mainichi,* another newsweekly, on gang wars in Tokyo. The ultranationalists are not known for their sense of humor. In 1993, a prominent rightist clad in kimono stormed into Asahi's Tokyo headquarters, drew a pair of pistols, and killed himself to protest a cartoon mocking him.

Among the more worrisome arenas of yakuza political involvement is the underworld's strident support for a remilitarized Japan. The yakuza, to be sure, are but one voice—or set of voices—on the right clamoring for a rapid buildup of Japan's armed forces. Historically, though, the gangs have been keen and active supporters of a potent military in Japan: in ultranationalist groups in the 1920s and 1930s, pushing the country into World War II; in "land development" programs to settle occupied Manchuria during the war; and after the war, in paramilitary units designed to help police and the military battle leftist groups. As noted earlier, the postwar era's highly politicized yakuza alliances—Zen Ai Kaigi and Seishi-kai, for example—have included at the top of their agendas a call for repeal of Article IX of Japan's postwar constitution, an antiwar clause that has limited the growth of the Japanese military.

The danger these groups pose is not immediate. But should events in East Asia spin out of control—a nuclear North Korea, a belligerent China —or the world economy lapse into depression, these groups could well play a destabilizing and potent role.

The steady push toward rearmament by the Japanese right has produced some impressive results. Prodded by the LDP's conservative wing—and by pressure from Washington—Japan's military has undergone a complete transformation. Once the butt of jokes among both Japanese and foreign officers, by the 1990s the country's so-called Self-Defense Forces ranked third worldwide in military spending, behind only the United States and Russia, and fielded an impressive 243,000 active troops. In 1998, the Japanese navy ran the sixth largest submarine fleet, and its fifty-five frigates and destroyers ranked second in the world. With 270 combat aircraft, Japan's air force was also one of the world's largest, and its defense industry ranks among the biggest and most advanced.

Talk of Japan's rearmament causes great consternation among neighboring countries that still vividly remember the brutality of imperial Japan's East Asia Co-Prosperity Sphere. The push to a stronger military has alarmed many Japanese as well, who see it as part of a larger drift back to the old, ultranationalist right. Japanese legislators have repeatedly tried to revise much more in the present constitution than just the antiwar clause. Proposals have included giving the emperor a "more than symbolic" role and restoring state support of certain Shinto religious functions. Both measures hark back to the fanatic days of the prewar era. Other worrisome signs are the nation's continued failure to accept responsibility for its wartime aggression and atrocities.

Although fears of a full-scale ultranationalist revival in Japan seem remote today, even political conservatives concede that if such an event should occur, the yakuza would be in the vanguard. Indeed, yakuza influence apparently extends to high levels of the Japanese military. In the mid-1980s, one yakuza boss was photographed with the current chairman of the military's Joint Staff Council. In 1995, Kyodo News Service revealed that another, retired JSC chief served as chairman of a gang of yakuza-backed financial racketeers, and a retired director general of the Defense Agency served as adviser to the group. Kuromaku like Kodama and Sasakawa long bragged about the tens of thousands of young Japanese men at their disposal. Kodama spoke of his gangster-rightist groups as part of "an anti-Communist popular front." Sasakawa, through his chairmanship of some thirty organizations, laid claim to "my private army of 8 million" ready to strike against leftists for the fatherland.

As long as Japan stays affluent and productive, there is little to fear from a resurgence of fascism in the country. Opposition parties and the liberal wing of the LDP still wield enough power to block any truly outrageous demand from the far right. In addition, the public generally views rightist methods with distaste. Furthermore, most yakuza gangs, despite their public vows of allegiance to the rightist cause, will continue to use the movement primarily as a front for other activities. Indeed, the yakuza's political influence will be felt foremost in terms of money and self-interest. The syndicates will simply be defending their long-held turf: the continued control of gambling, drugs, and other vice crimes, and of their increasingly varied financial rackets. Their primary motivation, like that of organized crime elsewhere, will be profit.

One clear sign of this trend away from ideology is the passing of that great figure in Japanese history: the ultranationalist kuromaku. With Kodama and Sasakawa both gone, the stage has shifted for Japan's "black-curtain wirepullers." Certainly there is no replacement for Kodama. The kuromaku mold is much more apt to be filled by men like Osano and Tanaka, postwar businessmen with cunning and connections, but who hardly qualify as ultranationalist godfathers. As Sasakawa, sensing the end of an era, told *Newsweek*'s Bernard Krisher back in 1976, "I am one of the last fools in this world."

The passing of Kodama and the others, though, signals much more than the changing nature of Japan's power brokers. Kodama's fall from power, together with the Lockheed scandal and Tanaka's resignation, formed a milestone in the development of Japan's still-young democracy. These events had a cleansing effect, if only temporarily, sweeping away for a moment the thickest portions of the black mist enveloping Japan. And if the mist returned quickly, in the form of yakuza payoffs and political connections, the corruption of the country's politics was forced deeper underground, for the press and the public were growing increasingly less tolerant of the old ways.

Kodama's passing also marked another, equally important milestone. Japan's rapid economic growth, technological sophistication, and rise to world power would thrust upon the yakuza new problems and opportunities. For even before Yoshio Kodama's last breath, the situation in the streets, among the disciplined bands on which he depended for support— this, too, was rapidly changing.

PART III

THE MODERN YAKUZA

CHAPTER FIVE

THE SYNDICATES

HE WAS A MAN THE SICILIANS WOULD HAVE CALLED THE *CAPO DI TUTTI CAPI.*
At sixty-five, he reigned as the nation's most powerful gangster thanks to the
help of friends like Yoshio Kodama and to his own extraordinary abilities.
He was Kazuo Taoka, third boss of the Yamaguchi-gumi and overlord of
12,000 yakuza throughout the Japanese islands.

Taoka radiated confidence and power as he rested at his table in the Bel
Ami nightclub. The club sat nestled in a crowded entertainment district
of Kyoto, Japan's ancient capital and cultural center and long a Yamagu-
chigumi stronghold. On stage, a limbo dance was nearing a climax and
about fifty guests were applauding. It was early on a Tuesday evening in July
of 1978.

A young man in a white shirt arose from his seat and slowly walked toward
the table near the stage where Taoka and five bodyguards were sitting. He
came no closer than fifteen feet, slipped out a .38-caliber pistol, and blasted
away at Taoka, leaving a hole in the godfather's neck. As the assassin fled for
his own life, Taoka was rushed into a bulletproof Cadillac and sped with police escort to a nearby hospital.

Taoka's assailant, twenty-five-year-old Kiyoshi Narumi, belonged to a
gang in the Matsuda syndicate, a bitter Yamaguchi rival also active in
western Japan. When a Matsuda boss died in a 1975 turf war with the
Yamaguchi-gumi, Narumi and other Matsuda gang members had swallowed
the ashes of their murdered oyabun in a pledge of revenge. Taoka, however,
survived, as he had other assassination attempts. His assailant was not so
lucky; he was found brutally murdered several weeks later on a mountain-
side near Kobe, headquarters to the Yamaguchi-gumi.

The assassination attempt sparked a gang war right out of Chicago in the
1930s. Gangsters fought gangsters in broad daylight, attacking each other

on the streets and raiding each other's offices. At least five more yakuza affiliated with the Matsuda-gumi were murdered in the bloody retaliations that followed.

The shooting swept Taoka out of action for several months, but more important, it signaled the long-term decline of the great godfather and the gravest challenge yet to the immense syndicate he had built. The Yamaguchi-gumi could handle an upstart rival like the Matsuda gangsters, but pressures within the syndicate were changing the face of Japan's biggest crime group. The Yamaguchi-gumi—an alliance of more than five hundred gangs—owed much of its strength to Taoka's charismatic leadership, which suddenly seemed highly vulnerable. Taoka had been suffering from an increasingly serious heart ailment for ten years; by the time of his shooting, the godfather found his lieutenants already struggling for succession.

Another problem facing the syndicate was a growing generation gap between older and younger gang members, with far too few middle-aged mobsters to help fill the void. Yakuza elders, not only in the Yamaguchi-gumi but in gangs throughout Japan, began complaining that their formidable yakuza tradition, unquestioning loyalty to the boss, was no longer blindly accepted by the younger soldiers. Other values, too, were being questioned—of strategy, of leadership—and not just by the underlings, but by the senior bosses themselves. In the Yamaguchi-gumi alone, as many as twenty-three bosses of affiliated gangs were expelled or disciplined for opposing syndicate policy. Police theorized that the Yamaguchi-gumi, which pioneered the modern Japanese crime syndicate, had simply grown too big—and too dependent on Taoka's leadership.

Another new development was the open fighting in the streets. For years the yakuza credo dictated that fights among the gangs would be settled outside the realm of legitimate society; it was part of the image of the noble gangster never to involve in gang business the common people, the *katagi no shu* (literally, "citizens under the sun"). But recent gang battles had erupted with little regard for anyone, least of all the general public, and the Japanese were growing tired of the open violence and disregard for custom. So outraged was the public that police launched a much-heralded eighty-day battle to end the gang war, fielding 1,100 officers in what was then the largest mobilization in postwar history. During the first two months of the crackdown, authorities rounded up 2,000 gangsters, including 518 senior members of the Yamaguchi-gumi. Officials went after Taoka's number two man, Kenichi Yamamoto, nicknamed Yamaken, eventually putting him away for three and a half years of hard labor on charges of firearms possession and intimidation. Prosecutors further pressed a number of old cases against Taoka that included violation of tax laws and blackmail of construction and steamship companies.

Responding to the growing pressures on his huge syndicate, within a year of the shooting Taoka fashioned an uneasy but effective truce with the Yamaguchi-gumi's most bitter enemies. To make sure the public got the message, Taoka did what any modern, self-respecting Japanese godfather would have done: he called a press conference. Under the glare of television lights, some sixty newsmen crowded into Taoka's plush home, sitting cross-legged on tatami mats. For over an hour the reporters listened to Yamaken, flanked by two other gang leaders. (Taoka himself was conspicuously absent.) The boss's right-hand man began by reading from a prepared statement in formal, flowery Japanese. Reporters were able to check his words against copies of the speech distributed earlier as part of a press kit. In the nationally televised address, the Yamaguchi-gumi declared an end to the bloodshed and solemnly apologized to the public and police for the "trouble" caused them. Following the press conference, events finally began to slow down for Japan's largest gang—but not for long.

Yamaguchi-gumi: Death and Succession

Taoka stayed out of public life for much of the following year. He later reemerged for a series of appearances in 1979 to quash rumors that his health was failing, but the yakuza boss looked pale and thin. In the sensational weeklies that chart the movements of Japan's far-flung underworld, Taoka's appearance only increased speculation about who would be his successor, the fourth boss of the Yamaguchi-gumi.

Despite its problems, the Yamaguchi-gumi still stood as Japan's most formidable crime syndicate. As one newspaper remarked, the gang's rhombus-shaped golden pin remained "a persuasive lapel ornament." In much of Japan, the showing of one's pin, combined perhaps with the baring of a tattoo, could get trucks moved, goods discounted, and hallways cleared. Other gangs show off their own badges, of course. Each syndicate wears a different design, proudly displaying its colors on official occasions, much as if they were Rotary brothers. In Japan, where the group, not the individual, defines much of daily life, the pins are an easy mark of identification.

The pins cannot always work their magic, however, particularly when their bearers are faced with police or other gangsters. The emblems were part of the matching outfits worn by Yamaguchi members as the gang made a well-publicized attempt in 1980 to expand its territory to Hokkaido, Japan's northernmost island. Nearly two hundred gang members, clad in white blazers and black polo shirts, flew to the capital city of Sapporo for the formal opening of their branch office. They were met at the airport by eight hundred members of local underworld gangs who had banded together to keep the Yamaguchi-gumi out of their territory. A nervous contingent of some 2,000 riot police kept the two groups apart. Officials stopped the

Yamaguchi-gumi gangsters from opening their office by quarantining the entire delegation in their hotel at a ski resort; a day later, their mission a failure, the gangsters returned to Osaka on a single flight of All Nippon Airways.

Far worse news awaited the Yamaguchi hierarchy than their failure in Hokkaido. One year later, the event long dreaded by the syndicate arrived. Kazuo Taoka's thirty-five-year rule ended with a final heart attack in July 1981. A quiet, private service was held for the immediate family and friends one week later. But a second funeral—an official one—was deemed necessary by the gang. Despite repeated police warnings, after three months of preparation, syndicate leaders arranged to give Taoka an elaborate Buddhist send-off in the best yakuza tradition. Police responded by raiding gangster homes and offices nationwide, and arresting nearly nine hundred gang members. Among the contraband seized: 102 guns, 192 swords, and 2 pounds of amphetamines. But the crackdown didn't work: to the Yamaguchi-gumi, the funeral was a matter of honor. On a Sunday in late October, some 1,300 yakuza from two hundred gangs gathered in Kobe to honor their departed boss. The service took place at a site where a "Taoka Memorial Hall" was to be built, adjacent to the godfather's home in a posh residential area. Three doors down sat the Hyogo Prefecture District Court, located amid the offices of Kobe's most respected lawyers. Surrounding those offices—and the gangsters—stood about eight hundred helmeted riot police armed with metal shields. Another five hundred police checked the arriving visitors at sixteen different places, including major airports and train stations.

Flowers arrived from all over the country—from other mob leaders, from prominent businessmen, and from Taoka's old friend Yoshio Kodama, then slowly dying in a Tokyo hospital. For those who came to pay their respects personally, body searches by police were the rule. Among those in attendance was an all-star cast of Japan's entertainment industry: singers, actors, musicians. Said one star, Yoshio Tabata, "From the late fifties to the late seventies, what entertainer in Japan was not helped by Taoka?" Also at the wake appeared Japan's leading man of the cinema, heartthrob Ken Takakura, who, among his numerous roles in yakuza movies, had played Taoka in a film trilogy about the godfather's life.

Taoka had reportedly chosen his ruthless number two man, Yamaken, as his successor. But shortly after the press conference, Yamaken was thrown into prison and not due out until late 1982. The syndicate, meanwhile, was in such disarray that few could tell who was in charge. Police thus watched closely to see who would fill the spot of chief mourner at the funeral, a role traditionally assumed by the syndicate's new boss. Much to their surprise, it was the godfather's widow, sixty-two-year-old Fumiko Taoka.

It was, perhaps, a measure of the near panic Yamaguchi leaders felt that, in the heavily macho world of the yakuza, they had openly turned to Fumiko, long a silent power in the organization. Her role was to be a temporary one, bridging the gap until a strong male leader emerged. But in a land where women held few top jobs and Western-style feminism had made little progress, the appointment was nothing short of remarkable. The place of women in the yakuza has long centered around their roles as prostitutes, hostesses, and housewives for the gangs. Occasionally, though, they amass considerable power in the Japanese underworld. As one gang member explained to a Japanese weekly, "There are women oyabun (bosses), but they don't openly show their faces in the yakuza world. Women don't go about brazenly in a man's world. . . . (Fumiko) will probably be there to act as receiver for others."

For a while, then, the 12,000 men of Japan's largest crime syndicate were led by a woman. Fumiko reportedly occupied her late husband's seat at top-level meetings and passed judgments on intra-gang disputes. With Yamaken due out of prison within months, most gang members expected a relatively smooth transition. They were mistaken.

Before he was a free man again, Taoka's heir apparent paid for his long years of heavy drinking. Seven months after his boss's death, Yamaken too succumbed—to cirrhosis of the liver. Suddenly, the entire structure of the Yamaguchi-gumi was thrown into unrelenting confusion. The work of a generation of gangsters—a complex blend of feudalism and corporate management—was now at risk.

During his thirty-five-year rule, Kazuo Taoka had run his syndicate with that famous Japanese knack for using innovative techniques while preserving traditional values. Despite the Yamaguchi-gumi's control of more than 2,500 businesses, sophisticated gambling and loan-sharking operations, and heavy investment in the sports and entertainment fields, the organization still functioned along feudal patterns that had existed for three hundred years. Day-to-day management of the syndicate—as with other yakuza groups—depended on the ancient relationships of oyabun-kobun, with fictive kinships extending from the highest "parent" to the lowest "child." These feudal vestiges certainly didn't hurt the gangs as they adapted to a modern, corporate world. By the time of his death, Taoka's organization was grossing well over $460 million annually, according to police. American executives from General Motors to the Mafia would no doubt give a great deal to manage such fervently dedicated workers as those of the Yamaguchi-gumi.

Above it all, Taoka reigned as an underworld shogun. But as is often the case, the godfather was removed from the daily affairs of the syndicate. That was left to his second-in-command, Yamaken, who had served as a kind of chairman of the board for the Yamaguchi "Corporation." On the fifth day of each month, Yamaken held a meeting with twelve leading bosses who functioned as a board of directors, deciding on syndicate policy and carving up the spoils of underworld Japan.

In all, there were 103 Yamaguchi bosses of various rank from more than five hundred separate gangs. The bosses held office according to the parlance of the oyabun-kobun relationship: at the top ruled four *shatei,* or "younger brothers" to Taoka. Also atop the pyramid served the other eight directors, the *wakashira-hosa* (assistant young leaders), one of whom would be appointed a *wakashira* (young leader). Equivalent to the Mafia's *consiglieri,* or counselors, were six members of a senior consultative group, the *sanro-kai.* Below this hierarchy lay a series of lesser offices: one *kambu atsukai* (executive), and eighty-three *wakashu* (young men), each of whom commanded his own legion of *kobun* (children) or *kumi-in* (enlisted men). Within these individual gangs existed a maze of similar relationships, all based on the oyabun-kobun system. In addition, there were large numbers of apprentices and fringe persons to oversee.

Vast sums of money flowed through this feudal hierarchy. The major affiliated gangs and the syndicate itself each issued an annual financial report. The gangs were required to send monthly amounts to the syndicate headquarters, often in the thousands of dollars. In addition, payments were made as New Year's gifts, for funerals (Taoka's brought in nearly $500,000), for each gangster released from prison, and for inspection visits by the Yamaguchi brass. By one police estimate, Taoka received annual tribute from his varied gangs totaling more than $2.1 million. (That figure would jump over the next decade. By the early 1990s, Yamaguchi-gumi headquarters brought in nearly $13 million in tribute money and fees from affiliated gangs. The top 110 bosses each paid monthly membership fees ranging from nearly $6,000 up to $8,000, according to various accounts.)

Those beneath Taoka also fared well. In a revealing 1984 interview with the *Mainichi* newspaper, a Yamaguchi boss let the public know just how well: "A boss of medium rank will make about $130,000 [annually], but when you get to the godfather class, you're probably talking more than $400,000. A syndicate head with 1,000 men under him can count on bringing in $43,000 a month. . . . Even if you deduct, say, $13,000 for entertainment and office expenses, that still leaves him with $30,000; that's a good $360,000 a year. And he can use it any way he likes." The money, moreover, was typically tax free.

These figures were supported by a National Police Agency survey in 1988, which found that top bosses earned an average of nearly $220,000 annually, while soldiers received a mere $27,000. A similar 1978 survey found that the yakuza rank-and-file typically made about the same as an average salaried worker in Japan. Members who controlled the earnings of women, such as pimps or club managers, fared much better, but the big money remained with the men at the top.

"Remember," said the Yamaguchi boss, "a gang leader's income depends on the number of soldiers he has under him. People say the Yamaguchi-gumi controls the Japanese underworld, but we didn't plan it that way. Competition between bosses for a bigger piece of the action has led them to expand their turf, until suddenly the syndicate is everywhere."

To the Japanese on the street, it did indeed seem like the Yamaguchi-gumi was everywhere. In the traditional business of the yakuza world, Taoka's mob commanded the field in western Japan. Its varied gangs controlled day laborers at the ports and in construction jobs; monopolized hundreds of street stall operators; extorted cash from local bars and national corporations; and ran gambling rackets from street-corner numbers operations to high-stakes card games worth millions of dollars a night. They organized political parties and worked as campaign aides for rightist candidates. And they ran nightclubs and cabarets, complete with hostesses, prostitutes, and virtually anything the public wanted but wasn't supposed to have.

Kazuo Taoka's greatest contribution, though, was in forcing open Japan's fast-growing economy to a rapidly modernizing underworld. In 1953, the Yamaguchi-gumi ran some twelve companies, largely tied to longshoring. By the early 1960s, Taoka himself had become vice-chairman of the National Longshoremen's Association, but that was just the beginning. By the early 1970s, the syndicate had expanded into professional boxing, sumo, and Western-style wrestling. Along with other leading syndicates, it controlled some one hundred production companies in the entertainment business. In addition, scores of talent agencies and booking firms were under yakuza influence. Many performers could not venture onto a stage without the blessing of their yakuza sponsors. Movie companies, too, with their insatiable appetite for yakuza films, fell under the influence of the gangs.

But the Yamaguchi-gumi also led the way into areas beyond entertainment. Despite a formal ban by the big syndicates on the sale of narcotics, Taoka's men turned to drug dealing as an easy way of meeting their monthly payments. The trade in methamphetamines, the drug of choice in Japan, exploded, providing the gangs with a lucrative and growing source of income. By the 1970s, police estimated nearly half the yakuza's income was generated by sales of speed. Other fields, too, proved especially lucrative.

There were, of course, the old standards of gambling dens and tekiya booths. High-stakes gambling could still bring in a hefty sum, and popular tekiya stands could each gross up to $1,000 a day. Police shut down thousands of the stalls each year at festivals, sports games, and other public gatherings. As much as one-fifth of yakuza gangs still earned their primary living by the stalls. Pachinko was another longtime money maker. Hundreds of the ubiquitous pinball-like parlors were tied to the yakuza across Japan, filling gang coffers with millions of dollars. Gangs typically received protection money and ran a street racket converting pachinko prizes into cash. But those traditional rackets increasingly seemed less attractive than the many new fields being pioneered by the Yamaguchi-gumi and other top syndicates. The gangs moved into moneylending, smuggling, and pornography in big ways. Their front companies made bids on huge public works projects, including subways and airport construction. They rigged baseball games, horse races, and public auctions for foreclosed property.

Enterprising yakuza began to move in wherever they could find an opportunity. They seized control of hospitals, English schools, amusement halls, and fortune-telling parlors. They bought into real estate, video games, trucking, waste disposal, and security services. They manufactured or distributed counterfeit Japanese stamps and bills, U.S. dollars, Cartier watches, and even brand-name food products. And no syndicate excelled better at the criminal end of business than the Yamaguchi-gumi. "The Yamaguchi-gumi is like a department store," said one cop in describing the group's diversified revenues. Perhaps mob expert Kenji Ino put it best. Taoka's sprawling crime syndicate, he observed, "had perfected the art of converting violence into money."

It took all of Taoka's immense power to bind these varied scams together. The Yamaguchi-gumi was not a monolith; gangs often acted independently of one another, and despite Taoka's unchallenged authority, divisions continually surfaced within the syndicate. Factions developed between militant gangs—anxious for expansion and eager to use violence—and more dovish and neutral groups. Differences existed as well between tekiya and bakuto bosses, and among newer occupations such as financial racketeering and drug dealing. But on important issues—mergers, key promotions, territorial wars—the cabinet was always consulted. And behind every decision stood the authority of the most powerful man in the Japanese underworld. To the yakuza in the street, there seemed to be no problem that godfather Taoka could not solve.

This, then, was the tightly knit structure thrown into confusion by the deaths of Taoka and Yamaken. The once invincible Yamaguchi-gumi suddenly found itself under assault from all sides. Police took the opportunity to launch an "eradication" campaign against the syndicate, arresting many of its top leaders. Squabbling broke out within the organization over how to best manage the conglomerate's vast resources. At the same time, rival gangs, long annoyed by the syndicate's power, began harassing Yamaguchi members, infringing on their territory and picking fights.

To counter these problems, an elite group of eight was selected to run the syndicate's affairs, with guidance and mediation from Taoka's widow,

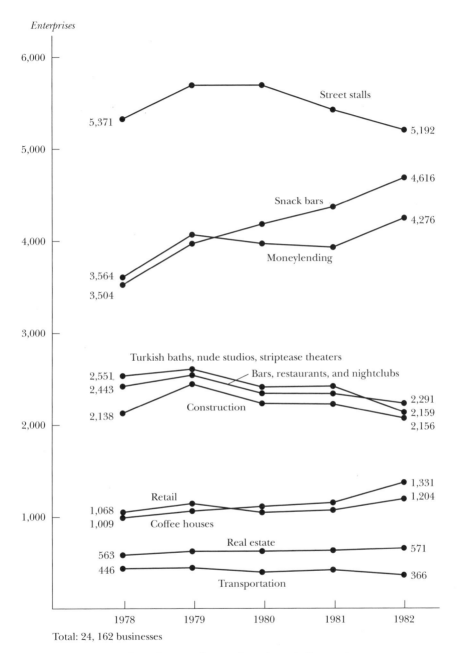

Figure 1. Number of enterprises under yakuza-influenced management, 1978–1982. (Source: National Police Agency, 1982.)

Fumiko. For a time their efforts at collective leadership were successful. Despite all the syndicate's troubles, from Taoka's death in 1981 to 1983 the Yamaguchi-gumi actually grew in size to a peak of 13,346 gangsters. A record 587 gangs comprised the syndicate, stretching into thirty-six of Japan's forty-seven prefectures.

It was clear, though, that the organization would soon have to select a new godfather, and that he would come from the group of eight. Among these eight bosses, men largely in their late forties and fifties, competition already was keen over who would grab the top spot. Feuding broke out. As tempers in the mob reached the breaking point, the contest came down to two veteran mobsters. The first: fifty-eight-year-old Hiroshi Yamamoto, a relative moderate and close associate of Yamaken. Among Yamamoto's qualifications was leading the syndicate in its successful drive into Kyushu, the southernmost island, during the early 1960s. The second candidate: fifty-year-old Masahisa Takenaka, an extremely aggressive but popular leader and longtime friend of the Taoka family. Fumiko reportedly favored Takenaka's militancy over Yamamoto's *interi* (intellectual) yakuza. Among Takenaka's qualifications: eleven convictions for extortion, battery, and other crimes, and pending charges on illegal gambling and tax evasion.

In the end, the selection was made in the finest tradition of gangland democracy, with intense lobbying and several votes by the 104 bosses. Amid charges of bribery and intimidation, a final tally was at last reached: the day had gone to Takenaka, 57 to 19, with numerous abstentions. Playing the role of final kingmaker was Fumiko, who then bestowed the full blessings of the Taoka family on the new leader. But more trouble lay ahead. When Fumiko summoned the defeated Yamamoto to ask his cooperation, the yakuza boss refused to become Takenaka's subordinate.

Within days, Yamamoto was calling his own press conference, and in a short address told all of Japan that the moment of truth had arrived: "I cannot agree to seeing Takenaka become the fourth head of the Yamaguchi-gumi," he announced. "I told [Mrs. Taoka] that I regretfully could not accede to her request. That is my frank and final decision." With that said, on June 19, 1984, at one of Kobe's leading restaurants, Yamamoto and eighteen top lieutenants formed the Ichiwa-kai, taking nearly half the syndicate's 13,000 men and instantly creating one of Japan's top three crime syndicates. The Ichiwa-kai bosses, dressed in dark blue suits, cemented their new relationship in a lengthy ceremony of sakazuki, with each man exchanging drinks of sake as a symbol of blood brotherhood.

Not to be outdone, Takenaka staged an even more elaborate ceremony on Shikoku Island to assume his position as the fourth Yamaguchi-gumi godfather. Some three hundred fellow mobsters attended, immaculately dressed in black suits with white ties, polished syndicate pins shining from their lapels. At a traditional Japanese inn, Taoka's widow solemnly handed a dagger to the new boss, symbolically marking Takenaka's ascension to the Yamaguchi throne.

For the next six months, tensions remained high between the two syndicates. Slowly, though, the Ichiwa-kai began to lose ground. The parent Yamaguchi-gumi promised amnesty to all those who would rejoin. The syndicate even instituted a new benefit for its members—retirement pay—and awarded the first amount, about $42,000, to a seventy-one-year-old bookie with the gang since 1948. The efforts seemed to work. The Yamaguchi-gumi steadily recaptured much of its lost membership, its ranks swelling to some 10,000, and again became Japan's largest crime organization. The Ichiwa-kai, meanwhile, had been reduced to 2,800 men. Worried by the increasing defections, the Ichiwa-kai's Yamamoto took action.

The ambush occurred on January 26, 1985, a Saturday night. At least four Ichiwa-kai hit men arrived in a black car at the Osaka apartment of Takenaka's mistress. As Takenaka and his two highest gang bosses stepped into an elevator, a hail of bullets ripped through their bodies. All would soon die from their wounds. In one attack, the Ichiwa-kai had swept away the top leadership of the Yamaguchi-gumi—but had begun a murderous gang war.

In the midst of more raids and executions, the Yamaguchi-gumi took time to pay respects to Takenaka. In a nationally televised funeral, more than 1,000 black-suited gangsters gathered again at Taoka's mansion. Black-and-white bunting covered the home, and a procession of Mercedes and other foreign luxury cars stretched down the street. The mobsters were in no mood for mourning, however. "We must kill," muttered one to a reporter. "Total slaughter," rumbled another.

By early February, the eighty-three bosses of the Yamaguchi-gumi had met and unanimously elected sixty-two-year-old Kazuo Nakanishi as their new leader, and then declared open war on the Ichiwa-kai. An immediate bloodbath was averted only by the rapid mobilization of 660 riot police to 184 gangland homes and offices. Over the next month, officials arrested more than 990 mobsters and confiscated some fifty handguns and rifles, among them at least one U.S. Army M-16 automatic. Nonetheless, more than two hundred armed attacks between the two syndicates erupted over the next year, leaving twenty-six gangsters dead. But the biggest surprise was yet to come.

Although the Yamaguchi-gumi held a commanding lead in sheer numbers, the Ichiwa-kai's men had made off with most of the syndicate's arsenal when they seceded. The price of handguns shot up from $3,000 to as much as $5,000. Desperate for firepower, the Yamaguchi hierarchy embarked on an ambitious and ill-fated journey, according to U.S. law enforcement.

Events reached a peak in September 1985, when U.S. undercover agents in Honolulu arrested Takenaka's powerful brother, Masashi, and Hideomi Oda—the syndicate's reputed "financial controller"—for conspiring to buy three rocket launchers, five machine guns, and one hundred handguns from what they thought were Hawaiian organized crime figures. As part of a related deal, claimed U.S. officials, Yamaguchi-gumi members sold or conspired to sell fifty-two pounds of amphetamines and twelve pounds of heroin to the Americans (with a total street value of $56 million). In addition, Takenaka and company were charged with trying to hire one of the undercover agents to assassinate Yamamoto of the Ichiwa-kai, to whom their own members could not get close. It seemed a remarkable coup for U.S. officials, the payoff from a yearlong multinational investigation involving six federal agencies and local police in Honolulu and Hong Kong. But for the Yamaguchi-gumi the venture was a complete disaster. Instead of gaining a fat arsenal and a foreign assassin, the syndicate had lost a great deal of money, "face," and, pending trial, two of its highest-ranking members to American jails.

Billed as the largest U.S. case yet against the Japanese mob, the trial made headlines in America and became one of the year's biggest stories in Japan. U.S. officials claimed the top yakuza planned to hire the Hawaiians, who would use the rocket launchers to blast apart the Ichiwa-kai's heavily fortified headquarters. But in court, the yakuza bosses claimed they were in Hawaii only to push their plan to bring pop superstar Michael Jackson to Japan. Although prosecutors produced an undercover tape showing the yakuza seemingly agreeing to the drugs-for-weapons deal, the defense argued forcefully that all this was a terrible cultural misunderstanding. One cross-cultural expert explained that in Japanese, the word *yes* ("hai") does not always mean "I agree," but only that "I hear what you're saying." The jury already was wary of the prosecution's key witness, a former pro wrestler and longtime drug informant who had been picked up for extortion during the trial and had indeed tried to make some kind of questionable deal to book Michael Jackson. Suspecting entrapment, the jurors found the Yamaguchi-gumi's top brass not guilty and sent them home.

Despite the Yamaguchi-gumi's eventual victory in Honolulu, back in Osaka the Ichiwa-kai had accomplished its primary task, throwing the Yamaguchi-gumi into a state of utter confusion. The gang war continued to rage over the next year, but the Ichiwa-kai kept losing ground. Attempts at mediation, spearheaded by the neutral Inagawa-kai, came and went. After an Ichiwa-kai member broke one cease-fire in late 1985, his boss cut his finger tip and presented it to the Inagawa-kai.

The Yamaguchi-gumi had lost more than its arsenal to the Ichiwa-kai. The upstart syndicate had absorbed many of the Yamaguchi-gumi's more business-minded dons, among them Hideo Shiragami. The sixty-three-year-old Osaka boss ran various companies and had big plans for the Northern Mariana Islands, a U.S. commonwealth near Guam. His enemies in the Yamaguchi-gumi caught up with him, however. That February, Shiragami's battered body was found in the sea off Saipan, near Banzai Cliff, the chilling spot where forty-three years earlier hundreds of Japanese men, women, and children had plunged into the rocky waters below rather than be taken prisoner by American troops. Shiragami was no more fortunate. His corpse bore plentiful marks of torture, with the ears, tongue, and middle finger cut off, the ribs crushed, and a bullet shot through the head.

Shiragami's brutal slaying apparently sickened even the Yamaguchi-gumi leadership. Six days later, the syndicate called an emergency meeting and then announced they were ceasing hostilities. The Ichiwa-kai followed suit. The two-year conflict had been Japan's bloodiest gang war ever, with more than three hundred shootings, twenty-five dead, and a fortune wasted on firearms, legal fees, security, and funerals. As the months passed, the Yamaguchi-gumi continued to regain its dominance, as the Ichiwa-kai lost both members and momentum. By 1989, the once huge Ichiwa-kai was reduced to a mere gang, and what few yakuza still belonged to it finally disbanded. The Yamaguchi-gumi had won.

Soon the Yamaguchi-gumi membership rolls topped 20,000, and Kazuo Taoka's once-threatened mega-syndicate appeared more formidable than ever before. Leadership of the criminal combine was taken up by Yoshinori Watanabe, a onetime noodle-maker whose tough but crafty management pushed the gang into forty-three of Japan's forty-seven prefectures. Police stumbled across an eighteen-page internal telephone directory showing how Yamaguchi-gumi influence extended into nearly every part of the nation. "Joining it is like taking out insurance," the gang's former attorney, Yukio Yamanouchi, told a reporter. "It's like working for Sony. You're part of the leader in your field." Indeed, its diamond-shaped lapel pin carried more cachet than any other symbol of the Japanese underworld. As the Yamaguchi-gumi celebrated the millennium, the great syndicate boasted nearly 34,000 members and close associates—by far the largest in Japan, comprising nearly half of all yakuza identified by police.

Families, Federations, and the Sumiyoshi-kai

The Yamaguchi-gumi is not the only big syndicate to experience rapid growth. Despite police claims of more than halving the number of yakuza since their peak in the early 1960s, Japan's three top syndicates all have continued to expand. The smaller gangs have borne the brunt of police crackdowns and changing times, succumbing to police pressure, new anti-racketeering laws, and absorption by the great syndicates. In 1963, the police counted 184,000 yakuza; by 2001, officials counted some 84,000 members and associates. But at the same time that yakuza ranks were being cut in half, the largest syndicates steadily increased their share of the underworld. The trend was especially strong in the 1980s and 1990s. From 1979 to 1998, Japan's top three crime groups—the Yamaguchi-gumi, Sumiyoshi-kai, and Inagawa-kai—grew from 40 to 82 percent of all formal yakuza members.

There are important structural differences among the big yakuza syndicates. Kazuo Taoka had run his Yamaguchi-gumi in the traditional way, structured in pyramid fashion, with enormous control vested at the top in a boss of bosses. By contrast, the Sumiyoshi-kai has long been a federation of crime families. Although both syndicates share many characteristics, they traditionally have represented the two organizational poles of gang structure in the yakuza world.

The Sumiyoshi-kai comprises a league of gangs. The pyramid of power in the Yamaguchi-gumi comes to a fine point, headed by a single man. The top of the Sumiyoshi pyramid is broader; while a powerful oyabun reigns over the syndicate, he is only one of several bosses, all considered equal partners. The Yamaguchi-gumi's pyramid more closely resembles that of traditional Italian Mafia families. The Sumiyoshi-style federation is a more modern development: less money goes to the top as tribute, less authority is vested in the godfather, and, consequently, more autonomy lies with the individual gangs. The Yamaguchi-gumi appears to be moving toward this structure. Since Taoka's death and the syndicate's remarkable growth, the Yamaguchi-gumi increasingly functions as an umbrella organization, with large degrees of autonomy among the various gangs. In return for regular payments to headquarters, they can call on the broader organization for help in case of gang wars, legal trouble, or other problems.

The more decentralized structure long practiced by Sumiyoshi gangs hasn't hurt their moneymaking ability: in the mid-1980s, officials conservatively estimated that the syndicate brought in more than $276 million per year. Indeed, much as the traditional Yamaguchi-gumi resembles early Mafia families, the makeup of the Sumiyoshi-kai closely follows that adopted by the American mob when it modernized during the 1930s. It was then, under the leadership of Lucky Luciano and others, that U.S. gangsters first created a national federation of crime families that law enforcement agencies would call La Cosa Nostra, but insiders would simply refer to as the Commission.

Both types of yakuza groups, despite differences in structure, possess the same basic tenets governing gang life. What is more striking is that these unwritten laws are similar to those traditionally held by the American and Sicilian Mafias:

1. Never reveal the secrets of the organization.
2. Never violate the wife or children of another member.
3. No personal involvement with narcotics.
4. Do not withhold money from the gang.
5. Do not fail in obedience to superiors.
6. Do not appeal to the police or the law.

Despite the similarities, though, even the traditional Mafia in America is less intricately structured than comparable yakuza syndicates. There are fewer officers and less control over the varied gangs. Crime families in the United States need this greater autonomy to help ensure the invisibility and mobility on which the American mob depends. The Mafia may be a social institution in the West, but unlike the yakuza, it has little or no public standing and must remain unseen. This also bears on why the U.S. Mafia is so much smaller than the yakuza: years of secrecy have helped pare the mob down to an estimated 1,000 initiated members in twenty-five families across America—a fraction of the Yamaguchi-gumi's size alone (although with associates the Mafia may number as high as 20,000).

Traditionally limited to those of southern Italian extraction, the Mafia is only one facet of organized crime in the West. Like the United States itself, American crime syndicates are diverse and multi-ethnic, ranging from drug-dealing motorcycle gangs to small-town bookmakers. The organization of the yakuza, by contrast, is fairly standardized, particularly among the traditional bakuto and tekiya gangs. Even within the "modern" Sumiyoshi-kai, for example, one finds yakuza tradition alive and well. Consider the thoughts of Shotaro Hayashi, eighth boss of the syndicate's Doshida gang and one of the Sumiyoshi-kai's leading powers.

In a 1984 interview, Hayashi held forth for the authors on the virtues of gang life in Japan. At the time, the Doshida family was a Tokyo-based clan of some two hundred gangsters. Hayashi, though, was related through kinship ceremonies to six other yakuza bosses; among them, the six "brothers" controlled about 1,000 of the Sumiyoshi's 6,700 members. Hayashi's daughter by blood was married to an American, perhaps the reason he was willing to entertain journalists from abroad.

At the residence-office of the gang, the red carpet was rolled out for the foreign guests. The shoes were removed first, of course, and then the visitors were led past a paneled hallway into a room quite large by Japanese standards. Framed photos covered the walls, of old godfathers, of the Doshida family, of Hayashi posed with Masao Hori, the head of Sumiyoshi-kai. Also displayed were fine artworks, and a complex organizational chart that traced the Doshida-gumi back through at least several generations of gamblers. The seating was on the floor, cross-legged, at an elegant wood table toward the center of the room.

Hayashi-san appeared shortly, wearing traditional Japanese garb. He was beginning to show some of his fifty-five years or so, but still looked like he could handle himself on the back streets of Tokyo. He had a hard face and stern eyes that peered from behind a pair of thick glasses. There was a hint of kindness there as well, the look of a leader who takes care of his own.

The resident historian, Fujita, was present, and he remarked quietly on the wealth around him. Hayashi was one of the richest men in the Sumiyoshi-kai, he confided. More than a gang leader, Hayashi was an entrepreneur who owned perhaps one hundred buildings on a busy suburban train line out of Tokyo. "There are no stations around at which he doesn't own property," assured Fujita.

Introductions were exchanged, and the host suddenly shouted something in guttural Japanese toward the next room. On cue, sixteen immaculate, crew-cut yakuza—his top captains and lieutenants—entered the room in a line against the wall. His men seated themselves on the floor, in martial arts style. They were wearing three-piece suits and looking unamused. Hayashi began:

> "The real yakuza existed until only the start of the Showa era [1925]. The way they're trained now is different. It's questionable whether real yakuza exist today. There was more chivalry in those days. The times have changed.
>
> "I have been a gambler since I was eighteen. We are gamblers. But then the government passed this unworkable law making assemblies of gamblers illegal. It forced us to expand to other business. They suddenly put us out of work. But the regulations backfired. The gamblers spread to the tekiya business, and things got mixed up."

It was now clear that this was an audience, not an interview, and that our godfather was holding court. It was an important opportunity for Hayashi, a traditionalist, to explain before the clan what is important within the yakuza world. His men remain seated, motionless, listening attentively to every word.

> "My life as a yakuza began with difficulty, when as a young delinquent I joined a gang. The oyabun didn't like me, though. I wanted to be a gambler, but for a long time after joining the family I wasn't allowed to gamble. First I helped with the cooking and cleaning, because the families back then didn't have help or many women. Men did all the housework except clean the toilet—that the women did. The boss had two rooms—one for his wife, the other for his mistresses."

As Goro Fujita and others later explain, his apprenticeship was not very different from what occurs today, although many bosses—including Hayashi—are critical that the training periods have become too short and are sometimes neglected altogether. Still, today's yakuza recruits typically spend from six to twelve months in training, doing menial tasks such as serving guests, answering phones, cooking, cleaning, chauffeuring the boss and his family. The most common complaint is boredom. Perhaps the greatest difference is that the modern yakuza now frequently carries a cell phone to help him stay on twenty-four-hour call six days and nights a week. Absence during a time of urgency can cost a fingertip. Hayashi's hands appear unscathed.

> "After some months of cleaning duty, I got a position doing *tachiban* [standing guard], but on cold winter days it was difficult. Finally, when new members joined our gang, I was able to do *zoriban* [arranging shoes in order]. These moves were important. For the first time I was not in the house, cleaning. Unless you take these steps, you could not become a card dealer.
>
> "You join this kind of business because you like your boss. What can you do unless you believe your oyabun is the second most powerful man in the world next to the emperor?
>
> "In the old days you had to cut your own skin in a sake glass to join. So this is the world of outlaws. The oyabun can't teach you anything unless you learn yourself. But one must pledge total obedience. To do that you must receive sake from the boss, with a third person as a witness. It is a very important ceremony. . . .
>
> "Yakuza tradition will never cease because we're different from ordinary people. That's why we joined this world. And we share the same idea that if we make one big mistake we die together."

Hayashi's chief complaint, like that of other oyabun, was that the old ways are dying, that the great values of giri-ninjo, of obligation and compassion, have faded. He bared one other complaint as well. He was detained by Customs officials in the United States recently while on a tour organized by a bank. "I was held for two hours, and always followed after that. Tell the Americans that those stories about us operating in the United States are untrue."

The audience was nearly over. Hayashi was feeling pensive. "The yakuza are a necessary vice for Japanese society. But in the future our biggest task is to become entrepreneurs, to become clean and pay taxes. The age of the tekiya is over; you have to do it aboveboard now. Business will be our main way to survive. As long as you pay taxes you're okay."

The interview ended. The sixteen yakuza—still motionless, still lined up against the wall—finally began to move. The party shifted upstairs to a long, narrow dining room set for twenty-five. A sumptuous feast had been prepared for the visitors. Amid slices of exotic Pacific fish and drinks of sake, Hayashi encouraged his top men to question his guests about the Mafia in America. Few spoke up, however. Those that did based their impressions

Major Yakuza Syndicates, 2001

No.	Name	Address of main office	Godfather	Member-ship
1	Yamaguchi-gumi	4-3-1 Shinoharahon-machi Nada-ku Kobe-shi, Hyogo	Yoshinori Watanabe	17,500
2	Sumiyoshi-kai	6-4-21 Akasaka Minato-ku, Tokyo	Shigeo Nishiguchi	6,200
3	Inagawa-kai	7-8-4 Roppongi Minato-ku, Tokyo	Kakuji Inagawa	5,100
4	Kyokuto-kai	1-29-5 Nishiikebukuro Toshima-ku, Tokyo	Kyu Hwa Cho	1,700
5	Matsuba-kai	2-9-8 Nishiasakusa Taito-ku, Tokyo	Chun Song I	1,500
6	Aizukotetsu-kai	176-1 Iwataki-cho Agaru Kaminokuti Higashitakasegawasuji Simogyo-ku Kyoto-shi, Kyoto	Toshitsugu Zukoshi	1,100
7	Dojin-kai	6-9 Torihigashi-machi Kurume-shi, Fukuoka	Seijiro Matsuo	530
8	Kokusui-kai	4-3-1 Senzoku Taito-ku, Tokyo	Kazuyoshi Kudo	520
9	Kudo-kai	1-1-12 Kantake Kokurakita-ku Kitakyushu-shi, Fukuoka	Satoru Nomura	520
10	Soai-kai	5-9-9 Nishi Tatsumidai Ichihara-shi, Chiba	Myong U Sin	460
11	Okinawa Kyokuryu-kai	2-6-19 Tsuji Naha-shi, Okinawa	Kiyoshi Tominaga	370
12	Kyokuto Sakurai Soke Rengokai	1787-1 Higashioki Aza Hara Numazu-shi, Shizuoka	Yasuyuki Serizawa	360
13	Fukuhaku-kai	5-18-15 Chiyo Hakata-ku Fukuoka-shi, Fukuoka	Makio Wada	340
14	Kyosei-kai	2-6-5 Nihoshin-machi Minami-ku Hiroshima-shi, Hiroshima	Isao Okimoto	280
15	Sakaume-gumi	2-6-23 Higashi-shinsaibashi Chuo-ku Osaka-shi, Osaka	Kin Zaikaku	280
16	Kyokuryu-kai	4-301-6 Ishimine-cho Shuri Naha-shi, Okinawa	Yoshihiro Onaga	270
17	Goda-ikka	3-14-12 Takezaki-cho Shimonoseki-shi, Yamaguchi	Kanji Nukui	190
18	Kyodo-kai	3-1170-221 Shintakayama Onomichi-shi, Hiroshima	Kazuo Morita	180

Major Yakuza Syndicates, 2001 *(continued)*

No.	Name	Address of main office	Godfather	Member-ship
19	Azuma-gumi	1-11-8 Sanno Nishinari-ku Osaka-shi, Osaka	Kiyoshi Kishida	170
20	Nakano-kai	12-4 Ikutama-cho Tennouji-ku Osaka-shi, Osaka	Taro Nakano	170
21	Taishu-kai	1314-1 Yugeta Oaza Tagawa-shi, Fukuoka	Raitaro Oma	130
22	Asano-gumi	615-11 Kasaoka Kasaoka-shi, Okayama	Yoshiaki Kushita	120
23	Kozakura-ikka	9-1 Kotuki-cho Kagoshima-shi, Kagoshima	Kiei Hiraoka	120
24	Shinwa-kai	2-14-4 Shiogami-cho Takamatsu-shi, Kagawa	Kunihiko Hosotani	70
25	Yamano-kai	180-1 Hayakawa Oaza Kousa-cho Kamimashiki-gun, Kumamoto	Tetsuo Ikeda	70

SOURCE: National Police Agency, 2001.

largely on viewings of *The Godfather,* an immensely popular film in Japan, and particularly so among the yakuza of Doshida-gumi.

The yakuza have been studied perhaps more than any other type of organized crime in the world. National Police Agency bureaucrats are sticklers for statistical data, and from their analyses we know that the yakuza dominate not only organized crime in Japan, but much of crime in general there. Between 1960 and 1992, yakuza members were responsible for 15 to 20 percent of all homicide cases, 10 to 20 percent of the burglaries, 15 to 25 percent of assaults, 30 to 40 percent of blackmail, and 40 to 50 percent of intimidation. They also fill Japan's penal institutions, comprising some 40 percent of the prison population.

More striking than crime statistics is the detailed knowledge of yakuza inside workings that researchers have found. It may seem strange that one can administer questionnaires about gang finances and lifestyle to mob soldiers and godfathers alike, but scholars in Japan have succeeded in doing just that. This is due in no small measure to the gangs' relative openness and to the efforts of a dedicated group of social scientists at Tokyo's National Research Institute of Police Science, a think tank tied to the National Police Agency. A 1993 NRIPS survey, for example, involved interviews with 1,440 randomly selected yakuza arrested during a three-month period. Asked about the keys to promotion in a yakuza gang, senior members stressed long service, followed by sociability and the ability to raise money for the group. Soldiers stressed sociability and sacrifice for the gang. A similar 1987 survey focused on the background and motivation of Japan's gangsters. Interviews with 925 yakuza revealed some not too surprising patterns: many came from broken homes, tended to fight often with wives and girlfriends, kept irregular hours, and were motivated by "hedonistic pursuits" and making big money. We even know that in the late 1980s, 34 percent of yakuza car owners preferred foreign automobiles (confirming the widespread suspicion that mobsters are Detroit's best market in Japan).

Among the more ambitious, and controversial, studies by NRIPS is one on yakuza income. In the late 1980s, researchers surveyed 917 gang members on how much money they made, where it came from, and how much they spent on living expenses. Based on the gangsters' answers, overall annual income for the yakuza was estimated at 1.3 trillion yen in 1989, just over $10 billion at the time. Critics thought the number far too low, particularly in light of figures for the U.S. Mafia of between $50 billion and $120 billion. (The U.S. illegal drug trade has been estimated at $50 billion.) Outside yakuza experts contend the study was far too conservative in accounting for income from various sources, among them narcotics, sokaiya and related acts of extortion, associate members, and front companies. Independent estimates have put annual income for the Japanese mob at anywhere from $45 to over $70 billion.

Given the controversy, the NPA has not issued new figures since then. Nonetheless, the study was quite illuminating. Researchers estimated the percentage earned by various yakuza rackets, and found that drug sales, particularly methamphetamines, were by far the largest source of revenue for the gangs—a multi-billion-dollar industry that accounted for roughly 35 percent of yakuza income. Following that were "legal" businesses at 20 percent, particularly loan sharking, construction, and real estate. Gambling notched next at 17 percent, followed by protection payments at 9 percent and "dispute resolution" at 7 percent.

Other NRIPS studies shed further light on the background of gang members and on economic relations among the gangs. One 1985–86 survey, focusing on 392 "made" members of major national syndicates, found that many gangs were not strongly tied to the parent organization. More than 60 percent of the gangs studied received no financial support whatsoever from the parent syndicate, and some paid no tribute at all. Loyalty was strongest to one's local gang and immediate boss, and lower-ranking gangsters were typically responsible for earning their own living.

Figure 2. Estimated breakdown of yakuza annual income, 1989. (Source: National Police Agency White Paper, 1989.) Independent analysts believe these figures to be quite conservative; their estimates of Yakuza annual income range from $45 billion to more than $70 billion.

The NRIPS studies also found that the offering of a surrogate family was often what attracted recruits to the ranks of the yakuza. The varied gangs serve as a kind of safety valve for tightly structured Japanese society, in which not having a steady job or an upstanding family can ruin one for life. Indeed, most new recruits were poorly educated, nineteen to twenty years of age, and were living alone when they joined, according to NRIPS data. Forty-three percent had lost one or both parents.

As much as one-third of the yakuza's recruits come from the infamous hot-rod gangs or *bosozoku* (literally, "speed tribes"), part of the postwar increase in Japanese juvenile delinquency. Like the yakuza, the bosozoku are highly organized within their troublesome groups. Police in 1999 estimated there were 28,000 bosozoku active in hundreds of gangs, loosely affiliated under several nationwide federations. Sporting swastikas and similar paraphernalia in imitation of Western biker gangs, they bear names like Medusa, Black Emperor, Fascist, and Weatherman, as often as not quite unaware of their symbols' true meaning. A bosozoku specialist with the National Police Agency explained to Tokyo reporter Michael Uehara: "They've created their own world. It's nothing like the world of other kids their age. There are rules and regulations, badges, uniforms of sorts . . . some groups even have membership fees and punishment for members who break rules."

The bosozoku are in fact a mirror of yakuza society, but their members are often no more than adolescents. More than three-quarters are under the age of twenty, nearly 60 percent between sixteen and eighteen years old. Most of them are dropouts from Japan's fiercely competitive school system who soon find themselves frozen out of the country's rigid job market. There are female clubs, as well, with names like the White Snake Ladies of Fukui and the Black Rose Racing gang from Fukuoka. The gangs stand behind a juvenile crime wave that shocked Japanese in the 1990s. NPA data show that in 1999 bosozoku were tied to more than 80 percent of serious juvenile crime, including murder, assault, extortion, and robbery. Between 1996 and 2000, serious bosozoku crime more than doubled.

Relations between yakuza and bosozoku are not necessarily amicable. Japan's bona fide gangsters tend to look down upon the young hoodlums, secure in the knowledge that they sit atop the criminal hierarchy. Young delinquents are frequently referred to by the term *chimpira*, which appears to be derived from the Japanese word for penis; this term is used on the streets as Americans might use the word *prick*. The hot-rodders are notoriously unruly and have given rise to "bosozoku riots" in which they trash neighborhoods and fight police. In one 1999 riot in Hiroshima, some 1,000 bosozoku fought police with rocks and Molotov cocktails for three days and nights. Still, though lacking the discipline of the yakuza, the bosozoku remain key sources of recruits, and most speed tribes have ties to the syndicates. The "retired" leader of one teen gang in Tokyo estimated that some 80 percent of area gangs pay the yakuza tribute of anywhere between several hundred and several thousand dollars each month.

The Medusa and other bosozoku gangs are not the only sources of recruits for the nation's underworld. There are the poor and disadvantaged, the dropouts and misfits who find a home in the gangs. But the yakuza's biggest employment pool likely comes from minority groups in Japan—a subject of extreme sensitivity. The ranks of the yakuza, in particular, are filled with large numbers from two groups that have suffered relentless discrimination in today's Japan: the nation's nearly 700,000 ethnic Koreans and its 2 to 3 million burakumin—the members of Japan's ancestral untouchable class described earlier. Similarly, although to a lesser extent, some of the more than 200,000 resident Chinese are also driven into the yakuza. The issue is sensitive enough that police will not officially estimate the numbers of these groups within the yakuza, nor will either the news media or criminologists openly discuss it. Indeed, a brief discussion of the subject helped stop publication of the first edition of this book in Japanese. Protests and harassment from these groups can be intense and have ensured that a frank discussion of crime problems among burakumin and minority groups in Japan is virtually impossible. Moreover, the very real problems of discrimination against these groups have given rise not only to a legitimate civil rights movement, but also to an industry of sham grievance groups eager for payoffs—many of them, ironically, tied to the yakuza. In the mid-1980s, one newspaper reported over two hundred fake *dowa,* or burakumin liberation, groups.

Unofficially, police and independent yakuza experts will venture estimates of the number of burakumin and minorities within the underworld. In congressional testimony, an FBI official stated that Koreans comprise some 15 percent of all yakuza, an estimate that Japanese police quietly support. Contrast this with the fact that Koreans comprise only 0.5 percent of the population. An FBI report further notes that in the early 1990s, eighteen of ninety top bosses in the Inagawa-kai—20 percent—were ethnic Koreans. NPA officials have further suggested that in the Yamaguchi-gumi, burakumin comprise some 70 percent of the membership, and Koreans 10 percent. Some caution observers to greet these numbers with skepticism, as they may be yet another unfair stigma put upon Japan's disadvantaged. But even if those numbers are high, to seasoned yakuza observers it is painfully clear that the number of Koreans and Chinese in the Japanese underworld is well in excess of those groups' ratio to the general population. Indeed, the fact that some gangs are largely Korean and that many tekiya groups are largely burakumin is an open secret.

For these minorities, for the bosozoku, and for the nation's poor, the gangs can easily seem like the only way out of an otherwise miserable life. Like the Mafia in America, the yakuza provides a vehicle for upward mobility. Children of successful gangsters are invariably given first-class educations and encouraged to get legitimate jobs. Such are the attractions of adoption into a yakuza family.

The paternalistic structure of the Japanese underworld is not out of character with Japanese society. American anthropologist David Stark, who spent a full year in a remarkable field study of a Japanese gang, wrote that "much of what appears so exotic about the gang's organization is actually shared by many of Japan's modern organizations." Stark cites the example of a Japanese bank managed under the principle of *daikazoku,* or "one great family." In a scene reminiscent of yakuza rituals, during the company's annual entrance ceremony, the parents of young recruits symbolically transfer the guardianship of their children to the "family" of the bank. The new workers are given company badges that, like the yakuza's, bear the company logo and list their rank and office within the organization.

There are other similarities. Like Japanese corporations, the yakuza gangs can boast all the trappings of belonging; business cards, used far more widely in Japan than in the United States, are routinely issued to members, embossed with the gang's emblem and clearly identifying the bearer's syndicate, rank, and name (although this practice has faded somewhat in recent years). Other symbols are widely used as well, such as flags and lanterns, and even official songs. Anthropologist Stark's host gang, on the Inland Sea, prominently displayed large, round sofa pillows emblazoned with the group's emblem, stuffed in the rear window of the boss's Lincoln Continental.

So organized are the yakuza that the larger syndicates even issue their own publications. The Yamaguchi-gumi, for example, for years published the monthly *Yamaguchi-gumi Jiho* and sent it to all gang members. The magazine resembles periodicals published for employees of large corporations and other organizations in Japan, including the prefectural police. In one 1973 issue, a two-page article with photos reported on the meeting of the National Narcotics Banishment and Purification Homeland League, a group composed of uniformed Yamaguchi gangsters from western Japan. Another section, "The Law Classroom," provided four pages of legal advice. There were even two pages of poetry written by gang members, followed by photos and announcements of initiation rites, jailings, prison releases, and funerals. In a later issue, godfather Taoka explained the moral guidelines of the syndicate. "I urge the Yamaguchi-gumi members to do their utmost to avoid being hated by people," he wrote. "Try to have an attitude of gentleness and mildness and always show a smile and act with sincerity."

The gangs use other means as well to ensure cohesiveness. In addition to various rituals, heavy slang—difficult for many Japanese to understand—has been practiced widely for generations; today the words vary even from gang to gang. Certain customs, such as tattooing and finger-cutting, also play a major role, marking the yakuza for life. To demonstrate that infractions of policy are not to be taken lightly, many gangs prominently display the severed fingers, preserved in spirits, at the group's headquarters.

The sense of belonging to the group—so important in Japan—does not come easily in the yakuza world. Indeed, the commitment to the gang is perhaps greater than that demanded by any other group in Japan. Many would-be yakuza fail the requirements of gang life and quit or are expelled. There is a 10 percent annual turnover, but those who survive the first few years adapt as successfully as any Japanese in a society where lifetime employment is an institution.

Inagawa-kai—A Talk with the Godfather

The magazines, badges, and other trappings of gang life in Japan mean very little without the presence of a great boss to hold the group together. If the strength of the yakuza derives in large part from its role as surrogate family, then it is the surrogate father who guides the clan on its way.

With Kazuo Taoka—the godfather of godfathers—gone from the Yamaguchi-gumi, and no one from the syndicate able to fill his shoes, the attention of Japan's seasoned yakuza watchers shifted to the leaders of the other syndicates. Few could match Taoka's experience and seniority in the crime world. Worse, there was no longer a Yoshio Kodama who could mediate among the syndicates and plan great alliances. Although the huge size and aggressive style of the Sumiyoshi-kai brought the federation considerable attention, it was not to that syndicate that both police and yakuza looked. It was instead to the Sumiyoshi-kai's longtime Tokyo rival, the enterprising Inagawa-kai, and its remarkable godfather, Kakuji Inagawa.

It was a measure of Inagawa's greatly increased stature that, at Taoka's funeral, he had served as head of the godfather's funeral committee, a unique position for a boss from another syndicate. But Kakuji Inagawa had good reason to be there. In a land where age and seniority are not to be treated lightly, the sixty-six-year-old boss carried with him the heart of the yakuza tradition. It was Inagawa who had helped organize Kodama's yakuza army to guard the streets for Ike's 1960 visit; who had served as head of the 13,000-strong Kanto-kai federation—Kodama's unfulfilled vision of a national alliance of rightists and gangsters; who had formed a historic truce with the Yamaguchi-gumi in 1972; and Inagawa again, the skilled fighter and gambler, who had built a postwar band of ragtag street toughs into Japan's fourth-largest crime syndicate, stretching into twelve prefectures and across the Pacific. With Taoka's death, Kakuji Inagawa had become a senior statesman of the yakuza.

The Japanese were not the only ones taking note of Inagawa's accomplishments. U.S. Customs officials, in a 1981 intelligence report on Inagawa-kai members setting up shop in Hawaii, warned about the organization's abilities:

> Although this 4,600 member gang with its one hundred sub-groups is not the largest OCR [organized crime] entity in Japan, it is possibly the most efficiently organized and more than compensates for its relatively small numerical strength through a combination of "political" skills at the strategic level and the uninhibited employment of muscle at the tactical levels. . . . The

power of the Inagawa-kai is also significantly enhanced by its close alliance with Japan's largest OCR organization, the Kansai-based Yamaguchi-gumi.

Like the Yamaguchi-gumi, the Inagawa-kai is structured in traditional pyramid fashion and lays great stress on the familial ties among its members. Smaller than the mammoth Yamaguchi-gumi, the syndicate enjoys greater discipline and tighter organization, while at the same time remaining more flexible. The Inagawa-kai, though, is by no means a small organization. Its more than 4,000 members make it larger than the Italian American Mafia in the United States.

Another factor strengthening the Inagawa-kai is the composition of its membership. Inagawa-kai gangsters traditionally come from bakuto, or gambler, stock. The Yamaguchi-gumi, by contrast, throws together all three of Japan's traditional gangster classes—gamblers, street stall operators, and hoodlums. The Sumiyoshi-kai can also claim bakuto roots, but because of its structure as a federation of gangs, it lacks what one NPA official called "the strong binding power" of the Inagawa pyramid.

A main source of income for the Inagawa-kai continues to be gambling: bookmaking, running high-stakes casinos, and organizing offshore gambling tours. The syndicate long ago expanded into other typical mob businesses as well, including loan sharking, drug dealing, and various forms of racketeering. According to a 1979 police estimate, the Inagawa gangs ran 879 legitimate businesses, including construction and entertainment companies, bars, cabarets, and restaurants. Officials believed the syndicate's combined annual income was nearly $200 million, and that was very likely a conservative estimate.

Like other syndicates, the Inagawa-kai runs on tribute extracted from its member gangs. "Compulsory" donations from within the syndicate totaled at least 580 million yen (about $2 million) from just one bank account monitored by the Tokyo Metropolitan Police in 1974. Top bosses paid 250,000 yen a month (about $1,300); less was demanded from the lower ranks. In the mid-1980s, the syndicate was composed of 119 gangs, from which twelve bosses were selected to act as a board of directors. Among those who sat at the top was Inagawa's own son, Yuko, who would eventually succeed him as godfather—an unusual development in modern yakuza gangs. A videotape of the succession ceremony in which Chihiro took command featured Inagawa's son shaking hands with the Yamaguchi-gumi's top don; the tape was sold to gang members and "supporters" for about $1,000.

Until his retirement in 1986, Kakuji Inagawa was considered by many to be Japan's most powerful godfather. Getting in to see such a man proved a difficult, at times precarious, task. Introductions from proper go-betweens were required, and one had to pass muster in a tense preliminary interview by the boss's top lieutenants. In addition, "face" must be saved by all parties involved, a complicated task because not all middlemen can be present at the final meeting. Compounding the problem is that such values as saving face, already treated quite seriously in Japan, assume new heights within the yakuza world. So arcane are some of the yakuza customs that even well-educated Japanese often do not understand the ways of this subculture. Attempting such an interview plunges one into a world of invisible strings and obligations that a foreign visitor can only stumble through noisily.

Inagawa did, however, meet the press on occasion, and apparently the interest of American journalists aroused his own curiosity. The final, deciding factor, according to one go-between, was Inagawa's personal fortune-teller, a seventy-eight-year-old sage who advised the powerful boss that such a meeting would be an auspicious one. The authors finally met Inagawa, then at the peak of his power, on a winter's day in 1984.

The gathering took place on the thirty-ninth floor of the posh, forty-floor Akasaka Prince Hotel in Tokyo. Inagawa-san held court that day in the hotel's executive suite, an elegant room bound by large windows and a fine view of the central city. Inagawa's top three lieutenants, who had conducted the pre-interview, were there again, stern-faced and businesslike.

Inagawa, though, was friendly, and offered a warm welcome. At seventy years of age, he looked remarkably well kept, perhaps ten years younger. A short, stout man, he wore a bit of a belly (but carried it well) and radiated confidence, success, and leadership. His balding, muscular head sat fastened onto a two-inch-high neck built like an anvil. Like his lieutenants, he was dressed in a dark blue three-piece suit.

The group was seated around a large, fragile glass table. Young, crew-cut servants from the gang rushed in and out with a procession of refreshments: green tea, delicate sweets, and, finally, coffee. These lay untouched.

"I like casual conversations," Inagawa began, "but it's difficult to do interviews. I don't want to become a showpiece. We're part of society's hidden world and not meant to be more."

There was nothing casual about this conversation, however. Inagawa-san lectured in a traditional manner, dictating philosophy to his students, throwing in his own anecdotes and little jokes. Still, the godfather tried hard to put his guests at ease, showing off his many scars from over the years. Part of an ear was cut off; there was a chest wound; and, most important, he pointed to the back of his head.

"Part of my brains were blown off, and I died, but somehow the doctors revived me. After that there was a new life for me and a change in my heart. Until then I was strong in physical strength—too strong in my younger days—and then my life changed, I went through a conversion."

Since that time, Inagawa-san had earned the reputation of a peacemaker among the yakuza gangs. His underworld diplomacy helped make him a very wealthy man. But the seasoned godfather had not forgotten his origins.

"I grew up in a poor home, with no heating and few conveniences. Our meals were meager, just pickles and rice." His father, a graduate of prestigious Meiji University, lost everything to gambling. Said Inagawa, who never completed elementary school: "Now I've reversed that."

His father also was involved in a left-leaning farmers' group, although that had little appeal to the boy. As a teenager, the young Inagawa studied martial arts at a local judo school, until one day his teacher recommended him to a local yakuza boss in need of strong-arms. "Fighting was my business then. I was very simpleminded—I wanted to be strong."

The yakuza life surprised him, though. "I was just cleaning the floors. I didn't know yakuza did that sort of thing. I was up at five A.M. every day, washing the sliding doors with my hands and cold water during the winter. Before, yakuza training was severe. Our business changed drastically after the war."

Inagawa traced back the Inagawa-kai's all-important family tree to the Hansho-kane, a gang he calls the University of Tokyo of the Yakuza, roughly akin to a Harvard for the Mafia. But it was only in 1945, after his service in the war, that he founded the Kakusei-kai, predecessor to the modern-day Inagawa-kai.

As a sign of Inagawa's new status, he proudly related an anecdote about the Tokyo Metropolitan Police: "Each year we personally travel to police headquarters to give our traditional New Year's greetings. And each year the police ask, 'When are you going to disband your group?' But in 1983, for the first time I was encouraged to live a long life and play lots of golf [a favorite pastime]. It's interesting to hear the police celebrate my longevity now. They said I'm the only one now to chair the yakuza system and keep the peace. They want me to live a long life because they depend on me and I feel thankful and would like to help them." (Tokyo police denied any such statements were made.)

Inagawa loved golf. Every third and fourth Monday, he sponsored a golf competition at the Lakewood course in Kanagawa Prefecture, inviting professional golfers and well-known entertainers. He also enjoyed taking his game on the road, traveling from one end of Japan to the other, at times followed by as many as seventy subordinates. The golf tours did more than improve his game: they were an opportunity to demonstrate his power to local gang bosses. At each stop, Inagawa gave banquets, inviting the region's reigning yakuza powers to dine with him. His travels weren't limited to the golf circuit, though. He often showed up at the VIP rooms of horse racing tracks as well. According to *Shukan Mainichi*, a weekly, wherever he went, the yakuza boss was always followed by a guardsman holding a large cash-filled paper bag.

Inagawa had a reputation for generosity—he collected hats and white shirts, and then gave them out to his younger members. Sometimes he would give $40 to a follower for a pack of cigarettes. He offered his visitors some sage advice: "Beware of the weak, for the strong will take care of themselves. And don't take any percentage from your direct subordinates; don't be greedy."

He was reflective about his old teacher, Yoshio Kodama. "It was unfortunate that Kodama-sensei was implicated in Lockheed, because we lost a great kuromaku. Yoshio Kodama was a great man and the world will never see the likes of him again." Indeed, Inagawa saw the end of the kuromaku era. "There will be no more kuromaku. This is the age of democracy. We needed kuromaku in an age of transition . . ."

Inagawa-san complained that the Western press has never written anything favorable about the yakuza; he expressed the hope that this would change. "I like books that have a favorable aspect to the yakuza," he said pointedly, and suggested that the authors might want to submit their manuscript to him so it could be checked for wrong "assumptions." He proposed as a model an apparently endless series about him in the sensational weekly *Asahi Geino,* in which the author kindly submitted his articles to Inagawa prior to publication. In one story, explained Inagawa, the author's assumptions were so wrong he had to edit out half the piece. The *Asahi Geino* series was a tribute to Inagawa's greatly increased stature in the yakuza world, but according to journalists familiar with the situation, the magazine could not stop publishing the serial even if it wanted to. Inagawa-san displayed the thirtieth installment; his aides later assured him that many more were on the way.

More than two hours had passed, and the boss indicated that the audience was nearly over. "I'm sure there are things that will give you a bad impression, but we're trying. Our problem today is how to be more liked by the community, or at least not hated . . ."

One of his top lieutenants, Keizo Tanaka, stressed a second point: "We'd like you very much to grasp the fact that our leader is a gentleman." Indeed he was. One could not help but be struck by the fine dress, polite manners, and hospitality shown by these top yakuza.

Before the meeting ended, however, Inagawa spent considerable time railing over a familiar theme among yakuza bosses: the young gangsters— less loyal, harder to control. "I can foster and educate the young people, and they hopefully will do so with the next generation," he said. "But beyond that it's difficult to grasp."

Inagawa was a traditionalist, a firm believer in the values of giri-ninjo and gangster chivalry. But he also saw room for change in many of the old customs, and had become something of a reformer among yakuza godfathers. He had, for example, shortened the once lengthy initiation rites entailing sakazuki, the formal exchange of sake. There were some rituals, though, such as the funeral ceremony, that he wouldn't touch. Others, like finger-cutting, he proved less successful at changing. As noted earlier, if the Inagawa-kai is typical, 39 percent of its members were missing at least one finger joint. Because of the high turnover within yakuza gangs, a lot of former gangsters were walking around with nine fingers. This concerned the yakuza boss, who was fond of telling the story of how he tried to stop the practice within his own gangs.

A lowly soldier in the Inagawa army had committed some grievous error, so his immediate boss demanded he slice off a fingertip as punishment. When Inagawa learned of this, he was enraged, and berated the boss for ordering such an act. The boss, humiliated and ashamed, responded in the only way he knew how: he cut off his finger and presented it to Inagawa.

The godfather was more successful at changing other long-held yakuza traditions. One reform that gained Inagawa wide attention in Japan was his abolition of the infamous *demukai,* the prison-release ceremony. When one of Inagawa's four arrests for gambling finally landed him in jail, his liberation, like most yakuza jail releases, was an occasion of great pomp. Hundreds of gang members arrived in dozens of expensive foreign cars. Once at the prison, the syndicate members carefully lined up according to gang, subgang, and personal rank. In Inagawa's case, as with other high-ranking yakuza, representatives of affiliated gangs were also present to pay their respects.

Demukai is an important rite of passage to the yakuza, a symbol that the state's rehabilitation effort has failed. Typically, the released gangster is given a significant promotion for doing his time for the gang. The gang publicly displays its commitment to its members and also engages in some recruitment, offering an opportunity for marginal members and potential recruits to interact with the organization.

Perhaps most important, the ceremony allows the gang to show off its power with a convoy of foreign luxury cars. There is something about large, black Cadillacs, Continentals, and Mercedes that has great appeal to the yakuza. Indeed, in Japan, where after taxes and refitting the price of a U.S. car doubles, the gangsters are Detroit's best customers. So closely identified are American cars with the yakuza that for years some parking lots banned the vehicles and police advised the public to steer clear of those inside them.

Clad in their flashy outfits, with their close-cropped hair and aggressive driving style, the yakuza in their foreign cars are readily identifiable on the highways of Japan. In a land where the biggest vehicle usually determines right-of-way, the yakuza driver commands the road, sweeping past normally combative truck drivers and anyone else who dares get in the way. Like a renegade funeral procession, these criminal convoys converge on unsuspecting rest stops and neighborhoods, tying up traffic and scaring local residents out of their wits. As one might imagine, such blatant displays of gang power have dismayed both the police and the general public. It was in response to this, Inagawa explained, that he decided to do away with the ceremony.

Befitting Inagawa's role in the yakuza, a movie based on the godfather's life was released in 1984 entitled *Shura no Mure* (A band of daredevils). As with many movies made about the yakuza, the Inagawa-kai helped with production of this feature film. Inagawa must have felt that his turn had arrived; a decade earlier, the Yamaguchi-gumi had seen to it that a trilogy on Kazuo Taoka's life was produced.

Inagawa's life story joined a central, firmly established cinematic tradition in Japan: the yakuza film. These films, descendants of the old samurai epics, bear little resemblance to American or European gangster movies; they are closer to the Western, in which cowboy and outlaw clearly define a code of morality. From the samurai, the yakuza has inherited the role of the last defender against the decadence and corruption ushered in by modernization and contact with the West.

Unlike the Western, though, yakuza films are as highly stylized as the Kabuki theater of a century earlier. The movies are "probably the most restricted genre yet devised," according to director Paul Schrader, writing in *Film Comment* magazine. "The characters, conflicts, resolutions, and themes are preset. . . . Yakuza films are litanies of private argot, subtle body language, obscure codes, elaborate rites, iconographic costumes and tattoos."

So similar are many of the films, with the same actors and the same stories, that often it is difficult to tell them apart. Japan's leading actor, Ken Takakura, who won his fame starring in gangster roles, made one yakuza classic—*Abashiri Bangaichi* (Abashiri Prison)—more than a dozen times, according to Schrader.

Typically, a traditional yakuza film opens with the outlaw's release from prison, the noble gangster having served years behind bars to spare his gang a police investigation. Other requisite scenes follow: the gambling den, the baring of the tattoo, the blood brother ritual, the evil oyabun, plenty of finger-cutting, and a final battle bloodying the screen with dazzling swordplay. Throughout, the film stresses the twin themes of giri-ninjo, as the yakuza hero struggles between his deeply felt virtues of absolute duty to his crooked gang and compassion for the oppressed. In the end, he dies a violent, but honorable, death. There is in these sagas an almost unrelenting obsession with death, a fatalism that runs through nearly every film. As one gangster on the big screen declared, "There are only two roads for a yakuza, prison and death."

If the human conflicts sound elaborate, the films themselves are not.

Yakuza movies were mostly low-budget endeavors that Japan's big studios threw together within a matter of weeks. Schrader traces back the first authentic yakuza film to 1964, a movie titled, appropriately enough, *Bakuto* (Gambler). The genre quickly came into its own, and by the mid-1970s, one hundred yakuza films a year were being churned out. And the Japanese loved them. Yakuza-film addicts range across the political spectrum, from leftist student activists to the ultranationalists of author Yukio Mishima's private army.

Toei Studios became the Warner Brothers of the yakuza movie industry, making well over three hundred of the films, most with the same plot structure. The studio owed much of its success to its general producer, Kouji Shundo, who pioneered the genre. Shundo learned about his subjects firsthand; he was a former yakuza. Present-day yakuza are employed in the industry as well. Most Japanese actors labor under contract to one of the country's four big studios, a system not unlike the worst days of old Hollywood. To enforce their will, some studios have reportedly hired gangsters over the years, resulting in a number of highly publicized assaults on Japan's leading stars.

Not surprisingly, the yakuza became the yakuza films' biggest fans. On the big screen, they could see themselves portrayed as the noble gangsters they so rarely are. But these are mostly the older works, from the heyday of the genre in the 1960s and early 1970s. First, a newer subgenre emerged, which struck somewhat closer to reality. This was the *Jitsuroku Eiga* (true document films), in contrast to the more orthodox *Ninkyo Eiga* (chivalry films). In this later group, there is less honor and more treachery, less swordplay and more gunfire. The modern yakuza cinema expanded along with the gangs; later films were set in Hong Kong and the Philippines. Complained godfather Inagawa in 1984, "In the movies nowadays, the yakuza is depicted as interesting, but he always loses to the authorities in the end. It's impossible to make a movie that's 100 percent pro-yakuza."

Times then grew even worse for yakuza movie fans—people stopped going to see the films. Japanese moviegoers were more interested in high-budget U.S. features laden with special effects. At the same time, the yakuza's image steadily eroded as the number of scandals, shootings, and other crimes tied to the gangs mounted. Unable to turn a profit, studios stopped producing yakuza films. In 1994, Toei, the last big studio in the business, announced that its new yakuza movie—*The Man Who Did in the Don*—would be its last. The movie was Toei's 252nd yakuza film since 1963.

Ironically, the yakuza film that would make the biggest profit in recent years was an anti-gang movie: *Minbo no Onna,* variously translated as "Mob woman" or "Extortion woman." Made by the brilliant director Juzo Itami, the 1992 feature parodied the yakuza while championing the struggle against them. The movie so enraged the gangs that three yakuza showed up on Itami's doorstep and slashed his face with knives.

The attack on Itami only stirred more outrage against the gangs by the public, who were steadily losing patience with their nation's misguided gamblers and peddlers. Indeed, like their fading heroic images on the screen, by the 1980s Japan's real-life outlaws were rapidly shedding their honorable image. The ruthless expansion pioneered by Taoka and his Yamaguchi-gumi, matched by Inagawa and the others, had made the public weary of the ever-present gangs. The widespread drug dealing, extortion, racketeering, and violence were affecting more people than ever before. But just as the Japanese thought they had seen it all, the corruption fostered by the yakuza spread to places even they didn't expect.

CHAPTER SIX

CORRUPTION, JAPANESE-STYLE

LIKE MANY GOOD CRIME STORIES, THIS ONE BEGAN BY ACCIDENT. IN MARCH of 1982, a middle-aged woman strode into the Osaka District Prosecutor's office and lodged a complaint against her boyfriend for physically assaulting her. The alleged offender was a retired sergeant of the local police. Japanese officials did not look kindly upon one of their own involved in domestic violence, or, for that matter, in other crime. Since the war, law enforcement in Japan had won the admiration and respect of not only the Japanese people, but police forces around the world. The accomplishments of Japan's police seemed to go hand in hand with those of the nation's "economic miracle." Women could safely walk the streets of Tokyo alone at night; rates of violent crime were among the lowest in the industrialized world; and the police had become a disciplined, dependable force of professional lawmen.

It was this image that was marred when the retired sergeant went about beating his girlfriend. Upon further investigation, officials learned that the former cop also worked for a gambling machine–leasing company, the kind that rents out computer-operated poker games. There was nothing illegal in it per se, but, as with similar games in the United States, regulation has proved difficult for Japanese authorities. Under certain owners, and with a small adjustment, the machines can transform an amusement arcade into a gambling hall.

Still, there was no reason to suspect foul play beyond the morally reprehensible actions of an ex-cop. Before long, however, the case would utterly transform the image of the Osaka police and raise for the first time in recent memory the specter of widespread systemic corruption within Japanese law enforcement, a corruption influenced, and at times inspired, by the yakuza.

It was while local investigators were checking into the ex-sergeant's background that they first smelled something rotten within the ranks. Their suspect, apparently, was using his old police cronies to tip off contacts in the gambling business about upcoming police raids.

As Osaka police probed further, the broad outlines of a major scandal came into view. The tip-offs were being made not only by the former sergeant, but by a growing number of police on active duty. And they were receiving payoffs not only from gambling bosses, but from the operators of striptease theaters as well. The respected officers of Osaka's Finest—the prefectural police—appeared to be working hand in hand with the local mob, a shocking development for the Japanese.

Osaka is a town that, like Chicago, has always played second city to Japan's New York—Tokyo. Osaka's 3 million people live within a sprawling metropolis of 19 million, in one of Asia's leading centers of commerce. For three hundred years, while the country's political and cultural life centered in Tokyo, Osaka concentrated on business and industry.

Also, like Chicago, Osaka became a mob town. Particularly hard hit was the adjacent port city of Kobe, home base of the legendary Yamaguchi-gumi, the largest crime syndicate in the country. The Yamaguchi-gumi had cash and political clout, and its 13,000 members had made organized crime a fact of life throughout the region. So it was, perhaps, only a matter of time before such power corrupted the local police.

Investigators took eight months to build their case, but by November of 1982 they were ready. On the first of the month, the initial collars were made: a senior policeman and the manager of a game center were arrested on bribery charges.

The next day, a veteran police sergeant, apparently unconnected to the inquiry, committed suicide, claiming his innocence in a final, handwritten note. More arrests followed over the next week, including that of the retired sergeant whose domestic assaults first sparked the investigation.

Later the same week, on the morning of November 12, 1982, Tadashi Sugihara, former chief of the Osaka police, tied a sash to the central beam running along the ceiling of his storehouse. Around the sash's other end he snugly wrapped his neck and proceeded to commit suicide in its most commonly practiced form in Japan. Unlike the sergeant earlier that week, Sugihara left no note. Those closest to him knew only that he had recently made a volley of phone calls to Osaka and had grown increasingly concerned about the police scandal.

Sugihara's reign over Osaka headquarters had lasted two years, until his promotion three months before his death to president of the National Police Academy. When he died, he was one of the highest-ranking policemen in all Japan. An elite bureaucrat with a bright political future, Sugihara was being groomed for the position of deputy minister of justice in the Nakasone cabinet.

Veteran Japanese cops were killing themselves because it was the only "honorable" way out of an unbearable situation. They had brought immeasurable shame to Japanese law enforcement, and their continued existence—not to mention their testimony—would only bring further humiliation upon those they had served so long. Sugihara, furthermore, was clearly under suspicion. He had been seen with another high-ranking police official frequenting almost nightly the expensive bars in a renowned Osaka entertainment district, according to an article in *Bungei Shunju,* a leading monthly. A typical night of such festivities—including a couple of restaurants and a nightclub—could easily have cost them $2,000. A convicted police investigator would later testify he had given some $16,000 to Sugihara to bribe his way out of a transfer. Other evidence would also implicate Sugihara in bribes from local mob-controlled Turkish bath houses. These *toruko,* as they were then called, were nothing more than houses of prostitution.

Although Sugihara's death firmly tied the scandal to the department's highest-ranking officers, it still wasn't clear how far the case would spread. Many citizens had long suspected that large-scale official corruption existed—even in the police departments. But the Japanese had felt that such problems were best swept under the tatami mat. Perhaps that was finally changing, for the Lockheed revelations were still fresh in the country's memory. Speculation on the police scandal was running rampant in the press, and seasoned reporters were betting that, with Sugihara's suicide, much more would be revealed. They were right.

By the beginning of 1983, the bribery scandal had snowballed. Investigators implicated scores of men from throughout the Osaka police force, and disclosed payoffs to individual cops as large as $20,000. When the dust finally settled, a record 124 lawmen had been fired or otherwise disciplined, enough officers to police a Japanese city of nearly 70,000. And still there was more.

In December, the national daily *Mainichi Shimbun* reported that two LDP politicians—including Akira Hatano, the justice minister in the newly appointed Nakasone cabinet—had acted as consultants to game machine associations whose members were linked to the Osaka bribery case. Hatano protested his innocence, explaining that he had never received any money for his services, and that he had assumed the organization was engaged in "wholesome forms of amusement." But despite Hatano's claims, suspicion lingered around the justice minister, whose campaign for the Diet in 1980 had attracted donations from a Tokyo yakuza-rightist political party. A former Tokyo police superintendent, Hatano would later comment that seeking morality from a politician is like "asking for fish at a vegetable shop."

By February of 1983, the Osaka bribery scandal had spread to neighboring Hyogo Prefecture, home to the national headquarters of the

Yamaguchi-gumi in Kobe. Authorities arrested a fifty-six-year-old vice squad chief and launched probes into the affairs of more than ten other officers. In what had become a familiar pattern to investigators, the vice chief, in return for bribes of about $1,000 to $2,000, leaked information on police raids to gambling machine operators. He would pass on payments of $50 to $100 to his subordinates to dissuade them from investigating the gambling shops, and invited officers of neighboring police stations to dinners and drinking parties with the machine agents and operators. Also part of his routine were visits to police stations, at times in the company of gamblers, who would arrive laden with gifts for the precinct's ranking officers.

The operations were as massive as they were corrupt. One gambling chain ran more than ten shops with some eight hundred machines; the company employed more than three hundred people and grossed above $350,000 daily. The shops, furthermore, stayed open twenty-four hours and most were located prominently along the region's major highways. Neon signs even advertised the machines to passing motorists. Yet despite this openness, only two of the company's shops were ever raided during its three-year existence. One day before an intensive, long-overdue police crackdown in November 1982, the operator abruptly closed all his shops, removed the machines, and disappeared.

One final, ominous blow would strike before the Osaka scandal faded from Japan's newspapers. In March, *Mainichi* reporters revealed the existence of a nationwide tip-off syndicate, run by retired police officers and businessmen and linked to the yakuza. The operation provided information on police raids to gambling clubs in twelve prefectures, including Tokyo, Osaka, and Hyogo. The syndicate, at least six years old, had gained a reputation for accuracy and timeliness, being able to warn its customers three to ten days before a raid. One contract with the Tokyo-based organization reportedly cost some $12,000, plus a monthly fee of between $500 and $2,000. Among the organizers was a prominent gangster who ran numerous "Turkish baths" in the Tokyo area, a man whom reporters identified only by the nickname "Emperor of the Night."

The World's Best Cops

The Osaka bribery scandal is not the only problem to have surfaced within the ranks of Japan's postwar police force. While most Japanese police departments maintain records to be envied by any large U.S. city, enough cases have arisen to suggest widening cracks within the system. The same year as the Osaka police scandal, for example, a former sergeant in Kyoto shot and killed a policeman and a bank employee before making off with about $2,300; months later, officials arrested a former Tokyo police captain for double murder and possession of nearly $80,000 worth of precious stones. Also that year were cases involving past and present lawmen in fraud, forgery, and kidnapping.

More recent reports reveal police officers dining and playing golf with gang bosses, accepting bribes, and even recommending yakuza chiefs to businessmen to help settle contract disputes. In 1999, the busy Kanagawa prefectural police, just outside Tokyo, were racked by a series of scandals that surpassed those of Osaka years before: officers were accused of extortion, drugs, assault, sexual harassment, violent hazing of new recruits, and an ensuing cover-up. Such incidents, when publicly revealed, tend to be dealt with harshly, resulting in reprimands, firings, and indictments. But too often, as in Osaka, the roots of corruption and indifference run deep. In 1990, press reports alleged what workers in Osaka's skid row had long suspected: that yakuza gangs bribed local police to help maintain control of the local labor racket. So incensed were the district's day laborers that they rioted for days, shocking much of Japan. Other apparent victims of police misconduct are Japan's numerous immigrant workers; Japanese cops are by now notorious for ignoring the plight of foreign hostesses and prostitutes, and for their often brutal treatment of illegal aliens.

Aside from a handful of reports on the yakuza, for years Western accounts about crime in Japan have been generally awash with praise for the police. Such points are usually made for good reason. The Japanese police in general do have a high standard of discipline, and violent crime is far lower than in the United States. A country with half the population of the U.S., Japan had only 1,282 murders in 1997. (There were 769 that year in New York City alone, and 15,289 in the United States—a thirty-one-year low.) According to official statistics, Americans are twenty-two times more likely to be raped, and five times more likely to be victimized by property crime. Perhaps most striking of all is the fact that from 1948 to 1973, official crime totals in Japan followed a downward curve. In other words, during a period of unprecedented economic and urban growth, while crime rates in America shot upward, those in Japan actually went down.

The Japanese police have appropriately taken their share of credit for this admirable accomplishment, and long prided themselves on being the world's best cops. Yet, so notable are their many achievements that it becomes difficult to understand the most persistent, overwhelming problem confronting law enforcement in Japan: How can nearly 100,000 gangsters thrive on the islands?

The answer, in part, rests on the unique relationship that exists between Japan's cops and robbers. It is, in a Western sense, a much more far-reaching, more institutionalized form of corruption than anything suggested by the police scandals previously discussed. At regular intervals, for example, police have staged massive crackdowns on the yakuza, hauling in some 30,000 to 50,000 gangsters and associates each year. From reading newspaper accounts, one might easily surmise that officials have waged an unrelenting war on the underworld. But while they make for impressive reading, the raids are mostly a form of harassment and, in particular, of publicity, reminiscent of the police chief's order in the movie classic *Casablanca* to "round up the usual suspects." Questions about the effectiveness of these methods were raised years ago by anthropologist Walter Ames, who spent eighteen months in Japan doing fieldwork on the police. In his 1981 book, *Police and Community in Japan*, Ames wrote that "these raids assume an almost ritual air because most of the gangsters are released in a few days through lack of evidence of criminal acts or because their offenses were minor." Ames further pointed out that the gangs usually receive warning before the huge raids, and that well before authorities arrive on the scene, virtually all contraband is concealed and the highest bosses have gone into hiding. The raids end with a uniquely Japanese twist: so the police can save face, the gangsters generally leave behind a few guns for the officers to confiscate. In one publicized case in 1995, three police went so far as to buy local yakuza several guns which they could then confiscate.

In keeping with the unusual openness of the gangs, there is a great deal of personal rapport between the yakuza and the police; local cops know local gangsters by name, and there is an easy familiarity between them. Such amicable relationships help form the bridge to police corruption. Departing precinct captains, for example, traditionally collect cash gifts from local merchants, much as retiring bureaucrats and company officials do with their own contacts. For the police chief, however, this can mean substantial gifts from local operators of massage parlors, gambling halls, and other gang businesses—but not if he has made life too uncomfortable for the community's wealthier "businessmen."

Police, though, are drawn to the yakuza for reasons other than bribery. Most Japanese lawmen are quite sympathetic to the highly conservative views held by the yakuza. Indeed, part of the rigorous routine investigation into the background of police recruits is to screen out anyone with possible left-wing leanings. Japanese leftists, unsurprisingly, have long accused police of going easy on the yakuza's often suspect political activity on the right.

There are other similarities as well. Like their criminal counterparts, many police have only high school educations and come largely from families of modest means. Also, more than a few Japanese cops admire and identify with the gangs' professed ideals of giri and ninjo, and similarly fashion themselves as a kind of latter-day samurai. These traditional values are expressed in a genre of moving ballads that frequently have yakuza or oyabun-kobun themes, and are quite popular among the police. "To understand the heart of Japanese people, you must understand the yakuza and ninkyo," one top narcotics control officer confided to the authors over drinks. "Not all yakuza are bad . . . I have friends who are yakuza—poor yakuza—and they are honorable, chivalrous people. They show the true spirit of the Japanese people."

For their part, the gangs traditionally have respected the police and understand their duty to enforce the law. After a gangland murder, for example, the guilty yakuza would turn himself in to the nearest police station and make a full confession. The deed having been done, he is fully prepared to suffer the consequences. As syndicate boss Kakuji Inagawa commented when asked about his gang's relationship with the police, "We believe in the Japanese police. If they say that the Inagawa gang is bad, then it is so. I don't want to say this, but they are a very capable lot. It is their duty to watch me. I respect them. Please convey my best regards to them."

This attitude of complicity is reinforced by the enduring links between high-ranking government officials and gang leaders, which have served to legitimize the position of the yakuza in Japanese society. What are police to think when a former prime minister and education minister guarantee the bail of a convicted murderer from the Yamaguchi-gumi? Police actions thus often seem tailored toward dealing not with a menacing underworld, but more with a somewhat misguided loyal opposition.

It is not simply that the yakuza are more accepted as crime syndicates than gangs elsewhere in the world; it is that the role of the gangsters is more publicly institutionalized. Yakuza perform various tasks that are left to lawyers or agents of the court in other societies, particularly when dispute resolution is involved. It is not well known in the West, for example, that as much as one-quarter of all bankruptcies in Japan are routinely handled by yakuza gangs. In 1995, the Japanese Bar Association estimated that one hundred *seiriya*—or "fixer" specialists—offered such services. Similarly, many yakuza or their associates set up shop as *jikenya* (incident specialists) or *jidanya* (settlement specialists). These fellows are often made use of by developers and landlords in tenant disputes, and by aggrieved parties in traffic accidents. At times the opposing party will bring in its own gang, and the two groups work out a deal that will at least ensure fat commissions for the gangsters.

Most Japanese do their best to avoid contact with the gangs, but often there are no alternatives. This, say legal scholars, is due largely to glaring holes in Japanese law and its enforcement, and most of all, to the state's deliberate cap on the number of attorneys. Japanese are famous for their lack of lawyers and supposed reluctance to litigate. Lawyers number about 1 per 8,500 people in Japan, compared to about 1 per 900 in Britain and 1 per 400 in America. Civil suits per capita are fewer than one-tenth of those in the Western common-law countries. But this may be due less to long-standing cultural values and more to institutional barriers—lack of legal support, high filing fees for civil suits, and poor enforcement of judgments. No wonder that some yakuza refer to themselves as *urashakai no ben-goshi* (lawyers from the dark side of society). Using yakuza can actually save money and time, notes law professor Mark West. A striking number of Japanese apparently agree. A 1993 poll found that 23 percent of men and 17 percent of women believed that hiring gangsters to collect money, obtain contracts, or settle disputes by threatening violence is "not bad" or "can't be helped." The reasons: the courts and police take too long or are too cumbersome to use. The gangsters were certainly easier to find than lawyers. In a 1988 survey, the number of Japanese admitting they knew yakuza members reached 11.3 percent—nearly 14 million people.

Perhaps the most remarkable aspect of the yakuza's public role is its function as a kind of alternative police force. Says criminologist Eric Von Hurst, a fifteen-year resident of Japan, "The one thing that terrifies Japanese police is unorganized crime. That's why there's so little street crime here. Gangsters control the turf, and they provide the security. If some hoods come around the neighborhood and start making trouble, chances are the yakuza will reach them first. Japanese police prefer the existence of organized crime to its absence." Among those who agree is former mob attorney Yukio Yamanouchi, who served for years as the Yamaguchi-gumi's counsel. "Japanese public security is very high," he told a reporter. "The crimes to be tolerated are a basic choice of the Japanese people."

The close ties between police and yakuza have broken down somewhat since the early 1990s. Stung by a series of scandals revealing yakuza ties to top levels of business and government, Japanese officials passed tougher laws aimed at racketeering by the gangs. Yakuza were so incensed at this violation of their long-held "understanding" with authorities that they responded by adopting the so-called Three No's Policy: no police allowed into their offices; no evidence offered or criminals delivered; and no confessing or offering information when arrested. Whether this is the beginning of a fundamental change in yakuza-police relations remains to be seen. At issue is not merely a well-worn truce between the authorities and the mob; the entire approach by Japanese law enforcement is at stake. In the West, police and prosecutors tend to speak of organized crime in warlike terms: the fight against the mob, the war against drugs. The attitude is one of eradication. Japanese authorities, in contrast, tend to favor containment: reining in the gangs, guiding the yakuza to more lawful activities. In Japan's group-centered society, the yakuza have their place like any other group. As one Tokyo business executive remarked, "If you destroyed the yakuza, where would all the criminals go?" The approach is not without merit. All modern societies host organized crime to some degree. Why not control the gangs as best as possible, instead of wasting resources in a fruitless attempt to destroy them?

The problem with this approach appears to be that it leads to precisely the kind of deep-seated corruption that has wracked postwar Japan for decades. Tolerance of organized crime breeds acceptance, and this in turn allows the underworld a greater opportunity to expand, to seek new venues and new businesses. The message of tolerance, moreover, is not merely received by organized crime, but by criminals and corrupt officials across that nation.

The Underground Economy

The unique symbiosis between Japanese authorities and the underworld is indicative of a much larger problem of structural corruption in the country. Some of it bears a strong resemblance to the grand old traditions of corruption in America's large eastern cities, where the politician, labor boss, and gangster got rolled into one well-greased machine. Other elements of graft and corruption in Japan, however, remain markedly different from those of the West, floating somewhere on the same cultural plane as the Japanese fusion between gangster and rightist.

To the distant observer, Japan's low crime rates can be misleading, depicting a society of completely law-abiding automatons. Even allowing for the highly defined role of the yakuza, a look at Japan's police statistics seems to reveal a people who simply don't break the law very much. The Japanese, however, can be just as devious and corruptible as Americans or Italians, even more so. They do not, for one glaring example, cooperate very much with the National Tax Agency, Japan's version of the IRS.

Like Americans, the Japanese support a massive underground economy, supported by legions of tax evaders, illegal workers, mobsters, drug users, and more. At the peak of Japan's booming Bubble Economy in 1990, underground economic activity reached an estimated 33.5 trillion yen, or about $230 billion, according to a study by the Yokohama Bank's Hamagin Research Institute. (A 1992 estimate by the IRS put America's underground economy at nearly $675 billion.) By 1999, years of recession had pushed that figure down by one-third, but Japanese officials still faced a huge and thriving black economy. Tax collectors unearthed a record 1.55 trillion yen (about $2.3 billion) in undeclared earnings in 1998. Topping the list of tax evaders are owners of bars, nightclubs, and pachinko parlors. Other groups with a penchant for avoiding the tax man include owners of hotels, hospitals, and loan companies, entertainers, physicians—and Buddhist monks.

At the urging of police in the early 1970s, the government finally began to tax the earnings of Japan's gangster class. It was hardly a novel idea. U.S. officials have used tax laws as a weapon against the mob since they put Al Capone away on income tax evasion in 1931. But Japanese officials, in their zeal to treat everyone equally under the law, announced in 1975 that gangsters were allowed to deduct "business expenses" from their income. "Included in the deductible expenses," read an Associated Press dispatch from Tokyo, "were rental for gambling places, per diem allowances to gangsters sent out for intimidation, payment to lookouts during gambling sessions and expenses of pimps."

Despite the liberal interpretations of tax law toward the gangs, the vast percentage of yakuza income remains uncounted and untaxed by Japan's official auditors. As in the United States, the gangsters are only following the rest of the population in hiding their billions of dollars from tax collectors. But if the Japanese penchant for tax dodging strikes a familiar chord with Americans, certain crimes in Japan take on a decidedly different flavor. Particularly distinctive are white-collar crime and related endeavors such as bribery and extortion.

When it comes to payoffs, Japan at times seems like a refined version of Mexico or the Philippines. If Japan does indeed have a serious problem of structural corruption, then it reaches its highest point here, in what appears to be a formalized system of endless payoffs. The demand for such payola ranges from multi-million-dollar corporate deals to apartment rentals and college entrance exams.

The concept of bribery in Japan is a muddy one, largely because the custom of gift-giving is so widespread and thoroughly institutionalized, to a far greater level than in the West. Gift-giving in Japan is a traditional, subtle art closely tied up with the obligations involved in giri, and pushing heavily against a thin line that separates it (usually) from outright bribery. Gifts are given when one is visiting another's home; twice a year—during July and December—to associates and to those for whom one feels giri; to employees who move or transfer jobs; when one returns home from a trip; and in a myriad of social situations that are often confusing and frustrating for the Japanese themselves. Gifts can range from inexpensive souvenirs to luxury items, or they can be crisp, clean bills sealed in special money envelopes. So deep-rooted is the practice that many households keep record books of gifts given and received with the prices listed. The Japanese recognize the importance of this custom with the saying that gifts are *junkatsuyu*—"the oil that lubricates society."

How does a Japanese recognize when a gift is in effect a bribe? Not easily. Police and others claim they can identify a bribe if the gift's value is excessive for the particular situation. But such judgments become easily confused; vice cops routinely accept free tickets from local porno show operators. Cash gifts—sometimes of $1,000 or more—are given to teachers by parents of students around final exams and admissions time; presents are offered each day by patients to doctors at elite university hospitals to obtain preferred treatment in Japan's socialized medical system. Writes anthropologist Harumi Befu of Stanford University, "It may be difficult for a Western observer to believe that one would not know when he is committing bribery, but . . . because gift-giving is so pervasive in Japan, and the obligations to give, to receive, and to reciprocate are so strongly entrenched . . . it is extremely difficult, if not impossible, to discern whether a gift is legitimate."

Often the bribery is so embedded in ritual that no questions can be asked. Japanese culture simply does not provide any appropriate way to refuse a gift once offered. A good example is the mah-jongg game. During contract negotiations between firms, the representative of one company is frequently invited by his counterparts in the other company to play the popular gambling game. Despite the skill of all the players, the hosts begin to lose huge bets in game after game to their client. Everyone knows what is going on, but the matter is never voiced. When the game ends, it is understood that the winner will do his best to get a contract with that firm.

According to Japanese law, it is a crime for public officials to accept any compensation, outside the legally specified salary, in connection with their recognized duties. The law relating to private citizens is much less clear. There is, in fact, no stated rule; judgment is based on what is socially acceptable. For example, company officials might entertain their business associates at $300 per night. The law allows for this. But if they spend such money on government officials, it can be considered a bribe. Practically, though, the law is seldom applied.

While prime minister, Kakuei Tanaka used the cover of traditional gift-giving to disburse his political funds. The politician's generosity was legendary: summer gifts, year-end gifts, bon voyage gifts, and various campaign contributions all came out of the prime minister's office. There are indeed times when the courts recognize that disbursement of funds has clearly gone beyond the realm of custom. But even then, it takes an event the stature of the Lockheed scandal to draw concerted public attention to the issue.

Many of Japan's more astute political observers readily concluded that the only unique element in the Lockheed case was that the officials were caught and prosecuted, and this only because the case involved a foreign company and large amounts of cash. Tanaka himself firmly believed that he had done nothing out of the ordinary, and that his political enemies had changed the rules on him. If true, then the relative absence of financial scandals in Japan may reflect not the workings of honest government, but a system's ability to cover them up.

How corrupt, then, is Japan? Anthropologist Befu jokes that to really enforce the law, the Japanese government would have to create a huge Department of Bribery Investigations. So pervasive is its use that virtually every major contemporary Japanese politician has had some brush with the nation's postwar bribery law at one point in his career. Some scholars suggest, however, that this may be changing. For many years, they argue, the Japanese public tolerated the sale of access by their politicians, but the Lockheed scandal seems to have signaled the start of a new era, in which the old ways of doing business are gradually being held to new standards.

If indeed the old ways are dying out, it will be a long process, for such cultural traits seldom change quickly in Japan. Those who have made clever use of bribery in the past—be it Yoshio Kodama with Lockheed or the Yamaguchi-gumi with the Osaka police—will have equally skilled successors. Furthermore, it is not only bribery that will have to meet new standards. Hand in hand with bribery and kickbacks go blackmail, extortion, and intimidation, crimes that seem to grow exceptionally well in the refined culture of Japan.

Sarakin and Saving Face

At least twice a week a small news story appears in the Japanese press that reads something like this: Mitsuru Takahashi, heavily in debt to creditors, can no longer bear the shame of being unable to pay off his loans. Rather than have his two children grow up penniless, he kills them and then tries unsuccessfully to take his own life.

The story appears with a number of variations throughout Japan. There was the insurance saleswoman from the west coast who drove her car into the sea, drowning herself and her family because she could not repay $40,000. Or the family of three in Nagano, in central Japan, who shot themselves to death over a $4,000 debt. And the story in Tokyo of the confessed killer of a prostitute who committed murder to escape his creditors by going to prison.

These are the victims of Japan's notorious *sarakin,* a word that literally means "salary man financiers" but that translates more directly as "loan sharks." In 1996, 3,025 Japanese killed themselves for financial reasons—many of them victims of mobbed-up loan companies who use public humiliation and strong-arm intimidation to handle debt collection. The problem has plagued Japan for years. Authorities reported that back in 1982 sarakin drove nearly 2,400 people to suicide, or about 11 percent of the nation's total suicide cases. The National Police Agency estimated that 7,300 others that year fled the sarakin by abandoning their families and their work, an almost unforgivable act in modern Japan. The practice still continues today. Those who vanish are called *johatsu*—"the disappeared people," or, literally, "evaporated."

At their peak in the mid-1980s, at least 42,000 sarakin firms operated in Japan, ranging from alleyway loan sharks to big consumer credit companies. These firms became as successful as they were notorious, largely because the country's mainstream financial institutions shied away from granting consumer credit. As a result, almost any adult Japanese could walk into a local sarakin office and—with nothing more than simple identification—walk out twenty minutes later with $2,000 in cash and a 60 percent annual interest rate.

Sensing an opportunity, U.S. firms in the early 1980s tried to move into the growing consumer credit market, only to find a business with "heavy gangster overtones," according to Richard Huber, then vice president of Citibank's Tokyo operations. In a *Business Week* story entitled "U.S. Bankers Take on the Japanese Mafia," Huber stressed that the major task facing American lenders was in persuading the Japanese that they don't run their businesses like the yakuza. "We're trying to convince consumers that we're different," he said, "that we won't break your kneecaps if you don't pay."

With a new generation keen to buy on credit, the consumer loan market exploding, and reports of abuse mounting, the government in 1983 passed long-overdue legislation aimed at cleaning up the industry. Legal interest rates, once as high as 110 percent annually, were limited to a still-hefty 40 percent, although penalties for loan sharking remained light. Pushed by government officials to transform their homegrown industry into a more respectable business, by the early 1990s the sarakin had been winnowed down to some 8,000 firms, with a handful of huge, more respectable lenders dominating the field. The fast-growing firms soon were counting billions of dollars in annual revenues and had become favorites for stock investors in Japan as well as overseas. One top lender, Shohkoh Fund, made owner Kenshin Oshima a billionaire. "This business has a rather dirty image in Japan, so it doesn't attract smart people," Oshima explained to *Forbes* magazine. "It is easier to compete with stupid people."

Many small lenders have continued their underground operations, lending to desperate consumers and enforcing their policies with fingerless bill collectors. These firms, dubbed *toichi*, are true loan sharks, with rates that reach 10 percent every ten days. And at least some of the more legitimate companies still use yakuza and strong-arm tactics to collect overdue debt. A 1990 TV program showed the reality of just how the mob collects money. The ten-minute segment followed a gang to a real estate agent's home, filmed him being kidnapped and hauled away to their office. There they beat the poor fellow and threatened to kill him unless he paid up. But even those crude tactics paled compared to what emerged in 1999, when the public learned of the methods employed by a collector for Nichiei Co., the nation's top sarakin for small business. The collector had called a retired steelworker who had guaranteed an acquaintance's loan, demanding he pay up. "You have to come up with the money," the man threatened. "Sell your house quickly. . . . Sell your clothes and all your belongings." But there was more: "Sell a kidney. You have two, don't you? Many of our borrowers only have one. You can get $28,000 for a kidney. You can get $9,500 for an eyeball." Frightened by the tone of previous calls, the retiree taped the conversation and the case quickly drew the attention of law enforcement and the media.

Behind such calls always lurks the threat of violence, which is why so many sarakin have found the yakuza useful partners. But the sarakin's collectors are skilled at using other techniques. Along with the implied violence, what Japanese debtors often fear most is the sarakin's power to repeatedly punch a sensitive nerve on which so much depends in Japan—saving face.

In its broadest sense, the ability to save face—or to "clear one's name," as some put it—remains a central fact of daily life in Japan. Businessmen devote enormous amounts of time to saving face, prompting more than a few Western salesmen to wonder how their Japanese customers ever earned their reputation for efficiency. It is of paramount importance, however, for such relations to be kept in balance. The loss of face displayed before the public—by noisy sarakin visits to one's home or office—pushes the Japanese to abandon their work and family, to commit suicide and even murder. Sarakin tactics are in fact typically designed to maximize loss of face. There was, for instance, the case when three sarakin charged into a wake and demanded that the bereaved widower pay up or they would disrupt the funeral. Or the case of sarakin express-mailing "reminders" of money due to debtors' children—care of their elementary schools.

Ironically, the sarakin themselves are also sensitive to loss of face. When *Gendai* magazine published an exposé of Yasuo Takei, the leading sarakin boss, in July 1983, all 300,000 copies of the issue disappeared within three days of release. *Gendai* editors accused Takei's outfit of buying up virtually the entire print run to keep the story from the public. The article, entitled "King of the Sarakin Business," detailed Takei's alleged career as a juvenile delinquent, black marketeer, and finally, sarakin boss. (Takei would later take his company Takefuji public, earn billions of dollars, and become one of the world's wealthiest men.)

The need of the Japanese to save face creates a unique climate in which a whole range of extortionist crimes can thrive. Much as gift-giving and giri contribute to the practice of bribery, so do these values make the Japanese particularly vulnerable to blackmail, intimidation, and a host of related acts. Extortion is, in fact, one of the yakuza's biggest money makers. A 1988 police survey estimated the gangs brought in nearly $1 billion annually from protection rackets. As Kusuo Kobayashi, a top Sumiyoshi-kai boss, explained, "I'm not a rich man. There's a lot of people who sympathize with what I am doing, and they make contributions."

Because of the emphasis on saving face, many crimes take on a different form than they would in the West, although the end is often the same. In 1984, for example, police in Tokyo accused four men of blackmailing a private dental college into handing over $85,000 by threatening to expose "back door" admissions of students with poor grades. The blackmailers, members of an obscure rightist "political party," vowed that unless payment was made, they would send a car equipped with a loudspeaker to the college campus to publicly denounce school officials.

In certain lines of business, the practice of extortion is particularly entrenched. A 1991 NPA survey of 3,000 major firms found that 41 percent had been targets of extortion. Hardest hit were companies involved in restaurants, securities, and insurance (70 percent), followed by construction (50 percent), banking (50 percent), and real estate (45 percent). The targets include some of Japan's best-known companies. A 1993 investigation by Osaka police found that All Nippon Airways had been pressured to give half-price tickets and priority seating to a Yamaguchi-gumi gang for the previous six years. Confronted with the charges, ANA declined to lodge a complaint.

Most victims are more down to earth, however. A 1995 survey by police of 60,000 bars, pachinko parlors, and other entertainment businesses in Tokyo found that some 18,000 were paying protection money. One popular scheme is an end-of-the-year racket in which yakuza go door-to-door selling New Year's decorations to small businesses. The decorations, usually a few sprigs of pine and bamboo, are ridiculously overpriced at hundreds of dollars; what is really being sold, of course, is protection for the new year. A favorite target is the so-called water trade—bars, restaurants, and nightclubs. Restaurant and bar managers quickly learn that their supply of *oshibori*—the hot hand towels in every Japanese eatery—are controlled by the yakuza; their supply of coffee, napkins, or ice may also be in the hands of the mob. The Yamaguchi-gumi even got national phone company NTT to print up phone cards with the gang's diamond-shaped insignia, which the gangsters promptly left at local shops and restaurants as a reminder to pay up.

With so much pressure to save face and so pervasive an extortion industry, it is not surprising that shakedowns have filtered down even to the schoolyard. Young students are routinely extorted by bigger classmates, who demand lunch money and payoffs to stop the harassment. Several cases garnered national publicity when the victims killed themselves. Particularly shocking was the 1994 case of a thirteen-year-old Hiroshima high school student who hanged himself after being forced to steal $10,000 from his parents to pay off bullying schoolmates. The widespread employment of extortion and intimidation has caused consternation among Japanese social critics. As one observer quipped: "Extortion is to Japan as snow is to the Eskimos. There are a hundred variations."

Sokaiya: "The General Meeting Mongers"

Japan's underworld showcase of extortion, however, is not in the schools, the water trade, or even the sarakin. It thrives among a remarkably brazen, professional class of corporate racketeers whose activities have tradition- ally centered around the company shareholders' meeting: the *sokaiya*. The word translates directly as "shareholders' meeting men" or "specialists," but the sokaiya gangs have been variously described in English as "financial racketeers," "general meeting mongers," "black gentlemen in the shadow," and "rent-a-thugs."

Virtually every company listed on Japan's stock exchanges has dealt with them. For years, they could be seen forming long queues in front of the gen- eral affairs bureau of any bank or securities firm. Most wore light-colored business suits similar to those of ordinary employees; others sported loud jackets adorned with wide neckties. At the larger banks, they would check to ensure their names were still officially listed in a special registry, enabling them to receive payoffs at least twice annually. Some made daily rounds through Japan's business districts, visiting several hundred corporations each year. At one major shipping firm, as many as eighty sokaiya visited each morning. They would be serviced by a company official who had been pay- ing off sokaiya for twenty-five years. At another firm, a leading bank, some 2,000 persons, including known gangsters and rightists, were registered to receive twice-annual payments of typically between $20 and $200; certain callers were quietly handed as much as $15,000. One 1999 study noted that Japanese firms pay sokaiya an average of $2,000 per year, and twice that for "expert" sokaiya, with fat bonuses around meeting times. Top sokaiya have been known to rake in tens of millions of dollars annually.

After a long-delayed crackdown by authorities, the sokaiya stopped lin- ing up at company general affairs departments in the early 1980s. But if these racketeers no longer operate as overtly as they once did, Japan's so- kaiya industry remains alive and well. And if they are not queuing up for corporate payoffs each morning, the sokaiya are still blackmailing the coun- try's largest businesses out of hundreds of millions of dollars each year.

Why are these extortionists paid off? Largely to leave the companies alone, to stop disrupting the staid world of Japanese business. Traditional sokaiya gangs operate by buying shares of a company's stock, digging up scandalous information, and then demanding hush money. They fer- ret out embarrassing facts about the company's performance and top man- agement: bookkeeping irregularities and payoffs, product liability claims and plant safety problems, officials who cheat on their income tax or keep mistresses. If the corporation refuses to pay up, at its next general meeting the sokaiya will appear armed with these unpleasant revelations and loudly berate the company management. These corporate "dissidents" can play rough. Fistfights have broken out at some meetings; at others, so-kaiya have sprayed paint, lit fires, and thrown whiskey bottles at the chair-man's desk. In at least one case, they have murdered a top executive.

Corporate officials, highly concerned over losing face before their em-ployees and the public, have traditionally anted up. As one police official put it, "It's not threats of violence that scare corporate executives. They're more afraid of damage to the reputations of friends and family members. We live in a culture of shame."

Although their stories don't appear in popular how-to books about Japa-nese management, their activities occupy a central place in the operation of Japan's largest corporations. The companies themselves are not always innocent victims. Occasionally, larger firms have played one sokaiya group against another, planting enough of "their" sokaiya in the audience to en-sure a smooth meeting. Dissident stockholders who dare protest company policy usually find themselves shouted down—or beaten up—by the bois-terous troop of mobsters on hand. More often the result is simply to render the Japanese shareholder meeting useless—a highly staged, sometimes far-cical performance that usually lasts less than twenty minutes. In 1996, more than 80 percent of the meetings lasted less than a half-hour.

Some scholars suggest that the sokaiya tradition can be traced back to the *ronin* (masterless samurai) of the Meiji era who went into the "protection business." The first actual sokaiya reportedly appeared after 1890, when the nation's original commercial code was enacted. Until the Occupation, though, few companies were publicly owned, and it was only with the rapid economic growth of the 1960s that the sokaiya business took off.

Among the leading bosses of the sokaiya world was, until his death, Yo-shio Kodama. He is said to have systematically advanced into sokaiya circles after 1965, starting his own racketeering groups and making alliances with others. Taking their lead from Kodama, the mainstream yakuza syndicates realized how lucrative the sokaiya rackets were and began moving into the field around 1972. The sokaiya were no match for the mobsters. Those who resisted yakuza payoffs or takeovers were forced to shave their heads as a warning to others.

With the mob's firm backing, the sokaiya business started to boom, in-creasing fourfold between 1972 and 1977. At their peak in 1981, a police survey revealed 6,800 sokaiya in five hundred separate groups extorting as much as $400 million annually. By 1987, police say, virtually all sokaiya were linking up with yakuza syndicates, and some 70 percent of the sokaiya's annual take was ending up in the hands of the mob. At least one sokaiya, though, was careful to mark the distinction between the two crime groups. "I don't like people to use the terms 'sokaiya' and 'yakuza' interchangeably," said Jiro Morimoto, boss of a thirty-member sokaiya group. "Yakuza are

Occupational Background of Yakuza

Occupation	Full-status members	Marginal-status members	Total	
Bakuto (gamblers)	26,960	5,148	32,108	(31%)
Tekiya (peddlers)	21,438	2,570	24,008	(23%)
Gurentai (hoodlums)	9,861	1,639	11,500	(11%)
Seaport racketeers	3,221	0	3,221	(3%)
Sokaiya (corporate racketeers)	47	2,417	2,464	(2%)
Scandal sheet extortionists	41	803	844	(1%)
Prostitution gangsters	495	74	569	(1%)
Others	39	29,202	29,241	(28%)
Totals	62,102	41,853	103,955	(100%)

SOURCE: National Police Agency, 1980.
NOTE: These categories are fluid; there are frequent crossovers. For example, many bakuto and tekiya may act as sokaiya or as other racketeers. Also, many sokaiya and right-wing gangsters are not counted as yakuza in official statistics and do not appear here.

inheritors of the old bushido, the samurai spirit, who stick to one principle. On the other hand, sokaiya could tell a story in ten different ways."

The scams devised by the sokaiya over the years are as ingenious as they are lucrative. Some set up booster clubs that seek "donations" from the companies for a range of rather dubious causes. Another favorite tactic is to host "parties" at which businessmen are expected to bring cash gifts. Other bands of sokaiya have branched into more enterprising efforts. One group arranged a beauty contest that companies were persuaded to "sponsor." Another organized a golf tournament for Tokyo businessmen—with exorbitant entrance fees. A third group hosted an "irresistible" Kabuki play at which tickets cost five times their normal price.

Often they pose as legitimate consultants from "economic research institutes," gathering corporate intelligence and, with the help of private detectives, maintaining dossiers on leading executives—down to the names and addresses of their mistresses. One notable success could be found in Eiji Shimazaki, president of the Shimazaki Economic Research Institute, with offices in the Tokyo and Osaka areas. In the 1980s, Shimazaki's outfit boasted a staff of sixty and a $6 million annual budget spent on conducting research, analyzing corporate finances, and publishing magazines. "It is well within my power to make or break corporate mergers," he once said, "let alone change board line-ups." Among the many achievements he cites is the merger of three large Mitsubishi firms into the present Mitsubishi Heavy Industries. A former teacher, Shimazaki's motto was "Be strong, just, and cheerful." Shimazaki's reach was long, indeed. Back in 1973, a police raid turned up documents detailing three years' worth of unsecured loans to his group, totaling nearly $3 million *from sixty-three banks nationwide,* including many of Japan's largest. Shimazaki's leverage over the lenders: threatening to disrupt their shareholders' meetings.

Another favorite sokaiya scam is posing as publishers of small magazines and newsletters—publishers who are only too happy to accept money for "subscriptions" and "advertising" in exchange for not printing scurrilous stories or causing other trouble. Management views such scandalous press with the same horror as threats against its general meetings. The contents of such stories are typically leaked to the company before the issue is distributed, and the company buys up all the copies, often at premium rates. Again, the companies are at times complicit; some firms buy sokaiya reports on rival companies, using them as competitive intelligence. In the late 1990s, such major corporations as Kirin Brewery and Nomura Securities admitted to paying for hundreds of these publications each year; Japan's large city banks on average subscribed to no less than 1,000 of them.

The practitioners of the sokaiya's varied exploits fall into several classes. Those who run sophisticated organizations—working at times closely with company management—receive salaries comparable to the best-paid corporate executives. They are chauffeured around town in limousines and maintain powerful political connections. Most sokaiya, though, are petty thugs hoping for an easy payoff. Their members come from varied walks of life: taxi drivers, tradesmen. Some are former student radicals, who see little wrong in preying on Japanese corporations. There are even the reputed "bartender sokaiya," former barmen who switched to extortion after listening to conversations between top executives over drinks. Also in the lower ranks of the business is the so-called banzai sokaiya, who walks around company offices shouting the exclamation "Banzai!" When questioned, he states that he has just become a shareholder and is merely expressing his joy and desire to encourage greater worker productivity. Several thousand yen is usually enough to convince him that his joy is better expressed elsewhere.

So lucrative is the field that some corporate officials who once dealt regularly with sokaiya have switched roles and turned up as sokaiya at company meetings—much to the surprise of management. The sokaiya's rationale, like that of the yakuza in general, is that they play a critical role in society. "The stockholders' meeting is a solemn function," one sokaiya told the newspaper *Yomiuri.* "We help it proceed smoothly and protect the interests of the innocent shareholders. We are the prop men of modern capitalism."

As with their yakuza brethren, the openness of the sokaiya can sometimes be jarring. One Japanese publisher even sends out questionnaires to the extortionists and puts out an annual directory based on the results. While it's hard to imagine a New York publisher asking local mobsters which restaurants and contractors they extort, the sokaiya eagerly respond. The 1997 edition of the guide lists 650 sokaiya, complete with addresses, phone numbers, targeted firms, affiliated yakuza gangs, and helpful hints on their tactics. Retailing for some $250, the guide is purchased by corporate officials, investigators, and the sokaiya themselves. Among the characters profiled: Tatsuki Masaki, head of a Tokyo "debating club" who posts the latest corporate scandals on his website; Makoto Kanehira, a rightist from the Comrades of the Great Japanese Kamikaze; and Ichiro Yamate, described as a six-foot-tall delivery van driver from Hiroshima with a "booming voice." There are even a few foreigners listed, who are reportedly sent to annual meetings to demand answers from embarrassed executives in English.

That both law enforcement and corporate officials allow such a corrupt and criminal industry to flourish is difficult to fathom, particularly for Westerners. One reason for the sokaiya's effectiveness is the Japanese fondness for avoiding confrontation. Decisions are made through behind-the-scenes talks; management will go to great lengths to avoid head-on clashes. Therefore, the *sokai*—or general meeting—should be only a legal formality, a harmonious gathering to recognize what is a fait accompli. At the heart of this love of order and calm lies the concept of *wa*. The accepted translation of *wa* is "harmony," but that word is somewhat misleading, because *wa* encompasses a far broader concept. Wa is emphasized not just in business but throughout Japanese life, and manifests itself in such ways as the Japanese reluctance to give negative answers. If dissident shareholders sharply question management, it is considered disharmonious—a serious violation of wa. But if the company hires yakuza to assault and silence the shareholders, the violation of wa would not be as great.

Still, the glaring success of an entire industry of corporate extortionists is due to more than simply a Japanese love of harmony. Western scholars who have studied the sokaiya believe these racketeers depend on a dismal pattern of poor disclosure by Japanese companies, lack of oversight by government officials, and a general lack of accountability. Ownership of corporate stock in Japan is more concentrated than in the United States. Much of a corporation's stock is typically owned by a tight web of cross-shareholding with affiliated banks and other companies. This handful of big investors traditionally frowns on public disclosure. Even when scandals and appalling mismanagement come to light, there is little securities fraud litigation in response. Regulators and the laws they rely on are weak and disorganized. Convictions for sokaiya shakedowns are punishable by a mere six months in jail—or less—and $2,600 in fines. Japan's Securities and Exchange Surveillance Commission investigated a total of only eighteen cases between 1992 and 1998—for violations of any kind. In contrast, the U.S. Securities and Exchange Commission investigates an average of 150 to 200 cases each year. Indeed, of the scores of prosecutions involving sokaiya payoffs between 1982 and 1999, only five sokaiya were sentenced to prison— and not a single executive.

The lack of disclosure and accountability feeds on itself, and it has helped create a climate of secrecy within corporate Japan. This, in turn, has fed the extortionate appetites of sokaiya and their ilk. Poor disclosure makes companies in any culture easy targets for blackmail—and will continue to do so in Japan, Inc., until its businesses become more transparent. As Tetsuo Tsukimura, chief economist with Smith Barney International's Tokyo office, told a reporter, "Accountability, as Western management understands it, is still virtually nonexistent in corporate and bureaucratic Japan."

Were the activities of the sokaiya limited to exposing the sexual affairs and tax scams of Japan's executives, the impact of these racketeers might be more easily overlooked. But the reach of these full-time extortionists goes deep into the heart of corporate responsibility and social policy. Just as Japan's largest corporations have been used by racketeers, so have they employed sokaiya and yakuza strongmen in controlling the unwanted airing of the most heinous corporate crimes. Nowhere is this better seen than in the historic Minamata case.

The Case of Minamata

For over a generation, the Chisso Corporation dominated the political and economic life of Minamata, a country town of 36,000 on Japan's southern island of Kyushu. The long-established fertilizer company had grown since the war into a leading manufacturer of petrochemicals. From its Minamata plant—a huge gray complex of pipes, towers, and tanks—the company had for years routinely dumped its lethal by-products into the heavily fished waters of Minamata Bay.

The Chisso Corporation had run into pollution problems before. Three times—in 1926, 1943, and 1954—the company paid local fishermen for losses caused by its dumping practices. But by 1953, the early effects of a far more serious development could be seen—the outbreak of one of the world's largest environmental poisoning disasters.

In their book about environmental problems in Japan, *Island of Dreams*, authors Norrie Huddle and Michael Reich describe the chilling progression of what would come to be called "Minamata disease":

> Birds seemed to be losing their sense of coordination, often falling from their perches or flying into buildings and trees. Cats, too, were acting oddly. They walked with a strange rolling gait, frequently stumbling over their own legs. Many suddenly went mad, running in circles and foaming at the mouth until they fell—or were thrown—into the sea and drowned. Local fishermen called the derangement "the disease of the dancing cats," and watched nervously as the animals' madness progressed.

Soon the malady spread to the fishermen and their families. The symptoms of the disease were horrible to watch. Although it was still undiagnosed, physicians knew the disease attacked the central nervous system and the brain, crippling its victims and eventually rendering them bedridden and incoherent. Forty percent of those poisoned died. Autopsies showed that their brains had become spongelike as cells were eaten away. Hundreds of families were affected, while medical authorities warned that thousands more were in danger.

By 1958, the victims and their families, treated as pariahs by a fearful public, demanded compensation and better pollution control at the Chisso plant. The company, however, resolutely denied that its operations were responsible, as it would for the next fifteen years. Yet, as early as 1959, Chisso knew from its own secret tests that its massive discharges of organic mercury were the cause of Minamata disease. A long-overdue official government report would much later reveal that for thirty-three years—until 1965—Chisso dumped a total of eighty tons of mercury into the shallow waters of Minamata Bay, mixed in with 600,000 tons of sludge.

To local fishermen, who had watched the number of victims grow as their catch steadily declined, Chisso's conduct was inexcusable. In a series of protests, they stoned the factory, at one point holding the executive director hostage overnight and causing extensive damage to company buildings. After the Japanese press picked up the story, the company eventually agreed to pay a small amount in compensation money to those affected. The Chisso Corporation, however, never admitted any responsibility in the matter.

Despite misgivings among the victims, the issue remained dormant until 1965, when another outbreak of mercury poisoning occurred far to the north in Niigata Prefecture. This time the cause was a Showa Denko Corporation factory, employing an industrial process identical to that of Chisso's Minamata plant. Niigata victims organized and took the historic step of filing the first large-scale suit against a polluter in postwar Japan.

In September 1968, fifteen years after the poisonings first appeared, the Japanese government officially recognized organic mercury as the cause of Minamata disease. Before another year passed, Minamata victims followed the lead of those from Niigata and filed suit against Chisso. Supporters of the Minamata group, however, went a full step farther. They took their cause directly to Chisso's corporate headquarters and stockholders' meetings in Tokyo and Osaka. This was as good as a declaration of war to Chisso, and the company promptly enlisted the help of two groups closely associated with the underworld—the sokaiya and the *hosho kaisha*, or "security companies."

Borrowing a tactic from the sokaiya, Minamata victims and supporters began purchasing single shares of the company's stock, entitling them to attend Chisso's general meetings and introduce motions. Although some five hundred members of the Minamata delegation arrived at the company's meeting in November 1970, few got much farther than the front door. The activists were barred by a line of guards who looked as if they'd been recruited from the seediest realms of the Tokyo underworld. One protester who did make it inside found his attempts at amending a management proposal futile. Waiting for the man were a host of sokaiya, who easily drowned him out with a chorus of jeers and promptly called the meeting to a close. Total time of Chisso's shareholder meeting: five minutes.

The company's next general meeting, in May 1971, took place in an atmosphere of increasing tension. Minamata victims and their supporters grew increasingly frustrated as their lawsuit dragged through the courts. Chisso, meanwhile, stood as resolute as ever, and came to its stockholders' meeting prepared to do battle.

In a replay of the November meeting, the protesters were met at the door by a menacing line of guards, sokaiya, and members of local ultranationalist gangs, and were again shouted down. The meeting lasted twelve minutes.

Outraged by the abrupt conclusion this time, the protesters remained at the site, arguing fiercely with company shareholders and sokaiya. Suddenly, about twenty guards stormed into the hall and attacked the Minamata contingent, smearing the green seats of the auditorium with blood. Within two minutes they were gone, leaving behind a shaken and battered group, and sending one badly injured youth to a hospital emergency room.

Police until now had stood by, letting Chisso and the protesters fight it out. But such a blatant attack—with wide press coverage and serious injuries—prompted a raid on the offices of Chisso's specially hired guard services. That Chisso's guardsmen had strong underworld ties should not have surprised the police. The yakuza-dominated security companies were a suspect lot, frequently called on by firms to harass striking workers during labor disputes.

Chisso's next shareholders' meeting took place in November 1971. This time, both sides came prepared. Nearly three hundred protesters, each owning one share of Chisso stock, slept on the concrete outside the convention hall the night before. At about 8:15 A.M., company supporters, including a mass of sokaiya and what one newspaper described as "eighteen members of a local rightist group," were allowed into the hall through two back doors.

The main entrance, where the protesters stood assembled, remained locked. As Chisso corporate officials arrived, skirmishes broke out between protesters and the company's hired musclemen barring the entrance. Some two hundred riot police moved in and broke up the fighting, evicting protesters from the entrance and making a number of arrests.

Meanwhile, inside the building, the handful of protesters who had made it in were unable to introduce motions or even be recognized by the chair. Frustrated, they threw their bodies together and stormed the stage, shouting "Murderer!" and "You swallow mercury!" The burly troops of sokaiya lining the front rows responded, and as in a lopsided football scrimmage, the activists were violently thrown back.

Shielded from the battle below him, the chairman called for a vote on the company's audit report, and a "unanimous" approval echoed through the hall. With no more items on the agenda, the proceedings were promptly adjourned. Total duration of Chisso's forty-fourth shareholders' meeting: nine minutes.

The scene was a bit too much for journalist Bo Gunnarsson of the large Swedish daily *Expressen*. At a Chisso press conference later that day, Gunnarsson, accompanied by his Japanese wife and small daughter, confronted the corporation's president, Kenichi Shimada. "I saw the stockholders' meeting for the first time, and it was terrible," insisted Gunnarsson. "Do you mean to say you have money to pay gangsters but not patients?"

Shimada, composed and polite, preserved his humble posture with a modest smile, although his eyes began to twitch. "I think it's a misunderstanding," he replied cautiously. "I believe we are taking full responsibility toward the patients."

If that responsibility entailed unleashing its hired thugs, Chisso clearly didn't mind. Indeed, it appears that the company made a careful decision to escalate this undeclared war. At its Minamata plant two months later, Chisso guards and company union thugs surrounded and viciously attacked a patients' negotiating group. Among the victims was W. Eugene Smith, the eminent fifty-three-year-old American photographer whose images had focused worldwide attention on the Minamata tragedy. In what Smith later described as "a deliberate company setup," Chisso toughs singled him out, destroyed his cameras, beat him, and smashed his body into the pavement, crushing several vertebrae and causing serious damage to his most valued photographic asset—his eyesight. Smith, the veteran photographer for *Life, Collier's,* and the *New York Times,* never fully recovered, although he and his wife remained in the city to finish their devastating photo essay, *Minamata.*

The assault on Smith was a serious mistake by Chisso, for it brought a barrage of criticism both in and out of Japan. Chisso, however, seemed undaunted. At its stately Tokyo headquarters, workmen installed iron bars at the front door and hired twenty-four-hour guards. Meanwhile, outside, a militant faction of the so-called victims' groups pitched a scraggly tent on the pavement alongside the entrance. Despite constant threats by police and ultranationalist groups to tear it down, the tent stood for months as a haunting reminder to the company, the press, and the public.

In what was becoming an almost ritual confrontation, Chisso's forty-sixth general shareholders' meeting took place in December of 1972. The number of protesters had by now dwindled to fifty, although the company came well prepared with what the *Japan Times* called "a horde of pro management shareholders." Once again, Chisso's critics were prevented from introducing a motion by the jeers and cheers of sokaiya on hand. With each item voiced from the president came a resounding "No objection" from the audience, despite attempts by protesters to scale the speaker's platform and demand an emergency motion. As the president declared the meeting closed, about twenty protesters rushed the stage, shouting "Down with Chisso!" and running straight into the lines of company guards and sokaiya; chairs flew, tables overturned, and police soon moved in. Total time of the meeting: four minutes, possibly a sokaiya record.

Justice finally prevailed on March 20, 1973, when a federal judge found Chisso guilty of gross negligence and ordered damages paid to the plaintiffs. Still unclear, though, was Chisso's attitude toward those not directly represented in the suit. Nearly four hundred victims had so far been officially identified, although some medical authorities put the total number at more than 13,000.

With momentum now on the victims' side, a series of tense, emotional negotiations followed. Two days after the verdict, Chisso management relented by agreeing "to accept all responsibilities concerning Minamata Disease . . ." But those who for so long had fought Chisso's corporate irresponsibility, its delaying tactics, and its use of the underworld were still not satisfied. The company's offer was accepted only after Chisso president Shimada, in a classic act of Japanese contrition, got on his hands and knees and formally apologized to the victims of Minamata. A day later, the iron bars blocking the company's main office were removed.

On July 9, 1973, twenty years after Minamata residents first noticed "the disease of the dancing cats," Chisso Corporation signed a final, public statement agreeing to pay compensation to all recognized victims. By early 1975, the company had paid out over $66 million to Minamata sufferers, and a new chapter in environmental protection had begun in Japan.

Extortion, Inc.

Ironically, the role of the sokaiya was virtually unaffected by the Minamata case. Indeed, the sokaiya's effectiveness may well have opened the way for their expansion, by proving their value to corporate Japan. Companies made growing use of the racketeers—and vice versa—for another decade. It was only after some twenty years of pressure for reform, largely by scholars and influential journalists, that the Diet finally cracked down in 1982 by tightening up the nation's commercial code. The new regulations made it illegal for companies to pay off sokaiya where no tangible service is rendered, and limit participation in annual meetings to persons holding 1,000 or more shares of stock. Company managements, furthermore, are required to stop evading questions from common stockholders at their general meetings.

At first the new laws seemed to work. Early police reports indicated that the number of sokaiya had dropped dramatically. (Scores of "retiring" sokaiya, of course, demanded and received "severance pay" from their corporate victims.) Companies vowed to break relations with the gangs and hold their meetings regardless of the outcome. But the sokaiya weren't backing down, and their influence remained strong. In one example, after the boss of a major sokaiya gang was hospitalized for hepatitis in 1983, pointed phone calls went out to Tokyo's largest corporations advising them of the hospital's location and a date for an appointment with the ailing boss. Police suspected some one hundred companies of sending representatives to the gang leader's bedside, many bearing cash gifts of between $100 and $200. Resisting the racketeers at shareholders' meetings proved equally difficult. In a key confrontation in early 1984, Sony Corporation's meeting lasted for a record thirteen and a half hours, as officials were grilled by angry sokaiya and other shareholders until almost midnight. So embarrassing was the meeting to Sony officials that it scared off many companies from breaking free of the sokaiya. By the summer of 1984, the *Asian Wall Street Journal* was reporting that "the sokaiya are on the comeback trail" and that "a majority of companies listed on the Tokyo stock exchange had either resumed payoffs or begun to seriously consider doing so."

The new laws did successfully drive many sokaiya out of the general meeting business. From their peak of 7,000 in the late 1970s, police reported they numbered fewer than six hundred in the late 1990s. But the marked reduction was due more to a sleight of hand by the authorities; as many as 4,000 were simply reclassified from sokaiya to *minbo,* or extortionists, and business was booming. In 1989, police reported the number of corporate shakedowns had more than doubled in the past decade. The crackdown on the "general meeting mongers" had merely forced the highly adaptable sokaiya into new ventures. Many of the racketeers began to lean more heavily on publishing scandal sheets. By the mid-1990s, several hundred of these extortion-minded publications still circulated, with companies typically paying between $1,000 and $2,000 per subscription. Other sokaiya homed in on hospitals, threatening to expose details of faulty care unless they were bought off. Some merely shifted gears and began receiving their payoffs from the overseas offices of targeted firms or took their gifts in company goods instead of cash. Some reinvented themselves, rather laughably, as shareholder advocates, private investigators, and financial consultants. And still others, in a time-honored tradition, founded right-wing political groups, disguising their payoffs as political contributions, or formed burakumin liberation groups demanding favors and compensation.

The sokaiya's reach also began to entangle several Western companies in Japan. The approaches ranged from clumsy attempts at newsletter subscription to more sophisticated shakedown schemes. "There's been a growing trend of extortionists targeting foreign firms," noted David Bong, former director of the Tokyo office for investigative firm Kroll Associates. Among those encountering the gangs was T Boone Pickens, the Texas oilman and corporate raider. In 1988, Pickens had allied himself with a notorious property developer in Tokyo as part of a hostile takeover attempt of Japanese car parts maker Koito. After becoming Koito's top shareholder, Pickens demanded a seat on the board, but company management gave the American a cold shoulder. Used to getting his way in America, Pickens showed up at Koito's shareholders' meeting to press his demands, only to be met by a squad of tough-looking fellows with flashy outfits and tightly permed hair. It was, recalled the Texan, "the most unusual shareholders' meeting I've ever attended in my life." Pickens denounced the alleged mob influence at hand, but Koito quickly hit back in an unusual press conference. If anyone had mob ties, said Koito officials, it was Pickens's Japanese partner, whose ties to the yakuza were well known. "It's the first I've heard of it," Pickens told the *Wall Street Journal.*

One sokaiya outfit that has stayed active is Rondan Doyukai, often called the largest in the industry. The group reportedly boasts some forty members holding shares in three hundred listed companies. The firm has done its best to enter the high-tech age, and has computerized its files on companies and boasts its own web page. But its tactics are anything but sophisticated. Rondan Doyukai is reportedly tied to the Sumiyoshi-kai and police have arrested its associates in several high-profile extortion cases. At a March 1991 shareholders' meeting of Sansui Electric, a Rondan man reportedly leapt onto the stage and slapped the chairman before being hauled away by police.

Those acts pale, however, compared to what other sokaiya have done. As they moved into other areas of extortion, a handful have gone to extremes that shocked the Japanese public. Among the most notable was the 1984 assault on former foreign minister Kiichi Miyazawa, then a candidate for prime minister. Miyazawa's assailant was a fifty-four-year-old racketeer who had first tried blackmailing the politician by writing stories on his private life for sokaiya-style newspapers.

The day following the attack, one prominent newspaper in a scathing editorial branded Miyazawa's attacker one of the "Hyenas of Nagatocho" (Nagatocho being the home of Japan's parliament). The editors complained that "these political leeches can be found roaming inside the Diet," and that although politicians are quick to denounce them, "they quite contrarily use such leeches to supply bits of juicy gossip and scandals with which to attack their political enemies. . . . In short, the politicians themselves are fostering this hotbed of corruption."

One month after the Miyazawa incident, another sensational case began making headlines across Japan. To Americans, the episode bore a striking resemblance to the poisoning of Tylenol pain relievers a year and a half earlier. The case involved a clever band of shakedown artists who, for more than a full year, became an obsession with the Japanese police and public. In letters mailed to the media, the blackmailers identified themselves as "The Man with 21 Faces," taken from the name of a popular series of children's mystery books and television shows in the 1950s. Demanding millions of dollars in ransom money, the group threatened to place cyanide in the products of six major food companies, causing bankruptcies and huge financial losses. At least eighteen boxes of cyanide-laced candies were in fact found on store shelves in various cities. Attached to each package was a typewritten note warning: "Danger. Contains poison. Eat this and die.— The Man with 21 Faces." The gang also kidnapped the president of top candy-maker Ezaki Glico and demanded a ransom of 1 billion yen and 100 kilos of gold bullion.

Glico's president escaped as a massive police investigation took hold. Through circumstantial evidence, including rumors in the sokaiya community, authorities became convinced that a sokaiya gang was behind the extortion attempts. But the sokaiya rackets had never escalated to this level before; these were renegades. One police expert called the case "a new type of crime for Japan."

Japan's police departments came under unprecedented criticism for their inability to apprehend the gang. Added to their frustration and loss of face was a constant stream of letters from the group itself, ridiculing police efforts before the nation. The gang addressed its notes to "Fools of the Police Force" and referred to officials as "poor, stupid cops." One letter mailed to the NHK-TV network sarcastically asked how many persons could be killed by a thirty-gram lump of cyanide, and suggested that answers be mailed to the Osaka Metropolitan Police. Ten winners, said the note, would be selected by lots, and awarded prizes of Morinaga candy—one of the targets of their cyanide poisoning campaign. In another note, the extortionists apologized to the director of the National Police Agency, saying they were sorry to have caused the balding director to lose even more hair over their activities.

For at least five consecutive weeks in 1984, police mobilized more than 44,000 officers on the case. At one point in late October, nearly half the nation's police force—130,000 officers—participated in a door-to-door search of 3.2 million homes and offices in the Osaka-Kyoto area. But Japan's finest were still unable to track down the extortionists, and leads soon dried up. The case remained unsolved for ten years, long enough for the statute of limitations to run out on the crimes. Officials admitted that their inability to solve the case imperiled police credibility as never before.

Crimes and Confessions

The Man with 21 Faces gang was not the only case challenging police credibility. Since the early 1970s, a growing number of journalists, lawyers, and social scientists have drawn attention to a nagging question posed by the existence of such a vast underworld—is Japan really as crime-free as police say? The country's rates of violent crime are clearly far lower than in the United States. All an American need do is walk the streets of Japan's largest cities at night to notice the difference. But what about white-collar and related crimes, particularly in such areas as bribery and extortion, where a vast number of acts go unreported?

The Japanese propensity for saving face influences not only the nation's susceptibility to certain crimes but also the reporting of those crimes. To prove an extortion case in Japan is quite difficult without causing considerable embarrassment to the individual or company involved. Much as loan sharks employ public embarrassment as a means of intimidation, so do so-kaiya and other extortionists depend on the risk of losing face to keep their victims silent. Certainly blackmail and extortion exist in America, but the crucial importance of saving face creates far more fertile ground in Japan for such crimes.

The society's emphasis on apologies and resolving disputes outside the police and the courts is another factor influencing the country's reported crime rates. One unhappy foreigner learned the hard way how the country's criminal justice system worked when he and two friends were attacked with fists and beer bottles by a pair of thugs in 1981. After summoning police and confronting their assailants, the foreigners were surprised to learn that the officers showed little interest in pursuing the case.

"You could choose to prosecute and that is your right," explained the police to the three victims. "However, you may not be able to prove your case ... so we suggest you pursue a more Japanese approach and accept an apology. We realize how you feel and an apology may seem inadequate to compensate you for the harm you have been done, so you will, naturally, only accept a sincere apology."

The victims were a bit surprised, to say the least. "There was really no choice," one said. "We shook hands with our assailants and accepted their 'sincere' apology."

For years, women's rights activists have argued that the underreporting of sexual assault and harassment is particularly extreme in Japan, and there are now data to back them up. A 2000 survey by the Justice Ministry, for example, found that only 10 percent of women reported crimes of sexual assault or harassment. A 1995 survey of female junior high and high school student commuters found that fully 76 percent reported being molested on trains—yet only 2 percent had reported the incidents to police. The experience of a Westerner again sheds light on the issue. In 1998, Raelyn Campbell, a fluent Japanese speaker and former aide to a Diet member, was sexually assaulted at her home in Tokyo. Intent on pursuing a rape case against her assailant, she found an almost medieval lack of sensitivity and action on the part of Japanese police. Perhaps it is not a surprise, then, that a mere 1,687 cases of rape and indecent assault were presented to the courts in 1998.

What, then, is the actual rate of crime in Japan? Like all statistics, figures on crime can be manipulated to say whatever those employing them would like to say. Authorities admit that, as in America, much crime in Japan goes unreported. They caution, furthermore, that their own data on under-reporting are dated and may be inaccurate. A Justice Ministry research center estimated that only some 30 percent of robbery cases were reported to police. Statistics on bribery, which may be the most unreported crime in Japan, are not available.

Crime rates are not the only official statistics in question. Also under attack is another critical crime figure: Japan's extraordinarily high rate of convictions of suspects taken to trial, which hovers around 99 percent year after year. (It reached 99.9 percent in 1998.) There is no such directly comparable U.S. statistic; one survey of the nation's seventy-five largest state courts during May 1996 found a conviction rate of 70 percent. Central to Japan's success is the remarkable fact that most suspects brought to court sign confessions during interrogations by police and prosecutors. Indeed, confession rates have run as high as 89 percent.

Although confessing one's errors occupies an important place in Japanese culture, some observers believe officials have gone much too far in trying to obtain confessions. Since at least the early 1980s, reports by human rights groups, legal associations, and others have branded Japan's justice system among the most backward in the modern world. A 1984 report by a group of Tokyo lawyers is typical of the charges made: marathon interrogation sessions lasting fourteen hours or more occur in many cases; suspects placed in tiny, brightly lit cells known as "birdcages" and forced to sit cross-legged on the floor, forbidden to lean against the wall; defense attorneys not allowed in interrogation rooms. Police, furthermore, can routinely detain suspects for twenty-three days without charging them, and sometimes re-arrest them on a series of separate charges, thus extending detention time as needed. (Some European countries, it should be noted, allow detention for as long as six months for crimes deemed serious enough.) Some Japanese judges even refuse to grant bail until a suspect confesses.

So great is the pressure to gain a confession, say critics, that police routinely use physical abuse against suspects during interrogations. Japan's immigration police are particularly notorious for their violent disdain toward illegal aliens. In some cases, police stand accused of forcing detainees to sign blank confessions. Authorities deny these charges and have claimed that such criticisms are motivated by "leftist ideology." But the confession-based system has led to numerous incidents of false imprisonment, including a string of widely publicized cases that resulted in overturned verdicts after years of imprisonment.

Unreported crimes and forced confessions are only part of law enforcement's problems in Japan, of course. The endless payoffs and tolerance of organized crime have exerted a steady, corrosive effect on Japanese society. Indeed, the corruption encouraged by years of tolerating sokaiya extortionists, sarakin-style loan sharks, and quasi-legal crime syndicates would begin to show its true cost in the mid-1980s. It was then that the Japanese economy began an extraordinary ride that brought unprecedented wealth to the islands. In the process, Japan would become an undisputed financial superpower—and the yakuza a criminal one.

Mitsuru Toyama (seated, with beard), pioneer of the Japanese ultranationalist movement, with members of his Black Dragon Society, circa 1930. Seated second from right is student Yoshio Kodama, who would become the single greatest force in the yakuza's postwar resurrection.

A young Kodama (left) in the 1930s as the bodyguard of Wang Ching-wei, chief of the Nanking (China) puppet government controlled by Japan. Kodama grew fabulously rich during the war by looting the Chinese and supplying the Imperial Navy.

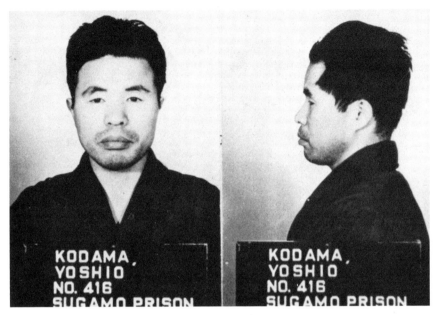

Kodama's mug shot from Sugamo Prison, after the war. He was designated a Class A war criminal and spent three years in jail, but was never tried; U.S. intelligence agents needed him elsewhere.

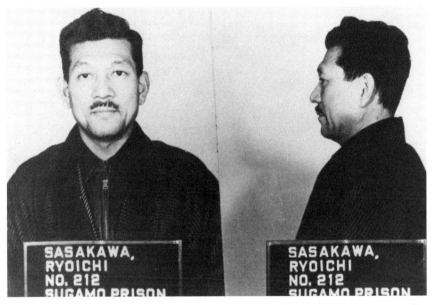

Ryoichi Sasakawa, the self-proclaimed "world's wealthiest fascist" and yakuza associate. Kodama's cellmate at Sugamo Prison, Sasakawa also was designated a Class A war criminal. He became one of Japan's richest men through his control of the incredibly lucrative speedboat racing industry.

Sasakawa with Benito Mussolini in 1939. Sasakawa continued to be a great admirer of Mussolini, whom he once called "the perfect fascist and dictator."

Major General Charles Willoughby, commander of U.S. Army Intelligence (G-2) under General MacArthur during the occupation of Japan. Willoughby's men recruited yakuza members to spy and disrupt the growing left and labor movements. (U.S. Army photograph)

Surveillance photo taken by a U.S. counterintelligence agent during a 1953 May Day parade in Nagoya. The Korean War greatly increased the work of U.S. intelligence agents in Japan, but their reliance on rightists and yakuza often produced mixed results.

Postwar ultranationalism at work: the dramatic 1960 assassination of Socialist Party Secretary-General Inejiro Asanuma by a young right-wing fanatic. The stabbing took place at a public gathering before television cameras, reporters, and a large audience. Asanuma's assassin later committed suicide in his police cell. (Provided by *Mainichi Shimbun*)

Kodama with Prime Minister Nobusuke Kishi in 1960. Kishi is looking over galley
proofs of Kodama's memoir, *Sugamo Diary,* before brushing his introduction into
the book. Kodama returned the favor that year by recruiting a 28,000-man army
of yakuza and rightists to protect the planned visit of President Eisenhower.

One of the last times Kodama is seen in public, as he is escorted to his only court appearance in the Lockheed bribery case in January 1984. (Provided by Kyodo News Service)

Kazuo Taoka, Japan's "godfather of godfathers," making one of his many appearances. Until his death in 1981, Taoka headed the nation's largest syndicate, the Yamaguchi-gumi, and was widely regarded as the most powerful mobster in Japan. (*Yomiuri Shimbun*)

Masahisa Takenaka, Taoka's successor as Yamaguchi godfather, in 1984. Takenaka was gunned down later that year by assassins from a Yamaguchi splinter group. (*Yomiuri Shimbun*)

Members of Zen Ai Kaigi, the fiery ultranationalist alliance, clash with police at the 1974 convention of their favorite target, the leftist Japan Teachers' Union. Zen Ai Kaigi's membership, like that of many far-right groups, is heavily yakuza. (*Yomiuri Shimbun*)

The 1985 funeral of slain Yamaguchi godfather Takenaka. Yakuza on right, riot police on left. (*Yomiuri Shimbun*)

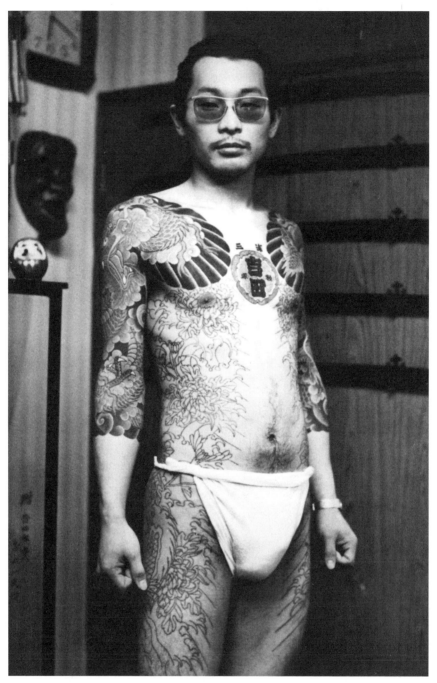

Yakuza with a partially completed tattoo. Many gang members still insist on traditional tattooing, done with a bamboo sliver in a long series of painful jabs. The full design can take months and, when completed, can cost more than $5,000. (Photo by Michio Soejima)

A scuffle involving sokaiya (financial racketeers) at a general meeting of Mitsubishi Shoji Corporation. Police crackdowns prompted the yakuza-dominated sokaiya to expand into a wide range of extortion and racketeering crime and to begin exploring opportunities overseas. (Provided by Kyodo News Service)

A large haul of amphetamines, discovered hidden in surfboards. The East Asian trade in "speed," or "shabu," has become one of the world's greatest drug routes, supplying as many as a million users in Japan and spilling into Europe and North American. (Provided by Kyodo News Service)

Hisayuki Machii, reputed godfather of the heavily Korean syndicate Towa Yuai Jigyo Kumiai (East Asia Friendship Enterprises Association). Machii and other yakuza allegedly helped arrange the 1973 kidnapping in Tokyo of political activist Kim Dae Jung by the Korean CIA. (Provided by Kyodo News Service)

CHAPTER SEVEN

THE KEIZAI YAKUZA

BABURU KEIZAI WAS THE NAME JAPANESE CAME TO CALL IT—THE BUBBLE Economy. And a great, speculative, devastating bubble it was. From the mid-1980s to 1990, the Japanese economy went on an extraordinary ride, with real estate and stock market values skyrocketing. The Bubble Economy would become one of the twentieth century's greatest speculative fevers. Its impact would transform much of Japan and, with it, the Japanese underworld.

The origins of the Bubble date back to a 1985 agreement among the G-7 nations to increase the yen's value against the dollar and other currencies. Frustrated by Japan's protectionist economy and constant trade surpluses, Western officials hoped the move would make Japanese exports more expensive while stimulating imports into that nation. Rise the yen did. Over the next two years, the Japanese currency doubled in value, jumping from 240 yen to the dollar to 120. The yen suddenly seemed the world's powerhouse currency. Japanese business—legitimate and not—found it now held tremendous buying power overseas.

At the same time, to spur domestic demand the central Bank of Japan slashed interest rates to a postwar record. Credit in Japan became available as never before. Investors plowed borrowed money into real estate and stock markets, shooting prices upward. Then they borrowed against their newly appreciated holdings and bought even more. The amount of capital held by the Japanese caught worldwide attention. Stoked by inflated assets and the powerful yen, nine of the world's top ten banks were now Japanese. In terms of sheer market capitalization, Tokyo became the world's largest stock exchange. Osaka bumped London to fourth place. The value of real estate in Tokyo, on paper, was said to exceed that of the entire

United States, while the grounds of the Imperial Palace equaled those of all California.

Japan's cities teemed with nouveaux riches; stories of excess became legendary, with news items of coffee and sushi dusted with gold. Japanese investors acquired a vast portfolio of trophy properties in the United States, ranging from Rockefeller Center to Columbia Pictures, while pundits predicted Japan's imminent eclipse of North America and Europe. Proclaimed the *Harvard Business Review* in 1989: "Japan sits on the largest cache of wealth ever assembled."

All this did not escape the notice of the yakuza. Gamblers at heart, Japan's most enterprising mobsters plunged into the booming real estate and stock markets and began making huge deals. The yakuza, in effect, became key absorbers of excess credit in Japan—and there was plenty to go around. Bankers competed with each other over who could hand out the most loans, and few bothered to look for missing fingers or tattoos. "The banks didn't check out their clients well," says a prominent Japanese banker with nearly forty years' experience. "There was no screening done. Any business could get loans—unknown finance companies, golf course developers, real estate firms." Much of the money was funneled through Japan's proliferating "nonbanks"—thousands of finance companies backed by the banking industry. Set up to invest in more speculative ventures, these largely unregulated lenders cared even less who their customers were.

Billions of dollars—trillions of yen—poured into yakuza coffers. Gang bosses began playing high-stakes roulette on the stock market, grabbing quick profits and threatening to seize control of prominent companies. Others speculated wildly in real estate and made investments at home and abroad. To Japanese who watched the gangs, it soon became clear that all this money was transforming the underworld. This new breed of criminal was dubbed the *keizai yakuza*, the economic gangster, and became the stuff of legend from Ginza nightclubs to Manhattan art auctions.

Economic Gangsters

As the Bubble inflated, the yakuza were well positioned to take advantage of the coming boom. First, the gangs themselves were not without a certain level of financial acumen and curiosity. Even before the Bubble, the major syndicates had become big business. Many gangs ran multi-million-dollar companies, particularly in construction and entertainment, and as the economy boomed, so too did the gangs' illicit portfolios: revenues from gambling, prostitution, and drug sales all were up. The smarter bosses already were getting advice from well-paid professionals and were pouring their profits into real estate and other assets. At the same time, the gangs' sokaiya rackets and work in bankruptcies had given them a back door into corporate Japan, and many could see the potential for big money. But what truly plunged the yakuza into the Japanese economy in an unprecedented way were two distinct sets of investors: Japan's stock speculator groups and property developers.

High-flying bands of stock speculators had shoved their way around Japanese markets for years. Most were loose alliances of like-minded investors. Typically, they would zero in on a vulnerable stock, push its value skyward, and then bail out before the stock crashed. Such practices were dubbed "ramping" and had become notorious on the Japanese exchanges. During the Bubble, ramping and speculation took on a new level as Japan's stock market soared to record highs each week. The speculator groups boasted an impressive membership of Japan's powerful and wealthy—businessmen, politicians, and, increasingly, yakuza bosses. Times were good for the gangs. Flush with money from the banks and their own portfolios, Japan's top mobsters learned firsthand the intricacies of stock speculation and greenmail, and then seasoned it with their own brand of blackmail.

The most notorious of the Bubble-era speculator groups was the Koshin Group, headed by the wily Mitsuhiro Kotani. Kotani had a habit of buying up huge chunks of company stock and then threatening to bring in the yakuza if things didn't go his way. The Tokyo-based investor ran into trouble with the law several times, most notably over the Koshin Group's investment in Janome, Japan's second-largest maker of home sewing machines. In 1987, Koshin bought some 20 percent of Janome's shares and Kotani, then forty-seven, was appointed a director of the company. But two years later, he threatened to sell his shares to the yakuza unless the company bought back his stock at the huge premium of $700 million. Kotani hinted that hit men from Osaka were in town, and that there might be trouble not only for the company but for its top backer, Saitama Bank. Members of an Inagawa-kai front company, meanwhile, showed up at Janome headquarters. "I heard you would invest in us," one told frightened executives.

Ultimately, Janome came through with payments of a still impressive $215 million. Kotani took his payoff—disguised as loans—and went on to raid other companies' stocks. Police later found that nearly a quarter of the Janome payment ended up in the hands of the Inagawa-kai. For his role in the case, Kotani was eventually arrested on charges of extortion and sent to prison. The presiding judge at his trial described Kotani's actions as "intentional, ingenious and wicked."

Kotani was but the most blatant of a whole set of stock speculators who took the yakuza under their wings. Top securities firms also welcomed their wealthy new customers and extended them credit, no questions asked. Soon Japanese godfathers were starting the day by checking their portfolios. In 1990, a Yamaguchi-gumi front company named Tensho Kogyo quietly became the largest shareholder of Kurabo, a respected textile firm with operations in Brazil, Indonesia, Thailand, and the United Kingdom. The crime syndicate grabbed hold of 15 million shares of the company's stock, worth some $140 million, before a frantic Kurabo bought them back. Behind the Kurabo deal was one Masaru Takumi, the reputed economic czar of the Yamaguchi-gumi. One of the leading keizai yakuza, Takumi reportedly controlled more than $500 million in gang assets.

Like the stock market, the real estate industry, too, had thrown open its doors to the gangs. Here, however, the path to riches was often much cruder—through mob-run eviction services dubbed *jiageya.*

Jiageya literally means "one who raises land prices," but the term is perhaps best translated as "land sharks," for they essentially are strong-arm thugs who force reluctant residents out of their homes. Typically, jiageya work directly or indirectly for big developers. Some jiageya buy up small plots of land to consolidate for large building projects; others simply scare the hell out of those in dwellings already owned by the builder. Developers have used yakuza as far back as the nineteenth century to clear title to land. Japanese law makes it quite difficult for landlords to evict tenants legally, even after the term of the original contract expires. But with the Bubble Economy, the stakes had escalated. As real estate values soared skyward, developers were in no mood to appease stubborn tenants.

Reports on jiageya incidents began to surface in 1985. By 1990, Osaka police had documented more than 1,600 jiageya cases, yet they seemed unable to do much about them. What authorities did learn was that the business is dominated by the underworld, and that the gangs are violent, relentless, and often ingenious.

Stories are legion about jiageya tactics. At first, polite negotiations and simple payoffs are offered. Those who refuse to move might find their new neighbors have missing fingers and keep noisy Dobermans on the front porch and smelly chickens in back. Reports of phone harassment, death threats, and abductions of tenants are common. In one Tokyo case, a thirty-one-year-old jiageya rammed a dump truck into a laundry run by a family that refused to move out of their building. Other jiageya have poured glue into keyholes, spread manure, and transformed the residence into a mob hangout. In Kyoto, the boss of the Kawamura-gumi moved his gang office into an apartment only to begin blasting out walls, digging up the basement, and using neighbors' parking spaces. When residents complained, they were beaten up; one was taken hostage for days.

The newspaper *Asahi* described the fate of a jiageya victim in Osaka during 1990. Tamako Nishiyama, a seventy-year-old widow, had refused repeated requests to vacate the two-story wooden home she had occupied for forty years. Over the next eight months vandals shattered most of the windows of her house, smashed in its front doorway, and covered the outer walls with red graffiti. Her front bell rang mysteriously at all hours of the night and delivery boys appeared seeking payment for Chinese food she never ordered. One evening she returned to find the first floor of her house crawling with poisonous centipedes.

Still, Nishiyama refused to budge. After months of this harassment, one night while she attended class at a nearby school, two men broke into her home, soaked its tatami mats with kerosene, and set the building afire.

The jiageya business was good to the yakuza. Shaking down a store owner might bring in hundreds of dollars, but a single jiageya job could net hundreds of thousands. The gangs typically charged 3 percent of a property's sales price; one 1987 estimate put jiageya earnings at $75 million annually, but that is likely a conservative estimate. Still, more important than the fees was the broad introduction into the real estate market it gave the yakuza. The jiageya business put them inside major developments in an unprecedented way. "This is when the keizai yakuza really became prevalent," observed attorney Seiji Iishiba, former head of the Tokyo police's organized crime unit. "Until the 1980s, the yakuza had mostly done joint ventures with real estate managers. This accelerated, then came the heavy real estate investment, and then they began to own companies."

A Japanese real estate developer—his identity hidden—explained how the business worked to a U.S. Senate investigative committee in 1992. Codenamed "Bully," the clearly knowledgeable businessman told of how he used yakuza contacts across Japan in his development business. To maintain good relations with the gangs, he constantly gave gifts to their bosses, including, on occasion, a Mercedes Benz. In the passages that follow, Bully refers to the yakuza as *boryokudan,* or violent groups, the name given them by police.

> "When the Boryokudan is called upon on behalf of a business, the Boryokudan boss will summon the developer to his office. They will negotiate, but typically will fail to reach agreement at this stage. The developer will then call on a rival of the Boryokudan boss with whom he has had past associations, and the negotiations will be left entirely to the gangsters.
>
> "The Boryokudan earn large commissions from such dealings, and this mediation service represents a significant portion of the gangs' yearly income. While such deals are typically free of conflict, Boryokudan have been known to use strong-arm tactics to force deals to their advantage [*sic*], if things do not go their way.
>
> "The involvement of organized crime does not end when the developer is cleared to develop the property. His Boryokudan contact will introduce him to friends who are in the construction business. At each stage in the develop-

ment of a piece of land, the Boryokudan will own companies or be closely affiliated with companies that bid on certain jobs in the project."

If a firm does not want to work with the gang, said Bully, it has two options: pay off the yakuza boss with a handsome cash gift, or set up a front company to insulate the firm from direct contact with the gang. "Many of Japan's most well-known companies deal with the Boryokudan indirectly through such fronts," Bully testified.

Construction and the Mob

The jiageya were not the mob's only path into real estate. For more than two hundred years, yakuza gangs have worked closely with construction companies, until the two groups are at times indistinguishable. As the economy boomed, crime syndicates found big money in the building trades.

Fueled by huge public works projects, construction is Japan's largest single industry. It employs some 7 million people, or about 10 percent of the nation's total workforce—nearly twice the percentage in the United States. The industry is notorious for corruption, with persistent charges of bid-rigging, insider deals, payoffs, and mob ties. It ranks at the top in Japan for undocumented spending, say tax authorities, and accounts for nearly half of all corruption cases. Its political clout and off-the-books generosity are legendary. Shimizu Corporation, Japan's largest contractor, admitted in the early 1990s that it doled out some $20 million annually to Japanese politicians in return for favored treatment on public works projects. Other companies have done much the same. "Paying off local politicians is much like committing a traffic offense," commented Shimizu chairman Teruzo Yoshino. "You know it's against the law, but it's not seen as unethical."

The industry's mob ties were tougher to defend. Japan's big construction firms are not controlled by the yakuza, but the relationship between them is deep and historic. Yakuza involvement in the construction trade dates back to feudal times, to roadside bands of laborers the gangs recruited and organized. The *daimyo*—Japan's feudal lords—looked to the gangs not only for workers but to run gambling dens to retrieve the wages they had just paid. To this day, construction firms and yakuza gangs often use the same word at the end of their names—*kumi* or *gumi*—meaning group. "People say the yakuza invaded the construction industry," explained one prominent public prosecutor. "But this is wrong. Ordinary people invaded the construction industry."

As the Bubble Economy picked up steam, gang income shot upward through their work for the industry as labor brokers, subcontractors, and fixers. By 1990, the yakuza ran as many as nine hundred construction firms across Japan, according to police. Most were small to medium-size companies, offering services that ranged from ready-mix concrete and gravel to waste disposal. Money also flowed to the gangs through kickbacks and contract-skimming. Gangs routinely rake in between 1 and 5 percent of the total value of public works projects, say yakuza watchers. In Kyoto and other cities, local gangs have reportedly enforced a ".8 percent rule," in which they receive that portion of any construction project. "The structure is such that construction projects can become difficult without paying cooperation money to the gangs," says Raisuke Miyawaki, a former chief of the NPA's organized crime unit.

The Kansai region, encompassing Kobe, Osaka, and Kyoto, has been particularly hard hit by the gangs. A 1993 survey by police found that nearly half of Osaka Prefecture's 566 construction firms had dealt with the yakuza. Among those paying off the mob, ironically, were seven companies belonging to an anti-Mafia association of local builders. Officials of two of those companies served as the association's vice president and auditor. Further evidence came with the seizure that year of an account book from a gangster's home, which showed the region's largest construction firms routinely made payoffs to the Yamaguchi-gumi.

The money raked in from Bubble-era projects was enormous. Police believe the gangs made tens of millions of dollars off huge construction projects like Kansai International Airport. Ironically, these were the same projects then targeted by U.S. officials, who complained that American companies were being shut out of Japan's huge construction market. But when trade officials in Washington complained of "non-tariff barriers," few imagined burly godfathers with tattoos and missing fingers. Perhaps they should have. The yakuza, to be sure, are not the only force at work. The bid-rigging and payoffs that pervade the industry are not generally due to the underworld. But developers clearly would have to answer to the mob if they awarded significant contracts to foreign firms and the gangs began losing revenue.

Construction is not the only protected industry infested by the mob. As Ushio Chujo, a Keio University economics professor, told the *Wall Street Journal,* "No one talks about it, but the yakuza are as much a roadblock to reform as the farm lobby and small-business owners." Until the mid-1980s, when U.S. officials intervened, the gangs played a major role in the booming pirate video industry. As much as 80 percent of American films and videos sold in Japan were, in effect, stolen. When Japanese authorities finally cracked down, U.S. sales reportedly ballooned to $300 million. Similarly, foreign shippers have long complained about the cumbersome and exclusionist practices on the Japanese waterfront. Such conditions are due largely to the iron grip on the docks by the Japan Harbor Transportation Association, which has long been linked to the yakuza. Change may come slowly. When trade officials press for easier access to Japan's port facilities, the yakuza may not be present at the negotiating table, but their interests will be hard for the Japanese side to ignore.

Gorufu and the Viper

As the Bubble Era progressed, the yakuza were not content to merely skim the cream off construction contracts. With big money flowing into gang coffers, increasingly they were investing in the projects themselves. The investments varied, but one property attracted the yakuza again and again: golf courses. Billions of dollars poured into Japanese golf course development, both at home and abroad. The yakuza did not control all of it, but clearly the gangs were behind a substantial share. "We suspect most golf course developments are yakuza-tied in some way," confided a top NPA official.

The Japanese are a golf-crazed people. So popular is *gorufu* in crowded Japan that its 12 million fans must sometimes reserve a spot months in advance just to play. With little room for sprawling courses, city skylines are dotted with hundreds of towering, netted driving ranges dubbed "birdcages." So coveted are golf club memberships that they are traded like stocks on a special exchange, with their own brokers and a weekly index issued by Nikkei. In 1990, at the height of the Bubble, a top yakuza boss reportedly offered $3.8 million for a membership at Japan's most exclusive club, just outside of Tokyo. He was turned down—not because he was a mobster, but because no one would sell.

Among the sport's biggest fans are the yakuza. Japan's mobsters love to play—and for high stakes. Gambling on the greens is taken seriously, with bets as high as $1,000 per stroke. Prizes might include foreign cars, tailored suits, and trips overseas. Top Japanese golf pros have repeatedly drawn embarrassing media attention for joining generous mob bosses on the greens. But others have learned to stay clear of the mobsters, who are notorious for beating up fellow golfers who play too fast or slow. Such behavior has prompted some clubs to issue "no gangster" rules. One region even formed a Council to Rid Chiba Golf Courses of Gangsters, complete with a twenty-page pamphlet railing against "flowers of evil that spoil our greens."

The golf clubs might make a public show of these efforts, but getting yakuza off the greens was nearly impossible—particularly when the gangs increasingly owned the courses. By 1992, Japan was home to 1,850 golf courses, with 300 others under construction and plans for 1,000 more. With space at a premium, the need was never greater for yakuza intervention to clear the land, provide protection, and make the requisite payoffs. Gaining approval for a golf course is not easy, and a determined developer must grease hands all along the way. Going prices are said to be $10,000 for a local councilman and $100,000 for a prefectural or national politician. An average golf course developer might spend $5 million on such bribes. For their help, some gangs took a financial interest in the development. Others, though, moved into the business themselves. By the end of the 1980s, golf development had become one of the most mobbed-up industries in all Japan.

Stock purchases, real estate deals, golf course development . . . there was no shortage of projects catching the underworld's eye. With money to spend, gang bosses paid less attention to the vice rackets in the streets and more to business and finance. Not all was invested, of course. Vast sums were simply spent, on women, cars, and fast living. But the interests of Japan's top mobsters clearly had changed. Indeed, the keizai yakuza no longer saw themselves as mere speculators and developers; they had become art connoisseurs as well.

Fine Western art became quite the rage among Bubble-era investors. From 1985 to 1990 art imports into Japan jumped more than twentyfold, worth an impressive $3.6 billion. From the nation's top banks to its *nouveau riche* yakuza, art purchases joined real estate and stocks as the favored investments of the time. Partial to impressionist paintings, the new collectors paid amounts that shocked the art world, throwing prices to extraordinary new levels.

No fewer than three hundred new dealers opened offices in Tokyo's posh Ginza district, and they, like so much of Japanese business, didn't ask where their clients' money came from. Many of the purchases were legitimate, of course, but by 1991, some dealers believed that up to 90 percent of the money flowing into Japan's art market was of dubious origin. There were tax evaders who found it a convenient way to hide assets, wealthy donors who used it for disguising political contributions, and yakuza who found it attractive as both an investment and a money laundry. In a 1992 report, the FBI noted that the yakuza were in fact affiliated with several galleries and that the gangs took control of numerous paintings through their work as loan sharks, seizing the art as collateral from debtors.

Among the new collectors making waves in the art market was one Yasumichi Morishita, who had made a fortune with his sarakin firm, Aichi Finance. Morishita's aggressive loan collecting had not endeared him to the Japanese press, which dubbed him the "King of Shady Money" and "The Viper"—the latter for allegedly slithering up to debt-ridden companies, taking them over, and killing them. Morishita's criminal record and reputed yakuza ties also earned him notoriety. In the early 1970s, he was convicted of loan sharking and tax evasion. He was arrested, but not indicted, on at least three other occasions for assault and unlawful confinement, securities fraud and forgery, and extortion. In 1987, his home in Tokyo's posh Denenchofu neighborhood was shot at.

Morishita's appetite for fine art seemed insatiable. In just four years, this Japanese—virtually unknown in the West—became one the world's largest buyers. During one buying spree in 1989, he reportedly paid $100 million for one hundred impressionist and postimpressionist paintings in New York. He liked the paintings so much, in fact, he even bought the seller, acquiring a 6.5 percent share in Christie's, the auction house. (While shopping abroad, he also picked up two golf courses in California and a third in Arizona.) Morishita boasted of spending in all nearly $1 billion on art, including some twenty Renoirs and paintings by van Gogh, Monet, Degas, Vuillard, Gauguin, and at least two Picassos: *La Maternité* and *Au Lapin Agile*.

Asked by a reporter about his alleged yakuza ties, Morishita was blunt: "I do not socialize with them." Indeed, Morishita claimed the very idea of yakuza involvement in the art market was far-fetched. "Even if the yakuza had the money, they don't have the ability to collect these paintings," he said. They did, however, have the ability to collect loans for Morishita, according to U.S. officials. Federal law enforcement reports depicted Morishita as a yakuza associate, and a 1992 U.S. Senate investigation alleged that his loan company used Sumiyoshi-kai members for debt collection. Published reports further claimed that his company's favorite gang for handling overdue loans and foreclosures was the Kobayashi-gumi, one of the Sumiyoshi-kai's top gangs.

Entrepreneurial Yakuza

When they weren't buying art, ramping stocks, and evicting tenants, Japan's top gangs concentrated on expanding their territory. This was particularly true of the Yamaguchi-gumi, which by 1990 towered in size over rival syndicates. For decades, an unofficial pact had ruled the Japanese underworld—that the Yamaguchi-gumi would stay out of Tokyo. It was understood that while the heart of Yamaguchi country was Kobe and Osaka, the nation's capital was the turf of the Inagawa and Sumiyoshi syndicates. But as the Bubble's wealth spilled out of Tokyo, the Yamaguchi-gumi was keen to move in on the city, with its huge property and stock markets, its corporate headquarters, and its 30 million people.

Like any good business intent on expanding its territory, the Yamaguchi-gumi offered incentives to its employees. Gang members received up to $10,000 to start businesses in the capital, plus monthly payments of between $1,500 and $2,000. The strategy worked. By 1990, the Yamaguchi-gumi boasted more than forty offices in Tokyo, with interests in gambling, loan sharking, extortion, and video pornography. From virtually nothing, the Yamaguchi-gumi had built up a Tokyo base of some five hundred members.

The Tokyo gangs were furious. Not only had the Yamaguchi-gumi broken the pact, but the big syndicate was attracting new members by routinely ignoring a long-held yakuza rule prohibiting recruitment of renegade or dismissed gang members. Particularly incensed was the Sumiyoshi-kai, then Tokyo's second-largest syndicate. "We will never let them cross the Tama River," declared a Sumiyoshi boss, referring to the waterway that separates central Tokyo from nearby communities. The Sumiyoshi-kai amassed a war chest, built up its arsenal, and sent members to the Philippines for target practice. At the same time, its leaders rallied at least eight other syndicates into an anti-Yamaguchi-gumi alliance. The transgression was serious enough that among the alliance's members stood the Inagawa-kai, despite its long-standing truce with the Yamaguchi-gumi.

The tension erupted into gang war. In 1990, drive-by shootings and face-to-face assassinations killed more than a dozen people, including three innocent bystanders. The tabloids filled with "Tokyo as Chicago" stories. In the suburb of Hachioji, gun battles made streets so unsafe that authorities offered maps showing children "safe detours" to take on their way to school. But the Yamaguchi-gumi had made its point: it was in Tokyo to stay.

That the Yamaguchi-gumi moved into Tokyo through its own business incentive program was but a sign of the times. The Bubble helped spark a burst of entrepreneurial activity by the yakuza, always among Japan's more innovative businessmen. In one worrisome marriage, gangsters made deals with the *otaku*, Japan's fervent high-tech youngsters, to do freelance hacking. Reports are scarce, but point to young hackers working with the gangs to steal funds and data by computer. Other yakuza pushed into Japan's distribution system, moving fish and marine products. Some bought into private hospitals, while still others supplied plastic Buddhas to the new religions springing up across the islands. Then there were the so-called *gakkoya* (school specialists), who applied their dubious talents to the financial affairs of private schools. One enterprising yakuza even posed as a commercial attaché for the Central African Republic in a ploy to enter that nation's diamond mining industry. Apparently the gangster got carried away with his role: by the time police found him, he was riding around Tokyo in foreign cars bearing that nation's flag and running an office with a gold-plated sign denoting an "official residence" of the embassy.

To handle these varied exploits, the yakuza needed what crime syndicates everywhere need: durable front companies. In Japan, these front operations were dubbed *kigyou shatei*—business brothers—and they proliferated like weeds during the Bubble. At the Bubble's peak, Tokyo police counted some 740 offices run by the underworld in that city alone, ranging from finance and real estate to waste disposal and artwork. Flush with cash, the gangs found they now had little trouble attracting professional help. Not just lawyers, but respected bankers, brokers, even ex-cops went to work for the yakuza. Many companies were quasi-legitimate; as the firms laundered money or funneled profits into gang coffers, the true owners kept their distance. As one gang manager proudly told Japanese TV, "Our employees don't even know we're members of the Yamaguchi-gumi." The yakuza had come far from forty years before, when Kazuo Taoka ordered his followers to run stevedoring companies on the Osaka-Kobe docks.

Those who decided to pull away from the gangs found the yakuza were like flypaper—very sticky. The gangsters are extremely skilled at exploiting the web of debt and obligation that binds so much of Japanese society together, observes Raisuke Miyawaki, the former top yakuza watcher for the NPA. "Members of the business world and the underworld became involved in each others' deals and indebted to each other," he says of the Bubble days. "Once gangsters became immersed into the financial system, they were very hard to disengage." Leaned on by their yakuza contacts, corporations soon found themselves hiring employees tied to the gangs and lending more and more money to mob-run enterprises.

The gangs, meanwhile, were joined in the feeding frenzy by other, sometimes less sophisticated, crooks. Some were independents—embezzlers out to make a quick killing, fraud artists searching for the right angle—but most seemed tied to yakuza crime syndicates in some way. Indeed, the Bubble strung together perhaps as never before the disparate parts of the Japanese underworld: yakuza, rightists, sokaiya, and other gangs of thugs and extortionists. These keizai yakuza could be seen in the lobbies of first-class hotels in Tokyo practicing what was soon dubbed "lobby diplomacy." Amid drinks of tea and whiskey, they exchanged tips on interest rates, ripe targets for extortion, and the hottest property developments. The hotels and police seemed powerless to do anything about the gatherings.

Buoyed by their seeming acceptance by the business world, the yakuza sensed a change in their social status. "The gangs no longer felt inferior," says Miyawaki. "Once they saw the crooked activities of supposedly legitimate businessmen and bankers during the Bubble Era, the yakuza began to discard their traditional sense of guilt." Others in the business community sadly agree. "It used to be that the yakuza economy and the legitimate economy were separate," bemoaned one Mitsubishi Bank executive. "Now they have come together."

The risks of that coming together would become apparent soon enough. In 1988, the investment community was shaken by the disappearance of Kazuo Kengaku, a bright Japanese fund manager known for his ties to the Yamaguchi-gumi. Kengaku and his Cosmo Research had made fast profits for their clientele by ramping stocks and greenmailing companies, but losses mounted after the market crash of October 1987. A year after the crash, Kengaku was finally found, buried in concrete and dumped in a field near Kyoto. Police suspect Kengaku's fate was tied to his investors' poor stock performance.

Kengaku's murder was but an omen of the trouble ahead. As the Bubble inflated and then collapsed, the scandalous tales of crime and collusion would seem endless. None, though, could match the exploits of Susumu Ishii, the Tokyo godfather who would come to epitomize the success and failure of Japan's new breed of gangster.

The Gangster with the Golden Touch

Susumu Ishii was no ordinary crook. He was the elite of the keizai yakuza, Japan's top economic gangster. And the sheer volume of money he would attract was unparalleled. First came the corporate loans and loan guarantees, one after another. Then the huge advances from securities houses. Next, the golf course membership fees. When Ishii added it all up, he must have been the wealthiest gangster in all Japan—perhaps in the world. Before it ended, Japan's largest corporations would give 325 billion yen— $2.3 *billion* at the time—to one of the nation's best-known crime figures, and then turned the other way.

Ishii had the golden touch—quite literally, according to a favored psychic he consulted. Akio Matsui, a well-known soothsayer, was renowned for his ability to see gold powder around those with strong luck, a longtime Japanese superstition. And Matsui claimed he often saw the magic dust around Ishii, once even on a small Buddha near the godfather.

While other gangsters swaggered about Japan, flashing their tattoos and intimidating their countrymen, Susumu Ishii pursued a more refined path. Tall and slender with silver hair, the soft-spoken Ishii dressed in immaculate business suits and preferred "persuasion" to violence. By the mid-1980s, with the Bubble Economy at hand, the gangster with the golden touch had risen to chairman of Japan's second-largest yakuza syndicate, the Inagawa-kai. With some help from his friends, he was now prepared to take the Japanese mob into business on a scale never before seen.

It all began modestly enough. Born in Tokyo in 1924, Ishii moved with his family to nearby Kamakura, where they ran a small noodle shop near the main highway. Neighbors remember the boy as a slight and shy fellow, but by his early teens he had become a force to be reckoned with. After gaining entrance to the respected Kamakura Middle School, he jumped into a knife fight and was expelled. With the Pacific War looming, the young Ishii went to work as a factory hand at a local naval arsenal and then entered nearby Yokosuka Navy Communications School. He graduated at the top of his class and found himself made a signalman with a *kaiten,* a human torpedo unit, in the spring of 1945. These fifteen-meter-long mini-subs were the marine equivalent of the kamikaze, designed to carry a ton and a half of explosive and one ill-fated sailor. The war ended, however, without Ishii's unit getting the call.

With the economy in ruins, Ishii found work wherever he could. He soon was hanging out with a Yokohama gang, which ran rackets in the booming black market and along the waterfront. His bosses found the young lad had a talent for making money. Before long, Ishii was put in charge of running the gang's recruitment of day laborers, a job at which he excelled. But after a decade of small-time rackets, Ishii was ready for something bigger. In 1958 he joined forces with the Inagawa-kai, an aggressive crime family then expanding into Tokyo and beyond. His ability to make money marked him as leadership material, and as the Inagawa-kai grew into one of Japan's top gangs, Ishii's power and influence grew with it.

Ishii was coming of age just as the yakuza were maturing into modern crime syndicates. His penchant for business eventually led him to Kenji Osano, the corporate magnate later convicted of perjury for his role in the Lockheed scandal. Osano took a liking to the ambitious Ishii, who responded by offering the syndicate's protection and support. For this Osano was grateful, and he rewarded the Inagawa-kai with lucrative construction projects and access to his resort empire. "Mr. Ishii had free entry into the chairman's office," recalled Koki Nishiyama, a longtime rightist who knew Ishii over the years. "He was a man of strict manners, who would wait patiently outside while the chairman was gone."

It was under Osano's wing that Ishii learned about the world of high finance—both at home and abroad. In Hawaii, the yakuza boss accompanied Osano on a buying spree during the early 1970s that netted the tycoon nearly half the top hotels in Waikiki. Ishii would use the opportunity to help pioneer the yakuza's expansion overseas. In Korea and Hawaii, he arranged high-stakes gambling junkets for Japanese businessmen, feting them with first-class airfare, hotels, and female escorts. Using marked cards, his men stole millions of dollars in crooked games, and then forced their terrified victims to pay up back home. In Hawaii, Osano's hotels became such notorious landing spots for the Inagawa-kai that Honolulu police put them under surveillance.

By now, Ishii had risen to number two in the Inagawa-kai, second only to Inagawa himself. But Ishii's increased visibility began attracting the attention of police at home as well. In 1978, the law finally caught up with him, and he was thrown into jail for the Korean gambling tours. He was fifty-four, and would spend the next seven years of his life in prison. His time there was a turning point for the graying gangster. "We cannot succeed in the yakuza world unless we are very active and aggressive until our early forties," he would say. "After that, we have to adapt our lives to ordinary society. We cannot always be so forceful."

There were, he reasoned, smarter ways to make money.

Susumu Ishii left prison in 1984, but the Japan he reentered was becoming a new place. Within two years, the Bubble began to inflate and business opportunities loomed everywhere for enterprising yakuza. It was here that Ishii got his first taste of the riches of the new era, by playing a key role in the 1986 takeover of troubled Heiwa Sogo Bank. Heiwa Sogo had been Japan's sixth-largest mutual savings and loan bank, with 101 branches nationwide. But in a hint of what was to come, in the early 1980s the bank had been plundered to near bankruptcy by shady developers, mobsters, and its own management. Saddled with $1.2 billion in unsecured and off-the-books loans, the bank sorely needed a rescuer. The government was not about to let Heiwa Sogo become Japan's first postwar banking failure.

Ishii's job was providing protection to Heiwa's management, and he found himself in the middle of a takeover battle over the scandal-plagued bank. "In the world of banking, the word was that when you dealt with the management of Heiwa Sogo, you dealt with Susumu Ishii as well," reported *Tokyo Insideline,* a respected political newsletter. Ishii worked at first to stop a buyout by Sumitomo Bank, but after a call from former prime minister Kishi, the gangster decided his interests in the matter had changed. He ended up switching sides—and was well rewarded for his efforts. After the sale, Ishii ended up with ownership of the Iwama Country Club, a thirty-six-hole, luxury golf course development just north of Tokyo.

Ishii needed financing to finish Iwama, and for that he turned to a booming package delivery service called Tokyo Sagawa Kyubin and to its president, Hiroyasu Watanabe. A hard-driving high school dropout, Watanabe had faced his own share of run-ins with the law, including convictions for embezzlement and tax evasion. In recent months, Ishii had done several favors for Watanabe, among them putting an end to scandal sheets looking into not one, but two families he kept on the side. Watanabe now responded generously, guaranteeing millions of dollars in bank loans to Ishii's development company.

Some months later, Watanabe again asked Ishii's help, this time for a more weighty task. The situation concerned one of Watanabe's political contacts, LDP powerhouse Noboru Takeshita, with whom he was anxious to gain favor. Takeshita had a good shot at becoming Japan's next prime minister, but he had somehow incurred the wrath of an obscure rightist gang, the Nihon Kominto (Japan Emperor's People Party). For six months, the group had harassed him with loudspeaker vans in a concerted campaign of *homegoroshi* (damning with praise), blaring sarcastic statements about Takeshita's ethics and career. The rightists claimed to be upset that Takeshita had broken from Kakuei Tanaka's faction just as the ex–prime minister had fallen ill. The embarrassment to Takeshita was considerable, and police, ya-kuza, and several Diet members all had tried to make the group stop, to no avail. Behind the request for help, Watanabe stressed, was none other than the LDP's Shin Kanemaru, widely considered the most powerful man in Japanese politics. A blunt power broker credited with engineering the last administration, Kanemaru was keen to see Takeshita as the next prime minister.

Ishii made short work of the rightists. The harassment soon ended and Takeshita's path to power was clear. Kanemaru himself then met with Ishii at an exclusive Tokyo restaurant to thank the gang boss for his efforts. "I met him because of my own sense of obligation," Kanemaru later testified before the Diet. "I knew, of course, that it was not a good thing, but I did it anyway." Several weeks after the dinner, in November 1987, Noboru Takeshita did indeed become prime minister of Japan, aided and abetted by one of the nation's top crime syndicates.

The World's Richest Gangster

Ishii's success left Sagawa officials feeling extraordinarily obliged and grate-ful to the mob boss. And Ishii took full advantage. As his longtime psychic later observed, "The fortunes greatly favored him at first."

Tokyo Sagawa began offering loans and loan guarantees to Ishii's com-panies, with not a single asset to secure the deals. By now the Bubble was fully inflated and lenders were practically throwing money at their clients. Backed by Sagawa's assurances, Ishii and his pals gained access to amounts that make the American mob's raiding of the Teamsters' pension fund look like shoplifting. By 1988 he had accumulated a whopping 230 billion yen, at the time worth some $1.66 billion. Ishii promptly poured the money into real estate, the stock market, and a tangled web of more than a dozen com-panies at home and abroad.

At the heart of the new business was golf. The Iwama Country Club was but the beginning; to become king of the fairways seemed to the yakuza boss a great and worthy pursuit. Backed by the Sagawa guarantees, Ishii pumped hundreds of millions of dollars into Iwama and two other developments. Others looked on in awe. Ishii soon earned notoriety as the Zaitech Ya-kuza—the Financial Engineering Mobster.

Not all the money, of course, was going where it should. Ishii began form-ing companies left and right, and was spending money furiously. In addition to development firms for the three golf courses, there were Toko Finance, Seisho Leisure, Keisan Industries, and at least eleven other corporations. Ishii loaded up a half-dozen companies with ghost employees made up of top syndicate officials and his own relatives. At the same time, large sums were being shoveled into Japan's overheated stock market, invested in firms like NTT, Nippon Steel, and Mitsui Metals. His men also took delivery of a "flying limo," a $6 million helicopter to ferry gang bosses to and from their new investments, while more than $30 million found its way into the international art market, bringing home a collection of masterpieces by Renoir, Monet, and Chagall.

Then there were the parties, posh affairs at Tokyo's finest hotels and clubs. Entertainers, athletes, and businesspeople all lined up to be feted by Mr. Ishii's lavish entertainment. Photos of one party, obtained by the newspaper *Yomiuri,* reportedly show Ishii clad in a dinner jacket with other top gang officials, mixing it up with the Tokyo glitterati. Among those in attendance, the paper noted, "were two big-name actors, famous singers, including a one-time winner of the Recording Grand Prix, three young pop singers, a foreign TV personality and a former world-class boxing champion." Another memorable gathering was a ten-day, all-expense-paid trip for TV personalities and a half-dozen professional golfers to a Mexican resort. Still another was a twenty-man tour of Latin America that included stops in Rio for Carnival and an audience in Panama with then-president Manuel Noriega.

Ishii's money went overseas along with his guests. In Panama he allegedly handed the drug-dealing Noriega $360,000, for reasons unknown. Other investments proved easier to trace. Through one affiliate, West Tsusho, he sent $40 million abroad to at least three countries, according to police records. Nearly $3 million went as down payment for a luxury resort in Macao, funneled through Rock of Japan, Ltd., a new Ishii subsidiary in Hong Kong. With his partner Aoki Construction, plans called for a two-hundred-room hotel, casino, golf course, and tennis complex. Another fast million went to buy land in South Korea—again for golf course development.

But the plans for America were his most ambitious overseas. Some $20 million flowed to the U.S., about half of it to buy into a New York finance firm and a Houston-based software company; the other $10 million purchased a one-hundred-acre site in Rockland County, New York—for yet another golf course development. Ishii's men put golf legend Gary Player on a lucrative retainer to oversee their development plans. Player, unaware of who was behind the money, even appeared at a packed Manhattan reception to launch what Ishii and company were proudly calling the New York Country Club.

Player was a great catch for these rich Japanese mobsters, but soon they couldn't believe their luck. Within months of George Bush's 1988 election as U.S. president, Ishii's front men managed to hire Bush's elder brother, Prescott, as an adviser. Prescott Bush, unaware of his clients' true background, was well paid for his efforts: he received a $250,000 finder's fee for aiding their purchase of Asset Management International Financing and Settlement, a New York firm, and stood to make another $750,000 from the other deals. The mobsters, though, wanted more: they wanted a meeting with the president himself. This didn't happen, but Ishii and company remained unfazed. If they played their cards right, they felt, the Japanese yakuza just might end up in the American White House.

By 1989, Susumu Ishii could see the outlines of a multinational, multibillion-dollar corporate empire under his direct control. Inspired, the yakuza boss pushed even harder. His latest brainstorm: advance marketing of the membership rights to his first golf club, Iwama, due to open in the fall of 1990. He would use the proceeds, he told friends, "for a one-time risk in the stock market."

One by one, Ishii and company approached their backers and associates throughout corporate Japan and pointedly asked for buyers. Again the money poured in. It was an impressive list: Tokyo Sagawa topped the group, spending nearly $60 million on two hundred memberships. The huge Aoki and Hazama construction companies also made major buys, as did affiliates of top securities houses Nikko and Nomura. Ishii had struck gold yet again: another $280 million flowed into his company accounts.

True to his word, Ishii now turned to the stock market, where, incredibly, he gained access to even more capital. By now, the Inagawa-kai's godfather had become a welcome customer at Nomura and Nikko, with contacts that extended to Nomura's board of directors. This was no small feat, as Nomura had become the world's largest securities firm. Nomura's president later admitted the company had known Ishii was a gangster and that there was "quite a large gap between Nomura's and society's way of thinking." But Ishii "looked like he was going to become an important customer."

An important customer, indeed. Finance affiliates of Nomura and Nikko gave Ishii an astonishing $255 million credit line to buy Tokyu Railway stock—with the stock itself as the only collateral.

Advising Ishii to get into Tokyu stock was none other than Mitsuhiro Kotani, the high-flying speculator behind the notorious Seibi Group. Ishii was soon in the middle of a classic ramping operation, with Nomura heavily promoting the stock and Ishii and friends pouring money in. Police later found at least nine Inagawa-kai members with Nomura accounts purchasing Tokyu stock, including retired godfather Inagawa himself.

Tokyu was not simply a transportation outfit, but the flagship company of a vast $21 billion combine whose holdings included hotels, real estate, and shopping centers. By November of 1989, Ishii had become Tokyu's largest single shareholder, amassing 32 million shares, or some 3 percent of company stock. He watched as its price soared from his first purchases of 1,610 yen per share to over 3,000. As the year drew to a close, the yakuza boss stood to make a killing of $275 million on the Tokyu stock alone.

Ishii's achievements were extraordinary. When it was all added up—the fees, the loans, the loan guarantees—the Tokyo godfather's working capital amounted to $2.3 billion. Meanwhile, the Inagawa-kai had become the largest crime syndicate in Tokyo. Beneath Susumu Ishii toiled 7,500 men, engaged in drug dealing, extortion, gambling, and a hundred other rackets. In the United States, an outfit like the Inagawa-kai would almost surely be indicted under racketeering and money-laundering laws, its assets seized and entire leadership thrown in jail. Yet in Japan, the business community of the world's second-largest economy had thrown open its doors, unlocked the safes, and even cheered the gangsters on. Perhaps most disturbing is how deep Ishii's backing extended. It was not only Sagawa Express and the big Nomura and Nikko brokerage houses. Aoki and Hazama Construction, two of Japan's top contractors, had joined in, as had affiliates of at least twenty-seven speculative nonbanks financed by Japan's top banks. There is no parallel in U.S. history. It is as if Merrill Lynch, Federal Express, and the Bechtel Corporation handed $2 billion to New York's Gambino family. Given the sustained notoriety of Ishii and the Inagawa-kai, it is almost inconceivable these companies did not know with whom they were dealing. In the case of Sagawa Kyubin, which guaranteed much of Ishii's borrowing, court records show that top officials in Tokyo were well aware of their partner's background.

A 1988 police report provides a measure of Ishii's accomplishment: researchers estimated total yakuza annual income at 1.3 trillion yen—or about $10 billion at the time. Yet here was one gangster gaining access to nearly a quarter of that amount in working capital—none of it accounted for in the police statistics. Moreover, it is clear that other yakuza across Japan were engaged in similar activity. No wonder independent researchers have put yakuza income between $45 and $70 billion.

Mr. Ishii had taken the keizai yakuza to undreamed-of heights in just three years. "Given the choice of a rich or poor life, people tend to go for rich," Ishii once said. But even one with the gift of gold dust cannot control the world economy. For it is in the nature of bubbles that eventually they will pop—and the Japanese economy was no exception. By early 1990 the Bubble was collapsing, and Susumu Ishii was in trouble.

Even before the Tokyo stock market crash, there were warning signs; they concerned not the health of the economy, but of Ishii himself. In early 1990 the yakuza boss collapsed while traveling in Mexico and was diagnosed with a brain tumor. He returned home in a wheelchair, only to be greeted with more bad news: the market was crashing.

Ishii had nearly $400 million tied up in Tokyu stock, and its value was plummeting. He flatly refused to sell, confident the market would rebound.

But the stocks kept falling. From its record high at the end of 1989, the Nikkei index lost nearly half its value over the next nine months—a loss, on paper, of some $2 *trillion*. Land prices, too, began to dive. And along with the land and stocks went business in general, as Japan fell into its worst economic slump in forty years. The Bubble had collapsed.

Top officials at Sagawa Express began to panic about the huge loans they had guaranteed Ishii and his companies, and asked for a detailed repayment plan. But late that January, Ishii was hospitalized for the tumor, and there was no more talk about the loans. When he was finally released weeks later, the situation had grown critical.

Ishii's companies were now falling behind in interest payments to the nearly two dozen banks and finance firms he had borrowed from, and his lenders were starting to demand their money. So large was the debt that the monthly interest payments alone totaled some $36 million. Making matters worse, in March the Japanese press revealed that Ishii's key investment vehicle, Hokuto Development, was a mob front, and reporters tied the company to Sagawa Express and the Tokyu stock. The authorities would soon be asking questions.

Suddenly, Ishii was finding it hard to get new loans, which worsened an already serious cash flow problem. Desperate for capital, he began threatening the Tokyu Group, demanding they purchase his shares at inflated prices. But Tokyu wasn't buying. By early April, the company's stock had plunged below Ishii's purchase price.

Ishii's balance sheet was looking worse and worse. On paper, his various companies had outstanding loans of over $700 million, with assets of only some $425 million. And the majority of those assets were the plummeting Tokyu stocks, most of which were already pledged as collateral and could not be touched. Meanwhile, his golf course developments were beset by a range of problems: poor cash flow, construction delays, lack of financing. He had borrowed so heavily for the Gold Valley Country Club—nearly $300 million—that even when ready to sell memberships it would never turn a profit.

Ishii's solution to all this was to return to the source. Incredibly, he approached Tokyo Sagawa and pointedly asked for yet more loan guarantees, explaining he needed the funds to remain solvent until the economy bounced back. Just as incredibly, Sagawa agreed. Officials there had their reasons. Should Ishii's enterprises fail, the weight of all those debts would fall squarely on their company. Moreover, Sagawa's deep involvement with the gang would become public, along with the fact that their top officials had guaranteed a fortune in reckless loans to the mob.

Thus began a whole new round of financing. Court documents reveal how every few weeks, Ishii's people visited Tokyo Sagawa, asking for new guarantees. By the end of 1990, their efforts had somehow secured another

$132 million in loans from four nonbanks as well as from Tokyo Sagawa itself. Most of the money went to paying interest on the previous debt, but as before, other huge portions simply disappeared into other projects. Like the gambler he was, Ishii was back playing the stock market, this time pouring nearly $20 million into a bid for control of Honshu Paper. But the funds he needed were now out of his reach. The Bubble had popped, and with it Ishii's budding empire. "He really wasn't a very good businessman," concluded a police detective who tracked his investments for three years. "He was good at raising money, but not at managing it."

By this time his health was failing badly. Increasingly impaired by his brain tumor, beset by financial woes, in October 1990 Ishii resigned as chairman of the Inagawa-kai and officially retired. That spring he entered a hospital for extended treatment, but the prognosis was not hopeful. His companies, meanwhile, were for all practical purposes bankrupt, and they were threatening to take Tokyo Sagawa Express with them. Months later, Tokyo Sagawa's top managers were fired by the parent company's board of directors, prosecutors indicted them for breach of trust, and the broad outlines of the full scandal at last came into view. The public—and the police—was stunned. Stories filled the news media about "The Sagawa Scandal," and hard questions were being put to the securities houses, the banks, and the Inagawa-kai.

By now, Ishii was beyond caring. His hair and beard had grown long, he dressed like a monk, and he waited to die. The godfather with the golden touch would hang on long enough to see his sixty-seventh birthday. But the end came soon after. On September 3, 1991, Ishii passed away in his hospital bed. Six thousand mourners paid tribute to the fallen yakuza boss, filing past the wooden gates of Tokyo's Honmonji Temple, many stopping to bow deeply before a giant photo of the man.

Susumu Ishii was dead, his companies bankrupt, and his lenders in shock. As investigators unraveled the Byzantine financial webs he left behind, they wondered where all the money had gone. Soon they would be asking that question about a trillion dollars in bad loans left by the Bubble's collapse.

CHAPTER EIGHT

THE COLLAPSING BUBBLE

THE BURSTING OF THE BUBBLE ECONOMY STUNNED THE JAPANESE. AFTER A four-year party, Tokyo woke up to a massive hangover of bad loans, bankruptcies, and its worst economic crisis since the late 1940s. As the stock market plummeted to half its value, land prices steadily followed. Dozens of golf course developments were put on hold. The trophy properties bought overseas for top dollar were now unloaded at huge losses. Japan's once high-flying banks found themselves holding so much bad debt that it threatened their stability. Shaken by the damage, the government and news media began a much-belated look at the corrupt mess before them.

The wreckage left by the Bubble's collapse exposed the seamy side of Japanese business and politics as never before. Rapid deflation of the economy was followed by nearly a decade of scandal: insider deals, influence peddling, massive bank fraud, mob-looted companies, and more. And, while there were plenty of independent crooks and corrupt politicians, the scandals showed most strikingly how far yakuza penetration of Japanese society had gone.

By the time the Sagawa scandal broke in 1991, Nomura, Nikko, and other top brokers already were under fire for reimbursing favored clients for stock losses. The secret payments confirmed what many investors in Japan and abroad had long believed—that the Japanese stock market was a rigged game, incredibly profitable for insiders and perilous for everyone else. Nomura had been called the world's most powerful securities house and its officials had earned a well-deserved reputation for arrogance. When the 1990 book *House of Nomura* alleged the firm had ramped share prices, dealt with sokaiya, and used insider information, Nomura sued author Al Alletzhauser for libel in British court. But now Japan's entire national media were reporting that Nomura had reimbursed clients for losses, ramped shares of Tokyu Corporation, and put a fortune in the hands of organized crime. Nomura quietly dropped the libel case.

The reimbursements by Japan's big brokers caught most of the attention overseas, while the implications of what Nomura and Nikko had done for the yakuza were largely lost. But the fact that two of their nation's three largest brokers had given a $255 million line of credit to the mob did not get past the Japanese. The public was outraged and the police dumbfounded. The presidents of both firms resigned, and the Finance Ministry ordered Nomura, Nikko, and two other top brokerages to close down their corporate sales divisions for one to three weeks.

For the Japanese public, the surprises were just beginning. As the Sagawa trial began in 1992, prosecutors revealed the sensational news that the Inagawa-kai had played a key role in the birth of the Takeshita administration. Takeshita had lasted less than two years as prime minister, forced out by an earlier, influence-peddling scandal. Still in the Diet, he now had to explain how a crime syndicate had helped clear his path to power. The former prime minister denied any knowledge of help from the yakuza, but most Japanese remained skeptical. News that Sagawa Express had lavished questionable funds on scores of politicians only inflamed the press and popular opinion.

Along with Takeshita, attention focused sharply on Shin Kanemaru, the LDP kingmaker who had asked for the Inagawa-kai's help. Kanemaru had received millions of dollars annually in secret contributions, investigators found, largely from the construction industry and Sagawa Express. A search of Kanemaru's home revealed some $50 million in cash, bearer bonds, and gold bullion stashed in his closets and desk drawers. Yet prosecutors let off Kanemaru with a mere slap on the wrist: a $1,600 fine for violating the campaign contributions law. The public was incensed. Citizen protests, unusual for Japan, appeared nationwide, with protesters clutching brooms and calling for a clean sweep of the nation's filthy politics. More than one hundred local governments passed resolutions calling for tough investigations and a crackdown on corruption. There were hunger strikes and, in a chilling throwback, a Japanese Army major even called for a coup d'etat. "Our country has been made to look ridiculous," complained the newspaper *Mainichi*. Disgraced and subject to unrelenting attack, Kanemaru resigned from the Diet in October 1992.

Next it was the construction industry's turn. Following the money trail from Kanemaru, investigators traced millions of dollars in bribes, kickbacks, and secret donations to politicians across Japan. Authorities arrested top officials of four major construction companies for bribery on public works projects and traced the flow of secret cash to scores of influential Dietmen, governors, and mayors. But again the punishments were modest: virtually all involved received suspended sentences.

The courts were less kind to stock speculator Mitsuhiro Kotani, whose mob ties had helped make his Koshin Group among the most feared corporate raiders in Japan. Convicted for extorting the Janome Sewing Company, Kotani was sentenced to seven years in prison. His Koshin Group, meanwhile, went out in spectacular fashion. In 1992, the group collapsed with a billion-dollar debt in one of Japan's largest ever bankruptcies.

Yet another sordid story came from Itoman, a respected one-hundred-year-old trading company based in Osaka. In 1991, the Japanese public learned that the firm had been virtually taken over and looted by mob associates. The company had made the grave error of allowing a top jia-geya to become a board member and head of its then-fast-growing real estate section. More than $3 billion quickly flowed out of Itoman, lost to insider deals, outright theft, and dubious investments in artwork and property development. Authorities arrested three Itoman executives, including the former president, and found the company's executive managing director dead in his bathtub, an apparent suicide.

"The sight of contrite company presidents bowing in apology and of police leading away embarrassed executives has become almost a staple of the evening news," observed the *Nikkei Weekly* in August 1991. But there was much more to come.

The Yakuza Recession

The Japanese banking industry was hit terribly hard. Bad loans piled up at lenders of every sort: big international banks, city banks, housing lenders, credit unions, agricultural cooperatives. The first signs of the chaos underlying the big banks arrived in the summer of 1991. Top officials of Fuji Bank—Japan's fourth-largest—admitted that three of their Tokyo branches had issued forged certificates of deposits worth some $2 billion. The CDs, in turn, were used as collateral by twenty-three companies to borrow money, largely for property speculation. Several of the firms were believed tied to the yakuza. Days later, two other banks—Tokai and Kyowa Saitama—found similar forged CDs used to secure hundreds of millions of dollars more in credit.

By fall of that year, those scandals had been eclipsed by another billion-dollar fraud, this time tied to the staid and proper Industrial Bank of Japan (IBJ). Again the story involved bogus CDs, but the tale was one of the strangest to come out of the Bubble era. At the center of the crime was Nui Onoue, a sixty-one-year-old Osaka restaurateur and self-styled mystic. She was Japan's largest individual investor and, at one point, one of the world's wealthiest people, with a portfolio worth $4.4 billion. Yet Onoue's background remains obscure, as does the original source of her wealth. Japanese press reports speculate she was associated with the Yamaguchi-gumi's

Takumi gang, whose members frequented her restaurants; among her many investments was plowing $200 million into the Inagawa-kai's ramping of Tokyu stock. But no firm evidence ever emerged that Onoue worked with the yakuza and she denied it forcefully to banking officials. What is clear is that her fortune, like so many others during the Bubble, was built on credit, and when the Bubble collapsed she turned to massive fraud to stave off bankruptcy. Desperate for funds, she forged certificates of deposits to obtain backing from IBJ, and then used them to borrow a whopping $1.3 billion from twelve other lenders.

Christened by Japan's press "The Bubble Lady," Onoue came to symbolize the excesses of the time. In 1991, she went bankrupt with an extraordinary debt of over $3 billion and was indicted for fraud and breach of trust. She later received twelve years in prison.

Across the lending industry, evidence of the yakuza's hand was hard to miss. The newspaper *Asahi* in 1991 traced loans and loan guarantees to Yamaguchi-gumi properties and businesses by seventeen financial institutions and four other businesses. On the list: banks, credit unions, brokerages, two real estate firms, one construction company, and an auto importer. Then there was the case of Gifu Shogin, a regional credit union about 180 miles west of Tokyo. Gifu Shogin largely serviced Japan's ethnic Korean community, but during the Bubble it became in effect a private bank for the mob. The boss of a Yamaguchi-gumi affiliate, the Sakahiro gang, actually gained a seat on the board of directors. By the time regulators pored over the bankrupt co-op's books, they found that nearly all the credit union's $110 million in outstanding loans had been made to crime syndicates—most of them poured into dubious real estate deals. When Gifu Shogin tried calling in the loans, the gangs did more than refuse—they threatened the bank managers, who had to bring in police for protection.

What befell Gifu Shogin's managers was occurring across Japan's battered financial landscape. After loaning the underworld vast sums during the Bubble, the nation's lenders found they simply could not collect. The yakuza were making it clear that the risks would be much too high. Consider the fate of Tomosaburo Koyama, a vice president of Hanwa Bank, a regional lender outside Osaka. Koyama was in charge of collecting the bank's bad loans. One morning in August 1993, he was getting into his car when a gunman murdered him in cold blood. Police believed the killing was tied to a local yakuza gang enmeshed in one of the bank's bad loan deals.

Koyama's murder was part of a larger crime wave against corporate Japan following the Bubble's collapse, ranging from vandalism to Molotov cocktails to slashings in the night. Much of it, authorities believe, was tied to business deals involving organized crime. Between 1992 and 1995, police logged twenty-one shooting attacks on homes of corporate executives. In the previous three years, only one such attack had been reported. A 1994 survey by public broadcaster NHK found that of 205 major companies responding, forty-six said their executives had been victims of violent threats or acts, from blackmail to shootings.

It would have been hard for Sumitomo Bank to miss the mob's message. One of the world's largest banks, Sumitomo had been among the Bubble's most aggressive lenders. The bank had amassed over $10 billion in bad loans it was now anxious to clear, but apparently not all its customers agreed on the terms. Between February and May 1993, Sumitomo group companies were virtually under siege, with twenty-two incidents of shooting, blackmail, arson, and harassment. Molotov cocktails were thrown at the homes of the bank chairman, the bank vice president, the chairman of Sumitomo Real Estate, and the chairman of Sumitomo Corp. Two bank branches were shot at and a third firebombed. None of the crimes was solved.

With police apparently impotent, the attacks escalated. In September 1994, Sumitomo bank manager Kazufumi Hatanaka answered an early morning call at his condominium home. He was gunned down in his doorway, execution-style, with a bullet to the head. Hatanaka was not your ordinary bank manager. He was a member of the big bank's board of directors and head of its operations in Nagoya, the nation's third-largest city. A seventy-three-year-old ex-con later confessed he had shot Hatanaka in an aborted burglary attempt, but officials remained unconvinced.

In the wake of the scandals, some companies moved to break all ties with organized crime, including the sokaiya. But like other Japanese businesses, the gangs watched their income plummet, and the sokaiya were in no mood to lose customers. One firm that had cut off the racketeers was Fuji Photo Film. Its new general affairs chief, Juntaro Suzuki, courageously enforced a complete end to sokaiya payments in 1991. Over the next year, Fuji Film's shareholders' meetings became long, drawn-out affairs, constantly disrupted by sokaiya. Then one night in February 1994, Suzuki answered the door of his suburban home and was stabbed to death with a cooking knife. Two gang members were arrested for the murder, one of them affiliated with the Yamaguchi-gumi. If Suzuki's murder wasn't a clear enough sign, weeks later, after Asahi Breweries announced it, too, would cut off sokaiya payments, Molotov cocktails were thrown at the home of its honorary chairman.

The Bubble apparently had changed the rules. Traditional yakuza—the "chivalrous gangsters"—boasted of living by a code of conduct that meant never harming the ordinary people. They certainly didn't shoot at them. Whether this had ever been true, the code had now lost all its meaning. The worlds of crime and commerce had simply become too entwined. At times it looked like the gangs had declared war on the Japanese. In 1994, the largest gang in Kitakyushu—a city of over 1 million—went on a shooting spree, firing at banks, hotels, and other businesses thirteen times during one month. The group, police said, had been stung by the recession and companies cutting off the flow of cash.

Japanese lenders remained the biggest target. In September 1993, shots were fired at the home of the president of Tokai Bank. In November 1994, the wife of a Hyakujushi Bank executive opened her front door and was stabbed in the head, neck, and wrist by an unknown assailant. In June 1995, two rightists shot up an Ibaraki Prefecture credit union after its officials refused to drop their claim on real estate owned by one of the gang's associates. Other banks had similar stories to tell. Between 1997 and 2000, suspicious "suicides" befell seven Japanese either investigating financial irregularities or ready to testify about them. Among the victims was Tadayo Honma, Nippon Credit Bank's new president, who faced cleaning up hundreds of millions of dollars in loans to mobbed-up companies.

The events left such an atmosphere of fear within the banking industry that virtually no banker would speak publicly about the issue to reporters. "These guys are a nightmare to deal with," said one Tokyo banker responsible for collecting bad loans, explaining why he wouldn't grant an interview. "The pool of people involved here is sufficiently small—bankers and yakuza—that they could figure out who you are without too much difficulty."

As the tally of bad loans reached into the hundreds of billions of dollars, the issue of collecting them grew increasingly serious during the 1990s. The problem was not without irony. In a corporate environment in which business often uses the mob to collect debts, what happens when the mob itself holds massive debt? "It's impossible for the banks to collect the bad loans—their exposure to the yakuza is too strong," observed Raisuke Miyawaki, ex-head of the NPA's organized crime unit and one of the few people to speak out on the issue. Bankers and Finance Ministry officials began referring to the problem as *moraru hazaado*—moral hazard.

Just how much did the Japanese underworld owe? "Nobody knows," said Miyawaki. "And nobody is trying to find out." Officials at the NPA and the Finance Ministry quietly confirmed Miyawaki's statement. The National Police Agency, confided an embarrassed official, "does not keep that kind of data." Sources in the Finance Ministry said they had ideas about certain companies, but no overall picture. Given that the Inagawa-kai's Ishii alone grabbed $2.3 billion, it seems reasonable to assume the total was in excess of $10 billion.

Miyawaki and others suggest the amount was much, much larger. Some 10 percent of the bad loans left by the Bubble's collapse were tied directly to the yakuza, Miyawaki estimated, and another 30 percent were "gray," with indirect ties to the gangs. Even taking 10 percent as the amount for all yakuza-tied loans—an amount that banking analysts find realistic—the implications are extraordinary. After years of playing down the debt, in 1999 the Finance Ministry finally admitted that the amount of bad loans held by Japanese banks was 80 trillion yen—or $720 billion. Many analysts believed the actual figure was closer to $1 trillion or more. With Japan's economy battered by years of recession, the number of bad loans may have actually grown; in 2001, investment bank Goldman Sachs put the total nearly three times higher—at an extraordinary 237 trillion yen—comprising some 39 percent of all corporate loans.

Even taking the government's more modest figure of $720 billion, that is still more than twice the size of America's savings and loan debacle—in an economy half the size. Now consider the yakuza's share: at $720 billion, if the underworld's portion were indeed 10 percent, that puts the mob's debt at 72 billion yen—approaching the gross domestic product of Israel or Singapore. And it's more than five times the official figure for the yakuza's annual income. If, as Miyawaki argued, the overall figure of mob-tied loans was close to 40 percent, that puts the yakuza's share at a whopping $288 billion—larger than the combined GDPs of Singapore and Switzerland.

The stakes were high not only for Japan but for the world economy. After years of recession in East Asia, policy makers in the West hoped a financially stronger Japan would pull the region out of a deflationary spiral that could affect profits and jobs worldwide. But the key to reviving Japan's economy lay in clearing away the mountain of bad loans—and the key to that lay in dealing with the yakuza. The gangs had come a long way from the petty black markets and gambling dens that followed the war. So central were the gangs to the crisis that Miyawaki branded Japan's economic woes a "yakuza recession."

One of Tokyo's top banking analysts, who insisted on anonymity, argued that the yakuza's biggest impact was in relatively minor interests the gangs had gained in various properties. "Within the individual pieces of collateral, you'll often find at the bottom of the lien structure some 'problem money' or yakuza interest—a loan, a property share, or some holding that allows that group control," he explained. "To get your hands on the collateral, you need agreement of all the parties with a financial interest in the property. But if the man at the bottom is a yakuza, he may make it a lot more difficult to gain his agreement. His lending size may be small, but his influence can be extraordinary. That kind of yakuza connection probably runs into several trillion yen—easily."

While a full picture was lacking, the extensive role of the yakuza was tough to hide, particularly when Japanese banks began offering bad loan portfolios to the public. One 1999 government study of 116 construction-related loans found that 42 percent were tied to organized crime. Attracted by the fire sale prices, U.S. and European buyers moved in with billions of dollars, but the foreigners often didn't like what they saw. In one portfolio examined by Kroll Associates, the investigative firm, 40 percent of those borrowers had ties to organized crime, and 25 percent had criminal records ranging from disrupting auctions to assault, extortion, and rape. A similar portfolio of 108 properties was offered in 1998 by Mitsui Trust and Banking Company, one of Japan's largest banks. Thirteen of the properties—including condos, undeveloped land, and parking lots—were held by Azabu Building, a company long tied by police to the yakuza. In 1998, Azabu president Kitaro Watanabe received two years in prison for hiding some $18 million in assets from creditors. Azabu properties are notorious for being protected by the Sumiyoshi-kai. One investigator who ventured onto one of the properties was promptly held hostage for an hour by the "tenants," until the gang boss telephoned the man. "Next time you come out here, come with the proper introductions!" shouted the godfather. "Go home, wash your face, and come visit us again." Similarly, two Japanese investigators working for Kroll were checking ownership of a club-packed low-rise in Tokyo's teeming Akasaka entertainment district. After making discreet inquiries, the men were suddenly accosted by four young toughs, demanding to know who sent them. Before they could answer, the thugs jumped them, smashing in one's teeth and bloodying the other.

The gangs devised ingenious ways to guard their interests. The Japanese underworld produced yet another brand of "specialists"—the *songiriya,* or loss-cutting specialists—a shadowy industry of squatters, extortionists, and investors. One favorite tactic was to file false liens against a property and then demand payoffs to relinquish their claims. Others preferred to invest by scaring off potential buyers and then coming in at the last moment to buy the property at a rock-bottom price. In perhaps the favorite technique, an indebted owner leases or sells the building to a gang, which then fills the place with yakuza. These tattooed squatters use threats and violence to avoid foreclosure, gain a better settlement, or extract huge payoffs to move. Some yakuza occupied office buildings in major cities for years during the 1990s. So brisk was the business, say police, that it created an active secondary market among the gangs, in which one songiriya group sold out to another. Many buildings had been owned by the yakuza outright, obtained through investment, fraud, or as "payment" from some hapless victim. The gangs weren't going to give up such valuable real estate so easily. One prominent godfather, Tokutaro Takayama, boss of Kyoto's Aizu Kotetsu syndicate, took offense that the gangs would become squatters for a mere payoff. "It was not true that yakuza entered into buildings haphazardly to occupy them illegally," he told a reporter. "Even for yakuza, if we loan, it would be natural that we try to secure credit, wouldn't it?"

The mobbed-up property market posed unusual problems for foreign investors. Some U.S. companies had made big profits buying cut-rate real estate after the crash of America's S&L industry. But the S&Ls were looted largely by white-collar crooks, not violent crime syndicates. Outsiders needed to be careful who their partners were. U.S. investment fund Lonestar, for example, found the going tough after it bought Eventail, a golf course management company allegedly tied to the yakuza. In 2001, Lonestar's Tokyo office was besieged by rightists apparently angry at the fund's plans for a golf club in Tochigi Prefecture. More trouble hit U.S. agribusiness giant Cargill, among the first foreign firms to buy the bad loan portfolios. In 1997, a mysterious fire struck the home of its top executive in Japan, prompting executives to call in police to investigate.

At least one prominent Tokyo businessman, Ryuma Suzuki, was bullish on foreign money coming in. "Japanese banks are acting like cowards," said Suzuki, who helped run a $1 billion organization with 7,000 employees. "I want to encourage U.S. banks to come to Japan. There's a huge business opportunity here, and it would help the trade deficit." Unfortunately, Suzuki's "company" was the Sumiyoshi-kai. In a 1998 interview, Suzuki, a top Sumiyoshi-kai boss, disputed that the yakuza were the source of trouble and offered his services to help clear the properties for new investment. "We're not the problem," he argued. "The authorities are slow to clean up the mess, so they're looking for a scapegoat. But we can help. We would work our butts off because there's a commission." And what kind of commission did Suzuki charge? "I believe the going rate is 30 to 40 percent," he said.

Faced with the yakuza infesting so much of the property market, foreign investors were indeed finding it hard to resist paying them off. As godfather Suzuki advised: "On the big discounted properties, you may have to cooperate with organizations like mine. Things can get a little rough out there." But paying off the gangs is likely to put foreign businesses in precisely the same situation as their Japanese counterparts, making the companies vulnerable while infusing the yakuza with cash. As Japan's banking industry found, the gangs do not easily go away. "The yakuza aren't going to back down," observed Kroll's Harry Godfrey, a former head of the FBI's Tokyo office. "In the short term you're getting an opportunity to make a profit, but you're exposing yourself to paying off organized crime, and that could spill over to the rest of your business." As the Japanese like to say, dealing with the yakuza is like feeding a tiger. If you try to stop, the tiger will eat you.

Where Are the Cops?

Where in all this were the police? To say Japanese law enforcement was unprepared for the Bubble and its aftermath is putting it kindly. Few cops understood the impact of the Bubble's rise and fall until the damage had been done. Moreover, Japan's organized crime detectives had never encountered this level of financial fraud before. "If you look at the Lockheed scandal, the money would fit in a suitcase," recalled Bill Rice, who ran the FBI's Tokyo office in the Bubble years. "If you look at the Sagawa scandal, the money would require a truck." It wasn't even clear which ministry had jurisdiction. "The mistake was that while the police investigated the Inagawa-kai's pimps and gamblers, they ignored Ishii and the people at the top," says Seiji Iishiba, the former chief of the Tokyo police yakuza unit. "The Japanese police only have a system to combat traditional yakuza. But the economic yakuza don't even share the same territory as the police—it's the Finance Ministry that must act on this. And the Finance Ministry doesn't have a system to investigate underground money."

The Tokyo Metropolitan Police did form a fifty-person task force, dubbed, appropriately enough, "The Special Investigation Headquarters for Probing into Illegal Business Activities of Banks and Securities Following the Burst of the Bubble Economy." But the problems derived from such deep-seated corruption demanded a response beyond what the cops could offer. Stung by the battered economy and the constant scandals, voters finally ended the LDP's corrupt, thirty-eight-year reign over Japanese politics. The reform-minded coalition that took power soon failed, however, and within a year the LDP was back in power. Still, even the LDP recognized the glaring need for change.

To better police the unruly stock markets, in 1992 the government created a Securities and Exchange Surveillance Commission. But the real crisis lay with the blanket of bad loans smothering the economy. To clean up the banking mess, Tokyo established scaled-down versions of America's Resolution Trust Corporation, which liquidated the bulk of S&L properties in the United States. Japanese law enforcement, however, launched no great crackdowns or campaigns. While publicly supporting the cleanup effort, police proved reluctant to intervene in what they saw as civil matters—a reaction to the pre–World War II days when authorities seemed to intervene everywhere. Disputes over contracts, liens, and tenants were best left to the private sector, they argued. Missing, too, was the kind of legal assault on negligent lenders that U.S. officials set up in the wake of the S&L failures. In cleaning up the S&L industry, prosecutors indicted more than 1,850 people, resulting in nearly 1,600 criminal convictions. In contrast, by 1998 Japanese authorities had brought fewer than one hundred indictments tied to the bad loans.

One major problem was that penalties for the gangs are too light, according to Kohei Nakabo, the outspoken head of Japan's Housing Loan Administration. The HLA was charged with collecting the worst of the bad loans—$50 billion of debt left by the collapse of Japan's housing lenders—and Nakabo was frustrated. His loan collectors were threatened repeatedly by mobsters and Nakabo himself received round-the-clock protection from Japan's secret service. Criminals can get ten years in jail for assault, he noted, but they face less than two years for hiding assets or impeding loan collection. The bad-loan cases take time, too, and all this makes the payoff seem small to law enforcement. "The police are uninterested," he complained. "Only the criminals think it's worthwhile."

Nakabo was not the only one frustrated by Japanese police. Their poor response was symptomatic of a larger crisis facing Japanese law enforcement: antiquated laws and procedures, tolerance of organized crime and corruption, a lack of initiative and leadership. "Japan has a nineteenth-century police force trying to fight twenty-first-century crime," a reporter once joked to a top NPA official. "No," the official replied. "We have a 1940s police trying to fight 1990s crime."

Whatever era it hailed from, Japan's police force was no match for the crimes of the 1990s. As the Bubble collapsed, Japanese law enforcement lacked the basic tools for fighting organized crime and corruption that officials in most other advanced nations took for granted. There were no laws against racketeering or money laundering. Police could not conduct electronic surveillance or stage controlled deliveries. Prosecutors could not authorize undercover operations or offer immunity to witnesses. This was, again, partly a reaction to the bad old days of the prewar Tokko, the Thought Police. Japanese officials rightly feared that granting such powers to police would stir an outcry by civil libertarians and the left. But there were other reasons at work.

One measure that surely would have helped clean up the Bubble mess was strong money-laundering legislation. Billions of dollars had been pilfered through fraud and intimidation by the gangs and other crooks, and much of that had been funneled into art, property, and securities. But with so much "black money" flowing to Japanese politicians from big industries like construction, authorities were not keen to crack down. As one official put it: "Money laundering is a way of life in Japan."

Pushed by U.S. pressure and a 1988 U.N. pact, Japan became the last of the G-7 nations to enact a money-laundering law in 1991. It was clear to foreign officials, however, that Japan's version lacked teeth. The measure dealt only with drug offenses, and the penalties were relatively weak, as were requirements that banks report suspicious activity. Even so, the law offered a potent weapon against the yakuza—the gangs take in an estimated one-third of their income from drug dealing—yet officials barely used it. After six years on the books, the law resulted in seizures of a mere $7 million in drug money. Typical was the response by authorities when confronted by Colombians eager to launder dirty cash in Japan. At least three times, sources say, Japanese police declined to launch a sting operation even to learn who was behind the attempts. A 1998 report of the international Financial Action Task Force on money laundering called Japan's efforts "virtually ineffective." Similar criticism came from the U.S. State Department's annual narcotics report that year. The report noted that Japan was suspected of being a major money-laundering center, but the nation's anti-laundering law remained "largely untested and unused."

At least Japan now had a money-laundering statute on the books, and some prosecutors were indeed interested in learning to use it more effectively. For the first time, the law also authorized controlled deliveries—allowing investigators to follow drugs to their ultimate destination, and thereby take down an entire narcotics ring. But here, too, authorities seemed unsure of themselves. Different agencies were not eager to cooperate with each other. Investigators from Japan's Customs Bureau and the Health Ministry's Narcotics Police were jealous of the NPA's sweeping authority. With competing turf and the need for building consensus, one prosecutor noted dryly that over one hundred officials had to be consulted on a single controlled delivery.

Some critics believe the problem lies in the very structure of law enforcement in Japan. All Japanese police function under a single entity—the National Police Agency. It is as if every U.S. city cop, county sheriff, and state trooper worked for the FBI. Yet there is no national investigative force like the FBI; the NPA itself is a largely administrative agency, filled with managers, statisticians, and report writers. Policing is left to the prefectures. The NPA dispatches its elite bureaucrats to head the prefectural police departments, and that, critics say, is where the problems begin. Rarely do these officials have any investigative experience, yet they routinely make decisions on the course of key cases. "They know a lot about managing their careers and very little about managing their investigations," complained Wayne Drew, who spoke out after serving two tours as the Drug Enforcement Administration's attaché in Tokyo. Drew worked on numerous cases with Japanese authorities, but left Tokyo dismayed with the "golden boys" of the NPA. "They leapfrog over experienced investigators to become assistant inspectors. They have no understanding of crime, of how it's committed. They have no understanding about motives, techniques, they've never arrested anyone, never interrogated anyone, never managed an investigation."

Drew's frustration is typical of what other Western law enforcement officials say privately about dealing with Tokyo. The criticism, moreover, extends to other areas of Japanese policing. "There's no national criminal intelligence database in this country," Drew said. "They don't have any intelligence analysts. It's incredible. You don't get to where you want to go by being innovative. If the boss is not on the scene, without him around they cannot act. It's better to do nothing than to make a mistake."

Despite its shortcomings, Japanese law enforcement is filled with dedicated professionals, but as Drew's comments suggest, it is a difficult system to reform. There are splits between internationalist and domestic factions at the NPA, between street-level investigators and career bureaucrats, and between traditionalists tolerant of the yakuza and would-be crusaders ready for a historic crackdown. Some of Japan's cops privately complain about the snail-like pace of reform within their own agencies. Others put the blame on public support. "We would like nothing better than eradicating the yakuza," confided a top Tokyo cop. "But the rest of society is not ready to make that commitment."

Perhaps so, but clearly the police have had much to do to rebuild their own credibility in the post-Bubble era. The aftermath of the Bubble Economy showed in embarrassing detail—month after month, scandal after scandal—the failure of law enforcement to contain the yakuza. But even that would pale compared to the impact a bizarre religious cult would have on the reputation of Japanese cops. Over the course of several months in 1995, the Aum Supreme Truth sect almost single-handedly destroyed the great sense of security that Japanese so treasured about their society. In March that year, Aum grabbed world headlines with its unprecedented nerve gas attack on the Tokyo subway. As no other case did, the investigation of Aum raised troubling questions not only about the approach, but about the general competency of Japanese law enforcement.

Long before the subway attack, while the Bubble was at its peak, Aum embarked on an extraordinary, six-year crime spree. The cult's law breaking knew no bounds: massive consumer fraud, land fraud, medical malpractice, extortion, drug dealing, firearms and explosives violations, manufacture of biological and chemical weapons, kidnapping, murder, and mass murder. Year after year this went on, nearly all of it within seventy miles of Tokyo. The response of Japanese law enforcement is a virtual case study on what not to do in fighting terrorism and organized crime. Leads were missed or never followed up, witnesses and evidence ignored, and agencies refused to cooperate with each other. Perhaps Japanese cops had come to rely too heavily on confessions, for the case revealed a striking lack of basic detective work and forensic science. Authorities were warned repeatedly about the cult—from concerned parents, defecting cult members, and crusading journalists. But no action was taken, until one day Tokyo cops awoke to find the world's busiest subway attacked with nerve gas at the height of rush hour.

The Aum case has important implications for Japan's battle against organized crime. The Aum cult, with its weapons smuggling, its drug dealing and systematic violence, often resembled a profit-hungry racketeering gang more than a fanatic doomsday cult. That Japanese cops had failed so badly on such an important menace suggested their success against the yakuza would also be mixed at best.

Faced with an uninspired police force, the citizens of Japan increasingly were taking matters into their own hands. The passive reputation no longer fit for Japanese who had tired of the yakuza's constant intervention in daily life. The number of citizen requests for police help against the gangs more than doubled between 1981 and 1991, to nearly 21,000. Demonstrations against the yakuza became more common, as did lawsuits.

In Okinawa, after a gang shooting at a mob headquarters mistakenly killed a high school student, locals banded together and persuaded police to shut down the office. In another neighborhood, residents used spotlights and video cameras to track visitors to a gang office. In Kyoto, residents took on local gangsters who had moved into their building and were blasting out walls and roughing up tenants. The angry apartment dwellers filed suit to force the gang to give up ownership of the complex. But the gangs would not go quietly, as pachinko parlor operators found in the early 1990s. A move by the parlors to cut yakuza ties resulted in threats and violence, including one operator finding a bloodied pig head in her doorway one morning. Another much publicized battle erupted in the late 1980s in Hamamatsu, about fifty miles from where the legendary Jirocho of Shimizu once held sway. Locals tried to evict a Yamaguchi-gumi gang from a fortress-like office building just up the street from an elementary school. After two years of violence, lawsuits, and protest, the citizens' group won, but the costs were high. The group's chief lawyer had been stabbed in the back with a fruit knife; others had their homes set afire or smashed up with a baseball bat. Never short of chutzpah, the yakuza even sued the local residents for "mental anguish."

Reaction to the gangs reached a peak with the 1992 release of *Minbo no Onna* (The extortion lady), a movie mocking the yakuza's work as jiageya and shakedown specialists. The film, by Japan's brilliant, satirical director Juzo Itami, portrayed a hard-boiled female lawyer and the timid staff of a major hotel trying to dislodge a tough gang from their property. Unlike the Robin Hood–like images depicted by earlier films, Itami showed the yakuza as crude thugs and bullies. Much to the delight of audiences nationwide, it also made the gangsters look like fools who would back down if only the public stood up.

It was too much for the gangs. One week after the movie's release, Itami was brutally attacked in a parking lot near his home by a half-dozen yakuza. The gangsters slashed wounds two inches deep on his face and arms. From his hospital bed, Itami was unbowed and called for a citizens' revolt against the underworld. Police, meanwhile, traced a car at the scene to the Goto-gumi, a three-hundred-man gang tied to the Yamaguchi-gumi. A raid of Goto-gumi headquarters in central Japan found a six-and-a-half-foot Japanese bear, locked in a cage, and a dozen Tosa dogs, a fierce Japanese fighting breed akin to a pit bull. Five gang members were eventually charged for the attack and received jail terms of four to six years.

The repercussions of Itami's movie continued for months. A former Sumiyoshi-kai boss, Soichi Konoike, went on TV and suggested the attack was not worthy of the yakuza. "Had the attackers been gangsters, they would have waged a more thorough attack, such as killing him or forcing him to apologize for the film," Konoike said. Days later, Konoike himself was the victim of a drive-by shooting while out walking his dog. Nor was Itami's work spared. When his next movie appeared in May 1993, a young rightist mounted the stage and slashed a twenty-nine-foot rip in the screen with a samurai sword.

A New Law in Town

As the yakuza's extraordinary reach grew clearer, top NPA officials eventually concluded that stronger measures were indeed called for. The billion-dollar scandals, the pervasive corruption, the yakuza's constant harassment and bloody gang wars all had taken their toll. For nearly three centuries, the yakuza have existed in a kind of social contract with the Japanese people— they were allowed to ply their vice crimes and fight their gang wars, as long as the *katagi no shu*, the common people, were not too deeply affected. But it was clear the contract had broken down as the gangs had grown in political and economic power.

What Japan's top police bureaucrats came up with was titled the Law Concerning Prevention of Unjust Acts by Boryokudan Members—perhaps better translated as the Organized Crime Countermeasures Act. Enacted in 1991, it is an unusual law, deemed "uniquely Japanese" by one of its proud authors at the NPA. Many of its provisions are vague and aimed at gray areas that authorities had found tough to control, such as the yakuza's endless extortion schemes. The new law set up a series of prefectural public safety commissions that can formally designate yakuza gangs as crime syndicates; the commissions can then issue desist orders for certain crimes and order punishment.

The law bans eleven types of racketeering activities, among them collecting protection fees and other extortionate acts, demanding contracts and loans from businesses, and working as jiageya, loan sharks, and "incident specialists." A 1993 revision expanded the measure's reach, addressing more of the fallout from the Bubble's collapse. The gangs were prohibited from disrupting auctions and from demanding that companies and brokers sell discounted shares or offer credit. It also barred gangs from stopping members from quitting by demanding money or severed fingers, and from forcing juvenile recruits to be tattooed.

The law was not without its critics. Much of what it attacks was already illegal, and the law's scope and penalties are relatively limited. Japanese officials had studied stronger anti-racketeering statutes in Italy and the United States, but opted not to incorporate measures that could target entire criminal organizations. The new law, for example, lacks the tough penalties and conspiracy laws behind America's RICO statute (the Racketeer Influence and Corrupt Organization Act), which allow officials to indict the leadership of a crime syndicate as a "continuing criminal enterprise." Nor does it target mob finances, provide for asset seizure, or offer witness protection. Nonetheless, the law was something of a breakthrough for Japanese law enforcement. For the first time, Japan had a legal definition of yakuza crime syndicates, a law that identified these groups as a social evil, and special measures with which to rein them in.

The yakuza reacted to the law in true form: they staged public protests and filed lawsuits. Mob bosses testified at hearings on the law, claiming the statute was discriminatory and interfered with their civil rights. In Kobe, the Yamaguchi-gumi's number two man, Masaru Takumi, complained that the new law violated the constitutional guarantee of freedom of assembly. In Tokyo, Sumiyoshi-kai president Shigeo Nishiguchi said his organization was actually not a criminal gang at all, but "a group that values the traditional Japanese virtue of a chivalrous spirit." A 1992 demonstration even featured yakuza wives and girlfriends, complete with placards and chants. Read one sign: "The husband may be a yakuza, but his wife and child are not criminals!" Groups from Japan's far right joined with those from the far left in a strange alliance against the law. Mobbed-up fronts like the Chivalrous Citizens' Union attended rallies and hearings with leftists like the Action Faction and the ultranationalist Issui-kai.

At first the new law appeared to have a dramatic impact. Police trumpeted reports of thousands of yakuza members retiring and scores of gangs disbanding. Newspapers ran stories about doctors removing tattoos and transplanting little toes to replace severed pinkies. Other reports featured reformed mobsters organizing groups like the "Council to Return Gangsters to Society" and even born-again yakuza finding Christ. But as is so often the case in Japan, the private reality proved rather different from the public face.

The new law did succeed in driving tens of thousands of mobsters out of their gang headquarters and off official gang rolls. But most did not leave the underworld; they merely shifted into harder-to-track associate and freelance roles. The law did help pare down overall numbers of yakuza by some 10,000, according to police statistics. By 1994, however, gang membership had stabilized at 80,000; nearly half were now designated "associates." These yakuza fellow-travelers were soon responsible for more crimes and arrests than "made" members.

Similarly, the news that many gangs were disbanding was no cause for celebration. Most of the groups were small and inconsequential. The new law had the unintended consequence of actually strengthening the big syndicates, which offered the legal and financial resources to withstand the challenges posed by authorities. The three most influential yakuza groups— Yamaguchi-gumi, Inagawa-kai, and Sumiyoshi-kai—increased their share of made members from 45 to 65 percent of all yakuza.

The big syndicates were well prepared by the time the law came into effect. The Yamaguchi-gumi issued members a manual entitled *How to Evade the New Law* and faxed instructions to its 116 affiliated gangs to set up corporations. Other syndicates used a similar strategy, and soon hundreds of new front companies were incorporated across Japan. Ownership of gang headquarters, local offices, and the homes of godfathers was transferred to the new companies. The doorplate outside the Yamaguchi-gumi's main office was changed to read Yamaki (Shining Mountain) Corporation, a company purportedly involved in real estate, golf club management, and artwork. The plaque outside the Inagawa-kai's headquarters now read Inagawa Industries. One gang, the Ono-gumi, incorporated as a cultural center, wedding hall, funeral parlor, retirement home, construction business, and real estate company. Their real business, according to Osaka police, was drugs. Another group, the Towa-kai, incorporated as a sports facility operator and a trading company for cosmetics and oils. And the yakuza fell back on their old standby, registering as right-wing political parties. One gang even took over a defunct religious organization, the Church of Peace and Morals, and installed its godfather as chief priest.

While the anti-yakuza law undoubtedly has had some harassment value, it also backfired in serious ways. The consolidation of the big syndicates was one development, but some experts believe the crackdown also gave the gangs new incentive to explore opportunities overseas, particularly in Asia. Perhaps most important, the law has driven much gang activity underground and made intelligence gathering more difficult. Yakuza bosses vowed to halt any cooperation with officials, including the old tradition of turning over killers to police. Combined with the jump in associate members and front companies, this change brought Japan's very public crime syndicates a giant step closer to their more private cousins in Sicily and America.

As Japan's stubborn recession persisted into the twenty-first century, its yakuza godfathers had more on their minds than anti-racketeering laws. "The members have had some trouble because of this law," a Yamaguchi-gumi boss told the newspaper *Asahi*. "But the crash of the economy has been a much bigger problem." Indeed, the yakuza faced the same dilemmas as the rest of Japanese business: how to restructure and regain their momentum. The easy money and fast life of the Bubble years were gone. Revenues from such traditional yakuza pursuits as gambling and extortion also were down. One study found that the nation's underground economy had shrunk by one-third between 1991 and 1999. The downsizing prompted by the anti-gang legislation was probably overdue, as the big syndicates, fed by the Bubble, had grown top-heavy. Bosses needed to retire and be replaced by a younger, leaner generation. Recognizing the loss in revenue, top syndicates slashed their demands for tribute money from affiliated gangs; the Yamaguchi-gumi cut its monthly levy by 50 percent to a bargain $10,000 each month. One boss, desperate for new members, simply advertised in a Yokohama paper for "drivers and general clerks," and picked up twenty new members that way. Few could have doubted the nature of their new jobs; outside the group's office hung a paper lantern inscribed with the words "Okamoto Gang."

What the yakuza needed most, though, were new markets and new profit centers. The post-Bubble years offered their own opportunities. There was big money to be made not only in shaking down real estate deals, but in handling bankruptcies and debt collection. Authorities pointed to an epidemic of loan sharks targeting small and medium-sized companies desperate for credit. Takeovers of indebted companies became a specialty. Gangs would buy the notes on a bad debt, forgive the loan, and then extend their own credit to the borrower. When their own loans weren't repaid, the yakuza's own "executives" showed up to take charge.

Clearly the gangs weren't going away. Police statistics for 1994 give an idea as to the continuing scope of yakuza business. That year, authorities brought cases against 279 mob fronts—more than half of them owned by the Yamaguchi-gumi. The largest number were in construction, followed by finance and insurance, restaurants, wholesale and retail, real estate, sex, transportation, waste disposal, and manufacturing. Some yakuza members returned to the gangs' most durable money makers: amphetamines and prostitution. Offices staffed by ex-yakuza "incident specialists" multiplied, many disguised as trading or advertising companies. On the northern island of Hokkaido, police tied some seventy fires to an arson-for-profit ring run by a local gang. But the yakuza's biggest money maker through the 1990s may well have been the Japanese government. Throughout the decade, Japan tried to spend its way out of recession, largely through a massive program of public works projects. In what has been called the largest program of its kind, between 1991 and 2000 the government spent a whopping $3.5 trillion on public works projects. Such projects, of course, are among the yakuza's favorite lines of work. By one estimate, some 30 to 50 percent of all public works projects involve gang payoffs. Given that the yakuza routinely skim between 1 and 5 percent of these contracts, this suggests that at a minimum, the gangs raked in $10.5 billion, and possibly as much as $87.5 billion.

Godfathers and gangs that had made killings in the stock and real estate markets—and held onto those assets—waited for the economy to revive. Among the more intriguing questions left by the Bubble's collapse was what happened to the $10 billion worth of artwork sold to the Japanese. Much of it was reportedly sold off at a fraction of the previous price, but many pieces apparently ended up in the hands of the yakuza, stored away in gangland basements or on display at the boss's home. A 1992 FBI report provided one hint. "When Gekkoso, a famous Ginza art gallery, went bankrupt recently," the report noted, "most of its nearly one hundred world-famous oil paintings were purchased by a Tokyo gallery affiliated with the Sumiyoshi Rengo Kai." Some masterpieces may not be seen again for years. The notorious sarakin Yasumichi Morishita lost his $1 billion collection when his Aichi Finance went belly up in 1997. The paintings will probably be tied up in Japanese courts for years, for the wily Morishita allegedly used them as collateral—twice. Less is known about the fate of Picasso's *Les Noces de Pierrette*. Bought for $53 million in 1989 by Tomonori Tsurumaki, a property tycoon who went bankrupt in 1993, the painting was later rumored to be in the hands of the yakuza.

Stubborn Sokaiya

While their yakuza brothers were hijacking companies and fleecing construction contracts, the sokaiya were staying busy, as well. After the Bubble-era scandals, many thought that huge corporate payoffs to the underworld would end. The onslaught of shootings and murders in the early 1990s, however, ensured that the sokaiya could not be so easily dismissed. One sign came with news of a Tokyo banquet in 1991, hosted by a top sokaiya. In attendance, according to the newspaper *Asahi*, were seventy racketeers and representatives of top firms, including Asahi Beer, Kirin Beer, and Mitsubishi Materials.

A year later, an assassination attempt on power broker Shin Kanemaru led police to Seiwa-kai, a rightist group deeply implicated in sokaiya activity. A raid on the group's office revealed that 103 companies were paying some $20,000 annually in subscription fees. Police ordered the companies to stop. Two years later, in a blackmail case, Tokyo cops again raided the group. Searching through account books, they found that the payments had actually gone up, to $25,000, from eighty firms.

Respected companies with reputations for disclosure and sound management were being caught red-handed. In 1992, the spotlight fell on Ito-Yokado Company, owner of 7-Eleven convenience stores in the U.S. and the most profitable retailer in Japan. Company executives reportedly paid sokaiya nearly $220,000 at meetings in an exclusive restaurant, an elevator, and a public toilet. Next to be implicated were officials of Kirin Brewery, who were arrested for handing the racketeers nearly $300,000. Clearly there was still money to be made shaking down Japan's largest companies. A 1994 investigation by Tokyo police found 730 sokaiya holding stock in nearly 12,000 companies. With so much scandal in the air, the gangs intensified their digging for dirt. In 1993, the Yamaguchi-gumi set up a "financial research association" overseen by a dozen top bosses. The syndicate issued a nationwide directive to gang members: identify local financial institutions, develop informants, and gather compromising material.

The scandals, the anti-gang law, the cleanup of the bad loans—none of these had fundamentally changed the course of Japanese organized crime. Before the Bubble, the yakuza already were modernizing, becoming more business-like and sophisticated. Having had a taste of high finance, the gangs weren't going back to the way it was before. Nowhere was that clearer than in the case of a Tokyo sokaiya named Ryuichi Koike.

Ryuichi Koike made his sokaiya debut at age twenty-eight. It was 1971, and he had joined up with Kaoru Ogawa, whose notorious Ogawa Group ranked among the top sokaiya gangs. One of Koike's teachers in the extortion trade had worked as an aide to Yoshio Kodama himself, so Koike was no doubt well schooled. That first year he was arrested for causing a melee at the Oji Paper Company shareholders' meeting, and worked for Mitsubishi Heavy Industries roughing up students who protested the firm's weapons contracts. By 1975, the young sokaiya already had made his mark. In May that year, Koike held one of the sokaiya's notorious "parties," to which invited businessmen are expected to bring cash gifts. Koike's gathering attracted no fewer than six hundred executives from 450 leading companies. Police estimated that the young sokaiya raked in more than $100,000 that night. Koike was unable to attend his own party, however. He had been arrested earlier that day—for threatening to kill the president of a vinyl company. For that, Koike received a suspended sentence and was soon back out on the streets. Two years later, he set off on his own and opened the Koike Economic Institute.

Koike established ties to many of Japan's most prestigious companies: makers of electronics and heavy machinery, securities firms, banks. Like other racketeers, he prospered during the Bubble, but Mr. Koike is more notable for his later exploits. Five years after the Bubble's collapse, he managed to repeat what Susumu Ishii had done five years earlier: obtain a veritable fortune from Japan's top companies.

Koike's primary target was the Dai-Ichi Kangyo Bank. At the time DKB was the world's fifth-largest bank, with over $400 billion in assets. DKB officials were willing to pay a handsome price for Koike not to disrupt their shareholders' meetings. Koike wanted credit, and the bank meekly obliged. Between 1994 and 1996, Koike raked in over $100 million in loans from DKB—loans bank officials later admitted they knew might never be repaid. Koike then used that money to purchase shares in other companies to speculate and to shake down new managements. Among the firms he approached: the big four securities brokerages—Nomura, Nikko, Daiwa, and Yamaichi. The brokers, in turn, paid Koike more than $5 million not to disrupt their own meetings, and they allegedly arranged illegal stock deals for him.

Prosecutors did not charge Koike with the full amount he'd extorted, as the statute of limitations had run out. Press accounts reported DKB had made as many as eighty-four separate loans to Koike dating back to 1989. The full amount may well have reached an incredible $272 million.

The Japanese press and public found the news hard to believe. After all the scandals of the Bubble years, corporate Japan still had not learned. Even as taxpayers funded a trillion-dollar effort to break out of what some were calling a "yakuza recession," their nation's leading companies continued to pour huge sums into the pockets of organized crime. Authorities arrested more than a dozen officials from DKB and the big securities houses, the companies' board members resigned, and the stock market plunged.

The revelations were too much for DKB's former chairman, Kunji Miyazaki. After being questioned by police and seeing his colleagues arrested, Miyazaki hanged himself. The scandal also proved fatal for Yamaichi Securities. The once venerable, hundred-year-old brokerage was already reeling from Bubble-era losses. Eleven top executives, including the Yamaichi chairman and the president, resigned or had been arrested. Clouded by controversy, the firm found its customers staying away and short-term funding difficult to arrange. Mortally wounded, the firm collapsed later that year in postwar Japan's largest-ever bankruptcy.

But there was more. Threatened with a hefty jail term, Koike talked, and soon police and prosecutors were following a trail that led to a *Who's Who* of Japan, Inc. Within months of Koike's arrest, prosecutors revealed that Mitsubishi Motors and other Mitsubishi Group companies had funneled money to sokaiya to keep their meetings quiet. Tokyo police revealed that the sokaiya extorting Mitsubishi also were leeching money from Asahi Bank, Dai Nippon Printing, and at least six Hitachi Group companies. Other revelations showed that Japan Air Lines, Toyota, and Nissan had also paid off the gangs, as had Hitachi, Toshiba, and food-maker Ajinomoto.

Japan's top department stores, too, were implicated in paying millions of dollars to sokaiya. Daimaru, Takashimaya, Matsuzakaya—these huge retailers were household names in Japan. The revenues of upscale Takashimaya were higher than McDonald's or Federal Express. Affiliated finance companies of Takashimaya and Daimaru allegedly made loans of nearly $7 million each to a construction firm run by the boss of a local gang. Relations with the boss were so cozy that Takashimaya let him dole out nearly $1 million annually to various sokaiya groups, and the department store's president attended the wedding of his son.

The scandals revealed that even the nation's political leaders were paying off the gangs. Until exposed by the press in 1997, a group of LDP lawmakers in the Gifu prefectural assembly subscribed to "newsletters" published by sokaiya and rightist groups, including a $1,000 payment to an ultranationalist gang that had thrown a firebomb at the LDP's local headquarters.

The newsletters and scandal sheets were of course a favorite tool for extorting money, but the corporate payoffs were laundered in impressively diverse ways. Nomura Securities transferred fake profits into Koike's private account. Mitsubishi Motors rented a sokaiya-owned beach house that none of its employees dared use. Mitsubishi Electric and Asahi Glass bought overpriced ads in a magazine for a stewardess-training school—run by the wife of a sokaiya. Japan Air Lines, Toyota, and Nissan paid exorbitant fees for office plants from a sokaiya-run "leasing" company.

The sokaiya scandals lasted through the year. By the end of 1997, some ninety top executives of Japan's most powerful corporations had resigned; fifty were arrested. In the fall of that year, after yet another wave of arrests, an editorial in the newspaper *Mainichi* summed up popular sentiment: "What? Another racketeering scandal? More embarrassment? Another reason for the rest of the world to scoff at us?" If not scoffing, foreigners certainly were puzzling over the tolerance for organized crime shown by the Japanese. "No other industrialized economy has lived with corporate blackmail the way Japan has," wrote *Business Week* after surveying the sokaiya scandals. Mark West, a legal scholar at the University of Michigan, tried to sum up recent events for an American audience. "The nearest U.S. equivalent to the recent Japanese scandals," he wrote, "would be if directors and mangers of Citicorp, Ford, General Electric, Motorola, Intel, Sara Lee, Macy's, Bloomingdale's, Merrill Lynch, Lehman Brothers, Salomon Smith Barney, and Morgan Stanley were all arrested in the same year for paying members of the Gambino and Lucchese crime families to keep their shareholders' meetings short."

Police and prosecutors were applauded for finally cracking down. A handful of critics, though, noted that although investigators had gone after dozens of corporate executives, relatively few sokaiya had been arrested; most of the revelations stemmed from Koike and one other prominent sokaiya. Moreover, the penalties were benign, to say the least. Koike received a nine-month sentence and a $6 million fine. All of the executives found guilty received suspended sentences. Dai-Ichi Kangyo Bank was fined a mere $4,200 and banned from underwriting public bonds and from opening new branches or accounts until year's end. Contrast that with the $300 million fine levied against Drexel Burnham Lambert for insider trading and market-rigging in 1989, or the $290 million fine and two-month license suspension that Salomon Brothers received for trying to corner the government bond market in 1992.

The sokaiya scandals added to a growing sense of crisis within Japanese law enforcement. The much-vaunted anti-gang law had done nothing to stem the transfer of hundreds of millions of dollars from corporate Japan to the sokaiya. The yakuza's influence over business and government appeared unabated. Foreign crime syndicates, drug dealing, and alien smuggling all were on the rise. And the Aum sect's murderous six-year crime spree revealed that Japanese detectives sometimes lacked the most basic investigative skills.

Again, Japanese lawmen and legislators went to work on the legal code. First, in 1997 revisions were made to Japan's commercial code, to sections governing corporate crime. Penalties and fines were strengthened for both sokaiya and those who would pay them. That same year, the Organized Crime Countermeasures Act was revised for the second time. This time it made clear that gang activity would include yakuza associates and front companies. In 1998, regulatory oversight of the financial industry was stripped from the scandal-ridden Finance Ministry and vested in the new Financial Supervisory Agency.

Perhaps most significant for the yakuza, a major crime bill passed the Diet a year later, formally authorizing police to conduct electronic eavesdropping against organized crime. At the time, Japan was the only large industrialized nation without such a measure. Given the government's past abuses in spying on the left, the law was highly controversial and limited to only four areas of illegal activity: guns, drugs, murder conspiracy, and illegal alien smuggling. The new law also expanded the reach of Japan's money-laundering law beyond drug offenses to include some two hundred different crimes, and gave judges greater discretion to protect the relatives and associates of witnesses. Officials moved as well to create a financial intelligence unit to better monitor suspicious capital flows. Other reforms occurred within the National Police Agency. Japan's premier investigative agencies, the Tokyo and Osaka police departments, could now assist other prefectures on important cases. New units were established for international and computer crimes.

It was an impressive, if belated, show of resolve. Japanese law enforcement had joined the twentieth century just in time to greet the twenty-first.

How effectively the laws will be implemented remains a big question. Certainly in the case of the sokaiya, it is unclear whether the get-tough attitude will work. In a survey conducted after penalties were increased, 79 percent of auditors and 75 percent of managers said they would be unable to cut sokaiya ties within ten years. The sokaiya, moreover, weren't going to disappear. In one sign of the times, a sokaiya web page—www.sokaiya .com—enabled like-minded extortionists to discuss suitable targets and dish the latest dirt. More telling evidence, perhaps, came with two incidents as the 1990s drew to a close. In 1998, after Nomura Securities announced it was cutting all sokaiya ties, a top executive received a note with the words "Your grandson is very cute" and a map showing the boy's route to school. Equally chilling were the words of Koike's old boss, Kaoru Ogawa, to a Japan Air Lines shareholders' meeting in 1999. Shots had recently been fired at the home of JAL's former president, and company officials already were on edge. Ogawa claimed to have reformed himself into the Japanese Ralph Nader, but his tactics sounded disturbingly familiar: "If the management does not improve," he announced, "then bam, bam—there will be more shootings."

The ever-adaptable gangs, meanwhile, were not standing still. By the late 1990s, the yakuza were charting a move into high tech. Underworld characters with cash to loan became financiers for Japanese start-up companies, which lacked the kind of venture capital available to start-ups in America. Japan's Mothers stock exchange opened in 1999, offering a new arena for small companies to sell stock, but before long police had blocked several mob-tied start-ups from listing there. The case of Liquid Audio Japan, the first company listed on the new exchange, generated particular notoriety. The firm, which specialized in digital delivery of music over the Internet, was run by its dashing thirty-two-year-old president, Masafumi Okanda, who mixed easily with TV personalities and music producers. But Okanda's earlier career had been spent at a car sales firm tied to the yakuza, according to press reports, and he may have picked up some bad habits. In 2000, police arrested him for allegedly working with five other men to kidnap one of Liquid Audio Japan's former directors, who was planning a U.S. trip that might have threatened Okanada's hold on the firm. The man was hit in the face, blindfolded, handcuffed, and released in a forest two days later, said police, who also noted that Okanda kept business cards of top yakuza bosses on his desk. After the incident, Okanda's alleged victim quit the company and joined rival Digicube, where employees soon found bullet holes in a door at their headquarters. In court, Okanda admitted he disliked the man, but he claimed he was innocent of any kidnapping or assault. By now, though, the damage had been done to the reputation of Japan's Internet industry, and rumors swirled around the markets of other allegedly mobbed-up firms. Observed the newspaper *Asahi:* "Concerns about the entry of criminal elements into the new market have become a reality."

Indeed, from low-brow extortion to high-tech investment, the yakuza seemed well prepared for the millennium. If more proof was needed of the mob's staying power, it came with yet another revelation of yakuza involvement in the economy. In 1999, the press reported that Tadamasa Goto, boss of a top Yamaguchi-gumi gang, had bought a million shares in Japan Air Lines and had become its second-largest individual shareholder. The news seemed a fitting end to the decade. As the twentieth century drew to a close, Asia's largest airline counted among its top investors the Yamaguchi-gumi.

PART IV

THE MOVE ABROAD

CHAPTER NINE

METH, MONEY, AND THE SEX TRADE

POLICE OUTSIDE OF JAPAN WERE PUZZLED. FOR YEARS, THEIR COUNTERPARTS in Japan refused to admit what seemed patently obvious: the yakuza had gone international. Since the late 1960s, Japanese mobsters had popped up from Paris to Paraguay, New York to Hong Kong. They were engaged in a growing number of rackets ranging from money laundering to extortion and gunrunning. Yet in the 1980s, asked by foreigners how many yakuza were operating abroad, the NPA's official answer was simple: there were none. Japanese officials rationalized their statements by simply declaring that all those who had left the country for extended periods were no longer "registered members" of their respective syndicates.

This was a face-saving gesture. After the hard knocks Japan's proud police force had taken, it must have been difficult to admit that their nation's worst crime problem—the yakuza—was being exported alongside television sets and automobiles. Japanese law enforcement gradually earned a reputation among foreign police for a wariness and lack of cooperation that left more than one overseas cop frustrated. The NPA did not open its first center for gathering foreign criminal intelligence until 1987. "The main intelligence on yakuza overseas is from diplomats posted abroad and from foreign diplomats in Japan," confided a top NPA official in 1995. "There is no intelligence system at the national or prefectural level."

The results of all this were far-reaching. Japanese law enforcement's delay in checking the international expansion of the yakuza helped ensure that underworld connections were made for much more than smuggling guns, drugs, and other contraband. By the mid-1970s, it was already apparent that the yakuza had made some very powerful friends outside Japan, both economically and politically. By the 1980s, it was clear that Japanese gangs were becoming a major force in a new era of global organized crime.

The yakuza had ventured abroad earlier in their history. In the 1920s and 1930s, during the heyday of ultranationalism, Japanese gangsters joined with rightist groups like the Black Dragon Society in raising havoc across mainland Asia. And, during the war, they went to China and helped pillage the continent, paying special attention to the opium trade. But in the postwar era, the yakuza were relatively late in exploring opportunities overseas, compared to their criminal cousins in the Sicilian Mafia and Chinese triads. The move abroad finally began in the late 1960s. Through much of that decade, as the Japanese economy grew into a world power, the yakuza kept to the homeland, feuding over territory and sharing in the riches of an increasingly affluent Japan. The first big push abroad would hit a nation nearby that already had borne the brunt of Japan's dark side: the Republic of Korea. Ethnic Koreans in Japan, a poorly treated minority, had joined the gangs in substantial numbers. As Japan and Korea normalized relations, these gang members opened the criminal doors to their homeland. The results would affect the future not only of Korean crime, but of Korean politics as well.

The Kim Kidnapping

A worried look seemed permanently drawn on the face of Kim Dae Jung. It was the summer of 1973, and the future president of South Korea was acting like a fugitive. Kim had become the leading opposition figure in the repressive world of South Korean politics; his demands for democracy had earned him worldwide recognition, but that hadn't stopped the often violent attacks of the Korean government. It didn't matter where Kim traveled: Korea, Japan, the United States. At each stop, it seemed, there were government-hired goons following him, breaking up his political rallies, preventing him from reaching appointments with key supporters. For three years this had gone on. Kim had just arrived in Tokyo from the United States, and the harassment was now intense. Every public gathering seemed a target of these government squads—criminal gangs of ethnic Koreans who since the war had gained a permanent place among the Japanese yakuza.

Kim's major sin was to have challenged Korea's strongman, Park Chung Hee, in a 1971 presidential election, a contest that Park won, it is widely acknowledged, only through massive government fraud and manipulation. Even after the election, the immensely popular Kim remained a major headache for the Park regime, as he toured the United States and Japan speaking out for human rights and democracy in Korea. It was no accident that, just after the election, a large truck smashed into Kim's car, killing three people and causing Kim serious hip injuries that left him with a severe and permanent limp. Korean officials later acknowledged that the attack was the work of the regime's notorious KCIA—the Korean Central Intelligence Agency.

The KCIA, established in the wake of Park's 1961 coup d'etat, had become the most feared means of repression wielded against South Korea's 35 million people. The organization employed more than 100,000 agents, according to some estimates, and its influence extended to every walk of Korean life. Few doubted the allegations of torture, kidnapping, and murder made against the corrupt agency. The KCIA, bluntly put, was an instrument of terror unleashed against any Korean who dared to challenge the authoritarian rule of Park Chung Hee.

Following the 1971 election, as Kim predicted, Park issued an emergency decree, abandoned the constitution, and placed the nation under martial law. Kim, who was out of Korea at that time, decided that to return home at this point would be risking death. Instead, the forty-nine-year-old politician sought audiences with influential figures in the United States and Japan, and addressed overseas Korean groups regarding the dangers he saw awaiting his country. His demands for democracy and free elections only incensed the Park regime even further. By 1973, Kim was gaining more international attention and prestige than ever, and in July of that year he was invited to Tokyo to address a powerful group within the LDP.

"When I arrived in Tokyo," Kim recalled, "my friends warned that Korean yakuza members were seeking to hurt me, so they asked me to be careful. They said there was some kind of plot against my life, and that they had received the information from sources close to the yakuza. The Koreans in the yakuza had a strong connection with Mindan [the South Korean residents' association] and with the KCIA."

Kim took the advice to heart. Upon his arrival in Tokyo, he led the life of a fugitive. Every two to three days he changed hotels, using false Japanese names to avoid his enemies. But on August 8, 1973, the KCIA finally caught up with him.

At about 11 A.M. on that day, Kim knocked on room 2211 of Tokyo's Grand Palace Hotel. He was there to meet with a fellow opposition politician, Yang Il Tong, then in Japan for medical treatment. About two hours later, Kim left the room and headed into the hallway for the elevator. Suddenly, six or seven powerfully built young men appeared in the corridor, shoved Kim into an adjacent room, beat him, and pushed a cloth saturated with anesthetic onto his face. Four of the men then dragged him into an elevator and down to a waiting car in the hotel basement. For the next five to six hours, still conscious despite the drug, Kim was kicked in the stomach and forced to kneel down in the back of the car with his mouth stuffed and his face held against his assailants' laps. Evading police roadblocks, the kidnappers stopped near Osaka, where they bandaged with masking tape first Kim's hands and feet, then his face so thoroughly that only his nose showed through. Shoving their prize into a second car, they drove for at least an hour to the oceanside.

It was an elaborate, well-planned abduction. Kim was placed aboard a small motorboat, which sped from Japanese waters, and then he was transferred to a larger, more powerful vessel. As the ship moved farther out to sea, Kim—still bound, gagged, and blindfolded—had weights tied to his hands and feet and heard crewmen talking of how to ensure that his body would never rise to the surface. A devout Catholic, Kim began saying his final prayers.

Suddenly, a helicopter or plane appeared overhead, causing a great deal of commotion among the crew. After considerable debate, Kim's abductors unexpectedly removed the weights and loosened his bonds. Apparently, someone had changed the day's agenda. Most observers credit rapid actions by outraged U.S. and Japanese officials with saving Kim's life that evening.

The next day the ship landed somewhere in South Korea, and after another journey by road, switching cars twice, they arrived in Seoul. There Kim was held for two days and, still blindfolded, finally released at night about sixty-five yards from his home. The Korean government welcomed Kim back by placing him under house arrest and subjecting him to years of persecution, including a jail term and a death sentence nearly carried out by President Park's successor, Chun Doo Hwan.

Shortly after the abduction, Tokyo police tied the kidnapping to the KCIA. At the kidnapping site, investigators found the fingerprints of Kim Dong Woon, first secretary of the Korean embassy and believed to be the Tokyo-area KCIA director. They further identified one of the getaway cars, tracing it to the Korean vice-consul in Yokohama. Japanese officials believed that as many as four groups were involved, totaling twenty to twenty-six men. Reports from former government officials in both the United States and Korea would later confirm KCIA involvement at the highest levels, and implicate President Park himself. What never became clear, though, was the widely suspected role played by leading members of the yakuza. Japanese officials have not been anxious to shed light on the controversy. Twenty years after the abduction, police were still questioning Kim about what happened.

At the center of suspicion stood Hisayuki Machii, said to be the most powerful Korean yakuza in Japan. Machii—blood brother to late Yamaguchi-gumi boss Kazuo Taoka, oyabun of Tokyo's notorious Tosei-kai and close ally of Yoshio Kodama—was the leader of a whole generation of Korean gangsters operating in Japan since the war. A report in the respected *Far Eastern Economic Review* cited "informed sources" who had "clearly identified a big Korean operator in Japan, Chong Gwon Yong, alias Hisayuki Machii . . . as a leading participant in the abduction" of Kim. Machii's alleged role was to have "leased" virtually the entire hotel floor from which

Kim was taken, and made the rooms available to the KCIA. These allegations were never proven. The suspicions were enough, though, to have prompted *Newsweek* Tokyo bureau chief Bernard Krisher to wire his home office: "Machii . . . appears to have been behind the Kim Dae Jung kidnapping, having worked closely with the Korean CIA, but no Japanese newspaper has been willing to run this, for Machii's henchmen don't hesitate to torture or even kill their detractors."

Two other prominent ethnic Korean gangs in the yakuza have been implicated in connection with the kidnapping—both reportedly part of the Yamaguchi-gumi. One of them, the Yanagawa-gumi, headed by Jiro Yanagawa, is of particular interest, as the gang boss reportedly played a key role in leaking to the Japanese press a defamatory report on Kim from the Korean government. According to journalist Takao Goto, a Japanese expert on the Kim kidnapping, it is likely that Yanagawa—like other underworld characters in Japan—obtained contacts in Korea through one key man: Yoshio Kodama.

The close links between Korean intelligence and the mob were readily apparent to those who investigated at any length. In 1978, Pharis Harvey, then a Tokyo-based consultant to the Christian Conference of Asia, researched the KCIA's connections in Japan at the request of the U.S. House Subcommittee on International Organizations. This was the high tide of America's "Koreagate" scandal. Congressional hearings were focusing on influence peddling and harassment in the United States by the KCIA and such friends as Tongsun Park and Sun Myung Moon. Harvey came away convinced that the "KCIA and the Korean yakuza were certainly intermingled, so it was never certain what was an official KCIA initiative and what was from a mobster organization."

If the yakuza were making deals with the KCIA, it was not wholly surprising to seasoned observers in Japan or Korea. The yakuza were merely continuing a tradition that stretches back to the nineteenth century.

The Korean Connection

The relationship between Japan and Korea has been a complex and often tragic one. Geography alone ensured that the history of these two peoples would be intertwined. Separated by as little as 120 miles across the Korean Strait and Sea of Japan, these two economic powers of Asia have come to a mutually beneficial, if at times uneasy, truce. Great animosity remains between Koreans and Japanese, dating back at least to the 1895 assassination of the Korean queen by members of the Dark Ocean Society. That murder helped create the pretext for Tokyo to order an invasion of Korea; the Japanese would not leave until their defeat by the Allied powers in 1945. During their forty years of occupation, the Japanese ruled ruthlessly over Korea.

By 1945, hundreds of thousands of Koreans had been shipped to Japan for forced labor.

Many Koreans who stayed in Japan after the war turned to the black markets and organized crime, forming gangs that were eventually absorbed into the larger Japanese syndicates. The yakuza, in fact, have been among the few institutions to open their doors to the Koreans in Japan. Even second- and third-generation Korean Japanese, most of whom speak Japanese far better than they speak Korean, suffer severe discrimination in employment, housing, and education. Although the majority of Japan's nearly 700,000 ethnic Koreans were born in Japan, they are legally still considered aliens.

Such conditions have driven large numbers of Korean Japanese into the yakuza, with some surprising effects. As Japan and South Korea finally moved toward normalized diplomatic relations in the mid-1960s, among those ready to act as intermediaries were top Korean yakuza bosses in Japan. Perhaps the most successful of those Korean bosses was the man thought by many to have been involved in Kim Dae Jung's kidnapping, Hisayuki Machii.

Machii was born in Japanese-occupied Korea in 1923 and lived in Japan a number of times before settling there permanently after the war. The son of a small-time steel merchant, he was a college dropout who felt more at home on the streets than in the classroom. As soon as the Occupation began, he moved into the lucrative black market activity and just as quickly ran afoul of the law. He was charged with one murder and was believed to have committed at least one other, but managed to avoid any time in prison for the alleged crimes.

Machii formed Tosei-kai (Voice of the East Gang) in 1948, a largely Korean band of yakuza. It was during these tumultuous postwar years that he and his men seized control of Tokyo's famed Ginza entertainment district. So thoroughly did Tosei-kai run the area that they were known as the Ginza Police, and undoubtedly they outnumbered the district's civil police in manpower and strength. Machii himself became known as the Ginza Tiger and the Ox, among other titles. He and his gang supplied concessions to the burgeoning, pinball-like pachinko industry, and soon moved on to control restaurants and bars. Police also suspect that the Tosei-kai moved into the booming methamphetamine trade in the early years, never to let go.

Machii also capitalized on his status as a non-Japanese to make connections under the Occupation. He served American authorities as a strike-breaker and an anti-Communist thug. Through the U.S. Army's Counter Intelligence Corps, Machii was reportedly introduced to Yoshio Kodama, and the two men began a long and mutually profitable relationship. Machii, in fact, became close to a number of prominent rightists. A common enemy,

Communism, plus the chance to make money, did much to smooth over race relations.

Later, Machii would claim that Tosei-kai had never been more than a political strong-arm group. "As some of our members broke the law, the police referred to us as gangsters," he told the newsweekly *Shukan Shincho*. Machii was not arguing a point; he was lying. Between 1946 and 1958 Machii would be arrested ten times, for crimes ranging from extortion and fraud to robbery and assault; he received three prison sentences, but served very little time. Some Japanese journalists believe Machii's early luck with the law was due to his work with G-2 in strikebreaking and attacking leftists. As for his Korean gangsters, they were hardly angelic either: in 1964 Tokyo police raided the Ginza headquarters of the Tosei-kai and found a sizable cache of firearms and explosives. The newspaper *Mainichi* called the gang "one of the most feared and strongest underworld organizations."

Machii paid special attention to the problems of Koreans in Japan. Placing his gang at the disposal of key leaders, he quickly became a major power within Japan's Korean community. Machii's role became even more pronounced during the Korean War, as Koreans in Japan fought violently over which Korea to support. Two groups grew out of the turmoil in Japan: Chongnyon, supporting Communist North Korea; and Mindan, supporting South Korea. Machii, of course, threw in his lot with the staunchly anti-Communist Mindan, and through his work of providing bodyguards began to meet agents of the KCIA.

By 1960, Machii had built up his Tosei-kai to some 1,500 members. Although it never rivaled the other major syndicates in sheer numbers, it achieved prominence through ferocity, position, and connections. Among Machii's connections was Yoshio Kodama, who recruited his Korean friend for the yakuza army being massed to protect Eisenhower during the 1960 security treaty disturbances. Later, under Kodama's auspices, Machii would befriend former prime minister Kishi and forge an alliance with Kazuo Taoka that would allow the Yamaguchi-gumi to move into Tokyo. It was Machii, again, who served as "auditor" of the yakuza-ridden Japan Pro-Wrestling Entertainment Company, with Taoka as vice-chairman and Kodama as chairman. Kodama was good for other matters, too. By investing with Kodama in a series of highly questionable real estate deals, Machii would become an extremely wealthy man.

In 1965, stung by police crackdowns, Machii formally disbanded his infamous Tosei-kai, but he immediately founded a "legitimate" successor organization, the Towa Yuai Jigyo Kumiai (East Asia Friendship Enterprises Association). Two years earlier, he had formed Towa Sogo Kigyo (East Asia Enterprises Company), with Kodama as chairman of the board, and out of these two organizations Machii would build a financial empire.

It was at about this time that Machii's foreign diplomacy ventures blossomed, with help again from Kodama. The ever-present kuromaku and Machii reportedly played an active role in promoting approval of the Republic of Korea–Japan Normalization Treaty, which mandated Japanese reparations to Korea and restored full diplomatic relations. Thanks to this new alliance, Machii and Kodama were soon meeting with leading Korean politicians, and finally with President Park himself, who apparently liked what he saw. With the blessings of Park, and the help of such friends as Kishi and Kodama, in 1970 Machii won control of the major ferry line between Pusan, South Korea, and Shimanoseki, Japan—the heavily traveled shortest route between the two countries.

By now Machii had become what one Japanese weekly called "a political merchant," a kuromaku of Japanese-Korean relations. Since the treaty normalizing relations between the two countries, Japanese businessmen were swarming into Korea, and vast amounts of graft, political contributions, and questionable payments of all sorts flowed both ways across the Sea of Japan. Machii set up new clubs and cabarets in Seoul and refurbished old ones in Tokyo; they would serve as meeting places for top Korean and Japanese officials, providing all the comforts available in an exotic "hostess" bar. While Machii was hobnobbing with the powerful, though, his gang members were still plying their traditional trades, now in both countries, enough so that Japanese officials considered the Towa Yuai Jigyo Kumiai one of the nation's top ten yakuza syndicates.

On a summer evening in 1973, Machii staged the gala opening of his new TSK-CCC (Celebrities' Choice Clubs), a multi-million-dollar reception at his new seven-story entertainment complex in Tokyo's fashionable Roppongi district. More than twenty-five star entertainers and sports figures celebrated his lavish new facility along with 7,000 other people, among them corporation presidents, the head of the Tokyo Bar Association, and a leading editor of the huge *Yomiuri* newspaper. Machii had made it big. TSK-CCC featured high-class restaurants, cabarets, discos, saunas imported from Finland, a Beverly Hills beauty salon, and much more. Machii, it was reported, had personally overseen the design of each room. Membership in TSK-CCC featured access to sixteen "deluxe private clubs" in Tokyo's Ginza. In addition, a giant recreation center for members was in the works, including a ski area, a thirty-six-hole golf course, an amusement park, and a housing development. The cost to get in on the ground floor of Machii's venture was a mere $700 per person, $1,900 per company. The genial Korean host called his creation "an oasis in the desert of dry, contemporary human relationships."

Machii, by now fifty, had become the archetypal refined syndicate boss. A multi-millionaire with a taste for Picasso and fine antique porcelain, he had taken TSK into entertainment, restaurants, real estate, tourism, even oil. Some 1,500 employees worked under him, from the operators of the Pusan ferry to the Korean "hostesses" in his bars. But there were storm clouds gathering.

On the same day in 1976 that Yoshio Kodama hobbled into his first and only Lockheed court appearance, TSK-CCC went bankrupt. In fact, Machii's dream collapsed in the wake of revelations spilling over from investigations of the Lockheed scandal and of Kodama. Saddled with a $72 million debt, TSK could no longer meet the payroll; the press, meanwhile, began asking pointed questions about the company's odd financial transactions. Of particular interest was the 1969 sale of vast tracts of land from Machii's planned giant recreation center. TSK's own directors admitted that Kodama had forced the company to sell the land at far below market cost to a favored company, then apparently embezzled more than $3.3 million of the money in a subsequent deal.

Despite his losses, by the mid-1980s the Ginza Tiger still wielded considerable power in both Japan and South Korea. Although he would "retire" from his Towa Yuai organization, he was still honorary director of the syndicate, a fact not lost on authorities when Machii's investments expanded beyond East Asia. Machii's old gang caught the attention of U.S. authorities, who noted the group's "extensive involvement in drug trafficking." In a 1992 report, the FBI called Towa Yuai "a virtual enigma" because of its small size (850 members) coupled with its extraordinary reach—into some twenty prefectures in Japan and abroad.

Hisayuki Machii's greatest legacy may well be helping to criminalize his homeland. Thanks to the Korean boss's diplomacy, South Korea became a yakuza playground, refuge, and investment center. Fugitives from Japanese justice would steal across the Sea of Japan, hiding out in the coastal cities of Korea until the heat passed. Syndicates like the Inagawa-kai set up casinos and arranged high-stakes gambling tours of the country, shaking down corporate executives in cooperation with their new Korean friends. In major cities like Seoul and Pusan, money was laundered in the traditional yakuza "water trades" of bars, cabarets, and restaurants. By autumn of 1974, the Inagawa-kai was busily gaining a foothold in construction by setting up a gravel business on the large southern island of Cheju, a Korean province long popular as a resort. And all the major syndicates appeared to have their fingers in two key areas: prostitution and drugs.

Despite the presence of so many Koreans within the yakuza, establishing the Korean connection was not always easy, due largely to the different characteristics of organized crime in Korea. Until Korea's democratization in the late 1980s, criminal gangs there were small and limited in scope. An unwritten rule appears to prevail in highly authoritarian societies: organized crime is successful only when the government allows it to be. As one knowledgeable U.S. official in Seoul noted in 1984, "Between the KCIA, the civil police, and military intelligence, you've got such a powerful security state here that it's impossible for organized crime to operate without official sanction. If it exists, it's state-sponsored or state-sanctioned."

Instead of large syndicates, small crime rings arose, and these formed the hard core of the yakuza's Korean connection. These enterprising bands, comprising from five to twenty-five people, took their chances in smuggling, the black market, pickpocketing. Their gang names came from hometown cities, smuggling boats, or whatever struck their fancy: names like Seoulpa, Pusanpa, and Insonghopa. The black market was an especially lucrative niche, fueled by the presence of 40,000 American GIs. One PX on a U.S. base, according to embassy officials, actually sold more merchandise than the combined salaries of its customers. Controls on imports also encouraged widespread smuggling of everything from electronics to Chinese medicine. Korean officials were too often on the receiving end of these deals to seriously consider cracking down.

As Korean society liberalized, the nature of organized crime changed. Korean crime syndicates grew larger and more sophisticated—and, perhaps not surprisingly, more like the yakuza. As in Japan, the gangs have disguised themselves as social organizations, or even religious groups. Their portfolio is also similar: widespread extortion, loan sharking, gambling, drugs, and influence over the entertainment and construction industries. By the early 1990s, Korean gangs controlled the supply of liquor to the entertainment business and had formed working alliances with yakuza syndicates.

The Japanese influence on Korean gangs was so large that yakuza were even training them to be gangsters. When police in Pusan raided Korea's White Tiger gang in 1990, they found evidence that its leaders had attended a ten-day seminar on being mobsters at Yamaguchi-gumi headquarters in Kobe. The Korean crooks went through a kind of yakuza boot camp, in which they shaved their heads, listened to lectures on yakuza traditions and moneymaking techniques, and trained to use guns during a midnight shooting session. Tuition was free. Apparently the yakuza expected to be paid in other ways.

As Bubble-era money flowed to the yakuza, the spillover into Korea was substantial. Long the Japanese mob's favorite foreign destination, Korea attracted thousands of yakuza for good times and cheap investments. While the Yamaguchi-gumi made deals with Pusan's White Tigers, the Sakaume-gumi tied up with another Pusan gang and bought real estate there. One Korean journal claimed in 1995 that 5,000 yakuza visited annually, and that yakuza investors had bought a twelve-story luxury hotel in Pusan, a department store in Ulsan, and real estate in Seoul. Other reports had yakuza buying securities and hiring Korean hit men to murder Japanese. By the 1990s, Korea found itself with a major organized crime problem, plagued not only by increasingly capable local gangs, but also by the yakuza as well as Russian and Chinese syndicates.

The Yakuza and Sexual Slavery

The yakuza's early experiences in Korea convinced many that their talents were best plied on an international scale. By the late 1960s, other forces, too, were tugging at the gangs to move abroad. Some had become managers of multi-million-dollar companies, who watched with fascination as their legitimate counterparts circled the globe making trade deals and investing capital. The gangs' younger members were better educated and more internationally minded; some had even picked up the mandatory English taught in Japanese schools. The greatest incentive, though, was the explosion of the nation's tourist industry in the late 1960s and 1970s. With a strong yen, the easing of currency export controls, and increasing amounts of disposable cash in their pockets, the Japanese traveled abroad as never before. But few travelers saw tourism as a means of building cross-cultural bridges. Instead, men from around the country lined up for prostitution junkets across much of East Asia. As many as two hundred Japanese men at one time would descend from their jumbo jets into these cities, on prearranged three-day junkets whose sole purpose was an orgy of drinking and whoring. The "sex tour" was born.

The Japanese sex tours encouraged the yakuza to follow the excesses of their countrymen across East Asia. Yakuza began showing up not only in Seoul, but also in Taipei, Manila, and Bangkok. The tours introduced the gangs to the international trade in sexual slavery, a merciless enterprise that they would soon help expand around the Pacific. It is a trade that affects hundreds of thousands of mostly poor Third World women and children, forcing them into prostitution at home and abroad. Activists have broadly defined the international trade in women to include sex tourism, prostitution around military bases, traffic in women and children, "mail order" marriages, and pornography. The yakuza have had a hand in nearly all of these, helped out by conniving local crime syndicates in the poorer countries of East Asia.

The sex industry in the West simply does not compare to the massive scale of prostitution now practiced in many of these developing countries, a condition closely related to the rise in tourism from the world's wealthier modernized countries. Until the mid-1970s, Western Europe had served as the slave traders' main market, with the countries of the Middle East not far behind; by the 1980s the international focus had shifted to East Asia, with Japan and the yakuza playing a key role.

The early signs of the boom in the East Asian sex trade could be seen in Taiwan by the end of the 1960s, as planeloads of Japanese men arrived in special tours to take advantage of the nation's cheap brothels. Geopolitics interrupted that trade in 1972, as Japan resumed diplomatic relations with mainland China. With flights into Taiwan curtailed, the Japanese tour companies quickly shifted their operations to the increasingly popular nocturnal attractions of Korea. Tourism had mushroomed in Korea after the nation normalized relations with Japan in 1965, with more than 650,000 Japanese visitors annually by the late 1970s. Few of the tourists were visiting temples, however. In a survey by the Korean Ministry of Tourism, no less than 80 percent of the men cited "kisaeng parties" as "what was most impressive about Korea." The word *kisaeng* historically applied to professional female entertainers, quite similar to Japan's highly refined tradition of geisha. But today the term is synonymous with prostitute.

In every major Korean city, large, government-registered "kisaeng houses" sprang up. One pair of houses sat in a wealthy area of Seoul, on either side of the Japanese ambassador's official residence. Each could accommodate eight hundred men at one time. The owner was reportedly a top politician with past service in the KCIA. Along with the official kisaeng houses arose hundreds of brothels and tens of thousands of prostitutes.

The sex tours became big business, prompting large hotels, tourist agencies, and airlines to jump into the trade. Japan Air Lines, which was flying about one-third of all Japanese international travelers by the end of the 1970s, coaxed its passengers rather directly. Read one JAL guidebook: "In order to embellish and relish the nights of Korea, you must start, above all else, with a Kisaeng party. . . . There is no doubt whatsoever about the well-established reputation that a night spent with a consummate Korean girl dressed in a gorgeous Korean blouse and skirt is just perfect. . . . Every travel agent organizing trips to Korea makes it a must to include a Kisaeng party in his client's itinerary."

The realities of the kisaeng houses were somewhat less pleasant. Generally, the women were impoverished migrants from the countryside, sold as minors on the black market for as little as $200 and forced into a life of prostitution. In the highly structured society of Korea, they were forever marked as "unpersons," a status comparable to that of India's untouchables. Managers raked off much of their pay, acts of violence against them were frequent, amphetamine use was widespread, and the living conditions were inhumane. There was a slave market atmosphere in some kisaeng houses, where the women stood half naked in large rooms by their lockers as the Japanese men paraded by and picked out their lady of the night.

The sex tours became so popular during the 1970s that, despite a resurgence of tourism to Taiwan and the booming trade with Korea, the Japanese began exploring other lands. They set their sights on the countries of

Japanese Overseas Travel, 1979

Country	Visitors	Men	Women
Republic of Korea	525,326	93.7%	6.3%
Taiwan	618,538	91.4%	8.6%
Philippines	190,637	83.7%	16.3%
Thailand	80,140	78.9%	21.2%
United States	1,410,320	59.4%	40.6%
France	166,622	50.5%	49.5%

SOURCE: Immigration Bureau, Ministry of Justice, Tokyo.

Southeast Asia, an easy hop from their old haunts in Taiwan. It was here that the sex trade—and the yakuza—would reach new heights, creating huge, industrial-scale centers of prostitution. Much of the market lies only a four- to five-hour plane ride from Tokyo, and the ravages of Third World poverty, combined with the power of the Japanese yen, fostered the massive sex trade, possibly involving as many as 80 percent of the 1 million Japanese men traveling abroad each year during the late 1970s.

Thailand and the Philippines bore the brunt of the assault, with considerable help from Hong Kong. As the richest country in Asia, Japan's role as lead buyer in the sexual slave market of East Asia could have been predicted. The aggressiveness of Japanese businessmen had already prompted taunts of "economic animal" throughout the region. Now to that was added a host of new names, including "sex animal" and "sex imperialist." Drunk, rowdy Japanese stumbling through the streets with their "girls" on arm renewed old hatreds in places like the Philippines, where Japanese atrocities during the war are not forgotten. In much of Asia, the Ugly American had found his match. Farmers, doctors, dentists, realtors, gangsters, and others lined up at Tokyo's Narita Airport for jets bound not only for Seoul and Taipei, but for Bangkok and Manila as well.

Here again, the women involved may be sold directly into prostitution by their families in the countryside; in Thailand, daughters from remote areas may be sold for a pittance. Some women go off willingly, seeking work in the big cities but finding no doors open but those of the local sex clubs. They tell their faraway parents they are working as "receptionists," a long-standing joke among prostitutes in Manila. Typically, they will support their entire family, sending home from one-third to one-half of their earnings. Most of the money they make, however, ends up in the hands of tourist agencies, hotels, club owners, pimps, and organized crime syndicates. It is not a good life for the women. As in Korea, drug use is high, sexually transmitted disease rampant, and violence commonplace.

Many of the brothels do, in fact, resemble slave auctions. In the largest of these flesh markets, as many as several hundred women sit in huge warehouse-like buildings, with numbers pinned to their dresses. Some clubs have one-way glass show windows so customers can "shop" at ease, "rather as you would select a fish from the tank in a seafood restaurant," explained one guidebook to Thailand.

Critics point to the establishment of U.S. military bases and the Vietnam War as the first great catalysts for prostitution in the region. It was the tourist industry, though, that brought the Asian sex trade to the fore in the 1970s. Thailand in particular has earned a reputation among travelers as the brothel of Asia, although the Philippines has also vied for that dubious honor. A 1998 study by the UN's International Labor Office concluded that in much of the region prostitution has become a major industry, with substantial economic impact on tourism, entertainment, and the rural poor. Estimates vary of how many prostitutes work in the various nations of East Asia. The Philippines may host nearly a half-million sex workers, according to the ILO study, while Thailand is home to between 200,000 and 300,000. Thousands more depend on the industry for their livelihood— owners, managers, pimps, cleaners, cashiers, parking valets, security guards, and more.

The yakuza did not originally create these conditions, nor do they control most of the local action, which is handled by various bands of native gangsters, pimps, and businesspeople. But the yakuza do play a key role in the trade in several ways. They have accompanied the tours, setting up contacts with local pimps and guiding their fellow Japanese toward women, drugs, or whatever else they desire. In many cases, they have financed the clubs, particularly those catering to Japanese. And they play a major role in trafficking the women overseas.

A measure of how entrenched the sex tours were is offered by none other than Ryoichi Sasakawa, the yakuza-connected Sugamo cellmate of Kodama who built up a fortune in motorboat racing. Sasakawa, a personal friend of then Philippines president Marcos, founded in 1979 the World Safari Club, a private, Japanese-only tour operation with exclusive rights to develop the unspoiled island of Lubang into a "tourist paradise." Sasakawa's advance advertisements in Japan touted unlimited fishing, hunting, diving, and "nudist areas" that of course included "private companions." But his plans for the island were soon discovered by women's and church groups, which claimed the resort amounted to a giant outdoor brothel. Bowing to the unfavorable publicity, Sasakawa and company canceled the project in 1981 "to avoid misunderstanding."

Big Japanese employers have also backed the region's sex industry, even arranging for their workers to go on the tours. In one celebrated incident, the Casio Company in 1979 held a banquet in a Manila hotel for its two hundred leading salesmen of the year. After wining and dining them, and inviting the elderly among them to call it a day, a huge folding screen parted to reveal two hundred "hostesses" for the night, each one bearing a number on her corsage.

While the Japanese were the most obvious offenders, the sex tours also attracted Europeans from West Germany and the Netherlands. Worst of all, the women's own governments have been complicit. With tourism as the third- or fourth-largest earner of foreign exchange in these countries, and most of the visitors men, for years local government officials condoned and even boosted the sex trade as a means of gaining hard currency. A 1984 report by the respected Korea Church Women United condemned the nation's kisaeng houses as "an auction block where girls are bartered in exchange for foreign money." Indeed, these critics charged that the sex trade had become so pervasive that without it Korea's all-important tourist trade would collapse—and with it a startling percentage of the cash needed to pay off the nation's foreign debt. Despite a 1947 ban on prostitution, claim the church women, Korean tourism officials even sponsored ideological lectures for the prostitutes about patriotism and the importance of the foreign exchange they earned.

Despite the apparent government sanction of the sex trade, opposition to the Japanese tours grew. In 1973, Korea's highly politicized student groups began protests at Kimpo Airport outside Seoul. They were joined by Christian women's organizations, which soon linked up with their Japanese counterparts. Opposition within Japan was spearheaded by the 4,000-member Women's Christian Temperance Union, a seasoned band of activists who had played a key role in the passage of Japan's antiprostitution laws in the 1950s. In the Philippines, a coalition of women's and church groups began organizing as well, and in 1980 filed its first formal protest with the Japanese embassy in Manila. This was at the height of the sex junkets, as the tourist industry pushed more than 1.8 million Japanese into the region.

Then, in June of 1981, a chain of carefully planned demonstrations followed Prime Minister Zenko Suzuki around his heavily publicized tour of Southeast Asia. By the time the prime minister reached Jakarta, he was willing to admit something was seriously wrong with Japanese tourism in the area. So effective were these protests that Thailand and the Philippines reportedly experienced a 25 percent drop in Japanese male tourists over the next few months.

The demonstrations and continued protests forced a number of overdue changes. Travel associations in Japan and the Philippines jointly condemned the sex tour business. Japan's Ministry of Transportation, after ignoring the trade for a decade, threatened to publicly name and chide the tour operators. In 1981, Japan's four major labor organizations finally joined in to stop the national embarrassment, appealing to the prime minister's office to halt the sex tours. And advertisements in the Japanese media, once filled with blatant references to the beautiful ladies of Manila and Bangkok, now stressed the countries' natural beauty. But Japanese demand for foreign prostitutes would not be so easily defeated. The tours did not stop; they simply became less blatant, with lesser-known operators moving smaller groups abroad. At the same time, the yakuza began to reverse the trade—instead of exporting men, they would import women.

Trafficking in Women

It was no coincidence that in the early 1980s, as the protests turned back the worst of the sex tours, the yakuza moved in force to another, equally exploitative aspect of the sex trade—the international traffic in women. The Japanese gangs began luring to Japan tens of thousands of women throughout Asia with the promise of legitimate jobs and good money, a practice that continues to the present. But instead of a new start, their victims are plunged into a world of forged passports and faked visas, and ultimately into sexual slavery, forced to work as poorly paid prostitutes in the brothels of Japan.

Trafficking in women, observed one UN crime expert, "is the world's biggest violation of human rights." Experts estimate that between 700,000 and 2 million women and children are trafficked globally each year—nearly a third of them from Southeast Asia, the yakuza's prime hunting ground. Another quarter comes from the nations of Eastern Europe and the former Soviet Union, a growing source for Japanese recruiters. The trafficking of women in East Asia is a multi-billion-dollar business, stretching from recruiters in the Burmese countryside to the nightclubs of Osaka. Unlike drugs and guns, a prostitute's service can be sold again and again. Not only is the sex business profitable, but penalties are less severe than those for moving guns or drugs.

The "import" of foreign women into Japan is not new to the yakuza. Police records show "white slavery," as the Japanese also call it, dating back to the early 1970s. The trade took off in the early '80s, and the gangs showed renewed interest in the '90s as the Bubble Economy's easy money disappeared. The practice has now become big business, and it has enraged its Japanese critics even more than the sex tours. The reason in part lies in a sensitive bit of Japanese history: around the end of the nineteenth century, Japan itself was a victim of the very same trade. By the late 1800s, impoverished Japanese families in large numbers were selling their daughters to international slave traders, who shipped the young women throughout East Asia and even to Hawaii and California. Other women, like the yakuza's modern-day victims, were tricked into the trade by being promised well-paid, legitimate jobs, only to be forced into prostitution upon leaving Japan.

The government even supported the trade, encouraging the slavers to follow the conquest of the Japanese Imperial Army and Navy across Asia, and "drafting" as many as 200,000 Korean women to "entertain" imperial troops at the front.

These unfortunate women were called the *karayuki-san;* the Japanese today have modified the term to describe the foreign women now ensconced in yakuza bars and brothels in Japan. They are called the *Japayuki-san,* Japan-bound prostitutes. Japanese authorities have been slow to act on this more recent manifestation of the sex trade, as the trade is widely tolerated by the nation's male-dominated institutions. Even when police do act, their efforts have not been very successful, due in good part to the attitudes of the principal supplier nations across East Asia.

For the worst victims, conditions are indeed terrible. Impoverished women, lured to Japan on various pretexts, find themselves at the mercy of gangsters who confiscate their passports and valuables and then force them to work as prostitutes, dancers, and hostesses. Without friends and unable to speak Japanese, they are packed into tiny rooms and find themselves trapped in a life of virtual slavery. Many enter the country as "entertainers" under Japanese immigration law; as such, they are considered guests, not workers, and so are unprotected by Japanese labor laws. Not all the women are abused, and many enlist in the trade knowing full well what awaits them. But the horror stories are so legion, and the exploitation so institutionalized, that the trade has become an enduring scandal for the Japanese. Fueling the traffic is a tremendous demand for foreign prostitutes. Estimates vary, but most experts believe that at any one time, some 100,000 foreign sex workers reside in Japan, the majority of them from the Philippines and Thailand. Growing numbers come from poorer nations such as Burma and China.

The business is incredibly lucrative. In Japan, an average session with a foreign prostitute cost some $200 during the late 1990s. With 100,000 foreign prostitutes doing at least one trick per day, that alone works out to $7.3 billion per year the foreigners are earning for their pimps, bar owners, agents, and, eventually, themselves. An entire industry has evolved around the traffic: recruiters, middlemen, immigration fixers, translators, forgers, travel agents, and mobsters from local Thai pimps to Osaka gang bosses. Native recruiters target remote areas, searching for naive or desperate families with young daughters. Some donate funds to local temples to gain acceptance of village leaders or organize beauty contests to lure potential recruits. They employ mobile phones and faxes to send the women's details to brokers in Bangkok and negotiate their prices on the spot. So lucrative is the trade that feuds in Thailand over control of the traffic have led to phone threats, including a bomb hoax, against the Japanese embassy in Bangkok.

Reliable figures are hard to come by, but interviews and published reports give an idea of the economics involved. In the hills of northwest Thailand and along the Burmese border, families may be offered as little as $300 for the sale of a daughter. The recruiter, in turn, sells the woman to a broker for $1,000 to $1,500, yielding a hefty profit. From there the woman is handled by various middlemen—a sleazy class of promoters and fixers who profit most from the trade, say analysts. Bedecked in designer suits and clutching cell phones, they jet regularly from Japan to Southeast Asia. Many are ethnic Chinese with contacts across East Asia, who play key roles in moving the women from agencies in Bangkok or Manila to their yakuza-tied handlers in Japan. More than a few are college graduates with good English. A 1991 investigation by the Philippine embassy in Tokyo found at least 280 talent companies and 74 agencies involved in the trade across the Philippines, most of them in Metro Manila. Another 403 similar outfits were identified in Japan, spread through some forty-two cities and prefectures. The traffic in illegal workers brought Thai agents some $100 million to $150 million annually during the mid-1990s, according to a study by economists at Bangkok's Chulalongkorn University.

One Thai trader claimed that he was paid $14,000 for each woman he recruited and got into Tokyo. His expenses—stylish clothes, air tickets, documents—cost around $5,000, so the profits were enormous. Other figures range as high as $30,000 per woman. Once in Japan, the women are told they must first recoup the price paid to the middlemen—which typically takes about one year. Additional "commissions," loans, rent, and other expenses may be tacked on, making some women indentured sex servants. They may be "resold" to other clubs by brokers in Japan, adding further to their indebtedness. "Men who recruit prostitutes come to me regularly and ask if I need new women to run my establishments. . . . It is as simple as . . . delivering a bowl of noodles," bragged one Japanese hotel operator. In 1984, the Asian Women's Association in Japan asserted that actual slave auctions occurred along a row of cheap hotels lining Showa Avenue in Tokyo's Ueno district. During one auction, dealers allegedly came from around the country to make their bids, which ranged from $3,000 for six months' service to $800 for "one little black girl."

A series of arrests over the years suggests the scope of the trade:

- In 2001, one Sumiyoshi-kai trafficker boasted of having forced over one hundred Southeast Asian women into the sex trade since the early 1980s. Working with a Thai broker, at least six times a year the yakuza picked up handfuls of women from the airport and drove them to Tokyo's Kabukicho red-light district, earning some 10 million yen for each one he delivered.
- Between 1994 and 1996, some sixty Thai women were smuggled into Japan packed into large suitcases by a smuggling ring dubbed the

"Company." The group consisted of about ten Thai and Japanese men, plus another twenty Japanese men who carried the suitcases through airport checkpoints.

- In 1996, three Mexican women escaped from a brothel in Hirosaki, northern Japan, and alerted authorities to a decade-long smuggling ring. Mexican police arrested two Japanese men on suspicion of smuggling some 3,000 women into Japan over the past decade. The men ran ads for Mexicans to work as hostesses in Japan.
- In 1993, immigration police in the southern Thai city of Hat Yai smashed one ring in which sixty women were waiting to be sent to Japan. Agents seized 206 forged passports from eight countries, including Thailand, Japan, Malaysia, Britain, and Ireland.
- In 1990, two Thais outside Tokyo were arrested for running a prostitution ring that had lured 1,000 Thai women to Japan. The two women paid some $10,000 for each prostitute, and then "sold" the women to bars and clubs for $20,000 each.
- In 1984, police in Thailand arrested a Japanese man and his Thai wife for sending some two hundred Thai women to Hong Kong and Japan via Macao. Over the previous two years, the couple had moved as many as two groups of eight women each month. Police also seized videotape equipment used to send "samples" of the women to interested parties.
- In 1973, police in Hong Kong uncovered a ring operating out of a tailor shop and tour agency, coaxing about fifty women per month to Tokyo from Hong Kong and Southeast Asia. Once the women arrived in Japan, they were forced into work as strippers and prostitutes.

Various scams are used to move the women into Japan. The simplest technique, noted one Thai smuggler, is to dress the woman in expensive clothes, accompanied by a fake husband on a trip to Japan. Counterfeit or stolen passports are widely used. As visas are tough to forge, many buy passports on the black market with visas already issued, and then change the photo. To enhance the illusion, brokers can purchase false bank statements for small fees in Bangkok, and route the couple through Hong Kong, Seoul, Beijing, or the U.S. first. Sometimes respectable-looking foreigners are recruited for $500 to act as spouses.

Sex-trafficking gangs can be as crude as they are criminal. One group based in Manila specialized in the export of young girls—ten to seventeen years old—to Singapore, Kuala Lumpur, and Tokyo. All were branded with an identical tattoo on their right thigh. The smugglers are enterprising, to say the least. Recruiters in Bangkok have run newspaper ads offering bogus jobs and scholarships to obtain college graduates for their schemes.

By the late 1990s, the trade was sufficiently established that most Filipinas, and many Thais, knew what they were getting into. "The slave trade stories are about 30 percent true," said Tatsuo Saito, a Manila correspondent for Kyodo News Service in the 1980s. "I've interviewed almost five hundred women here over a three-year stay. More than 90 percent who were in Japan want to return. The money is excellent for them and they got along with the yakuza just fine." Activists disagree sharply with those figures, and their arguments received a boost from a 2000 study by Japan's Social Security Research Foundation. The study reportedly surveyed 257 foreign women, most of them questioned by police after their arrests, and found that nearly two-thirds said they had been forced to work in the sex trade.

Still, the trade undeniably exerts a strong economic pull, and many women do indeed complete more than one tour of Japan. Some are lucky enough to have jobs as hostesses, in which their principal duties consist of conversing with customers and getting them to buy drinks. Those with a good boss make as much as ten times what they could in their native countries, and much of that money goes back home to their families. Thriftier Thais can save $3,000 or more a year—a considerable amount in Thailand, close to the starting salary of an economics professor. Yet, despite the demand for these women, they usually receive half of what their Japanese counterparts make, and few are prepared for the often brutal treatment meted out by their yakuza caretakers.

Several sensational cases hit the news media during the 1990s, in which foreign sex workers were brutally murdered or killed their pimps. In June 1990 alone, four were murdered, two committed suicide, and one was stabbed. The widespread abuse produced various martyrs, none more famous than twenty-two-year-old Maricris Sioson. In the summer of 1991, she arrived at Tokyo's Narita airport with a six-month visa as an "entertainer," hoping to earn money for her family in the Philippines. Driven by her handlers to Fukushima Prefecture, she found herself in a club with conditions so brutal that nine women had already escaped. Only weeks later, on September 14, Sioson was dead. A Japanese autopsy attributed her death to hepatitis B, but after her body was returned to the Philippines, a postmortem concluded that she had died from head wounds. Adding to the outrage that year were revelations from another case in southwest Japan. Police there arrested seven bar operators for locking up eighteen Filipina dancers in a small shack by day and forcing them to work in sex clubs by night. The group had confiscated the women's passports and return plane tickets, officials said. For two months, the women had been forced to work and were beaten if they refused to work twelve-hour days as prostitutes, with no days off.

Sioson's death sparked widespread anti-Japanese protests in Manila and prompted crackdowns on both visiting yakuza and the number of Filipinos allowed to go to Japan on entertainment visas. But the crackdowns succeeded only in pushing more business to Thailand. From 1991 to 1995, some 10,000 to 15,000 Thai workers flowed to Japan each year, the majority of them women bound for the sex industry. By 1994, four hundred of them each month were approaching the Thai embassy in Tokyo asking to be sent home. Authorities in Thailand have been particularly blind to the suffering. As many as one hundred cops are involved, according to press reports, including police lieutenants and captains. "Are you kidding?" snorted a Thai smuggler when asked if his business involved kickbacks to immigration agents. "That's the essential part . . ."

Within Japan, authorities, too, have been slow to deal with the problem, although police in 1984 created a special office to deal with illegal women workers in the country. The trade is widely winked at by authorities in Japan's male-dominated society. Japanese women's groups have made important progress in exposing the trade and lobbying for change. Some have formed shelters across Japan, but they have not had easy going. Most are poorly funded; several have been vandalized by yakuza thugs and forced to change locations and operate undercover. Some gangs reportedly post photos of escapees, encouraging associates to turn them in if found. "The women are mentally and physically exploited to the limit, and in worst cases, their lives are deprived," says longtime activist Yayori Matsui. "The global trafficking in women is a modern form of slavery."

The Meth Capital of the World

Although the sex trade first lured the yakuza abroad in large numbers, it is the drug trade that has proven the most lucrative. And the drug of choice for the Japanese, and increasingly elsewhere, is methamphetamine, known on the streets of America as speed, crank, and meth, and on the streets of Japan as *shabu* and S. The Japanese prefer a potent form of crystal meth, often called ice in English, which they smoke or inject. It has made the yakuza a fortune.

The East Asian meth trade is unquestionably one of world's most massive drug routes, a multi-billion-dollar dope connection that is changing the face of organized crime and drug abuse in the region. So great is the demand for the drug, and so lucrative are its sales, that Japanese police believe that meth sales account for one-third of yakuza income. Criminologist Masayuki Tamura, an expert on Japanese drug trafficking, believes the meth trade has been central to the Japanese mob's success. Starting in 1970, he says, the drug trade's huge profits acted as the cash engine that allowed Japan's big syndicates to expand nationally.

To foreigners accustomed to the image of Japan as crime-free, the number of meth abusers may come as a shock. Since the 1980s, estimates have typically put the number in Japan at some 500,000, roughly the number of known heroin users in the United States. But other estimates range as high as 1 million, and a 1998 survey shocked officials, indicating that 2.2 million Japanese either use or have used stimulant drugs. As one Tokyo drug abuse expert put it, "Japan is the meth capital of the world." A Japanese scientist is credited with having discovered methamphetamine, and the Japanese have endured a fifty-year affair with the drug. "Japan is the type of society that needs methamphetamine," remarked one longtime resident of Tokyo. "The treadmill is very fast and people use it to stay on." Indeed, at least one psychological study indicated that the pace of life in Japan is measurably faster than in such countries as England, Taiwan, and the United States—a fact to which resident foreigners in the country will readily attest. But the drug comes with a terrible physical and mental cost. Speed freaks, suffering from lack of sleep and delusions, can be violent and disoriented, lapsing into behavior typical of paranoid schizophrenia.

Meth is a yakuza business. The gangs are believed to control virtually the entire market in Japan. The big syndicates, notably the Yamaguchi-gumi and Inagawa-kai, run vertically integrated networks for meth production and distribution. Top bosses are well insulated, as drug deals are handled by local gangs and lower-ranking yakuza, but the traffic provides a major source of the capital moving through gang offices. Some enterprising yakuza have even strived for one-stop shopping. One Kanagawa gang gained access to a large supply of syringes and needles after a top member became an authorized dealer of medical equipment. By the time authorities caught up to them, they had already distributed over 1,000 syringes and needles.

Methamphetamine abuse in Japan dates back to the war, when the government doled out the drug to workers and soldiers, including kamikaze pilots. During the Occupation, it became popular as an over-the-counter drug until being banned in 1948. During the early 1950s, the drug's continued popularity led to an underground boom in stimulant abuse, as yakuza gained access to government stockpiles of the drug and then set up their own clandestine laboratories. Stung by concerted crackdowns at home, the gangs eventually moved the often smelly labs to Korea. Through the 1970s and early 1980s, at least 70 percent of the yakuza's meth supply came from South Korea. At secret locales scattered throughout Korea, local crime gangs—typically with yakuza financing—manufactured vast stores of the drug. The huge supply of Korean meth sparked what one newspaper called a "Blizzard of White Powder" from abroad. From 1975 to 1983, the number of drug-related arrests tripled in Japan. Among the leading offenders: housewives, students, taxi drivers, firemen, and soldiers. The prime smuggling route lay between Pusan—South Korea's second-largest city—

and the nearby Japanese port of Shimanoseki. Pusan, a bustling seaport and trading center, is a favorite haunt of the yakuza. It is a smuggler's paradise, teeming with thousands of seamen, small boats, and Japanese tourists.

For years, despite repeated Japanese requests for a crackdown, Korean officials winked at the enormous traffic, influenced by well-placed bribes as well as by anti-Japanese feelings within the government. This hands-off attitude gradually changed as speed use spread to the Koreans themselves. Finally, as the 1988 Olympics neared, Korean law enforcement staged a concerted campaign against the meth industry, weeding out corrupt police and driving scores of the labs overseas.

The Korean crackdown drove the trade to Taiwan, solidifying ties between criminal gangs there and the yakuza. Korean chemists even visited the island to train their Taiwanese counterparts in how to "cook" the high-quality crystal meth the Japanese demand. Tons of the stuff arrived in Japan, smuggled from Taiwan in everything from frozen tuna to cans of fruit and boxes of tea. But as meth use rose to alarming levels on Taiwan, authorities there, too, cracked down. This time, production moved to the Chinese mainland and North Korea, sparking Japan's third and largest boom in meth abuse. During the 1990s, record shipments poured into Japan, driving down the price and fostering wide acceptance of meth use among young people. So plentiful was the supply that the price for a thirty-milligram dose plunged from 10,000 yen in the 1980s to 2,000 yen in 1998. "Until the early '90s, deals were made cautiously," said one narcotics detective. "Now anyone can get it. The yakuza started selling at bargain prices, looking for small profits and quick returns."

China's entry into the region's narcotics trade held major implications for Japan. China is a major producer of the ephedra plant, which is widely used for processing into ephedrine, the organic base for methamphetamine. As China opened its markets, drug traffickers from Hong Kong and Taiwan moved into the southern provinces. There they found vendors eager to provide ephedrine and other chemical precursors, and police forces that were lax, corrupt, or both. The opportunities on the Chinese mainland attracted a whole new class of criminal entrepreneur. Among the pioneers was Lee Chau-ping, a shrewd Hong Kong businesswoman dubbed the Ice Queen by the press. Lee did for ice what other entrepreneurs have done for legitimate goods—took advantage of cheap labor, lax regulation, and a fast-growing economy. In Guangdong and Fujian provinces, she set up a series of plants that may have been the world's largest meth enterprise. "Where others built laboratories, Lee built factories," said Sgt. Tom Hansen of the Royal Canadian Mounted Police, who tracked her operation to Hong Kong and China. Between 1989 and 1992, Lee's operation produced a whopping 4.5 metric tons of the drug, which Hong Kong dealers then sold off largely

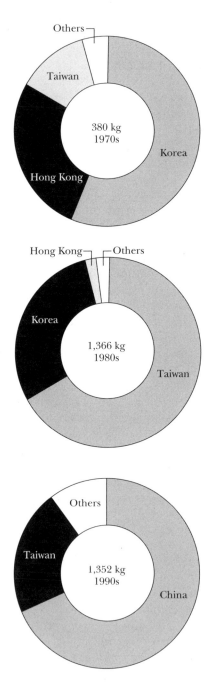

Figure 3. Countries of origin of the methamphetamine seized in Japan from the 1970s through the 1990s. (Source: Japan Customs Bureau.)

in Japan and the Philippines. Each factory employed fifteen to twenty people working sixteen-hour shifts. Lee eluded authorities in five countries; she is believed to have settled along the Thai-Burmese border, where she has helped build up another meth industry that has caused a near epidemic of abuse in Thailand and neighboring countries.

As meth seizures in Japan hit record levels, police began tracking shipments not only from southern China, but also from its northeast provinces, near the North Korean border. Eventually, it dawned on investigators that many of the shipments were actually from North Korea, and that the impoverished, xenophobic state had entered the drug trade in a major way. Reports from defectors, seizures from North Korean ships, and arrests of North Korean smugglers made it clear that the Communist state had become more than merely a new source of illegal narcotics; it was actually sponsoring the trade. Beset by famine and desperate for hard currency, the North Korean government had entered the dope business, funding poppy fields and meth labs. Even worse, North Korean officials had in effect criminalized their diplomatic corps, using embassies as fronts for distributing drugs and other contraband.

One survey found a record of criminal complaints against North Korean diplomats in sixteen countries between 1994 and 1999. North Korean officials have been implicated in smuggling everything from counterfeit U.S. dollars and fake CDs to tobacco and endangered species parts. Authorities in at least nine countries have nabbed North Korean diplomats with a virtual pharmacy of illegal drugs: opium, heroin, cocaine, hashish. Investigators in 1999 traced orders for fifty tons of ephedrine to North Korean front companies; that quantity is twenty times more than the nation's legitimate needs. "We've rarely seen a state use organized crime in this way," says Phil Williams, a University of Pittsburgh professor and editor of the journal *Transnational Organized Crime.* "This is a criminal state not because it's been captured by criminals but because the state has taken over crime." By 1999, North Korea was earning as much as $500 million from narcotics and other illegal activities, according to intelligence analysts—equal to its entire income from legitimate exports.

Among the early signs was a surprising seizure in April 1997 at a small port in southern Japan. There a lone customs inspector wondered about the twelve large cans of honey that crew members hand-carried from a North Korean freighter. It seemed strange, the inspector thought, that North Korea was exporting food in the midst of a famine. A check found the cans crammed with 130 pounds of meth. More large seizures followed, and the prognosis was not good. Within two years, the North Koreans were supplying nearly 20 percent of Japan's multi-billion-dollar meth market.

The yakuza also peddle other drugs, ranging from heroin to paint thinner, but these pale compared to the estimated seven tons of meth they sell each year. Distribution of other drugs tends to break down along ethnic lines, with foreign crooks handling much of the supply. Southeast Asians peddle marijuana and heroin, Iranians opium, and the Israelis ecstasy and a bit of everything else. In the early 1980s, U.S. drug enforcement officials were alarmed by reports the yakuza were moving into the Southeast Asian heroin trade. With the yakuza's manpower, money, and organization, and the massive trade between Japan and the rest of the world, huge quantities of the drug could be moved to the United States, Australia, Europe, and Japan itself. But the threat failed to materialize. Opiates never developed much of a following in Japan. Of greater interest to the gangs was another drug then plaguing the world, one more suited to the high-strung tastes of Japanese drug users—cocaine.

The Great Cocaine Scare

It was the kind of news that gave nightmares to the best international crime fighters: an alliance between Japan's Yamaguchi-gumi and Colombia's Cali Cartel. Yet that was what intelligence reports were showing in 1990. Representatives of Colombia's top drug syndicate—the most sophisticated criminal organization in Latin America—had made contact with Japan's largest yakuza gang, and together they were plotting to move huge amounts of cocaine into Japan. The potential of a working alliance between the best criminal minds of Colombia and Japan was disturbing, to say the least.

Investigators had tracked ties between the yakuza and Latin American cocaine traffickers since the mid-1980s. But by 1988, Colombia's business-savvy drug cartels had undertaken a major effort to establish a market for cocaine in Japan. The attraction was not hard to understand. The North American market was saturated and pressure from law enforcement was relentless. The Japanese, meanwhile, loved stimulants, the yakuza already ran an ideal distribution system, and the potential profits were huge. The wholesale price of coke in Japan ran some 40 to 70 percent higher than in the United States, according to a 1990 DEA assessment.

Early reports suggested that coke traffickers in Japan were mostly independent, although the yakuza were clearly watching to see if cocaine's popularity took off. Law enforcement officials, too, were watching closely, and the news was not good. Seizures of cocaine in Japan went from a mere 208 grams in 1988 to 69 kilos in 1990—still modest compared to the tons being seized in North America, but enough to spark headlines about coke's growing popularity and alarm among police. "The same South American ships we raided and found cocaine on in Antwerp, I have seen in Japanese harbors," Stanley Furce, the DEA's man in Tokyo, told a reporter in 1990. "There is no question in my mind that Japan is a new target market for cocaine." Tsukasa Saito, director of the Tokyo police's drug section, told the newspaper *Asahi,* "The Colombian cocaine bosses are making their Japanese connections now."

Investigators found top Japanese banks and brokerage houses were being used by the Medellin Cartel to launder money. The rival Cali Cartel was thought to have set up distributors in Tokyo, Osaka, Yokohama, and Kobe, and was trans-shipping the drug from such unlikely ports as Los Angeles and New York. Smuggling and selling the coke was a panoply of Latin Americans—Colombians, Venezuelans, Peruvians, Bolivians. The Colombians seemed determined to show they could be just as ruthless in Japan as they were at home. Following arrests of cocaine traffickers in 1990, anonymous letters claiming to represent the Medellin Cartel threatened to murder then prime minister Toshiki Kaifu and top police investigators unless Colombians in jail were freed. More letters arrived the following year—each laden with four grams of cocaine—threatening media outlets, auto companies, banks, and securities firms.

But then, strangely, the threat disappeared. Police had braced for a blizzard of cocaine that never came. No one was quite sure why the Colombians never followed through. It seems the Japanese authorities did little to stem coke imports directly. The impact of the Bubble-era scandals and the new anti-mob law had forced the gangs to adopt a lower profile; perhaps the big syndicates sensed that mass introduction of a new and dangerous drug would bring further scrutiny and prosecutions. The collapse of the Bubble Economy also likely diminished the public's appetite—and pocketbook—for new drugs. Since World War II, meth had been Japan's drug of choice, and even as meth seizures jumped through the '90s, cocaine seizures remained modest.

Adding to the puzzle is that drug agents were tracking huge shipments of coke bound for Japan. In 1995, for example, Brazilian authorities seized a whopping 510 kilos of cocaine en route to Japan, and arrested a Colombian tied to the Cali Cartel who had spent the two previous months in Japan. Noting that they had seized only thirty-six kilos for that entire year, Japanese police suggested that such a large shipment must have been for trans-shipment. DEA agents thought them rather naive, but until further proof arrives, cocaine's trafficking in Japan will remain more a novelty than an industry.

If not a blizzard of white powder, though, what the cocaine threat did show was how quickly organized crime was changing in Japan—and how multinational it had become. If the sex tours and meth trade had pulled the yakuza through East Asia in the '70s, the Bubble Economy yanked them around the world in the '80s. Japanese mobsters began showing up from Shanghai to Chicago, from Paris to Sao Paulo. And the gangs were not just moving yakuza-style rackets and investments overseas; they were exporting yakuza-style corruption. Shady Japanese businessmen were offering huge amounts of money to get things done, using fixers and front companies, with additional cover provided by big banks, brokers, and development firms. At the same time, the criminal map of East Asia was changing, with the emergence of China and the fall of the Soviet Union—and growing numbers of foreign racketeers were ending up on Japanese shores. All this would have a far-reaching impact on the yakuza and the world of Asian organized crime.

CHAPTER TEN

OLD MARKETS AND NEW

AT THE HEIGHT OF THE BUBBLE ECONOMY, POLICE IN CHIBA PREFECTURE, home to Tokyo's Narita International Airport, finally started keeping tabs on just how many yakuza were heading overseas. The officials identified 2,916 yakuza traveling abroad in 1988, and 3,696 during the first nine months of 1989. Those numbers are likely conservative, given the yakuza who undoubtedly slipped through uncounted. The newspaper *Asahi* reported that of some 87,000 yakuza in 1989, an estimated 10,000 went abroad. Half of the gangsters identified by Chiba police were headed to South Korea, followed by the Philippines, Thailand, Hong Kong, Taiwan, Saipan, and Guam. Only thirty-five said they were going to the United States, a likely response to tougher screening by U.S. Customs and Immigration officials. Asked why they were traveling abroad, most said they were tourists, traveling for golf, sex, gambling, and gun-firing practice. Chiba officials duly notified Japanese Customs to target the gangsters on their return home, yet oddly no notice went out to law enforcement overseas. The insular Japanese police opted not to alert foreign officials that several thousand gangsters were heading their way.

With scant help from Japanese authorities, the U.S. Customs Yakuza Documentation Center embarked on its own attempt to document the extent of yakuza travel overseas. During the early 1990s, working with Customs and Immigration agents in Australia and other nations, the YDC compiled a record of yakuza forays by copying passport pages of suspected gangsters and entering their visits into a database. The results were eye-opening. The team inspected passport stamps from nearly two hundred yakuza and associates largely between 1986 to 1993. The agents found hundreds of entries into twenty-one nations, ranging from Pacific Island nations to such distant locales as Turkey and India. The most popular ports of entry were, unsurprisingly, in East Asia, but many ventured to Australia, Western Europe, and North America. Some evidently had business in the Bahamas, Buenos Aires, Bogotá, and Mexico City; others, in Macao and Shanghai. At least eight U.S. cities were visited; not just the likely targets in Hawaii and the West Coast, but also New York, Chicago, Detroit, Miami, and Washington, D.C.

After years of denying that the yakuza had gone international, by 1990 the NPA had changed its tune. That year, an NPA official would tell an international police conference that the yakuza "are considered to be traveling abroad as an everyday affair." Three years later, the agency's annual *White Paper* acknowledged that yakuza were expanding overseas through arms and drug trafficking, real estate investment, and the sex trade. An NPA survey that year found that thirty-five Japanese companies in twelve nations were victims of harassment and shakedowns by yakuza and sokaiya, mostly in Southeast Asia but also in the United States, the United Kingdom, and France. Activities included demands for money, business cooperation, and hotel accommodations. Other intelligence reports placed the yakuza in the Northeast Asian fishing industry, in Southeast Asian development projects, and in golf course resorts in North America. Police found that the gangs were even expanding abroad through restaurants, moving into the training of Japanese chefs and directing their employment overseas. Yet another report placed them in Ulaanbaatar, Mongolia, extorting a pack of Korean businessmen. Backed by a strong yen and their gangs' ample resources, the yakuza's impact would be felt worldwide. But it was Japan's neighbors in East Asia that would feel the full brunt of their push overseas.

The Philippines: A Second Home

Since arriving with the sex tours of the 1970s, the yakuza have found the Philippines their home away from home in the tropics. Indeed, the islands have become a center of the Japanese mob's international operations, second only to South Korea. It is an exciting place for the younger, more aggressive yakuza. A former American colony, the Philippines is a hazy, humid, sweat-soaked archipelago of 7,000 islands centered around the more than 10 million residents of Metro Manila. English is widely spoken, and, with a developing economy and widespread corruption, it is a land where the dollar and the yen will go very far indeed.

Employing some well-honed techniques from Japan, the yakuza have made important political connections among those who rule over the Philippines' 80 million people. The gangs have bribed their way into a lucrative, long-term relationship with both local businessmen and bureaucrats. Through well-placed "gifts," the more enterprising yakuza have avoided jail as well as extradition, maintained dubious business ventures, and repeatedly cleared Customs with no questions asked.

By the mid-1980s, senior members of the Yamaguchi-gumi, Inagawa-kai, and Sumiyoshi-kai had opened luxurious offices in Makati, the so-called Wall Street of Manila, according to a confidential U.S. Drug Enforcement Administration report. Makati's complex of skyscrapers, malls, and international hotels, set alongside some of the city's worst slums, makes an ideal home to the import-export firms and travel agencies the yakuza prefer using as fronts. Other yakuza gangs have taken root as well. The Korean syndicate of Hisayuki Machii, according to press reports, acquired "coral reef exploration rights" in the country. But the gangs' biggest early investments were made in the city's Ermita district, the sleazy center of the Philippine sex trade. In 1982, the *Times-Journal*, a leading Manila daily, cited police officials as saying that at least thirty clubs and restaurants in the area were yakuza-owned. The businesses, with Filipino dummy owners, were said to serve as fronts for gunrunning, drug smuggling, and trafficking in women.

By the early 1980s, Manila newspapers were abuzz with sensational reports of yakuza activity. One daily even ran a huge box on "Spotting a Yakuza," complete with photos of a tattooed back and a hand sans pinkie. Another paper ran banner headlines, YAKUZA SLAVE TRADERS HUNTED. Manila police, meanwhile, drew a confession out of one resident yakuza who claimed that up to several hundred of his ilk were active in the Philippines at any given time. In 1988, a top Philippine official estimated that one hundred yakuza were active in the country, mostly around Manila.

Working with the increasingly sophisticated Filipino gangs, the yakuza expanded into gambling, fraud, and money laundering. But next to the sex trade, the Japanese gangs have prized the Philippines most as a base for smuggling operations. With thousands of islands, most of them undeveloped, the Philippines offers convenient locales for the yakuza's foul-smelling meth factories. Of even greater interest are handguns, which are illegal in Japan but abundant in the Philippines. The country became a major source of firepower for the yakuza, supplying thousands of handguns to Japan. Yakuza money even helped spark development of a cottage gunsmith industry around the seaside town of Danao, on the central island of Cebu. As many as 5,000 artisans worked in the region, making cheap knock-offs of Magnums, Uzis, Colts, and Berettas. The biggest market was domestic, with clients ranging from Communist and Muslim rebels to local warlords and crooks of various persuasions. But the yakuza were also frequent buyers. In 1988, Kyoto's Aizu Kotetsu syndicate even recruited five of the Filipino gunsmiths, who set up an underground factory in Japan. The operation lasted only two years before being raided by Japanese police. By then, though, the group had produced some 160 guns and earned the syndicate some $600,000.

A glimpse of the arms market came into world view in October 1986, when an explosion rocked the rear of a Thai Airways jet heading from Manila to Osaka. The blast sent the plane reeling into a steep dive, plummeting four miles in minutes and catapulting passengers about the cabin. More than one hundred people were injured before the plane made an emergency landing. Behind the blast, investigators found, was a Yamaguchi-gumi member returning from the Philippines with a smuggled hand grenade aboard. The yakuza had retreated to the toilet to wrap the U.S.-made grenade to smuggle it past Customs, police said, but he accidentally pulled the pin as the aircraft lunged through a pocket of turbulence.

Hand grenades and other assorted weaponry are available from crooked soldiers or on the black market in the Philippines. When Manila police raided the headquarters of one gunrunning ring, dubbed the "Manila Connection," they reportedly discovered machine guns, automatic rifles, fifty pistols, enough ammunition for a small siege, and various drugs. The mastermind of the gang, one Hiroaki Kumitomo, a thirty-one-year-old yakuza, had earlier been found dead in a parked car in suburban Manila. Police believed the murder was linked to an abortive drug deal. Several other yakuza have been found floating in the murky rivers of Manila following disputes with their own groups or Filipino partners. Indeed, many Filipinos on both sides of the law deeply resent the entry of Japanese gangsters into their homeland. At one point, yakuza were even targeted for execution by Philippine guerilla groups.

Sometimes the victims are innocent Japanese who got in the way of ill-fated scams. For years, the Philippines hosted a series of contract killings arranged by Japanese. During one spate from 1978 to 1981, police tied at least four Japanese homicides to murder-for-insurance schemes there. First, the gangs would intimidate businessmen in Japan into taking out huge insurance policies, listing the gang members as beneficiaries. Then, after somehow luring their victims to Manila, the yakuza hired Filipino assassins for as little as $2,500. After the fourth homicide of a visiting Japanese, authorities finally got wind of the scam, and in 1981 police and soldiers raided a training camp for the assassins in a town south of Manila. Officials seized eight suspects, targets, shells, and a small arsenal of handguns.

There is no shortage of rackets for yakuza in the Philippines. One alleged gangster, Kikyoki Ouki of Kobe, reportedly used his fluent Tagalog and a .38 caliber revolver to pose as a Philippine immigration agent while shaking down Japanese investors in Manila. Counterfeiters are another attraction of the Philippine underworld. Police in Japan have seized fake international driver's licenses, certification stamps used by the government, and Japanese 100-yen notes made in the Philippines. Still other attractions can be found in Cebu, with its resorts and direct flights to Japan. There, the yakuza can shop for guns and women and get needed rest and relaxation, too.

In the early '90s, so many Japanese mobsters were frequenting the place that it prompted charges the gangs were bringing back the sex tours.

Philippine authorities have staged crackdowns over the years, giving an idea of the scope of yakuza activity there. Smuggling boats have been seized, fugitives tracked down, contraband seized, and mobsters deported. Between 1975 and 1983, according to press reports, police arrested and deported eighty-three yakuza suspects. Another crackdown in 1990–91 resulted in dozens of yakuza being arrested or deported. Among the crimes: drug dealing, illegal weapons possession, overstaying visas, traffic in women. Concerned by the influx of shady characters from Japan, in 1991 authorities established a yakuza profile, alerting immigration agents to look for flashy clothes, expensive jewelry, punch-perm haircuts, arrogant manners, severed pinkies, and striking tattoos. That year, more than one hundred yakuza were turned away. In one day, airport authorities refused entry to a visiting group of sixteen Japanese with missing fingers and tattoos. But pressure to allow in the Japanese was soon applied. A new immigration commissioner claimed the practice interfered with the civil rights of the visiting Japanese. But too many officials seemed more concerned with easy payoffs than civil liberties. "Corruption is rampant," explained one top immigration official, frustrated by the job. "Inspectors and top officials take bribes, while the airport police run a side business 'escorting' visitors through the airport." The escorts conveniently bypass immigration inspectors.

Thailand: A Tropical Wild West

From Manila, it is a short plane ride to Bangkok, the teeming capital city and marketplace of Thailand. Like elsewhere in Southeast Asia, the yakuza were originally attracted to Bangkok by the sex trade. But Thailand is a bit like the Wild West set in the tropics, and, like the Philippines, it exerts a strong pull on the more adventurous Japanese gangsters. Since the 1950s, Thailand has been surrounded by armed conflict. With guerilla movements still in neighboring Burma, opium barons to the north, and rampant corruption throughout the nation, it is a land of opportunity for enterprising mobsters. Indeed, with its vast prostitution industry, lucrative arms traffic, and thriving drug trade, there seems no criminal need that Thailand cannot fill. A 1998 study by economists at Thailand's respected Chulalongkorn University estimated that six illegal activities—all tied to organized crime—earned between $8 and $13 billion annually, equivalent to 8 to 13 percent of the entire Thai gross national product. By far the largest was illegal gambling, followed by prostitution and drug trafficking, and then, roughly, arms trading, diesel oil smuggling, and trafficking in people. If other rackets are thrown in—illicit logging, trading in protected species, other smuggling—the amount could reach 20 percent of GNP, the scholars estimated.

By the early 1980s, the yakuza already were well ensconced in Bangkok. Operating out of first-class hotels, the gangsters moved into nightclubs, jewelry shops, and import-export firms, using them as fronts for smuggling guns and drugs. Some gang members showed interest in the heroin trade pouring out of the Golden Triangle, that no-man's land of opium barons and warlords that borders Burma, Laos, and Thailand. Far more attractive to the yakuza, it turned out, is the region's booming meth industry, also centered along the Thai-Burma border. But the yakuza find Thailand intriguing for much more than drugs. One operation, for example, involved a Saitama gang boss who ran a construction business and exported tractors to his Chinese customers in Thailand. The yakuza businessmen received his payment in guns, gold bars, jewels, and wristwatches. Others have moved sokaiya-style operations to Bangkok, targeting Japanese firms. Stolen cars are another big scam, with Japanese crooks running stolen luxury vehicles to Thailand, selling them off or breaking them down in Thai "chop shops"— and then selling the parts back home. In 1994–95, police traced the export of as many as 130 stolen vehicles worth more than $5 million to a single gang in the Tokyo area. Other reports claim the gangs are moving stolen construction equipment—including earthmovers—out of Japan for sale in the region.

Another racket is smuggling endangered species and exotic animals. One ring shipped 110 lemurs, which the yakuza hoped to sell for some $2,000 each. One gun smuggler shipped handguns crammed into seven boxes of seventy poisonous snakes, including fifteen cobras and thirty chain vipers. Somehow the shipment cleared Japanese Customs, but police soon panicked the entire city of Hakone when they disclosed that the gangsters had dumped the snakes into a local river.

By 1990, at the height of the Bubble Economy, more than two hundred yakuza and associates were believed active in Thailand. Every major syndicate from Japan was represented, as was nearly every crime: kidnapping, drugs, extortion, prostitution. The gangs not only expanded in Bangkok, but moved to Chiang Mai and other cities. So influential were the yakuza that in 1993, when Japanese police held a seminar for their countrymen in Bangkok on how to deal with the gangs, more than 140 companies sent people.

Cracking down on the Japanese mob is not a high priority for Thai law enforcement, who have enough trouble policing themselves. Corruption reaches extraordinary levels among the police, who make as little as $200 per month. Many have come to count on payoffs and sexual favors from brothels, but often their criminal involvement is far more serious. High-ranking police have been implicated in big-time gambling, the drug trade, and human trafficking. Over a dozen top cops were implicated in the theft or cover-up of the theft of $20 million in Saudi royal jewels in 1989. Seven Thai cops were implicated in the murders of seven Asian visitors in the early 1990s, including a Japanese executive. The reason the yakuza presence is not larger in Thailand, quipped one scholar, is that they met a bigger mafia: the Bangkok police.

The Chinese Triads

In the mid-1970s, reports began filtering in to Japanese police of gang activity not just in Thailand and the Philippines, but throughout Southeast Asia. Yakuza members were sighted in Indonesia, Malaysia, Singapore, Hong Kong, and Taiwan. In most places, they have practiced a familiar pattern: the procurement of guns, drugs, and women; the investment and laundering of cash from Japan. As they have expanded, though, the yakuza have also had to learn a kind of underworld diplomacy, for their travels have introduced them to another, equally powerful set of criminal organizations: Chinese triad societies.

Triads are not the strict, hierarchical kind of crime families one sees in the yakuza or the Italian Mafia. At the street level, smaller triad gangs do tend toward a more close-knit structure, centered around a single leader, but the big triads are more like criminal brotherhoods—fraternal associations through which one receives support and protection. The differences were spelled out in hearings before the U.S. Congress in 1992, by a triad member whose past included heroin smuggling and work as a Hong Kong policeman:

> "I was not required to pay any percentage of my profits to our leadership. The rules for the triads are that we do favors for each other, we protect each other, we assist each other and make introductions and engage in criminal activities together. But triads are not strict discipline organizations like the Italian mafia."

Indeed, the world of Chinese organized crime is a complex one. Not all triad members are gangsters, nor are all Chinese gangsters triad members. There are tongs, street gangs, drug rings, and alien smugglers, among others, which may involve crooks from more than one triad, or from none at all. But it is the big triad societies, based largely in Hong Kong, but also in Taiwan, China, and overseas, that are the most sophisticated and influential criminal organizations in the region.

The linkup of the Japanese mob with Chinese triads ranks among the more ominous results of the yakuza's move into East Asia. Bound by ethnicity and codes of silence, the triads exist in various forms in Hong Kong and Thailand—where they finance much of the world's heroin trade—and wherever most of the world's 30 million overseas Chinese have settled. The triads, in fact, comprise one of the key links in global organized crime today, with connections ranging from Sydney, Singapore, and San Francisco to Amsterdam, Yokohama, and New York. Their range of criminal activity rivals that of the yakuza: gambling, drugs, prostitution, counterfeiting, fraud, extortion, loan sharking, and smuggling of all sorts, as well as major interests in finance, construction, and the film and entertainment industries. As such, it is of no small importance that alliances have been struck, and business begun, between the yakuza and the triads—the largest criminal organizations of the world's largest continent.

The danger here is not of a monolithic Asian Mafia invading the West. Such ideas are at best misinformed. Differences in language, custom, and history ensure that no great mergers will occur within the Asian underworld; indeed, the varied groups are as likely to be fighting among themselves as cooperating. Nevertheless, alliances do occur between powerful crime syndicates, particularly in narcotics and human trafficking. More important, informal networks are created that become the basis for much of the criminal activity that crosses borders.

To understand the significance of the triads and their relationship to the yakuza, some history is in order. The Chinese gangs exhibit many of the same traits as their Japanese counterparts: ancient rituals, loyalty and secrecy, and a history dating back some three hundred years. The triads similarly have carried a Robin Hood image through the years and are romanticized in movies and television series. And, like the yakuza, the triads have a history of heavy political involvement. Some Chinese scholars trace Chinese secret societies, from which the triads arose, to as far back as 21 A.D. Most accounts, though, cite the year 1674 as the legendary beginning of the first triad society, when a group of Buddhist monks at a monastery in Fujian province became a rallying point against that nation's oppressive Manchu rulers. The monks refined a highly effective form of self-defense that came to be called kung fu, and though their cause was a lost one, they founded a set of secret societies that would endure for generations. Years later, when Sun Yat-sen established the Chinese Republic in 1911, the triads were there to help him. In his bid to control China, Sun's successor, Chiang Kai-shek, repeatedly turned to the triads, which by then had become largely a criminal force with a heavy involvement in the opium trade. Chiang, in fact, was himself a triad member, and relied so heavily on his underworld allies that they served as generals, soldiers, spies, businessmen, and hired thugs in his Kuomintang (KMT), the Chinese Nationalist Army.

Mao's 1949 victory spelled death for the triads in mainland China. Smugglers, dealers, and hardened crooks of all sorts were summarily rounded up and imprisoned; many were simply shot. The Communist takeover of China, it is generally agreed, ended the nation's long ordeal with opium ad-

diction. It did not, however, end the triads. Wherever Chiang's Nationalist Army fled, the triads went along—to Hong Kong, Taiwan, and from the
south of China into Burma, where they built up the Golden Triangle heroin trade.

Hong Kong already had a serious problem with triad societies, thanks in
part to the Japanese. After Hong Kong fell to Japan during the war, the
colony's new masters formed the cooperative triads into the Hing Ah Kee
Kwa, the "Aid Asia Flourishing Association," and used them to help keep order. The Japanese shared with their collaborators the profits from prostitution and gambling, and allowed the gangs to control the opium trade in the
colony. The occupying Japanese, like the British before them, relied heavily on opium addiction to keep the population docile.

After the war, the triads sank their roots deeper into Hong Kong (again
in British hands), aided by the mass exodus of fellow members from the
mainland. The British then banned opium in the colony, which immediately gave rise to a thriving black market and a steady source of income
for postwar gangs. Soon the local triads were playing a central role in the
world's narcotics trade and were expanding rapidly. By the 1980s, despite
three decades of police crackdowns, Hong Kong's syndicates stood at
80,000 strong, with a solid core of professional criminals estimated at
12,000. By the late 1990s, Sun Yee On, the largest triad, claimed at least
30,000 members, rivaling the Yamaguchi-gumi.

Considering Hong Kong covers only 403 square miles and has a population of 6.7 million, the colony must have among the highest per capita
number of gangsters on the face of the earth. With its heavy presence of
Japanese business, trade, and tourism, Hong Kong is a natural for the yakuza. The tiny colony is at the same time one of the world's busiest ports,
a leading financial center, and a magnet for visitors. While the tourists are,
as always, a favorite target for vice, the companies have become a target
for the sokaiya, who, unsatisfied with returns at home, have moved their
unique brand of extortion abroad. More important to the gangs, though, is
Hong Kong's central role in exporting meth from southern China and
women from across Southeast Asia. As early as the mid-1970s, police say, the
Inagawa-kai, Sumiyoshi-kai, and other syndicates had set up nightclubs and
travel services in Hong Kong to facilitate their varied smuggling operations.

By 1980, police in Hong Kong were asking questions about the yakuza. A
confidential report that year by the Royal Hong Kong Police's Interpol Bureau concluded that the Sumiyoshi-kai was most active in the colony, but
warned of a serious lack of knowledge of yakuza activity. Citing the flood of
Japanese visitors and money pouring into the colony, officials wrote: "It
would be naive and shortsighted to assume that they are not active here. . . .
We have seen the ubiquitous line of Japanese tourists being led dutifully to
a particular shop. One wonders—just who is doing the leading?"

The yakuza may not have been leading the tours, but they found much in Hong Kong to keep them busy. Beginning in the early 1980s, the territory became a key trans-shipment point for methamphetamine, which by decade's end was available by the ton from southern China. Their key suppliers appear to be members of Hong Kong's infamous 14K triad, whose reach stretches from street gangs in San Francisco to drug kingpins in Amsterdam. The big triad is a favorite of the yakuza, supplying drugs, women, and whatever else their criminal brothers from Japan may desire. Another attraction for the Japanese mob is nearby Macao, the seedy gambling center plagued by bloody triad turf wars. Although crime is strictly a triad affair on Macao, police there report yakuza involvement in laundering money through the casinos, and in loan sharking and extortion.

The Taiwan Connection

After the Communist victory in China, the triads fled not only to Hong Kong and the Golden Triangle but also to Taiwan, although here they did not set up overtly criminal associations. By the 1970s, homegrown gangs had built themselves into formidable crime syndicates and had taken on the mantle of triad societies.

Taiwan, like Korea a Japanese colony for forty years, lies only seven hundred miles from the southern tip of Japan and holds a great attraction for the yakuza. This vibrant, modernized island of 22 million people served as one of the original sex tour destinations for Japan's male travelers, and continues to lure Japanese mobsters for various rackets. Taiwan became a favorite base for smuggling drugs, guns, and illegal aliens, and as a convenient hideout for fugitives. The gangs, meanwhile, invested heavily in real estate and various import-export companies, moving everything from carrots and bananas to folk art.

Unlike their counterparts in Thailand and Hong Kong, Taiwanese gang members handle only small amounts of heroin, but they moved heavily into meth production during the 1980s. Police believe the "Taiwan Connection" first began in 1975. Officials got an idea of the scope of the operation when in 1984 they uncovered a ring of smugglers that in a five-month period moved an estimated 163 kilograms from Taiwan into Japan, an amount worth $135 million. The gang's leading courier was alleged to be one Tancredo Duluc, the ambassador to Taiwan from the Dominican Republic. The diplomat, according to Taiwanese officials, had made more than forty-eight trips out of Taiwan in the past year.

To engage in such large-scale smuggling, strong crime syndicates are needed, and these Taiwan has in abundance—with hundreds of different gangs, most of them grouped under a half-dozen major syndicates. The nation's leading triad is the powerful United Bamboo Gang, which counts some 10,000 members and associates. Along with the next-largest group, the Four Seas Gang, they control much of the nation's prostitution, gambling, and protection rackets. During their long rule over Taiwan, the Nationalist Chinese Party used the gangs for political purposes, much as they had in China. Through the 1970s, the gangs were employed to spy on and disrupt political opponents of Chiang Kai-shek and his son and successor, Chiang Ching-kuo. Then, in 1984, the Taiwan Defense Ministry's Intelligence Bureau recruited leading Bamboo Gang members to silence Chinese American journalist Henry Liu, whom they murdered in his suburban garage outside San Francisco. Such official sponsorship backfired badly, discrediting the government and allowing the gangs to gain deep footholds in the entertainment and construction industries. As Taiwan democratized, the organized crime only grew worse. By the 1990s, the Taiwan mob had grown so powerful that a handful of anti-gang legislators required police protection. In 1996, Taiwan's justice minister alleged that the underworld had ties to many as 10 percent of the national legislature and 30 percent of local elected officials. Among the lawmakers allegedly mobbed up: Lo Fu-chu, the self-proclaimed "spiritual leader" of Taiwan's third-largest triad, the Heavenly Justice Alliance, who ironically won a seat on the national assembly's Justice Committee.

Such conditions were like putting out the welcome mat to the yakuza. So close did relations grow between Japanese and Taiwanese crime syndicates that the different gangs entered into formal alliances. United Bamboo members, for example, admit to having formed an important pact with the Yamaguchi-gumi. The May 1988 funeral of an underworld boss attracted not only members of Taiwan's United Bamboo Gang and other local gangs, but also representatives of the Yamaguchi-gumi and Sumiyoshi-kai. One Japanese syndicate sent twenty yakuza decked out in black suits. Again, in April 1993, some five hundred underworld figures from Japan, Hong Kong, and Taiwan gathered in Taipei to attend the lavish funeral of Liu Huan-jung, a ranking Bamboo Gang member dubbed the "Cold-Faced Assassin." Liu had been executed by the state for his murder of five rival gangsters.

The Bamboo Gang is something of a pioneer in setting up overseas ventures. It has long had affiliated members in Los Angeles and other U.S. cities, and in the early 1980s the syndicate hosted a lavish reception in Hong Kong to clinch a peace pact with the local triads. Using as a front its Churan United Sports Association, the Bamboo hierarchy sent out engraved dinner invitations proclaiming, "We are all members of a big family." Details are sketchy about this meeting of the mobs, but varied reports assert that in attendance were some 350 well-heeled triad leaders representing virtually every major Hong Kong group. Such gang parleys worry law enforcement officials, who see in them the possibility for endless sources of trouble. Growing international activity on the part of both Chinese and Japanese crime syndicates, coupled with the increasing sophistication of the gangs, means that new avenues of cooperation will emerge—new types of crimes, new investment scams, new smuggling routes. Some experienced lawmen, however, are cautious about how far-reaching the changes might be. "The alliances are mostly personal relationships," said a ranking Hong Kong police inspector with many years experience in combating the triads. "The links between organized crime groups in Asia depend on initiative— by the criminals, and by the police to stop them. It's not a static situation."

Initiative, unfortunately, is not lacking among Asia's great crime syndicates. And by the late 1980s, a great new opportunity appeared on radar screens of the region's mob bosses: the People's Republic of China was open for business. Both the triads and the yakuza responded in force.

China and the Yakuza

China's opening to the world in the 1980s brought more than just trade and industry; it ushered in levels of corruption and organized crime not seen since the pre-revolution days of Shanghai's infamous Green Gang. Pay-offs, shakedowns, counterfeit goods, prostitution, and gambling all became part of urban China as the gates to development and crime were thrown wide open.

As China moved to recover its lost territories of Hong Kong and Macao, concern grew that triad members from the colonies would flee to the West. While some criminal migration did indeed occur, the concern was largely misplaced—the triads found opportunity aplenty in the homeland and flocked into rackets across southern China. Hong Kong gangs spread through nearby Guangdong province, while gangs from Taiwan pushed into Fujian province, where they share common dialects. China's Communist leaders even made it clear that some triads would be considered "patriotic," prompting some analysts to warn of a budding alliance between organized crime and the Communist Party. Such fears proved well founded. By the late 1990s, the People's Liberation Army jointly owned a string of nightclubs with the Sun Yee On triad, while the Public Security Bureau—which includes China's police force—ran several high-class brothels. One of Hong Kong's most notorious businessmen, an alleged triad member, counts China's Ministry of Justice among his top stockholders.

The impact for Japan, and the rest of East Asia, was considerable. During the postwar era, China had figured hardly at all as an element in Japan's criminal troubles. But by the 1990s, China was altering the criminal balance of East Asia much as it was shifting the region's military and economic balance. By the early '90s, Japan had become China's chief trading partner, its largest foreign aid donor, and one of its top investors. China, meanwhile, had become Japan's biggest source of criminal headaches from abroad.

Movements of illegal drugs, arms, and aliens streamed out of the PRC, heading across Asia but in particular to lucrative markets in Japan. In 1991, police began seizing large numbers of Chinese-made Tokarev pistols, used by the PRC military. Through most of the decade, Japanese officials confiscated more Tokarevs than any other handgun model. Just one gang, a Matsuba-kai affiliate, smuggled in 2,300 Tokarevs between 1988 and 1991. So many Tokarevs spilled into Japan that the price plunged from some $2,000 to as little as $700. Other seized weapons included Chinese-made machine guns and at least one bazooka. China's southern Yunnan province, meanwhile, joined Burma, Laos, and Thailand as the fourth leg of what had become a Golden Quadrangle, with tons of heroin being trans-shipped for export abroad. Of greater impact for Japan was the meth trade, as Chinese drug lords set up factories in the south and northeast to feed underground markets in Tokyo and Osaka. "Snakeheads"—local agents and recruiters along the southern coast—also set up lucrative rackets in people smuggling.

All this offered the yakuza golden opportunities. Flush with money from the Bubble years, the gangs began building bases in China to augment their smuggling rackets. Japanese mobsters made investments in joint ventures, karaoke bars, and hotels. A study by Professor Su Zhiliang of Shanghai Normal University reportedly found large-scale yakuza investment along the Yangtze River, centering on Shanghai, but stretching into the cities of Zhenjiang, Nanjing, and Wuhan. Su found dozens of yakuza active in the region, providing the capital for businesses like nightclubs and karaoke pubs, working with local gangsters and triad members from Taiwan and Hong Kong. The booming Chinese market also attracted Japan's top sokaiya gang, Rondan Doyukai, which donated two eight-hundred-book "libraries" on Japanese business to Beijing University. Analysts believe the move was a ploy to recruit people to dig up dirt on Japanese corporations in China.

China was not the only emerging market attracting yakuza interest. As borders fell and markets opened in the post–Cold War world, opportunities abounded for enterprising gangsters. The yakuza had worked with Southeast Asian triads since the '70s, and the growing underworld in China was indeed enticing. Another criminal force, however, had entered the world stage. Russian crooks were knocking on Japan's door, and the yakuza were curious.

Russian Mob Ties

Perhaps no development has changed the face of global organized crime more than the rise of the Russian Mafia. From the rubble of the Soviet empire has sprung a far-reaching criminal class comprised of several thousand gangs, whose influence extends from major banks and businesses to the ruling councils of former Soviet republics. They have played key roles in stripping those countries of billions of dollars in currency, precious metal, natural resources, and more. While less organized than Italian or Japanese crime syndicates, Russian mobsters have shown an enterprise and a ruthlessness that has enabled them to expand worldwide at alarming speed. And it is not only the Russians at work, but a panoply of violent ethnic gangs: Georgians, Chechens, Ukrainians, and more. Former KGB and police agents are behind many of the gangs, and they have blazed a multinational trail that has brought them into contact with the world's top crime syndicates—including the yakuza.

Russia and Japan remain distant neighbors, due largely to the dispute over Soviet seizure of Japan's northern islands at the end of World War II. Trade between the Russian Far East and Japan has nonetheless increased rapidly, so it was no surprise that eventually the Russian and Japanese mafias would meet up. The ties remain tentative, but the future offers great opportunity for Russo-Japanese criminal activity. The early signs already are clear, with stolen cars and consumer goods heading to Russia, while arms, women, and pilfered seafood head to Japan.

At Japan's northernmost ports, Russian sailors have offered various arms—including automatic weapons and hand grenades—in exchange for cash, cars, or consumer goods. Others bring illegal shipments of marine products to port, or trade them at sea. Much of the rackets is apparently based out of Vladivostok, which serves as portal to the Russian Far East. It is also one of Russia's most mobbed-up cities. In one 1997 case, Japanese cops busted a car theft ring so well organized that a Russian broker in Vladivostok gave orders for the model and color of each vehicle to be stolen. Run by a former yakuza boss, the gang shipped over $20 million worth of cars before authorities caught up with them. By the end of the '90s, Japanese prosecutors believed more than 17,000 cars had left Japan in questionable deals.

Russian women have now joined Southeast Asians in the international sex trade. Tens of thousands of Russian women from the former Soviet Union are being sent overseas each year, to Macao, Dubai, Germany, the U.S.—and Japan, where they are seen as exotic and command high fees. The scope of the trade can be seen in the number of visas for "entertainers" (long a euphemism for bar girls or prostitutes) granted to Russians by Japanese officials—nearly 5,000 in 1995, accounting for one in five of all Russian visas. As they have with Southeast Asian women, Japanese police have shown little inclination to interfere with the trade, and it is left to churches and nonprofit organizations to offer what little assistance there is.

Working with the Russians can be hazardous, as a Sumiyoshi-kai boss learned in 1994. The owner of a seafood trading firm, he was murdered while on a business trip to Sakhalin, the big Russian island northeast of Japan. But that hasn't deterred other business-minded yakuza. One Yamaguchi-gumi boss all but announced his intention to work with the Russian mob, telling *Mainichi* reporters that he planned to spend six months in Russia learning the language and meeting his criminal brethren. "As a nation is in trouble, there must be sources of income," he explained. "We would like to research the market."

La Yakuza Latina

Researching the market was something the yakuza appeared keen to do worldwide. By the mid-1980s, the yakuza's travels already had taken them far beyond East Asia—to South America, Western Europe, and the countries on the farther reaches of the Pacific Rim. Indeed, the gangs have shown an eagerness to make connections in virtually every nation where an opportunity has presented itself. Little is known about the yakuza's activities in many of these places. Few of the crimes get reported, and local police seldom know what to look for. Missing fingers and body tattoos are not regularly on the minds of Customs inspectors in Sydney and Sao Paulo.

Like Chinese mobsters, though, the yakuza tend to congregate mostly where large ethnic communities tied to the homeland reside. Nowhere is this truer than in the case of Brazil. Japanese have been migrating in large numbers to Brazil since the 1930s, when many went to work as agricultural laborers. After the end of World War II, a huge wave of immigrants arrived, many of them former soldiers who, once repatriated to Japan, left their war-torn homeland to seek a new life abroad. As a result, today there are over 1 million ethnic Japanese living in South America. More than three-quarters of them live in Brazil, making it the largest Japanese settlement outside of Japan. Another 80,000 reside in Peru, 30,000 in Argentina, and 10,000 in Bolivia. The enormous number living in Brazil has helped make that country one of Japan's top centers of foreign investment. It has also helped nurture a Japanese underworld, both imported and homegrown.

Brazil has its share of organized crime problems without the yakuza: a rising cocaine trade spilling over from nearby Bolivia and Peru, active associates of the Italian Mafiosi, and down-and-out members of the country's varied ethnic groups. The yakuza have found their niche in the heart of Brazil's Japanese community, the Liberdade (Liberty) district of the huge city of Sao Paulo. Some 250,000 Japanese live there, squashed into twenty square blocks of that city of more than 17 million.

The yakuza apparently first caught the attention of the Brazilian media in the late 1970s, when violence erupted between Japanese and Korean gangs in Liberdade. Those involved have rightly been called *gurentai,* or hoodlums, by the Japanese community there. These young gangsters don't cut off their fingers or go in for tattooing. But many have kept up ties with yakuza in Japan, and much of their criminal activity sounds surprisingly familiar. In tandem with yakuza from abroad, they have set up commercial businesses as fronts, with a preference for restaurants, bars, import-export companies, and floral shops. They are heavily into smuggling—Brazilian goods out of the country, and Japanese goods (mostly electronic items, on which Brazil has strict quotas) into the country. Within the Liberdade area they control gambling, drugs, prostitution, and protection rackets. Other reports suggest that the Brazilian yakuza have moved into vending and slot machines and construction.

The yakuza made another media splash in Brazil in 1979, when police cornered two gangsters involved in a murder-for-insurance scheme strikingly similar to those occurring in the Philippines at about the same time. After fleeing to Taiwan, Paraguay, and Sao Paulo, the yakuza eventually made their way to the town of Araguaia outside Brasilia, where they died in a shootout with federal agents. But it was not until the 1980s that ties between the yakuza and their Brazilian cousins mushroomed, when Japan imported more than 100,000 Brazilians to help ease a labor shortage. Some seventy recruitment agencies sprang up in Japanese cities, many of them targeting Japanese Brazilian men and Brazilian women of all kinds. The sex trade took off, as did gun and drug smuggling. In 1994, Brazilian police were stunned to find a genuine yakuza boss from the Yamaguchi-gumi hiding out in the southern state of Parana. The oyabun, complete with missing finger and full-body tattoos, was believed to be running cocaine, prostitutes, and laborers to Japan, as well as laundering money through real estate transactions.

The yakuza have caused troubles elsewhere in Latin America, notably in the sex trade. Recruiters of prostitutes and hostesses have conned women from Mexico to Brazil into trips to Japan. In 1996, when Mexican authorities announced they had uncovered a decade-long sex trafficking operation, the ring sounded all too familiar. In typical fashion, Japanese agents set up offices to recruit "entertainers" and sent as many as 3,000 women to Japan under the guise of hostesses in nightclubs. One recruiter, when caught by Mexican police, had a list of 1,200 women with him. Another group operated in the early 1990s out of San José, Costa Rica, recruiting more than one hundred women not only from across Latin America but also from Canada and Germany.

The region is a source of guns as well. Yakuza gunrunning operations have been tied to Argentina, Bolivia, Panama, and, most of all, to Brazil. Brazilian-made handguns were the source of one of Japan's largest-ever smuggling cases, stretching from Yokohama to Capetown, South Africa. During the early 1990s, yakuza associates smuggled more than 1,000 of the Brazilian guns and over 10,000 rounds of ammunition into Japanese ports aboard tuna boats from Capetown. Most of the guns were sold to major crime syndicates; several ended up being used in some of Japan's most notorious crimes, including the attempted robbery of an armored truck in 1992, a rightist assassination attempt that year against LDP vice president Shin Kanemaru, and various yakuza shooting incidents.

It remains unclear what other activities Japan's shadier businessmen are up to in Latin America. The yakuza have forged ties with Colombia's cocaine cartels, although, as noted earlier, this has yet to result in a flood of coke reaching Japanese shores. Police suspect considerable yakuza money has found its way to the region, but little is known about the precise investments. The gangs, though, may find Latin America ripe for expansion someday. Perhaps that's what the Bubble Era's top yakuza, Susumu Ishii, had in mind when he reportedly doled out $360,000 in cash to then-president Noriega in 1989. One of the Inagawa-kai godfather's backers, Aoki Construction, allegedly made $4 million in payoffs of its own to Noriega. Ishii and Aoki had plans for a huge golf and gambling resort in Macao, and perhaps similar plans were under way in Panama.

"Yakuza en Paris"

It is not surprising, perhaps, that if the yakuza made their way to Colombia and Paraguay, they would turn up in Western Europe. The Old World's many attractions have not escaped Japanese crooks. Shaking down their countrymen, smuggling guns and hard-core porn, stealing art, buying up real estate, and touring the Continent all have brought Japan's mafia to Europe. Intelligence gathered by U.S. Customs reveals that in the late 1980s and early 1990s, yakuza and their associates visited at least eight cities across the region: Barcelona, Berlin, Bologna, Dusseldorf, Helsinki, London, Nice, and Paris.

While not as plentiful as in the United States or parts of Asia, Western Europe's gun dealers have long attracted the yakuza. As early as 1965, an Air France pilot was caught smuggling guns to the yakuza. Italian guns later proved popular among the gangs. In 1982, Japanese police stopped a twenty-eight-year-old member of the Kyosei-kai and charged him with smuggling three hundred .25-caliber Garesi handguns and 20,000 bullets he had picked up in Milan. A year later a second smuggler was nabbed with thirty-seven of the guns. More recent seizures have been traced not only to Italy but to Germany, Spain, and Belgium. In one 1995 case, police seized 1,300 miniature pistols imported from Austria.

The gangs have turned to Europe for drugs as well. Germany has been a source of meth and France of ecstasy (MDMA) for the gangs. Germany has also attracted yakuza-owned trading companies specializing in the export of expensive cars to Japan. Cases of slave trading are suspected as well, on the basis of the yakuza's central role as broker for the Southeast Asian women so popular among Dutch and German men. Sometimes European cities are used merely as a back door for the sex trade. In one particularly heinous case, Italian authorities in 1997 uncovered an international pedophilia racket tied to Japanese and Chinese mobsters. Customs police nabbed a Japanese man and Chinese woman coming in from Bangkok after a twelve-year old girl with them pleaded for help. The girl claimed she had been taken from her parents in China and forced to work as a prostitute in Thailand. The couple claimed to be the girl's relatives, but officials found they had false passports and had made multiple trips through Italy bound for the United States. Europe's huge pornography industry also holds an attraction for the Japanese gangs. Back in 1980, Sumiyoshi-kai associates were smuggling out of Northern Europe hard-core porno films, which were then banned in Japan.

Investigators are convinced the yakuza have made substantial investments in Europe, particularly during the Bubble, but hard intelligence is tough to find. Unconfirmed reports allege that yakuza invested in a French castle; one reliable source claims a top yakuza syndicate invested along with the now-defunct Heiwa Sogo Bank in Vatican holdings.

Unsurprisingly, the yakuza have found Europe attractive for what is perhaps their favorite scam: fleecing Japanese corporations. Pushed by the crackdown on sokaiya in Japan, a handful of these professional extortionists have explored Europe as a new hunting ground. Japanese companies, always conscious about their public image, have proved easy targets for sokaiya clever enough to relocate abroad. Seiji Hamamoto, a notorious practitioner of the trade, opened a "foreign correspondent office" in London in the fall of 1981. Police in Tokyo lost little time in labeling it a front for blackmailing subsidiaries of Japanese companies. Other sokaiya also found London a convenient haunt, with its bustling financial markets and plentiful numbers of Japanese bankers and brokers. Authorities suspected Japanese mobsters had set up shop at several nightclubs and restaurants, and were engaged in not only extortion but also insider trading.

One leading sokaiya group, Rondan Doyukai, seems partial to the Continent. During the early 1980s, the gang invested thousands of dollars in the stock of at least three large European firms: Rotterdamsch Beleggings Consortium, Compagnie Française des Petroles, and Compagnie Financiere de Paris et des Pays Bas (PARIBAS). The group followed up its investments in 1984, when, fresh from shaking down the Isetan department store in Japan, it sent eleven of its members on a whirlwind tour of Europe, taking in the sights of London, Paris, Geneva, and Rome.

France holds a special place in Japanese hearts, and the yakuza are no exception. French food and fashion are prized in Tokyo, and Paris is a popular destination for Japanese heading abroad. Still, it was a shock to a Japanese police commissioner visiting Paris for a seminar when he bumped into several leading members of the Yamaguchi-gumi. That was back in the 1970s, but the yakuza have kept up their affinity for things French. In 1988, a French television show even invited top yakuza from two Yamaguchi-gumi gangs to appear on national TV. Before 3.5 million viewers, the pinkieless gangsters spoke confidently of their work as sokaiya, rightists, and investors in a top corporation. "We try to teach the Japanese spirit to the Japanese," explained Masaru Fujii of the Fujii-gumi. "We break up labor strikes and we march to demonstrate opposition to the leftists." The event prompted coverage by one Japanese weekly, under the title "Yakuza en Paris."

So popular has Paris been with the Japanese mob that Masaru Takumi, the notorious number two boss of the Yamaguchi-gumi, tried to enter the city in 1992. Out on bail for breaking currency exchange laws, Takumi got an Osaka court to grant a one-month reprieve to visit France for treatment of diabetes and a liver ailment. But Takumi apparently had more on his mind than the high state of French medicine. Japanese police learned he had planned to meet in Paris the Yamaguchi-gumi godfather himself, Yoshinori Watanabe, and two of his top deputies. The group, police said, had planned a European junket that would take them to Milan, Venice, Geneva, and London, where they would check into "business opportunities."

French authorities had other ideas, however. On learning of Takumi's visit, officials turned away the yakuza boss at Orly airport, sending him back to Tokyo that same day. With word of their visit in the press, the other yakuza bosses quietly canceled their European tour.

The French had good reason to keep Takumi and his pals out of their country. The few Japanese crooks hanging around were already causing them headaches, ranging from art theft to money laundering. By the mid-1980s, Japan had become a popular market for stolen art; not only did the Japanese have money and a taste for French paintings, but Japanese law made it almost impossible to recover them once they were stolen. Police traced one 1984 theft back to two French nationals and a Japanese ex-con who had done time in French prison. The gang had stolen four paintings by Camille Corot from a museum in eastern France, but these were recovered in Japan three years later. While in Japan to recover the paintings, investigators from the French police's Office for the Repression of Art Theft found the yakuza actually helpful regarding the fate of another famous theft. These yakuza had been approached by sellers hoping to unload nine paintings stolen at gunpoint from France's Mermotten Museum in 1985, including the Monet masterpiece *Impression—Sunrise*. The painting, which gave impressionism its name, depicts dawn over the French port of Le Havre. Tipped off by the yakuza, French cops eventually tracked down the stolen art in a Corsican villa.

Fine art is not the only French product that has attracted Japan's gangsters. In April 1992, authorities shut down what they claimed was a sophisticated money-laundering ring run by the yakuza in Paris. Over six years, the group washed some $75 million in cash by smuggling and wiring gang profits to France, which they used to buy French designer luxury goods. Each day, the gang sent Japanese students, and sometimes Chinese or Vietnamese as well, to shops in posh neighborhoods to buy handbags and clothing made by Hermes, Louis Vuitton, Chanel, and Lancel. The students reportedly held bankrolls of 500-franc notes the gang had withdrawn from banks in Luxembourg, Switzerland, and the Channel Islands. Working through a front company, the group then exported the goods to Japan and sold them at a small loss—leaving the yakuza with plentiful cash that was now "clean." French police arrested four Japanese and three accomplices, including a corrupt French Customs official, and seized 2,500 luxury items worth $2.3 million.

The Gold Coast

Australia, too, has proved an attractive destination for the yakuza, as it has for Japanese generally. The flight there takes eight hours, but one arrives in eastern Australia from Japan without crossing any time zones and in the opposite season. It's a big country with plenty of space and low prices. Maybe that's why half a million Japanese make the trip each year. And among those half-million legitimate tourists are a number of yakuza. In fact, the yakuza have taken an interest in Australia since the early 1980s. They have invested millions of dollars in real estate, set up various front companies, and continued to visit. Sometimes it's just to play, and sometimes it's all business.

The yakuza have shown a particular fondness for Queensland's Gold Coast. The southern coast of Queensland is tropical and warm, with a laissez-faire attitude. Moreover, Queensland cops have had a nagging problem with corruption, illegal gambling, drugs, and prostitution. So it's not surprising that yakuza have shown up in police intelligence reports. For instance, in the tourist mecca of Surfers Paradise, yakuza have attempted to extort money from Japanese tourists. And in 1988 the NPA reported that about thirty Yamaguchi-gumi members entered Australia on tourist visas and were surveilled as they frolicked on the Gold Coast beach. In 1990, a group of fourteen others gambled away $1 million in four days. Later, the Yamaguchi-gumi bought and maintained at least three corporate beach-front holiday villas in Queensland.

But it has been the money the yakuza bring with them that's excited the interest of Australian authorities. Police have observed yakuza with huge amounts of cash—in the million-dollar range—visiting casinos and hob-nobbing with casino management. At first, officials thought the Japanese mob was using couriers to launder money in casinos. But there was more. Police noticed that top yakuza bosses had gambled away millions at casinos across Australia: Diamond Beach in Darwin; Jupiter's at the Gold Coast; Bertwood in Perth.

By the late 1980s, this yakuza activity was squarely on the radar screen, and by 1989, it had stirred an ugly debate. Aussies, already nervous over billions of dollars in foreign investment streaming into their land, needed little encouragement to get overly excited over the yakuza. One Liberal MP called for a ban on tattooed Japanese with severed fingers. While the reaction was tinged with racism and certainly overblown, local concern was legitimate. By 1995, Japanese had bought nearly $4 billion of land comprising over 166,000 hectares, including hotels, golf courses, and resorts—and many Australians deeply resented it. But whether the yakuza represented a significant proportion of those purchases was open to question.

In the mid-1990s, there was a major debate within the law enforcement community over the degree of threat posed by Japanese organized crime. By 1994, Australian police had launched five major investigations into yakuza activity, from corporate investment and moves to enter the nation's construction industry to extortion and defrauding of local Japanese companies, as well as luring Australian women into the sex racket in Japan. But no major cases were made, and a 1995 parliamentary report was cautious, concluding that "there appears to be no hard direct evidence of illegal activity by yakuza gangs in Australia."

On the other hand, Australian officials found that at least two hundred known yakuza had entered the country during the decade from 1986 to 1996. Other intelligence reports revealed that at least twenty-eight yakuza and associates from seven major gangs traveled to Australia on at least sixty-five occasions between 1986 and 1993. Most had gone to Sydney and Brisbane, but others had ventured to Cairns, Melbourne, Perth, and Townsville, as well as to Auckland, New Zealand. And then there remained the question of high-ranking yakuza hanging around.

In May 1990, Chun Yong I, a boss of the ethnic Korean gang Toa Yuai, entered Australia with nearly $100,000 in cash. Police noticed that he was short a couple of fingers, but they did not catch the fact that Chun neglected to check off his twenty-seven legal offenses and thirteen years in jail on his visa application. Nor was Chun the only one. A top Sumiyoshi-kai boss, head of the Shino-gumi, visited Australia six times, three of them as a guest of the Conrad Jupiters Casino. Each time he was accompanied by bodyguards and arrived holding a leather bag with a reputed $1 million in cash stuffed inside. He was observed making various investments in land and Australian companies.

Or take Masaru Takumi, the notorious number two man in the Yamaguchi-gumi, one of the most successful keizai yakuza, nicknamed "the man who never sleeps." Takumi made a considerable effort to insinuate himself into Australia. In 1987, he was granted a four-year multiple-entry visa to the country. He purchased, through Takumi Enterprises Pty Ltd., a penthouse at Surfers Paradise on the Gold Coast worth A$880,500. According to law enforcement, Takumi's next-door neighbor in Surfers Paradise was Suemitsu Ito, who would later be indicted for his alleged role in the mob-looting of Itoman and Company. Ito and Takumi were apparently more than neighbors; Takumi flew to Guam on Ito's private jet, according to law enforcement sources. All told, Takumi visited Queensland five times: twice in 1987, twice in 1988, once in 1992. In 1991, Australian authorities even approved his request for a new visa, despite his record of having been jailed five times in Japan.

But Takumi's reputation finally caught up with him. After hard questions were raised in parliament in 1993, Australia's immigration minister revoked Takumi's visa. His pal Ito fared just as badly. Ito had purchased a vacant block in the center of Surfers Paradise where he intended to erect a grand hotel. Ito was big-time, and worked with Minoru Isutani, a major shareholder in the Gold Coast's biggest development, the massive Hope Island project. But Ito was charged with fraud and embezzlement in the Itoman scandal, and his ambitious plans for Australia crashed along with Itoman.

So, too, ended Mitsuhiro Kotani, the notorious stock speculator who worked with the Inagawa-kai's Ishii during the Bubble. Kotani bought a huge Gold Coast golf course resort—five-star hotel, condos, the works. He also bought apartment buildings, vacant lots, and land in the nearby countryside. But again, the properties were never developed after Kotani fell into trouble back home.

Others were keen on entering Australia's gambling industry. In 1991, a yakuza front company nearly obtained a casino license in the capital city of Canberra. After investigating the yakuza's Bubble-era investments, authorities suspected the yakuza held a significant share of the nearly $8 billion believed laundered through Australia each year. Not all were top-dollar investments, of course, but most of them were lavish. One yakuza boss paid twice the going rate for a run-down sheep farm, which he hoped to turn into a kind of yakuza retreat for his men. In the end, he was deported for concealing his criminal record.

There were indications that the yakuza might be committing more than financial crimes, though. In 1992 and again in 1994, Japanese couriers were nabbed with Southeast Asian heroin. Both times, the couriers had ties to Yamaguchi-gumi; one was a Tokyo yakuza member, another a retired cop. They were not small-time: the 1994 case involved a yakuza coming into Melbourne from Kuala Lumpur with thirteen kilograms of heroin. Others committed crimes more bizarre. Consider the case of Akiko Kitayama, who with her sixty-two-year-old ex-yakuza husband retired on the Gold Coast. The Kitayamas had done well enough to post a $530,000 bond to secure residency, but hubby had been hobbled by a severe stroke. Apparently anxious to move on, Mrs. Kitayama allegedly murdered her husband, chopped up his body with an electric saw in the bathroom, and left his remains for the garbagemen to collect.

But perhaps the strangest link between Australia and the yakuza was the case of John Joseph Hills. The twenty-one-year-old native of Sydney was raised in Japan, attended a Japanese school, and called himself Jo Kodama. In Japan, he fell into bad company and followed a route many homegrown yakuza had tread: sniffing and selling glue ingredients and being sent to a reform center for stealing. Eventually, he joined the Sumiyoshi-kai, becoming a driver and front man for a gang company until being charged with the forced detention and sexual abuse of a seventeen-year-old Japanese girl.

No one thinks Jo Kodama set a pattern for the Australians. Few Aussie crooks are likely keen on becoming members of the Japanese mob. There was money to be made with the yakuza, though, and hundreds of foreigners were ready to try their luck, not only overseas but, like Jo, within Japan itself.

A Foreign Crime Wave Hits Japan

In a fitting bit of irony, while the yakuza were exploring criminal opportunities overseas, foreign crooks were returning the favor. The same forces of globalization that were drawing the yakuza abroad—new markets, a strong yen, cheap travel—also were attracting waves of outsiders to insular Japan. Some found Japan, with its safe streets and trusting ways, ripe for a crime wave.

The trouble began in the mid-1980s, when those in the sex trade were joined by waves of other foreign workers, attracted by the strong yen and the promise of plentiful jobs. Japanese found themselves with a powerhouse economy, a labor shortage, and young people unwilling to do work involving the three K's: *kitanai, kitsui, kiken* (dirty, demanding, dangerous). More than 200,000 Latin Americans of Japanese descent poured into Japan during the 1990s. Other visitors came from Southeast Asia, Pakistan, Bangladesh, China, and Iran. From 1990 to 1993, the number of foreigners overstaying their visas nearly tripled to some 300,000, according to Justice Ministry statistics. By 2000, the number had reached a half-million.

The influx of foreign workers—many of them illegal—sharply expanded the underground networks of human trafficking to Japan. The varied smuggling rings boosted an underground economy of false papers, money-making scams, and other crime that lent itself to yakuza control and influence. Passports could be had for some $2,000, a bogus marriage to a Japanese man for $5,000. Once in Japan, foreign workers from poorer nations often found themselves at the mercy of yakuza-run employment agencies, which raked off as much as half of an immigrant's wages as commission. One gang running a group of Thai construction laborers took $70 from their daily wage of $170. The yakuza had pocketed some $200,000 by the time police began asking questions.

By the mid-1990s, the traffic in human cargo had turned heavily Chinese. Again, the yakuza were heavily involved, working with notorious Chinese brokers dubbed "snakeheads." Yakuza helped arranged boats, booked passage within Japan, and secured the aliens in safe houses. With the collapse of the Bubble Economy, human trafficking proved a lucrative and reliable source of income. One Hong Kong gang boasted an 80 percent success rate in smuggling people into Japan. The supply of Chinese hoping to book passage, moreover, was huge. Japan ranks close behind the United States as a favored destination for Chinese illegal migrants, and the sea journey to Japan is far shorter and cheaper than heading to the New World. The boat trip from China's Fujian province to southern Japan takes about a week, and the cost to would-be immigrants is some $25,000 to $30,000, compared with as much as $45,000 to the U.S. As with the traffic in sex workers, the migrants typically enter a kind of indentured servitude, paying back the fees at painfully slow rates once they arrive in Japan. Horror stories abound of those who fail to pay: the chopping off of ears and fingers, women forced into prostitution, kidnappings until family back in China comes up with the money.

Along with the growth in illegal immigration came the spread of foreign crime gangs. For the Japanese, who like to think of their society as homogenous, it came as a shock that organized crime in Japan was no longer the exclusive domain of the yakuza. In a sign of the times, Tokyo police in 1991 found over 1,000 foreigners active as members or associates of the city's yakuza gangs. Most were Korean, followed by Chinese, but the survey also noted a number of Filipinos and Thais, seven Americans, a Russian, a Turk, and an Australian.

By the mid-1990s, it was clear that crime in Japan's biggest cities had gone international. The South Koreans were involved in everything from pickpocket gangs to the meth trade. Thai gangsters were smuggling drugs and, working with yakuza, running gambling dens for illegal Thai workers. Police had tied Vietnamese crooks to stolen jewelry, vehicle theft, and heroin traffic. Iranian hustlers were doing a brisk business in counterfeit phone cards. Nigerian con artists were busy at work fleecing unwitting Japanese. Small-time Israeli racketeers began arriving in the mid-1980s, and gained a tough reputation. Soon they were involved with yakuza in drugs, arms, counterfeit goods, and stolen property. Even the French were taking part. In 1987, while the yakuza were dealing in stolen French art and laundering money through Paris, a French gang apparently returned the favor by pulling off Japan's largest bank robbery.

It was the Chinese, though, that posed the biggest headache for Japanese law enforcement. The first wave arrived in the 1980s from Taiwan. Gangsters from the island's top two syndicates, United Bamboo and Four Seas, opened restaurants in Tokyo, using them as fronts for drug deals, prostitution, and gambling. Hong Kong's top triad societies soon followed: by the late 1990s, the Sun Yee On and 14K had established strong bases in Japan's big cities, relying on alliances with major yakuza syndicates. The more sophisticated gangs flew in members from Hong Kong and mainland China to commit crimes and then flee. But it was the influx of often desperately poor immigrants from China itself that filled the ranks of the most troublesome gangs. Hundreds of thugs from Shanghai, Beijing, and Fuzhou set up rackets in Japan, with turf wars erupting at times into bloody conflict. The Chinese gangs spun a growing web of organized crime. Their widespread theft of jewelry, watches, and designer clothes led to a thriving industry for fenced goods, stretching from Shanghai's boutiques to corner discount stores in Tokyo. Other crimes included credit card fraud, pachinko fraud, software piracy, armed robbery, kidnapping, murder, and the smuggling of drugs and illegal aliens. "The mainland Chinese are learning from the Hong Kong gangsters," observed Mo Bang-fu, a Chinese crime expert in Japan.

Between 1992 and 1996, crimes by foreigners jumped nearly fivefold in Japan. Police were arresting record numbers of them—and nearly half were Chinese. The foreign crime wave fed a growing backlash to the presence of so many immigrants among the insular Japanese, prompting alarmist calls for crackdowns on illegal aliens and foreign crooks. In 1993, rightists in Tokyo plastered the city with swastika-marked posters, calling for the expulsion of all immigrants. One flier warned that foreign workers were "threatening our culture, history and lifestyle" and vowed to "take action" against them. Sensational media reports told of how ruthless Chinese thugs had pushed the yakuza out of their old haunt of Kabukicho, a sleazy nightlife district in Tokyo. "Kabukicho," asserted one breathless tabloid, "is no longer part of Japan." Added the weekly *Sunday Mainichi:* "The day when Japan is run by the world's gangsters may not be far off." One 1992 Japanese movie, *Heavenly Sin,* featured Iranians setting fire to police cars, leering Filipinas and Africans, and gangs of foreign laborers pillaging the streets of Tokyo under a local Chinese gang ruled by an Arab. Adding to the alarm was none other than Tokyo mayor Shintaro Ishihara, who in 2000 publicly warned of riots by foreigners should an earthquake strike the city. Police, too, have played on Japan's well-worn xenophobia, with report after report warning of an invasion of criminals from abroad. After seizures of Chinese illegal aliens doubled in 1997, the NPA told a Diet committee the trade was becoming "a threat to national security."

Such fears, however, are overblown. While foreign gangs are making their mark in Japan, organized crime there remains very much a yakuza affair. Indeed, the various bands of foreign crooks serve largely at the Japanese mob's pleasure. They are far smaller, less organized, and relatively un-sophisticated. As one streetwise Iranian gangster told the *Japan Times,* "Over here, we Iranians can't do anything without help from the yakuza." They are a success because the yakuza allow them to be. The Japanese mob contin-ues to be Japan's tried and true equal opportunity employer, working with Chinese snakeheads, Israeli drug dealers, or Iranian fraud artists. The vast majority of racketeering, extortion, and organized vice crime remains very much in the hands of the yakuza. What the foreign gangs have done, how-ever, is add a dangerous new element to the mix. With yakuza operating overseas in significant numbers, and foreign gangsters now based in Japan, the opportunities for cooperation have never been greater. Moreover, the advent of foreign gangs within the country poses new challenges to Japa-nese police, who were never noted for their international outlook. The cops' lack of language skills and informants is worrisome enough, but the foreign crooks have proved frustrating for another reason: unlike yakuza, few foreign suspects ever confess.

As police played catch-up to the new crooks in Japan, the yakuza continued to explore opportunities overseas. Despite their attractions, South America and Europe are still somewhat far afield for the Japanese mob. China and Australia beckon, and Southeast Asia remains a favorite haunt. But like other Japanese businessmen, the more ambitious yakuza and their front men long ago set their sights on the United States. It should not have come as a surprise, then, when tattooed men from Japan began showing up on the beaches of Hawaii and Guam, and on the U.S. mainland itself. By the early 1970s, the yakuza were already setting up bases in the United States, em-barking on a sometimes sloppy campaign of crime that would take them first to America's Pacific islands, and then on to Los Angeles, San Francisco, New York, and nationwide.

CHAPTER ELEVEN

ACROSS THE PACIFIC

FRED GUSHIN HAD NEVER HEARD OF THE YAKUZA. THE NEW JERSEY NATIVE had spent seven years as head of enforcement for his state's Casino Control Commission, and he had seen his share of mobsters, con men, and other crooks. But in 1991, Gushin unwittingly put himself on a collision course with the Japanese mob. That was the year he quit his job and began looking for a new challenge. An ad had caught his eye, for a position advising a new gambling commission in Tinian.

Tinian?

Gushin soon found himself 7,000 miles from home in the western Pacific, on a speck of land ninety miles from Guam. Tinian, along with Saipan and Rota, was part of the CNMI—the Commonwealth of the Northern Marianas Islands, U.S. possessions that were closer to the Philippines and Japan than even Hawaii. Tinian's 3,000 residents had decided they wanted a world-class gambling industry, and they wanted talent like Gushin to help make it happen. Gushin took the job, and set about putting together a top-notch enforcement division. If major gambling money was coming to the CNMI, Gushin wanted to ensure that it was clean.

That, it turned out, was the last thing its developers wanted. Before it was over, Gushin would battle front men for Japan's biggest crime syndicates, as well as his own employers, and would end up fleeing the islands after just a year.

Trouble at Broadway and 42nd

It's a little difficult to believe that any Japanese would have wanted to see the Northern Marianas after the war. First, there was the Battle of Saipan, which claimed 40,000 Japanese lives, including some 9,000 civilians who chose to fling themselves over what is known as Banzai Cliff rather than be captured by the Americans. Then, neighboring Tinian played host to the B-29 squadron, including the famed *Enola Gay*, which laid waste to Hiroshima. Yet, a few decades later, Japanese tourists filled jumbo jets to make the three-hour flight south to the balmy Marianas.

Much of Saipan, with a population of 50,000, was turned into a huge beach club and shopping mall catering largely to the Japanese. On the other side of the island, out of sight of tourist eyes, were dozens of fenced-off garment factories employing thousands of Chinese and Filipinos who labored for sub-minimum wages in sub-minimum conditions. Although this was nominally U.S. land, the Northern Marianas are a commonwealth, and customs and immigration are run by locals.

All this was music to yakuza ears. The gangs had been scouting the Pacific for congenial landing spots, and officials had traced yakuza forays as far afield as New Caledonia, Tahiti, and the Marshall Islands. On Guam, the ya-kuza were involved in their usual rackets of laundering money and smuggling guns and drugs. One venture in Palau, about five hundred miles east of the Philippines, had not worked out so well. According to Bill O'Reilly, who as an FBI agent chased yakuza through the region in the 1980s, the Japanese found that Palau's local officials could be just as crooked and conniving as they were. During the mid-1980s, one gang joined with a top politician to finance the building of an airport hotel, only to lose control of the project over "permit problems." A few years later, the U.S. DEA joined with other authorities in Operation Fruitbat, which indicted forty-six people around the Pacific on smuggling charges. Those arrested included yakuza and Palauan officials.

But it seemed that luck would improve in the Marianas. In 1991, the island of Tinian decided to move forward in licensing gambling casinos. Despite its small size and minuscule population, Tinian had big-time aspirations. Perhaps that was because Tinian from the air resembles the island of Manhattan. So much so that when conquering American GIs laid out streets in 1945, they named the north-south thoroughfare Broadway, and the east-west street 42nd. On the other hand, Tinian, like Saipan and nearby Rota, also claimed to be home to the largest per-capita consumers of Budweiser, Spam, and Tabasco sauce. In any case, there was little doubt that casinos would drastically alter, if not obliterate, the tranquillity of the island. But the leaders of Tinian were determined.

Immediately, yakuza-connected Japanese tried to buy their way to casino ownership. The yakuza had been active in the Marianas and Guam since the late 1970s, and had tried before to bankroll a gambling center in the CNMI. This time they must have sensed a golden opportunity. It was the height of the Bubble Economy and there was money to buy both casinos and local fixers. What the gangs hadn't counted on was an honest regulator from New

Jersey. Determined to screen out any mobbed-up applicants, Fred Gushin hired top-notch private investigators to do background checks and consulting firm Arthur Anderson to go over the books of prospects. Gushin was soon shocked at what they were finding. Before long, he concluded that the Japanese mob was making a major push to control the new gambling industry, setting up operations to skim casino funds, launder money, own legitimate fronts, and develop a back door into the United States. He found that of seven applicants, none had any experience in the gaming industry, and all had problems with either yakuza ties, integrity issues, or ability to raise capital.

These were not impulsive actions, but were carefully planned. One was a Ginza real estate company tied to the boss of Sumiyoshi-kai. The front company established a local branch in Saipan, then purchased a Saipan bank and changed its name to Marianas Bank. With that entity as the firm of record, it tried to get a license, and failed. Gushin's investigators visited another applicant and found a Sumiyoshi-kai insignia on its office wall.

One of the best-prepared applicants was Hiroyuki Asai, who as head of ASA, sought to build a $300 million casino hotel. But Asai had a few blemishes on his record. He was an investor in what he listed as the "Money Lending Relief Center," and in 1979 he was convicted of loan sharking. From the mid-1980s to the time of the hearing in 1991, his primary business was jiageya—the yakuza-run business of forcing tenants off their land. Investigators also found witnesses placing him in the company of gun-runners and yakuza sex trade smugglers in the Philippines. If that wasn't enough, his company liabilities exceeded the assets, and Asai claimed that he received only $82,000 a year in salary, yet somehow lived a lavish life. Confronted with the evidence, ASA requested that the commission simply ignore it and issue the license anyway. Oddly, members of Gushin's own gaming commission appeared sympathetic.

Gushin marshaled publicity and federal law enforcement officials, and, after four hours of debate, the commission reluctantly turned down ASA's application, concluding that "Mr. Asai and his company have associations with the Japanese yakuza, namely the Yamaguchi Gumi. . . . Essentially, Mr. Asai and ASA are a front for the Yamaguchi Gumi . . ."

During the hearing, however, locals in the pay of Asai stood outside the two-story hearing center carrying signs demanding that the commission license the casino. At first, Gushin found the events hard to believe, but later found it typical of how things got done on the islands. "At best, government and the yakuza peacefully coexisted in the CNMI," he concluded. "At worst, they were in business together."

To say the least. The commission chairman was arrested by U.S. Customs for marijuana possession, and in the office Gushin noticed his eyes were often glazed and his attention span short. The mayor of Tinian, who was also the chairman's older brother, "was attempting to shake down a partner of ASA" and then influence its case before the commission. The vice-chairman twice accepted sex tours to the Philippines, Gushin charged, accompanied by the CEO of ASA and the mayor. A third commissioner allegedly worked less than half time, yet instructed his staff to record full-time attendance, and was suspected of drug use. Another commissioner had a record for embezzlement in Guam. And the executive director was suspected by law enforcement of drug use and distribution. "Some of the commissioners could probably not qualify for licensure under their own statute," Gushin wrote in a memo.

Gushin began to fear for his safety and in 1992, after fourteen months, left Tinian and its gaming commission behind. By then, he had stopped or stalled the yakuza bids long enough for the Bubble Economy to collapse, drying up whatever funding the applicants once had. But he remained pessimistic about the yakuza's future impact on the region, calling it "a disaster waiting to happen." Indeed, that year, an FBI report observed that yakuza activity in the U.S. and its possessions had become a major concern, noting that the gangs were now "entrenched in Guam and the Commonwealth of the Northern Marianas Islands." They would not be leaving anytime soon.

But there are bigger prizes in the Pacific than Saipan or Tinian. For instance, the biggest city between Tokyo and Los Angeles is just teeming with opportunities, and the yakuza were not about to let those go undeveloped.

Gangsters in Paradise

Like their fellow Japanese, the yakuza have found Hawaii a congenial spot. Prior to World War II, the Japanese went to Hawaii for vacations, but following the war, as soon as prosperity settled upon Japan, tourists returned in much larger numbers. By the mid-1990s, nearly 2 million Japanese visited the islands annually, spending a hefty $3 to $4 billion each year. So popular is Hawaii as a destination for Japanese that some in that country have taken to calling it the forty-eighth prefecture, as an American might dub Canada the fifty-first state. And, like tourists everywhere, many Japanese leave not only their cares at home, but also their inhibitions.

Massage parlors openly advertise in the newspapers. "Beach boys" pass out cards with telephone numbers advising of the location of American women. Apartments, hotels, and condominiums serve as floating whorehouses. And given that prostitution is part of the tourism industry, law enforcement isn't generally too severe on violators of the law. Some judges won't touch a prostitution case unless drugs are involved as well.

While Hawaii isn't a particularly dangerous place, there's an impressive number of crime gangs for a state so small. The state's major industry, tourism, provides both cash and victims for criminal organizations. The soldiers come from an ethnic smorgasbord as diverse as the islands: Hawaiians, Samoans, Koreans, Filipinos, Chinese, Japanese Americans, *haoles* (whites), and blacks. Despite this apparent glut of gangs, the yakuza have had little difficulty joining the ranks of Hawaiian mobsters.

By the early 1970s, yakuza could be seen sunning themselves in full-body tattoos on the beaches of Waikiki. It didn't take long for the gangs to move into business, at first preying on the tourist trade. The evidence wasn't hard to find for those strolling along Waikiki's Kalakaua Avenue. Along with the Pizza Huts, Japanese shopping plazas, and other mundane emporia, one found as fine a collection of massage parlors, bottomless clubs, porno movie houses, and adult book stores as exists between San Francisco's Tenderloin district and Tokyo's Kabukicho.

Many of the massage parlors maintained some relationship to the yakuza. A sweeping investigation conducted by the Honolulu Police Department back in 1981 revealed that half of the fourteen parlors raided had Japanese-surnamed operators, and of those seven, two were definitely linked to the yakuza. One, a diminutive porn shop operator named Tsuyoshi "Bambi" Bamba, was tied to the Inagawa-kai and was subsequently deported. Another was linked to a major yakuza operator, and owned a sushi bar and a gun shop as well as a porno shop with a live sex show. Others bought protection or gave kickbacks to yakuza or their associates.

The yakuza were early on drawn to the sex industry. They certainly had the background for it, and, it turns out, they had a few connections. As early as 1973, there were ties between Mafia pornographers and the yakuza. Among their contacts, according to an FBI report, was Michael Zaffarino, then acting boss of the Bonanno Mafia family.

But today the yakuza in Hawaii have ventured far beyond pimping and pornography. They are into gunrunning, gambling, drugs, and perhaps most important, money laundering and major league investment.

For decades now, the yakuza have been faced with the problem that plagues all highly successful criminals—what to do with all that money. The huge profits that the yakuza wring out of their various investments pose to them the same problem that cocaine profits do to Colombians and Mexicans. One solution that occurred to the yakuza was simple: invest it in Hawaii. There they have found plenty of Hawaiians who will sell to Japanese with cash, no questions asked.

And, for the yakuza, as for other crime syndicates, the investment doesn't necessarily have to turn a profit to be successful. "If the yakuza get $1 back for every $2 invested," said former Honolulu detective Bernie Ching, "they're happy." The reason, of course, is that now the $1 is clean, and can be used or returned to Japan. The money is simply declared as a profit or sale of a legitimate business, or just moved to Japan by wire transfer with no explanation. Japanese bankers, as a rule, are not particularly curious as to the source of funds. Even under new money-laundering laws, Japan remains a rather easy country in which to invest unsourced money.

But most yakuza did not arrive as high-level money launderers, or even as criminals—at first. The yakuza originally entered Hawaii sometime in the late 1960s, as restaurateurs, cooks, dishwashers. They often took any kind of menial job that would enable them to look around unobtrusively. Later, in the early '70s, they began meeting people from the local crime syndicates and worked out alliances, or at least nonaggression pacts. Interestingly, when in Hawaii, members of different yakuza syndicates often worked together. Perhaps it was the Aloha spirit, or maybe it was necessity.

In any case, the initial wave of yakuza did not seem to pose a threat to Hawaiian criminals. They were, in fact, a generally graceless and inept lot, certainly not the finest of Japan's 250-year gangland tradition. But they did, if nothing else, pave the way for others.

The First Wave

By 1973, the police were keeping a handful of yakuza under surveillance, and were beginning to conclude that their presence was no fleeting phenomenon. If they needed further proof, it came in the form of Wataru "Jackson" Inada, an all-around criminal who rather flamboyantly, and not too effectively, set up headquarters in Honolulu and proceeded to run a series of scams that led to his premature death in 1976.

Inada, a member of the Tokyo-based Takahashi-gumi—a Sumiyoshi-kai affiliate—wandered into Hawaii in 1972. Shortly after his arrival, he teamed up with a local gangster of Korean descent named John Chang Ho Lee, a man who knew just about everyone in the Honolulu underworld. Together the two hoods formed Mitsui Tours, which catered exclusively to Japanese visitors, and which probably originated the now-common junket of hauling tourists to gun ranges. There, Japanese could indulge in the forbidden pleasure of shooting handguns. The idea was a worthwhile one, but in July 1974, at the Koko Head range, one of the gun-happy shooters accidentally put a .45 bullet through his heart, and Inada was out one shooting range.

Over the next two years, Inada would begin a prostitution racket, a gambling casino, and a shakedown of local porno shops. Back in 1973, though, Inada saw that there was really big money to be made in the heroin business. With his cash reserves, his Asian connections, and Lee's distribution network, he could make a fortune. It didn't work out that way.

Inada had no trouble finding the heroin in East Asia, but sales proved trickier. Inada and Lee enlisted the help of reputed Los Angeles Mafia boss Peter John Milano, who, for $100,000, promised to run a kilo of heroin through LA and on to a buyer in the Midwest. It was to be the beginning of a regular operation. But by late 1973, Lee had been arrested for selling heroin to an undercover agent and, in return for a reduced sentence, agreed to testify against his former partners in future trials. As a result of the Lee case, Milano and six other mainlanders were arrested and tried.

Inada persisted and in July of 1975, he was arrested for the sale of $165,000 worth of the drug to yet a different undercover agent. Lee was scheduled to testify against his old friend, but he never got the chance. Five days before the scheduled beginning of the trial, Inada, then forty-three, and his Korean girlfriend were found shot in the head. The murder was never officially solved, although police have long suspected the hit was arranged by Lee, who did not want to be branded a snitch.

If Jackson Inada was a bungler, he was also a pioneer. In barely over three years, he had put together virtually every tourist scam that the yakuza would later use, and some that went beyond the tourist game. Like many pioneers, though, Inada will be best remembered for his efforts rather than for the results.

The one operation that Inada never got around to was gun smuggling. That was left to another Takahashi-gumi thug, a former boxer named Takatsugu Yonekura. Yonekura was not a typical yakuza. He had attended college and had been on the Japanese Olympic boxing team. In Japan, he met and married an American woman; they emigrated to the United States, where he obtained legal residency and a green card from Immigration. It was in 1975 or so that Yonekura went into the gun business, but he didn't last very long. In May of 1976, U.S. Customs arrested Yonekura in Hawaii with a cache of fifty Raven .25-caliber automatics and six hundred rounds of ammunition. In December of that year, Yonekura was convicted and sentenced to a term in Halawa Correctional Facility in Hawaii. (At his sentencing hearing, Yonekura's attorney insisted that the tattoos covering his client's body were merely the result of a "deep depression," and had no connection with the yakuza.)

While on parole, Yonekura displayed the same brazen lack of judgment that his friend Inada had shown, running gambling games, shaking down businesses, and exporting bullet-proof vests to Japan. He then visited Japan, only to return minus the top knuckle of his right pinkie, but $10,000 richer. Yonekura evidently apologized in the time-tested way for his bungling in America, and was rewarded with a new allowance from his Takahashi boss. U.S. officials were unimpressed, seized his $10,000, and gave him five years in federal prison for currency violations. Yakuza are known for stoically doing their time in prison, but this was America, and Yonekura apparently didn't feel bound by such customs. In 1981, he left his confining accommodations at the federal prison at Lompoc, California, and expertly disappeared. For all his ineptitude as a thug, Yonekura showed great ingenuity as an escapee, and U.S. marshals searched Los Angeles in vain for him. Six months later, he showed up in Mexico City, where he complained bitterly to a Japanese reporter before disappearing again. Five years, said Yonekura, was a wholly unjust sentence for currency violations, as was undoubtedly true. The sentence also failed to deter any incoming yakuza.

The Three Mules

On May 9, 1979, customs line inspector Yenlyn Shadowens was checking out an incoming Japanese air passenger at Honolulu International Airport. She looked over Satoshi Meguro and asked him for his passport. It showed, according to Customs, extensive travel to and from Bangkok, Honolulu, and Guam, pivoting around Tokyo. Meguro had been in Bangkok only a week before his arrival in Honolulu. Shadowens summoned a Customs inspector and voiced her suspicions.

Meguro was hustled into the interrogation area and, through an interpreter, told Customs that he worked at a bar in Japan. He had with him only a small valise and a duty-free bag containing a bottle of Remy Martin and a carton of Dunhill cigarettes. When inspectors opened the Dunhill carton, they found packets of white powder. Two other companions of Meguro's, Tamotsu Omori and Yasuhiro Ono, were located in different parts of the air terminal—after they had passed inspection. A second search yielded duty-free bags containing Dunhills and a white powder.

The powder turned out to be #4 heroin—a high-quality Southeast Asian brand—a pound to each carton. The DEA was called in and found a fourth man, Kiyoshi Yoshioka, in a Waikiki hotel. This man was believed to be the team leader, but no evidence could be turned up to hold him. Tokyo police revealed that Yoshioka was a member of another Sumiyoshi affiliate, the Seishi-kai. The Japanese police searched the residences of the three drug runners, or "mules." Among the seized papers were detailed schematic drawings of customs facilities at Bangkok, Hong Kong, and Tokyo airports, and instructions on how to most easily clear those facilities.

But most fascinating among the seized papers was a meticulous set of instructions on required behavior for mules. Naturally, unquestioning obedience was demanded, but in return the compensation and expenses were precisely laid out. Said the code of practice:

> You should obey whatever you are told to do by your group leader. You have no choice, you cannot refuse or complain of the leader's instructions. The above instructions are given at the request of the financier in order to protect ourselves and to accomplish our work. Therefore, if you want to work and get paid for it, you should follow instructions.

[The pay schedule is] $5,000 for the trip plus $500 more or less for your
pocket money.

Your group leader will determine the amount. You must pay for your souvenirs yourself.

Your leader will pay for your hotel and three meals. He will also pay for
your drinks, up to $75.

Although the flat payment was the same whether the couriers had to go
to America or Southeast Asia, instructions for trips to the United States
placed a curious restriction on the mules: "Your group leader will pay for
your tickets, hotel and meals. You will have to pay for your other expenses,
like drinks or snacks."

And, concluded the missive, "If you have any objections, it means you will
be out. You are again advised that you will not get a penny if you fail to obey
instructions given by the financier or the middlemen." Many U.S. or South
American drug dealers must have often wished for that kind of deference
on the part of their runners.

On August 28, 1979, the trio of hapless mules were sentenced to terms
ranging from ten to twelve years in federal prison for their part in the heroin scheme. Their fellow gang members and associates back home, who had
undoubtedly cashed in on the previous trips, weren't touched. Whatever the
final outcome for the runners, it is clear that Americans have not seen the
last of yakuza drug smugglers. Police have since monitored a host of suspect
Japanese couriers working their wares through such ports of entry as Los
Angeles, San Francisco, and Vancouver. If officials needed any further
proof, it came in the 1985 seizure of twelve pounds of heroin and fifty-two
pounds of methamphetamine in Honolulu and Hong Kong. Police in the
two cities arrested seven Japanese and three Chinese in connection with the
case—including two of the highest-ranking bosses of the Yamaguchi-gumi,
as well as associates of the notorious Hong Kong 14K triad.

The runners each drew ten or more years in federal prison. Perhaps it
had a deterrent effect: the yakuza never became major players in the Asian
heroin trade, although their Korean associates later became active in introducing crystal meth into Hawaii. But the case had another important effect.
The three mules helped sound an alarm that made U.S. law enforcement sit
up and start asking questions about the yakuza. For the first time, American
cops were taking Japanese organized crime very seriously.

The Front Lines

It was January 1982. From 6 A.M. to 10:30 A.M., plainclothes customs patrol
officers (CPOs) Al Gano and Bill Sweet studied the crowds of Asian visi-

tors as they queued up behind the Customs inspection line at Honolulu's sprawling airport. During these hours, 747s arriving from Taipei, Manila, Osaka, and Tokyo disgorged their passengers into the controlled bedlam of the international arrival area. The passengers were tourists, immigrants, businesspeople, . . . and yakuza.

"There's a couple of ways you can spot a yakuza," Gano said. A trim, alert man with a thin mustache, sharp eyes, and a New Jersey accent, Gano had spent a lot of time looking them over. "For one thing, your average Japanese tourist . . . well, walks humbly. Yakuza, they strut. Another easy sign is when they arrive in a group. The boss—the oyabun—is usually surrounded by his boys—the kobun—and they're carrying his bags, lighting his cigarette, and saying, 'hai! hai!' (yes, yes)."

Bill Sweet offered an observation: "Of course, you might get lucky and spot a missing pinkie."

Missing pinkies, though, are awfully hard to spot at ten or twenty yards; dress styles were a better clue. "They used to all wear crew cuts," Gano said. "But now a lot of them wear punch perms. Of course, so do a lot of people who aren't yakuza."

They spied a knot of yakuza-looking types on the departure deck. A few were sporting punch perms—short, frizzy hair—but what stood out were the tough, expressionless faces and a lot of flashy polyester clothing. They looked like a couple of nightclub owners with their hired help.

Back on the line, an inspector moved across the vast waiting area and murmured to the CPOs, "We've got a hit."

Another CPO escorted a stocky, smiling Japanese male into one of the back rooms. His wife, looking worried, was asked to wait outside while her husband was led into the Yakuza Documentation Center (YDC).

Sweet began interrogating the man in fluent Japanese. Except for his punch perm and black slacks, though, the man didn't look very criminal, and he was far from sullen, cheerfully answering all questions. "That doesn't mean anything," said Gano. "Even the oyabun are ridiculously polite."

Sweet didn't get very far in filling out the form when he realized that this "hit" was a false alarm. The man owned a small construction firm in Hokkaido—a fact occasionally consonant with yakuza ties or even membership—but the subject was not their man. He just happened to have the same name as a known yakuza. It's a common error.

Over the years, the unassuming, raspy-voiced Sweet managed to build data on the yakuza from virtually nothing into a sophisticated criminal intelligence system. But there was the very basic problem of names. The man from Hokkaido was just one of an almost constant stream of incorrectly identified suspects. The problem is built into the language. It's not unusual even for well-educated native speakers of Japanese to fail to properly read a given name from the written characters, or to correctly "spell" a name after hearing it. The *kanji,* Chinese-based ideograms that form the basis of written Japanese, are not phonetic; they can typically be read several different ways. Korean names in Japanese can be even more difficult to interpret properly. (According to Bill Sweet, there are thirty-five different kanji just for the Korean name "Lee.")

Even if the name is translated correctly, the path remains bumpy. Due to diplomatic considerations, requests for information have to go first to the Customs attaché at the U.S. embassy in Tokyo, who then hand-delivers it to bureaucrats at the National Police Agency. If all goes well, Customs receives a return answer within thirty-six hours, but many requests take considerably longer.

Things began to change after 1982. Until then, American policy toward the yakuza was still relatively laissez-faire, and minor visa and currency violations did not usually keep yakuza out of the United States. By 1983, though, those who arrived to run rackets increasingly came under official scrutiny. By 1985, U.S. officials in Hawaii had brought charges against thirty-one yakuza and associates, mostly for visa fraud. By 1993, YDC had indexed over 30,000 names of yakuza and hard-core associates. Having labored in obscurity until 1986, Bill Sweet must have been gratified when the YDC's warnings finally began to set off alarms. Perhaps the most visible evidence of Sweet's hard work came when the more savvy Immigration inspectors actually started touching each finger to ensure it was real.

The Big Time and the Mongoose

To some influential Hawaiians, a yakuza contact brings with it a certain cachet. There's the tangible benefit of links to muscle and money as well as yakuza connections in Japan that can often result in lucrative contracts— legal and illegal. For another, hanging out with the yakuza is in some ways exotic, and Japanese mobsters are known for lavish entertaining. The yakuza themselves gain access to business connections and legitimacy. A high-ranking Yamaguchi-gumi boss, when asked about his syndicate's interest in Hawaii, said, "We came here first to buy property; then we buy the people."

One of the first rich Hawaiians who sought out the yakuza was Charles Higa. Having dissipated the multi-million-dollar shipping fortune built up by his father and grandfather, Higa ran his own trucking business into the ground. Then he began keeping company with Samoan thugs and Japanese gangsters. To make money, Higa tried shaking down marginal businesses. On September 22, 1983, he and two others were arrested and charged with extortion and conspiracy, specifically for attempting to pry $300 a month from the manager of the Tsukoba Book and Video Store in Waikiki, a porno operation.

In the court proceedings following his indictment, Higa admitted to links with organized crime. According to reporter Jim Dooley, writing in the *Honolulu Advertiser,* Higa was quite candid about those ties:

> [Higa] said he first met the yakuza in Japan in the late 1950s. He said his family trucking business in Japan depended on a labor force controlled by the yakuza and he complied with local custom by making a gift—money or sake—to yakuza representatives. Since that time, he said, he has met with other yakuza leaders. He acknowledged a personal acquaintance with the top three leaders of the Sumiyoshi-rengo, a large Tokyo-based yakuza group which has been active in Hawaii in recent years. And he said he had met twice in Hawaii with Kazuo Taoka, the now-deceased boss of Yamaguchi, the single largest yakuza organization. Higa also said he was acquainted with Kaoru Ogawa, identified by Tokyo police as Japan's "most influential racketeer."

Higa received a five-year sentence for extortion, and whatever favors he may have done for the various yakuza oyabun were never made public at his trial. By the time Higa admitted to knowing the notorious sokaiya Kaoru Ogawa, the Japanese racketeer had already left Hawaii. But in 1978, Ogawa returned, moving his family from Japan to Hawaii and indulging in a variety of investments. He was soon embroiled in a struggle to control stock in the City Bank of Honolulu, and accused of intimidating bank employees in an apparent attempt to squelch their testimony.

Another visitor to the islands was Hisayuki Machii, the "retired" boss of Towa Yuai Jigyo Kumiai, the ethnic Korean gang based in Tokyo. On a 1982 trip to Hawaii, Machii claimed that he had simply come for the purpose of having oral surgery, but managed to find the time to visit alleged Towa associate Ken Mizuno, investor and Las Vegas restaurateur. Police believed that Machii invested some of his millions in the islands.

Investigators were often stunned by the company kept by visiting yakuza. Perhaps no one raised more questions than billionaire Kenji Osano. During the 1970s, Osano was the major Japanese investor in Hawaii. Osano was often spoken of in the same breath as fellow fixers Kodama and Sasakawa, but excepting his major role in the Lockheed scandal, he maintained a cleaner public image. In 1976 he began buying property as if he was playing Monopoly. By the time he finished his mainland and Hawaiian buying spree, Osano owned five Waikiki hotels: the Sheraton Waikiki, Royal Hawaiian, Surfrider, Moana, and Princess Kaiulani, plus the Sheraton Maui on that island.

Honolulu police noted that Osano kept company with Susumu Ishii, then the Inagawa-kai's number two man. Ishii had apprenticed himself to the hotel baron, gaining knowledge that would pay off during the Bubble years. On other trips to Hawaii, Osano was seen in the company of top officers of the same syndicate. A Honolulu detective further claimed that Osano's hotels served as landing spots for yakuza, although he didn't say that Osano personally intervened for the gangs. "They'll get a job there, work for a while, and then go into their own hustles."

By the mid-1980s, it was clear that the yakuza had firmly established themselves in the islands. According to some police sources, the Japanese gangs became the second most powerful criminal syndicate in the state, right behind the native Hawaiians. But the yakuza were gradually pulling away from the petty street-level rackets pioneered by characters like Jackson Inada. "There is a new breed of yakuza out there," announced Honolulu city prosecutor Keith Kaneshiro in 1992. "You won't find them with missing fingers and with body tattoos. You'll find them in business suits making multi-million-dollar deals." U.S. Customs' Bill Sweet agreed. "Everything we see seems to involve investments and money laundering," he said two years later.

The excesses of Japan's Bubble Economy hit Hawaii with full force. Across the islands, money was talking, and it was speaking Japanese. On beaches, hillsides, shopping malls, and other valued properties, the Japanese were buying, building, or otherwise doing business. As a result, land values and assessments followed the impossibly steep curve of Tokyo's inflated real estate. By 1989, Japanese investors owned all but one of the seafront hotels in Waikiki, and that year alarm bells began to ring loudly. Many Hawaiians made money from the Bubble, but the torrent of yen also provoked persistent fears of Japanese invasion. In 1989, Honolulu mayor Frank Fasi took the unprecedented step of calling for a ban on foreign (read Japanese) investment in the islands.

Of course, Hawaii was merely the most afflicted such state. Japanese armed with bulging portfolios were snapping up properties throughout the United States, principally in New York and California. In 1987, Japan replaced Britain as America's top foreign investor, which caused a great outcry, much of it colored by racism and intolerance. High-profile purchases such as major Hollywood studios and Rockefeller Center exacerbated anti-Japanese sentiment, but some Americans discounted the threat. As one critic asked, "Who cares if the Japanese invest in a few pieces of overpriced Manhattan real estate?"

In fact, the observation was sound. By 1992, many Japanese had pulled out of the U.S. market after losing their shirts. The U.S. economy was beginning to heat up, but the real estate market stayed put. Investors couldn't pay for their loans. Minoru Isutani, for instance, remained the controversial owner of Pebble Beach for just seventeen months. After all the excitement he wound up losing nearly $350 million.

The Hawaiian tumble, though, was even worse.

Take the case of Asahi Juken, Japan's second-largest condo builder. The construction firm was a leading builder in the Osaka region with 1,500 employees and $1.5 billion in gross income in 1991. Like many other Japanese firms, Juken sought to move into foreign markets and chose Hawaii for a major construction venture.

But Asahi Juken was no ordinary builder. The privately held firm was headed by Kizo Matsumoto, who founded the company shortly after resigning from the Yamaguchi-gumi, and by his brothers, Takeo, Takao, and Kihachi—also allegedly linked to the syndicate. Kizo and Kihachi were tied to the Yamaguchi-gumi's Shiragami gang, whose boss, Hideo Shiragumi, had been beaten and tortured to death on Saipan in 1987.

In 1988, Asahi Juken, already active in Thailand, announced plans for a $1 billion development on Guam. But the firm's reputation preceded it. The island's governor, Joseph Ada, flatly told the press, "We want nothing to do with Kizo Matsumoto."

Undeterred, Matsumoto also had his sights set on Hawaii, where he bought an entire block of downtown Honolulu for over $100 million. That was just an appetizer, though. That same year, Matsumoto purchased the 486-room Turtle Bay Hilton and Country Club on Oahu's north shore. To round it out, he then bought part of the adjacent eight-hundred-acre Kuilima Resort, and announced that another $1 billion would be sunk into new development plans.

But the Matsumotos' reputation soon caught the attention of U.S. law enforcement in Hawaii. Takeo and Takao, who also ran a security company technically owned by Asahi Juken, were indicted in Hawaii on visa fraud charges after lying about their criminal records. And, soon after the billion-dollar announcement, Kizo was stripped of his visa and forced to return to Japan. The news was no better there. The Bubble was collapsing, leaving Asahi Juken awash in bad loans. By 1991, the company was mired in nearly $4.5 billion of debt.

Federal officials grew increasingly concerned about the fate of Hawaii's golf industry. The cost of playing golf in Japan had become so high that it could actually be cheaper to fly to Hawaii or Southeast Asia than play at home. Billions of dollars poured in to buy and develop Hawaiian golf courses. By 1988, the Japanese held all privately owned golf courses on Oahu that were open to the public, except for one. Local activists worried about harm to the environment, while local golf enthusiasts fretted over prohibitive prices brought by the Japanese. But what most concerned law enforcement were persistent reports about the criminal records of several big-time developers. As one senior U.S. law enforcement official noted at the time: "Golf is a big moneymaker and it's a great way to launder money."

At a 1992 U.S. Senate hearing, a protected witness nicknamed Bully described just how extensive yakuza investment in the islands had become. Early yakuza investments, he said, had focused on art and Hawaiian real estate, but in recent years the purchases had zoomed to a new level. Bully claimed to have personal knowledge "of at least five major properties in Hawaii which were bought with money generated illegally" by the yakuza. Moreover, he estimated that there were probably closer to fifty major properties in Hawaii, including resort hotels and golf courses, that were outright property of Japanese crime syndicates. Sumiyoshi-kai, he noted, "has been particularly active in international real estate development, and uses sophisticated methods to take control of property."

Among other operations, Bully detailed the machinations of Hachidai Sangyo, a company run by alleged mob associate Katsuhiro Kawaguchi. In the 1980s, Kawaguchi bought up $26 million in Hawaii real estate, including a Waikiki shopping mall and the Coconut Island resort. The company, backed by the mobbed-up trading firm Itoman, even tried to purchase Honolulu's $45 million St. Augustine Church. But Kawaguchi, whose home and housekeeper were shot up by a yakuza in 1987, was charged with visa fraud and, in 1988, deported from Hawaii.

Others met with similar fates. Between 1986 and 1988, Kitaro Watanabe, a reported protégé of Kenji Osano, spent more than $500 million on Hawaiian real estate. Watanabe, president of Azabu USA Inc., had been tied to a rightist front group used by Tokyo's Kobayashi-gumi, a gang in the Sumiyoshi-kai. Watanabe invested in six major Hawaii hotels and became the second-largest owner of hotel rooms on the Islands. But Watanabe fell into financial trouble and received a two-year jail term in Japan for hiding assets from creditors. Big-time Osaka developer Yasuo Yasuda, who hoped to develop a large golf course facility, was forced back to Japan in 1989 for not disclosing his criminal record. One gang boss, Hitohiro Nishikawa, reputed head of the Nishikawa-kai, reportedly cleared nearly $1 million with his investment in a beach-side home. But he came under investigation for allegedly bribing a U.S. Customs official to gain entry.

By the early 1990s, it was clear that the Bubble Economy's collapse had also left the Hawaiian economy reeling. Visits by Japanese tourists plummeted, while business in general took a dive. Billions of dollars in speculative investment were written off, with mob-tainted investors suffering the same fate as legitimate Japanese. But not every investment was misguided or overspeculative, nor did every shady developer go bankrupt. The Bubble brought unprecedented interest from top mobsters and their most powerful associates in Japan, and the setbacks of the Bubble era are unlikely to stem the gangs' long-term interest in Hawaii. The islands are too close, too rich, and too lucrative to be ignored. The locals proved themselves more than willing to take money from suspect investors, knowing that when the yakuza made money, they too would profit. The only people who lose are ordinary Hawaiians, who see property values pushed out of reach, drugs and vice increase, and corruption spread across their fair land.

Hawaiians may find that the yakuza are similar to another visitor from Asia, the mongoose. Years ago, Hawaiian sugar growers brought the mongoose to the island to rid the cane fields of a previous import, the rat. The weasel-like mongoose, however, failed to make a dent in the rat population, but did take a liking to Hawaiian chickens and other livestock. Today it has become an ineradicable pest. The yakuza, welcomed by some for the money they bring in, may prove to be as larcenous and parasitic in the long run as the mongoose, and just as hard to dislodge.

CHAPTER TWELVE

TO AMERICA

IN 1975, AN UNUSUAL GANGSTER FILM STARRING ROBERT MITCHUM AND Japanese actor Ken Takakura opened in the United States to generally indifferent audiences. The unconvincing plot, the strange and highly stylized Japanese acting, and the exotic setting didn't send Americans flocking to the box office. But viewers were probably amused by the outlandish and anachronistic swordplay, and found the finger-cutting sequences both compelling and gruesome. In any case, the movie, entitled simply *The Yakuza,* enjoyed a short run to nearly empty houses. It deserved better. It still plays occasionally on late-night television and it's on home video, but in 1975 Americans neither knew nor cared about the subject matter—Japanese organized crime.

By the early 1980s, that had begun to change. Americans other than Hawaiians were slowly becoming aware of the yakuza through the news media, and indirectly because of the new posture of U.S. law enforcement. Press reports of official statements about the yakuza conveyed a note of panic, with headlines like "Japanese Organized Criminals Invading West," and "FBI Chief Warns of Japanese Crime Ring."

A number of top Washington law enforcement officials, including Ronald Reagan's attorney general, William French Smith, and FBI chief William Webster, warned on several occasions that the yakuza presented a threat to the nation that warranted swift action. Partly as a response to this clamor, members of the Reagan administration decided to include the yakuza in the agenda of the 1983 President's Commission on Organized Crime. Some previous panels, like the Kefauver and McLellan Senate committees, had made a discernible impact on organized crime by putting pressure on law enforcement and increasing citizen awareness. But the Reagan commission was the first to expand the definition of organized crime, observing that it was no longer the exclusive domain of the Mafia—not that it truly ever was.

California authorities recognized this change rather early, owing perhaps to the weak position of traditional Italian syndicates in that state. In the 1980s, state authorities paid less attention to the Italian groups and more to the "nontraditional" gangs, which include everyone else. In its 1981 report to the legislature, the California Bureau of Organized Crime and Criminal Intelligence (BOCCI) devoted as much space to Israeli, Vietnamese, and Japanese groups as to the Mafia. By 1984, it had become clear that this broader version of organized crime was firmly entrenched on the national level, and that it included the yakuza.

The president's commission held its second public hearing in New York in March 1984, focusing on money laundering, a requisite task of all organized crime groups, including the yakuza. Cash, according to commission director James Harmon, is "the life-support system without which organized crime cannot exist." The commission discovered that the money to be laundered for the $50 billion annual U.S. drug trade, for example, comes from all points of the compass—East Asia as well as Latin America—and that many U.S. bankers have been only too willing to oblige organized crime.

Finally, in its third hearing, held on October 25, 1984, the commission gathered in New York to address the issue of Asian organized crime, and the yakuza were to occupy one-third of the agenda. Certainly, the attention was by then justified. Verifiable police reports placed yakuza from Roanoke, Virginia, to Arizona to Seattle. The yakuza were highly involved in the Japanese tourist industry, were smuggling guns and pornography out of the country, allying themselves with American gangsters and gamblers, and laundering funds. They were, in short, getting well entrenched in America, and it was time to place them under closer scrutiny.

The first witness called before the president's commission appeared shrouded in a black robe and hood, looking somewhat like a ninja. He was led across the floor of the high-ceilinged, columned hall to a seat behind a screen that shielded him from the press and audience. Chief Counsel Harmon then revealed to the commission and audience that the man was an oyabun, or leader, in a major Japanese organized crime gang. The twelve commission members present listened carefully as the witness described tattooing and yubitsume, or ritual finger-cutting, and provided a graphic account of how that painful act is accomplished. "The actual procedure is to take . . . what they in Japanese yakuza call little silver knife—on a table—and you pull it towards you and bend over and your body weight will snap your finger off. . . . The finger that is severed is put in a small bottle with alcohol and your name is written on and it is sent to whoever you're repenting to as a sign that you are sorry."

The nameless oyabun also elaborated on the organizational charts of the

Yamaguchi-gumi and Sumiyoshi-rengo that the commission had provided, and explained how the yakuza are active in his own specialty, economic crime. Gangsters in Japan, he told the panel, try to find companies in financial trouble, and engage in a number of schemes to take them over. Through bogus notes and threats to company officials and creditors, they assume control of the ailing business, sell off the assets, and profit from the failure.

This yakuza had personally run high-stakes card games two or three times a month in Japan. Because of his status, he retained 40 percent of the profits, which amounted to $40,000 to $60,000. After expenses, he realized about $16,000 per game. Money, though, had to be passed up to the very highest echelons; yakuza leaders maintained control through money, and lower members rose by passing it on. Nonetheless, said the witness, "I would say that I lived a very good life, probably equivalent to the presidency of a company employing three hundred to five hundred people."

Later in the day, another hooded witness made an appearance. Also a Japanese national, this anonymous informant had been a U.S. resident for ten years, and he described yakuza activity in New York. Card games, with stakes in the many thousands of dollars, were being run by a combination of yakuza, yakuza associates, and Italian American hoodlums. The customers were both Japanese nationals and Japanese Americans. He believed that the Italians, who wore guns and sold stolen goods at the games, were actually in charge of the action.

Less dramatic than the hooded witnesses, perhaps, but equally revealing was the testimony of three American policemen, all knowledgeable in the workings of the yakuza in the United States: Inspector John McKenna of the San Francisco Police Department; Detective George Min of the Los Angeles Police Department; and Bernard Ching of the Honolulu Police Department. The three intelligence cops described in brief how the yakuza were gaining crucial footholds in their respective communities.

Bernard Ching described the Hawaiian yakuza scene in much the same terms he had used to reporters nearly three years earlier: gun smuggling, prostitution, pornography, extortion, and drugs. What was new to some observers, however, was the admission that yakuza activity was not confined to the islands. Detective Min of Los Angeles presented an impressive list of yakuza activities in the large Japanese communities of Southern California. "I have seen many crimes instituted by the yakuza," he told the panel. "We have cases of homicide, prison escape, gun smuggling, money laundering . . ." Inspector McKenna, for his part, added that the SFPD had identified members of the Sumiyoshi-rengo in the San Francisco area. He believed that a pattern of intimidation and extortion existed within the Japanese business community.

None of the testimony by police, and little by the witnesses—except the finger-cutting and other exotic Japanese customs—was particularly startling crime news. Activities from money laundering to murder are, of course, the basic stuff of organized crime. No, the news was that it was Japanese, and it was occurring both in Japan and in the United States, and it contradicted popularly held beliefs. The public, to the extent that they thought about it at all, believed that the Japanese had virtually no crime problem, and that Japanese Americans were the most law-abiding of citizens. Now the issue of yakuza coming to America would stir up some ugly ghosts from the past.

Ron Wakabayashi, the national director of the Japanese American Citizens League, told the *New York Times* that yakuza-hunting could "fan anti-Asian sentiment," and given the American predilection for periodic attacks on Asians, it was a well-founded warning. Because of economic competition from Japan, many Americans had begun to blame Asians—any Asians—for their problems. In 1982, for instance, two disgruntled and intoxicated auto workers in the Detroit area attacked a bachelor party of Chinese Americans, killing the prospective bridegroom with a baseball bat. The assailants' defense hinged in part on their having mistaken the victims for Japanese, and the court handed down extremely lenient sentences.

From government commissions and committees, from news reports, books, articles, and movies, the subject of organized crime from across the Pacific had crept into the U.S. consciousness . . . and onto the agenda of law enforcement. By the late 1980s, Asian organized crime had become a priority for the FBI and other U.S. law enforcement agencies. Yakuza money launderers, Chinese drug smugglers, Korean prostitution rackets, and more were now of pressing interest to American cops. New hearings were held before the U.S. Congress in 1992, in which the yakuza's reach into the United States was detailed. The billion-dollar developments in Hawaii were highlighted, as were similar investments on the mainland from New York to California. It had taken U.S. law enforcement some fifty years to acknowledge the existence of the Mafia; now, some twenty years after the modern yakuza had landed in America, the Yamaguchi-gumi was suddenly a topic of national discussion.

That year, the FBI publicly warned that yakuza activity had reached a major level of concern. Japanese crime syndicates exert "a growing influence on the state of Hawaii, and are significantly represented coast to coast on the U.S. mainland," the bureau said in a report. Officials identified the Yamaguchi-gumi, Sumiyoshi-kai, Inagawa-kai, and Towa Yuai as all being active in the U.S., and warned of the threat they posed "through the laundering of ill-gotten gains and the infiltration of legitimate businesses in the United States." DEA intelligence reports, meanwhile, suggested that Japan had become a major trans-shipment point for narcotics. It was an ideal situation for smugglers. Because of Japan's squeaky clean image, U.S. Customs did few if any checks on cargo coming from there. DEA agents in Tokyo found that between 1987 and 1989, at least 750 kilograms of heroin were shipped through Japan to the U.S. by Thais, Chinese, Nigerians, Americans, and Japanese.

Over the years, American law enforcement gained an education in Japanese organized crime and began to realize that this was no passing fad. By 1994, for instance, the FBI had eight Japanese speakers on its payroll. Police bulletins informed intelligence units of developments in the yakuza, and law enforcement groups devoted to Asian crime were meeting regularly. All this began to produce results. During Japanese holiday seasons, alert Customs and Immigration officials have stopped hundreds of yakuza attempting to enter the United States. One watchful Customs inspector even found a yakuza with a false fingertip. A few years earlier, these characters would have slipped by undetected. By the end of the '90s, yakuza investigations had occurred in Los Angeles, San Francisco, Las Vegas, Honolulu, New York, and Denver. Police had even identified yakuza tactics such as jiageya under way in areas like San Francisco.

Yet there was still something of a fad in the approach to tackling Japanese organized crime. Instant experts abounded in law enforcement, often with little clue of how the gangs really operated. This held true regarding much of Asian organized crime, which for too long had been shielded in America by a bamboo curtain that separated immigrant communities from the rest of the country. Few cops on Asian gang squads were even aware, for example, that Japanese crime syndicates not only had a future in America, they had a past.

The Cotton Connection

The history of Japanese organized crime in America actually dates to the early twentieth century. As in other immigrant communities, organized crime arose nearly as soon as the Japanese population grew large enough to support permanent gangs. By and large, those gangs controlled vice, principally gambling. By 1910 there were over 70,000 people of Japanese descent in the United States, with at least a third of those living in and around Los Angeles. The center of Japanese activity in the United States was in the downtown LA community of Little Tokyo. And controlling all the gambling, as well as other aspects of the community, was the Tokyo Club, situated atop a three-story building at Jackson Street and Central Avenue.

Based in Los Angeles, the Tokyo Club had branches—or more correctly, franchises—all over the West, from Seattle to the Mexican border. The bulk of the operation was in California, with eight Tokyo Clubs in the Central

Valley alone. It was a very successful operation. In the 1920s, it counted a profit of more than $1 million a year, a considerable sum in those days. Because it held the biggest accumulation of capital in the Japanese community, the Tokyo Club functioned as a bank as well. It also supported sports teams and lined the pockets of police and city officials.

The men who ran the Tokyo Club were businessmen-gangsters. Recalled Howard M. Imazeki, the late editor of *Hokubei Mainichi,* San Francisco's Japanese American daily, "We didn't call them yakuza then, but now I think that's probably what they were." Power struggles frequently occurred within the club, sometimes erupting into gunfire.

Wrote criminologist Isami Waugh, "In the cases of insubordination and disobedience Club President Itatani was severe in meting out the penalty; he sent his gang of powerful burly men to take care of these rebels in the Chicago gangland manner. . . . In two or three extreme cases, so the grapevine reported, men were actually murdered and their bodies were disposed of so well that even the police detection failed."

Small-time rackets were not the only criminal interests of America's forgotten yakuza. Americans may find it difficult to believe, but in the 1930s, Japan held a position similar to that which Colombia holds today—the heart of the narcotic menace. Harry J. Anslinger, the crusading and fervent chief of the U.S. Bureau of Narcotics for much of its existence, commented that, in the prewar years, "We should not be far short of the mark if we said that 90 percent of all the illicit 'white drugs' of the world are of Japanese origin, manufactured in the Japanese Concession of Tientsin, around Tientsin, in and around Dairen, or in other cities of Manchuria, Jehol, and occupied China, and this always . . . under Japanese supervision."

A slightly more academic 1942 study by the Institute of Pacific Relations and the Foreign Policy Association, entitled *Japan and the Opium Menace,* described Japan's domination of the drug trade. After invading China in the '30s, the Japanese government wielded control over much of the world opium trade. "During these years (1932 to 1937)," wrote the authors, "the Japanese Concession in Tientsin became the headquarters for a vast opium and narcotic drug industry. Whole sections of the Concession, particularly along Hashidate Street, were honeycombed with narcotic drug dens and small laboratories manufacturing various types of heroin powder and cigarettes." Moreover, opium dens in occupied China were also run by the Japanese, or by associated Taiwanese and Korean drug dealers. "Armed Japanese gangsters," noted the study, "were often stationed outside dens to prevent interference with their operation."

Unfortunately, a good deal of prewar propaganda colored evaluations of Japanese criminal activity, but even if Chief Anslinger exaggerated by two or three times the percentage of Japanese-manufactured narcotics, that still left a lot of white drugs. And some of them found their way into the United States.

The Bureau of Narcotics began to notice Japanese morphine, called "cotton morphine" because of its appearance, as early as 1932, just one year after the Japanese takeover of Manchuria. The following year, the grave concern voiced by the bureau began to show signs of justification, although the quantities seized were still rather small. Japanese were arrested with cotton morphine in Tacoma, Washington; Portland, Oregon; and Hawaii. All the arrests involved Japanese residents of America. In Portland, four tins seized in a February 24, 1933, raid bore the label "Japan Pharmaceutical Establishment" and contained morphine hydrochloride. The other arrests involved a similar type of morphine.

For the next five or six years, there were numerous arrests of Japanese passengers and crew members of steamships, most sailing under Japanese flags. They brought in morphine, heroin, and sometimes even cocaine. There were also functioning American distribution networks, headed by Japanese.

In April of 1935, California authorities arrested Fujiyuki Motomura, a major San Pedro drug trafficker, with over $5,000 worth of cocaine and morphine, about ten pounds in those days. Police believed that Motomura was tied to an additional fifty pounds of drugs found elsewhere in Southern California. The following year, California authorities again made a major arrest when state narcotics police in Los Angeles arrested Toshiyoshi Nagai for attempting to sell five pounds of morphine to undercover officers. Nagai told the prospective buyers that his brother owned a morphine factory in Japan and that he, Toshiyoshi, could supply any amount the buyers wanted. The smugglers were apparently using a number of routes, most of them successful; in 1938, the American representative at the Geneva drug conference told the assembled officials that 650 kilos of heroin from Japan had been captured by American agents on the West Coast. Using the usual law enforcement formula of ten to one—for every pound or kilo seized, police assume that ten get through—the Japanese may have accounted for some 6,500 kilos of heroin in the period described.

In addition to their own operations, the Japanese were responsible for supplying huge amounts of heroin to the biggest drug rings in the United States. These gangs at the time were under the control of Jewish and Italian gangsters operating all over the country. In San Francisco, for instance, mobster Mario Balestreri, successor to the mob run by "Black Tony" Parmagini, decided to increase his take and buy directly from the producers. He sent his men to purchase from Japanese dealers in Kobe, Japan, and Shanghai, China, then in Japanese hands. In 1939, police discovered that two of Louis "Lepke" Buchalter's lieutenants, Yanis Tsounias and George

Mexis, had fled to the Japanese Concession at Tientsin and set up a heroin operation. The two were shipping enough to the United States to supply 10,000 addicts for a year, according to the Bureau of Narcotics.

Japanese racketeers and drug traffickers ceased doing business in America once war began. Japanese and Korean drug dealers continued to work in the occupied territories of Asia, but few if any shipments made their way to the States. The gangsters who ran the Tokyo Club and the drug smuggling rings, meanwhile, were interned along with the rest of the Japanese population early in 1942. Like the yakuza in Japan, many of them appeared to harbor ultranationalist sentiments. Openly rightist Japanese in the camps were sent to a special section at the camp in Tule Lake, California, and many of these were repatriated to Japan after the war. There have been no follow-up studies on the Tokyo Club leaders, but it's more than possible that many of them returned to their ancestral land. In any case, after the Tokyo Club closed its doors in 1941, it never reopened.

With the criminal leadership gone, and the post-internment community far too traumatized to engage in open lawlessness, organized crime in the postwar Japanese American community was at a virtual standstill. Study after study reported a phenomenally low arrest rate among Americans of Japanese ancestry through the 1950s and 1960s. Gambling did not disappear, of course, and the Japanese were part of the poker clubs that made their appearance in the Los Angeles suburb of Gardena, but these were legalized operations. It was, according to Los Angeles police, not until the late 1960s that Japanese Hawaiian gamblers drifted over from the islands and began to set up illegal bookmaking operations.

Southern California Yakuza

Los Angeles has a lot to attract the yakuza. Besides the climate, the money, and the glamour, Los Angeles has the largest Japanese community on the mainland. All told, over 200,000 people of Japanese descent reside in the LA area. More than 99 percent of these have no connection with the underworld, but a growing number of yakuza have slipped into the Japanese community there, and some are doing quite well.

As early as 1981, the California Department of Justice warned of growing yakuza activity in an annual report:

> Law enforcement authorities have noted during the past several years that a number of Japanese organized crime members have immigrated from Japan and are now residing in the San Francisco and Los Angeles areas. There are approximately fifty gang members and associates now living in California.
>
> Law enforcement sources indicate that Japanese organized crime groups are operating tour agencies, Japanese gift shops and night clubs. Their crim-

inal activities include extortion of Japanese businesses, harassment of Japanese tourists, prostitution, gun and pornography smuggling, narcotics distribution and laundering money.

In 1982, one who surfaced was Tetsuo "Leo" Orii, who ran the Club Niji, a modern-day successor to the Tokyo Club. A hostess bar that offered an assortment of barely clad Asian and other women as companions, Niji catered mostly to businessmen from Japan. Orii was involved in various business ventures in and around Los Angeles, and at least one police intelligence report called him "the most influential figure of the Japanese organized crime faction" in the city.

Orii was quite open and respectful of his links with the yakuza. "I've entertained the oyabun of Sumiyoshi when they come here," he boasted. "We are brothers of the same family. When the chief of Sumiyoshi came to the U.S., he stayed at my house. They come to my bar."

Orii said he joined the yakuza at age sixteen and spent the next ten years fighting his way through prison and the tough Sumiyoshi-kai gangs that dominate much of Tokyo. He made a name for himself by extorting money out of college kids in Tokyo's busy Ginza district. But, he says, after a decade with the yakuza, he'd had enough. "The only way out was to leave Japan, but I'm still in. They won't let you out."

So young Tetsuo arrived in America, went into legitimate business, and claimed he kept up his unbreakable link with the yakuza only by putting up oyabun at his Pacific Palisades home. Even if he wanted to, he said, he could not be a real yakuza in America. He admitted there was some yakuza activity in Hawaii, but not on the mainland. "Yakuza are not into California because it's not profitable," he argued. "They can make twice as much money in Japan. They can't speak English very well, so they go where the Japanese are."

The problem, maintained Orii, was the police. The LAPD's Asian Task Force, he said, picked him on because "they need to show a reason for their existence." Most gangsters, of course, like to claim that they are simply honest citizens who just happen to have a few shady associates. Orii, however, got caught. In 1975 he and his partner, Tomonao Miyashiro, a.k.a. Tony Kawada, were arrested and convicted of shaking down a Japanese businessman. LAPD brought charges of conspiracy, extortion, kidnapping, and assault with a deadly weapon against Miyashiro, who tried to shoot the victim. Orii, apparently not present at the shooting, was charged only with attempted extortion.

Time, apparently, did not wither Orii's ambition. A 1993 intelligence report on the Sumiyoshi-kai in LA asserted that it engaged in drugs, extortion, prostitution, pornography, gambling, weapons smuggling, money laundering. Among their alleged number was one Leo Orii, considered by federal intelligence officials to be "the most influential figure of the Boryo-kudan in Los Angeles." Orii, though, is only one individual in a rather fluid group of yakuza-connected Japanese in the Los Angeles area. Members of this group allegedly engage in racketeering and investment scams. Names appear and reappear on various watch lists, but there are few arrests.

For deeply held cultural reasons, and because they are strangers in the United States, Japanese nationals here are extremely reluctant to talk with American police about their troubles with the gangsters. Victims of yakuza shakedowns will most likely just suffer the loss and try to forget it. One group in Los Angeles that tried hard to break through this barrier is the LAPD's Asian Task Force. Criticized by some as a public relations outfit, the task force has indeed put a lot of effort into simply maintaining a presence in the various Asian communities in Los Angeles, including the Japanese. One problem it found in dealing with the yakuza is that they had not caused nearly as much trouble as local Chinese or Vietnamese gangs, and therefore did not lead police to spend the time or money to pursue them.

Nonetheless, as the exploits of Orii's partner, Miyashiro, demonstrated, the yakuza in California were not necessarily delicate in their tactics. A pair of unsolved crimes, reminiscent of the Tokyo Club killings of fifty years earlier, were evidence that the yakuza had to be taken seriously. Two Asian male bodies found in remote parts of Southern California, one in a shallow grave near Oxnard on the coast north of LA, and a second found near Castaic Lake in the Angeles National Forest, pointed strongly to yakuza skull-duggery. "We never could identify the bodies," said LAPD detective George Min, "but one was heavily tattooed, and the other was also believed to be yakuza."

Another Japanese murder victim surfaced in 1984, and was also believed to be the victim of yakuza violence. Hiroshi Eto, reportedly running from massive gambling debts in Japan, had been found strangled in his room at the Los Angeles Hilton. A Japanese newspaper reported that Eto, a "dating club" operator, had heavily insured his life with an American carrier prior to his leaving Tokyo. Upon Eto's death, a Taiwanese male stood to collect about $315,000 in yen in what is by now a standard, and gruesome, yakuza method of collecting back debts. Some yakuza in LA apparently make their living as hit men for this and similar tasks.

Beyond the shakedowns and outright murders, a key yakuza activity in Southern California is money laundering, a tough operation for police to detect. Here, as in Hawaii and elsewhere, the easiest, most efficient money laundry is a high-volume cash business, such as a bar, restaurant, or gift shop. But the yakuza have also invested in non-cash businesses in the Los Angeles area, investigators say. As in East Asia, investment and import-export firms are favorites of the gangs, and the LAPD has kept watch over a number of Japanese-owned firms. As officials in Hawaii noted, though, law enforcement can trace money back to Japan and run into a stone wall. "Japanese bankers," said one Honolulu official, "are like Swiss bankers. They reveal nothing."

Such frustration was echoed in a report by detectives Jimmy Sakoda and Yoichi Ikuta. Sakoda, an investigator with the LA County District Attorney's Office, and Ikuta, with the LAPD's organized crime intelligence unit, are two of the most respected, savviest yakuza investigators in the U.S. Wrote Sakoda and Ikuta:

> Over the years, United States law enforcement have expressed frustration over not being able to confirm whether or not a Japanese investor is associated in any way with JOC [Japanese organized crime]. Strict privacy laws and dummy companies made it difficult, if not impossible, for United States law enforcement to trace the flow and sources of investment funds. Creating further confusion and complications, under Japanese laws it was not illegal for a gangster to take his gambling or extortion proceeds and invest it in real estate or any other legitimate business venture.

The largest U.S. firm with known ties to a yakuza or former yakuza has for years been headquartered in the Los Angeles area. This is Machii-Ross Petroleum, an investment of one of Japan's best-known yakuza leaders, the ubiquitous Hisayuki Machii. Apparently, when the Korean head of the Towa Yuai Jigyo Kumiai decided to invest in an American enterprise, he chose a prestigious type of business, and one that is decidedly non-yakuza: oil.

Machii-Ross was incorporated in 1970 as an oil exploration company and invested in wells principally in the Wattenburg field in central Colorado. From its Santa Monica offices, the company has also explored in Texas and, through a subsidiary operation, built and run a natural gas processing plant. Machii invested over $1 million in the business, which seems to have paid off handsomely.

The American partner of the company is Kenneth Ross, a genial former lobbyist and California state assemblyman. Ross claimed that he was a little surprised when informed of his partner's colorful background. "When we began the company," said Ross, "all I knew was that he was a wealthy Korean living in Japan. I had never heard of the yakuza."

Over the course of their partnership, Ross got to know Machii quite well, despite the fact that they needed a translator to communicate. Machii's criminal activities, said Ross, are in the past, and his partner regretted the reputation he must carry. Nonetheless, Machii told Ross, "I'm proud of what I did. Proud of my activities fighting Communism." Machii, of course, fought Communism so successfully that he was able to amass considerable wealth. "Machii," said Ross in 1984, "lives almost like Howard Hughes, in a huge five-story home that he rarely leaves. I suspect that he's worth well over a billion dollars . . . maybe twice that."

Machii's American investments do not represent, then, a significant part of his overall fortune. They did, however, attract the attention of U.S. officials. Ross, who has been regarded by American police as clean, was visited a number of times by both local and federal authorities and questioned about Machii. No specific charges or even allegations came out of these visits.

In a police intelligence report, however, an unnamed but remarkably similar company was accused of using suspect funds. The report referred to a "Japanese-based oil leasing and exploration company with offices in California and Colorado." The suspicions were anything but vague: "It is suspected that money made from illicit drug trafficking is being funneled through this company." Other police intelligence placed Machii-Ross in a network of yakuza-related enterprises, without leveling specific charges.

Ross, who has run the American end of the business without much help or interference from Machii, denies any possibility of wrongdoing. He pointed to the reputably obtained audits of the firm, and the records of funds transferred from Japan to the United States by way of Mitsui and Manufacturers Hanover banks. He did not know the exact source of the funds invested, but added, "As far as I know, the [gang] disbanded in 1967."

The West Coast Sex Trade

For many American and European men, Asian women hold a special allure. Likewise, for many Japanese men, Caucasian women are the object of sexual fascination. Call it the lure of the exotic.

In the early 1980s, Tokyo-based journalist Jean Sather investigated the trade and the special attraction white women hold for Japanese men. Sather, then with the Asahi newspapers, wrote:

> Many expensive clubs, and their customers, prefer the "exoticism" of Western women. This is part of a general tendency in modern Japan to see Caucasian women as more beautiful and much sexier than Japanese women. Caucasian models are used heavily in advertising, porno films that feature white women are popular, and many Japanese women still visit plastic surgeons to have their eyes made rounder and their noses more prominent.

Gyo Hani, then executive editor of the *Japan Times*, told Sather:

> Attitudes are not really changing towards Caucasians. They're not creatures from outer space, but close to it. Asian aliens look like us, but if you have a woman who's fair-skinned, blue-eyed, with blond hair, then you have a treasure.

Japanese technology is still incapable of filling this particular domestic need, and thus Japan, in this case, requires imports. To meet the demand, the women must somehow be attracted to the homeland, either with their consent or, as often, through subterfuge and trickery. The former Soviet republics have become a major source of the traffic in Caucasian women, but the Japanese sex industry is always eager to recruit Americans. The so-called white slave trade from North America is relatively small, but it exists and has proved nightmarish for those who have fallen victim.

The yakuza, naturally, are only too willing to attempt to cash in on the market, but they have a problem: few yakuza speak English well enough to entice women to come to Japan. They have, therefore, tended to operate through fronts or paid agents on the West Coast. According to various police reports, these agents usually obtain women by placing ads for singers and dancers in the entertainment press, publications such as LA's *Dramalogue.* These have listings for "cattle call" drama auditions, as well as for seamier performances, such as nude modeling and porn pictures. Talent agents design these ads to appeal to the starving actress or singer. Some agencies have recruited farther afield, in San Francisco and Portland, Oregon, among other cities.

What happens to the women in Japan varies. Some of the women, having worked as prostitutes at home, are under few illusions about what the ad is actually seeking, but others have expected straight jobs as singers or dancers, only to be forced to add tasks ranging from "hostessing" in bars to outright prostitution. Treatment can be brutal and escape difficult. One American woman recruited from Los Angeles told her story to the *Japan Times* just hours before she fled Japan. Her stay included two attempted rapes as well as violations of her contract. Her employer, one Kanji Chiba, "insisted that she relinquish her [return air] ticket for 'safekeeping,' which she did." Some of the women are duped into cooperating with their exploiters, ever hopeful for a better future. Said one: "A lot of the mistakes have been mine. You're naive, vulnerable, ambitious—you dream. That's what these people capitalize on—your dreams."

Women who return from what is often a hellish experience in the yakuza clubs often seek revenge, but usually get little satisfaction. Few of the recruiting agents can be located, and the victims have little in the way of legal recourse against those few who can be found. American law holds that the agents must have knowingly sent the women to houses of prostitution, and this is difficult, if not impossible, to prove. A number of civil suits were launched by women against the talent agents in the 1980s. After seeing an ad in the *San Francisco Chronicle* for entertainers, aspiring singer Lisa Petrides went to a San Francisco agency for "a very professional audition," but wound up at the Little Club in Tokyo, where her yakuza bosses insisted that she forget about singing and concentrate on hostessing. She called the agency from Japan, but her former agent refused to help her. When Petrides returned to California, she sued the agency and got a small out-of-court settlement. The agency remained in operation.

Another victim of the talent ruse, Kristina Kirstin of Los Angeles, filed a $15 million lawsuit in 1982. She named three defendants: her American agent, the agent's counterpart in Japan, and Alexander Haig, then secretary of state. Haig was charged because Kirstin alleged that the U.S. embassy in Japan refused to help her when she wished to flee Japan. The embassy, maintained Kirstin, was indifferent to her plight at the Mil Members Club in Kyoto, even though it was a known yakuza operation. U.S. officials at the State Department had told her that, by law, she was on her own and they could do nothing.

Bad publicity has helped curb the number of "entertainers" heading to Japan, although not before their number reached into the hundreds. A few agencies are still around, say police, searching for new victims. As one investigator noted, "The demand for Caucasian prostitutes is so great over there it can't be filled."

The Arming of Japan

When one thinks of the trade in precision machinery between the United States and Japan, the flow seems to be heavily toward the States. But there is one instrument that is entirely an export item from the United States to Japan. Thanks to a combination of high quality, availability, and minimal legal encumbrances, American firearms are sought and acquired by the Japanese. The distributors, and in this case the customers, of the product are primarily the yakuza. Americans have competition from various foreign producers, but they are by far the yakuza's largest single source of weaponry—providing one-third of all handguns seized between 1994 and 1998. This is twice the amount provided by the nearest rival source, China. The United States is, in effect, arming the Japanese underworld.

Eddie Kurimata (not his real name) is typical of the yakuza's mainland connections. A Japanese American, naturalized here, he was no stranger to the world of crime before he met any yakuza. After he did time for drugs, he met a few Japanese gangsters in San Francisco and took them up on what he thought was an excellent offer. He became a gun scout for them. "I'm straight now," he insisted. "But I've made money off the yakuza here. They need us. There's no way they can get all the guns they need in Japan."

For three years, Eddie traveled to scores of gun shops throughout the Bay Area. He'd purchase three pistols in Daly City, four in Oakland, two in San Rafael. A good sale to his yakuza customers could be as few as twelve guns, but it paid off. "I worked for them," he said, "but just for the money. It was too good to pass up." Kurimata could realize a profit of $1,000 per handgun.

The possibility of such profits exists largely because of the discrepancy between Japanese and American gun laws. For all practical purposes, guns aren't allowed in Japan, and they are freely permitted in the United States. This, in turn, creates a huge price differential. A pistol that sells legally for $250 will command up to ten times that amount in Japan. Ammunition frequently sells for $5 to $12 a bullet there.

While the United States rarely imports illegal firearms, it is a key source of illegal exports for those overseas. For gun buyers, America is a wide-open gun supermarket with few restrictions. As one West Coast official of the U.S. Bureau of Alcohol, Tobacco, and Firearms (ATF) put it, "Most foreign police regard American gun laws as a joke." Japanese laws, however, are anything but a joke.

The idea of a civilian population with easy access to firearms flies in the face of a Japanese tradition that stretches back nearly four centuries. For two hundred years, the Japanese conducted a remarkable social experiment by banning all firearms on the islands. It began in the early seventeenth century, largely as a reaction to the cold-bloodedness of combat with firearms, and as a gesture of commitment to the sword, an enduring symbol of honor and stature in Japan. It was also an expeditious way to maintain power in the central government.

As Noel Perrin details in his fascinating book *Giving Up the Gun,* Japan's gunsmiths were summoned to a single city in 1642, forced to work for a government monopoly, and slowly starved out of business. Japan's feudal rulers impounded massive numbers of firearms, and for the next two hundred years the development of modern weaponry virtually stopped. When Commodore Perry arrived in 1853, his sailors wryly noted that the Japanese shore batteries defending Tokyo harbor could fit inside and be fired out of their ships' cannons.

A tradition of gun control survived the Industrial Revolution and even World War II. In 1958, the Diet enacted the Firearms and Swords Control Act, which had the effect of making Japan relatively free of handgun murders. Even with a sharp increase over the past decade, Japan remains among the safest countries in the world. In 1998, for instance, firearms were used to kill 30,708 in the United States. That year in Japan, twenty-two people died as a result of firearms.

There are virtually no legal handguns in Japan at all, except those used by military and police. Only a few dozen civilians—all sportsmen—have permits to own arms. By contrast, there are an estimated 260 million firearms in private hands in the U.S. The scarcity of guns has helped make them a source of fascination to the Japanese. Tourists, along with movie stars, writers, cops, and crooks, make visits to firing ranges a standard stop while traveling abroad. An entire magazine is devoted to expensively detailed, high-tech fake weapons, some of which run to hundreds of dollars and only shoot

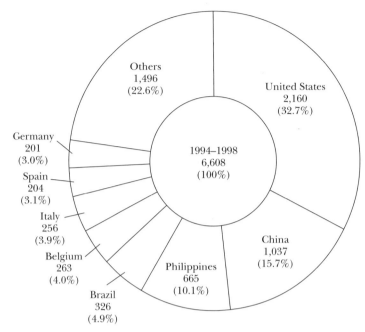

Figure 4. Countries in which handguns seized in Japan were manufactured. (Source: National Policy Agency.)

plastic pellets a few yards. The lack of guns has caused some inventive ya-kuza to actually refit the plastic replicas; others have ingeniously fashioned ballpoint pens into pistols that shoot a .22 caliber bullet by pressing the clip.

But it is the real model that Japanese crooks want. To help Japan with its gun gap, the yakuza have moved tens of thousands of handguns illegally into Japan. Guns smuggled into Japan do not go to collectors or to citizens interested in protecting their homes; they typically go to the gangs. A 1981 NPA report noted that 89.5 percent of all handguns seized came from "criminal syndicates." But as handguns poured into Japan in the 1990s, the gun market started attracting other customers. The proliferation of cheap handguns and a rash of public shootings in the 1990s sparked reports that illegal arms were spreading from yakuza to petty crooks and unstable indi-viduals. Indeed, once-rare handguns became a common accessory for Jap-anese criminals. A 1989 NPA *White Paper* noted that the ratio of yakuza to handguns had been ten to one, but was now closer to one to one. Police be-lieved as many as 150,000 illegal handguns were in circulation. The fall in price itself suggests the boom in gun sales. A Smith & Wesson .38 caliber re-volver, bought for $275 in the U.S., fetched as much as $4,000 on the back streets of Tokyo in 1990; by 1997, the price had fallen to as little as $500.

Americans have been involved in gun smuggling ever since the first days of the postwar firearms ban. For gun couriers, the varied syndicates have employed Japanese Americans, Guamanian Americans, U.S. military, tourists, students, and anyone else who might slip through Customs with a small arsenal. Officials have tracked the shipment of thousands of U.S.-made guns to Japan from Chicago, Tucson, Los Angeles, and other cities. Many of the yakuza's American partners have been military personnel. This is hardly surprising, considering the tens of thousands of U.S. troops stationed in Japan. Many of them are bored, lonely, and low on cash, and many have access to stores of American weapons. In one 1989 case, soldiers of an eighty-man Green Beret unit were accused of smuggling over two hundred guns, Thai gold, jewelry, and pharmaceutical drugs to an Okinawa yakuza gang.

A key point of contact for American gunrunners, suggested a DEA report, is the off-base bars where GIs and others go for drink, women, and drugs. Just how this connection can work was revealed to law enforcement officials by Air Force veteran James Anthony Bridgeport. In early 1983, a joint operation by ATF, Japanese Customs, and the U.S. Air Force broke up a twelve-man smuggling ring headed by Bridgeport. Based in Tucson, Arizona, the ring had been sending guns to Japan via military air transport. Bridgeport began his association with the yakuza while stationed in Japan. "It basically started with little favors, money loans," Bridgeport later testified. "I just got in over my head, began to meet people, and borrow. And it ended up where I was a little bit deeper than I should have been. And then when I tried to get out, it was impossible."

Bridgeport claimed that he had been pressured by the yakuza into smuggling—first amphetamines, then guns. When he failed to recover a package of amphetamines—his first assignment—Bridgeport was beaten by yakuza members and threatened by having a gun placed in his mouth. He later succeeded in smuggling a shipment of speed from Korea to Japan. When he returned to the United States, the yakuza tracked him down and forced him to move guns. All told, over a two-year period, Bridgeport netted a total of $250,000 for gunrunning. Although the money was sweet, he lived in fear, until one of his cohorts was seized in San Francisco with thirty-eight handguns and revealed the operation.

The majority of gun shipments to Japan, though, have been handled by civilians rather than military people. Some of the smuggling methods show a great deal of ingenuity. Guns are taken from the United States into Japan in false-bottom bags, inside folk craft articles, in CD players and travel irons, in television cameras, and even inside pineapples, an item commonly carried by Japanese returning from Hawaii. Larger quantities require roomier conveyances, and in 1980 Japanese police discovered five pistols in the gas tank of a British Jensen automobile arriving from the United States.

American-built cars are used as well, and it is perhaps no coincidence that yakuza oyabun are the principal purchasers of imported American cars.

The trans-Pacific gun route was, by 1985, sufficiently well developed that smugglers could respond to particular crises in Japan with special orders for guns. For instance, when Masahisa Takenaka, newly crowned oyabun of the Yamaguchi-gumi, was assassinated in January 1985 by a hit team from the recently splintered Ichiwa-kai, U.S. police knew that shipments of guns would soon be leaving for Japan. DEA agents were able to turn early leads into a yearlong investigation of gunrunning, drug dealing, and murder conspiracy that ended with the arrest of two of the Yamaguchi-gumi's highest-ranking bosses in Honolulu. But even this, police agree, made only a small dent in the yakuza's gun purchasing.

Three years later, the U.S.-Japan pipeline made news. In August 1988, the Panamanian ambassador to Japan received four heavy attaché cases by diplomatic pouch from Oklahoma. Inside, to his surprise, were twenty handguns and 866 rounds of ammunition. The ambassador duly reported the shipment to Japanese authorities, who found the ambassador's own secretary was involved with the yakuza in running guns to Japan. The twenty guns, all .38s, would have likely fetched $100,000 or more on the black market.

It is a dismal way to alleviate the foreign trade crisis: Japanese gangsters buying American handguns and hiring American entertainers and prostitutes. But the yakuza, as recent events have shown, are not content simply to buy American. Like good businessmen everywhere, they have become investors, and they have expanded activities here in part due to a strong foothold in their favorite base of operations abroad—the tourist trade.

The Tourist: An Easy Mark

Along with oranges and grapes, Japanese tourists ought to be considered lucrative cash crops for the state of California. Hundreds of thousands of Japanese visit the state each year, leaving behind hundreds of millions of dollars. Yet much of this booming tourist industry tends to be a closed system. Tourists typically fly in aboard Japan Air Lines, stay at Japanese-owned hotels, eat in Japanese restaurants, shop at Japanese-owned boutiques, ride about in Japanese tour buses, and patronize Japanese purveyors of drink, guns, and vice. Police suspect yakuza involvement in a good deal of the racket. As early as 1981, state investigators noted that the gangs had apparently launched a drive "to dominate the Japanese tourism industry in San Francisco and Los Angeles." The report described a common pattern of accosting cash-laden Japanese tourists and, through deception or intimidation, forcing them to participate in selected tours.

Police on the West Coast are aware of questionable practices in the Japanese tourist trade, but they have been largely unable to make many cases, due in part to the reluctance of witnesses to come forward. Another problem is figuring out exactly what is going on in the often sleazy tourist districts. In one incident, police got a notion of just how dangerous Japanese tourism can be. An entrepreneur named Stuart "Steve" Conn opened a gift shop called Nikkaido in downtown San Francisco that catered to Japanese tourists. The store offered Western wear, which for a time the Japanese loved. And, in a separate room in the back, there was a huge selection of pornographic magazines, films, videotapes, and plastic paraphernalia. The operation was typical of Japanese tourist traps up and down the West Coast. According to one police report, Conn also adopted the hard-sell techniques of many tourist traps. "Japanese are lured into the shop by Japanese-speaking 'hustlers,'" it read. "Once inside the shop, they are intimidated into buying gifts at very high prices. Victims rarely complain to police for fear of retaliation and losing face among their people."

In July 1984, the pugnacious Conn was found by police near the city's Japan Town with bullet holes in his leg and shoulder. From his bed in San Francisco General Hospital, Conn claimed to any who would listen that his assailants were yakuza. Because Conn had numerous enemies, police weren't convinced that yakuza were, in fact, the gunmen. But it also turned out that Conn had a silent partner in the operation: the son of Japanese speedboat racing czar, neofascist, and yakuza friend Ryoichi Sasakawa.

The Wrong Side of Japanese Business

Sasakawa had already rung alarms by trying to buy into American business, and it was bigger than a gift shop. In 1978, Takashi Sasakawa, Ryoichi's second son, publicly joined with well-known Japanese restaurateur, speedboat racer, and balloonist Hiroaki "Rocky" Aoki to announce plans to lease the aging Shelburne Hotel in Atlantic City and turn it into a casino. The gambling boom was hitting the East Coast, and Sasakawa, for one, wanted to be in on it. Aoki, owner of the famed Benihana chain, felt he could add an exotic touch to the Jersey Shore.

The actual deal was a hopelessly complicated affair involving several paper corporations in both America and Japan, and several hundred million dollars. Of this, Takashi openly owned 47 percent of the enterprise, although no knowledgeable observer believed Takashi was the real investor. His New York attorney asserted to the press that Takashi's father was "far removed from the deal," but few were convinced.

Within months, the U.S. Securities and Exchange Commission charged Takashi Sasakawa and Aoki with insider stock trading. The two men had purchased 60,000 shares of the Hardwicke Company, knowing that they would later engage that company to manage the planned Shelburne Benihana. This move inflated the value of the stock, a patently illegal move. Sa-sakawa was forced to make restitution to the sellers of the original Hard-wicke stock.

The Sasakawas were reportedly quite taken aback by this wrinkle; Ryoichi was used to manipulating stock values for his own profiteering without a peep from the Japanese government. Following that unpleasantness, Sasa-kawa continued to pump money into the Shelburne project, but without his previous enthusiasm. There were indications that the casino would not fly, and not only because the SEC was on his tail. Sasakawa's seedy background had caught up with him. Because of Sasakawa's dossier, American banks re-fused to "anchor" the project with domestic loans, and New Jersey law en-forcement let it be known that any project with the Sasakawa name on it would have a hard time getting a casino license. If New Jersey wanted to keep mob-connected Americans out of Atlantic City, it could hardly open the door to yakuza-connected Japanese.

Sasakawa's interest in Atlantic City made a good deal of sense, and he brought to it plenty of expertise. The boat racing czar already knew the gambling business from the ground—or the water—up, and could run large-scale betting operations as well as anyone. Some law enforcement people worried that, had it succeeded, it could have served as the biggest Japanese-owned laundry in the United States, which is why they helped scuttle the deal. By the time the Sasakawas, Aoki, and the silent partners bailed out—selling their interest to a Philadelphia real estate developer in 1981—they had lost an estimated $27 million.

Undaunted, in February of 1983, Ryoichi arrived in San Francisco to re-ceive the Linus Pauling Medal for Humanitarianism for his generous dona-tion of $770,000 to the Linus Pauling Institute of Science and Medicine. The man who once called himself "the world's wealthiest fascist" was now out to become the world's greatest philanthropist.

Sasakawa's efforts at self-aggrandizement were boggling. Prior to the black-tie dinner given by the Pauling Institute, he held a luncheon at San Francisco's posh Bohemian Club—which is anything but—and spent the morning giving interviews to the local media. At the luncheon, Sasakawa re-ceived the guests bowing like a buoy in a rough sea and smiling continu-ously. His publicist, flown out from the giant New York firm of Doremus, told the assembled that Sasakawa was, among other things, a patriot, a man unashamed to love his country and his mother. In fact, Sasakawa erected a statue in Japan of himself carrying his aged mother on his back, but the ob-ject of his veneration was less the mother than the bearer.

He also denounced any hint of his ultranationalist past. When the au-thors pointed out to him at a San Francisco press conference that U.S. Army documents were quite explicit about his plundering in China, he proclaimed, "I have not exploited one yen or one penny. What I did was to donate several million tuberculosis injections to China." Any other stories were "Communist-inspired." He was equally vehement in denying any relations with the yakuza, conveniently forgetting that he had publicly boasted of including the late Yamaguchi-gumi boss Kazuo Taoka among his drinking companions.

In spite of Sasakawa's indifferent results in cleaning up Japanese history and his place in it, the grand old kuromaku continued to make a name for himself as a philanthropist and promoter. By 1994, his Japan Shipbuilding Industry Foundation was bringing in nearly $1.4 billion annually, and had doled out more than 1 trillion yen around the world. The aging ultranationalist had become the largest private donor to the United Nations and was funding international health centers, Ivy League universities, and even the presidential library of Jimmy Carter, who praised his "good work for peace."

Sasakawa's most ambitious giveaway in America was the United States–Japan Foundation, headquartered in New York and begun in 1980 with a generous $48 million endowment from Sasakawa. To orchestrate its efforts, the foundation's original American working group included such luminaries as Henry Kissinger; Chairman Angier Biddle Duke, former ambassador to four countries and heir to a tobacco fortune; James A. Linen, former president of Time, Inc.; former RCA chairman Robert Sarnoff; and former New York mayor John Lindsay. Among its "honorary advisers" were Jimmy Carter and Gerald Ford.

The expressed goal of the U.S.-Japan Foundation was to enhance, through grants and education, cooperation between the two countries, primarily of an economic nature. But there was another, more covert goal, and that was to raise the value of Sasakawa's personal stock among the movers and shakers. According to Rocky Aoki, Sasakawa's former business partner, the old ultranationalist was angling for the Nobel Peace Prize, and he was willing to spend almost any amount of money to get it. He even set up an office in Oslo, Norway, in order to better lobby the Nobel Committee, and in 1985 he was actually nominated for a prize.

Despite all his do-gooding and donating, Sasakawa remained a gambling czar with strong ties to the extreme right in Japan, and with less overt but definite ties to the yakuza. In his native Japan, Sasakawa remained terribly controversial, with many organizations reluctant to go near his money. In 1993, when a reporter for Japan's most respected journal, *Bungei Shunju,* ran a six-month investigation of Sasakawa's power, he received death threats and went into hiding. Sasakawa's reputation proved tough to shake, and even in the West many institutions, such as National Public Radio, engaged in public handwringing over whether to accept his money. If, as

Dr. Linus Pauling said of Sasakawa's philanthropy, "Perhaps he's just trying to make up for past misdeeds," he never entirely succeeded.

In 1996, Ryoichi Sasakawa finally passed away. He was nearly a century old, and had reinvented himself as few have in recent history. Today, the most tangible evidence of Sasakawa is a life-size statue of the man covered with adoring children of all races, which stands outside the Sasakawa Peace Foundation on L Street in Washington, D.C. There it continues to puzzle or amuse passersby, most of whom haven't a clue as to who is decorating their sidewalk.

Sasakawa was not the only questionable Japanese financial figure to arrive in North America. Since the early 1980s, the United States and Canada have hosted a rogues' gallery of gamblers, racketeers, and money launderers from the Land of the Rising Sun. Among the more curious are the sokaiya, who apparently have wondered if their extortionate ways might take root in America.

On April 21, 1982, the manager of the powerful sokaiya group Rondan Doyukai, a gentleman named Shigeru Kobayashi, attended a stockholders' meeting at the Chase Manhattan bank in New York. Kobayashi sat through Chairman David Rockefeller's opening remarks, and forty minutes of questioning from the floor—undoubtedly fighting the urge to silence the dissenters—and then turned and addressed the crowd. Said Kobayashi: "We represent your stockholders from Japan. I am happy to be here at your general meeting. Now I have the honor of seeing Chairman Rockefeller. . . . He is a great man because he met with His Majesty the Emperor when he visited Japan a couple of years ago, and very few people in Japan can shake hands with the Emperor. I would also like to express my sincere appreciation for your high dividends."

Kobayashi's statement probably amused those stockholders present, but some were also puzzled. Why should Rondan Doyukai send one of its top people to New York merely to flatter the company? Kobayashi later told a Japanese newspaper: "We rode into New York to show them what Japanese sokaiya are. But, just before the meeting, the *Wall Street Journal* carried a sensational article with banner headline saying, 'The Sokaiya are coming, the Sokaiya are coming,' as if the Japanese gangsters were invading the U.S. This raised a stink. We know that the public peace is bad in New York, so we thought we might be eliminated by the Mafia."

Kobayashi somehow avoided a trip to the bottom of the East River, but he needn't have worried in the first place. Nearly six years earlier, in equally violent Los Angeles, another sokaiya group had made its appearance. In 1976, according to police sources, fifty Japanese executives filed into one of the ballrooms of the Biltmore Hotel in downtown LA. They were the top-ranking officers of the largest Japanese corporations operating on the West Coast, and they had come to pay their respects to a group of visiting sokaiya (who had neglected to announce their presence to the press). Police at the same time observed sokaiya Masato Yoshioka making a tour of Los Angeles to present himself at Japanese-owned banks, conglomerates, and securities investment firms, possibly to hit any companies missed at the Biltmore meeting. Although the businesses were reluctant to talk about the incident, informants revealed to law enforcement agents that, as in Japan, it was cheaper to pay up than to risk the consequences.

Rondan Doyukai also had made earlier trips to America. It had sent representatives to the 1981 annual meeting of the Bank of America in San Francisco. They were, in the words of corporate secretary John Fauvre, "polite but insistent." The group approached the microphone, said Fauvre, with their own photographer and translator, and introduced themselves with lengthy formality. The sokaiya then did little more than wish the bank good luck, much as Kobayashi would do to Chase Manhattan a year later. Rondan Doyukai's interests extended to other Western companies, as well. The group invested $232,000 to gain shareholder status in a strategic handful of American and European companies, according to the *Wall Street Journal* report that so terrified Kobayashi. Among those targeted besides Chase and Bank of America were General Motors, IBM, and Dow Chemical.

Other sokaiya operations got under way. Los Angeles and New York City police discovered that sokaiya-type scandal sheets were being used to extort money from Japanese corporations, and sokaiya continue to remain a threat to American branches of Japanese companies, particularly the smaller ones. In the early 1990s, at least one sokaiya group formed in the Los Angeles area, calling itself the Japanese Defense Society. And a report from Japan warned that some gangs are believed to have sent some of their brighter members to pursue advanced business degrees in American universities, to prepare for sokaiya-style rackets in the United States.

Meeting of the Mobs

As awareness of yakuza spread to the New York Police Department in the early 1980s, the local cops had a hard time keeping track of Japanese mobsters there. Said one Chinese American officer in a heavy New York accent, "There's only one Japanese American on the whole force, and he doesn't speak Japanese."

Nonetheless, Asian cops in the intelligence division had noted reports of yakuza shakedowns of Japanese businesses and individuals. The NYPD was dubious of any large-scale ongoing criminal operations in the area, though. Said one officer at the time: "If there were any rackets, like prostitution, the Five Families would be interested. You can't do anything for very long in

New York without the traditional mob becoming aware of it. In the bar business, you have to deal with them. They're in restaurant supply, in liquor, and related activities. I think New York is just geographically inconvenient for the yakuza to get anything going in. That's one reason they have done so much better in L.A.—less structured organized crime."

Less than a year after this pronouncement, the President's Commission on Organized Crime revealed that the New York mob was perfectly willing to play ball with Japanese gangsters in organizing gambling setups. The NYPD was correct up to a point: the mob doesn't want competitors in its territory, but it loves to have more customers. The yakuza didn't then and don't now pose a threat to American organized crime groups anywhere on the mainland, but they certainly can form alliances with gangsters in the United States, alliances that will benefit both parties.

It is, in fact, precisely these alliances that have given American law enforcement the jitters. Ties between American and other mobs have always increased the strength of domestic gangsters. In some ways, U.S. organized crime went international at the turn of the century, when arriving Sicilian gangsters kept in touch with their cousins in the old country, and Jewish and Greek drug smugglers maintained ties to relatives in strategic locations. Over the years, the Americans became more involved in the international drug trade and, during Prohibition, in bootlegging. After World War II, big-time American gangsters took gambling operations to Havana, the Bahamas, and Europe.

The relative decline of the Italian American Mafia has meant that there are more players in the game today. Yakuza gangs have the opportunity to join forces with any number of ethnic and regional gangs on an opportunistic basis.

The power of such alliances has truly worried American officials. Warned former U.S. Attorney Michael Sterrett, who first alerted federal law enforcement to the yakuza: "There are now shadow governments in the U.S. and Japan that collect their own taxes, make their own rules, and enforce their own laws. An alliance between the yakuza and U.S. organized crime means that drugs and guns and huge amounts of money will be moving across the world accountable to no one but the mobs themselves. It means an international shadow government."

Perhaps the major difficulty the mobs face in cementing such a union is a large cultural and linguistic barrier, as well as the absence of any long-term, binding ties. Few American gangsters have cousins in the yakuza, and not many speak even pidgin Japanese. Consequently, the element of trust is lacking, and it is impossible to set up a cross-Pacific theft or smuggling scheme without that trust. In organized crime, several million dollars does not change hands on the basis of a written contract.

What the two mobs need, then, is a place to meet and get to know one another—maybe a place to relax, to eat, to drink, maybe to whore and gamble; to exchange, even through an interpreter, the amenities that bring about the aura of trust required before business can be planned. This place ought to be open enough to ensure that these meetings don't raise too much suspicion. Fortunately for the mobs, there is such a place: Las Vegas.

Japanese mobsters and high rollers came to Las Vegas in the 1970s as participants in gambling junkets. Pleasure has clearly led to business. As long ago as 1975, American and Japanese investigators believe they uncovered a link between Caesar's Palace in Las Vegas and organized crime in Japan. In 1973, Caesar's, then suspected of being under the direct control of mob families, appointed an allegedly yakuza-connected movie producer, Kikumaru Okuda, to help find customers and to collect debts owed to the casino. Two years later, according to Japanese press reports, Okuda associates threatened a number of debtors who together owed more than $200,000. The collectors would, they said, have the yakuza kill them if they didn't pay up. Caesar's Palace officials denied that Okuda had any mob connections on either continent, but the case in Japan was strong enough to send Okuda and two others to jail for extortion. More meetings followed between mobbed-up Japanese and Americans. At an early '80s golf tournament in State Line, Nevada, police surveilled known yakuza being hosted by Mafia associate Allen Dorfman, who had lent his financial acumen to raiding the Teamsters' pension fund. Dorfman didn't have time to pursue his new contacts. Soon after, he was gunned down with eight bullets to the head in suburban Chicago.

The Japanese, though, found that they could profit from a permanent base of some sort in Las Vegas, and they have made several attempts to secure one. As early as 1971, billionaire Kenji Osano began negotiations to purchase the Sands Hotel and Casino. Like Sasakawa seven years later, Osano knew that a giant casino operation, with its enormous flow of cash, its facilities, and its location in a gambling capital, could only help him and his friends in the gambling business. Osano, however, was forced to withdraw from the deal when his troubles with Lockheed began.

In this case, Japanese were not discriminated against; until 1987, *no* foreigner had ever owned or operated a Nevada casino. After that date, though, a procession of Japanese buyers strode into Las Vegas—gamblers, real estate speculators, nouveaux riches—each hoping to stake a claim in the legendary gaming capital. Nevada gaming authorities found themselves stumped as they investigated their new applicants—stumped by Byzantine records and financial transactions, cultural differences, and a nation where mob ties often seemed just another cost of doing business. Like other foreign investigators, Nevada gaming officials soon learned that Japanese authorities were not overly helpful. "The Japanese police system is such that it's difficult to get information," William A. Bible, chairman of the Nevada

Gaming Control Board, told a reporter. In private, Bible's investigators would use far tougher language.

Several Japanese did receive casino or liquor licenses, despite allegations of yakuza ties. But the license generally turned out not to be a license to print money, but to lose it. Few stories were more colorful than that of Ken Mizuno.

The High Rollers

A flamboyant gambler and high-stakes grifter, Ken Mizuno was one of the biggest losers of the Bubble Economy. Yet years afterward, people in Las Vegas still spoke of him with awe. A former pro baseball player in Japan, Mizuno gained a reputation for his golfing expertise and his ties to the yakuza. He first surfaced in Las Vegas in 1982, where he attempted to secure a liquor license for a Japanese restaurant in the Tropicana Hotel and Casino. According to the *Las Vegas Valley Times,* Mizuno entered the United States with $3 million in traveler's checks—an unusual way to transfer money. Police, however, claimed that he had not $3 million, but $100 million at his disposal, and charged furthermore that it was yakuza money. Over the protests of the cops, Mizuno nonetheless received his license and moved on to bigger game.

As the Bubble took off, Mizuno's profile in the city grew larger and larger. Between 1988 and 1991, he would fly in from Tokyo in his private DC-9, often accompanied by dozens of friends, and drop in at the baccarat pits at the Mirage Hotel and Casino. The high-rolling Japanese was capable of gambling away millions of dollars at a time. Soon he'd become a Las Vegas fixture and was put up in a free suite reserved for high-stakes gamblers. But it wasn't only Vegas that drew his attention. Ken Mizuno was one of the Bubble era's yen-crazed Japanese, jetting around the Pacific developing golf courses and resorts. It was a remarkable spending spree. At various times, he owned the Olomana Golf Links in Hawaii and the Royal Kenfield Golf Course in Henderson, Nevada. But his prize was the Indian Wells Golf and Country Club, a famed PGA tour stop near Palm Springs, California. All told, through Ken International, Mizuno owned the Indian Wells Country Club, the Indian Wells Racquet Club, six acres of adjacent land, and the swanky new Hotel Indian Wells, for which he paid an extravagant $24 million—or an average of $160,000 for each of the 150 guest rooms.

It was in Las Vegas, though, where Mizuno's reputation grew fastest. He was a legendary tipper when he won, a favorite among hotel staff. But the hotel made its real money when he lost. And the losses were extraordinary.

According to gambling records obtained by the newspaper *Yomiuri,* Mizuno visited the Mirage twenty-nine times between December 1989 and October 1991. Posing as Thomas Anderson, Mizuno eventually accrued losses of almost $65 million, mostly by playing baccarat. Records show that Mizuno's largest win was $4.3 million; his biggest loss, $11.24 million. That's a lot of money, even in a bubble economy. The problem was, according to U.S. and Japanese law enforcement officials, the money wasn't his to spend.

In one of the Bubble's great frauds, Mizuno and his partners set about developing the Ibaraki Country Club outside of Tokyo. In 1988, promising golf-starved Japanese they could play any time, they began selling memberships to the public for $14,000 each. But with every new offering, they hiked the prices until they had more than tripled the price within three years. The offering was a huge success, with Mizuno and company selling 52,000 memberships. The problem was that the club could only accommodate 1,830 members.

The sales generated some $800 million, over half of which Mizuno used for his buying spree of golf courses, hotels, and gambling, police said. Much of the money ended up in the U.S.—in Nevada, California, and Hawaii. Flush with the cash from the membership scam, between 1989 and 1991, Mizuno sent wire transfer after transfer—forty-seven in all, say prosecutors—to the States. More funds came by courier, until Machii had moved a whopping $260 million to America. Investigators traced the money not only to country clubs, but to vacant lots, luxury homes, a Rolls Royce convertible, a red Mercedes Benz, and that $5 million DC-9 on which he flew into Las Vegas. Plus, an unspecified amount of money was disbursed to nationalist politician Shintaro Ishihara and other sympathetic LDP members. Somehow, in the midst of this spending spree, Mizuno never got around to finishing the Ibaraki Country Club.

So outrageous was the scam that even Japan's normally docile investors complained—and took action. Buyers of the bogus memberships joined together in groups, hired lawyers, and filed suit against Mizuno and his sales agents. A Japanese judge branded the memberships "as valuable as plastic fruit."

But Mizuno was the target of more than civil actions. He was investigated in both the U.S. and Japan, and he was hit hard. Indeed, the Mizuno case became a rare model of cooperation between authorities in Japan and the IRS and Customs in the States. Mizuno's corporation pled guilty and agreed to forfeit its assets, including the Indian Wells resort, to the U.S. government. It was the second-largest non-drug forfeiture case in U.S. history. The resulting sale netted $50 million to the Treasury Forfeiture Fund, which was returned to the victims in Japan.

But the law wasn't finished with him. In March 1997, Mizuno, then sixty-three, was convicted in Japanese court of fraud and tax evasion and sentenced to eleven years in prison.

Ken Mizuno, of course, was not the only questionable Japanese pouring money into American golf courses. Bubble money was fueling Japanese golf course development from Saipan to South Carolina. Japanese investments in U.S. golf courses ballooned from less than $10 million annually before 1988 to over $1 billion in 1990. By 1991, the number of Japanese-owned golf course developments jumped to 120, over half of them in Hawaii and California. Some investors were blatant fronts for the mob, such as West Tsucho, the firm used by the Inagawa-kai's Susumu Ishii, who spent $10 million to develop a course in upstate New York. The alleged ties of others were less clear. The buying of high-profile courses touched a nationalistic nerve, much as did the purchase of Rockefeller Center and Columbia Pictures, and it didn't take much for people to suspect the worst.

Perhaps the best-known case was that of Pebble Beach, near Monterey, California. One of the finest, most beautiful championship courses in the world, Pebble Beach was home to the Bing Crosby Open and a highly desirable vacation spot. In 1990, Minoru Isutani's Cosmo World bought the course for an unheard-of $841 million, and immediately controversy arose over plans to make the famous course an exclusive, private club catering to Japanese. Soon rumors of yakuza involvement were in the air.

A former encyclopedia salesman who had become one of Japan's top developers, Isutani was also investing in a $200 million golf resort on the Kona coast of Hawaii and a $50 million one in LA. But media reports claimed he had shady connections, and Isutani became the target of several probes and eventually a Senate hearing. His financing for the Pebble Beach purchase was extraordinarily complex. The sale had been guaranteed by Itoman and Company, then being looted by yakuza associates, and investigators were never clear on where the original money came from. Still, no proof ever emerged that the money was in fact dirty. Mired in controversy, Isutani's plans for Pebble Beach stalled until the Bubble's collapse killed any chance of him moving forward. By the time he sold the course, Isutani had lost a mind-numbing $340 million.

North of the Border

The yakuza's spending spree in North America wasn't confined to the United States. There were bargains just north of the border, and the yakuza were eager to shop. By the early 1990s, investigators had tracked yakuza visits to Edmonton, Montreal, Toronto, and Vancouver. Wealthy British Columbia, police found, holds a special attraction for the gangs. Once the cops started checking, they managed to tie Vancouver crime figures to yakuza in Hawaii and Japan going back to the early 1980s. By the time the Bubble Economy peaked, top-ranking mob bosses of Japan were meeting at local sushi restaurants, buying multi-million-dollar homes, and investing in local businesses. Police found other yakuza were involved in narcotics. A former top member of Tokyo's Matsuba-kai was implicated in smuggling some twelve kilos of heroin into Canada. Another case suggested yakuza were trans-shipping cocaine through Vancouver from South America to Japan.

The best-known yakuza on Canada's West Coast was none other than Yamaguchi-gumi financial czar Masaru Takumi—"the man who never sleeps." It was the same Takumi who had invested on Australia's Gold Coast, visited Paris and Guam, and served as the great syndicate's second in command. Takumi, it turned out, was also bullish on Canada.

Takumi funded and was president of T.M. Canada Investment Corporation and owner of E.M. Tours of Canada, a Vancouver travel agency located one floor beneath the cabinet offices for the British Columbia provincial government. By 1993, E.M. boasted 6,000 clients in Japan and was managed by a Bangladeshi immigrant named Mohammed Rahman. The manager claimed he had met Takumi in Edmonton in 1991, on an eleven-day cross-Canada tour that included sightseeing at Niagara Falls, golfing in Banff, and a visit to Victoria. "He just told me one thing," Rahman later said to the *Vancouver Sun*. "'Canada is a heaven.'"

Because of his business dealings in British Columbia, Takumi purchased a C$400,000 home in Vancouver, not a very expensive house. When news of a yakuza boss's purchase attracted curious visitors to look over his Vancouver home, Takumi grew angry. Rahman recounted that Takumi was worried he would lose face by having bought a relatively modest home. "They will think the Japanese mafia is poor," Rahman heard him say. "He said it would be better to buy one hundred houses, then they can see Japanese mafia is very rich." Canadian authorities were not amused, and let it be known that Takumi was not a particularly welcome investor. Embarrassed Japanese officials soon arrested the underboss in Osaka, charging him with failing to obtain approval before opening a large foreign bank account. Takumi would not pose a threat for much longer, though. After ordering the Nakano-kai, a violent Yamaguchi-gumi faction, to cease a gang war, its members ambushed him in 1997. When the shooting ended, Takumi's dead body lay sprawled on the bloody floor, with seven bullets pumped into the head and chest.

The Cultural Barrier

Given the colorful nature of organized crime generally, and the yakuza in particular, it's hard to understand the dreary nature of most U.S.-Japan police conferences. One can at least give them credit for trying, for cops from both ends of the Pacific have been meeting together since the early 1980s. There are parleys between Customs officials, drug agents, prosecutors, the FBI, and the NPA. American police chiefs have flown to Japan to study the success of Japan's *koban*, or police boxes, and its community-based policing system. Japanese cops come to America to study money-laundering and anti-racketeering laws. Yet despite all this effort, relations between U.S. and Japanese cops have never been good. The Americans complain that the Japanese are less than cooperative, too timid, and too worried about face. The Yanks cannot even get arrest records, let alone detailed financial information. Japanese law enforcement, they say, is a closed system, much like the nation's commercial markets.

The Japanese, in turn, find the Americans boorish, uninformed, and linguistically challenged. Unqualified federal agents are posted to Tokyo, and then removed before trust can be established. Confidential documents are passed along that end up in U.S. courts or in the press. Given Japan's history with an overreaching state, new laws on surveillance and conspiracy must be introduced with care and consensus—a dilemma about which impatient Americans seem clueless.

Such conflicts could fill the pages of a cross-cultural handbook. Given this state of affairs, it seems remarkable that the yakuza are not more entrenched in the United States. Fortunately, there are bright spots. The best Western and Japanese cops have always found ways to cooperate. Informal relationships, long the basis of trust in law enforcement, have taken hold among the more committed and curious cops. The more perceptive officials understand that organized crime has transformed itself since the Cold War, respecting few laws and no borders; for law enforcement to keep pace, it, too, must learn to adapt quickly.

A handful of key cases and watchful eyes at the border may well have averted a major yakuza presence in North America. High-profile prosecutions like those of Ken Mizuno and Masaru Takumi let the Japanese mob and its associates know they would not have an easy time of it. The yakuza have not given up—many simply bypass the efficient airport checkpoints in Honolulu and Los Angeles, flying instead to gateways where inspectors won't know a yakuza from a Hmong tribesman. Nonetheless, the prosecutions have made headlines in Japan and impressed the gangs. Even Kakuji Inagawa, founder of the Inagawa-kai, felt moved to complain. "Please tell the American people we wish them no harm," he told the authors. "All we want to do is go to Hawaii and play golf."

Just play golf? The evidence suggests otherwise. But the yakuza's future in the West is not yet written. The gangs maintain an active presence and now understand how to do business overseas. At the turn of the twenty-first century, they continue to work the tourist trade; shake down Japanese business; smuggle guns, women, and drugs; and above all, launder and invest funds. During flush times—as in the Bubble years—many Americans were all too willing to aid and abet the yakuza with scant regard for the public good.

By virtue of their immense cash resources, the yakuza may make further inroads by buying acceptance. Clearly, the Bubble-era investments proved the potential of this approach. Had more of those investments taken hold, we probably would have seen the gangs become more deeply ingrained in North America. We have seen it before. Certain subtle rulings and policies can, for instance, make it easier for "investors." Police officials might receive quiet advice that there are higher priorities than pinkieless gangsters from across the sea. Friends in and around government will help yakuza front men obtain necessary licenses and permissions to do business. Very little will be overt, and if the yakuza are lucky, next time little will come to the attention of the press or public.

On the other side of the fence, American mobsters will find that those who play ball with the yakuza stand to make a lot of money in one way or another—in gambling, for instance, or perhaps in drugs—and there is no need to view the Japanese with suspicion. Those Americans who can broker deals for the yakuza and their friends will also find that they can make small fortunes.

To succeed in America, the yakuza do not have to take over the place. Indeed, they cannot. But if they proceed with caution and ally themselves with the right people, they can do extremely well. And that is the danger. By the time they succeed, the gangs will have come to be regarded as simply part of the cost of doing business, as they are in Japan.

A NEW YAKUZA

"ULTIMATELY, THE YAKUZA WILL BECOME LIKE THE U.S. MAFIA," EXPLAINED
Kakuji Inagawa, Japan's most esteemed godfather. "In the future," he said,
"there'll be one national mob. Like my organization, the bigger firms will
take over. You can see the move toward a more corporate structure."

Inagawa, though, was clearly not happy about this turn of events. "The
Mafia will kill for profit," he warned. "The yakuza must respect morals and
regulations and obey them—but that tradition is fading. . . . It would be easy
if we could turn back the pages of time. It is because of the generation gap
that I worry."

Inagawa is not alone. The most common complaint among Japan's underworld chieftains today is that the new yakuza are more violent, less obedient, and interested in honoring fat profits, not feudal traditions. As longtime Kyoto boss Tokutaro Takayama told a reporter, "Today, they don't care
anymore about obligations, tradition, respect and dignity. There are no
rules anymore." Perhaps worst for the aging godfathers, there is little they
can do about it. They are no longer in full command of a generation raised
with jet travel, biker gangs, television, leisure time, and growing consumer
credit.

The yakuza are in the midst of a transformation. Their structured, insular world of giri-ninjo, tattoos, finger-cutting, total obedience, and all the
other trappings of gangster chivalry is in danger of obsolescence. In a way,
this change is long overdue. Few other Japanese run their lives by these
hoary tenets of feudalism, although bits and pieces of the oyabun-kobun
system persist in postwar Japan. As the samurai did a hundred years ago,
when they dropped their swords and picked up profit-and-loss statements,
the yakuza are finally shedding their medieval past, and the changes may be
equally far-reaching. Japan's gangsters have recently discovered that the

criminal world of the twenty-first century does not require ideology, chivalry, or absolute loyalty. Instead, the times seem to call for sophisticated crooks and cunning, adventurous schemers. As a result, for the first time the yakuza are beginning to act as much for themselves as for the gang as a whole, and it is changing the face of organized crime in Japan.

These are not changes that are occurring wholesale, as they did, for instance, in the early 1930s in New York. It was then that Charles "Lucky" Luciano engineered the elimination of the leading old-line bosses, and with them went all the "Moustache Petes," the Sicilian-born gangsters with their Old World ways. The modernization of the Japanese underworld began in the broken rubble of 1945, and has been going on ever since.

As early as 1954, an anonymous oyabun warned of the dangers befalling the underworld:

> What is happening today has never happened before. The traditional yakuza used to fight among themselves and sometimes steal, but it was only a matter of living in underworld society. If a yakuza caused injury to ordinary people, we used to punish him immediately. It was not permitted by our rules to hurt the weak; however, today, force is used against the weak people indiscriminately, and there is no longer a sense of order in the yakuza world.

Skeptics might ask if the yakuza were ever truly chivalrous. Throughout their long history, Japan's gangster class has acted foremost as an undeniably criminal force, extorting, bullying, and robbing those with the bad luck to fall in their path. But even the seasoned members of Japanese law enforcement will admit in confidence that their nemesis has a noble side. Like so much of the Japanese culture, the nation's organized crime syndicates exist in a maze of contradiction. The yakuza have played the role of that society's honorable opposition, integrated yet rejected, legal yet criminal. The answer is a qualified yes—the yakuza do have a chivalrous side, and that is indeed part of what has changed so dramatically. As the gangs arm themselves with America's handguns, and are increasingly unaccountable to both their bosses and the general public, the substance and the image of the noble outlaw are finally disappearing.

The breakdown in traditional lines of authority has much to do with the changing structure in many of the syndicates. No one really knows for sure if, as Inagawa believes, there will be one great national mob in the future. But like the Mafia, Japanese crime groups have consolidated into a handful of larger, more loosely knit syndicates. At the same time, they are working with huge numbers of associates and front companies, and they have burrowed further underground. Free-lance mob associates—drug dealers, racketeers, human traffickers—are now big business in Japan.

The Tokyo Metropolitan Police, who rank among their nation's most astute yakuza-watchers, publicly aired in 1984 what the gangs had long since realized. "There is a clear trend of declining solidarity and obedience" among the yakuza members, officials reported. "This stems from the retirement of aging gang bosses who maintained strict discipline as well as changes in the temperament of rank-and-file gangsters." No longer, it seems, will kobun say that the passing crow is white just because the oyabun so observes.

The issue of retirement is crucial, according to criminologist Kanehiro Hoshino, one of Japan's leading yakuza experts. Younger oyabun are moving into power, and they are steadily shifting the structure and tone of the gangs. The yakuza's move into high finance and expansion abroad occurred as the last of the great bosses, those who came to power during the Occupation, passed on. Once again, the comments of godfather Inagawa are revealing. "The yakuza in Hawaii are outsiders and misfits," he said years ago. "They cannot adapt themselves to Japan." These very misfits, however, have spearheaded the yakuza's move abroad. Most are the members of a new, more adaptable generation of Japanese criminals, far too busy making money in Honolulu or Hong Kong to worry about severed fingers and sake ceremonies. Regardless of whether they are full members or just knowledgeable associates, they continue to work in concert with the yakuza back home.

Not every restless yakuza is a misfit, however. Most are simply of another generation. The younger yakuza, those who came to crime not through the waterfront, the labor gang, or the black market, but through gangs of street punks and hot-rodders, are simply not very enamored of gangland tradition. They are less willing to obey their bosses at every step; few are ready to give their lives for some abstract devotion to duty. Much as *omerta*—the rule of silence—broke down within the Italian American Mafia, yakuza underlings have started to talk; some have even turned in their bosses for ordering hits, an unthinkable act years ago.

A 1993 police survey of the gangs confirmed how much priorities were changing. Success in the underworld used to be a top goal for yakuza, but even senior members and bosses now seem less enamored by the prospect. "Today, accumulating great wealth or succeeding at an enterprise has become their only goal," wrote researchers. Indeed, money is the key. "They really don't want to get caught these days," observed Hoshino, who oversaw the study. "The longer they're in jail, the more income they lose." And they're willing to do whatever it takes to make that income. The once rigid structure of gamblers and peddlers—the bakuto and tekiya gangs—has disappeared. "You can't tell who's who anymore," says Seiji Iishiba, who ran the Tokyo police's anti-mob unit. "It's now like a department store." Even the most common traditions are changing: the younger yakuza are forsaking the full-body pictorial tattoos. They opt instead for a simple line drawing or phrase on their upper arm, more similar to the tattoos of Western youths.

The reason, says researcher Hoshino, is not a change in aesthetics: the old-style tattoos cost a fortune, and are simply no longer worth either the physical or financial stress.

Nor is it worthwhile for the more aggressive yakuza to pay heed to the old tradition of never harming *katagi no shu,* "the citizens under the sun." This is the creed, as old as the yakuza itself, of never hurting the common people. The anonymous oyabun who railed about the underworld's lost sense of order in 1954 might keel over in disbelief at the state of affairs today. Fast profits and plentiful handguns have become the standards of power throughout the Japanese underworld, and the two have combined to cause an explosion of violence by the gangs.

Officials now complain that shootouts in broad daylight have victimized innocent bystanders. But the violence is not confined to gang wars, and even the cops have fallen victim to yakuza shootings—another break with the past. Gunplay is being used to back up everything from corporate shakedowns to loan sharking, a radical change for both the police and the yakuza. In his 1976 study of Japanese police, American scholar David Bayley could write that "Japan . . . is a totally disarmed society; criminals hardly ever carry firearms." So great are the changes that just eight years later they would lead one police official to say, "We are convinced that literally every yakuza owns or carries a handgun even on the streets, an entirely different situation from the past." Even allowing for overstatement, the National Police Agency knows now that the yakuza—thanks to the huge traffic in gun smuggling—are heavily armed in a society that forbids the ownership of handguns. Yakuza are carrying more guns in part because there are more guns to be had in Japan. The vaunted ban on handguns is becoming less effective, at least within the underworld. For this the U.S. bears some responsibility; America, with its 260 million firearms, is the primary source for smuggled guns among the yakuza.

Beyond the changes in structure, authority, and violence, the yakuza have come to resemble the American mob in at least one other way: more and more gangsters are opting for crimes of greater sophistication. There still is the bottom layer of simple-minded thugs, of course. But in the early 1980s, there emerged the *interi yakuza,* the so-called intellectual gangsters: white-collar crooks, financial racketeers, and the overlapping groups of sokaiya. Then came the *keizai yakuza,* the economic gangsters, which pushed the gangs far deeper into corporate Japan than few thought possible. Billions of dollars fell into the hands of the yakuza, in what must be one of history's greatest transfers of wealth to organized crime. The Japanese people will be undoing the financial damage for years to come.

The collapse of the Bubble Economy did force the yakuza to retrench. But like legitimate business, they have written off their losses and restructured their operations. Always among the most adaptable, most entrepreneurial Japanese, they have emerged from the Bubble with more assets and more business know-how. They now understand financial markets, corporate takeovers, and large-scale development projects, and they have solidified their influence over key segments of Japan's entertainment, leisure, and construction industries. What this means to their fellow Japanese is not good news. With greater assets, more companies, and a worldwide reach, the best for the yakuza may be yet to come—a great new wave of economic crime, in which the Japanese mob preys on legitimate business as never before. Fraud, looted companies, extortion, intimidation, money laundering, plus the old rackets of drugs, gambling, and prostitution—the potential is enormous.

These changes go hand in hand with other developments bearing on the future of the gangs: the newer yakuza have gone international. They are better educated and better traveled, and an increasing number can speak English, the language of commerce through much of the world. In the postwar world, the yakuza were quite late in moving overseas. They lagged behind other crime syndicates—Corsican, Italian, American, and Chinese—in part because the Occupation kept the gangs at home until 1952. But it was inevitable that the yakuza would eventually follow the striking successes of Japan's businessmen around the world. And follow they have. If the events since 1970 prove anything, it is that the yakuza have shown a willingness to expand wherever opportunities have presented themselves. As the twentieth century drew to a close, the yakuza owned properties in most of the world's major trade and resort centers, and they were continuing to invest. They had gained footholds in Japanese communities from Honolulu to Sao Paulo, and formed working alliances with Chinese, Colombian, and American crime syndicates. "The yakuza's overseas activities have just begun in earnest," warns Raisuke Miyawaki, the former head of the NPA's organized crime section. "By now, yakuza groups have learned what they needed to learn to build their operations overseas, and they have established support networks overseas to collect information and develop their moneymaking activities."

The shifts within the yakuza, however, are part of a broader set of changes occurring within Japan. It is not only organized crime that is undergoing a major transition; it is crime itself. Crime rates were reaching postwar highs by 2002, with record arrests for drugs and other offenses. Crimes by women, foreigners, and juveniles all posed unprecedented challenges to police. At the same time, crime in general has become more violent, leading the Japanese press to conclude that "Western-style" crime has finally arrived. Although most of these figures are still quite small by U.S. standards, many are comparable to those in Western Europe. They certainly represent a significant rise for the Japanese, and pose unwelcome questions about the future of public safety in that country.

The changes sweeping through the yakuza world, and through Japan as a whole, have also affected the underworld's place in Japanese politics. Few organized criminal groups in the world are as closely linked to a single political force as are the yakuza to the Japanese far right. Certainly in the United States, the idea of a politically extreme group interchangeable with a Mafia-like organization is all but unknown. But Japan of the twenty-first century is not the world of the Occupation, or even the world that spawned the huge rightist/gangster coalitions of the 1960s. The far right itself has changed, if not in purpose, then in impact and acceptability, to the public at large. To a degree, the Lockheed and ensuing scandals have made the rightists, particularly underworld rightists like the heirs of Kodama, a little less savory and a little more outside the ruling structure. And, for the time being, Japan's economic strength has meant that fewer Japanese than ever have heeded the call of the far right. Most people's expectations are being met, and any appeal that the ultranationalists might have to the masses has been blunted by paychecks and consumer goods.

Another milestone is that, much as the traditional yakuza godfathers are fading, the great rightist kuromaku—the power brokers of twentieth-century Japan—have passed away. Of the accused war criminals released in 1948, Kodama, Kishi, and Sasakawa all are dead. The new kuromaku of Japan are by trade businessmen, not ultranationalists. And while these men may have underworld ties, the times have changed since the heady days of the Drawn Sword Regiment and Ampo. There are no longer American Occupation officials in need of yakuza spies and strikebreakers; no longer justice ministers who make it their business to unite the underworld into an anti-Communist militia; no longer a Yoshio Kodama to organize a yakuza army to protect the visit of an American president.

Nevertheless, it would be a mistake to dismiss the far right in Japan. The underworld continues to be closely tied with the ultranationalist movement, and organizationally the far right is still alive and active. The danger for now is a potential one. Should Japan fall into economic ruin, should leftists come to power, or should the nation be threatened militarily, the far right could well become a major force in the country again. The rearming of Japan's long-dormant military makes this prospect more worrisome than ever in the postwar era. In 1960, Columbia University professor Ivan Morris, one of the foremost chroniclers of Japanese culture and the right wing, speculated on what the reaction might be to a leftist threat. His words are as appropriate today as they were back then. Wrote Morris:

> The fact that on the whole rightists have become far less radical and anti-capitalist in their stand would probably make it easier for them to cooperate with the conservatives than it was in the prewar days. A number of the postwar nationalist organizations have combined politicians, business men, and

professional rightists in their leadership and such groups would probably become more numerous and important. . . . The less respectable strong-arm groups could usefully cooperate with the police in breaking strikes and in obtaining information about leftists and trade unionists. In case a full-fledged police state should come into being many of them could profitably be mobilized as anti-Communist shock troops. As the government steadily came to adopt extreme undemocratic policies, prominent rightist personalities would be likely to gain positions of influence in the state, and many middle-of-the-road conservative leaders would probably become increasingly right wing in their orientation . . . virulent xenophobia and the various other irrational factors associated with extreme nationalism would come into play, and would tend to make the country's foreign policy unstable and unpredictable.

The deaths of Kodama and lesser kuromaku have helped make this a less likely scenario. Their passing, combined with the impact of the various postwar scandals, has at least partly diminished yakuza power at the governmental level. A surprising number of politicians still use the gangs to raise money and do dirty work, but political figures increasingly avoid any connection with gangsters, ultranationalists, and anything that smacks of the nation's corrupt "Black Mist."

A key element in this change is that the press and the public have become more aware of yakuza involvement in the seamier aspects of politics, and less forgiving to those involved as a result. That the yakuza helped clear the way to power for Prime Minister Noboru Takeshita truly outraged millions of Japanese. The yakuza's role in the failure of banks, trading houses, and other business also has left the public with less patience for the gangs. The news media, meanwhile, have grown bolder in exposing these types of incidents, and in looking for ties between the establishment and the underworld. This, combined with the continuing shakedowns of the country's biggest corporations, the mushrooming drug traffic, and the increasing violence, has finally begun to erode the longtime social acceptance of the gangs.

The police have responded to an increase in public pressure, and to a decrease in political protection for the gangs, by more freely attacking their most serious crime problem. There are new laws on the books and a more assertive stance by the public. But there is much to undo. Decades of tolerating organized crime have pushed the yakuza deep into the fabric of Japanese society, and the gangs will not retreat quietly. Yakuza have not counterattacked as blatantly as in Italy, where Mafiosi have dynamited and machine-gunned police, prosecutors, and priests who dared get in their way. But the corruption and violence are no less insidious. The yakuza feed into a corrosive, far-reaching corruption that has touched every corner of Japan, Inc.

For those overseas, the danger is that the yakuza will export their unique brand of crime and corruption. But for foreign observers, attempting to assess the yakuza's impact is not an easy task. One runs the risk of either over- or underestimating the Japanese gangs. It is very easy for Americans, when viewing a foreign "menace," to be misled by the outer trappings rather than the reality of the threat. Certainly the frightening images of tattoos, missing fingers, and suicidal loyalty all contribute to misunderstandings. It has happened before.

Perceptions of the Mafia have long been colored by ignorance and racism, both of which interfere with a sober assessment of the phenomenon. The tragedy of such a view is that other people of the same ethnicity are likely to be tarred with the same brush. On the other hand, it is likely that when the "threat" fails to live up to early expectations, it is then downplayed, and potential problems are ignored. The early Mafia grew exponentially during Prohibition, but some law enforcement people refused to take it seriously. The FBI's J. Edgar Hoover, throughout most of his forty-eight-year tenure, stoutly maintained that the Mafia did not exist.

Things have come a long way since 1976, when U.S. Strike Force attorney Michael Sterrett was told to delete observations about yakuza tattoos and finger-cutting, for fear his reports would not be believed. Many American law enforcement groups have today a passing knowledge of the yakuza, if not necessarily a clear plan of action. For some yakuza activities, though, such as large-scale money laundering, it may already be too late to stop operations even with a clear plan. For others, such as drug dealing and sexual slavery, well-informed and aggressive police action could prevent untold misery and save lives in a host of countries.

Most important for Americans, decisive moves taken today by law enforcement on both sides of the Pacific can stop the yakuza from becoming a permanent fixture of criminal life in the West. The early twenty-first century is a critical time for the yakuza as well as the police in the United States. The dominance of the Mafia over organized crime has eroded substantially, and other groups have the opportunity to step in. Black and Hispanic criminals stand to take over the lion's share, but on the West Coast and in New York, Asian gangs also have a chance to carve out a growing piece of the action, and among these the yakuza are certainly well organized, well financed, and ready to expand. It remains to be seen whether they can capitalize on this opportunity, and whether U.S. law enforcement can stop them in time.

Like the blind men examining the elephant, observers of organized crime "see" only a small part of the whole beast. It is inevitable; what comes to light at any one time may be important or may be trivial. Furthermore, the line between some kinds of criminal and legitimate commerce is often blurred, changing with the laws and the times. Racism, self-righteousness, political opportunism, and fear color perceptions of organized crime and render many appraisals suspect and indistinct.

But beyond the indistinction, opportunism, and bigotry, there is the raison d'être of organized crime. It lies under the patina of colorful characters, exotic rituals, nicknames, and legends. At the core lies one undying principle—theft. Gangsters may provide goods and services, but usually at a vastly inflated cost. In its most basic form, organized crime is simply institutionalized robbery. For the average citizen, the presence of gangsters—be they Japanese or American—adds an invisible tax to every dollar or yen. Gambling, bribery, extortion, prostitution, and drugs all demand a human and economic toll from society. In those areas in which organized crime holds a substantial interest—bars, restaurants, construction, entertainment, trash collection, longshore work—a direct cost is passed along to the public. Gangsters, unlike most businesspeople, are not content with reasonable profits, and they rarely put money back into the community in any constructive way. They want an exorbitant return, and they want it for nothing. They are, as the late Jonathan Kwitny once wrote, "a class of persons who live like kings but whose only contribution is to innovate new ways to steal the wealth produced by hard-working citizens."

Despite the greatest efforts of police and the public, this robbery of the commons continues unabated, and increasingly reaches into every corner of society. By serving as muscle for the worst elements in business and politics, organized criminals have impeded progress in everything from representative government to a clean environment. They have prevented new unions from protecting workers and have seriously compromised many existing unions. They have protected corporations from those seeking redress for dangerous and insensitive policies. They have worked as hit men and hired muscle for repressive governments and corrupt politicians. They have served in Japan, among other places, as the most virulent exponents of male dominance—buying, selling, and enslaving women for the sex trade. And they have robbed entire communities not only of their money but of their youth as well, spreading a deadly trail of narcotics addiction that stretches around the world. There is, quite literally, nothing that organized crime won't do for money.

The yakuza are an exceptional organized crime group. In the twentieth century, they were often a key to political power in Japan. They have carved out a secure niche for themselves and have arrogated an extraordinary degree of open wealth. In the West, one could look only to Sicily, perhaps, to find such overtly powerful gangland figures. Through the years, the Japanese have learned to live with the yakuza and to render unto them as much as necessary to keep the peace. This method has in the past provided a certain public harmony, but that social contract is finally breaking down.

All this should make for an intriguing world of Japanese crime in the twenty-first century. Given its progress in the last fifty years, one should not underestimate the potential of Japan's enterprising underworld. Since the

Pacific War, we have seen the yakuza go from gambling dens to the stock market, from construction gangs to real estate, from neighborhoods to national politics, and from local, feudal structures to multinational corporate ones. Whether the Japanese can use this period of flux in the underworld to dramatically alter some of the ancient relationships between the public and the yakuza, and to build a higher wall around the gangs, is impossible to foretell. Organized crime in Japan has grown remarkably powerful, and like organized crime everywhere, once entrenched it is nearly impossible to eradicate. It can, however, be contained, and it remains to be seen if the yakuza will be prevented from further applying their proven techniques to the rest of the world. What is clear is that over the past three hundred years, the yakuza have become one of the world's most successful criminal organizations, and that whatever the public does, these once honorable outlaws of Japan are apt to be around for another three hundred years.

A NOTE ON RESEARCH

RESEARCH FOR THIS BOOK BEGAN WITH WORK UNDERTAKEN BY THE AUTHORS for the Center for Investigative Reporting in early 1981. Acting on a tip that Japanese mobsters were active in the West Coast tourist industry, we began a wide-ranging probe of yakuza expansion overseas. The results of that initial investigation appeared one year later in a segment of ABC's *20/20* newsmagazine. The authors subsequently wrote a series of articles on the subject for a variety of magazines and newspapers, and eventually devoted full time to researching this book, which was first published in 1986. Over the years, the authors continued to monitor and report on the gangs, and in 1994 David Kaplan received a Fulbright grant to update the original edition.

The revised edition incorporates nearly 1,000 interviews worldwide over two decades. The authors met with diplomats, scholars, police officials, intelligence agents, businesspeople, political activists, journalists, and organized crime figures. Our reports and conclusions are based on these interviews and on extensive use of material from public and private libraries, government archives, and law enforcement files.

Few criminologists or legal scholars in Japan wish to venture into yakuza territory. An invaluable exception is the National Research Institute for Police Science in Tokyo, which hosts a dedicated group of social scientists who have done pioneering work on the culture, organization, and economics of organized crime. The writings of two former police officials—Seiji Iishiba and Raisuke Miyawaki—are also illuminating. The annual National Police Agency *White Papers* are useful as well, as are various speeches and papers by Japanese police officials. The work of several journalists and popular writers also stand out: Kenji Ino, Atsushi Mizoguchi, Goro Fujita.

Japan is a highly literate society with thousands of publications—daily newspapers, weekly magazines, journals, and newsletters—ranging the political spectrum from right to left. Whenever possible, we relied on direct translations from these publications, as well as from books, academic papers, and government reports. There is, unfortunately, no grand tradition of investigative reporting in Japan, as there is in the United States; critical, in-depth coverage of important issues occasionally finds its way into the big dailies, but more often ends up in the usually sensational weekly press. Where we have used weekly press accounts, they are typically backed up by other, more reliable, sources.

Of great help was the remarkably vital English press in Japan. Tokyo today can boast three English daily newspapers, more than most American cities; all but one are based on Japanese editions, and generally these papers cover the yakuza with interest. For copies of these stories and other relevant documents, the authors made use of various databases, the extensive clipping files at the Foreign Correspondents' Club in Tokyo, the back files of major publications, and the National Diet Library for hard-to-get documents. Most important, perhaps, was access to the private library of John Roberts, which now resides at the University of Hawaii's Center for Japanese Studies. This remarkable collection of indexed clippings, studies, and reports offers details on yakuza, rightists, and shadowy Japanese politics from the 1950s to the 1980s.

During various tours of East Asia and the Pacific, the authors also gained access to reports of yakuza activity in the region. Again, the English press in the capital cities of these countries proved most helpful, as did local journalists, government officials, businesspeople, and organized crime figures. Through a network of sources around the globe, we were able to garner reports of yakuza activity from other regions as well, including South America, Western Europe, and Russia.

Written materials in the West on the yakuza, once rather scarce, are growing in number and sophistication. Enterprising foreign reporters in Japan have repeatedly ventured into the Japanese underworld and produced an impressive range of stories. Of special note is the work of Brad Martin, Karl Schoenberger, and Eric Talmadge.

Until *Yakuza*, only one general book in English had appeared on the subject, *The Tattooed Men*, written by Florence Rome and published in 1975. Sections of other books pertained: "Underground Empire" in Harry Emerson Wildes's memoir of the Occupation, *Typhoon in Tokyo;* also parts of Mark Gayn's recollections of that same period, *Japan Diary.* A handful of key academic reports in English also provided an important introduction to the field for the authors and other researchers who followed. Particularly noteworthy are the field studies of anthropologists Walter Ames and David Stark, both sponsored by the University of Michigan at Ann Arbor; the research of George De Vos at the University of California at Berkeley; and, in Tokyo, the works of Glenn Davis while at Sophia University and of Kanehiro Hoshino and his associates at the National Research Institute of Police Science.

More recent studies have been done by Peter Hill at the University of Stirling in Scotland, Jacob Raz at Tel Aviv University, Ken Szymkowiak at the University of Hawaii, and Mark West at the University of Michigan Law School. Popular treatments of the gangs have appeared as well, most notably Chris Seymour's *Yakuza Diary*, Mark Schreiber's *Shocking Crimes of Postwar Japan*, Robert Whiting's *Tokyo Underworld*, and Junichi Saga's translated *Confessions of a Yakuza*. Various U.S. government documents also provide important background. Especially helpful were hearings before the President's Commission on Organized Crime in 1984 and the U.S. Senate Permanent Subcommittee on Investigations in 1991 and 1992.

We made use of a number of American libraries. Of particular help was the University of California at Berkeley, including the Bancroft Library and the various departmental libraries, and the Government Documents Section of Doe Library. The East Asia Section at the University of Maryland's McKeldin Library had the most extensive Occupation materials outside the government. The Gordon Prange and Justin Williams collections rest there, each containing bits of history ranging from critical documents to the flotsam of bureaucracy.

The most boggling trove of materials resides at the National Records Center in Suitland, Maryland. The NRC contains twenty acre-sized rooms, each filled with towering shelves of the most important and obscure records of the country. It is here that the bulk of American papers on the Occupation of Japan are stored. The records of the Supreme Commander of the Allied Powers, or SCAP, are still stored in the boxes in which they were packed in Tokyo in 1952. Indexing is crude at best, but these are the primary documents of a unique period in American and Japanese history. There are, as well, additional materials available, particularly the Embassy Post Files at the National Archives in Washington, D.C.

Other primary documents proved equally challenging to obtain. The authors filed numerous Freedom of Information Act requests to nearly a dozen federal agencies, some of which responded, and some of which were less than helpful. Court records, as well as FOIA materials, were useful for yakuza-related figures who had dealings in the U.S., and those we found in California and Hawaii. Finally, confidential law enforcement reports were made available to us; these often supplied key documentation of yakuza movements in Japan and abroad.

NOTES

Chapter One

Pp. 4–6: Historical material for this section is drawn from George Sansom, *A History of Japan 1615–1867* (1963), pp. 32–36, 57–60; George A. De Vos, *Socialization for Achievement* (1973), pp. 286–87; and *The East* magazine, vol. 17, October 1981, pp. 46–48.

Pp. 6–7: Chobei Banzuiin background is from *The East* magazine, vol. 17, October 1981, pp. 47–48; Sansom, *A History*, p. 60; and *Asahi Evening News,* January 31, 1979.

Pp. 8–10: Oyabun-kobun description is based on Kanehiro Hoshino, *The Recent Trend of Underworld and Organized Crime in Japan,* research paper of the National Research Institute of Police Science, Tokyo, 1979, p. 16; Iwao Ishino, "The Oyabun-Kobun: A Japanese Ritual Kinship Institution," *American Anthropologist,* December 1955, pp. 696–98; Hiroaki Iwai, "Delinquent Groups and Organized Crime," *Japanese Culture and Behavior* (1974), p. 390; Chie Nakane, *Japanese Society* (1973), p. 42.

P. 9: Mafia and triad initiation rites are described in Yiu Kong Chu, *The Triads as Business* (2000), pp. 31–35; W. P. Morgan, *Triad Societies in Hong Kong* (1960), chapter 8; Ed Reid, *The Grim Reapers* (1969), p. 26; Eric Hobsbawm, *Bandits* (1969), p. 34.

P. 9: Yakuza initiation rites are from Iwai, "Delinquent Groups," p. 388; Walter L. Ames, *Police and Community in Japan* (1981), p. 108; and Federal Bureau of Investigation, *An Analysis of the Threat of Japanese Organized Crime to the United States and Its Territories* (1992), pp. 7–8 and A-1 to A-3. For a description of modern-day succession rites, see Jacob Raz's impressive fieldwork in "Insider/Outsider: The Way of the Yakuza," *Kyoto Journal,* Summer 1990; Eric Talmadge's "Gangsters Use Succession to Display Underworld 'Tradition,'" Associated Press, March 10, 1991; and Bradley Martin's "Japan's Yakuza Are Devoted to Detail in Their Rituals," *Asian Wall Street*

Journal, June 2, 1986. Videotapes of yakuza succession rites are sometimes available, such as "The Installation Ceremony for the Fifth Successor to the Yamaguchi-gumi."

Pp. 10–11: Tekiya background is based on De Vos, *Socialization,* pp. 284–85; Kanehiro Hoshino, *Organized Criminal Gangs in Japan,* research paper for the National Research Institute of Police Science, June 1971, pp. 5–6, 11–12. See also Raz's "Insider/Outsider."

Pp. 11–12: Information on burakumin is from Mikiso Hane, *Peasants, Rebels, and Outcasts* (1982), pp. 139–43; Hoshino, *Organized Criminal Gangs,* p. 13.

P. 13: Origin of the word *yakuza* comes from Ames, *Police and Community,* p. 108; De Vos, *Socialization,* pp. 282–83; David Harold Stark, *The Yakuza: Japanese Crime Incorporated,* doctoral thesis (1981), pp. 27–28. Expulsion practices are described by Stark, *The Yakuza,* pp. 105–8.

P. 14: For a fuller description of finger-cutting customs and history see Hoshino, *Organized Criminal Gangs,* p. 8; Stark, *The Yakuza,* p. 111. The survey on the incidence of finger-cutting and tattooing was done by the National Research Institute of Police Science. A 1971 survey found similar results: 42 percent of bakuto members with severed fingers, and 10 percent with more than one finger severed.

Pp. 14–15: Tattooing information comes from *Asahi Evening News,* March 29, 1984; Hoshino, *Organized Criminal Gangs,* p. 10, and *The Recent Trend,* p. 22; Florence Rome, *The Tattooed Men* (1975), p. 54; Stark, *The Yakuza,* p. 117.

P. 16: The description of the "travelers" can be found in *The East* magazine, October 1981.

Pp. 18–20: Shimizu no Jirocho story is drawn from *Asahi Evening News,* January 6, 1975, and February 7, 1979; George De Vos, "Organization and Social Function of Japanese Gangs," in *Aspects of Social Change in Modern Japan,* ed. R. P. Dore (1967), pp. 290–91; Oliver Statler, *Japanese Inn* (1961), pp. 233–50, 271.

Pp. 21–22: Information on the early Toyama years is from Glenn Davis, *The Right Wing of Japan,* master's thesis (1976), pp. 6–8.

Pp. 22–23: Genyosha espionage activities are detailed in Richard Deacon, *Kempei Tai: A History of the Japanese Secret Service* (1985), pp. 40–41.

P. 23: Genyosha's role in the 1892 election is from E. H. Norman, "The Genyosha: A Study in the Origins of Japanese Imperialism," *Pacific Affairs,* September 1944.

Pp. 23–24: Other background on the Dark Ocean and Black Dragon Societies can be found in Davis, *The Right Wing of Japan,* pp. 5–15; I. I. Morris, *Nationalism and the Right Wing in Japan* (1960), especially p. 88; John Roberts, *Mitsui: Three Generations of Japanese Business* (1973), p. 134; and in an unusual two-part series by Andy Adams, "Behind the Mask of Japan's Black Dragon Society," *Black Belt* magazine, August and September 1969, pp. 44–47.

P. 25: Background on Takejiro Tokunami and the Great Japan National Essence Society is based on an interview with noted yakuza authority Kenji Ino on March 2, 1984, and on the following sources: *Uyoku Jiten* (The right-wing dictionary) (1970), p. 45; Morris, *Nationalism,* pp. 314, 338–39; Roberts, *Mitsui,* pp. 209–10.

P. 26: Reports on the yakuza in Manchuria are from Tetsuro Morikawa, *Chi no Senkoku: Don Taoka Sogeki Jiken* (Bloody verdict: The shooting of Don Taoka) (1979), p. 209; De Vos, *Socialization,* p. 299. Background on the Japanese wartime heroin trade can be found in Roberts, *Mitsui,* pp. 312–13; Jonathan Marshall's superb article "Opium and the Politics of Gangsterism in Nationalist China, 1927–1945," *Bulletin of Concerned Asian Scholars,* vol. 8, no. 3, 1976, pp. 22, 29, 39–42; and chapter 3 of Richard Friman's *NarcoDiplomacy: Exporting the U.S. War on Drugs* (1996).

Chapter Two

Pp. 31–32: Kades's press conference is from SCAP files, "Press Conference, Civil Information and Education Section," September 19, 1947; and from interviews with Mr. Kades, late 1984–early 1985.

P. 35: Sangokujin background is based on Rome's *The Tattooed Men;* Kazuo Taoka, *Yamaguchi Gumi Sandaime: Taoka Kazuo Jiten* (Yamaguchi-gumi third generation: The autobiography of Kazuo Taoka) (1973); and interviews with Kenji Ino and Goro Fujita, February–March 1984.

P. 36: Shupak investigation comes from SCAP, "Public Safety Division Oyabun-Kobun System Report," 1948.

Pp. 37–38: Ando story is from Mark Gayn, *Japan Diary* (1948); and Justin Williams Sr., *Japan's Political Revolution under MacArthur* (1979), p. 14. See also Robert Whiting's *Tokyo Underworld* (1999). Whiting writes that Ando "had a black book that reportedly contained the names of hundreds of Occupation officers he had befriended whom he could frequently be seen entertaining at one of the several Ginza nightclubs and Asakusa bordellos he owned."

Pp. 39–40: The record of SCAP's probe into the gangs is in Government Section's "Report of the Oyabun-Kobun Subcommittee," September 25, 1947; Military Intelligence Section's "Oyabun-Kobun Systems," October 1, 1947; and *Public Safety Division History,* vol. 1 (1948), pp. 165–83. Also useful are Harry Emerson Wildes's *Typhoon in Tokyo* (1954) and his "Underground Politics in Postwar Japan," *American Political Science Review,* vol. 42, 1948.

P. 41: Background on Occupation reforms is from Jon Livingston et al., *Postwar Japan: 1945 to the Present* (1973), pp. 10, 116–42.

Pp. 41–43: The gyakkosu debate is familiar to virtually all students of the Occupation. See, for example, Williams, *Japan's Political Revolution,* pp. 51, 71, 208.

P. 43: Status of the JCP comes from I. I. Morris, *Nationalism,* p. 60; and Livingston et al., *Postwar Japan,* p. 75.

P. 44: For a description of the CIA's secret war against the French Communists, see Alfred W. McCoy's *The Politics of Heroin* (1991), pp. 53–63. For another point of view, see Roy Godson's *American Labor and European Politics* (1976), pp. 120–22.

Pp. 44–45: The postwar involvement of U.S. intelligence in recruiting Japanese gangsters and ultranationalists is based on confidential interviews with former G-2 officials and, in part, on the following documents: John Dower, "The Eye of the Beholder," *Bulletin of Concerned Asian Scholars,* October 1969, pp. 16–25; Ann Crittenden, "CIA Said to Have Known in 50's of Lockheed Bribes," *New York Times,* April 2, 1976; Tad Szulc, "The CIA's Activities in Postwar Japan," *Asahi Evening News,* April 23, 1976; Minoru Omori, *Sengo Hisshi* (Postwar secret history), vol. 7 (1981).

P. 45: Willoughby background is from Frank Kluckhom, "Heidelberg to Madrid—The Story of General Willoughby," *The Reporter,* August 19, 1952. Also see Willoughby files at MacArthur Memorial Archives, Norfolk, Virginia.

Pp. 46–47: Information related to Matsukawa and the other incidents comes from Chalmers Johnson, *Conspiracy at Matsukawa* (1972), especially pp. 4–5 and 377–81; Seicho Matsumoto, *Nihon no Kuroikiri* (Black mist over Japan), vols. 1 and 2 (1974), especially pp. 224–25; Omori, *Sengo Hisshi,* vol. 7, pp. 195–99.

P. 47: For details of the Kaji case, see Morris, *Nationalism,* p. 220; and Johnson, *Conspiracy,* pp. 367–73.

Pp. 47–48: Details on the various secret organs can be found in SCAP files, miscellaneous documents, Record Group 331, National Records Center, Suitland, Md.; Morris, *Nationalism,* p. 221; *Shukan Bunshun,* April 15, 1976; Ei Mori, *Kuroikikan* (Black chamber) (1977), pp. 26–35; Omori, *Sengo Hisshi,* vol. 7.

P. 48: Machii incident is from Hisaakira Takemori, *Miezaru Seifu* (Invisible government) (1976), p. 72.

Pp. 49–50: G-2 use of ultranationalist groups is based on confidential interviews with former U.S. intelligence officers; Delmer M. Brown, *Nationalism in Japan* (1955), p. 248; Morris, *Nationalism,* pp. 13, 68–69; Omori, *Sengo Hisshi,* vol. 4, pp. 144–46.

Pp. 50–51: Early Kodama background is primarily from Yoshio Kodama, *I Was Defeated* (1951); and *Bungei Shunju,* January 1961. See also *Japan Times,* June 12, 1977; and Morris, *Nationalism,* p. 443.

Pp. 51–52: Kodama's wartime exploits are from *Yomiuri Shimbun,* April 26, 1976; David Boulton, *The Grease Machine* (1978), pp. 47–49; Jim Hougan, *Spooks* (1978), p. 415; and *Uyoku Jiten.*

Pp. 52–53: The quotation on Kodama is from a G-2 report, May 24, 1947, marked to the attention of Col. R. E. Rudisill.

P. 53: For Kodama's apparent deal with G-2, see *New York Times,* April 2, 1976; *The New Republic,* April 10, 1976; and *Asahi Evening News,* April 23, 1976. Also, "Kodama no Kage de Odoru Aru Fuikusa" (The fixer who danced in Kodama's shadow), *Asahi Jianaru,* October 1, 1976, and October 8, 1976; *Kodama Yoshio to wa Nanika?* (What is Yoshio Kodama?), *Bungei Shunju,* May 1976. Also see Jonathan Marshall's "Opium, Tungsten, and the Search for National Security, 1940–52," in *Drug Control Policy: Essays in Historical and Comparative Perspective,* ed. William O. Walker (1992).

P. 53: The *New York Times* story on U.S. covert backing of the Japanese right is dated October 9, 1994.

P. 53: Tsuji's background is from *Japan Times,* July 26, 1976; and SCAP, Government Section, "Memorandum for the Record," by Harry Emerson Wildes, August 16, 1946.

P. 54: Kodama's varied exploits are described in *Japan Times,* April 28, 1976; *New York Times,* April 2, 1976; and Takemori, *Miezaru Seifu,* p. 130.

Chapter Three

Pp. 56–57: These scenes are from a privately translated copy of rightist historian Bokusui Arahara's *Dai Uyoku Shi* (The great history of the right wing) (1966), pp. 483–85. The book is considered a classic among Japan's modern ultranationalists.

Pp. 57–58: Information on Tokutaro Kimura and his Drawn Sword Regiment comes from Kenji Ino in the respected monthly *Ekonomisuto,* February 26, 1976; Morikawa, *Chi no Senkoku,* p. 217; John W. Dower's biography of Prime Minister Shigeru Yoshida, *Empire and Aftermath: Yoshida Shigeru and the Japanese Experience* (1979); *Japan Times,* October 26, 1961; and U.S. Archives at the National Records Center in Suitland, Md., Record Group 331, Box 2275G.

P. 62: The similarity between yakuza and rightists in the 1950s is from Marius Jansen's "Ultranationalism in Post-War Japan," *Political Quarterly,* April–June 1956, pp. 141–51. The *Daily Yomiuri* article cited is from October 20, 1959.

Pp. 63–64: For Kodama in this period, see Morris, *Nationalism,* p. 444; *Asahi Evening News,* February 16, 1960; and *Japan Times,* June 12, 1977.

Pp. 64–65: Various Occupation-era documents on Sasakawa were obtained from the U.S. National Archives. The authors further received dozens of pages of later U.S. reports under the Freedom of Information Act. A key source of information on Sasakawa is also the superb work of the late Tokyo journalist John Roberts. See his story in the Hong Kong monthly *Insight,* April 1978, under the title "Ryoichi Sasakawa: Nippon's Right Wing Muscleman," and related pieces in *Far Eastern Economic Review,* June 18, 1973, February 17, 1978, and June 23, 1978. Also useful is Hanji Kinoshita's "Rightists on the March," in *Oriental Economist,* November 1952; the authors' own "Soft Core Fascism" in the *Village Voice,* October 4, 1983; and numerous clips from the Japanese daily press. Sasakawa's boast of being "the world's wealthiest fascist" is noted in *Time* magazine, August 26, 1974. Finally, we have relied on an October 2, 1976, interview conducted with Mr. Sasakawa by Bernard Krisher while he was *Newsweek* bureau chief in Tokyo.

Pp. 65–66: Kishi's rather questionable background is covered in George R. Packard III's *Protest in Tokyo: The Security Treaty Crisis of 1960* (1966); and in Roberts, *Mitsui.*

Pp. 67–68: Ohno's fondness for the yakuza is detailed in *Mainichi Daily News,* August 16, 1963, and July 18, 1964; and *Japan Times,* July 30, 1963.

P. 68: The quote on the Pine Needle Association appeared in the *Daily Yomiuri,* April 9, 1960. For an overview of the crisis, see Packard's *Protest in Tokyo.*

Pp. 69–70: The material on Kodama's organizing to protect Ike is from the late Koji Nakamura's "The Samurai Spirit," in *Far Eastern Economic Review,* October 16, 1971. Also see Kenji Ino, *Yakuza to Nihonjin* (Yakuza and the Japanese) (1993), pp. 254–58; and *Asahi Geino,* January 15, 1984. A decade after the Ampo battles, Nakamura and Ino were two of the few Japanese journalists willing to look critically at the collusion between the government and the rightist/yakuza groups.

P. 70: Ambassador MacArthur's remarkable notion about the Ampo demonstrators appeared in U.S. State Department telegram no. 4230, transmitted from Tokyo on June 15, 1960. Additional information on Ampo appears in Richard Storry's *A History of Modern Japan* (1960), pp. 274–76; and in Roberts, *Mitsui*, pp. 462–63.

Pp. 71–72: The only comprehensive look at Zen Ai Kaigi in English is in *The Right Wing of Japan* (1976), journalist Glenn Davis's prescient master's thesis at Tokyo's Sophia University. We have also relied on an April 2, 1976, unpublished interview by then Zen Ai Kaigi chief Takei by Mr. Davis and journalist Koji Nakamura, and on the following publications: *Kaibyaku* (the monthly newspaper of Zen Ai Kaigi), April 1983 and January 1984; Koji Nakamura's stories in *Far Eastern Economic Review*, October 16, 1971, and in *National Time* magazine (Australia), October 7, 1974; Donald Kirk's excellent look at the yakuza and the right in the *New York Times Magazine*, "Crime, Politics and Finger Cutting," December 12, 1976; and Kenji Ino's *Kodama Yoshio no Kyozo to Jitsuzo* (The image and reality of Yoshio Kodama) (1970).

P. 72: Even less exists on Seishi-kai than on Zen Ai Kaigi. See Ino, *Kodama Yoshio no,* p. 35; *Sandei Mainichi,* November 2, 1969; *Daily Yomiuri,* March 17, 1969; and *New York Times,* January 7, 1970.

Pp. 74–75: The early life and rise of Kazuo Taoka is presented in Florence Rome's lively account of her search for Japan's underworld, *The Tattooed Men*. Much of her material evidently comes from Taoka's own three-volume autobiography, *Yamaguchi Gumi Sandaime.* We have also relied upon a remarkable 1964 *Mainichi* newspaper series on the gangs (July 18–August 1, 1964) and on the *Mainichi Daily News,* May 24, 1982.

P. 76: Inagawa's early days are from a 1984 interview with him by the authors, and from numerous Japanese press clips. The U.S. cable on Inagawa's gang, dated August 9, 1950, is from the National Archives Embassy Post Files.

Pp. 78–80: All material and quotes on Kanto-kai are from a fourteen-part series on that coalition, the yakuza, and their links to Japanese politics that appeared in the newspaper *Mainichi* in 1964. The English version appeared in the *Mainichi Daily News* beginning July 18, 1964. It was a thorough and courageous look at the subject at a time when such investigative reporting was sorely lacking in the press.

Pp. 81–82: The alliance between the Yamaguchi-gumi and Inagawa-kai is described in the aforementioned *Mainichi* series and in Rome, *The Tattooed Men.*

P. 82: The sakazuki ceremony was reported in *Mainichi Daily News,* December 6, 1972.

Chapter Four

Pp. 83–84: For Church's statement, and background on the Lockheed scandal, see *Hearings of the Subcommittee on Multinational Corporations of the Committee on Foreign Relations,* U.S. Senate, February 4 and 6, 1976.

P. 85: Chalmers Johnson's quote is from his excellent three-part series on Kakuei Tanaka and the Lockheed scandal in the *Asian Wall Street Journal,* December 14, 15, and 16, 1983. A more detailed discussion of the scandal can be found in Johnson's "Tanaka Kakuei, Structural Corruption, and the Advent of Machine Politics in Japan," chapter 9 of his 1995 book, *Japan: Who Governs?*

Pp. 85–87: Kodama's dealings with Lockheed in the 1950s and 1960s are from the *New York Times*, March 1, 1976; and the *Sunday Times* (U.K.), March 7, 1976. His letter to Sato is cited in the *Asahi Evening News*, February 17, 1976.

Pp. 88–89: Kodama's ouster of ANA president Oba is described in the *Asian Wall Street Journal*, December 16, 1976; and *Asahi Evening News*, March 23, 1976.

P. 89: Sasakawa's role in the Lockheed scandal is reported in Robert Shaplen, "Annals of Crime: The Lockheed Incident," *New Yorker*, January 23 and 30, 1978.

Pp. 89–90: The flow of Lockheed money into Japan, the role of Deak and Co., and the CIA's possible involvement are explored in the *New York Times*, March 1 and April 2, 1976; and in Tad Szulc's "The Money Changer," *The New Republic*, April 10, 1976.

P. 91: Osano's statement about his relations with Kodama is quoted in the *Japan Times*, July 22, 1976.

P. 91: Osano's Las Vegas tours and Hamada's huge losses are from varied press reports. See especially *Asahi Evening News*, March 14, 1980; *Daily Yomiuri*, March 7 and April 11, 1980; and *Japan Times*, June 24, 1974, and April 11, 1980.

P. 91: Mob connections to the Osano/Hamada tours are reported in *Asahi Evening News*, March 25, 1980; *Daily Yomiuri*, March 13, 1977; *Japan Times*, April 12, 1980; and *Mainichi Daily News*, April 12, 1980.

P. 92: Hamada's background is from "Hamada's Shady Past," a three-part series in *Mainichi Daily News*, April 12, 13, and 14, 1980; *Yomiuri Shimbun*, March 7, 1980; *Japan Times*, April 11, 1980; and *Mainichi Daily News*, February 25, 1978.

Pp. 93–94: Maeno's kamikaze attack on Kodama's home is from *Asahi Evening News*, March 24, 1976; *Far Eastern Economic Review*, April 2, 1976; *The Times* (U.K.), March 24, 1976; and Boulton, *The Grease Machine*, p. 270.

P. 96: Kodama's final days and funeral are described in *Japan Times*, January 24, 1984; and *Mainichi Daily News*, January 19, 1984.

P. 98: Takayama's quote is from *Mainichi Daily News*, May 14, 1992.

P. 98: Kishi's dealings with the underworld are noted in *Shukan Asahi*, June 7, 1974; *Far Eastern Economic Review*, April 20, 1979; the *Los Angeles Times*, November 9, 1980; and *Mainichi Daily News*, October 9, 1971. A long list of prominent guests responding to the Taoka wedding invitation—including Kishi, Sasakawa, and Itoyama—is printed in the *Shukan Asahi* story. Itoyama's quote is from the *Washington Post*, April 11, 1999.

Pp. 98–99: On Mori's alleged ties to the gangs, see Kyodo News dispatches of June 20, June 21, and December 13, 2000; and Reuters, December 10, 2000. Kaifu's photo with the racketeer is noted in the *Times of London*, July 26, 1991. The visit by the DSP's Ouchi to the Inagawa-kai is reported in that story, as well as in *Mainichi Daily News*, July 5, 1991; and *Asahi Evening News*, July 17, 1991. Dietman Ueno's trip with the Sumiyoshi-kai boss was reported in *Japan Times*, March 12, 1992.

P. 99: The younger Ohno's mob connections are detailed in various press clips. See, for example, *Daily Yomiuri,* December 12, 1982; *Japan Times,* October 27, 1980, and April 3, 1983; and *Mainichi Daily News,* November 28, 1982, and January 1 and April 3, 1983.

Pp. 99–100: Rokusuke Tanaka's use of yakuza in his campaigns is from *Japan Times,* December 23, 1983; and *Mainichi Daily News,* February 8, 1979.

P. 100: Dietman Tsukuda's affections for the mob are reported in *Asahi Evening News,* October 26, 1981; *Daily Yomiuri,* June 21, 1982; and *Mainichi Daily News,* October 26, 1981. Dietman Motomura's alleged ties to the Dojin-kai were reported in *Japan Times Weekly,* February 28, 1987.

P. 101: Yakuza ties to local officials are detailed in numerous press reports. See, for example, *Asahi Evening News,* November 22, 1983; *Daily Yomiuri,* March 17, 1979, and February 7, 1981; and *Mainichi Daily News,* July 13, 1980. The Fukuoka incident is described in a Kyodo News Service report, September 18, 1998; the beating of the Saitama councilwoman is from *Mainichi Daily News,* October 27, 1992.

Pp. 101–2: The Eiji Sadaoka case comes from *Japan Times,* April 29, 1975.

P. 102: Information on Zen Ai Kaigi is from an interview by the authors with Donshyo Kawasaki, office manager of the association's Tokyo headquarters, March 8, 1984. See also Davis's *The Right Wing of Japan;* Karl Taro Greenfeld's "The Curious Clout of Japan's Right," *The Nation,* August 12, 1991; and an Agence France Presse dispatch of November 27, 1998.

Pp. 102–3: The expansion of yakuza political parties is reported in an *Asahi Shimbun* story, translated by the Asia Foundation and related to the U.S. press on September 21, 1981.

P. 103: Sasakawa's quote on rightists is from *Newsweek,* July 7, 1986. Kobayashi's quote is from *60 Minutes,* "Godfather of the Ginza," November 20, 1988.

P. 104: On the fate of Nagasaki mayor Motoshima, see the *New York Times,* August 20 and 26, 1990. On the far right's ability to shut down debate, see, for example, the case of Iris Chang's book, *The Rape of Nanking,* reported in the *New York Times,* May 20, 1999. Hakobu Konishi's quote is cited in Greenfeld's story in *The Nation,* August 12, 1991.

P. 104: The sending of a gun to Prime Minister Sato by a yakuza was reported widely in Japan. See, for example, *Daily Yomiuri,* November 17, 1971, and *Japan Times,* September 30, 1971.

P. 105: The threatening note to foreign securities firms was reprinted in the newsletter *Insideline,* June 2, 1992.

P. 107: Statistics on the military are drawn from *The World Almanac 2001.* See also the Center for Defense Information's summary of the debate over Japanese rearmament, "The Defense of Japan: Should the Rising Sun Rise Again?" *Defense Monitor,* vol. 13, no. 1.

P. 107: On mob links of top military veterans, see Japan Economic Newswire, May 22, 1995; and *Yomiuri Daily News,* July 25, 1987. On nationalist sentiment and the shifting mood toward rearmament, see a series of Pacific News Service dispatches dated April 29 and December 1, 1982, and November 7, 1983; and "War and Remembrance," *Far Eastern Economic Review,* August 25, 1994.

Chapter Five

Pp. 111–12: The Taoka shooting and its aftermath are described in numerous press clips. See, for example, *Asahi Evening News,* September 30, 1978; *Japan Times,* July 23, 1978; *Mainichi Daily News,* October 3, 1978; and *Shukan Jitsuwa,* August 13–20, 1978.

P. 113: The Yamaguchi-gumi press conference was covered widely. Clips were used from *Asahi Evening News,* December 16, 1978; *Daily Yomiuri,* October 12, 1978; and *Los Angeles Times,* November 9, 1978.

P. 114: Details of Taoka's death and funeral are from *Asahi Evening News,* July 25 and October 30, 1978; *Los Angeles Times,* November 9, 1978; *Mainichi Daily News,* October 21 and 27, 1981; and *Shukan Jitsuwa,* August 13–20, 1978.

P. 115: Fumiko Taoka's role is cited in *Mainichi Daily News,* June 16, 1982; and *Shukan Jitsuwa,* August 13–20, 1978. Journalist Shoko Ieda studied the wives of yakuza and those of politicians, and found them similar. "They are both totally devoted to their husbands' careers," she once observed. Her book on gangland women, *Gokudo no Onnatachi* (Gangsters' wives), became a best-seller.

Pp. 115–16: The Yamaguchi-gumi structure is described in *Mainichi Daily News,* June 3, 1981. Figures on the syndicate's income are from *Mainichi Shimbun,* February 13, 1984; *Mainichi Daily News,* April 16, 1977; and *Asahi Evening News,* March 29, 1979. On Yamaguchi-gumi fees paid by top bosses, see Eric Talmadge's fine work for the AP, printed in the *Los Angeles Times,* April 7, 1991; *Japan Times,* February 7, 1992; and a *Shukan Taishu* story translated in *Mainichi Daily News,* August 7, 1994. The Yamaguchi-gumi's economic interests are described in National Police Agency, *Yamaguchi-Gumi, Inagawa-Kai and Sumiyoshi-Rengokai* (1987), pp. 4–5.

P. 117: Taoka's position as head of the National Longshoremen's Association is noted in *Mainichi Daily News,* May 16, 1992. The importance of amphetamine sales to the big syndicates is noted in Tamura Masayuki, "The Yakuza and Amphetamine Abuse in Japan," in *Drugs, Law and the State,* ed. Harold H. Traver and Mark S. Gaylord (1992), pp. 102–3.

P. 117: Information on yakuza influence over the Japanese entertainment industry is from interviews; *Asahi Evening News,* June 9, 1976; and *Mainichi Daily News,* February 20, 1973. Kenji Ino's quote is from *Japan Times,* March 6, 1985.

Pp. 117–18: On the yakuza's long influence on the pachinko industry, see the National Research Institute of Police Science's *Pachinko Ten Gyokai ni Okeru Boryokudan Haijyo Katsudo no Jittai* (The reality of gang eradication activities in the pachinko industry), 1991. In 1994, police estimated that some 843 pachinko parlors in Tokyo were yakuza-affiliated, providing the gangs with nearly $150 million annually. See *Asahi Evening News,* February 5, 1994.

Pp. 120–21: The Yamaguchi-gumi election and subsequent splitting are reported in numerous press clips. See, for example, *Asahi Evening News,* July 4, 1984; and *Mainichi Daily News,* June 20, 1984.

Pp. 121–22: Background on the 1985 arrests of the Yamaguchi-gumi godfathers in Honolulu is from the criminal complaint filed in the case, no. 85-0207M in U.S. District Court, Honolulu, September 3, 1985; an attached affidavit by DEA Special Agent Robert A. Aiu; a related press release from the U.S. Department of Justice, also dated September 3; interviews with law enforcement officials in Honolulu, September 4–13, 1985; *Honolulu Advertiser,* December 31, 1989; and *The National Law Journal,* April 28, 1986. Although the top yakuza walked, two minor defendants were convicted: a lower-ranking yakuza in Honolulu and a Chinese supplier convicted of drug charges in Hong Kong. On the yakuza boss's claims about wanting to book Michael Jackson, see *Mainichi Daily News,* January 27, 1986; and *Honolulu Advertiser,* August 1, 1991. On the cross-cultural arguments used in the yakuza trial, see Gary Fontaine and Laurence J. Severance, "Intercultural Problems in the Interpretation of Evidence: A Yakuza Trial," *International Journal of Intercultural Relations,* vol. 14, 1990, pp. 168–69.

P. 123: On the end of the Yamaguchi-gumi/Ichiwa-kai gang war, see the National Police Agency's *White Paper,* 1989, p. 6. See also Hyogo Prefectural Police Headquarters, *Present Situation of Yamaguchi-gumi and Police Counter Measures,* December 6, 1989. A good profile of godfather Nakanishi is in Velisarios Kattoulas's "Taking Care of Business," *Far Eastern Economic Review,* November 30, 2000; Yukio Yamanouchi's quote is drawn from that story.

P. 124: Differences in syndicate structure were explained in an interview with Kanehiro Hoshino, chief researcher, National Research Institute of Police Science, Tokyo, March 7, 1984. The income of Sumiyoshi-rengo is cited in *Asahi Evening News,* March 29, 1979.

Pp. 124–25: Similarities between U.S. and Japanese organized crime groups are detailed in chapter 6 of anthropologist David Stark's *The Yakuza,* especially p. 241.

P. 125: Statistics on the number of U.S. Mafia members come from the FBI's Organized Crime Section, 2001; the President's Commission on Law Enforcement and Administration of Justice, *Task Force Report: Organized Crime,* 1967; and Charles Grutzner, "How to Lock Out the Mafia," *Harvard Business Review,* March–April 1970, p. 47.

Pp. 125–27: The interview with Shotaro Hayashi was by the authors in Tokyo, 1984. More background on the Sumiyoshi-kai comes from several internal police intelligence reports: "History and Activities of the Sumiyoshi Rengo-kai," December 2, 1987, and "The Activities of the Sumiyoshi Rengo-kai," December 6, 1989, Tokyo Metropolitan Police Department; and "The Sumiyoshi-kai," Joint Drug Intelligence Group, Los Angeles, February 3, 1993.

Pp. 127–30: Figures on the percent of crime cases attributed to yakuza are from a study by Kanehiro Hoshino for the National Research Institute of Police Science: *Boryokudan Hanzai no Henka to Tenbo* (Changes in boryokudan crime in the past and future), 1994. The NRIPS surveys on the gangs were done by Hoshino and his associates. The 1993 study is *Boryokudan no Boryokudan Fukujibunka e no Docho* (A study on the conformity of boryokudan members to boryokudan subculture). The 1987 study is *Boryokudan no Seikatsu Kozo no Kenkyo* (A study on the way of life of members of organized crime gangs). And the survey of 392 yakuza is *Koiki Boryokudan no Keito Keiretsu-Ishiki no Kenkyu* (A study on the attitudes of members of semi-national criminal gangs toward their association and subsidary association), 1985 and 1986.

P. 130: The percent of yakuza driving foreign cars is from the NRIPS study *Boryokudanin no Keizai-Kiban ni Kansuru Kenkyu* (A study of the economic basis of boryokudan members), 1988.

P. 130: The $10 billion estimate of yakuza income is from *Boryokudanin no Keizai-Kiban* and is also detailed in the NPA's *White Paper,* 1989. For other, larger, income estimates see, for example, Kyodo News Service, July 27, 1991; and *Washington Post,* April 11, 1999. On U.S. organized crime income, see "The 50 Biggest Mafia Bosses," *Fortune,* November 10, 1986; *Newsweek,* January 5, 1981; and *Time,* May 16, 1977. The study of 392 yakuza is *Koiki Boryokudan no Keito . . .* from 1985 and 1986.

Pp. 131–32: Information on the bosozoku comes from Velisarios Kattoulas's "Young, Fast and Deadly: Japan's Biker Gangs," in *Far Eastern Economic Review,* February 1, 2001; Michael Uehara's "Japan's Nocturnal Nuisance," *PHP Magazine* (Tokyo), January 1984; and the following clips: *Japan Times,* May 4, 1982; *Yomiuri Shimbun,* April 19, 1985; and *Mainichi Daily News,* March 10, 1998. For more on bosozoku, see the books *Speed Tribes* by Karl Taro Greenfeld and *Kamikaze Biker* by I. Sato. The estimate of over two hundred fake "dowa" groups comes from *Asahi Evening News,* March 6, 1985.

Pp. 132–33: Estimates of burakumin and minority membership of yakuza gangs are from interviews with various police officials over a fifteen-year period. See *Asahi Evening News,* April 17, 1985. The FBI testimony is from *Asian Organized Crime,* hearings before the U.S. Senate Permanent Subcommittee on Investigations, October 3, 1991, p. 21. The FBI report cited is *An Analysis of the Threat of Japanese Organized Crime to the United States and Its Territories,* July 1992, p. 15. The historical ties of tekiya gangs to burakumin is noted in Hoshino, *Organized Criminal Gangs in Japan.* While Japanese media refuse to deal with the issue openly, the Koreans have no such qualms. Unofficial police estimates were supported by one Korean magazine, which reported that 10 percent of all yakuza were ethnic Korean. See *Sisa Journal,* July 27, 1995.

Pp. 133–34: Stark's fascinating and gutsy field study was done as his doctoral thesis in anthropology at the University of Michigan, Ann Arbor, and is titled *The Yakuza: Japanese Crime Incorporated* (1981).

P. 134: The Yamaguchi-gumi's monthly magazine is described in Ames, *Police and Community,* pp. 119–20; and in the *San Francisco Examiner,* July 25, 1981.

Pp. 135–40: The interview with Kakuji Inagawa was by the authors in Tokyo, 1984. The income and structure of Inagawa-kai are described in *Tokyo Shimbun,* February 5, 1975; *Shukan Sankei,* late August–early September 1981; *Asahi Evening News,* March 29, 1979; *Daily Yomiuri,* November 27, 1974; and in two internal reports by the Fourth Investigation Section, Criminal Investigation Division, Kanagawa Prefectural Police Headquarters, "Recent Trend of Inagawa-kai," 1987, and "Inagawa Kai: Present Condition and Countermeasures," 1990. Note: Inagawa passed away on September 3, 1991.

Pp. 140–41: The information on gang funerals and yakuza driving habits is from Stark, *The Yakuza,* pp. 136 and 139; *Hokubei Mainichi* (San Francisco), January 25, 1985; *Shukan Asahi,* October 26, 1984; and *Focus,* October 19, 1984.

Pp. 141–42: Paul Shrader's thorough analysis of the yakuza film genre is entitled "Yakuza Eiga: A Primer," and appears in *Film Comment* magazine, January 1974. See also Ian Buruma's writings in the *Far Eastern Economic Review,* May 3, 1984, and in his book *Behind the Mask* (1984), especially pp. 189–90. On the drop in yakuza film popularity, see T. R. Reid's "The Sun Is Setting on Japanese Gangster Shoot'em-Up Flicks," *Washington Post,* January 14, 1994.

Chapter Six

Pp. 144–47: The story of the Osaka police scandal is based on numerous press clips and on a long article in the July 1983 issue of Japan's prestigious monthly *Bungei Shunju:* "Osaka Fukei Fushoku no Kozo" (The corroded structure of the Osaka Prefectural Police). Justice Minister Hatano's questionable actions, cited on pp. 159–60, are reported in *Japan Times,* December 15, 1982; *Mainichi Daily News,* December 10, 1982; and the *Los Angeles Times,* November 5, 1983.

Pp. 147–48: The accounts of police corruption are described in various interviews and press reports. Early accounts can be found in *Japan Times,* September 9, 1969, and June 30, 1976; *Daily Yomiuri,* January 25, 1970, and July 6, 1976; and *Mainichi Daily News,* May 27, 1982, November 25, 1984, and January 15, 1985. A good overview of more recent cases is in former prosecutor Takeshi Tsuchimoto's "Light and Shadow in Japan's Police System," *Japan Quarterly,* April 1, 2000. See also Asahi News Service, November 21, 1990, on the Osaka day laborer riots; "Mob Boss Took Police to Dinner," *Mainichi Daily News,* October 16, 1993; "2 Tokyo Police Officers Accept Gang Hospitality," *Daily Yomiuri,* February 18, 1990; "Hyogo Police Inspector Golfed with Gang Boss," *Mainichi Daily News,* November 16, 1993; and "Cop Canned for Using Assistance from Crime Boss," *Mainichi Daily News,* February 2, 1994. On the Kanagawa police scandals, see, for example, "Ex-police Chief 'Admits' Cover-up," *Daily Yomiuri,* November 8, 1999.

P. 148: Statistics on crime rates in Japan and the U.S. are drawn from the NPA's *White Paper,* various years; the FBI's Uniform Crime Reports, and Robert Thornton's *Preventing Crime in America and Japan* (1991), p. 13. No fewer than four books in English have appeared extolling the achievements of police in Japan. For a glowing account, see David H. Bayley, *Forces of Order: Police Behavior in Japan and the United States* (1976). Bayley wrote of Japan as "Heaven for a Cop" and dismissed corruption as being "almost nonexistent." A more balanced account is Ames's *Police and Community;* the remaining two are William Clifford, *Crime Control in Japan* (1976), and L. Craig Parker Jr., *The Japanese Police System Today* (1984).

Pp. 150–51: A 1979 survey found yakuza involved in 23 percent of company liquidations. On yakuza involvement in bankruptcy, see Frank Packer and Marc Ryser's

The Governance of Failure: An Anatomy of Corporate Bankruptcy in Japan, Working Paper No. 62, Columbia University, Center on Japanese Economy and Business, New York, April 1992. On the yakuza's role generally in dispute resolution, see the important work of Curtis J. Milhaupt and Mark D. West in "The Dark Side of Private Ordering: An Institutional and Empirical Analysis of Organized Crime," *University of Chicago Law Review,* vol. 67, no. 1, Winter 2000; and the *New York Times,* August 29, 1991. On related problems in the Japanese legal system, see Milhaupt and West, above, and Karel van Wolferen's *The Enigma of Japanese Power* (1990), pp. 212–16.

Pp. 149–51: The close relations between yakuza and police were detailed in confidential interviews with law enforcement officials in Tokyo; in Ames, *Police and Community,* especially pp. 107, 142, and 159; and by former mob lawyer Yukio Yamanouchi's "Yamaguchi-Gumi Komon Bengoshi no Shuki" (Notes of a Yamaguchi-gumi consulting attorney), *Bungei Shunju,* November 1984, p. 405. Yamanouchi's quote is from the *New York Times,* August 29, 1991.

P. 151: The survey on attitudes toward using gangsters was reported in *Japan Times,* April 19, 1993; and *Mainichi Daily News,* April 19, 1993. The number of Japanese knowing yakuza is from the NPA, *White Paper,* 1989, p. 25.

P. 152: On the Hamagin Research Institute study, see *Yomiuri Shimbun,* May 25, 2001; and Kyoto News, May 23, 2001.

P. 153: The section on bribery in Japan is based largely on the fascinating work of anthropologist Harumi Befu of Stanford University. See "Bribery in Japan: When Law Tangles with Culture," in *The Self and the System;* and "An Ethnography of Dinner Entertainment in Japan," *Arctic Anthropology,* vol. 11 Suppl., 1974. See also Richard H. Mitchell's *Political Bribery in Japan* (1996), p. 155; and Gerald L. Curtis's *Election Campaigning Japanese Style* (1983), pp. 238–24. Tanaka's use of gift-giving to disburse political funds is from Chalmers Johnson's series on the prime minister in the *Asian Wall Street Journal,* December 15, 1983.

P. 153: On Kakuei Tanaka being made a scapegoat, see Chalmers Johnson's discussion in *Japan: Who Governs?* pp. 198 and 350.

Pp. 155–56: Information on the sarakin in the early 1980s is from, among others, *Asahi Evening News,* April 12, 1984; *Daily Yomiuri,* November 2 and 5, 1983; *Asian Wall Street Journal,* October 30, 1984; and *Asahi Evening News,* November 28, 1998.

Pp. 156–57: Oshima's quote is from *Forbes,* July 18, 1994. The program on yakuza debt collection aired on the Tokyo Broadcasting System and was reported on by Kyodo News Service, May 16, 1990. The collector's demand that a debtor sell his kidney was widely covered. See, for example, *Washington Post,* November 5, 1999.

P. 157: The *Gendai* story comes from *Japan Times,* June 8, 1983; and *Mainichi Daily News,* July 9, 1983. Kobayshi's quote is from "Godfather of the Ginza," *60 Minutes,* November 20, 1988.

P. 158: The 1991 NPA survey on extortion is noted in *Nihon Keizai Shimbun,* May 5, 1991. The ANA extortion case is reported in *Daily Yomiuri,* November 30, 1993. On surveys of extortion among entertainment businesses, see *Japan Times,* April 7, 1995; *Yomiuri Report from Japan,* March 15, 1991; and *Daily Yomiuri,* January 14, 1980. The 1994 school suicide case is reported in *Japan Times,* December 3, 1994.

Pp. 159–62: Background on the sokaiya, once scarce, is now voluminous. The authors' own data come from interviews with sokaiya, Japanese police and corporate executives, and various law enforcement, academic, and press reports. Ken Szymkowiak's *Sokaiya* (2002) provides the most comprehensive treatment in English. On sokaiya ties to yakuza, see the NPA's 1987 report, *Boryokudan Criminalities in Japan and Police Measures against Them;* the FBI's *An Analysis,* p. 25; and "Sokaiya (Corporate Extortionists)," a speech by ex-NPA official Raisuke Miyawaki before the Foreign Press Center, Tokyo, June 1997. More generally, see *Nihon Keizai Shimbun,* January 10, 1978; *Daily Yomiuri,* August 30, 1978, and October 10, 1982; *International Management,* September 1983; *Asian Wall Street Journal,* June 12, 1984, and July 4, 1985; and *Chicago Tribune,* November 26, 1990.

P. 159: On amounts paid to sokaiya, see Mark D. West's impressive study, "Information, Institutions, and Extortion in Japan and the United States: Making Sense of Sokaiya Racketeers," *Northwestern University Law Review,* Spring 1999, pp. 774–75.

P. 160: Kodama's involvement in the sokaiya rackets is noted in *Asahi Evening News,* April 5 and June 7, 1976.

Pp. 161–62: Shimazaki's story is detailed in the *Daily Yomiuri,* February 20, 1973; and *Mainichi Daily News,* May 26, 1971.

Pp. 162–63: Details on the sokaiya guide are taken from Martin Fackler and Donald Macintyre's wonderful piece, "A Japanese Publisher Finds Profits in 'Who's Who' of Racketeers," *Bloomberg Business News,* June 27, 1997.

P. 163: The importance of wa to the sokaiya is explained in an unpublished paper by Eric M. Von Hurst, *The Sokaiya Syndrome,* 1973, pp. 2–3. For good analyses of how sokaiya depend on the lack of corporate transparency, see Mark West's "Information, Institutions, and Extortion in Japan"; Henry Laurence's "The Big Bang and the Sokaiya," *JPRI Critique,* August 1999; and "Sokaiya Scandals, Economic Woes Spotlight Japanese Corporate Governance," *JEI Report,* January 23, 1998.

P. 163: The statistics of securities cases investigated are from West, "Information, Institutions, and Extortion in Japan," p. 783. The quote of Smith Barney's Tsukimura is from Dow Jones News, August 9, 1997.

Pp. 164–65: Background on the early history of Minamata disease comes from Norrie Huddle and Michael Reich's important *Island of Dreams: Environmental Crisis in Japan* (1975), especially pp. 103–7, 115, and 129.

Pp. 166–68: Chisso's use of yakuza, sokaiya, and other thugs is described at length in the Japanese press. See, for example, *Asahi Evening News,* June 4, 1971; *Japan Times,* June 2, June 4, and November 30, 1971; *Mainichi Daily News,* January 12, May 27, and November 30, 1971. On the assault on Eugene Smith by Chisso's goons, see *Asahi Evening News,* April 10, 1974; and W. Eugene Smith and Aileen Smith's *Minamata* (1975), p. 135.

Pp. 167–68: The outcome of the Minamata tragedy is detailed in Huddle and Reich's *Island of Dreams,* pp. 129–31; and W. Eugene Smith and Aileen Smith's *Minamata* (1975), p. 135.

Pp. 168–69: On the impact of commercial code reforms and sokaiya moves into other areas of extortion, see Ken Szymkowiak's impressive 1996 dissertation, *Necessary Evil:*

Extortion, Organized Crime and Japanese Corporations; the NPA's *Present State of Boryo kudan and Our Crackdown Operations* (1983); *Asian Wall Street Journal,* June 12 and July 3, 1984; and *Daily Yomiuri,* October 10, 1982.

P. 169: On payments to sokaiya scandal sheets, see West, "Information, Institutions, and Extortion in Japan," p. 774; *Asahi Shimbun,* July 10, 1997; and *Asahi Evening News,* February 8, 1994.

P. 170: The T Boone Pickens encounter with the sokaiya was widely covered. His quote is from the *Wall Street Journal,* June 30, 1989. David Bong's quote is from an interview, December 1999.

P. 170: On Rondan Doyukai, see the *Times,* June 22, 1991; and "Blackmail!" *Business Week,* July 21, 1997.

Pp. 172–73: The 1981 assault on the three foreigners is described in a letter in *Japan Times Weekly,* December 19, 1981. The Justice Ministry survey on sex crimes is reported in Kyodo News Service, April 1, 2000; the 1995 survey is cited in *Mainichi Daily News,* May 13, 1995. Raelyn Campbell details her experience in "Raped (by the Cops) in Tokyo," *JPRI Critique,* February 1999.

P. 173: The figure on underreporting of robberies is noted in Kyodo News Service, October 14, 2000. Older data are described in "The Police and the Situation of Public Safety in Japan," a speech given before the 1984 Interpol conference in Cairo by Masaharu Saitoh of the National Police Agency. See especially table 3 of the appendix.

P. 173: Statistics on Japan's near-perfect conviction rate are cited in the annual *White Paper on Crime,* issued by Japan's Ministry of Justice. U.S. conviction rates are from the Bureau of Justice Statistics, U.S. Department of Justice. See http://www.ojp. usdoj.gov/bjs/fed.htm#Adjudication. The state court figure of 70 percent is from a May 1996 survey of the nation's seventy-five largest state courts.

Pp. 173–74: The controversy over confessions in Japan is explored in the *Los Angeles Times,* September 6, 1984; *Daily Yomiuri,* March 4, 1984; Ames, *Police and Community,* p. 136; and Chalmers Johnson, *Conspiracy at Matsukawa* (1972), chapter 4. On police forcing signatures to blank confessions, see, for example, *Japan Times,* November 29, 1994. On violence against foreigners, see "More Detainees Claim Abuse by Officials," *Japan Times,* December 30, 1994. On the problems of Japanese criminal justice, see *A Typical Example of Human Rights Violations under the Daiyo Kangoku System in Japan,* Japan Civil Liberties Union, July 30, 1991; and "Victims of a Safe Society," *Los Angeles Times,* February 27, 1992.

Chapter Seven

Pp. 175–76: Background on the Bubble Economy is drawn from various sources. Most helpful were Christopher Wood's *The Bubble Economy* (1992), especially pp. 1–12; and R. Taggart Murphy's "Power without Purpose: The Crisis of Japan's Global Financial Dominance," *Harvard Business Review,* March–April 1989.

P. 177: On Kotani and the Koshin Group, see James Sterngold's "In Japan, a Plundered Company," *New York Times,* November 19, 1993; *Nihon Keizai Shimbun,* April 30,

1991; *The Economist*, September 4, 1993. Kotani's fate is discussed in Japan Economic Newswire, March 25, 1997; and *Daily Yomiuri*, March 27, 1997.

Pp. 177–78: Information on the Yamaguchi-gumi's investment in Kurabo and Takumi's $500 million portfolio is from the Tokyo newsletter *Insider*, November 20, 1990, and February 6, 1991. See also *Asahi Evening News*, November 2, 1990; and *Daily Yomiuri*, December 12, 1990.

Pp. 178–79: Reports of jiageya activity are voluminous. See, for example, Asahi News Service, September 29, 1987, and June 24, 1990; *Forbes*, December 14, 1987. The story of Ms. Nishiyama was carried by Asahi News Service, April 13, 1990. Iishiba's comment is from an author's interview.

Pp. 178–80: Bully's illuminating testimony is from U.S. Senate hearings, *Asian Organized Crime: The New International Criminal*, June 18, 1992, pp. 89–90.

P. 180: Stories on corruption in the construction business are numerous. See, for example, *Nikkei Weekly*, August 23, 1993; *Mainichi Daily News*, August 18, 1993; and *Far Eastern Economic Review*, June 11, 1987. Shimizu chairman Yoshino's quote is from the *Far Eastern Economic Review*, October 7, 1993.

Pp. 180–81: On yakuza involvement in the construction industry, see *Asahi Evening News*, August 25, 1993; *Daily Yomiuri*, April 23, 1993; Kyodo News Service, March 16, 1993; *Japan Times*, February 5, 1994; *Forbes Global*, February 8, 1999; and author Kaplan's own "Gangs Sniff Quake Bounty," *Asahi Evening News*, February 5, 1995. The prosecutor's statement is from an author's interview, June 1994. The historic ties of yakuza to the construction industry are discussed in sociologist Kanehiro Hoshino's unpublished paper, *Organized Crime and Its Origins in Japan*, 1988, pp. 2–3. Yamaguchi-gumi involvement in the Kansai airport project is noted in an NPA unpublished report, *Yamaguchi-Gumi, Inagawa-Kai and Sumiyoshi-Rengokai*, 1987, p. 25.

P. 181: On yakuza as a factor in protectionism, see Norihiko Shirouzu's fine reporting job in "Pier Pressure: U.S.-Japan Ship Fight Is Being Complicated by Talk of Mob Ties," *Wall Street Journal*, October 21, 1997; *Asahi Evening News*, August 2, 1997; and *Fortune*, April 22, 1991.

Pp. 182–83: Yakuza ties to the golf industry are from NPA interviews and Eric Talmadge's AP story, "Japan Golf Courses Take Aim at Thugs," December 9, 1990. On golf gambling by yakuza, see "Boryokudan to Gorufu Jyo: Gorufu Tengoku Nippon no Byori" (Gangsters and golf courses: the sickness of golf heaven Japan), *Shukan Gendai*, August 24, 1991. On payoffs in golf development, see "Playing Golf on the Shady Side in Japan," *Japan Times*, August 4, 1994.

P. 183: On the yakuza's role in the art market, see *Forbes*, April 29, 1991; the FBI's *An Analysis*, p. 23; and Benjamin Fulford's "Japan's Art Collections Pay for Excesses of Bubble-Economy," *South China Morning Post*, January 25, 1998.

Pp. 183–84: Morishita's comments are from the *Washington Post*, December 11, 1989. On his background and art collecting, see that story as well as the *Far Eastern Economic Review*, January 17, 1990, and October 22, 1992; *Tokyo Insider*, October 20, 1989; and the *New York Times*, January 8, 1990. Morishita's alleged yakuza ties are described in confidential reports by the U.S. Joint Drug Intelligence Group and Customs Service; and in the U.S. Senate hearings, *Asian Organized Crime: The New International Criminal*, August 4, 1992, p. 52. See also the *Honolulu Advertiser*, August 22, 1988.

Pp. 184–85: On the Yamaguchi-gumi's move into Tokyo, see the FBI's *An Analysis*, p. 12; *Asahi Shimbun*, August 21, 1999; *Nihon Keizai Shimbun*, May 2, 1991; Reuters, December 13, 1990.

P. 185: On yakuza interests in the hospital industry, see *Shukan Diamond*, March 10, 2001. On the gangster who posed as a commercial attaché, see *Mainichi Daily News*, April 9, 1990.

Pp. 185–86: The gangs' transition to keizai yakuza is drawn from several interviews with Seiji Iishiba, as well as his "Structural Changes in Japanese Society and Boryokudan," *Jurisuto*, September 1, 1991. On yakuza use of obligation to enter big business, see the *Shukan Aera* translation in *Asahi Evening News*, July 1, 1997. Miyawaki's quote is from an author's interview, June 29, 1999. See also his "The Shady Side of Japanese Society," speech before the School of Advanced and International Affairs, Johns Hopkins University, June 29, 1999.

P. 186: The Mitsubishi Bank executive's quote is from *Institutional Investor*, International Edition, August 1991.

Pp. 186–87: On the fate of Kazuo Kengaku and Cosmo Securities, see "Japanese Fund Manager Found Buried in Concrete," *Financial Times*, October 19, 1988.

Pp. 187–89: Much of Ishii's early background, including the quotes of Abe and Nishiyama, is drawn from a superb series by Kyodo News Service, reprinted as "The Black Current" in the *Japan Times*, April 1, 1992. See also Eric Talmadge's Associated Press story of July 25, 1991.

P. 189: The Heiwa Sogo Bank scandal was widely reported in Japan. See, for example, *Japan Times*, November 15, 1986; *Daily Yomiuri*, July 9, 1986; *Financial Times*, July 10, 1986; *Asian Wall Street Journal*, August 19, 1986; and Aron Viner's *Inside Japanese Financial Markets* (1988), pp. 209–12. Ishii's involvement is described in *Tokyo Insideline*, December 24, 1992, and July 30, 1994; and in Atsushi Mizoguchi's *Gendai Yakuza no Ura Chishiki* (1993), pp. 116–25.

Pp. 189–95: Details of Ishii and his associates' financial dealings are set out in the indictment on the case, *Preliminary Petition regarding Infraction of the Commercial Law by Watanabe Hiroyasu, Jun Saotome, and Munenobu Shoji*, Tokyo Regional Public Prosecutor's Office, September 22, 1993; and in confidential interviews with detectives at the Tokyo Metropolitan Police Department. See also *Japan Times*, March 3, 1992, and October 27, 1992. On Ishii and the Sagawa scandal generally, see "Rishoku Boryokudan Inagawa-kai to 'Nomura Shoken' no Mitsu Getsu" (Money-making boryokudan, Inagawa-kai and honeymoon of Nomura stocks), *Bunka Hyoron*, November 1991; "Ishii Susumu Zen Kaicho wa Koushite 'Omote no Bijinesu' ni Noridashita" (How former boss Ishii Susumu moved into "legitimate business"), *Shukan Post*, August 9, 1991; Kei Yuasa's *Sandei Mainichi* story, translated in *Mainichi Daily News*, October 13, 1991; and author Kaplan's own "The Gangster with the Golden Touch," *Tokyo Journal*, September 1995.

Pp. 189–90: On Nippon Kominto's campaign against Takeshita, see an interview with its boss in *Asahi Evening News,* July 28, 1992; also *Asahi Evening News,* November 17, 1992; and *Daily Yomiuri,* November 21, 1992. Kanemaru's testimony is reported, among other places, in *New York Times,* November 29, 1992.

Pp. 191–92: Prescott Bush's involvement with Ishii's operation is from *Los Angeles Times,* August 1, 1991; Reuters, February 26, 1992; a Reuter-Kyodo dispatch in *Japan Times,* June 28, 1992; "It All Started in a Tokyo Chinese Restaurant," *Sunday Mainichi,* reprinted in *Mainichi Daily News,* July 9, 1991; *Wall Street Journal,* June 10, 1991; and Report from Japan, Inc. (a Yomiuri news service), September 16, 1991.

P. 192: On Ishii's ties to Nomura and Nikko, see "Nomura, Nikko Knowingly Dealt with Gang Boss," *Mainichi Daily News,* July 10, 1991; *Japan Times,* July 9, 1991; *Asahi Evening News,* August 30, 1991; *New York Times,* August 30, 1991.

P. 194: On the Bubble's collapse and the stock market's loss of $2 trillion, see Wood, *The Bubble Economy,* pp. 7–8; also *New York Times,* April 26, 1992.

Chapter Eight

Pp. 196–97: On post-Bubble fallout from the yakuza's economic impact, see author Kaplan's *Japanese Organized Crime and the Bubble Economy,* Occasional Paper 70, Woodrow Wilson Center, 1996; his article "Yakuza, Inc." in *U.S. News & World Report,* April 13, 1998; Brian Bremner's "Yakuza and the Banks," *Business Week,* January 29, 1995; and Velisarios Kattoulas's "The Yakuza Recession," *Far Eastern Economic Review,* January 17, 2002.

P. 197: The scandal surrounding Kanemaru was covered at length by the news media. See, for example, *Mainichi Daily News,* October 7, 1992; *Daily Yomiuri,* October 7, 1992, *Time,* October 5, 1992; and *International Herald Tribune,* October 16, 1992. On the construction industry scandal, see *Mainichi Daily News,* November 2, 1993; *Far Eastern Economic Review,* October 7, 1993; and *Tokyo Business,* November 1993.

P. 198: On the fate of Kotani and the Koshin Group, see *Mainichi Daily News,* April 9, 1992; *Asahi Shimbun,* March 26, 1997; and Dow Jones International News, March 26, 1997.

P. 198: On the Itoman scandal, see Wood, *The Bubble Economy,* pp. 134–39; Bully's testimony in the U.S. Senate hearings, *Asian Organized Crime: The New International Criminal,* p. 95; and *Japan Times,* September 10, 1991. The *Nikkei Weekly* quote is from August 3, 1991.

P. 198: The scandals involving bank CDs are from press reports and Wood, *The Bubble Economy,* pp. 142–43.

P. 198: The IBJ/Onoue scandal is described in Wood, *The Bubble Economy,* 146–56; *Japan Times,* September 14, 1991; *Mainichi Daily News,* January 25, 1992; *The Economist,* October 12, 1991; *New York Times,* August 14, 1991; *Wall Street Journal,* August 23, 1991.

Pp. 198–99: On Onoue's alleged ties to the yakuza, see *Tokyo Insider,* April 25, 1990.

P. 199: On the Asahi paper's probe of loans to the Yamaguchi-gumi, see *Asahi Evening News*, November 21, 1991. The Gifu Shogin case is from interviews with NPA officials. See also *Mainichi Daily News*, July 9, 1991; *Asahi Evening News*, November 21, 1991; *New York Times*, October 18, 1994; and *Business Week*, January 29, 1995.

Pp. 199–200: Mob attacks against Japanese firms are from interviews and the following clips: *Far Eastern Economic Review*, August 12, 1993; *Mainichi Daily News*, September 26, 1994, and February 28, 1995; *Los Angeles Times*, October 8, 1994; *Japan Times*, October 19, 1994; and *Daily Yomiuri*, June 28, 1995.

P. 200: The Suzuki murder is analyzed at length in Ken Szymkowiak's *Sokaiya* (2002), pp. 165–71. See also *Mainichi Daily News*, October 21, 1994, and *Daily Yomiuri*, October 20, 1994. On the Nippon Credit Bank case and other suspect "suicides," see Benjamin Fulford's "Buried in the Books," *Forbes*, January 8, 2001.

Pp. 201–2: On the size of the Japanese banking industry's bad loans, see, for example, *Wall Street Journal*, August 23, 1999; *New York Times*, July 30, 1993; and *Far Eastern Economic Review*, October 4, 2001. The 2001 Goldman Sachs report is discussed in the *Review* story. Estimates of the yakuza's bad loan share by Miyawaki and banking analysts are from authors' interviews.

Pp. 202–4: The 1999 survey of mobbed-up construction loans was by the Housing Loan Administration and is cited in "The Yakuza Recession," *Far Eastern Economic Review*, January 17, 2002. Data on the mob-tied bad loan portfolios came from confidential interviews by the authors with investigators and bank officials in Tokyo, February–March 1998.

P. 203: Godfather Takayama's quote is from "Hajime Takano's Interview Series—No. 1," http://www.smn.co.jp/interviews/0071i01e.html

P. 204: The comments by Sumiyoshi-kai boss Suzuki are from an author's interview, February 1998. The mysterious fire that hit Cargill was described in interviews with company officials. See also author Kaplan's "Yakuza, Inc." Lonestar's troubles are noted in "The Yakuza Recession," *Far Eastern Economic Review*, January 17, 2002. Harry Godfrey's comments are from an author interview, February 1998.

Pp. 205–6: Bill Rice's comments come from a 1991 author interview. Those of Seiji Iishiba and Kohei Nakabo are from author interviews in February 1998. Nakabo further describes his experiences in "Japan's Homework for the Twenty-First Century," *Japan Quarterly*, January 1, 2001.

Pp. 206–8: The comments of the NPA official and Wayne Drew are from author's interviews. On the lack of tools to fight organized crime, see David T. Johnson, *Why the Wicked Sleep: The Prosecution of Political Corruption in Postwar Japan*, JPRI Working Paper, No. 34, June 1997. On the failure to investigate the Aum cult, see Kaplan and Marshall's *The Cult at the End of the World* (1996), pp. 79–81 and 185–87.

Pp. 206–7: On Japan's slow response to money laundering, see Foreign Broadcast Information Service translation, *Shukan Toyo Keizai*, August 16, 1997, pp. 110–12, by T. Tateishi: "Is Japan a Money Laundering Paradise?—Backward Nation in Terms of Money Laundering"; Friman, *NarcoDiplomacy*, pp. 81–84; the U.S. State Department's *International Narcotics Control Strategy Report* (1998), p. 619; *Daily Yomiuri*, December 20, 1998; and Kyodo News Service, June 26, 1998.

P. 209: The number of citizen requests for police help on yakuza is from the NPA's *White Paper on Police,* 1992, p. 34. On the public's growing intolerance of the gangs, see Karl Schoenberger's "Yakuza—Japan Mobs under Fire," *Los Angeles Times,* March 18, 1988; and *Asahi Shimbun,* June 22, 1987. The anecdote of the pig's head left in a pachinko owner's doorway is from chapter 5 of the *Mainichi Shimbun's Soshiki Boryoku o Ou* (Tracing organized violence) (1992).

Pp. 209-10: Coverage of the Itami attack was voluminous. See, for example, Kyodo News Service, June 1, 1992, and December 3, 1992; Reuters, December 5, 1992; and *The Guardian,* August 17, 1993.

P. 211: On yakuza protests against the 1992 anti-racketeering law, see *Far East Economic Review,* March 2, 1992; Asahi News Service, April 10, 1992; and Associated Press, November 27, 1992.

Pp. 211-12: On the yakuza's reaction to the anti-gang law, see two 1993 reports by the National Research Institute of Police Science: *Boryokudan Taisakuhou Shikogo no Boryokudanin no Seikatsu Henka* (Changes in the way of life of boryokudan members after enforcement of the anti–organized crime law), and *Boryokudan Taisakuhou no Boryokudan ni Oyobosu Eikyo to Kumiin no Ridatsu* (The impact of the anti–organized crime law on boryokudan and their members' intentions to resign from the organization); and Peter Hill's 2000 doctoral thesis at the U.K.'s University of Stirling, *Botaiho: Japanese Organised Crime under the Boryokudan Countermeasures Law.*

Pp. 211-12: On the shift to associate status within the gangs, see Miyawaki, "The Shady Side of Japanese Society," *Ekonomisuto,* June 3, 1997, pp. 74–79. On the move to front companies, *Mainichi Daily News,* February 11, 1992, and January 29, 1993; *Daily Yomiuri,* June 14, 1992; and Reuters, February 18, 1992.

P. 212: On consolidation of the gangs, see Peter Hill's "Botaiho ka no Yakuza: Japanese Organised Crime under the Boryokudan Taisakuho," paper presented to the British Society of Japanese Studies annual conference, April 6, 1999; and his "Botaiho: Organised Crime Countermeasures in Japan," *Social Science Japan,* November 1998. Data on the shift come from editions of the NPA's *White Paper,* 1991–98.

P. 213: The study on Japan's underground economy was by the Hamagin Research Institute. See *Yomiuri Shimbun,* May 25, 2001.

P. 213: The Yokohama boss advertising for recruits was reported by Reuters, February 1, 1990. On mob takeovers, see the chilling story of how the owner of a thirty-store chain of clothing boutiques lost control of his firm in *Sunday Mainichi,* reprinted in *Mainichi Daily News,* March 31, 1993. The number of yakuza front companies charged in 1994 is from the NPA's *National Police White Paper,* 1995, p. 96.

Pp. 213-14: On the yakuza's take of public works projects, we're indebted to Benjamin Fulford's fine work in "The Yakuza's Revenge," *Forbes Global,* February 8, 1999. See also the author's own "Gangs Sniff Quake Bounty," *Asahi Evening News,* February 5, 1995; and *Asahi Evening News,* August 3, 1993.

P. 214: On the fate of Bubble-era artwork, see the FBI's *An Analysis,* p. 23; and Fulford's "Japan's Art Collections Pay for Excesses of Bubble-Economy."

P. 214: The Tokyo sokaiya banquet is reported in "Sokaiya to Kigyo no Tantosha no Aienkai" (Sokaiya and corporate managers at large banquet), *Asahi Shimbun,* June 22, 1991. The Seiwa-kai incident is from *Mainichi Daily News,* June 12, 1994.

P. 215: The figure of 730 sokaiya is from *Mainichi Daily News,* June 17, 1994. The Yamaguchi-gumi's "financial research association" was reported in "Yakuza Storming the Corporate Ship," *Tokyo Business,* April 1994. On the Kirin case, see Reuters, July 15, 1993; and on Ito-Yokado, see *New York Times,* December 13, 1992.

P. 215: On Koike's early background, see *Ekonomisuto,* June 3, 1997, pp. 74–79; *Japan Times,* May 14, 1975, and June 17, 1997; Laurence, "The Big Bang and the Sokaiya."

Pp. 215–16: Koike's dealings with DKB and the brokerages received heavy coverage in Japan. See, for example, *Daily Yomiuri,* June 11, 1997; and *Shukan Aera,* reprinted as "Koike Hurt by Incompetency," *Asahi Evening News,* November 8, 1997.

P. 216: On Koike's loans from DKB: Bloomberg Business News, June 27, 1997; *Daily Yomiuri,* June 7, 1997, and January 13, 1998; and *Japan Times,* January 27, 1998.

P. 216: On Yamaichi's bankruptcy, see *Los Angeles Times,* November 24, 1997.

Pp. 216–17: Coverage of the sokaiya scandals of the late 1990s was also heavy. Good overviews are Terry Ursacki's "The Sokaiya Incidents of 1997: Understanding Executive Malfeasance in Japan," *1998 Best Papers Proceedings of the Association of Japanese Business Studies Eleventh Annual Conference* (1998), pp. 65–81; Laurence, "The Big Bang and the Sokaiya"; and Bill Spindle's "Japanese Gangs Search for New Ways to Prey on Firms," *Wall Street Journal,* August 19, 1998.

Pp. 216–17: On the department store payoffs: *Business Week,* July 21, 1997; *Asahi Evening News,* June 12 and June 15, 1996; and *Daily Yomiuri,* June 13 and June 17, 1996.

P. 217: The *Mainichi Shimbun* editorial was reprinted in *Mainichi Daily News,* October 25, 1997. The *Business Week* comment is from July 21, 1997. The LDP group's sokaiya payoffs are noted in Japan Economic Newswire, November 30, 1997.

P. 217: West's quote is from his "Information, Institutions, and Extortion in Japan," p. 769.

P. 218: The comparisons with the Drexel Burnham and Salomon Brothers cases are taken from West, "Information, Institutions, and Extortion in Japan," p. 777.

Pp. 218–19: The survey on breaking sokaiya ties is from Japan Economic Newswire, March 25, 1998. On the wave of new anti-crime laws, see "New Laws Boost Tokyo's Anticrime Powers and Public's Privacy Concerns," *JEI Report,* August 29, 1999.

Pp. 219–20: Ogawa's quote is cited in the *Guardian,* June 30, 1999, and *New York Times,* August 11, 1999. On the case of Liquid Audio Japan, see, for example, *Asahi News,* December 12, 2000; *Daily Yomiuri,* October 26, 2000; *Mainichi Daily News,* October 26, 2000; Associated Press, October 29 and December 21, 2000; and *Far Eastern Economic Review,* November 30, 2000. On Yamaguchi-gumi investment in Japan Air Lines, see Associated Press, March 23, 1999; and *Washington Post,* April 11, 1999.

Chapter Nine

P. 223: Discussion of the attitudes of Japanese law enforcement toward yakuza operating abroad is based on numerous interviews with ranking officers of the Tokyo Metropolitan Police and the National Police Agency during the 1980s, as well as with both local and federal U.S. law enforcement officials.

Pp. 224–25: The events leading up to Kim's kidnapping are described in U.S. House of Representatives, *Hearings before the Subcommittee on International Organizations of the Committee on International Relations,* "Activities of the Korean Central Intelligence Agency in the United States," part 1, March 17, 1976, pp. 12–13. See also *San Francisco Chronicle,* January 13, 1985; and *Mother Jones,* May 1985.

P. 225: Background on the KCIA is drawn from U.S. House of Representatives, *Hearings before the Subcommittee on International Organizations,* p. 12; Robert Boettcher, *Gifts of Deceit: Sun Myung Moon, Tongsun Park, and the Korea Scandal* (1980), pp. 23–30; and *New York Times,* August 20, 1973.

P. 225: Kim's statements are from an interview with the authors in December 1984. His kidnapping is described in *Asian Wall Street Journal,* August 17, 1978; *New York Times,* August 15, 1973; *San Francisco Chronicle,* January 13, 1985; and a U.S. Department of State cable, U.S. Embassy (Seoul) to Washington, D.C., "Account of Kim Tae Chung's Kidnapping," August 1973.

P. 226: The KCIA's involvement in Kim's kidnapping is from Ranard's testimony in U.S. House of Representatives, *Hearings before the Subcommittee on International Organizations,* March 17, 1976; *Japan Times,* February 8, 1984; *Mainichi Daily News,* September 25, 1973; and *Asahi Evening News,* September 26, 1973.

Pp. 226–27: Machii's alleged role in the kidnapping is discussed in *Shukan Gendai,* August 30, 1973; Takao Goto, *Koria Uochiya* (Korea watcher) (1982), p. 94; and *Far Eastern Economic Review,* November 12, 1973, and May 13, 1974. Other possible yakuza involvement is cited in *Koria Uochiya,* p. 93; and *Mainichi Daily News,* February 8, 1977.

Pp. 228–29: Machii's early background was pieced together from interviews with his American business partner, Ken Ross, and with Tokyo Metropolitan Police officials. Also consulted were the following articles: "Kankoku Kara Kita Otoko" (The man came from Korea), three-part series in *Shukan Bunshun,* June 23, June 30, and July 7, 1977; *Shukan Shincho,* July 26, 1973; and *Mainichi Daily News,* November 20, 1964.

P. 230: Machii's contacts with high-ranking Korean officials are detailed in *Ekonomisuto,* March 16, 1976; *Shukan Shincho,* July 18, 1970; *Asahi Evening News,* March 20, 1976; and the leading Korean monthly, *Wolgan Chosen,* February 1984. His gang's continued criminal activities are noted, among other places, in *Yomiuri Shimbun,* June 8, 1975. The FBI report that discusses Towa Yuai Jigyo Kumiai is *An Analysis.*

Pp. 231–33: The yakuza's big move into South Korea is documented in interviews and reports in *Tokyo Shimbun,* February 12, 1975; and *Daily Yomiuri,* June 8 and October 20, 1975. See also the Korean journal *Wolgan Chosen,* February 1984. The influence of Korean gangs is from Korean Supreme Prosecutor's Office, *Organized Crime* *in Korea,* January 1994. On the Korean gangsters being trained by yakuza, see *Mainichi Daily News,* April 30, 1990; *Asahi Evening News,* December 29, 1990. See also Mainichi Shimbun, *Soshiki Boryoku o Ou,* pp. 123–25. The Korean journal noted is *Sisa Journal,* July 27, 1995.

P. 234: Information on kisaeng tourism in this section is drawn from confidential interviews in Seoul, and from Korea Church Women United, *Kisaeng Tourism* (1984), pp. 10–12, 19–20; the characterization of Korean prostitutes as "unpersons" is from Paul S. Crane, *Korea Patterns* (1978), pp. 29–30, 128.

P. 236: Estimates of the number of prostitutes in East Asia are from Lin L. Lim's 1998 study, *The Sex Sector: The Economic and Social Bases of Prostitution in Southeast Asia,* published by the International Labor Office; and for Thailand, from Pasuk Phongpaichit, Sungsidh Piriyarangsan, and Nualnoi Treerat, *Guns, Girls, Gambling, Ganja* (1998), pp. 197–201. For origins of the region's modern sex trade, see "Hospitality Girls in the Philippines," *Southeast Asia Chronicle,* January–February 1979; and "Prostitution in Asia," a background paper prepared by Sister Mary Soledad Perpinan, Manila, for the General Assembly of the World Council of Churches, 1983.

Pp. 236–37: Sasakawa's "tourist paradise" on Lubang is from *Action Bulletin,* March and July 1981; *Japan Times,* May 25, 1981; and *Mainichi Daily News,* April 15, 1981. The Casio story is from *New York Times,* August 5, 1979.

P. 237: On government complicity in the sex trade, see Korea Church Women United, *Kisaeng Tourism,* pp. 17 and 26; and *The Progressive,* February and March 1985.

Pp. 237–38: Background on the karayuki-san is from Hane, *Peasants, Rebels, and Outcasts,* pp. 207, 218–25.

P. 238: The number of women and children trafficked is noted in United States Central Intelligence Agency, Center for the Study of Intelligence, *International Trafficking in Women to the United States: A Contemporary Manifestation of Slavery and Organized Crime,* April 2000, p. 3.

Pp. 238–39: Background on the Japayuki-san is from "Women in Crisis in Japan," information sheet, Japan Women's Christian Temperance Union, Tokyo, undated (c. 1983); and *Daily Yomiuri,* August 5, 1984.

P. 239: On the estimate of 100,000 foreign sex workers in Japan, see Matsui Yayori, *Eliminating Trafficking in Asian Women,* undated paper posted on the following website in June 2000, http://www.alternatives.com/crime/ASIAWOM.HTML; and Phongpaichit, Piriyarangsan, and Treerat, *Guns, Girls, Gambling, Ganja,* p. 165. Other estimates range from 75,000 to 150,000; see, for example, the Human Rights Watch report *Owed Justice: Thai Women Trafficked into Debt Bondage in Japan,* September 2000; and "Human Trafficking: Bright Lights, Brutal Life," *Far Eastern Economic Review,* August 3, 2000.

P. 239: There are numerous reports on the plight of Southeast Asian women in Japan. For a look from the perspective of Japan's pioneering women's shelter, see Shizuko Ohshima and Carolyn Francis's book, *Japan through the Eyes of Women Migrant Workers* (1989). On the treatment of Thai sex workers in particular, see Human

Rights Watch's *Owed Justice;* and Phongpaichit, Piriyarangsan, and Treerat, *Guns, Girls, Gambling, Ganja,* p. 170. On Filipinas, see Ma. Rosario P. Ballescas, *Filipino Entertainers in Japan: An Introduction* (1992).

Pp. 239–40: Information on economics of the sex trade was garnered from interviews in Bangkok and Tokyo, and from numerous published reports. Particularly helpful was the work of journalist Kim Gooi in Bangkok. Also relied on were the following reports: the CIA's study, *International Trafficking in Women to the United States;* "Illegal Alien Smuggler Describes Business," *The Nation* (Thailand), November 9, 1994; *Time,* June 21, 1993; *Far East Economic Review,* October 14, 1993, December 14, 1995, and August 3, 2000; *Bangkok Post,* March 15, 1994; Reuters, December 22, 1988; and Abigail Haworth and Kyoko Matsuda's "Flesh and Blood," a two-part series exposing the sex trade's brutal realities in *Tokyo Journal,* July and August 1994. Threats against the Japanese embassy are noted in *Mainichi Daily News,* February 27, 1992.

P. 240: The slave auction was reported in *Asian Women's Liberation,* no. 6, 1984, Asian Women's Association, Tokyo. Prices for buying and leasing Filipinas are from *Mainichi Daily News,* February 24, 1985. The quote from a Thai trafficker in women is from "Illegal Alien Smuggler Describes Business," *The Nation* (Bangkok), November 9, 1994.

P. 240: The $30,000 figure for women trafficked in Japan is from Regan E. Ralph, Human Rights Watch, in *Hearings before the U.S. Senate Committee on Foreign Relations Subcommittee on Near Eastern and South Asian Affairs,* February 22, 2000. The study by the Chulalongkorn economists is Phongpaichit, Piriyarangsan, and Treerat, *Guns, Girls, Gambling, Ganja.* See especially pp. 155, 171, and 181.

Pp. 240–41: For specific trafficking cases cited, see, respectively, *The Nation* (Bangkok), April 13, 1999; the suitcase smuggling incident is noted in Phongpaichit, Piriyarangsan, and Treerat, *Guns, Girls, Gambling, Ganja,* p. 167; Japan Economic Newswire, May 4, 1996; *The Nation* (Bangkok), November 18, 1993; *Mainichi Daily News,* June 14, 1990; *Bangkok Post,* February 17, 1984; *Asahi Evening News,* September 7, 1974.

P. 242: The bogus scholarships are reported in *Mainichi Daily News,* July 28, 1989. The Social Security Research Foundation study is discussed in "Bright Lights, Brutal Life," *Far Eastern Economic Review,* August 3, 2000.

Pp. 242–43: The Sioson case was widely covered. See, for example, *Chicago Tribune,* November 17, 1991. On the number of Thai women heading to Japan, see Phongpaichit, Piriyarangsan, and Treerat, *Guns, Girls, Gambling, Ganja,* p. 155; and on the four hundred Thais asking to be sent home, *The Nation* (Bangkok), April 6, 1994.

P. 243: Yayori Matsui's quotes are from her essay at http://www.alternatives.com/crime/ASIAWOM.HTML.

P. 243: On meth money financing yakuza expansion, see Masayuki Tamura's "The Yakuza and Amphetamine Abuse in Japan," in *Drugs, Law and the State,* ed. Harold H. Traver and Mark S. Gaylord (1992), pp. 102–3. The estimates of 1 million meth users and seven tons of meth are from the U.S. State Department's *International Narcotics Control Strategy Report,* 1999. The survey finding 2.2 million users is noted in *Daily Yomiuri,* January 25, 1999; and *Shincho 45,* April 2000.

P. 244: For a good discussion of postwar official response to meth use in Japan, see chapter 4 of Friman's *NarcoDiplomacy*. The plunge in the price of meth is noted in Kyodo News Service, April 17, 1998; and *Mainichi Daily News,* April 29, 1998. For a general discussion on meth's growing popularity, see *Shincho 45,* April 2000. On meth use in Japan during the 1980s, see the NPA's *Drug Problem in Japan,* various years; and *Present State of Boryokudan.*

Pp. 245–47: On the Ice Queen's tale and China's emergence as a major meth producer, see author Kaplan's series in *Asia Times,* January 7–9, 1997. On meth problems in Thailand, see Bertil Lintner's "Speed Demons: Asia's Newest Drug Scourge," *Far Eastern Economic Review,* May 8, 1997. On North Korea's criminal activities, see author Kaplan's "The Wiseguy Regime: North Korea Has Embarked on a Global Crime Spree," *U.S. News & World Report,* February 15, 1999.

Pp. 248–49: The Yamaguchi-gumi/Cali Cartel ties are from interviews with drug intelligence agents with the NPA and DEA. See also *The Drug Trafficking Situation in Japan: A Strategic Assessment,* DEA Office of Intelligence, 1990, pp. 12, 20; "Mayaku Karuteru (Koronbia) Nippon ni Shinryakuchu" (Colombian drug cartel is coming to Japan), *Shukan Bunshun,* July 18, 1992; "Cocaine in Japan," *Japan Times Weekly,* August 18, 1990; *Japan Times,* January 30, 1993; and *Daily Yomiuri,* January 7 and February 20, 1991.

Pp. 248–49: Furce's comment is from Michael Berger's "Japan May Be Target for Cocaine Cartels," *San Francisco Chronicle,* June 11, 1990. On the Medellin Cartel's money laundering in Japan, see *Asian Wall Street Journal,* August 7, 1990; and *Mainichi Daily News,* September 8, 1990. On threatening letters from the Medellin Cartel, see *Daily Yomiuri,* May 21, 1991; *Mainichi Daily News,* June 6, 1990; *Asahi Evening News,* February 6, 1991.

P. 249: On the failure of Colombian drug merchants to penetrate Japan, see Friman's *NarcoDiplomacy,* pp. 80–81.

Chapter Ten

Pp. 251–52: The number of yakuza leaving Narita airport is cited in Fourth Criminal Investigation Department, Chiba Prefectural Police Headquarters, *Anti-Handgun Smuggling Measures,* 1989; and *Chicago Tribune,* May 17, 1992. The Asahi estimate is from *Asahi Evening News,* December 29, 1990. The NPA official's quote is from Fourth Investigation Section, Criminal Investigation Division, Kanagawa Prefectural Police Headquarters, *Inagawa Kai: Present Condition and Countermeasures,* 1990. The NPA survey of companies victimized by yakuza abroad is noted in "Japanese Gangs Target Firms Operating Abroad," *Daily Yomiuri,* November 4, 1993.

Pp. 252–53: The yakuza's early expansion into the Philippines is described in *Times Journal* (Manila), November 12 and December 8, 1982; and the U.S. Drug Enforcement Administration report, *A Brief History of Japanese Organized Crime,* 1979. Machii's syndicate investments are cited in *Daily Yomiuri,* June 8, 1975; and *Mainichi Daily News,* February 16, 1975.

P. 253: On the number of yakuza, see "General Says 100 Japanese Gangsters Are in the Philippines," Associated Press, March 18, 1988.

P. 253: On the Danao gun trade, see the fine piece by the Associated Press's David Thurber, June 11, 1997; also Reuters, January 17, 1992; and the *Mainichi Shimbun*'s book *Soshiki Boryoku o Ou*, pp. 126–30.

Pp. 253–54: On the grenade explosion aboard the Thai Airways jet, see *New York Times*, November 4, 1986; and Associated Press, November 8, 1986. The yakuza's attraction to Cebu is noted in "Philippines: Japanese Gangsters Bringing Back 'Sex Tours,'" Inter Press Service, February 19, 1992.

P. 255: On crackdowns by Philippine authorities, see, for example, Kyodo News Service, May 9, 1990; and *Manila Standard*, July 9, 1999. The Philippine immigration official's quote is from an interview, 1993.

Pp. 255–57: The Chulalongkorn study is Phongpaichit, Piriyarangsan, and Treerat, *Guns, Girls, Gambling, Ganja*; see pp. 7–8. On the yakuza's expansion into Thailand, see the *Bangkok Post* stories of October 21, 1990; and Reuters, October 14, 1990. On their involvement in endangered species smuggling, see *Japan Economic Journal*, July 15, 1989. On corruption among Thai police, see "Playing by the Rules," *Far Eastern Economic Review*, December 1, 1994; and the painfully amusing "How to Buy Your Own Police Station," in the now-defunct Thai magazine *Caravan*, August 1994.

P. 257: The yakuza's early expansion across East Asia is reported in *Tokyo Shimbun*, February 5, 1975; *Yomiuri Shimbun*, June 8, 1975; and *Daily Yomiuri*, December 22, 1981.

Pp. 257–59: A number of books detail the history of the triads. Of particular help were part 1 of W. P. Morgan's account, *Triad Societies in Hong Kong* (1960); chapters 2–3 of Ko-lin Chin's *Chinese Subculture and Criminality: Non-traditional Crime Groups in America* (1990); and Yiu Kong Chu's *The Triads as Business* (2000), pp. 11–21. On ties of the Chinese Nationalists to triads, see Pichon P. Y. Loh's *The Early Chiang Kai-shek* (1971), pp. 24 and 132–34; Brian Crozier's *The Man Who Lost China* (1976), pp. 125–26; and author Kaplan's own *Fires of the Dragon: Politics, Murder and the Kuomintang* (1992), especially pp. 227–32.

P. 259: The yakuza's early activity in Hong Kong is described in a confidential report by D. M. Hodson, Interpol Bureau, Royal Hong Kong Police, *Organized Crime in Japan*, December 12, 1980; *Daily Yomiuri*, March 4, 1978; *Far Eastern Economic Review*, December 27, 1984; and the NPA's "Drug Problem in Japan," 1983. More recent data come from interviews with the Royal Hong Kong Police, May 1996.

P. 260: Yakuza activity on Taiwan is reported in *Mainichi Daily News*, February 29, 1992; *Yomiuri Shimbun*, June 8, 1975; and *Mainichi Daily News*, February 16, 1975. The alleged involvement of the Dominican ambassador was reported by, among others, Kyodo News Service dispatch, August 2, 1984; and *Mainichi Daily News*, July 30, 1984.

P. 261: Information on the alliance between Taiwanese and Japanese syndicates was obtained in interviews with Bamboo Gang members in 1985 and 1988. The alliances were also noted in *Far Eastern Economic Review*, December 27, 1984. The United Bamboo Gang's "meeting of the mobs" in Hong Kong was featured in *Newsweek*, April 1, 1985. On the Cold-Faced Assassin's funeral, see Reuters, April 9, 1993. On alleged ties of assemblyman Lo to the triads, see "The Mob Takes a Fall," *Time International*, March 17, 1997.

Pp. 262–63: On Chinese government ties to the triads, see Fredric Dannen's excellent "Partners in Crime: China Bonds with Hong Kong's Underworld," *The New Republic,* July 14, 1997. On seizures of Chinese-made weapons in Japan, see, for example, *Japan Times,* November 10, 1994, and May 30, 1991; and the NPA's *White Paper,* various years.

P. 263: Prof. Su's study of yakuza in China is reported on in *Tokyo Shimbun,* July 7, 1994. Rondan Doyukai's donation to Beijing University is from a confidential source.

Pp. 264–65: On the Russian trade in stolen cars and other goods, see *Daily Yomiuri,* November 11, 1992; *Shukan Aera,* June 27, 1997; *Japan Times,* September 14, 1997; Kyodo News Service, September 13, 1997; and *Los Angeles Times,* January 6, 2002. The murder of the Sumiyoshi boss on Sakhalin was reported in *Japan Times,* July 22, 1994. On the traffic in Russian women generally, see the CIA's *International Trafficking in Women to the United States,* especially pp. 57–59.

Pp. 265–66: Early yakuza activity in Brazil is described in two of that nation's leading newspapers, *Folha de Sao Paulo,* September 18, 1983; and *Jornal do Brasil,* February 22, 1985; and in a series of 1984 interviews by our associate Michael Kepp with Antonio Carlos Fon of *Isto E,* Brazil's second-largest newsweekly; Ari de Moraes of *Diario Popular,* a Sao Paulo daily; and William Kimura, editor of *Diario Nipak,* a bilingual daily in Sao Paulo. More recently, see "Asiatic Crime in Brazil," *IAACI News,* International Association of Asian Crime Investigators, November 1992. On the yakuza boss in Parana state, see "Japan's Yakuza Gangs Making Their Way into Brazil," *Daily Yomiuri,* April 3, 1994; and "Yakuza Nabbed in Brazil," *Asahi Evening News,* March 10, 1994.

Pp. 266–67: The Mexican sex trade is reported in *Japan Times,* May 6, 1996; and the *Orange County Register,* May 4, 1996. On the Costa Rican recruiters, see Kyodo News Service, November 18, 1992. On the South African gun-smuggling ring, see *Daily Yomiuri,* July 18, 1995; *Mainichi Daily News,* July 19, 1995; and *Japan Times,* November 15, 1995. On Aoki Corp's alleged payments to Noriega, see "Bush Kin: Trading on the Name?" *Los Angeles Times,* May 10, 1992.

P. 267: The yakuza's early forays into Europe are described in an internal report by the U.S. Immigration and Naturalization Service, *Strategic Assessment: Asian Organized Crime,* March 1, 1985, and in various news stories. See, for example, *The Guardian,* May 20, 1979; *Asahi Evening News,* May 22 and 23, 1979; *Japan Times,* March 1, 1983; and *Daily Yomiuri,* December 29, 1982.

P. 268: The child prostitution ring in Italy is reported by Reuters, November 6, 1997. On sokaiya activity in the U.K., see "Police Fear Japanese Mafia Is Moving into Britain," *The Guardian,* September 28, 1992. Rondan Doyukai's European foray is reported in *Wall Street Journal,* April 16, 1981; and *Daily Yomiuri,* October 10, 1982, and June 4, 1984.

P. 269: Yakuza on French TV is from "Yakuza en Pari," *Asahi Jyanaru,* September 23, 1988. On the attempted visit by Yamaguchi-gumi bosses, see Agence France Presse, August 20 and September 3, 1992.

P. 269: On yakuza involvement in French art thefts, see "Yakuza Linked to Paris Painting Theft," *Mainichi Daily News,* October 25, 1987; "Watashi ni Todoita Mafia no

Shirei" (I received an order from the Mafia), *Shukan Asahi,* August 28, 1992; "Masterpiece Paintings, Stolen in 1985, Returned to Paris," Associated Press, December 6, 1990; "Art Crime Update: The Japanese Connection," in *Wall Street Journal,* March 23, 1990.

P. 270: On the yakuza's Paris money laundry, see an Agence France Presse dispatch dated April 4, 1992; "Yakuza Money Laundry Shut Down in France," *Washington Times,* April 8, 1992; and Jeffery Robinson's *The Laundrymen* (1996), pp. 256–57.

Pp. 270–73: The material on Australia comes from a variety of official sources: Queensland Police, Bureau of Criminal Intelligence, *Japanese Organised Crime in Queensland,* 1992; National Crime Authority, *The Boryokudan and Australia—National Strategic Assessment,* undated, c. mid-1996; Parliament of the Commonwealth of Australia, *Asian Organised Crime in Australia: A Discussion Paper by the Parliamentary Joint Committee on the National Crime Authority,* February 1995; U.S. Yakuza Documentation Center, *Japanese Organized Crime Overseas Financial Activities,* intelligence report, December 7, 1993; *The Yakuza: Australia's Response to Japanese Organised Crime,* report prepared by Julia Bruce, parliamentary intern for Mrs. Kathy Sullivan, MP, June 9, 1995. Also helpful were a number of Australian and other publications: "National Crime Authority Issues Japanese Mafia Warning," *Australian Financial Review,* February 19, 1997; "Can Australia Keep Out the Yakuza," *Courier-Mail,* June 15, 1991; *Japan Times,* February 3, 1996; "Shady Links," *Four Corners,* September 9, 1991. Earlier yakuza activity in Australia is based on a 1985 radio report by the Australian Broadcasting Corporation, Sydney, "Background Briefing: The Yakuza." On the Kitayama case, see Agence France-Presse, February 16, 2001. On the Australian yakuza member, see Gwen Robinson's "Prison Term Looms for an Australian Yakuza," in *Nikkei Weekly,* August 17, 1991; and Agence France Presse, "Australian Yakuza Nabbed in Japan," July 3, 1991.

P. 274: On snakehead traffic into Japan, see, for example, *Daily Yomiuri,* May 28, 1994; Kyodo News Service, April 11, 1997; *Far Eastern Economic Review,* May 14, 1998; *Asiaweek,* May 9, 1997.

P. 274: On the influx of foreign workers into Japan, see "The Japan That Can Say Yes," *Newsweek International,* June 5, 2000. On criminal elements among them, see, for example, "Crime by Illegal Aliens," *Japan Echo,* February 1998. The Tokyo police survey of foreigners in the yakuza is noted in "More Foreigners Join Japanese Yakuza," *Asahi Evening News,* August 17, 1991.

P. 274: On Vietnamese crooks in Japan, see Kyodo News of September 29, 1998; and *Japan Times,* February 10, 1996. Israeli criminal activity is reported by Agence France-Presse, November 16, 1991. On the French, see Reuters, April 5, 1988.

P. 275: On the reach of Chinese gangs in Japan, see Mo Bangfu's "Kyuzo Suru Zai-Nichi Chugokujin Mafia no Hanzai," *Sekai,* November 1997 (translated as "The Rise of the Chinese Mafia in Japan" and reprinted in *Japan Echo,* February 1998); *Asahi Shimbun,* June 24, 1999. Mo Bang-fu's quote is from "Sun Yee-On Pushes into Japan," *South China Morning Post,* December 13, 1999.

Pp. 275–76: On xenophobic reactions to the growth in foreign gangs, see *Asahi Evening News,* October 15, 1992; *The Economist,* November 7, 1992. Ishihara's remarks were widely reported. See Kyodo News of April 13, 2000. The *Sunday Mainichi* story is reprinted in *Mainichi Daily News,* May 3, 1992. The Iranian's quote is from *Japan Times,* November 29, 1997.

Chapter Eleven

Pp. 277–80: The Northern Marianas section is based in part on interviews with former Tinian Casino Gaming Control Commission official Fred Gushin and investigator Bill O'Reilly, as well as the experiences of book co-author Alec Dubro, who briefly served as a consultant to the commission. In addition, we drew material from the papers of the commission, including memos and press releases; "Casino Gaming Comes to Tinian—An Open Door for the Yakuza?" remarks by Gushin before the Fourteenth International Asian Organized Crime Conference in Calgary, Canada, July 16, 1992; and a DEA press release, Agana, Guam, July 13, 1989. See also *Japan Times,* February 26, 1987; and *Mainichi Shimbun,* March 5, 1992. Yakuza interest in the Pacific islands was noted as early as 1979 in the Drug Enforcement Administration's *A Brief History of Japanese Organized Crime.*

Pp. 280–81: On the roots of organized crime in Hawaii, see the 1978 report of the Hawaii Crime Commission, *Organized Crime in Hawaii.* The report was an excellent beginning for a state probe, but the commission trod on too many sensitive and important toes; power was withdrawn from it and its funding sharply cut after this report intimated that the commission could name names among the powerful in Hawaii with links to organized crime. For background on the commission, see James C. F. Wang, *Hawai'i State and Local Politics* (1982), pp. 523–28.

Pp. 281–82: During the 1980s, most day-to-day reporting on the yakuza in Hawaii appeared in the *Honolulu Advertiser* under Jim Dooley's byline. Dooley, a transplanted Californian, has become the premier crime reporter on Hawaii and has undoubtedly written more on the yakuza than any other American newspaper reporter. See Dooley's fine series, "Shadow Links: A Yen for Golf," *Honolulu Advertiser,* August 21–25, 1988.

Pp. 282–84 : Much of the reporting on Inada, Yonekura, and other yakuza in Hawaii appears in various articles by Dooley in the *Honolulu Advertiser.* See especially his four-part series on the gangs beginning March 19, 1978. We also relied on numerous interviews with Honolulu law enforcement sources; on a valuable internal 1979 U.S. Customs report, *Yakuza—Japanese Organized Crime;* and on the following press clips: Inada—*Honolulu Advertiser,* March 20 and December 17, 1980; *Penthouse,* April 1983; Yonekura—*Honolulu Advertiser,* March 19, 1980; *Rafu Shimpo* (Los Angeles), March 31, 1982; and a federal sentencing memorandum on Yonekura, U.S. District Court (Hawaii), Cr. P40. 79–00418.

Pp. 284–85: The Three Mules case is detailed in a U.S. Drug Enforcement Administration document obtained under the Freedom of Information Act, *Report of Investigation R4–76–0055,* May 11, 1979, Honolulu; U.S. Customs report, *Yakuza;* and Jim Dooley's August 29, 1979, article in the *Advertiser.*

Pp. 287–88: Background on Charlie Higa is based on confidential interviews with Honolulu law enforcement officials; the *Honolulu Star-Bulletin,* January 25, 1984; and Dooley's articles in the *Honolulu Advertiser,* September 22, 23, and 29, 1983.

P. 288: Background on Kaoru Ogawa is based on confidential interviews with police in Hawaii and Japan; *Mainichi Daily News,* January 19, 1980; *Shukan Yomiuri,* May 30, 1982; and *Honolulu Advertiser,* August 15 and 18, 1982.

P. 288: Osano's activities in Las Vegas are covered in chapter 4. For this section we've also drawn on confidential interviews with Hawaii law enforcement officials; *Asahi Evening News,* October 5, 1974; and *Japan Times,* June 24, 1974.

P. 289: Kaneshiro's quote is from *Honolulu Advertiser,* October 16, 1992. Sweet's comment is from an interview.

Pp. 289–91: Much of the section "The Big Time and the Mongoose" comes from U.S. Senate hearings, *Asian Organized Crime: The New International Criminal,* June 18 and August 4, 1992. On the Matsumoto brothers' alleged ties to the Yamaguchi-gumi, see *Asian Organized Crime: The New International Criminal,* p. 51; and the *Honolulu Advertiser,* August 23, 1988, and December 2, 1989. Kitaro Watanabe's alleged yakuza ties were reported in the *Honolulu Advertiser,* August 23, 1988, and July 7, 1989; and author Kaplan's "Yakuza, Inc."

Chapter Twelve

P. 293: The headlines are from *Los Angeles Times,* November 14, 1981, and *USA Today,* November 28, 1983, respectively. They were not the only inflammatory headlines to hit the stands.

P. 294: For years, the California attorney general's organized crime bureau issued an annual report. The quote is taken from *Organized Crime in California: 1981.*

P. 295: Testimony at the President's Commission on Organized Crime was recorded in the commission's preliminary transcripts, dated October 23, 1984, and in numerous press clips.

Pp. 297–98: Information on the Tokyo Club was gathered by Isami Arifuku-Waugh, primarily from reports in the rich Bancroft Library collections at the University of California, Berkeley. Arifuku-Waugh's findings were published in her 1978 doctoral thesis for the University of California (Berkeley) School of Criminology, *Hidden Crime and Deviance in the Japanese-American Community, 1920–1946.* See also James Oda's controversial self-published history, *Heroic Struggles of Japanese Americans* (1981); the Japanese American newspaper *Rafu Shimpo* (Los Angeles), October 20, 1930; and the authors' "California's Yakuza: Foothold in Little Tokyo," *Californian,* July–August 1987.

P. 298: The quote on Japanese morphine in North America is from the U.S. government's *Annual Report of the Bureau of Narcotics,* 1932, p. 10.

Pp. 298–300: Information on prewar Japanese narcotics dealing in the U.S. appears, for the most part, in the Bureau of Narcotics annual reports, 1930–42. These are not the most objective of reports, but they are based on arrest and court records. For a detailed and scholarly treatment of Chinese and Japanese involvement in the prewar heroin trade, see Jonathan Marshall's excellent study, "Opium and the Politics of Gangsterism in Nationalist China, 1927–1945," in *Bulletin of Concerned Asian*

Scholars, July–September 1977. See also Frederick T. Merrill's *Japan and the Opium Menace,* published jointly by the International Secretariat, Institute of Pacific Relations, and the Foreign Police Institute, New York, 1942. On Japan's deep involvement in the opium trade, see a paper by Kathryn Meyer at Lafayette College, "Japan and the World Narcotics Traffic"; and Friman's *NarcoDiplomacy.* For a propagandistic, but interesting, look at the Japanese narcotics trade, see Violet Sweet Haven's book *Gentlemen of Japan* (1944). Also see Harry J. Anslinger's *The Protectors* (1964), p. 31.

Pp. 301–2: The Leo Orii story is based on two interviews with Mr. Orii in 1982; on interviews with LAPD and other officials, 1982–85; and on confidential law enforcement reports, including ones in 1993 and 1996.

Pp. 303–4: Machii's activities in the U.S. are based on interviews with his American business partner, Kenneth Ross, in 1982 and 1985; on confidential law enforcement reports; and on a television segment from ABC's *20/20* newsmagazine, "Japan's Other Exports," May 27, 1982.

P. 304: Sather's quotes on the image of Western women in Japan are from *Hostesses* (1984), her master's thesis in journalism for the University of California at Berkeley.

Pp. 304–6: Reporting on the "white slavery" trade is from interviews with hostesses and entertainers in the U.S. and Japan by the authors and our associates, and from numerous press clips. See, for example, *San Francisco Examiner,* May 6, 1982, and August 10, 1983; *Los Angeles Times,* April 13, 1982; *Japan Times,* April 17, 1981, and June 13, 1982; *Hokubei Mainichi,* August 7, 1982; "White Slaves," *Playgirl* magazine, November 1982; and "Yakuza," *Penthouse,* April 1983. See also "Japan's Other Exports," from ABC's *20/20* newsmagazine, May 27, 1982.

Pp. 306–10: For a historical look at guns and gun control in Japan, see Noel Perrin's fascinating *Giving Up the Gun* (1979). Information on gun smuggling comes from numerous interviews with U.S. and Japanese law enforcement officials, the NPA's *Firearms Control in Japan* (1999), and various reports of the Japan Customs and Tariff Bureau. On specific cases, see *Japan Times,* July 15, 1966, December 20, 1980, April 17, 1981, and November 21, 1981; *Sankei Shimbun,* July 15, 1981; *Mainichi Daily News,* July 1, 1976; and *Asahi Evening News,* July 7, 1976.

P. 306: Eddie Kurimata's work is from an author's interview. The case of the Panamanian ambassador comes from a speech at the Japan-U.S. Conference on Measures against Organized Crime Groups, by the deputy director, First Safety Division, Crime Prevention Bureau, Tokyo Metropolitan Police Department.

P. 310: The case of the Green Beret smugglers was reported on Naha NHK Television, August 19, 1989; *Stars & Stripes,* August 24, 1989; and UPI, August 15, 1990.

P. 311: The Steve Conn case is drawn from interviews with law enforcement officials, Mr. Conn, and his publicist, Davy Rosenberg. See also *San Francisco Chronicle,* June 19, 1984.

Pp. 311–14: Sasakawa's activities in the U.S. were constant and fascinating. Our story is based on interviews with Mr. Sasakawa, Rocky Aoki, Richard Petree, and New Jersey law enforcement officials; various documents of the U.S.-Japan Foundation; and numerous press clips. Essential reading is Andrew Marshall's "In the Name of the

Godfather," *Tokyo Journal,* October 1994; and the *Bungei Shunju* series in 1993. See also the authors' "Soft Core Fascism," *New York Times,* July 11, 1978; and, for an in-depth look at Sasakawa and Atlantic City, John Mintz's report in the *Trenton Times* (New Jersey), February 8, 1981.

Pp. 314–15: Sokaiya activities in the U.S. are from confidential police reports; *Wall Street Journal,* April 16, 1981; *Shukan Bunshun,* May 7, 1981; and "The Yakuza Are Coming," by the authors in *California Living,* the Sunday magazine of the (now-defunct) *Los Angeles Herald Examiner,* February 6, 1983.

Pp. 317–18: Information on yakuza activity in Las Vegas comes from police sources and numerous press clips. See *Yomiuri Shimbun,* June 22, 1975; *Mainichi Daily News,* June 29, 1975; *Japan Times,* July 23, 1982, and October 19, 1975; Karl Schoenberger, "Japanese Tap Out in Las Vegas," *Los Angeles Times,* March 15, 1993.

Pp. 318–20: The information on Isutani is from the 1992 U.S. Senate hearings, *Asian Organized Crime: The New International Criminal,* pp. 52–53; and the NBC TV newsmagazine *Exposé,* May 30, 1991. The Mizuno case is based on a Department of Justice case summary, October 5, 1993; a U.S. Senate Judiciary hearing on asset forfeiture, 1997; and various press clips. See, for example, Jim Dooley's piece in the *Honolulu Advertiser,* July 19, 1982; *Los Angeles Times,* August 19, 1992, and October 5, 1993; *Mainichi Daily News,* October 16, 1992, and February 22, 1992; and *Japan Times,* June 11, 1992, and October 15, 1995.

Pp. 320–21: For information on Canada, we've relied on a paper by S/Sgt. L.D. "Smokey" Stovern (Royal Canadian Mounted Police), Coordinated Law Enforcement Unit, Vancouver, B.C., presented at the Fifteenth Annual International Asian Organized Crime Conference, March 30, 1993; and also on the fine reporting of David Hogben in the *Vancouver Sun,* August 6 and 8, March 20, 1993, and April 8, 1993. Takumi's assassination is described in a *Shukan Asahi* story translated in *Asahi Evening News,* September 3, 1997; *Shukan Gendai,* October 18, 1997; and *Mainichi Daily News,* October 8, 1997, and November 19, 1997.

Epilogue

P. 325: Inagawa's comments are from his Tokyo interview with the authors, February 9, 1984. Takayama's quotes are from the *Washington Post,* April 11, 1999.

Pp. 325–29: The changing nature of the yakuza was detailed in various interviews with Kanehiro Hoshino and in studies by him and his colleagues at Tokyo's National Research Institute of Police Science. For the 1993 survey on changing gang priorities, see NRIPS' *Boryokudan Taisakuhou no Boryokudan ni Oyobosu Eikyo to Kumiin no Ridatsu,* p. 26.

P. 326: The anonymous oyabun's quote is cited in George De Vos, *Socialization,* pp. 294–95.

P. 327: The quote from Tokyo police is taken from the *Mainichi Daily News,* February 9, 1984. Seiji Iishiba's quote is from an author's interview, 1997.

P. 329: Miyawaki's comments are from his speech, "The Role of the Yakuza in Japan Today," November 12, 1996.

Pp. 330–31: The Morris quote and related thoughts are from his landmark study *Nationalism,* pp. 421–23.

P. 333: The characterization of organized crime as theft is explored at length in Jonathan Kwitny's fine book, *Vicious Circles: The Mafia in the Marketplace* (1979). Kwitny's quote is from p. 70.

GLOSSARY

Baburu keizai Bubble Economy, the extraordinary speculative bubble that inflated Japanese stock and real estate prices during the late 1980s.

Bakuto Gambler, used especially to refer to the roadside bands of gamblers in feudal Japan. One of the three historic types of Japanese gangsters, along with tekiya and gurentai.

Boryokudan Literally, violence groups. Used by Japanese police to refer to yakuza.

Bosozoku Motorcycle and hot-rod gangs, a prime source of yakuza recruits.

Burakumin The members of Japan's ancestral class of outcasts, perennial victims of discrimination. Another prime source of yakuza recruits.

Daigashi An underboss of a yakuza syndicate, below the *oyabun* or boss.

G-2 U.S. Army Intelligence under the Occupation, headed by Major General Charles Willoughby. Used yakuza and rightists to spy on and disrupt the left.

Genyosha The Dark Ocean Society, Japan's first modern ultranationalist group, founded in 1881. Pioneered the fusion between gangsters and rightists.

GHQ General Headquarters of the Allied Powers during the Occupation of Japan, led by General Douglas MacArthur. The center of U.S. power in Japan from 1945 to 1952.

Giri Closest translation is debt or obligation, but the concept entails much more. Often used with the word *ninjo* by yakuza to describe the basis for their "honorable" traditions.

Gumi A suffix denoting association, company, or gang, commonly used by both yakuza groups and construction firms. Sometimes spelled *kumi*.

Gurentai Ruffian or hoodlum, the ruthless gangsters who grew amid the black markets of postwar Japan. One of the three historic types of Japanese gangsters, along with *bakuto* and *tekiya*.

Gyakkosu Or "reverse course." The abrupt political shift in U.S. Occupation policy beginning in 1947 that turned against the left and the labor movement.

Ikka A family or household, used as a suffix after some gang names.

Inagawa-kai One of Japan's top three syndicates, based in the Tokyo-Yokohama region. Inagawa-kai was among the first syndicates to venture abroad.

Jiageya A yakuza-dominated industry of thugs who force tenants off their land.

Jikenya Literally, incident specialists; typically yakuza-tied fixers who negotiate everything from traffic accidents to contract disputes. Similar to *seiriya*.

Kai A suffix denoting association or society, often used in gang names.

Kakuseizai Methamphetamine, Japan's favored drug of abuse. Also called *shabu*, S, and *piropon*.

Kanto-kai Yoshio Kodama's dream of a unified underworld fashioned into a national political force. A coalition of syndicates largely from Tokyo's Kanto plain, the Kanto-kai fell apart after fifteen months, in 1965.

Kigyo shatei Front company, used by yakuza to infiltrate the world of legitimate business.

Kobun "Child role," used in conjunction with oyabun ("parent role") to connote the familial relationship within most yakuza gangs.

Kokuryu-kai The Amur River Society, also known as the Black Dragon Society. A leading ultranationalist group founded in 1901 and a direct descendant of the Dark Ocean Society.

Kuromaku Literally, black curtain, a term from traditional Kabuki theater. Now used to connote a behind-the-scenes fixer, godfather, or power broker.

LDP Liberal Democratic Party, a coalition of largely conservative factions that have dominated Japanese politics since 1955.

Mizu shobai "Water business" or "water trades," meaning nightclubs, bars, restaurants, and related businesses.

Ninjo Compassion or empathy. Often used with *giri* (obligation) to describe the Japanese conflict between one's duty and one's feelings; a central theme in Japanese literature. Both are favorite terms of traditional yakuza.

NPA The National Police Agency, the central agency for administration and control of Japanese police, including all prefectural and local forces.

Oyabun "Parent figure," used with *kobun* to describe the familial relationship within the gang. Somewhat similar to the use of *godfather* in the West.

Prefecture The Japanese equivalent of a U.S. state, but geographically about the size of most U.S. counties.

Rengo A federation, used as a suffix with some yakuza syndicate names.

Ronin Masterless samurai, the source of countless legends about good and evil in medieval Japan.

Sangokujin "People of three countries." A name for the Taiwanese, Koreans, and Chinese who were brought to Japan as wartime labor. Yakuza fought pitched battles with them over control of black markets in the immediate postwar years.

Sarakin Literally, "salary man financiers," but often associated with loan sharks and strong-arm collectors.

SCAP Supreme Commander for the Allied Powers, the official title of General MacArthur's command during the U.S. Occupation of Japan, 1945 to 1952.

Seiriya "Fixer" specialists, a yakuza-dominated industry offering mediation services for accidents, bankruptcies, and disputes. Similar to *jikenya*.

Shabu See *kakuseizai*.

Sokaiya "General meeting specialists," Japan's unique breed of financial racketeer. Professional extortionists and strong-arm thugs who traditionally prey on shareholders' meetings, but are now diversified into wide areas of organized crime.

Songiriya "Loss-cutting specialists," a shadowy industry of squatters, extortionists, and investors who target bankrupt properties and bad loans.

Sumiyoshi-rengo The Tokyo-based federation of gangs with operations throughout much of Japan and abroad. The nation's second-largest yakuza group.

Tekiya Street stall operators and peddlers. One of the three historic types of Japanese gangsters, along with *bakuto* and *gurentai*.

Tokugawa era   Japan's final period of feudalism, ruled by a succession of shogun from 1603 to 1868. During most of this time, Japanese rulers deliberately isolated the nation from the rest of the world.

Towa Yuai Jigyo Kumiai   East Asia Friendship Enterprise Association, the heavily Korean yakuza syndicate founded by crime boss Hisayuki Machii. With fewer than 1,000 members, the group is still one of the most active overseas.

Triads   Chinese secret societies associated with criminal activity. With strong bases in Hong Kong, Taiwan, and China, triads are involved in narcotics, alien smuggling, and other rackets worldwide.

Yakuza   Literally, "8-9-3," the worst score in the card game *hanafuda*. Traditional term for Japanese gangsters.

Yamaguchi-gumi   Japan's largest crime syndicate, with some 34,000 members and associates in the 1990s, over a third of all yakuza. The syndicate is very active overseas.

Yubitsume   The ritual act within the yakuza of slicing off the little finger at the joint to atone for a mistake.

Zen Ai Kaigi   The fiery coalition of ultranationalist groups in Japan. Jokingly called Yakuza Kaigi because of its large gang membership.

BIBLIOGRAPHY

Sources: General

Alletzhauser, Al. *The House of Nomura*. London: Bloomsbury, 1990.

Ames, Walter L. *Police and Community in Japan*. Berkeley: University of California Press, 1981.

Anslinger, Harry J. *The Protectors*. New York: Farrar, Straus, 1964.

Aoyama, Koji. *Yakuza no Seikai: Kenka, Jingi, Tobaku, Sono Onna* (Yakuza society: Fighting, chivalry, gambling, and women). Tokyo: Kofusha, 1979.

Arahara, Bokusui. *Dai Uyoku Shi* (Great history of the right wing). Tokyo: Dai Nippon Kokumin To, 1966.

Arifuku-Waugh, Isami. *Hidden Crime and Deviance in the Japanese-American Community, 1920-1946*. Ph.D. diss., University of California School of Criminology, 1978.

Arlachi, Pino. *Mafia Business: The Mafia Ethic and the Spirit of Capitalism*. London: Verso, 1987.

Asakura, Kyouji. *Yakuza*. Tokyo: Gendai Shokan, 1990.

Ballescas, Ma. Rosario P. *Filipino Entertainers in Japan: An Introduction*. Quezon City, Philippines: Foundation for Nationalist Studies, 1992.

Barry, Kathleen, et al. *International Feminism: Networking against Female Sexual Slavery*. New York: Published by the authors, 1984.

Bayley, David H. *Forces of Order: Police Behavior in Japan and the United States*. Berkeley: University of California Press, 1976.

Beasley, W. G. *The Modern History of Japan*. New York: Praeger, 1963.

Benedict, Ruth. *The Chrysanthemum and the Sword: Patterns of Japanese Culture*. New York: World, 1946.

Berrigan, Darrel. *Yakuza no Sekai: Nihon no Uchimaku* (Yakuza society: Behind the Japanese curtain). Tokyo: Kindai Shisosha, 1948.

Boettcher, Robert. *Gifts of Deceit: Sun Myung Moon, Tongsun Park, and the Korea Scandal*. New York: Holt, Rinehart and Winston, 1980.

Bornoff, Nicholas. *Pink Samurai: Love, Marrage and Sex in Contemporary Japan.* New York: Pocket Books, 1991.

Boulton, David. *The Grease Machine.* New York: Harper and Row, 1978.

Bresler, Fenton. *The Chinese Mafia.* New York: Stein and Day, 1980.

Brown, Delmer M. *Nationalism in Japan.* New York: Russell and Russell, 1955.

Buruma, Ian. *Behind the Mask.* New York: Pantheon, 1984.

———. *The Wages of Guilt: Memories of War in Germany and Japan.* New York: Farrar Straus and Giroux, 1994.

Castberg, A. Didrick. *Japanese Criminal Justice.* Westport, Conn.: Praeger, 1990.

Chin, Ko-lin. *Chinese Subculture and Criminality: Non-traditional Crime Groups in America.* Westport, Conn.: Greenwood, 1990.

Chu, Yiu Kong. *The Triads as Business.* New York: Routledge, 2000.

Clifford, William. *Crime Control in Japan.* Lexington, Mass.: Lexington Books, 1976.

Craig, William. *The Fall of Japan.* New York: Dial Press, 1967.

Crane, Paul S. *Korea Patterns.* Seoul: Royal Asiatic Society, 1978.

Curtis, Gerald L. *Election Campaigning Japanese Style.* Tokyo: Kodansha, 1983.

Davis, Glenn. *The Right Wing of Japan.* Master's thesis, Sophia University, 1976.

Deacon, Richard. *Kempei Tai: A History of the Japanese Secret Service.* New York: Berkley Books, 1985.

De Vos, George A. *Socialization for Achievement.* Berkeley: University of California Press, 1973.

Dore, R. P., ed. *Aspects of Social Change in Modern Japan.* Princeton: Princeton University Press, 1967.

Dower, John W. *Embracing Defeat: Japan in the Wake of World War II.* New York: The New Press, 1999.

———. *Empire and Aftermath: Yoshida Shigeru and the Japanese Experience.* Cambridge: Harvard University Press, 1979.

———. *Japan in War and Peace: Selected Essays.* New York: The New Press, 1993.

Duus, Peter. *The Rise of Modern Japan.* Boston: Houghton Mifflin, 1976.

Fowler, Edward. *San'ya Blues: Laboring Life in Contemporary Tokyo.* Ithaca: Cornell University Press, 1996.

Friman, H. Richard. *NarcoDiplomacy: Exporting the U.S. War on Drugs.* Ithaca: Cornell University Press, 1996.

Fujita, Goro. *Koan Daiyoran* (Great directory of public security). Tokyo: Kasakura Shuppan, 1983.

———. *Koan Hyakunenshi* (The one-hundred-year history of public security). Tokyo: Koan Mondai Kenkyu Kyokai, 1979.

———. *Ninkyo Hyakunenshi* (The one-hundred-year history of chivalry). Tokyo: Kasakura Shuppan, 1980.

Gayn, Mark. *Japan Diary.* Tokyo: Charles E. Tuttle, 1948.

Gibney, Frank. *Japan: The Fragile Superpower.* New York: W. W. Norton, 1975.

Global Survival Network. *Crime and Servitude: An Exposé of the Traffic in Women for Prostitution from the Newly Independent States.* Washington, D.C.: Global Survival Network, 1997.

Goto, Takao. *Koria Uochiya* (Korea watcher). Tokyo: Gendai no Rironsha, 1982.

Greenfield, Karl Taro. *Speed Tribes: Days and Nights with Japan's Next Generation.* New York: HarperCollins, 1994.

Handelman, Stephen. *Comrade Criminal.* New Haven: Yale University Press, 1997.

Hane, Mikiso. *Peasants, Rebels, and Outcasts: The Underside of Modern Japan.* New York: Random House, 1982.

Haven, Violet Sweet. *Gentlemen of Japan.* New York: Ziff-Davis, 1944.

Hayashi, Norikiyo. *Soshiki Boryoku no Ichi Danmen* (Organized crime dissected: An investigator's journal). Tokyo: Tachibana Shobo, 1996.

Hill, Peter. *Japanese Organised Crime under the Boryokudan Countermeasures Law.* Ph.D. thesis, University of Stirling, May 2000.

Hobsbawm, Eric. *Bandits.* New York: Dell, 1969.

Hougan, James. *Spooks.* New York: William Morrow, 1978.

Huddle, Norrie, and Michael Reich. *Island of Dreams: Environmental Crisis in Japan.* Tokyo: Autumn Press, 1975.

Human Rights Watch. *Owed Justice: Thai Women Trafficked into Debt Bondage in Japan.* New York: Human Rights Watch, 2000.

Hyogo-ken Kensetsugyo Boryoku Tsuihou Kyogi-kai (Hyogo Prefecture Association for Removal of Boryokudan from the Construction Industry). *Boryoku Tsuiho no Tettei no Tameni: Kensetsugyo o Meguru Boryokudan tou no Jittai to sono Taiou ni Tsuite* (For the complete removal of violence: The reality of boryokudan in the construction industry and how to control them). Hyogo, Japan: Hyogo Prefecture Association for Removal of Boryokudan from the Construction Industry, 1988.

Ide, Hideo. *Jissho: Nihon no Yakuza* (Documented account: The Japanese yakuza). Tokyo: Tatsukaze, 1972.

Iiboshi, Koichi. *Kaigenreiku no Yamaguchi Gumi* (Yamaguchi-gumi under curfew). Tokyo: Gentaishi Shuppankai, 1983.

Ino, Kenji. *Botaiho ka no Yakuza* (Yakuza under the anti-gang law). Tokyo: Gendai Shokan, 1994.

———. *Kodama Yoshio no Kyozo to Jitsuzo* (The image and reality of Yoshio Kodama). Tokyo: Sokon Shuppan, 1970.

———. *Nihon no Uyoku* (Japan's right wing). Tokyo: Nisshin Godo Shuppan, 1973.

———. *Sengo Ninkyoushi no Kenkyu* (Studies on the postwar history of chivalry). Tokyo: Gendai Shokan, 1994.

———. *Yakuza to Nihonjin* (Yakuza and the Japanese). Tokyo: Gendai Shokan, 1993.

Iwaii, H. *Byori Shudan no Kozo* (The structure of pathological groups). Tokyo: Seishin-Shobo, 1963.

Jennings, John M. *The Opium Empire: Japanese Imperialism and Drug Trafficking in Asia, 1895–1945.* Westport, Conn.: Praeger, 1997.

Johnson, Chalmers. *Conspiracy at Matsukawa.* Berkeley: University of California Press, 1972.

———. *Japan: Who Governs?* New York: W. W. Norton, 1995.

Johnson, Elmer Hubert. *Criminalization and Prisoners in Japan: Six Contrary Cohorts.* Carbondale: Southern Illinois University Press, 1997.

Kaplan, David E. *Fires of the Dragon: Politics, Murder and the Kuomintang.* New York: Atheneum Books, 1992.

———. *Japanese Organized Crime and the Bubble Economy.* Occasional Paper 70. Washington, D.C.: Woodrow Wilson Center, 1996.

Kaplan, David E., and Andrew Marshall. *The Cult at the End of the World: The Incredible Story of Aum.* New York: Crown, 1996.

Kata, Koji. *Nihon no Yakuza* (The Japanese yakuza). Tokyo: Yamato Shobou, 1987.

Kelly, Robert J., ed. *Organized Crime.* Totowa, N.J.: Rowman and Allanheld, 1986.

Kent, Noel. *Hawaii: Islands under the Influence.* New York: Monthly Review Press, 1983.

Kodama, Yoshio. *I Was Defeated.* Tokyo: Robert Booth and Taro Fukuda, 1951.

———. *Sugamo Diary.* Tokyo: Taro Fukuda, 1960.

Korea Church Women United. *Kisaeng Tourism.* Seoul: Catholic Publishing House, 1984.

Kwitny, Jonathan. *Vicious Circles: The Mafia in the Marketplace.* New York: W. W. Norton, 1979.

Lebra, Takie Sugiyama. *Japanese Patterns of Behavior.* Honolulu: University of Hawaii Press, 1974.

Lebra, Takie Sugiyama, and William P. Lebra. *Japanese Culture and Behavior.* Honolulu: University of Hawaii Press, 1976.

Lee, Changsoo, George De Vos, et al. *Koreans in Japan.* Berkeley: University of California Press, 1981.

Lim, Lin L. *The Sex Sector: The Economic and Social Bases of Prostitution in Southeast Asia.* Geneva, Switzerland: International Labor Office, 1998.

Livingston, Jon, et al. *Imperial Japan: 1800–1945.* New York: Random House, 1973.

———. *Postwar Japan: 1945 to the Present.* New York: Random House, 1973.

Louis, Lisa. *Butterflies of the Night: Mama-sans, Geisha, Strippers, and the Japanese Men They Serve.* New York: Tengu Books, 1992.

Mainichi Shimbun. Soshiki Boryoku o Ou (Tracing organized violence). Tokyo: Mainichi Shinbunsha, 1992.

Matsumoto, Seicho. *Nihon no Kuroikiri* (Black mist over Japan). 2 vols. Tokyo: Bungei Shunju, 1974.

McCoy, Alfred W. *The Politics of Heroin.* New York: Lawrence Hill Books, 1991.

Mitchell, Richard H. *Political Bribery in Japan.* Honolulu: University of Hawaii Press, 1996.

Miyamoto, Teruo. *Yakuza na Hitobito* (Gangster people). Tokyo: Bunsei Shuppan, 1999.

Miyazaki, Manabu. *Totsupamono Retsuden* (Memoirs of crime). Tokyo: Chikuma Shobou, 1998.

Mizoguchi, Atsushi. *Chi to Koso* (Blood and battle). Tokyo: Sanichi Shobo, 1970.

———. *Gendai Yakuza no Ura Chishiki* (Secrets of the modern yakuza). Tokyo: Nihon Purintekusu, 1993.

Morgan, W. P. *Triad Societies in Hong Kong.* Hong Kong: The Government Printer, 1960.

Mori, Ei. *Kuroikikan* (Black chamber). Tokyo: Daiyamondo, 1977.

Morikawa, Tetsuro. *Chi no Senkoku: Don Taoka Sogeki Iiken* (Bloody verdict: The shooting of Don Taoka). Tokyo: Sanichi Shubo, 1979.

Morris, I. I. *Nationalism and the Right Wing in Japan.* London: Oxford University Press, 1960.

Nakane, Chie. *Japanese Society.* Berkeley: University of California Press, 1973.

Nelli, Humbert S. *The Business of Crime*. Chicago: University of Chicago Press, 1976.

Nihon Bengoshi Rengokai (Japanese Bar Association). *Minji Kainyu Boryoku: Chinou Boryoku to Tatakau Bengoshi* (Violent intervention in civil affairs: Lawyers struggling against intelligent violence). Tokyo: Shoji Homu Kenkyukai, 1995.

Nishi, Toshio. *Unconditional Democracy*. Stanford: Hoover Institution Press, 1982.

Oda, James. *Heroic Struggles of Japanese Americans*. Hollywood: James Oda, 1981.

Ohshima, Shizuko, and Carolyn Francis. *Japan through the Eyes of Women Migrant Workers*. Tokyo: Japan Women's Christian Temperance Union, 1989.

Omori, Minoru. *Sengo Hisshi* (Postwar secret history). Vol. 4, *Akahata to GHQ* (Red flag and GHQ). Vol. 7, *Boryaku to Reisen to Jujiro* (The crossroads of conspiracy and cold war). Tokyo: Kodansha Bunko, 1981.

Owen, John. *Authority without Power: Law and the Japanese Paradox*. New York: Oxford University Press, 1992.

Packard, George R., III. *Protest in Tokyo: The Security Treaty Crisis of 1960*. Princeton: Princeton University Press, 1966.

Packer, Frank, and Marc Ryser. *The Governance of Failure: An Anatomy of Corporate Bankruptcy in Japan*. Working Paper No. 62. New York: Columbia University, Center on Japanese Economy and Business, April 1992.

Parker, L. Craig, Jr. *The Japanese Police System Today*. New York: Kodansha International, 1984.

Perrin, Noel. *Giving Up the Gun*. Boston: Shambhala Publications, 1979.

Phongpaichit, Pasuk, Sungsidh Piriyarangsan, and Nualnoi Treerat. *Guns, Girls, Gambling, Ganja: Thailand's Illegal Economy and Public Policy*. Chiang Mai, Thailand: Silkworm Books, 1998.

Reid, Ed. *The Grim Reapers*. New York: Bamani Books, 1969.

Robinson, Jeffery. *The Laundrymen*. New York: Arcade, 1996.

Roberts, John. *Mitsui: Three Centuries of Japanese Business*. Tokyo: John Weatherhill, 1973.

Rome, Florence. *The Tattooed Men*. New York: Delacorte, 1975.

Saga, Junichi. *Confessions of a Yakuza: A Life in Japan's Underworld*. Tokyo: Kodansha International, 1991.

Sampson, Anthony. *The Arms Bazaar*. London: Coronet Books, 1977.

Sansom, George. *A History of Japan*. Tokyo: Charles E. Tuttle, 1963.

Sato, I. *Kamikaze Biker: Parody and Anomy in Affluent Japan*. Chicago: University of Chicago Press, 1991.

Schaller, Michael. *Altered States: The United States and Japan since the Occupation*. New York: Oxford University Press, 1997.

———. *The American Occupation of Japan: The Orgins of the Cold War in Asia*. New York: Oxford University Press, 1985.

Schonberger, Howard B. *Aftermath of War: Americans and the Remaking of Japan, 1945–1952*. Kent, Ohio: The Kent State University Press, 1989.

Schreiber, Mark. *Shocking Crimes of Postwar Japan*. Tokyo: Yenbooks, 1996.

———. *The Dark Side: Infamous Japanese Crimes and Criminals*. Tokyo: Kotansha International, 2001.

Seagrave, Sterling. *The Soong Dynasty*. New York: Harper and Row, 1985.

Seymour, Christopher. *Yakuza Diary: Doing Time in the Japanese Underworld*. New York: Atlantic Monthly Press, 1996.

Shukan Taishu Henshubu (Weekly Taishu Editorial Section). *Yakuza Dai Jiten* (Ya-kuza great dictionary). Tokyo: Futabasha, 1993.

Shunkan Shincho, ed. *Makasa no Nihon* (MacArthur's Japan). 2 vols. Tokyo: Shin-cho Bunko, 1983.

Skrobanek, Siriporn, Nattaya Boonpakdi, and Chutima Janthakeero. *The Traffic in Women: Human Realities of the International Sex Trade.* London: Zed Books, 1997.

Smith, Patrick. *Japan: A Reinterpretation.* New York: Pantheon, 1997.

Smith, W. Eugene, and Aileen Smith. *Minamata.* New York: Holt, Rinehart and Winston, 1975.

Stark, David Harold. *The Yakuza: Japanese Crime Incorporated.* Ph.D. thesis, University of Michigan, 1981.

Statler, Oliver. *Japanese Inn.* New York: Harcourt Brace Jovanovich, 1961.

Sterling, Claire. *Crime without Frontiers: The Worldwide Expansion of Organised Crime and the Pax Mafiosa.* London: Little, Brown, 1994.

Storry, Richard. *A History of Modern Japan.* Middlesex, England: Penguin Books, 1960.

Szymkowiak, Kenneth. *Necessary Evil: Extortion, Organized Crime and Japanese Corpo-rations.* Ph.D. diss., University of Hawaii, 1996.

———. *Sokaiya: Extortion, Protection, and the Japanese Corporation.* Armonk, N.Y.: M. E. Sharpe, 2002.

Takemori, Hisaakira. *Miezaru Seifu* (Invisible government). Tokyo: Shiraishi Shoten, 1976.

Taoka, Kazuo. *Yamaguchi Gumi Sandaime: Taoka Kazuo Jien* (Yamaguchi-gumi third generation: The autobiography of Kazuo Taoka). 3 vols. Tokyo: Tokukan Shoten, 1973.

Thornton, Robert Y., with Katsuya, Endo. *Preventing Crime in America and Japan.* Armonk, N.Y.: M. E. Sharpe, 1991.

Toland, John. *The Rising Sun.* New York: Random House, 1970.

Traver, Harold H., and Gaylord, Mark S., eds. *Drugs, Law and the State.* Hong Kong: Hong Kong University Press, 1992.

Uyoku Jiten (Right-wing dictionary). Tokyo: Shakai Mondai Kenkyu-kai, 1970.

Van Wolferen, Karel. *The Enigma of Japanese Power.* New York: Random House, 1990.

Ventura, Rey. *Underground in Japan.* London: Jonathan Cape, 1992.

Viner, Aron. *Inside Japanese Financial Markets.* Homewood, Ill.: Dow Jones-Irwin, 1988.

Walker, William O., ed. *Drug Control Policy: Essays in Historical and Comparative Per-spective.* University Park: Pennsylvania State University Press, 1992.

Whiting, Robert. *Tokyo Underworld.* New York: Pantheon, 1999.

Wildes, Harry Emerson. *Typhoon in Tokyo.* New York: Macmillan, 1954.

Williams, Justin, Sr. *Japan's Political Revolution under MacArthur.* Athens: University of Georgia Press, 1979.

Wood, Christopher. *The Bubble Economy.* New York: Atlantic Monthly Press, 1992.

Woodall, Brian. *Japan under Construction: Corruption, Politics, and Public Works.* Berkeley: University of California Press, 1996.

Yamanaka, Ichiro. *Heisei Yakuza* (Yakuza in the Hesei era). Tokyo: Chuo Aruto Paburasha, 1989.

Government Reports

California Department of Justice, Bureau of Organized Crime and Criminal Intelligence. *Organized Crime in California*, 1981.

———. Miscellaneous reports.

Financial Action Task Force on Money Laundering. Annual reports, various years.

Hawaii Crime Commission. *Organized Crime in Hawaii*. Vol. 1. August 1978.

Hyogo Prefectural Police. *Present Situation of Yamaguchi-Gumi and Police Counter Measures*, December 6, 1989.

Japan Customs and Tariff Bureau, Enforcement Division. *Country Report Japan: Recent Customs Seizures of Drugs and Guns in Japan*, 1998.

———. *Trends in Illicit Drug and Gun Smuggling in Japan*, various years.

Japan Ministry of Justice. *White Paper on Crime*, various years.

Japan National Police Agency. *Anti Drug Activities in Japan*, 1993–96.

———. *Boryokudan Criminalities in Japan and Police Measures against Them*, 1987.

———. *Comprehensive Strategies for Drug Control in Japan*, 1987.

———. *Drug Problem in Japan*, various years.

———. *Firearms Control in Japan*, 1999.

———. *Keisatsu Hakusho* (National Police white paper). Tokyo: Okurasho Insatsu kyoku, 1982–2000.

———. *Present State of Boryokudan* (Organized crime groups) *and Our Crackdown Operations*, 1983.

———. *White Paper on Police*, 1982–98.

———. *Yamaguchi-Gumi, Inagawa-Kai and Sumiyoshi-Rengokai*, 1987.

Japan National Research Institute of Police Science (Hoshino, Kanehiro, Ayako Uchiyama, and Choichi Shishido). *Boryokudan Haijyo Katsudou ni Taisuru Boryokudanin no Ishiki* (Views of gangsters on gang eradication activities), 1991.

———. (Hoshino, Kanehiro). *Boryokudan Hanza no Henka to Tenbo* (Changes in boryokudan crime in the past and future), 1994.

———. (Hoshino, Kanehiro, Fumio Mugishima, and Kenji Kiyonaga). *Boryokudan-in no Danshi to Shisei: Boryokudan no Dentoteki Fukuji Bunka no Kenkyu* (Tattooing and finger joint cutting by organized crime members), 1971.

———. (Mugishima, Fumio). *Boryokudanin to Dantai to no Kankei ni Kansuru Kenkyu* (Follow-up survey of organized crime members), 1974.

———. (Uchiyama, Ayako, and Kanehiro Hoshino). *Boryokudan no Boryokudan Fukujibunka e no Docho* (A study on the conformity of boryokudan members to boryokudan subculture), 1993.

———. (Uchiyama, Ayako). *Boryokudanin no Keizai-Kiban ni Kansuru Kenkyu* (A study of the economic basis of boryokudan members), 1988.

———. (Hoshino, Kanehiro, Ayako Uchiyama, Yutaka Harada, and Fumio Mugishima). *Boryokudan no Seikatsu Kozo no Kenkyo* (A study on the way of life of members of organized crime gangs), 1987.

———. (Tamura, Masayuki, Kanehiro Hoshino, Ayako Uchiyama, and Seiji Yonezato). *Boryokudan Taisakuhou no Boryokudan ni Oyobosu Eikyo to Kumiin no Ridatsu* (The impact of the anti–organized crime law on boryokudan and their members' intentions to resign from the organization), 1993.

———. (Uchiyama, Ayako, Kanehiro Hoshino, Masayuki Tamura, and Seiji

Yonezato). *Boryokudan Taisakuhou Shikogo no Boryokudanin no Seikatsu Henka* (Changes in the way of life of boryokudan members after enforcement of the anti–organized crime law), 1993.

———. (Tamura, Masayuki). *Kakuseizai no Ryutsu Kibo Suitei ni Kansuru Ichi Kosatsu* (A study on the estimated scale of distribution of stimulant drugs), 1990.

———. (Harada, Yutaka, Fumio Mugishima, and Kanehiro Hoshino). *Koiki Boryokudan no Keito Keiretsu-Ishiki no Kenkyu* (A study on the attitudes of members of semi-national criminal gangs toward their association and subsidiary association), 1985 and 1986.

———. (Hoshino, Kanehiro). *Organized Crime and Its Origins in Japan.* Unpublished paper, 1988.

———. (Hoshino, Kanehiro). *Organized Criminal Gangs in Japan: The Subcultures of Organized Crime Gangs,* June 1971.

———. (Uchiyama, Ayako, Kanehiro Hoshino, and Choichi Shishido). *Pachinko Ten Gyokai ni Okeru Boryokudan Haijyo Katsudo no Jittai* (The reality of gang eradication activities in the pachinko industry), 1991.

———. (Suzuki, Shingo, Kanehiro Hoshino, Yoshiaki Takahashi, Choichi Shishido, and Masayuki Tamura). *Rainichi Gaikokujin ni Yoru Hanzai* (Crimes by foreigners in Japan), 1990.

———. (Hoshino, Kanehiro). *The Recent Trend of Underworld and Organized Crime in Japan,* February 1979.

———. (Hoshino, Kanehiro, Fumio Mugishima, and Yutaka Harada). *Saikin no Boryokudan Kanyusha to Boryokudan-Yobigun-Shonen ni Kansuru Kenkyu* (A study on newly enlisted members and fringe members of organized crime gangs), 1981.

———. (Uchiyama, Ayako, Seijun Okeda, Kanehiro Hoshino, Yutaka Harada, and Fumio Mugishima). *Shonen ni Taisuru Boryokudan no Eikyo ni Kansuru Kenkyu* (A study on the influence of organized criminal gangs upon juveniles), 1992.

Parliament of the Commonwealth of Australia. *Asian Organised Crime in Australia: A Discussion Paper by the Parliamentary Joint Committee on the National Crime Authority.* Canberra, Australia, February 1995.

———. *The Yakuza: Australia's Response to Japanese Organised Crime: A Report prepared by Julia Bruce, Parliamentary Intern for Mrs Kathy Sullivan MP.* Canberra, Australia, June 9, 1995.

Royal Hong Kong Police Department, Interpol Bureau (D. M. Hodson). *Organized Crime in Japan,* December 19, 1983.

Supreme Command for the Allied Powers. *The Brocade Banner: The Story of Japanese Nationalism,* September 23, 1946.

———. Civil Information and Education Section. Press conference, September 19, 1947.

———. Civil Information and Education Section. Press conference, November 7, 1947.

———. Government Section. "Political Reorientation of Japan," September 1945– September 1948.

———. Government Section. "Oyabun-Kobun Subcommittee Report," September 25, 1947.

————. Military Intelligence Section. Miscellaneous interrogations and reports of Yoshio Kodama and Ryoichi Sasakawa, 1946–48.

————. Military Intelligence Section. "Oyabun-Kobun Systems," October 1, 1947.

————. Miscellaneous documents, especially Record Group 331, National Records Center, Suitland, Md.

————. Public Safety Division. *Public Safety Division History*. Vol. 1. 1948.

Tokyo Regional Public Prosecutor's Office. *Preliminary Petition regarding Infraction of the Commercial Law by Watanabe Hiroyasu, Jun Saotome, and Munenobu Shoji,* September 22, 1993.

United States Bureau of Narcotics, annual reports, 1932–40.

United States Central Intelligence Agency, Center for the Study of Intelligence. *International Trafficking in Women to the United States: A Contemporary Manifestation of Slavery and Organized Crime,* April 2000.

United States Commission on Wartime Relocation and Internment of Civilians. *Personal Justice Denied: Report of the Commission,* 1982.

United States Customs Service. Miscellaneous reports of Yakuza Documentation Center, Honolulu, Hawaii.

————. *Yakuza—Japanese Organized Crime,* 1979.

United States Department of State. *International Narcotics Control Strategy Report,* various years.

United States Drug Enforcement Administration. *A Brief History of Japanese Organized Crime,* 1979.

————. *The Drug Trafficking Situation in Japan: A Strategic Assessment,* 1990,

United States Federal Bureau of Investigation. *An Analysis of the Threat of Japanese Organized Crime to the United States and Its Territories,* July 1992.

————. *Oriental Organized Crime,* January 1985.

United States House of Representatives. Hearings before the Subcommittee of International Organizations of the Committee on International Relations. *Activities of the Korean Central Intelligence Agency in the United States,* March 17 and 25, 1976.

————. Report to the Committee on Foreign Affairs. *U.S. Narcotics Control Program Overseas: An Assessment,* February 22, 1985.

United States Immigration and Naturalization Service. *Strategic Assessment: Asian Organized Crime,* March 1, 1985.

United States Joint Drug Intelligence Group. *The Sumiyoshi-kai,* February 3, 1993.

United States National Security Council. *International Crime Threat Assessment,* December 2000.

United States President's Commission on Law Enforcement and Administration of Justice. *Task Force Report: Organized Crime,* 1967.

United States President's Commission on Organized Crime. Miscellaneous reports and memoranda, 1984–85.

————. Open Hearing Transcripts. New York, October 25, 1984.

————. *Organized Crime of Asian Origin,* Record of Hearing 3, October 1984.

United States Senate. Committee on Foreign Relations. Hearings of the Subcommittee on Multinational Corporations, February 4 and 6, 1976.

United States Senate. Permanent Subcommittee on Investigations of the Commit-

tee on Governmental Affairs. *Asian Organized Crime.* Hearing. October 3, No-
vember 5–6, 1991. Washington, D.C.: U.S. Government Printing Office, 1992.
———. *Asian Organized Crime: The New International Criminal.* Hearings. June 18
and August 4, 1992. Washington, D.C.: U.S. Government Printing Office, 1992.
———. *The New International Criminal and Asian Organized Crime.* December 1992.
Washington, D.C.: U.S. Government Printing Office, 1993.
———. *Statement of the Senate Permanent Subcommittee on Investigations Minority Staff
on International Narcotics Trafficking,* November 12, 1981.

Compositor: G&S Typesetters, Inc.
Text: Baskerville
Display: Syntax, Baskerville
Printer and binder: Thomson-Shore